ELEMENTS

OF

GEOMETRY AND TRIGONOMETRY;

WITH

PRACTICAL APPLICATIONS.

By BENJAMIN GREENLEAF, A. M.,

AUTHOR OF A MATHEMATICAL SERIES.

IMPROVED ELECTROTYPE EDITION.

BOSTON:

PUBLISHED BY ROBERT S. DAVIS & CO.

NEW YORK: MASON, BAKER, & PRATT, 142 GRAND STREET.

PHILADELPHIA: J. A. BANCROFT & COMPANY.

ST. LOUIS: HENDRICKS & CHITTENDEN.

CHICAGO: S. C. GRIGGS & CO.

Je 1904

GREENLEAF'S

NEW COMPREHENSIVE SERIES.

An ENTIRELY NEW MATHEMATICAL COURSE, *fully adapted to the best methods of Modern Instruction.*

GREENLEAF'S NEW PRIMARY ARITHMETIC.

GREENLEAF'S NEW INTELLECTUAL ARITHMETIC.

GREENLEAF'S NEW ELEMENTARY ARITHMETIC.

GREENLEAF'S NEW PRACTICAL ARITHMETIC.

GREENLEAF'S NEW ELEMENTARY ALGEBRA.

GREENLEAF'S NEW HIGHER ALGEBRA.

GREENLEAF'S NEW ELEMENTARY GEOMETRY.

GREENLEAF'S ELEMENTS OF GEOMETRY.

GREENLEAF'S ELEMENTS OF TRIGONOMETRY.

GREENLEAF'S GEOMETRY AND TRIGONOMETRY.

☞ *Other Books of a Complete Series, in preparation.*

⁂ KEYS to the PRACTICAL ARITHMETIC, ALGEBRAS. GEOMETRY and TRIGONOMETRY, in separate volumes.

RIVERSIDE PRESS:
PRINTED BY H. O. HOUGHTON AND COMPANY.

PREFACE.

THE preparation of this treatise was undertaken at the earnest solicitation of many teachers, who, having used the author's Arithmetics and Algebra with satisfaction, were desirous of seeing his series rendered more nearly complete by the addition of the Elements of Geometry and Trigonometry.

That there are peculiar advantages in a graded series of text-books on the same subject, few, if any, properly qualified to judge, will doubt. The author, therefore, feels justified in introducing this volume to the attention of the public.

In the Elements of Geometry, he has followed, in the main, the simple and elegant order of arrangement adopted by Legendre; but in the methods of demonstration no particular authority has been closely followed, the aim having been to adapt the work fully to the latest and most approved modes of instruction. In this respect, there will be found incorporated a considerable number of important improvements.

More attention than is usual in elementary works of this kind has been given to the *converse* of propositions. In almost all cases where it was possible, the converse of a proposition has been demonstrated.

The demonstration of Proposition XX. of the first book is essentially the one given by M. da Cunha in the *Principes Mathématiques*, which has justly been pronounced by the highest mathematical authorities to be a very important improvement in elementary geometry. It has, however, never before been introduced into a text-book by an American author.

The Applications of Geometry to Mensuration, given in the eleventh and twelfth books, are designed to show how the theoretical principles of the science are connected with manifold practical results.

The Miscellaneous Exercises, which follow, are calculated to test the thoroughness of the scholar's geometrical knowledge; and sufficient Applications of Algebra to Geometry are given to show the relation existing between these two branches of the mathematics.

The Elements of Plane and Spherical Trigonometry present a complete system, theoretical and practical, fully adapted to the wants of advanced classes.

The trigonometric functions, in this treatise, have been regarded as *ratios*, since this improved method has not only now superseded the ancient method in English and French works, but has been approved and adopted generally by the best American mathematicians. Reference, however, is made to whatever is especially valuable in the old method.

In the preparation of this work the author has received valuable suggestions from many eminent teachers, to whom he would here express his sincere thanks. Especially would he acknowledge his great obligations to H. B. Maglathlin, A. M., who for many months has been associated with him in his labors, and to whose experience as a teacher, skill as a mathematician, and ability as a writer, the value of this treatise is largely due.

BENJAMIN GREENLEAF.

Bradford, Mass., July 25, 1861.

NOTICE.

A Key, comprising the Solutions of the Problems contained in this work, is published, *for Teachers only;* and the same will be mailed, post-paid, to the address of any Teacher who will forward sixty cents in stamps to the Publishers.

CONTENTS.

PLANE GEOMETRY.

SOLID GEOMETRY.

PRACTICAL GEOMETRY.

BOOK XI.

BOOK XII.

BOOK XIII.

BOOK XIV.

TRIGONOMETRY.

BOOK I.

BOOK II.

BOOK III.

BOOK IV.

BOOK V.

BOOK VI.

ELEMENTS OF GEOMETRY.

BOOK I.

ELEMENTARY PRINCIPLES.

DEFINITIONS.

1. GEOMETRY is the science of *Position* and *Extension.*

The elements of position are direction and distance.

The dimensions of extension are length, breadth, and height or thickness.

2. MAGNITUDE, in general, is that which has one or more of the three dimensions of extension.

3. A POINT is that which has position, without magnitude.

4. A LINE is that which has length, without either breadth or thickness.

5. A STRAIGHT LINE, or RIGHT LINE, is one which has the same direction in its whole extent; as the line A B.

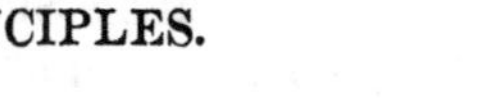

A————B

The word *line* is frequently used alone, to designate a straight line.

6. A CURVED LINE is one which continually changes its direction; as the line C D.

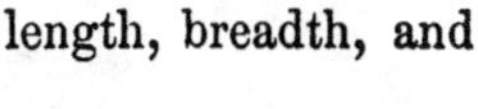

C⌒D

The word *curve* is frequently used to designate a curved line.

7. A Broken Line is one which is composed of straight lines, not lying in the same direction; as the line E F.

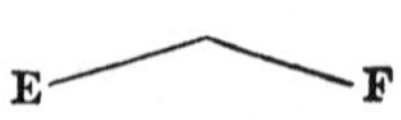

8. A Mixed Line is one which is composed of straight lines and of curved lines.

9. A Surface is that which has length and breadth, without height or thickness.

10. A Plane Surface, or simply a Plane, is one in which any two points being taken, the straight line that joins them will lie wholly in the surface.

11. A Curved Surface is one that is not a plane surface, nor made up of plane surfaces.

12. A Solid, or Volume, is that which has length, breadth, and thickness.

ANGLES AND LINES.

13. A Plane Angle, or simply an Angle, is the difference in the direction of two lines, which meet at a point; as the angle A.

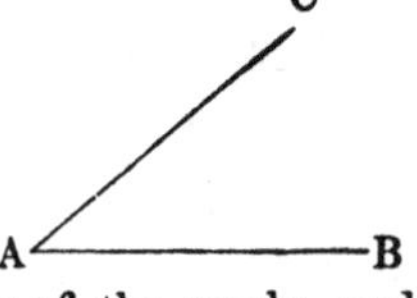

The point of meeting, A, is the *vertex* of the angle, and the lines A B, A C are the *sides* of the angle.

An angle may be designated, not only by the letter at its vertex, as C, but by three letters, particularly when two or more angles have the same vertex; as the angle A C D or D C B, the letter at the vertex always occupying the middle place.

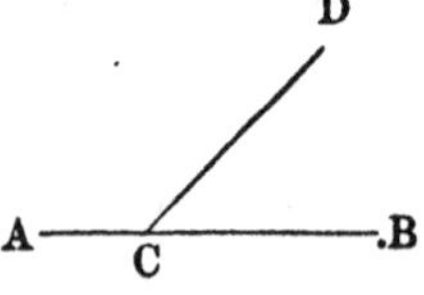

The *quantity* of an angle does not depend upon the length, but entirely upon the position, of the sides; for the angle remains the same, however the lines containing it be increased or diminished.

14. Two straight lines are said to be *perpendicular* to each other, when their meeting forms equal adjacent angles; thus the lines A B and C D are perpendicular to each other.

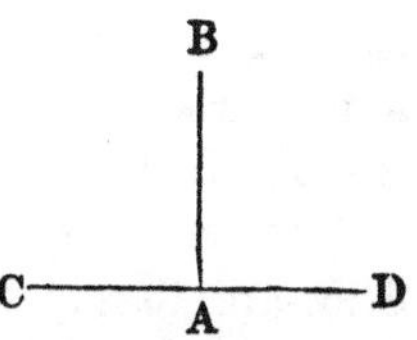

Two adjacent angles, as C A B and B A D, have a common vertex, as A; and a common side, as A B.

15. A **Right Angle** is one which is formed by a straight line and a perpendicular to it; as the angle C A B.

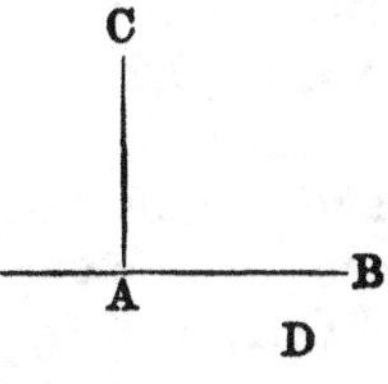

16. An **Acute Angle** is one which is less than a right angle; as the angle D E F.

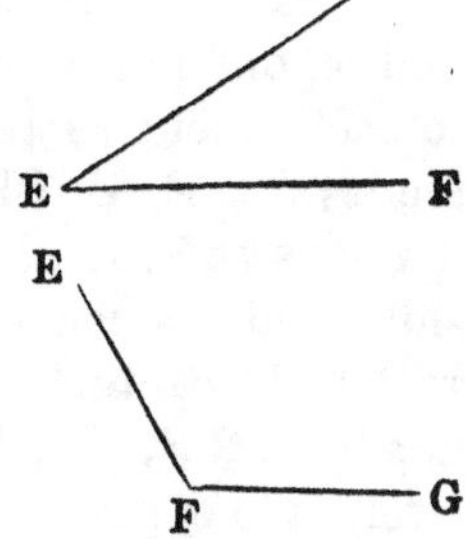

An **Obtuse Angle** is one which is greater than a right angle; as the angle E F G.

Acute and obtuse angles have their sides oblique to each other, and are sometimes called *oblique angles*.

17. **Parallel Lines** are such as, being in the same plane, cannot meet, however far either way both of them may be produced; as the lines A B, C D.

18. When a straight line, as E F, intersects two parallel lines, as A B, C D, the angles formed by the intersecting or secant line take particular names, thus:—

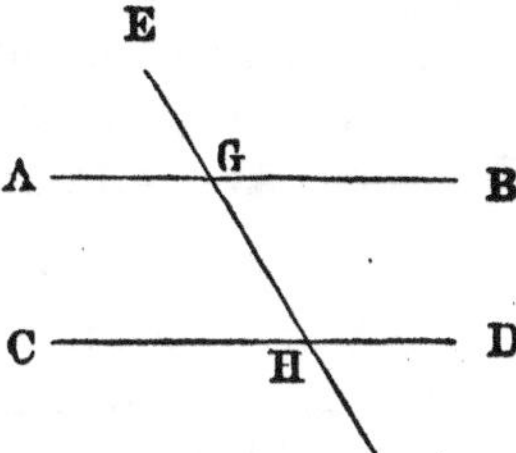

Interior Angles on the same Side are those which lie within the parallels, and on the same side of the secant line; as the angles B G H, G H D, and also A G H, G H C.

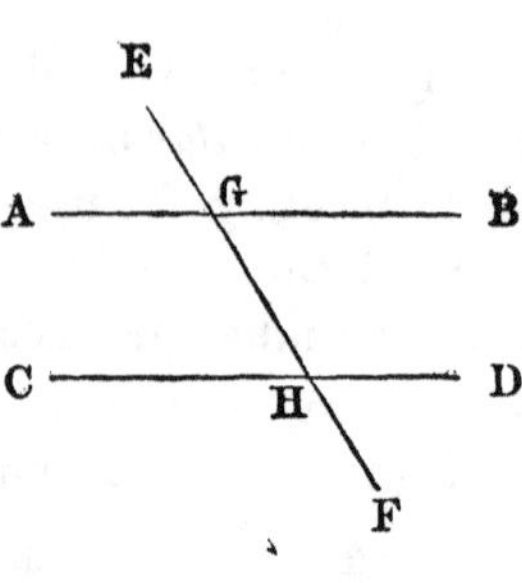

EXTERIOR ANGLES ON THE SAME SIDE are those which lie without the parallels, and on the same side of the secant line; as the angles B G E, D H F, and also the angles A G E, C H F.

ALTERNATE INTERIOR ANGLES lie within the parallels, and on different sides of the secant line, but are not adjacent to each other; as the angles B G H, G H C, and also A G H, G H D.

ALTERNATE EXTERIOR ANGLES lie without the parallels, and on different sides of the secant line, but not adjacent to each other; as the angles E G B, C H F, and also the angles A G E, D H F.

OPPOSITE EXTERIOR and INTERIOR ANGLES lie on the same side of the secant line, the one without and the other within the parallels, but not adjacent to each other; as the angles E G B, G H D, and also E G A, G H C, are, respectively, the opposite exterior and interior angles.

PLANE FIGURES.

19. A PLANE FIGURE is a plane terminated on all sides by straight lines or curves.

The boundary of any figure is called its *perimeter*.

20. When the boundary lines are straight, the space they enclose is called a RECTILINEAL FIGURE, or POLYGON; as the figure A B C D E.

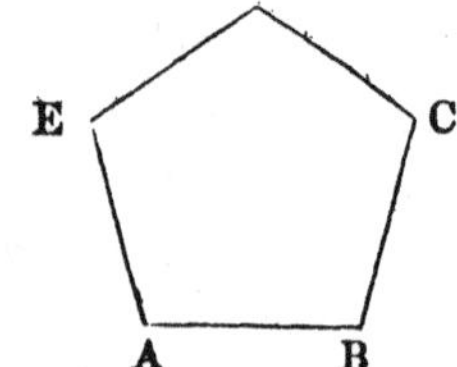

21. A polygon of three sides is called a TRIANGLE; one of four sides, a QUADRILATERAL; one of five, a PENTAGON; one of six, a HEXAGON; one of seven, a HEPTAGON; one

of eight, an OCTAGON ; one of nine, a NONAGON ; one of ten, a DECAGON ; one of eleven, an UNDECAGON ; one of twelve, a DODECAGON ; and so on.

22. An EQUILATERAL TRIANGLE is one which has its three sides equal ; as the triangle A B C.

An ISOSCELES TRIANGLE is one which has two of its sides equal ; as the triangle D E F.

A SCALENE TRIANGLE is one which has no two of its sides equal ; as the triangle G H I.

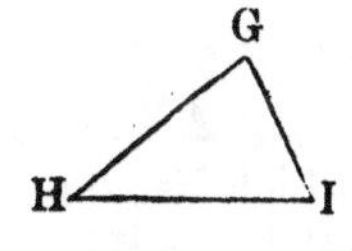

23. A RIGHT-ANGLED TRIANGLE is one which has a right angle ; as the triangle J K L.

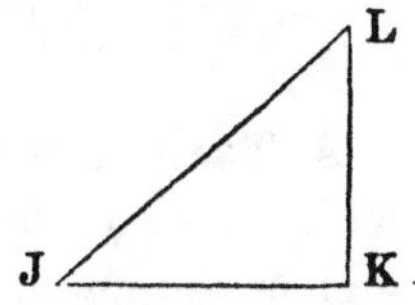

The side opposite to the right angle is called the *hypothenuse ;* as the side J L.

24. An ACUTE-ANGLED TRIANGLE is one which has three acute angles ; as the triangles A B C and D E F, Art. 22.

An OBTUSE-ANGLED TRIANGLE is one which has an obtuse angle ; as the triangle G H I, Art. 22.

Acute-angled and obtuse-angled triangles are also called *oblique-angled* triangles.

25. A PARALLELOGRAM is a quadrilateral which has its opposite sides parallel.

26. A RECTANGLE is any parallelogram whose angles are right angles ; as the parallelogram A B C D.

A **Square** is a rectangle whose sides are equal; as the rectangle E F G H.

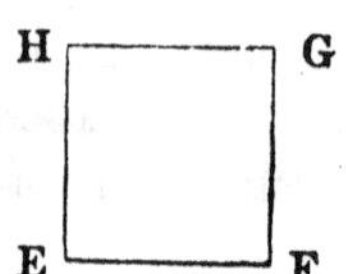

27. A **Rhomboid** is any parallelogram whose angles are not right angles; as the parallelogram I J K L.

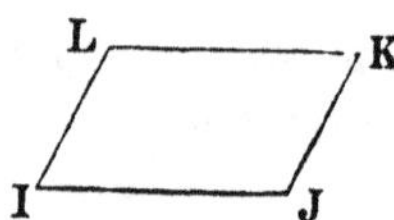

A **Rhombus** is a rhomboid whose sides are equal; as the rhomboid M N O P.

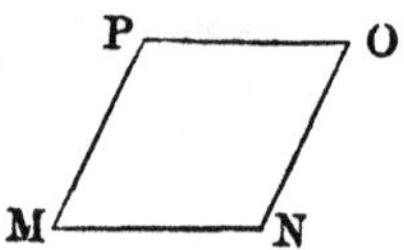

28. A **Trapezoid** is a quadrilateral which has only two of its sides parallel; as the quadrilateral R S T U.

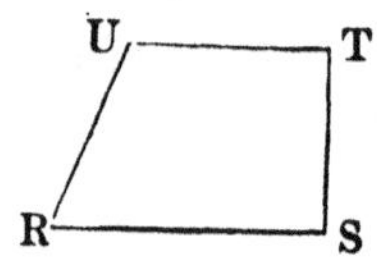

A **Trapezium** is a quadrilateral which has no two of its sides parallel; as the quadrilateral V W X Y.

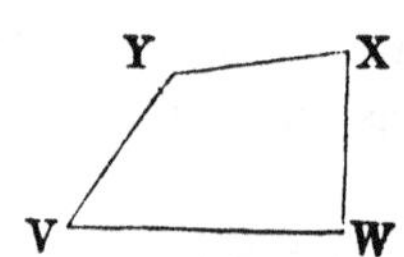

29. A **Diagonal** is a line joining the vertices of any two angles which are opposite to each other; as the lines E C and E B in the polygon A B C D E.

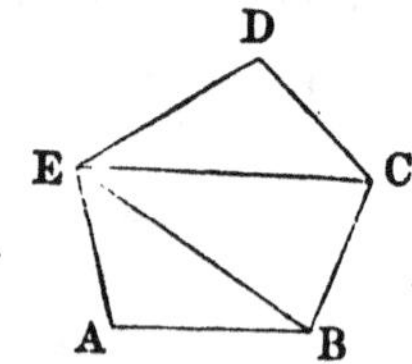

30. A **Base** of a polygon is the side on which the polygon is supposed to stand. But in the case of the isosceles triangle, it is usual to consider that side the base which is not equal to either of the other sides.

31. An *equilateral* polygon is one which has all its sides equal. An *equiangular* polygon is one which has

all its angles equal. A *regular* polygon is one which is equilateral and equiangular.

32. Two polygons are *mutually equilateral*, when all the sides of the one equal the corresponding sides of the other, each to each, and are placed in the same order.

Two polygons are *mutually equiangular*, when all the angles of the one equal the corresponding angles of the other, each to each, and are placed in the same order.

33. The corresponding equal sides, or equal angles, of polygons mutually equilateral, or mutually equiangular, are called *homologous* sides or angles.

AXIOMS.

34. An AXIOM is a self-evident truth; such as, —

1. Things which are equal to the same thing, are equal to each other.
2. If equals be added to equals, the sums will be equal.
3. If equals be taken from equals, the remainders will be equal.
4. If equals be added to unequals, the sums will be unequal.
5. If equals be taken from unequals, the remainders will be unequal.
6. Things which are double of the same thing, or of equal things, are equal to each other.
7. Things which are halves of the same thing, or of equal things, are equal to each other.
8. The whole is greater than any of its parts.
9. The whole is equal to the sum of all its parts.
10. A straight line is the shortest line that can be drawn from one point to another.
11. From one point to another only one straight line can be drawn.
12. Through the same point only one parallel to a straight line can be drawn.

13. All right angles are equal to one another.

14. Magnitudes which coincide throughout their whole extent, are equal.

POSTULATES.

35. A Postulate is a self-evident problem; such as,—

1. That a straight line may be drawn from one point to another.

2. That a straight line may be produced to any length.

3. That a straight line may be drawn through a given point parallel to another straight line.

4. That a perpendicular to a given straight line may be drawn from a point either within or without the line.

5. That an angle may be described equal to any given angle.

PROPOSITIONS.

36. A Demonstration is a course of reasoning by which a truth becomes evident.

37. A Proposition is something proposed to be demonstrated, or to be performed.

A proposition is said to be the *converse* of another, when the conclusion of the first is used as the supposition in the second.

38. A Theorem is something to be demonstrated.

39. A Problem is something to be performed.

40. A Lemma is a proposition preparatory to the demonstration or solution of a succeeding proposition.

41. A Corollary is an obvious consequence deduced from one or more propositions.

42. A Scholium is a remark made upon one or more preceding propositions.

43. An Hypothesis is a supposition, made either in the

enunciation of a proposition, or in the course of a demonstration.

PROPOSITION I.—THEOREM.

44. *The adjacent angles which one straight line makes by meeting another straight line, are together equal to two right angles.*

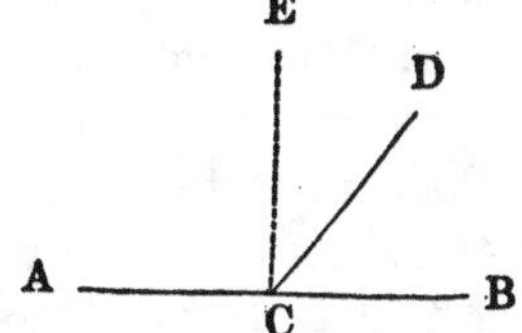

Let the straight line D C meet A B, making the adjacent angles A C D, D C B; these angles together will be equal to two right angles.

From the point C suppose C E to be drawn perpendicular to A B; then the angles A C E and E C B will each be a right angle (Art. 15). But the angle A C D is composed of the right angle A C E and the angle E C D (Art. 34, Ax. 9), and the angles E C D and D C B compose the other right angle, E C B; hence the angles A C D, D C B together equal two right angles.

45. *Cor.* 1. If one of the angles A C D, D C B is a right angle, the other must also be a right angle.

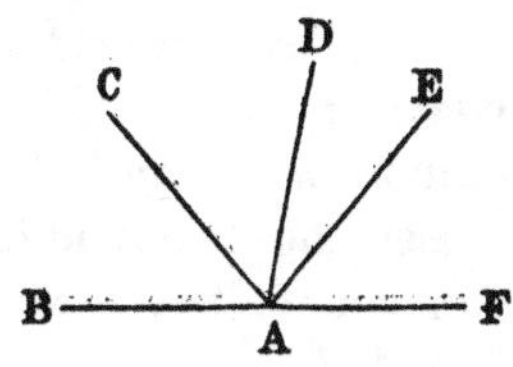

46. *Cor.* 2. All the successive angles, B A C, C A D, D A E, E A F, formed on the same side of a straight line, B F, are equal, when taken together, to two right angles; for their sum is equal to that of the two adjacent angles, B A C, C A F.

PROPOSITION II.—THEOREM.

47. *If one straight line meets two other straight lines at a common point, making adjacent angles, which together are equal to two right angles, the two lines form one and the same straight line.*

Let the straight line D C meet the two straight lines A C, C B at the common point C, making the adjacent angles A C D, D C B together equal to two right angles; then the lines A C and C B will form one and the same straight line.

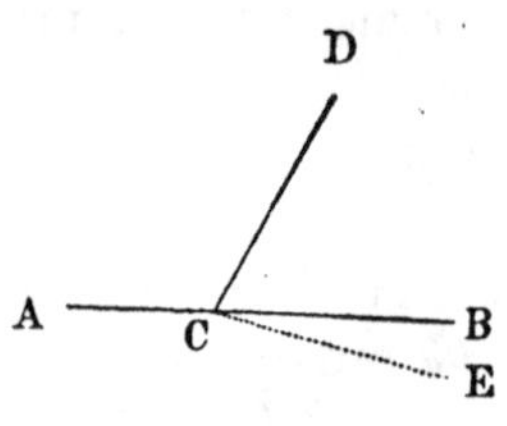

If C B is not the straight line A C produced, let C E be that line produced; then the line A C E being straight, the sum of the angles A C D and D C E will be equal to two right angles (Prop. I.). But by hypothesis the angles A C D and D C B are together equal to two right angles; therefore the sum of the angles A C D and D C E must be equal to the sum of the angles A C D and D C B (Art. 34, Ax. 2). Take away the common angle A C D from each, and there will remain the angle D C B, equal to the angle D C E, a part to the whole, which is impossible; therefore C E is not the line A C produced. Hence A C and C B form one and the same straight line.

Proposition III.—Theorem.

48. *Two straight lines, which have two points common, coincide with each other throughout their whole extent, and form one and the same straight line.*

Let the two points which are common to two straight lines be A and B.

The two lines must coincide between the points A and B, for otherwise there would be two straight lines between A and B, which is impossible (Art. 34, Ax. 11).

Suppose, however, that, on being produced, the lines begin to separate at the point C, the one taking the direction C D, and the other C E. From the point C let the line C F be drawn, making, with C A, the right angle A C F. Now, since A C D is a straight line, the angle F C D will be a right angle (Prop. I. Cor. 1); and since A C E is a straight line, the angle F C E will also be a right angle; therefore the angle F C E is equal to the angle F C D (Art. 34, Ax. 13), a part to the whole, which is impossible; hence two straight lines which have two points common, A and B, cannot separate from each other when produced; hence they must form one and the same straight line.

Proposition IV. — Theorem.

49. *When two straight lines intersect each other, the opposite or vertical angles which they form are equal.*

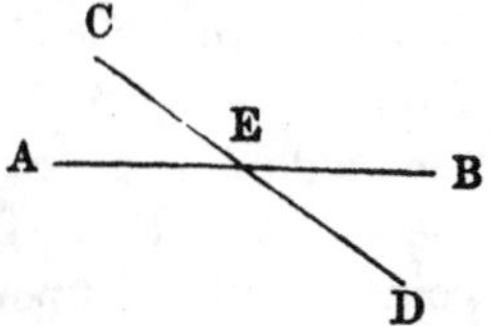

Let the two straight lines A B, C D intersect each other at the point E; then will the angle A E C be equal to the angle D E B, and the angle C E B to A E D.

For the angles A E C, C E B, which the straight line C E forms by meeting the straight line A B, are together equal to two right angles (Prop. I.); and the angles C E B, B E D, which the straight line B E forms by meeting the straight line C D, are equal to two right angles; hence the sum of the angles A E C, C E B is equal to the sum of the angles C E B, B E D (Art. 34, Ax. 1). Take away from each of these sums the common angle C E B, and there will remain the angle A E C, equal to its opposite angle, B E D (Art. 34, Ax. 3).

In the same manner it may be shown that the angle C E B is equal to its opposite angle, A E D.

50. *Cor.* 1. The four angles formed by two straight lines intersecting each other, are together equal to four right angles.

51. *Cor.* 2. All the successive angles, around a common point, formed by any number of straight lines meeting at that point, are together equal to four right angles.

PROPOSITION V.—THEOREM.

52. *If two triangles have two sides and the included angle in the one equal to two sides and the included angle in the other, each to each, the two triangles will be equal.*

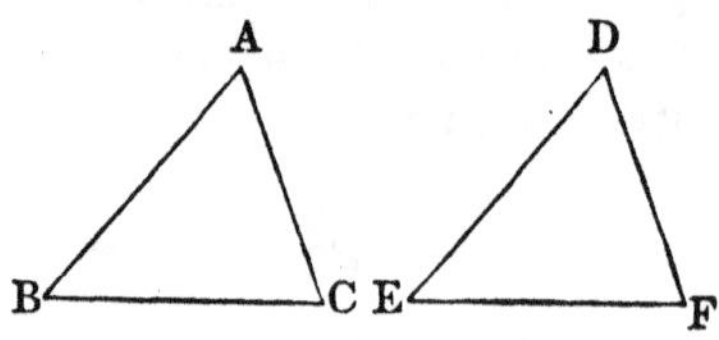

In the two triangles A B C, D E F, let the side A B be equal to the side D E, the side A C to the side D F, and the angle A to the angle D; then the triangles A B C, D E F will be equal.

Conceive the triangle A B C to be applied to the triangle D E F, so that the side A B shall fall upon its equal, D E, the point A upon D, and the point B upon E; then, since the angle A is equal to the angle D, the side A C will take the direction D F. But A C is equal to D F; therefore the point C will fall upon F, and the third side B C will coincide with the third side E F (Art. 34, Ax. 11). Hence the triangle A B C coincides with the triangle D E F, and they are therefore equal (Art. 34, Ax. 14).

53. *Cor.* When, in two triangles, these three parts are equal, namely, the side A B equal to D E, the side A C equal to D F, and the angle A equal to D, the other three corresponding parts are also equal, namely, the side B C equal to E F, the angle B equal to E, and the angle C equal to F.

PROPOSITION VI.—THEOREM.

54. *If two triangles have two angles and the included side in the one equal to two angles and the included side in the other, each to each, the two triangles will be equal.*

In the two triangles A B C, D E F, let the angle B be equal to the angle E, the angle C to the angle F, and the side B C to the side E F; then the triangles A B C, D E F will be equal.

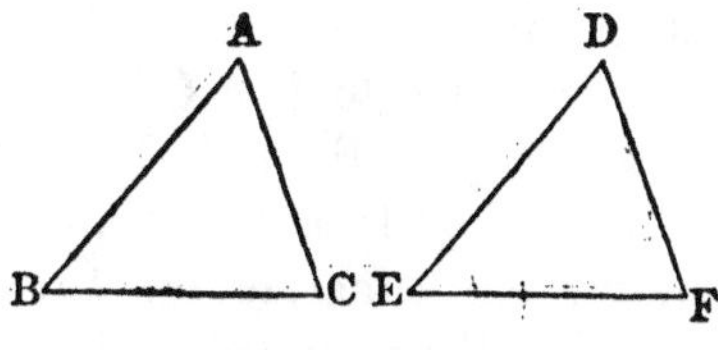

Conceive the triangle A B C to be applied to the triangle D E F, so that the side B C shall fall upon its equal, E F, the point B upon E, and the point C upon F. Then, since the angle B is equal to the angle E, the side B A will take the direction E D; therefore the point A will be found somewhere in the line E D. In like manner, since the angle C is equal to the angle F, the line C A will take the direction F D, and the point A will be found somewhere in the line F D. Hence the point A, falling at the same time in both of the straight lines E D and F D, must fall at their intersection, D. Hence the two triangles A B C, D E F coincide with each other, and are therefore equal (Art. 34, Ax. 14).

55. *Cor.* When, in two triangles, these three parts are equal, namely, the angle B equal to the angle E, the angle C equal to the angle F, and the side B C equal to the side E F, the other three corresponding parts are also equal; namely, the side B A equal to E D, the side C A equal to F D, and the angle A equal to the angle D.

PROPOSITION VII. — THEOREM.

56. *In an isosceles triangle, the angles opposite the equal sides are equal.*

Let A B C be an isosceles triangle, in which the side A B is equal to the side A C; then will the angle B be equal to the angle C.

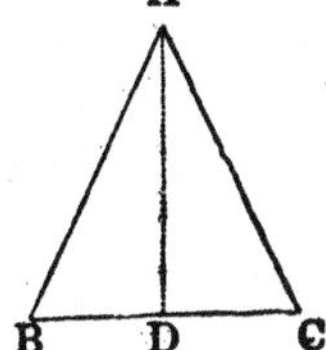

Conceive the angle B A C to be bisected, or divided into two equal parts, by the straight line A D, making the angle B A D equal to D A C. Then the two triangles B A D, C A D have the two sides A B, A D and the included angle in the one equal to the two sides A C, A D and the included angle in the other, each to each; hence the two triangles are equal, and the angle B is equal to the angle C (Prop. V.).

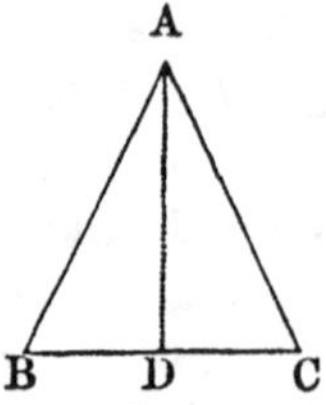

57. *Cor.* 1. The line bisecting the vertical angle of an isosceles triangle bisects the base at right angles.

58. *Cor.* 2. Conversely, the line bisecting the base of an isosceles triangle at right angles, bisects also the vertical angle.

59. *Cor.* 3. Every equilateral triangle is also equiangular.

PROPOSITION VIII. — THEOREM.

60. *If two angles of a triangle are equal, the opposite sides are also equal, and the triangle is isosceles.*

Let A B C be a triangle having the angle B equal to the angle C; then will the side A B be equal to the side A C.

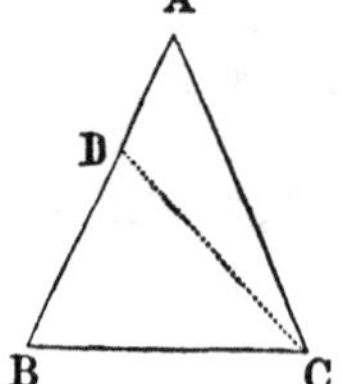

For, if the two sides are not equal, one of them must be greater than the other. Let A B be the greater; then take D B equal to A C the less, and draw C D. Now, in the two triangles D B C, A B C, we have D B equal to A C by construction, the side B C common, and the angle B equal to the angle A C B by hypothesis; therefore, since two sides and the included angle in the one are equal to two sides and the included angle in the other, each to each, the triangle D B C is equal to the triangle A B C (Prop. V.), a part to the whole, which is impossible (Art. 34, Ax. 8). Hence the sides A B and A C cannot be unequal; therefore the triangle A B C is isosceles.

61. *Cor.* Therefore every equiangular triangle is equilateral.

PROPOSITION IX. — THEOREM.

62. *Any side of a triangle is less than the sum of the other two.*

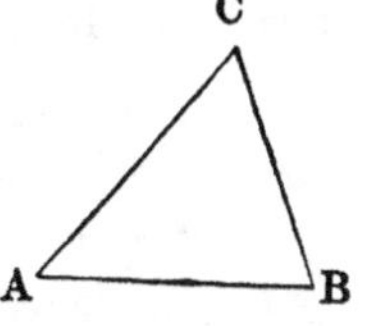

In the triangle A B C, any one side, as A B, is less than the sum of the other two sides, A C and C B.

For the straight line A B is the shortest line that can be drawn from the point A to the point B (Art. 34, Ax. 10); hence the side A B is less than the sum of the sides A C and C B.

In like manner it may be proved that the side A C is less than the sum of A B and B C, and the side B C less than the sum of B A and A C.

63. *Cor.* Since the side A B is less than the sum of A C and C B, if we take away from each of these two unequals the side C B, we shall have the difference between A B and C B less than A C; that is, *the difference between any two sides of a triangle is less than the other side.*

PROPOSITION X. — THEOREM.

64. *The greater side of any triangle is opposite the greater angle.*

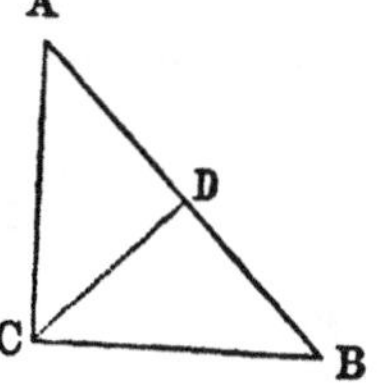

In the triangle C A B, let the angle C be greater than B; then will the side A B, opposite to C, be greater than A C, opposite to B.

Draw the straight line C D, making the angle B C D equal to B. Then, in the triangle B D C, we shall have the side B D equal to D C (Prop. VIII.). But the side A C is less than the sum of A D and D C (Prop. IX.), and the sum of A D and D C is equal to the sum of A D and D B, which is equal to A B; therefore the side A B is greater than A C.

65. *Cor.* 1. Therefore the shorter side is opposite to the less angle.

66. *Cor.* 2. In the right-angled triangle the hypothenuse is the longest side.

Proposition XI. — Theorem.

67. *The greater angle of any triangle is opposite the greater side.*

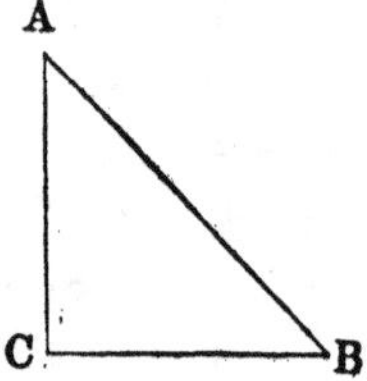

In the triangle C A B, suppose the side A B to be greater than A C; then will the angle C, opposite to A B, be greater than the angle B, opposite to A C.

For, if the angle C is not greater than B, it must either be equal to it or less. If the angle C were equal to B, then would the side A B be equal to the side A C (Prop. VIII.), which is contrary to the hypothesis; and if the angle C were less than B, then would the side A B be less than A C (Prop. X. Cor. 1), which is also contrary to the hypothesis. Hence, the angle C must be greater than B.

68. *Cor.* It follows, therefore, that the less angle is opposite to the shorter side.

Proposition XII. — Theorem.

69. *If, from any point within a triangle, two straight lines are drawn to the extremities of either side, their sum will be less than that of the other two sides of the triangle.*

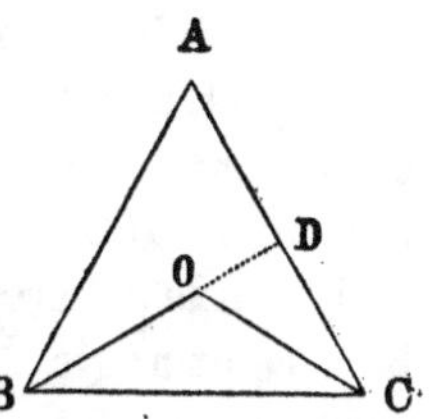

Let the two straight lines B O, C O be drawn from the point O, within the triangle A B C, to the extremities of the side B C; then will the sum of the two lines B O and O C be less than the sum of the sides B A and A C.

Let the straight line B O be produced till it meets the side A C in the point D; and because one side of a triangle is less than the sum of the other two sides (Prop. IX.), the side O C in the triangle C D O is less than the sum of O D and D C. To each of these inequalities add B O, and we have the sum of B O and O C less than the sum of B O, O D, and D C (Art. 34, Ax. 4); or the sum of B O and O C less than the sum of B D and D C. Again, because the side B D is less than the sum of B A and A D, by adding D C to each, we have the sum of B D and D C less than the sum of B A and A C. But it has been just shown that the sum of B O and O C is less than the sum of B D and D C; much more, then, is the sum of B O and O C less than B A and A C.

Proposition XIII. — Theorem.

70. *From a point without a straight line, only one perpendicular can be drawn to that line.*

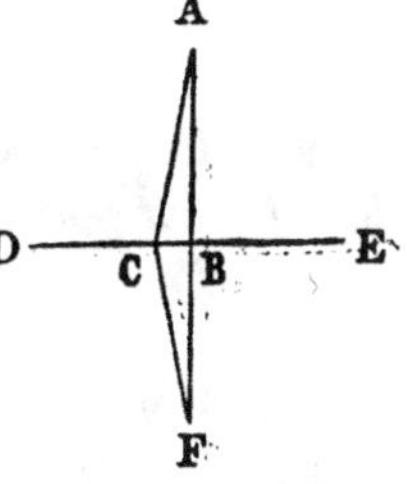

Let A be the point, and D E the given straight line; then from the point A only one perpendicular can be drawn to D E.

Let it be supposed that we can draw two perpendiculars, A B and A C. Produce one of them, as A B, till B F is equal to A B, and join F C. Then, in the triangles A B C and C B F, the angles C B A and C B F are both right angles (Prop. I. Cor. 1), the side C B is common to both, and the side B F is equal to the side A B ; hence the two triangles are equal, and the angle B C F is equal to the angle B C A (Prop. V.) But the angle B C A is, by hypothesis, a right angle ; therefore B C F must also be a right angle ; and if the two adjacent angles, B C A and B C F, are together equal to two right angles, the two lines A C and C F must form one and the same straight line (Prop. II.). Whence it follows, that between the same two points, A and F, two straight lines can be drawn, which is impossible (Art. 34, Ax. 11) ; hence no more than one perpendicular can be drawn from the same point to the same straight line.

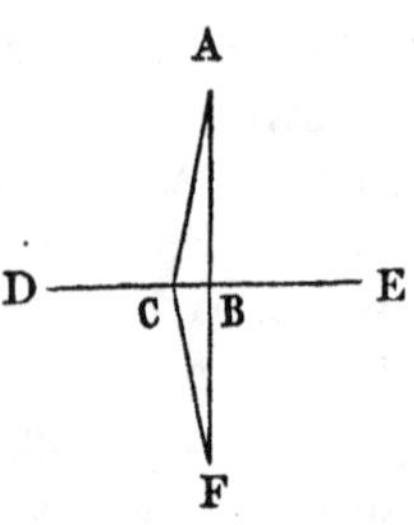

71. *Cor.* At the same point C, in the line A B, it is likewise impossible to erect more than one perpendicular to that line. For, if C D and C E were each perpendicular to A B, the angles B C D, B C E would be right angles ; hence the angle B C D would be equal to the angle B C E, a part to the whole, which is impossible.

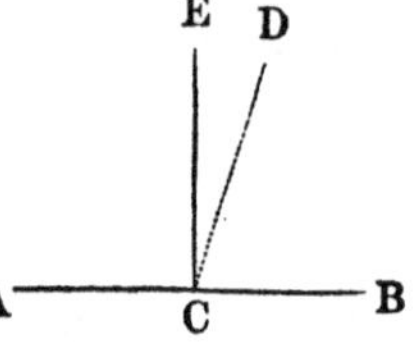

Proposition XIV. — Theorem.

72. *If, from a point without a straight line, a perpendicular be let fall on that line, and oblique lines be drawn to different points in the same line ;—*

1st. *The perpendicular will be shorter than any oblique line.*

2d. *Any two oblique lines, which meet the given line at equal distances from the perpendicular, will be equal.*

3d. *Of any two oblique lines, that which meets the given line at the greater distance from the perpendicular will be the longer.*

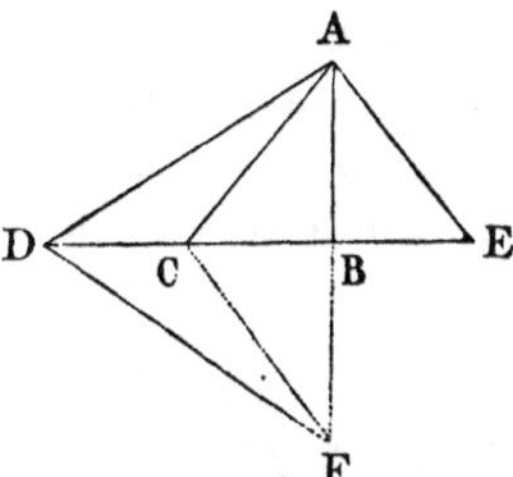

Let A be the given point, and D E the given straight line. Draw A B perpendicular to D E, and the oblique lines A E, A C, A D. Produce A B till B F is equal to A B, and join C F, D F.

First. The triangle B C F is equal to the triangle B C A, for they have the side C B common, the side A B equal to the side B F, and the angle A B C equal to the angle F B C, both being right angles (Prop. I. Cor. 1) ; hence the third sides, C F and A C, are equal (Prop. V. Cor.). But A B F, being a straight line, is shorter than A C F, which is a broken line (Art. 34, Ax. 10) ; therefore A B, the half of A B F, is shorter than A C, the half of A C F ; hence the perpendicular is shorter than any oblique line.

Secondly. If B E is equal to B C, then, since A B is common to the triangles, A B E, A B C, and the angles A B E, A B C are right angles, the two triangles are equal (Prop. V.), and the side A E is equal to the side A C (Prop. V. Cor.). Hence the two oblique lines, meeting the given line at equal distances from the perpendicular, are equal.

Thirdly. The point C being in the triangle A D F, the sum of the lines A C, C F is less than the sum of the sides A D, D F (Prop. XII.) But A C has been shown to be equal to C F ; and in like manner it may be shown that A D is equal to D F. Therefore A C, the half of the line A C F, is shorter than A D, the half of the line A D F ; hence the oblique line which meets the given line the greater distance from the perpendicular, is the longer.

73. *Cor.* 1. The perpendicular measures the shortest distance of any point from a straight line.

74. *Cor.* 2. From the same point to a given straight line only two equal straight lines can be drawn.

75. *Cor.* 3. Of any two straight lines drawn from a point to a straight line, that which is not shorter than the other will be longer than any straight line that can be drawn between them, from the same point to the same line.

PROPOSITION XV.—THEOREM.

76. *If from the middle point of a straight line a perpendicular to this line be drawn,—*

1st. *Any point in the perpendicular will be equally distant from the extremities of the line.*

2d. *Any point out of the perpendicular will be unequally distant from those extremities.*

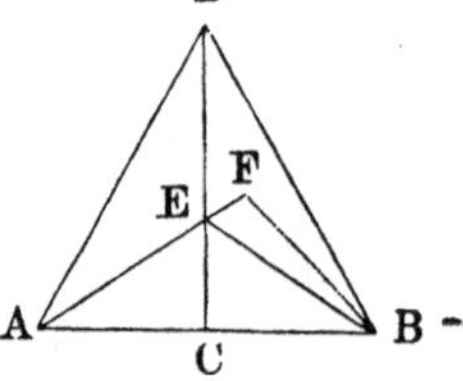

Let D C be drawn perpendicular to the straight line A B, from its middle point C.

First. Let D and E be points, taken at pleasure, in the perpendicular, and join D A, D B, and also A E, E B. Then, since A C is equal to C B, the two oblique lines D A, D B meet points which are at the same distance from the perpendicular, and are therefore equal (Prop. XIV.). So, likewise, the two oblique lines E A, E B are equal; therefore any point in the perpendicular is equally distant from the extremities A and B.

Secondly. Let F be any point out of the perpendicular, and join F A, F B. Then one of those lines must cut the perpendicular, in some point, as E. Join E B; then we have E B equal to E A. But in the triangle F E B, the side F B is less than the sum of the sides E F, E B (Prop. IX.), and since the sum of F E, E B is equal to the sum of F E, E A, which is equal to F A, F B is less than F A. Hence any point out of the perpendicular is at unequal distances from the extremities A and B.

77. *Cor.* If a straight line have two points, of which each is equally distant from the extremities of another

straight line, it will be perpendicular to that line at its middle point.

PROPOSITION XVI. — THEOREM.

78. *If two triangles have two sides of the one equal to two sides of the other, each to each, and the included angle of the one greater than the included angle of the other, the third side of that which has the greater angle will be greater than the third side of the other.*

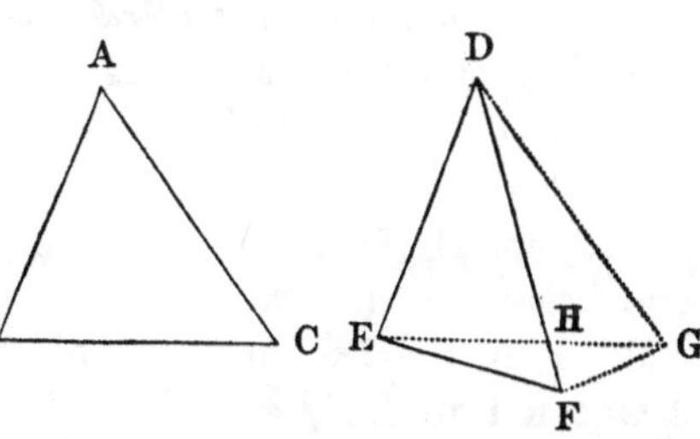

Let A B C, D E F be two triangles, having the side A B equal to D E, and A C equal to D F, and the angle A greater than D; then will the side B C be greater than E F.

Of the two sides D E, D F, let D F be the side which is not shorter than the other; make the angle E D G equal to B A C; and make D G equal to A C or D F, and join E G, G F.

Since D F, or its equal D G, is not shorter than D E, it is longer than D H (Prop. XIV. Cor. 3); therefore its extremity, F, must fall below the line E G. The two triangles, A B C and D E G, have the two sides A B, A C equal to the two sides D E, D G, each to each, and the included angle B A C of the one equal to the included angle E D G of the other; hence the side B C is equal to E G (Prop. V. Cor.).

In the triangle D F G, since D G is equal to D F, the angle D F G is equal to the angle D G F (Prop. VII.); but the angle D G F is greater than the angle E G F; therefore the angle D F G is greater than E G F, and much more is the angle E F G greater than the angle

E G F. Because the angle E F G in the triangle E F G is greater than E G F, and because the greater side is opposite the greater angle (Prop. X.), the side E G is greater than E F; and E G has been shown to be equal to B C; hence B C is greater than E F.

PROPOSITION XVII.—THEOREM.

79. *If two triangles have two sides of the one equal to two sides of the other, each to each, but the third side of the one greater than the third side of the other, the angle contained by the sides of that which has the greater third side will be greater than the angle contained by the sides of the other.*

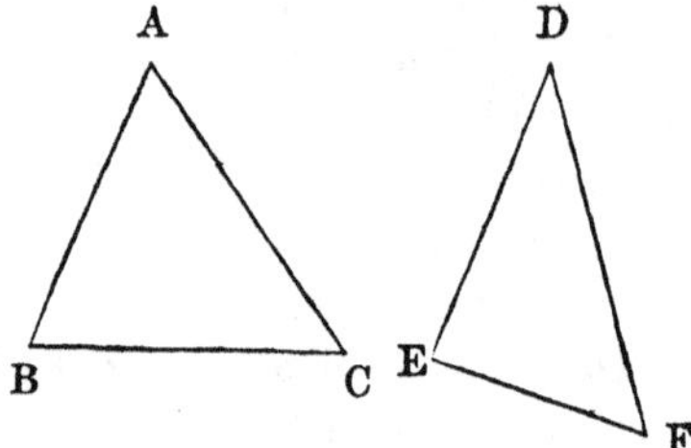

Let A B C, D E F be two triangles, the side A B equal to D E, and A C equal to D F, and the side C B greater than E F, then will the angle A be greater than D.

For, if it be not greater, it must either be equal to it or less. But the angle A cannot be equal to D, for then the side B C would be equal to E F (Prop. V. Cor.), which is contrary to the hypothesis; neither can it be less, for then the side B C would be less than E F (Prop. XVI.), which also is contrary to the hypothesis; therefore the angle A is not less than the angle D, and it has been shown that is not equal to it; hence the angle A must be greater than the angle D.

PROPOSITION XVIII.—THEOREM.

80. *If two triangles have the three sides of the one equal to the three sides of the other, each to each, the triangles themselves will be equal.*

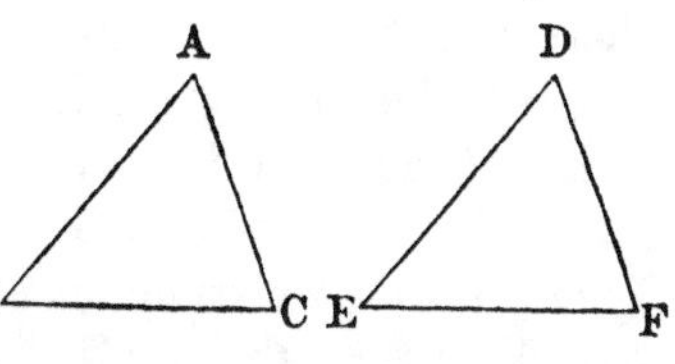

Let the triangles A B C, D E F have the side A B equal to D E, A C to D F, and B C to E F; then will the angle A be equal to D, the angle B to the angle E, and the angle C to the angle F, and the two triangles will also be equal.

For, if the angle A were greater than the angle D, since the sides A B, A C are equal to the sides D E, D F, each to each, the side B C would be greater than E F (Prop. XVI.); and if the angle A were less than D, it would follow that the side B C would be less than E F. But by hypothesis B C is equal to E F; hence the angle A can neither be greater nor less than D; therefore it must be equal to it. In the same manner, it may be shown that the angle B is equal to E, and the angle C to F; hence the two triangles must be equal.

81. *Scholium.* In two triangles equal to each other, the equal angles are opposite the equal sides; thus the equal angles A and D are opposite the equal sides B C and E F.

Proposition XIX. — Theorem.

82. *If two right-angled triangles have the hypothenuse and a side of the one equal to the hypothenuse and a side of the other, each to each, the triangles are equal.*

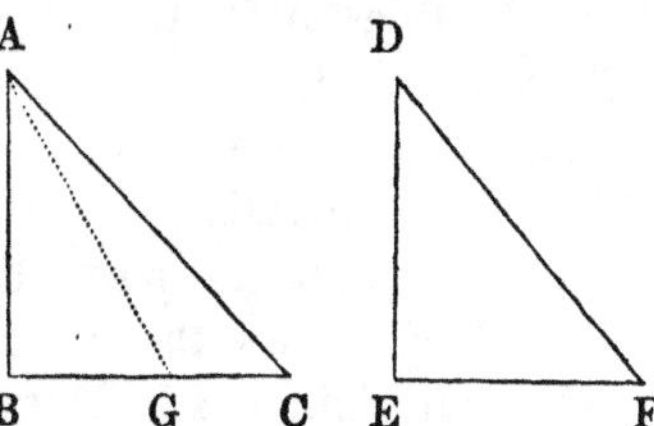

Let the two right-angled triangles ABC, DEF, have the hypothenuse A C equal to D F, and the side A B equal to D E; then will the triangle A B C be equal to the triangle D E F.

The two triangles are evidently equal, if the sides B C and E F are equal (Prop. XVIII.). If it be possible, let these sides be unequal, and let B C be the greater. Take B G equal to E F, the less side, and join A G. Then, in the two triangles A B G, D E F, the angles B and E are equal, both being right angles, the side A B is equal to D E by hypothesis, and the side B G to E F by construction; hence these triangles are equal (Prop. V.); and therefore A G is equal to D F. But by hypothesis D F is equal to A C, and therefore A G is equal to A C. But the oblique line A C cannot be equal to A G, which meets the same straight line nearer the perpendicular A B (Prop. XIV.); therefore B C and E F cannot be unequal, hence they must be equal; therefore the triangles A B C and D E F are equal.

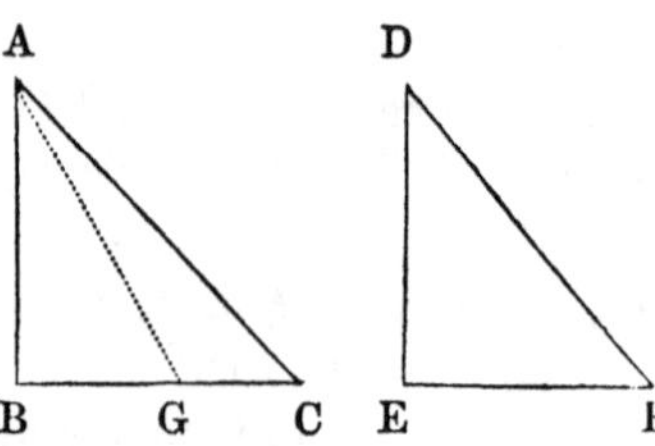

PROPOSITION XX. — THEOREM.

83. *If a straight line, intersecting two other straight lines, makes the alternate angles equal, the two lines are parallel.*

Let the straight line E F intersect the two straight lines A B, C D, making the alternate angles B G H, C H G equal; then the lines A B, C D will be parallel.

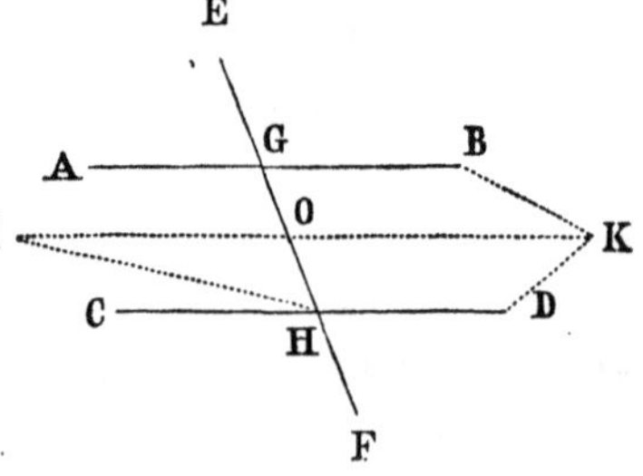

For, if the lines A B, C D are not parallel, let them meet in some point K, and through O, the middle point of G H, draw the straight line I K, making I O equal to O K, and join H I. Then the opposite angles K O G, I O H, formed by the intersection of the two straight lines I K, G H, are equal (Prop. IV.); and the triangles K O G,

I O H have the two sides K O, O G and the included angle in the one equal to the two sides I O, O H and the included angle in the other, each to each; hence the angle K G O is equal to the angle I H O (Prop. V. Cor.). But, by hypothesis, the angle K G O is equal to the angle C H O, therefore the angle I H O is equal to C H O, so that H I and H C must coincide; that is, the line C D when produced meets I K in two points, I, K, and yet does not form one and the same straight line, which is impossible (Prop. III.); therefore the lines A B, C D cannot meet, consequently they are parallel (Art. 17).

NOTE. — The demonstration of the proposition is substantially that given by M. da Cunha in the *Principes Mathématiques*. This demonstration Young pronounces "superior to every other that has been given of the same proposition"; and Professor Playfair, in the *Edinburgh Review*, Vol. XX., calls attention to it, as a most important improvement in elementary Geometry.

PROPOSITION XXI. — THEOREM.

84. *If a straight line, intersecting two other straight lines, makes any exterior angle equal to the interior and opposite angle, or makes the interior angles on the same side together equal to two right angles, the two lines are parallel.*

Let the straight line E F intersect the two straight lines A B, C D, making the exterior angle E G B equal to the interior and opposite angle, G H D; then the lines A B, C D are parallel.

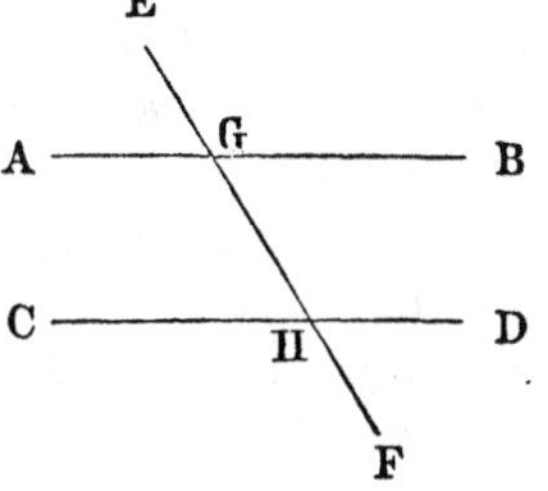

For the angle A G H is equal to the angle E G B (Prop. IV.); and E G B is equal to G H D, by hypothesis; therefore the angle A G H is equal to the angle G H D; and they are alternate angles; hence the lines A B, C D are parallel (Prop. XX.).

Again, let the interior angles on the same side, B G H, G H D, be together equal to two right angles; then the lines A B, C D are parallel.

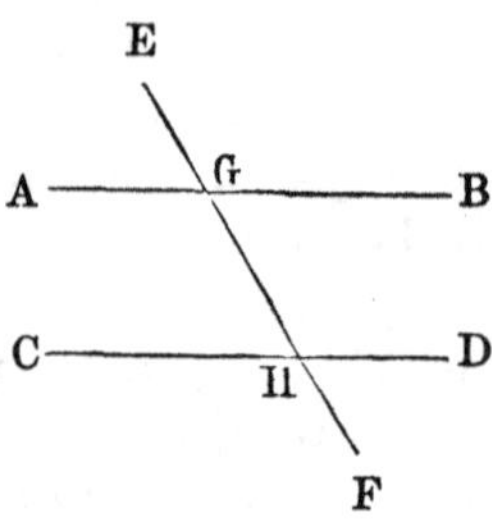

For the sum of the angles B G H, G H D is equal to two right angles, by hypothesis; and the sum of A G H, B G H is also equal to two right angles (Prop. I.); take away B G H, which is common to both, and there remains the angle G H D, equal to the angle A G H; and these are alternate angles; hence the lines A B, C D are parallel.

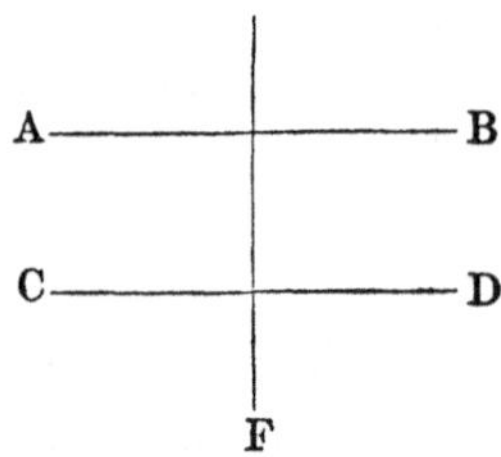

85. *Cor.* If two straight lines are perpendicular to another, they are parallel; thus A B, C D, perpendicular to E F, are parallel.

PROPOSITION XXII.—THEOREM.

86. *If a straight line intersects two parallel lines, it makes the alternate angles equal; also any exterior angle equal to the interior and opposite angle; and the two interior angles upon the same side together equal to two right angles.*

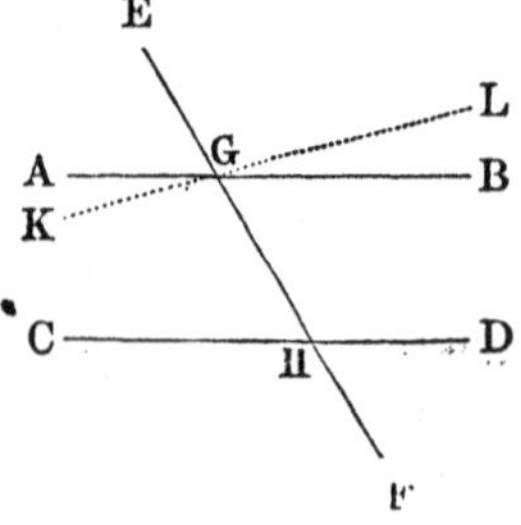

Let the straight line E F intersect the parallel lines A B, C D; the alternate angles A G H, G H D are equal; the exterior angle E G B is equal to the interior and opposite angle G H D; and the two interior angles B G H, G H D upon the same side are together equal to two right angles.

For if the angle A G H is not equal to G H D, draw the straight line K L through the point G, making the angle K G H equal to G H D; then, since the alternate angles G H D, K G H are equal, K L is parallel to C D (Prop. XX.); but by hypothesis A B is also parallel to C D, so that through the same point, G, two straight lines are drawn parallel to C D, which is impossible (Art. 34, Ax. 12). Hence the angles A G H, G H D are not unequal; that is, they are equal.

Now, the angle E G B is equal to the angle A G H (Prop. IV.), and A G H has been shown to be equal to G H D; hence E G B is also equal to G H D.

Again, add to each of these equals the angle B G H; then the sum of the angles E G B, B G H is equal to the sum of the angles B G H, G H D. But E G B, B G H are equal to two right angles (Prop. I.); hence B G H, G H D are also equal to two right angles.

87. *Cor.* If a line is perpendicular to one of two parallel lines, it is perpendicular to the other; thus E F (Art. 85), perpendicular to A B, is perpendicular to C D.

Proposition XXIII. — Theorem.

88. *If two straight lines intersect a third line, and make the two interior angles on the same side together less than two right angles, the two lines will meet on being produced.*

Let the two lines K L, C D make with E F the angles K G H, G H C, together less than two right angles; then K L and C D will meet on being produced.

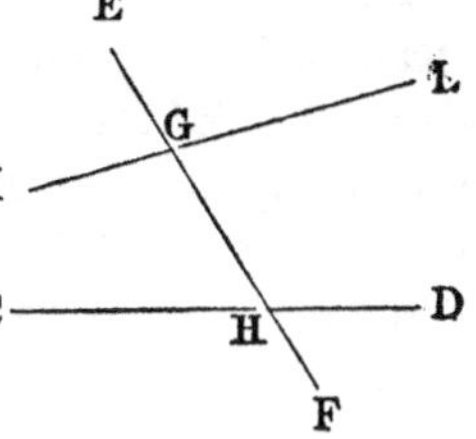

For if they do not meet, they are parallel (Art. 17). But they are not parallel; for then the sum of the interior angles K G H, G H C would be equal to two right angles (Prop. XXII.); but by hypothesis it is less; therefore the lines K L, C D will meet on being produced.

89. *Scholium.* The two lines K L, C D, on being produced, must meet on the side of E F, on which are the two interior angles whose sum is less than two right angles.

PROPOSITION XXIV. — THEOREM.

90. *Straight lines which are parallel to the same line are parallel to each other.*

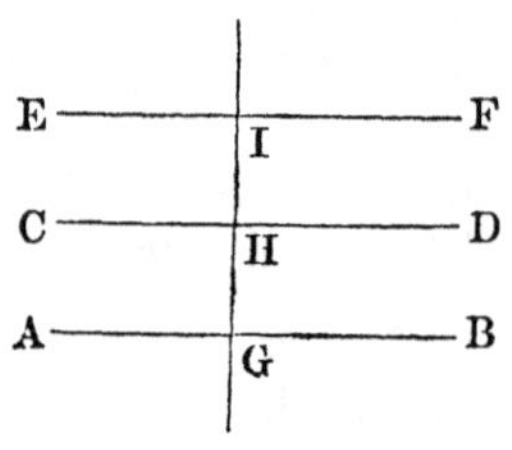

Let the straight lines A B, C D be each parallel to the line E F; then are they parallel to each other.

Draw G H I perpendicular to E F. Then, since A B is parallel to E F, G I will be perpendicular to A B (Prop. XXII. Cor.); and since C D is parallel to E F, G I will for a like reason be perpendicular to C D. Consequently A B and C D are perpendicular to the same straight line; hence they are parallel (Prop. XXI. Cor.).

PROPOSITION XXV. — THEOREM.

91. *Two parallel straight lines are everywhere equally distant from each other.*

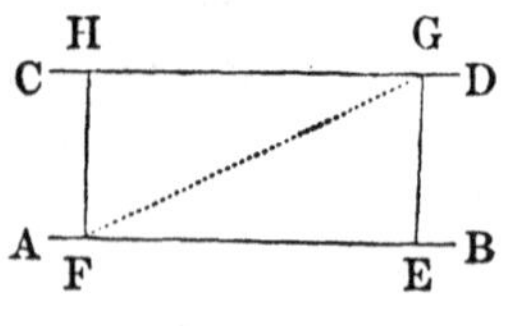

Let A B, C D be two parallel straight lines. Through any two points in A B, as E and F, draw the straight lines E G, F H, perpendicular to A B. These lines will be equal to each other.

For, if G F be joined, the angles G F E, F G H, considered in reference to the parallels A B, C D, will be alternate interior angles, and therefore equal to each other (Prop. XXII.). Also, since the straight lines E G, F H are perpendicular to the same straight line A B, and consequently parallel (Prop. XXI. Cor.), the angles E G F, G F H, considered in reference to the parallels E G, F H, will be alternate interior angles, and therefore equal. Hence, the two triangles E F G, F G H, have a side and the two adjacent angles of the one equal to a side and the two adjacent angles of the other, each to each; therefore these triangles are equal (Prop. VI.); hence the side E G, which measures the distance of the parallels A B, C D, at the point E, is equal to the side F H, which measures the distance of the same parallels at the point F. Hence two parallels are everywhere equally distant.

Proposition XXVI. — Theorem.

92. *If two angles have their sides parallel, each to each, and lying in the same direction, the two angles are equal.*

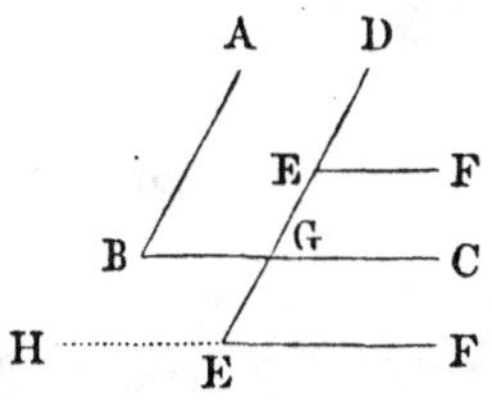

Let A B C, D E F be two angles, which have the side A B parallel to D E, and B C parallel to E F; then these angles are equal.

For produce D E, if necessary, till it meets B C in the point G. Then, since E F is parallel to G C, the angle D E F is equal to D G C (Prop. XXII.); and since D G is parallel to A B, the angle D G C is equal to A B C; hence the angle D E F is equal to A B C.

93. *Scholium.* This proposition is restricted to the case where the side E F lies in the same direction with B C, since if F E were produced toward H, the angles D E H, A B C would only be equal when they are right angles.

Proposition XXVII. — Theorem.

94. *If any side of a triangle be produced, the exterior angle is equal to the sum of the two interior and opposite angles.*

Let A B C be a triangle, and let one of its sides, B C be produced towards D; then the exterior angle A C D is equal to the two interior and opposite angles, C A B, A B C.

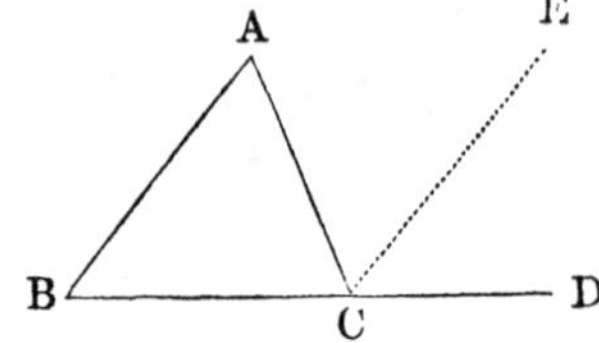

For, draw E C parallel to the side A B; then, since A C meets the two parallels A B, E C, the alternate angles B A C, A C E are equal (Prop. XXII.).

Again, since B D meets the two parallels A B, E C, the exterior angle E C D is equal to the interior and opposite angle A B C. But the angle A C E is equal to B A C; therefore, the whole exterior angle A C D is equal to the two interior and opposite angles C A B, A B C (Art. 34, Ax. 2).

Proposition XXVIII. — Theorem.

95. *In every triangle the sum of the three angles is equal to two right angles.*

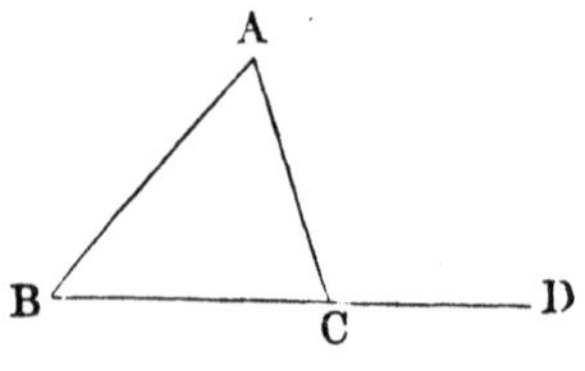

Let A B C be any triangle; then will the sum of the angles A B C, B C A, C A B be equal to two right angles.

For, let the side B C be produced towards D, making the exterior angle A C D; then the angle A C D is equal to C A B and A B C (Prop. XXVII.). To each of these equals add the angle A C B, and we shall have the sum of

A C B and A C D, equal to the sum of A B C, B C A, and C A B. But the sum of A C B and A C D is equal to two right angles (Prop. I.); hence the sum of the three angles A B C, B C A, and C A B is equal to two right angles (Art. 34, Ax. 2).

96. *Cor.* 1. Two angles of a triangle being given, or merely their sum, the third will be found by subtracting that sum from two right angles.

97. *Cor.* 2. If two angles in one triangle be respectively equal to two angles in another, their third angles will also be equal.

98. *Cor.* 3. A triangle cannot have more than one angle as great as a right angle.

99. *Cor.* 4. And, therefore, every triangle must have at least two acute angles.

100. *Cor.* 5. In a right-angled triangle the right angle is equal to the sum of the other two angles.

101. *Cor.* 6. Since every equilateral triangle is also equiangular (Prop. VII. Cor. 3), each of its angles will be equal to two thirds of one right angle.

Proposition XXIX. — Theorem.

102. *The sum of all the interior angles of any polygon is equal to twice as many right angles, less four, as the figure has sides.*

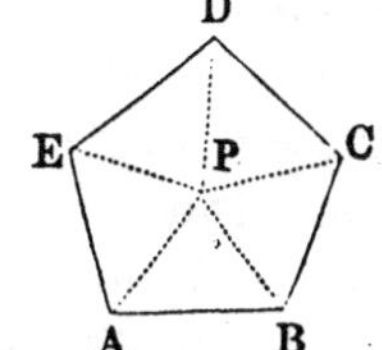

Let A B C D E be any polygon; then the sum of all its interior angles, A, B, C, D, E, is equal to twice as many right angles as the figure has sides, less four right angles.

For, from any point P within the polygon, draw the straight lines P A, P B, P C, P D, P E, to the vertices of all the angles, and the polygon will be divided into as many triangles as it has sides. Now, the sum of the three angles in each of these triangles is equal to two right angles (Prop. XXVIII.); therefore the sum of the angles of all these triangles is equal to twice as many right angles as there are triangles, or sides, to the polygon. But the sum of all the angles about the point P is equal to four right angles (Prop. IV. Cor. 2), which sum forms no part of the interior angles of the polygon; therefore, deducting the sum of the angles about the point, there remain the angles of the polygon equal to twice as many right angles as the figure has sides, less four right angles.

103. *Cor.* 1. The sum of the angles in a *quadrilateral* is equal to four right angles; hence, if all the angles of a quadrilateral are equal, each of them is a right angle; also, if three of the angles are right angles, the fourth is likewise a right angle.

104. *Cor.* 2. The sum of the angles in a *pentagon* is equal to six right angles; in a *hexagon*, the sum is equal to eight right angles, &c.

105. *Cor.* 3. In every *equiangular* figure of more than four sides, each angle is greater than a right angle; thus, in a *regular pentagon*, each angle is equal to one and one fifth right angles; in a *regular hexagon*, to one and one third right angles, &c.

106. *Scholium.* In applying this proposition to polygons which have *re-entrant* angles, or angles whose vertices are directed inward, as B P C, each of these angles must be considered greater than two right angles. But, in order to avoid ambiguity, we shall hereafter limit our reasoning to polygons with *salient* angles, or with angles directed outwards, and which may be called *convex* polygons. Every convex polygon is such that a

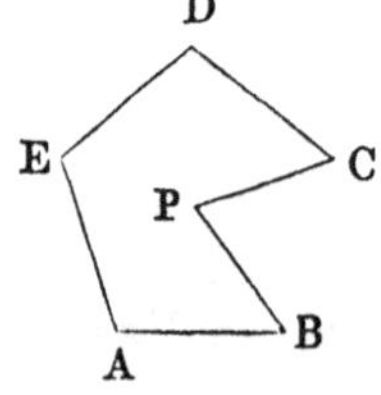

straight line, however drawn, cannot meet the perimeter of the polygon in more than two points.

PROPOSITION XXX. — THEOREM.

107. *The sum of all the exterior angles of any polygon, formed by producing each side in the same direction, is equal to four right angles.*

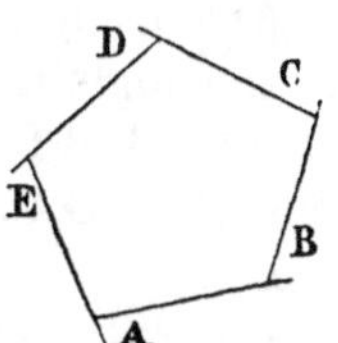

Let each side of the polygon ABCDE be produced in the same direction; then the sum of the exterior angles A, B, C, D, E, will be equal to four right angles.

For each interior angle, together with its adjacent exterior angle, is equal to two right angles (Prop. I.); hence the sum of all the angles, both interior and exterior, is equal to twice as many right angles as there are sides to the polygon. But the sum of the interior angles alone, less four right angles, is equal to the same sum (Prop. XXIX.); therefore the sum of the exterior angles is equal to four right angles.

PROPOSITION XXXI. — THEOREM.

108. *The opposite sides and angles of every parallelogram are equal to each other.*

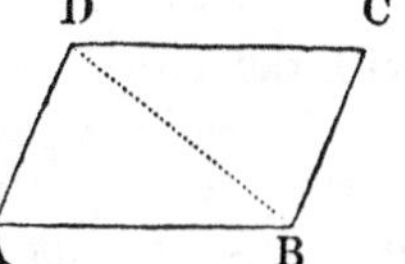

Let ABCD be a parallelogram; then the opposite sides and angles are equal to each other.

Draw the diagonal BD, then, since the opposite sides AB, DC are parallel, and BD meets them, the alternate angles ABD, BDC are equal (Prop. XXII.); and since AD, BC are parallel, and BD meets them, the alternate angles ADB, DBC are likewise equal. Hence, the two triangles ADB, DBC have two angles, ABD, ADB, in the one, equal to two angles, BDC, DBC, in the other, each to each; and since

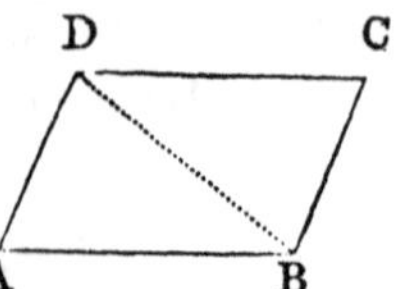

the side BD included between these equal angles is common to the two triangles, they are equal (Prop. VI.); hence the side AB opposite the angle ADB is equal to the side DC opposite the angle DBC (Prop. VI. Cor.); and, in like manner, the side AD is equal to the side BC; hence the opposite sides of a parallelogram are equal.

Again, since the triangles are equal, the angle A is equal to the angle C (Prop. VI. Cor.); and since the two angles DBC, ABD are respectively equal to the two angles ADB, BDC, the angle ABC is equal to the angle ADC.

109. *Cor.* 1. The diagonal divides a parallelogram into two equal triangles.

110. *Cor.* 2. The two parallels AD, BC, included between two other parallels, AB, CD, are equal.

Proposition XXXII.—Theorem.

111. *If the opposite sides of a quadrilateral are equal, each to each, the equal sides are parallel, and the figure is a parallelogram.*

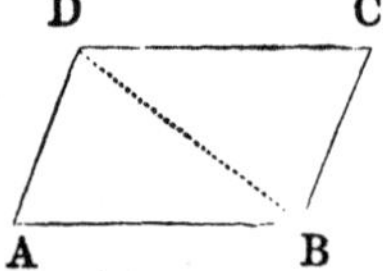

Let ABCD be a quadrilateral having its opposite sides equal; then will the equal sides be parallel, and the figure be a parallelogram.

For, having drawn the diagonal BD, the triangles ABD, BDC have all the sides of the one equal to the corresponding sides of the other; therefore they are equal, and the angle ADB opposite the side AB is equal to DBC opposite CD (Prop. XVIII. Sch.); hence the side AD is parallel to BC (Prop. XX.). For a like reason, AB is parallel to CD; therefore the quadrilateral ABCD is a parallelogram.

PROPOSITION XXXIII. — THEOREM.

112. *If two opposite sides of a quadrilateral are equal and parallel, the other sides are also equal and parallel, and the figure is a parallelogram.*

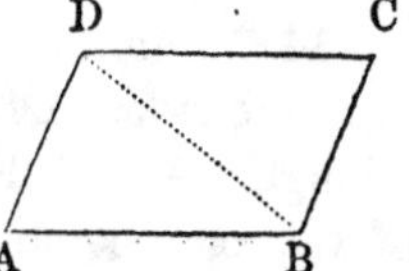

Let A B C D be a quadrilateral, having the sides A B, C D equal and parallel; then will the other sides also be equal and parallel.

Draw the diagonal B D; then, since A B is parallel to C D, and B D meets them, the alternate angles A B D, B D C are equal (Prop. XXII.); moreover, in the two triangles A B D, D B C, the side B D is common; therefore, two sides and the included angle in the one are equal to two sides and the included angle in the other, each to each; hence these triangles are equal (Prop. V.), and the side A D is equal to B C. Hence the angle A D B is equal to D B C, and consequently A D is parallel to B C (Prop. XX.); therefore the figure A B C D is a parallelogram.

PROPOSITION XXXIV. — THEOREM.

113. *The diagonals of every parallelogram bisect each other.*

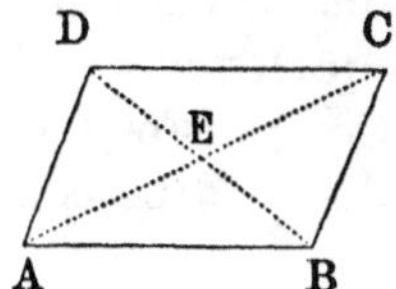

Let A B C D be a parallelogram, and A C, D B its diagonals, intersecting at E; then will A E equal E C, and B E equal E D.

For, since A B, C D are parallel, and B D meets them, the alternate angles C D E, A B E are equal (Prop. XXII.); and since A C meets the same parallels, the alternate angles B A E, E C D are also equal; and the sides A B, C D are equal (Prop. XXXI.). Hence the triangles A B E, C D E have two angles and the included side in the one equal to two angles and the included side in the other, each to each; hence the two triangles are equal (Prop. VI.); therefore the side A E opposite the angle A B E is equal to C E opposite C D E; hence, also, the sides B E, D E opposite the other equal angles are equal.

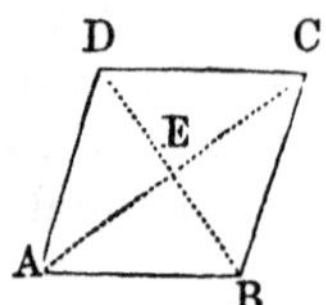

114. *Scholium.* In the case of a rhombus, the sides A B, B C being equal, the triangles A E B, E B C have all the sides of the one equal to the corresponding sides of the other, and are, therefore, equal; whence it follows that the angles A E B, B E C are equal. Therefore the diagonals of a rhombus bisect each other at right angles.

Proposition XXXV. — Theorem.

115. *If the diagonals of a quadrilateral bisect each other, the figure is a parallelogram.*

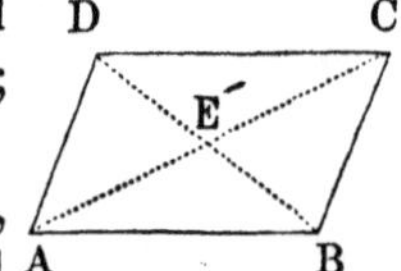

Let A B C D be a quadrilateral, and A C, D B its diagonals intersecting at E; then will the figure be a parallelogram.

For, in the two triangles ABE, CDE, the two sides A E, E B and the included angle in the one are equal to the two sides C E, E D and the included angle in the other; hence the triangles are equal, and the side AB is equal to the side CD (Prop. V. Cor.). For a like reason, A D is equal to C B; therefore the quadrilateral is a parallelogram (Prop. XXXII.).

BOOK II.

RATIO AND PROPORTION.

DEFINITIONS.

116. RATIO is the relation, in respect to quantity, which one magnitude bears to another of the same kind; and is the quotient arising from dividing the first by the second.

A ratio may be written in the form of a fraction, or with the sign : .

Thus the ratio of A to B may be expressed either by $\frac{A}{B}$, or by A : B.

117. The two magnitudes necessary to form a ratio are called the TERMS of the ratio. The first term is called the ANTECEDENT, and the last, the CONSEQUENT.

118. Ratios of magnitudes may be expressed by numbers, either exactly, or approximately.

This may be illustrated by the operation of finding the numerical ratio of two straight lines, A B, C D.

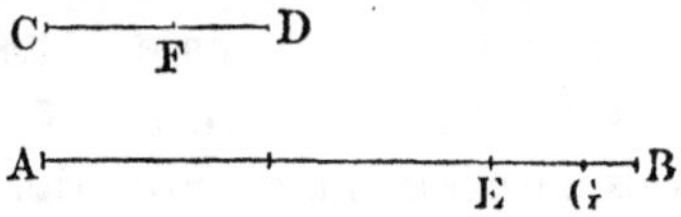

C—F—D

A——E—G—B

From the greater line A B cut off a part equal to the less C D, as many times as possible; for example, twice, with the remainder B E.

From the line C D cut off a part equal to the remainder B E as many times as possible; once, for example, with the remainder D F.

From the first remainder B E, cut off a part equal to the second D F, as many times as possible; once, for example, with the remainder B G.

From the second remainder D F, cut off a part equal to B G, the third, as many times as possible.

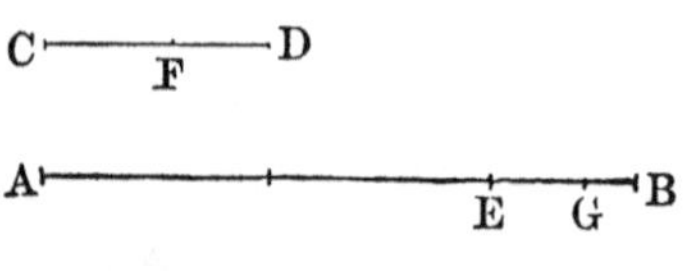

Proceed thus till a remainder arises, which is exactly contained a certain number of times in the preceding one.

Then this last remainder will be the common measure of the proposed lines; and, regarding it as unity, we shall easily find the values of the preceding remainders; and, at last, those of the two proposed lines, and hence their ratio in numbers.

Suppose, for instance, we find G B to be contained exactly twice in F D; B G will be the common measure of the two proposed lines. Let B G equal 1; then will F D equal 2. But E B contains F D once, plus G B; therefore we have E B equal to 3. C D contains E B once, plus F D; therefore we have C D equal to 5. A B contains C D twice, plus E B; therefore we have A B equal to 13. Hence the ratio of the two lines is that of 13 to 5. If the line C D were taken for unity, the line A B would be $\frac{13}{5}$; if A B were taken for unity, C D would be $\frac{5}{13}$.

It is possible that, however far the operation be continued, no remainder may be found which shall be contained an exact number of times in the preceding one. In that case there can be obtained only an approximate ratio, expressed in numbers, more or less exact, according as the operation is more or less extended.

119. When the greater of two magnitudes contains the less a certain number of times without having a remainder, it is called a MULTIPLE of the less; and the less is then called a SUBMULTIPLE, or measure of the greater.

Thus, 6 is a multiple of 2; 2 and 3 are submultiples, or measures, of 6.

120. EQUIMULTIPLES, or LIKE MULTIPLES, are those which contain their respective submultiples the same number of

times; and EQUISUBMULTIPLES, or LIKE SUBMULTIPLES, are those contained in their respective multiples the same number of times.

Thus 4 and 5 are like submultiples of 8 and 10; 8 and 10 are like multiples of 4 and 5.

121. COMMENSURABLE magnitudes are magnitudes of the same kind, which have a common measure, and whose ratio therefore may be exactly expressed in numbers.

122. INCOMMENSURABLE magnitudes are magnitudes of the same kind, which have no common measure, and whose ratio, therefore, cannot be exactly expressed in numbers.

123. A DIRECT ratio is the quotient of the antecedent by the consequent; an INVERSE ratio, or RECIPROCAL ratio, is the quotient of the consequent by the antecedent, or the reciprocal of the direct ratio.

Thus the direct ratio of a line 6 feet long to a line 2 feet long is $\frac{6}{2}$ or 3; and the inverse ratio of a line 6 feet long to a line 2 feet long is $\frac{2}{6}$ or $\frac{1}{3}$, which is the same as the reciprocal of 3, the direct ratio of 6 to 2.

The word *ratio* when used alone means the direct ratio.

124. A COMPOUND ratio is the product of two or more ratios.

Thus the ratio compounded of A : B and C : D is $\frac{A}{B} \times \frac{C}{D}$, or $\frac{A \times C}{B \times D}$.

125. A PROPORTION is an equality of ratios.

Four magnitudes are in proportion, when the ratio of the *first* to the *second* is the same as that of the *third* to the *fourth*.

Thus, the ratios of A : B and X : Y, being equal to each other, when written A : B = X : Y, or $\frac{A}{B} = \frac{X}{Y}$, form a proportion.

126. Proportion is written not only with the sign =, but, more often, with the sign :: between the ratios.

Thus, A : B :: X : Y, expresses a proportion, and is read, The ratio of A to B is equal to the ratio of X to Y; or, A is to B as X is to Y.

127. The *first* and *third* terms of a proportion are called the ANTECEDENTS; the *second* and *fourth*, the CONSEQUENTS. The *first* and *fourth* are also called the EXTREMES, and the *second* and *third* the MEANS.

Thus, in the proportion A : B :: C : D, A and C are the antecedents; B and D are the consequents; A and D are the extremes; and B and C are the means.

The antecedents are called *homologous* or *like* terms, and so also are the consequents.

128. All the terms of a proportion are called PROPORTIONALS; and the last term is called a FOURTH PROPORTIONAL to the other three taken in their order.

Thus, in the proportion A : B :: C : D, D is the fourth proportional to A, B, and C.

129. When both the means are the same magnitude, either of them is called a MEAN PROPORTIONAL between the extremes; and if, in a series of proportional magnitudes, each consequent is the same as the next antecedent, those magnitudes are said to be in CONTINUED PROPORTION.

Thus, if we have A : B :: B : C :: C : D :: D : E, B is a mean proportional between A and C, C between B and D, D between C and E; and the magnitudes A, B, C, D, E are said to be in continued proportion.

130. When a continued proportion consists of but three terms, the middle term is said to be a MEAN PROPORTIONAL between the other two; and the last term is said to be the THIRD PROPORTIONAL to the first and second.

Thus, when A, B, and C are in proportion, A : B :: B : C; in which case B is called a mean proportional between A and C; and C is called the third proportional to A and B.

131. Magnitudes are in proportion by INVERSION, or INVERSELY, when each antecedent takes the place of its consequent, and each consequent the place of its antecedent.

Thus, let A : B :: C : D ; then, by inversion,

$$B : A :: D : C.$$

132. Magnitudes are in proportion by ALTERNATION, or ALTERNATELY, when antecedent is compared with antecedent, and consequent with consequent.

Thus, let A : B :: D : C ; then, by alternation,

$$A : D :: B : C.$$

133. Magnitudes are in proportion by COMPOSITION, when the sum of the first antecedent and consequent is to the first antecedent, or consequent, as the sum of the second antecedent and consequent is to the second antecedent, or consequent.

Thus, let A : B :: C : D ; then, by composition,

$$A + B : A :: C + D : C, \quad \text{or} \quad A + B : B :: C + D : D.$$

134. Magnitudes are in proportion by DIVISION, when the difference of the first antecedent and consequent is to the first antecedent, or consequent, as the difference of the second antecedent and consequent is to the second antecedent, or consequent.

Thus, let A : B :: C : D ; then, by division,

$$A - B : A :: C - D : C, \quad \text{or} \quad A - B : B :: C - D : D.$$

PROPOSITION I. — THEOREM.

135. *If four magnitudes are in proportion, the product of the two extremes is equal to the product of the two means.*

Let A : B :: C : D ; then will $A \times D = B \times C$.

For, since the magnitudes are in proportion,

$$\frac{A}{B} = \frac{C}{D};$$

and reducing the fractions of this equation to a common denominator, we have

$$\frac{A \times D}{B \times D} = \frac{B \times C}{B \times D},$$

or, the common denominator being omitted,

$$A \times D = B \times C.$$

PROPOSITION II.—THEOREM.

136. *If the product of two magnitudes is equal to the product of two others, these four magnitudes form a proportion.*

Let $A \times D = B \times C$; then will $A : B :: C : D$.

For, dividing each member of the given equation by $B \times D$, we have

$$\frac{A \times D}{B \times D} = \frac{B \times C}{B \times D},$$

which, reduced to the lowest terms, gives

$$\frac{A}{B} = \frac{C}{D}.$$

Whence $A : B :: C : D$.

PROPOSITION III.—THEOREM.

137. *If three magnitudes are in proportion, the product of the two extremes is equal to the square of the mean.*

Let $A : B :: B : C$; then will $A \times C = B^2$.

For, since the magnitudes are in proportion,

$$\frac{A}{B} = \frac{B}{C},$$

and, by Prop. I.,

$$A \times C = B \times B, \quad \text{or} \quad A \times C = B^2.$$

PROPOSITION IV.—THEOREM.

138. *If the product of any two quantities is equal to the square of a third, the third is a mean proportional between the other two.*

Let $A \times C = B^2$; then B is a mean proportional between A and C.

For, dividing each member of the given equation by $B \times C$, we have

$$\frac{A}{B} = \frac{B}{C},$$

whence $$A : B :: B : C.$$

PROPOSITION V.—THEOREM.

139. *If four magnitudes are in proportion, they will be in proportion when taken inversely.*

Let A : B :: C : D; then will B : A :: D : C.

For, from the given proportion, by Prop. I., we have

$$A \times D = B \times C, \quad \text{or} \quad B \times C = A \times D.$$

Hence, by Prop. II.,

$$B : A :: D : C.$$

PROPOSITION VI.—THEOREM.

140. *If four magnitudes are in proportion, they will be in proportion when taken alternately.*

Let A : B :: C : D; then will A : C :: B : D.

For, since the magnitudes are in proportion,

$$\frac{A}{B} = \frac{C}{D};$$

and multiplying each member of this equation by $\frac{B}{C}$, we have

$$\frac{A \times B}{B \times C} = \frac{C \times B}{D \times C},$$

which, reduced to the lowest terms, gives

$$\frac{A}{C} = \frac{B}{D}.$$

whence $A : C :: B : D.$

Proposition VII. — Theorem.

141. *If four magnitudes are in proportion, they will be in proportion by composition.*

Let $A : B :: C : D$; then will $A + B : A :: C + D : C$.

For, from the given proportion, by Prop. I., we have

$$B \times C = A \times D.$$

Adding $A \times C$ to each side of this equation, we have

$$A \times C + B \times C = A \times C + A \times D,$$

and resolving each member into its factors,

$$(A + B) \times C = (C + D) \times A.$$

Hence, by Prop. II.,

$$A + B : A :: C + D : C.$$

Proposition VIII. — Theorem.

142. *If four magnitudes are in proportion, they will be in proportion by division.*

Let $A : B :: C : D$; then will $A - B : A :: C - D : C$.

For, from the given proportion, by Prop. I., we have

$$B \times C = A \times D.$$

Subtracting each side of this equation from $A \times C$, we have

$$A \times C - B \times C = A \times C - A \times D,$$

and resolving each member into its factors,

$$(A - B) \times C = (C - D) \times A.$$

Hence, by Prop. II.,

$$A - B : A :: C - D : C.$$

Proposition IX. — Theorem.

143. *Equimultiples of two magnitudes have the same ratio as the magnitudes themselves.*

Let A and B be two magnitudes, and $m \times A$ and $m \times B$ their equimultiples, then will $m \times A : m \times B :: A : B$.

For $$A \times B = B \times A;$$

Multiplying each side of this equation by any number, m, we have

$$m \times A \times B = m \times B \times A;$$

therefore

$$(m \times A) \times B = (m \times B) \times A.$$

Hence, by Prop. II.,

$$m \times A : m \times B :: A : B.$$

Proposition X. — Theorem.

144. *Magnitudes which are proportional to the same proportionals, will be proportional to each other.*

Let $A : B :: E : F$, and $C : D :: E : F$; then will

$$A : B :: C : D.$$

For, by the given proportions, we have

$$\frac{A}{B} = \frac{E}{F}, \text{ and } \frac{C}{D} = \frac{E}{F}.$$

Therefore, it is evident (Art. 34, Ax. 1),

$$\frac{A}{B} = \frac{C}{D}.$$

Hence $$A : B :: C : D.$$

145. *Cor.* 1. If two proportions have an antecedent and its consequent the same in both, the remaining terms will be in proportion.

146. *Cor.* 2. Therefore, by alternation (Prop. VI.), if two proportions have the two antecedents or the two con-

sequents the same in both, the remaining terms will be in proportion.

Proposition XI. — Theorem.

147. *If any number of magnitudes are proportional, any antecedent is to its consequent as the sum of all the antecedents is to the sum of all the consequents.*

Let A : B : : C : D : : E : F; then will

$$A : B :: A + C + E : B + D + F.$$

For, from the given proportion, we have

$$A \times D = B \times C, \quad \text{and} \quad A \times F = B \times E.$$

By adding A × B to the sum of the corresponding sides of these equations, we have

$$A \times B + A \times D + A \times F = A \times B + B \times C + B \times E.$$

Therefore,

$$A \times (B + D + F) = B \times (A + C + E).$$

Hence, by Prop. II.,

$$A : B :: A + C + E : B + D + F.$$

Proposition XII.— Theorem.

148. *If four magnitudes are in proportion, the sum of the first and second is to their difference as the sum of the third and fourth is to their difference.*

Let A : B : : C : D; then will

$$A + B : A - B :: C + D : C - D.$$

For, from the given proportion, by Prop. VII., we have

$$A + B : A :: C + D : C;$$

and from the given proportion, by Prop. VIII., we have

$$A - B : A :: C - D : C.$$

Hence, from these two proportions, by Prop. X. Cor. 2, we have

$$A + B : A - B :: C + D : C - D.$$

PROPOSITION XIII. — THEOREM.

149. *If there be two sets of proportional magnitudes, the products of the corresponding terms will be proportionals.*

Let $A : B :: C : D$, and $E : F :: G : H$; then will

$$A \times E : B \times F :: C \times G : D \times H.$$

For, from the first of the given proportions, by Prop. I., we have

$$A \times D = B \times C;$$

and from the second of the given proportions, by Prop. I., we have

$$E \times H = F \times G.$$

Multiplying together the corresponding members of these equations, we have

$$A \times D \times E \times H = B \times C \times F \times G.$$

Hence, by Prop. II.,

$$A \times E : B \times F :: C \times G : D \times H.$$

PROPOSITION XIV. — THEOREM.

150. *If three magnitudes are proportionals, the first will be to the third as the square of the first is to the square of the second.*

Let $A : B :: B : C$; then will $A : C :: A^2 : B^2$.

For, from the given proportion, by Prop. III., we have

$$A \times C = B^2.$$

Multiplying each side of this equation by A gives

$$A^2 \times C = A \times B^2.$$

Hence, by Prop. II.,

$$A : C :: A^2 : B^2.$$

Proposition XV. — Theorem.

151. *If four magnitudes are proportionals, their like powers and roots will also be proportional.*

Let $A : B :: C : D$; then will

$$A^n : B^n :: C^n : D^n, \quad \text{and} \quad A^{\frac{1}{n}} : B^{\frac{1}{n}} :: C^{\frac{1}{n}} : D^{\frac{1}{n}}.$$

For, from the given proportion, we have

$$\frac{A}{B} = \frac{C}{D}.$$

Raising both members of this equation to the nth power, we have

$$\frac{A^n}{B^n} = \frac{C^n}{D^n},$$

and extracting the nth root of each member, we have

$$\frac{A^{\frac{1}{n}}}{B^{\frac{1}{n}}} = \frac{C^{\frac{1}{n}}}{D^{\frac{1}{n}}}.$$

Hence, by Prop. II., the last two equations give

$$A^n : B^n :: C^n : D^n,$$

and

$$A^{\frac{1}{n}} : B^{\frac{1}{n}} :: C^{\frac{1}{n}} : D^{\frac{1}{n}}.$$

BOOK III.

THE CIRCLE, AND THE MEASURE OF ANGLES.

DEFINITIONS.

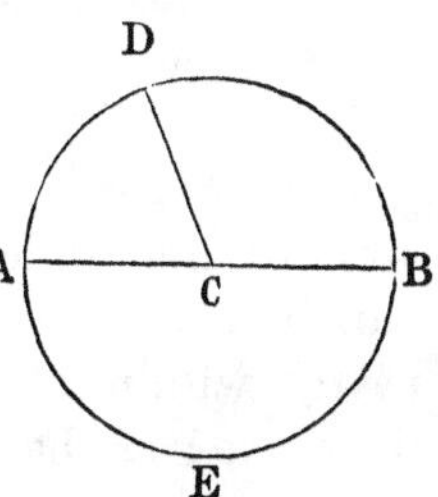

152. A CIRCLE is a plane figure bounded by a curved line, all the points of which are equally distant from a point within called the *center;* as the figure A D B E.

153. The CIRCUMFERENCE OF PERIPHERY of a circle is its entire bounding line; or it is a curved line, all points of which are equally distant from a point within called the center.

154. A RADIUS of a circle is any straight line drawn from the center to the circumference; as the line C A, C D, or C B.

155. A DIAMETER of a circle is any straight line drawn through the center, and terminating in both directions in the circumference; as the line A B.

All the radii of a circle are equal; all the diameters are also equal, and each is double the radius.

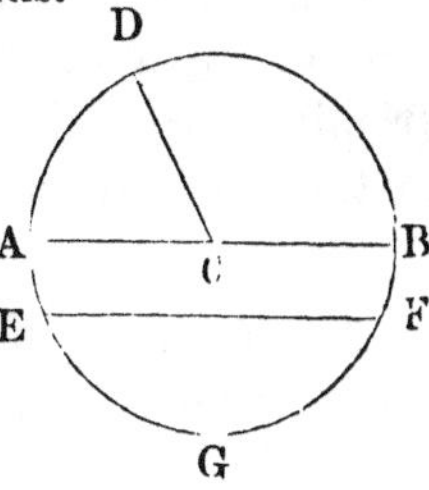

156. An ARC of a circle is any part of the circumference; as the part A D, A E, or E G F.

157. The CHORD of an arc is the straight line joining its extremities; thus E F is the chord of the arc E G F.

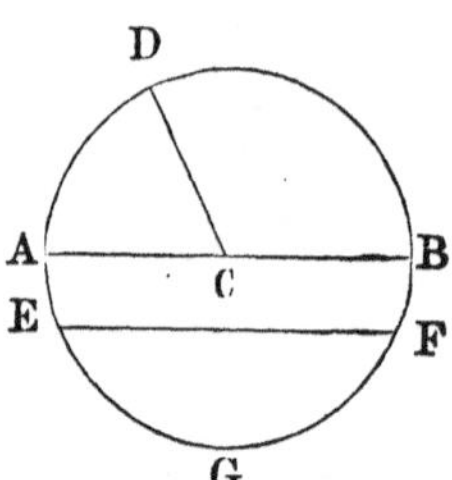

158. The SEGMENT of a circle is the part of a circle included between an arc and its chord; as the surface included between the arc E G F and the chord E F.

159. The SECTOR of a circle is the part of a circle included between an arc, and the two radii drawn to the extremities of the arc; as the surface included between the arc A D, and the two radii C A, C D.

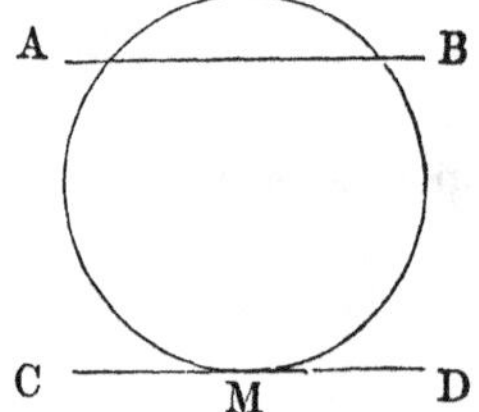

160. A SECANT to a circle is a straight line which meets the circumference in two points, and lies partly within and partly without the circle; as the line A B.

161. A TANGENT to a circle is a straight line which, how far so ever produced, meets the circumference in but one point; as the line C D. The point of meeting is called the POINT OF CONTACT; as the point M.

162. Two circumferences TOUCH each other, when they have a point of contact without cutting one another; thus two circumferences touch each other at the point A, and two at the point B.

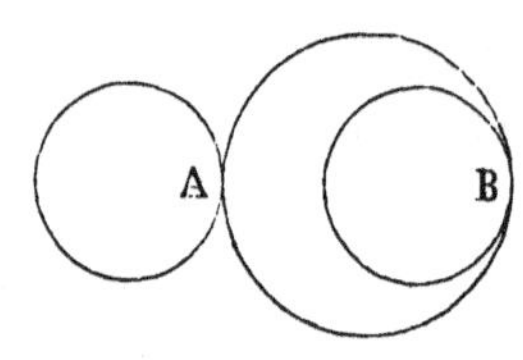

163. A STRAIGHT LINE is INSCRIBED in a circle when its extremities are in the circumference; as the line A B, or B C.

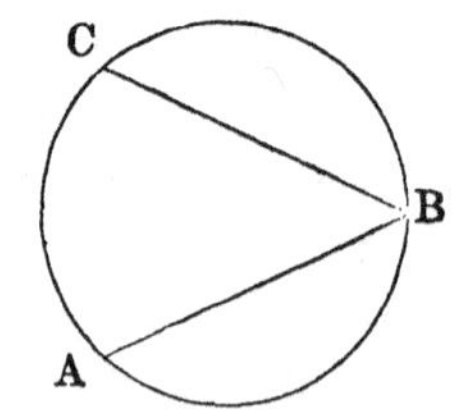

164. An INSCRIBED ANGLE is one which has its vertex in the circumference, and is formed by two chords; as the angle A B C.

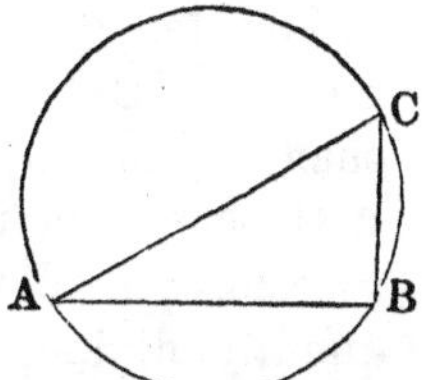

165. An INSCRIBED POLYGON is one which has the vertices of all its angles in the circumference of the circle; as the triangle A B C.

166. The circle is then said to be CIRCUMSCRIBED about the polygon.

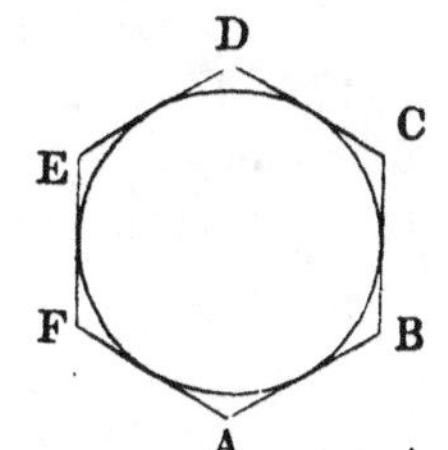

167. A POLYGON is CIRCUMSCRIBED about a circle when all its sides are tangents to the circumference; as the polygon A B C D E F.

168. The circle is then said to be INSCRIBED in the polygon.

PROPOSITION I. — THEOREM.

169. *Every diameter divides the circle and its circumference each into two equal parts.*

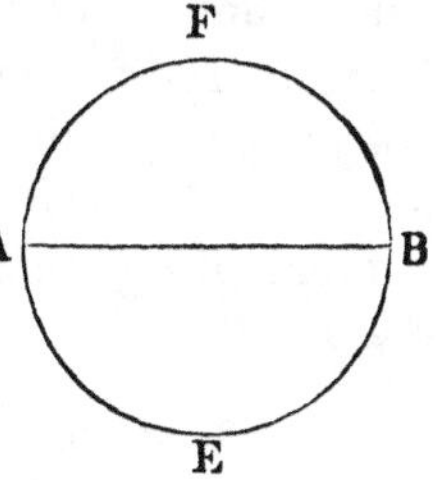

Let A E B F be a circle, and A B a diameter; then the two parts A E B, A F B are equal.

For, if the figure A E B be applied to A F B, their common base A B retaining its position, the curve line A E B must fall exactly on the curve line A F B; otherwise there would be points in the one or the other unequally distant from the centre, which is contrary to the definition of the circle (Art. 152). Hence a diameter divides the circle and its circumference into two equal parts.

170. *Cor.* 1. *Conversely*, a straight line dividing the circle into two equal parts is a diameter.

For, let the line A B divide the circle A E B C F into two equal parts; then, if the center is not in A B, let A C be drawn through it, which is therefore a diameter, and consequently divides the circle into two equal parts; hence the surface A F C is equal to the surface A F C B, a part to the whole, which is impossible.

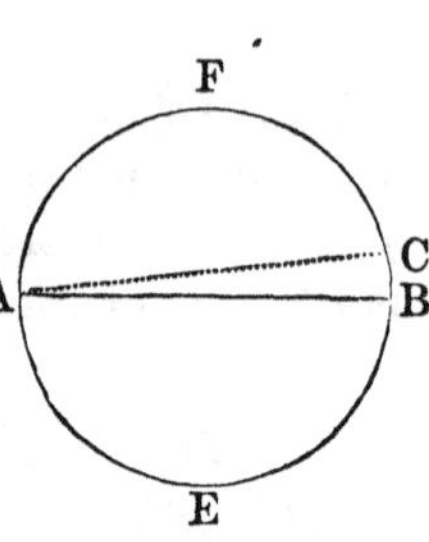

171. *Cor.* 2. The arc of a circle, whose chord is a diameter, is a semi-circumference, and the included segment is a semicircle.

Proposition II. — Theorem.

172. *A straight line cannot meet the circumference of a circle in more than two points.*

For, if a straight line could meet the circumference A B D, in three points, A, B, D, join each of these points with the center, C; then, since the straight lines C A, C B, C D are radii, they are equal (Art. 155); hence, three equal straight lines can be drawn from the same point to the same straight line, which is impossible (Prop. XIV. Cor. 2, Bk. I.).

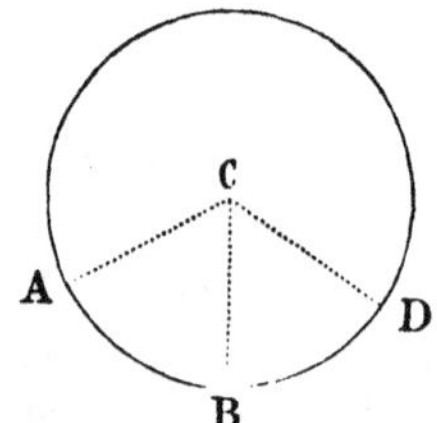

Proposition III. — Theorem.

173. *In the same circle, or in equal circles, equal arcs are subtended by equal chords; and, conversely, equal chords subtend equal arcs.*

Let A D B and E G F be two equal circles, and let the arc A D be equal to E G; then will the chord A D be equal to the chord E G.

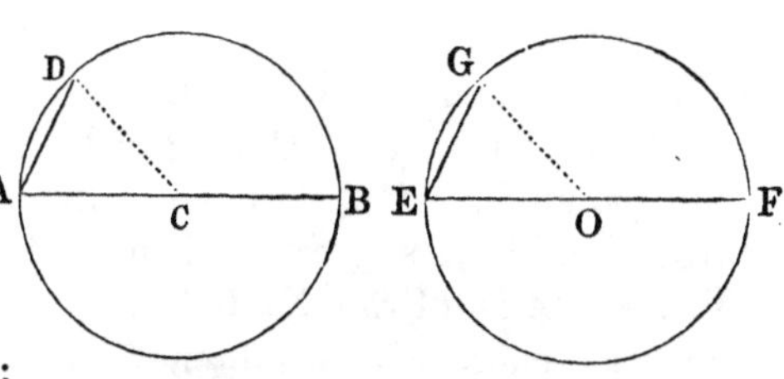

For, since the diameters A B, E F are equal, the semicircle A D B may be applied to the semicircle E G F; and the curve line A D B will coincide with the curve line E G F (Prop. I.). But, by hypothesis, the arc A D is equal to the arc E G; hence the point D will fall on G; hence the chord A D is equal to the chord E G (Art. 34, Ax. 11).

Conversely, if the chord A D is equal to the chord E G, the arcs A D, E G will be equal.

For, if the radii C D, O G are drawn, the triangles A C D, E O G, having the three sides of the one equal to the three sides of the other, each to each, are themselves equal (Prop. XVIII. Bk. I.); therefore the angle A C D is equal to the angle E O G (Prop. XVIII. Sch., Bk. I.).

If now the semicircle A D B be applied to its equal E G F, with the radius A C on its equal E O, since the angles A C D, E O G are equal, the radius C D will fall on O G, and the point D on G. Therefore the arcs A D and E G coincide with each other; hence they must be equal (Art. 34, Ax. 14).

Proposition IV. — Theorem.

174. *In the same circle, or in equal circles, a greater arc is subtended by a greater chord; and, conversely, the greater chord subtends the greater arc.*

In the circle of which C is the centre, let the arc A B be greater than the arc A D; then will the chord A B be greater than the chord A D.

Draw the radii C A, C D, and C B. The two sides A C,

C B in the triangle A C B are equal to the two A C, C D in the triangle A C D, and the angle A C B is greater than the angle A C D; therefore the third side A B is greater than the third side A D (Prop. XVI. Bk. I.); hence the chord which subtends the greater arc is the greater.

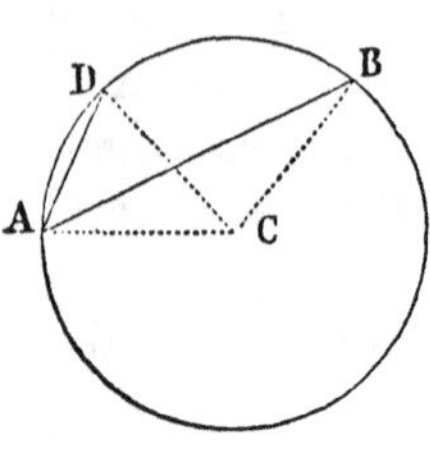

Conversely, if the chord A B be greater than the chord A D, the arc A B will be greater than the arc A D.

For the triangles A C B, A C D have two sides, A C, C B, in the one, equal to two sides, A C, C D, in the other, while the side A B is greater than the side A D; therefore the angle A C B is greater than the angle A C D (Prop. XVII. Bk. I.); hence the arc A B is greater than the arc A D.

175. *Scholium.* The arcs here treated of are each less than the semi-circumference. If they were greater, the contrary would be true; in which case, as the arcs increased, the chords would diminish, and conversely.

Proposition V.—Theorem.

176. *In the same circle, or in equal circles, radii which make equal angles at the centre intercept equal arcs on the circumference; and, conversely, if the intercepted arcs are equal, the angles made by the radii are also equal.*

Let A C B and D C E be equal angles made by radii at the centre of equal circles; then will the intercepted arcs A B and DE be also equal.

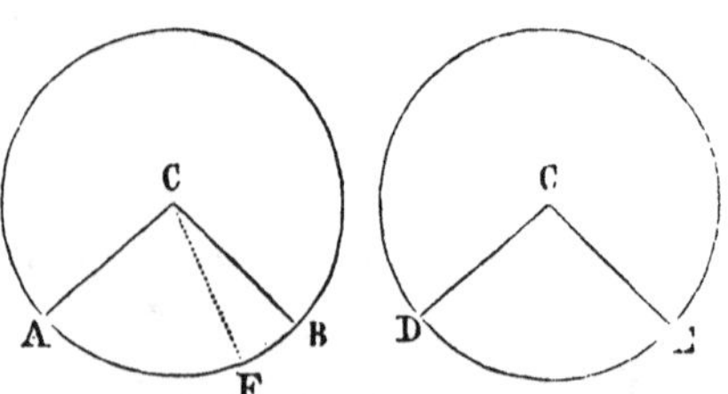

First. Since the angles A C B, D C E are equal, the one may be applied to the other; and since their sides, being radii of equal circles, are equal, the point A will coincide with D, and the point B with E. Therefore the arc A B must also coincide with the arc D E, or there would be points in the one or the other unequally distant from the center, which is impossible; hence the arc A B is equal to the arc D E.

Second. If the arcs A B and D E are equal, the angles A C B and D C E will be equal.

For, if these angles are not equal, let A C B be the greater, and let A C F be taken equal to D C E. From what has been shown, we shall have the arc A F equal to the arc D E. But, by hypothesis, A B is equal to D E; hence A F must be equal to A B, the part to the whole, which is impossible; hence the angle A C B is equal to the angle D C E.

PROPOSITION VI. — THEOREM.

177. *The radius which is perpendicular to a chord bisects the chord, and also the arc subtended by the chord.*

Let the radius C E be perpendicular to the chord A B; then will C E bisect the chord at D, and the arc A B at E.

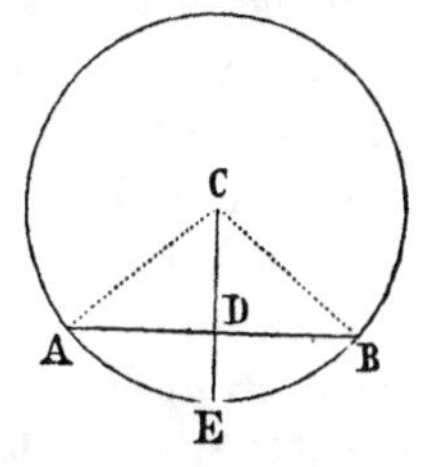

Draw the radii C A and C B. Then C A and C B, with respect to the perpendicular C E, are equal oblique lines drawn to the chord A B; therefore their extremities are at equal distances from the perpendicular (Prop. XIV. Bk. I.); hence A D and D B are equal.

Again, since the triangle A C B has the sides A C and C B equal, it is isosceles; and the line C E bisects the base A B at right angles; therefore C E bisects also the angle A C B (Prop. VII. Cor. 2, Bk. I.). Since the angles A C D, D C B are equal, the arcs A E, E B are equal

(Prop. V.); hence the radius C E, which is perpendicular to the chord A B, bisects the arc A B subtended by the chord.

178. *Cor.* 1. Any straight line which joins the centre of the circle and the middle of the chord, or the middle of the arc, must be perpendicular to the chord.

For the perpendicular from the centre C passes through the middle, D, of the chord, and the middle, E, of the arc subtended by the chord. Now, any two of these three points in the straight line C E are sufficient to determine its position.

179. *Cor.* 2. A perpendicular at the middle of a chord passes through the center of the circle, and through the middle of the arc subtended by the chord, bisecting at the centre the angle which the arc subtends.

Proposition VII. — Theorem.

180. *Through three given points, not in the same straight line, one circumference can be made to pass, and but one.*

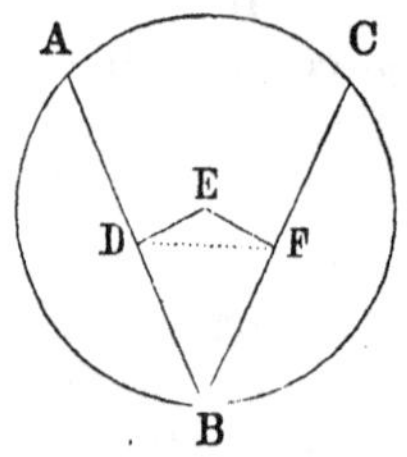

Let A, B, and C be any three points not in the same straight line; one circumference can be made to pass through them, and but one.

Join A B and B C; and bisect these straight lines by the perpendiculars D E and F E. Join D F; then, the angles B D E, B F E, being each a right angle, are together equal to two right angles; therefore the angles E D F, E F D are together less than two right angles; hence D E, F E, produced, must meet in some point E (Prop. XXIII. Bk. I.).

Now, since the point E lies in the perpendicular D E, it is equally distant from the two points A and B (Prop. XV. Bk. I.); and since the same point E lies in the perpendicular F E, it is also equally distant from the two points B and C; therefore the three distances, E A, E B, E C, are equal; hence a circumference can be described from the center E passing through the three points A, B, C.

Again, the center, lying in the perpendicular D E bisecting the chord A B, and at the same time in the perpendicular F E bisecting the chord B C (Prop. VI. Cor. 2), must be at the point of their meeting, E. Therefore, since there can be but one center, but one circumference can be made to pass through three given points.

181. *Cor.* Two circumferences can intersect in only two points; for, if they have three points in common, they must have the same center, and must coincide.

Proposition VIII. — Theorem.

182. *Equal chords are equally distant from the center; and, conversely, chords which are equally distant from the centre are equal.*

Let A B and D E be equal chords, and C the center of the circle; and draw C F perpendicular to A B, and C G perpendicular to D E; then these perpendiculars, which measure the distance of the chords from the center, are equal.

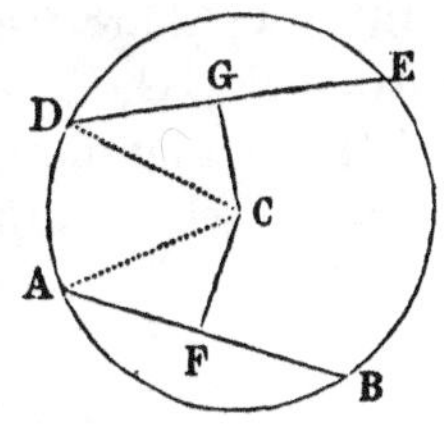

Join C A and C D. Then, in the right-angled triangle C A F, C D G, the hypothenuses C A, C D are equal; and the side A F, the half of A B, is equal to the side D G, the half of D E; therefore the triangles are equal, and C F is equal to C G (Prop. XIX. Bk. I.); hence the two equal chords A B, D E are equally distant from the center.

Conversely, if the distances C F and C G are equal, the chords A B and D E are equal.

For, in the right-angled triangles A C F, D C G, the hypothenuses C A, C D are equal; and the side C F is equal to the side C G; therefore the triangles are equal, and A F is equal to D G; hence A B, the double of A F, is equal to D E, the double of D G (Art. 34, Ax. 6).

PROPOSITION IX. — THEOREM.

183. *Of two unequal chords, the less is the farther from the center.*

Of the two chords D E and A H, let A H be the greater; then will D E be the farther from the center C.

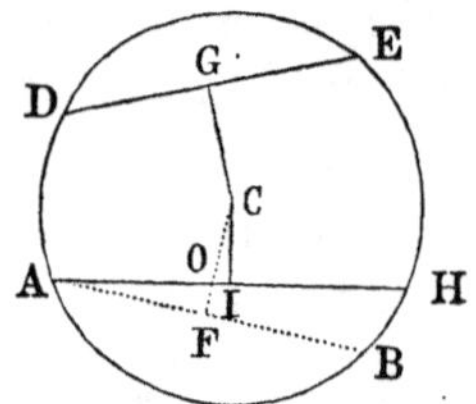

Since the chord A H is greater than the chord D E, the arc A H is greater than the arc D E (Prop. IV.). Cut off from the arc A H a part, A B, equal D E; draw C F perpendicular to this chord, C I perpendicular to A H, and C G perpendicular to D E. C F is greater than C O (Art. 34, Ax. 8), and C O than C I (Prop. XIV. Bk. I.); therefore C F is greater than C I. But C F is equal to C G, since the chords A B, D E are equal (Prop. VIII.); therefore, C G is greater than C I; hence, of two unequal chords, the less is the farther from the center.

PROPOSITION X. — THEOREM.

184. *A straight line perpendicular to a radius at its termination in the circumference, is a tangent to the circle.*

Let the straight line B D be perpendicular to the radius C A at its termination A; then will it be a tangent to the circle.

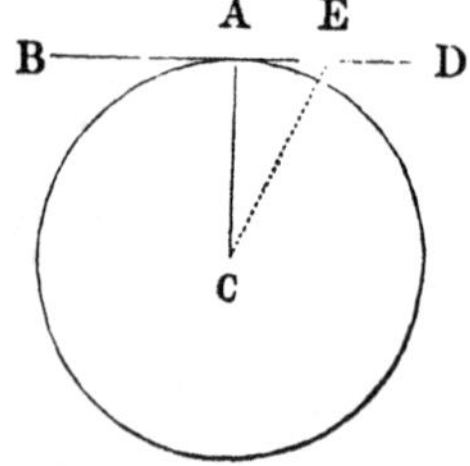

Draw from the centre C to B D any other straight line, as C E. Then, since C A is perpendicular to B D, it is shorter than the oblique line C E (Prop. XIV. Bk. I.); hence the point E is without the circle. The same may be shown of any other point in the line B D, except the point A; therefore B D meets the circumference at A, and, being produced, does not cut it; hence B D is a tangent (Art. 161).

Proposition XI. — Theorem.

185. *If a line is a tangent to a circumference, the radius drawn to the point of contact with it is perpendicular to the tangent.*

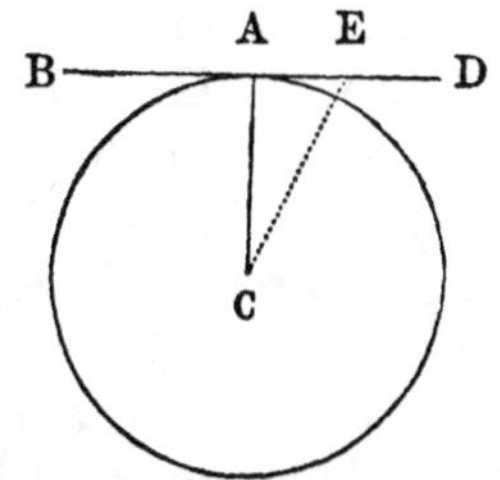

Let B D be a tangent to the circumference, at the point A; then will the radius C A be perpendicular to B D.

For every point in B D, except A, being without the circumference (Prop. X.), any line C E drawn from the center C to B D, at any point other than A, must terminate at E, without the circumference; therefore the radius C A is the shortest line that can be drawn from the center to B D; hence C A is perpendicular to the tangent B D (Prop. XIV. Cor. 1, Bk. I.).

186. *Cor.* Only one tangent can be drawn through the same point in a circumference; for two lines cannot both be perpendicular to a radius at the same point.

Proposition XII. — Theorem.

187. *Two parallel straight lines intercept equal arcs of the circumference.*

First. When the two parallels are secants, as A B, D E.

Draw the radius C H perpendicular to A B; and it will also be perpendicular to D E (Prop. XXII. Cor., Bk. I.);

therefore the point H will be at the same time the middle of the arc A H B and of the arc D H E (Prop. VI.); therefore, the arc A H is equal to the arc H B, and the arc D H is equal to the arc H E; hence A H diminished by D H is equal to H B diminished by H E; that is, the intercepted arcs A D, B E are equal.

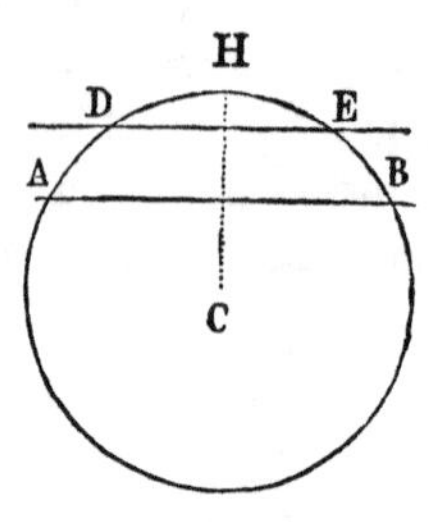

Second. When of the two parallels, one, as A B, is a secant, and the other, as D E, is a tangent.

Draw the radius C H to the point of contact H. This radius will be perpendicular to the tangent D E (Prop. X.), and also to its parallel A B (Prop. XXII. Cor., Bk. I.). But, since C H is perpendicular to the chord A B, the point H is the middle of the arc A H B; hence the arcs A H, H B, included between the parallels A B, D E, are equal.

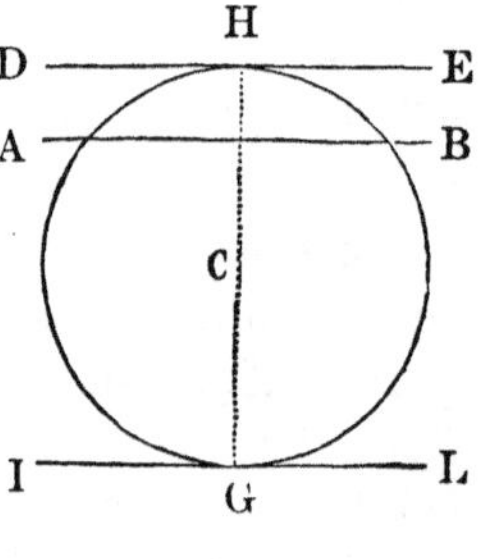

Third. When the two parallels are tangents, as D E, I L.

Draw the secant A B parallel to either of the tangents, and it will be parallel to the other (Prop. XXIV. Bk. I.); then, from what has been just shown, the arc A H is equal to the arc H B, and also the arc A G is equal to the arc G B; hence the whole arc H A G is equal to the whole arc H B G.

It is further evident, since the two arcs H A G, H B G are equal, and together make up the whole circumference, that each of them is a semi-circumference.

188. *Cor.* Two parallel tangents meet the circumference at the extremities of the same diameter.

PROPOSITION XIII. — THEOREM.

189. *If two circumferences touch each other externally or internally, their centers and the point of contact are in the same straight line.*

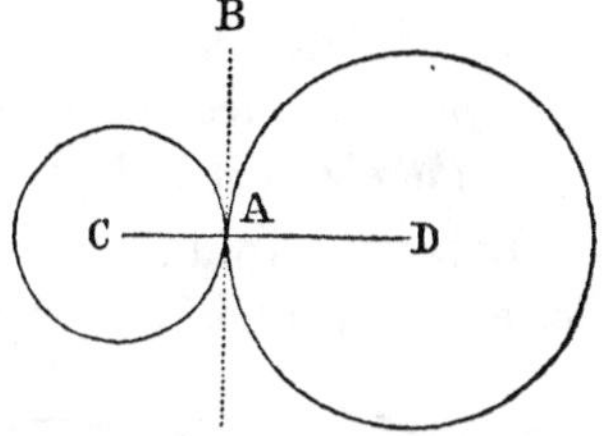

Let the two circumferences, whose centers are C and D, touch each other externally in the point A; the points C, D, and A will be all in the same straight line.

Draw from the point of contact A the common tangent A B. Then the radius C A of the one circle, and the radius D A of the other, are each perpendicular to A B (Prop. XI.); but there can be but one straight line drawn through the point A perpendicular to A B (Prop. XIII. Bk. I.); therefore the points C, D, and A are in one perpendicular; hence they are in one and the same straight line.

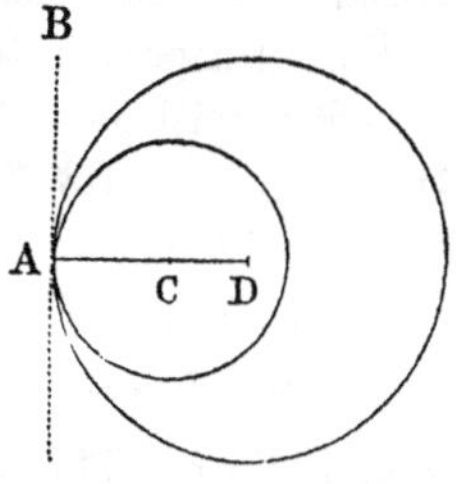

Also, let the two circumferences touch each other internally in A; then their centers, C and D, and the point of contact, A, will be in the same straight line.

Draw the common tangent A B. Then a straight line perpendicular to A B, at the point A, on being sufficiently produced, must pass through the two centers C and D (Prop. XI.); but from the same point there can be but one perpendicular; therefore the points C, D, and A are in that perpendicular; hence they are in the same straight line.

190. *Cor.* 1. When two circumferences touch each other externally, the distance between their centers is equal to the sum of their radii.

191. *Cor.* 2. And when two circumferences touch each other internally, the distance between their centers is equal to the difference of their radii.

Proposition XIV.—Theorem.

192. *If two circumferences cut each other, the straight line passing through their centers will bisect at right angles the chord which joins the points of intersection.*

Let two circumferences cut each other at the points A and B; then the straight line passing through the

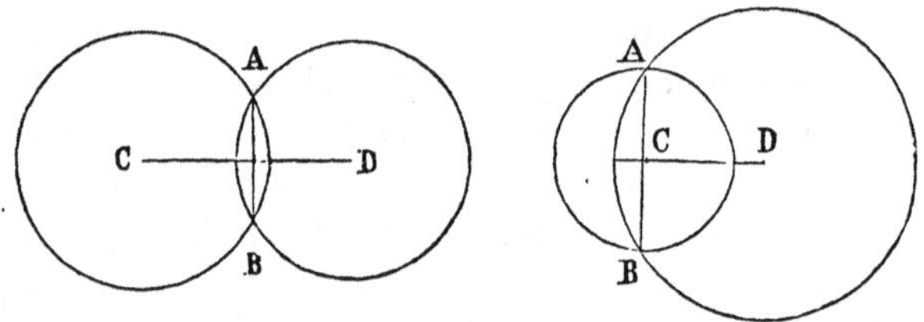

centres C and D will bisect at right angles the chord A B common to the two circles.

For, if a perpendicular be erected at the middle of this chord, it will pass through each of the two centers C and D (Prop. VI. Cor. 1). But no more than one straight line can be drawn through two points; hence the straight line C D, passing through the centers, must bisect at right angles the common chord A B.

193. *Cor.* The straight line joining the points of intersection of two circumferences is perpendicular to the straight line which passes through their centers.

Proposition XV.—Theorem.

194. *If two circumferences cut each other, the distance between their centers will be less than the sum of their radii, and greater than their difference.*

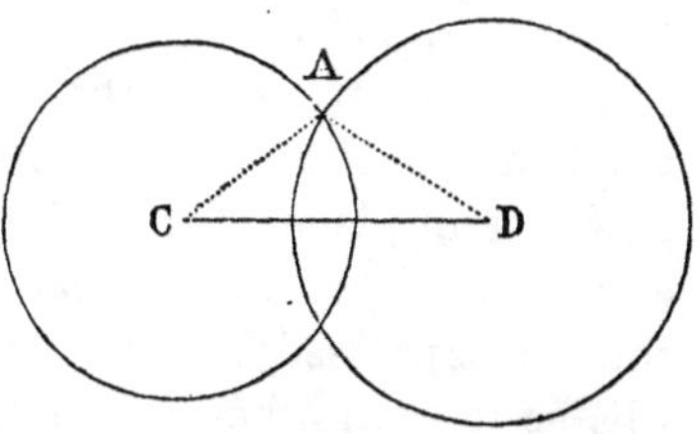

Let two circumferences whose centers are C and D cut each other in the point A, and draw the radii C A and D A. Then, in order that the intersection may take place, the triangle C A D must be possible. And in this triangle the side C D must be less than the sum of A C and A D (Prop. IX. Bk. I.); also C D must be greater than the difference between D A and C A (Prop. IX. Cor., Bk. I.).

Proposition XVI. — Theorem.

195. *In the same circle, or in equal circles, if two angles at the center are to each other as two whole numbers, the intercepted arcs will be to each other as the same numbers.*

Let us suppose, for example, that the angles A C B, D C E, at the center of equal circles, are to each other as 7 to 4; or, which amounts to the same thing, that the angle M, which will serve as a common measure, is con-

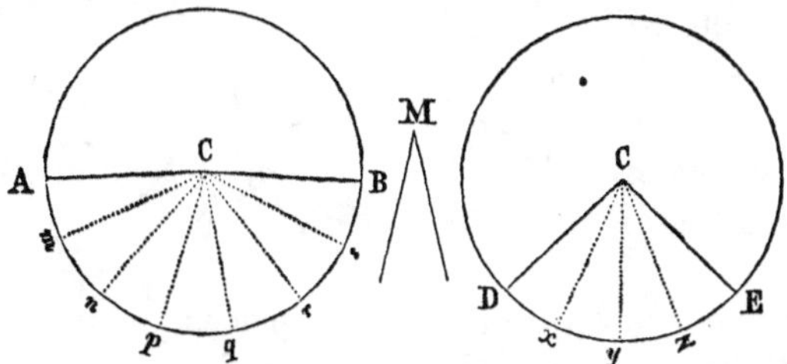

tained seven times in the angle A C B, and four times in the angle D C E. The seven partial angles A C *m*, *m* C *n*, *n* C *p*, &c. into which A C B is divided, being each equal to any of the four partial angles into which D C E is divided, each of the partial arcs A *m*, *m n*, *n p*, &c. will be also equal to each of the partial arcs Dx, xy, &c. (Prop. V.); therefore the whole arc AB will be to the whole arc DE as 7 to 4. But the same reasoning would apply, if in place of 7 and 4 any numbers whatever were employed; hence, if the ratio of the angles ACB, DCE can be expressed in whole numbers, the arcs AB, DE will be to each other as the angles ACB, DCE.

196. *Cor. Conversely*, if the arcs AB, DE are to each other as two whole numbers, the angles ACB, DCE will be to each other as the same whole numbers, and we shall have ACB : DCE : : AB : DE. For, the partial arcs Am, mn, &c. and Dx, xy, &c. being equal, the partial angles ACm, mCn, &c. and DCx, xCy, &c. will also be equal.

Proposition XVII. — Theorem.

197. *In the same circle, or in equal circles, any two angles at the center are to each other as the arcs intercepted between their sides.*

Let ACB be the greater, and ACD the less angle; then will the angle ACB be to the angle ACD as the arc AB is to the arc AD.

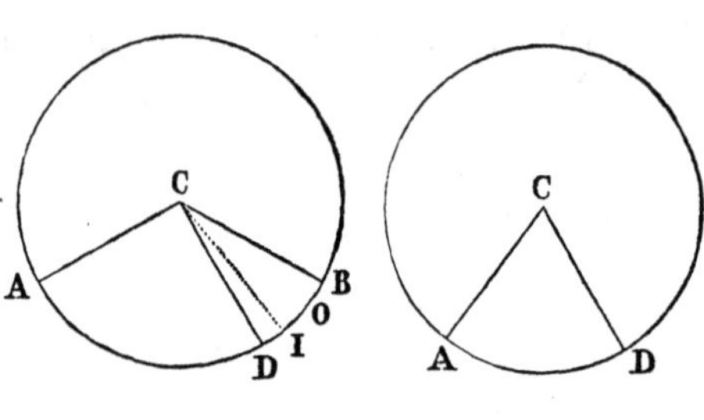

Conceive the less angle to be placed on the greater; then, if the proposition be not true, the angle ACB will be to the angle ACD as the arc AB is to an arc greater or less than AD. Suppose this arc to be greater, and let it be represented by AO; we shall have the angle ACB : angle ACD : : arc AB : arc AO. Conceive, now, the arc AB to be divided into equal parts, each of which is less than D O; there will be at least one point of division between D and O; let I be that point; and join C I. The arcs A B, A I will be to each other as two whole numbers, and, by the preceding proposition, we shall have the angle A C B : angle A C I : : arc A B : arc A I. Comparing these two proportions with each other, and observing that the antecedents are the same, we infer that the consequents are proportional (Prop. X. Cor. 2, Bk. II.); hence the angle A C D : angle A C I : : arc A O : arc A I. But the arc A O is greater than the arc A I; therefore, if this proportion is true, the angle A C D must be greater than the angle A C I. But it is less; hence the angle A C B cannot be to the angle A C D as the arc A B is to an arc greater than A D.

By a process of reasoning entirely similar, it may be shown that the fourth term of the proportion cannot be less than A D; therefore it must be A D; hence we have,

Angle A C B : angle A C D : : arc A B : arc A D.

198. *Scholium* 1. Since the angle at the center of a circle, and the arc intercepted by its sides, have such a connection, that, if the one be increased or diminished in any ratio, the other will be increased or diminished in the same ratio, we are authorized to take the one of these magnitudes as the measure of the other. Henceforth we shall assume the arc A B as the measure of the angle A C B. It is to be observed, in the comparison of angles with each other, that the arcs which serve to measure them must be described with equal radii.

199. *Scholium* 2. Sectors taken in the same circle, or in equal circles, are to each other as their arcs; for sectors are equal when their angles are so, and therefore are in all respects proportional to their angles.

PROPOSITION XVIII. — THEOREM.

200. *An inscribed angle is measured by half the arc included between its sides.*

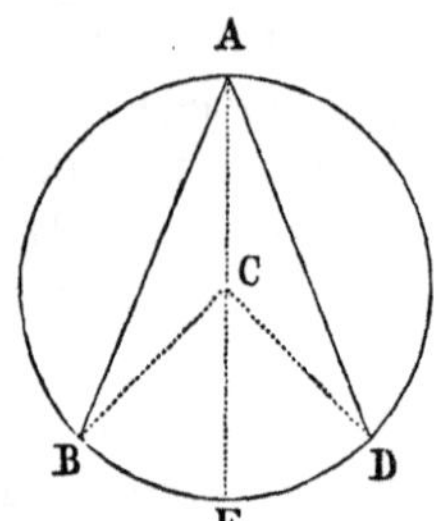

Let B A D be an inscribed angle, whose sides include the arc B D; then the angle B A D is measured by half of the arc B D.

First. Suppose the center of the circle C to lie within the angle B A D. Draw the diameter A E, and the radii C B, C D.

The angle B C E, being exterior to the triangle A B C, is equal to the sum of the two interior angles C A B, A B C (Prop. XXVII. Bk. I.). But the triangle B A C being isosceles, the angle C A B is equal to A B C; hence, the angle B C E is double B A C. Since B C E lies at the center, it is measured by the arc B E (Prop. XVII. Sch. 1); hence B A C will be measured by half of B E. For a like reason, the angle C A D will be measured by the half of E D; hence B A C and C A D together, or B A D, will be measured by the half of B E and E D, or half B D.

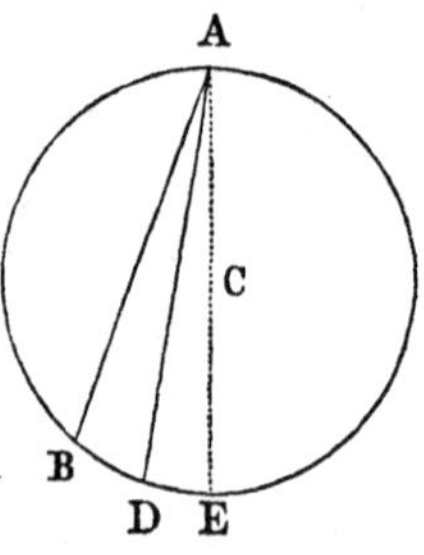

Second. Suppose that the center C lies without the angle B A D. Then, drawing the diameter A E, the angle B A E will be measured by the half of B E; and the angle D A E is measured by the half of D E; hence, their difference, B A D, will be measured by the half of B E *minus* the half of E D, or by the half of B D.

Hence every inscribed angle is measured by the half of the arc included between its sides.

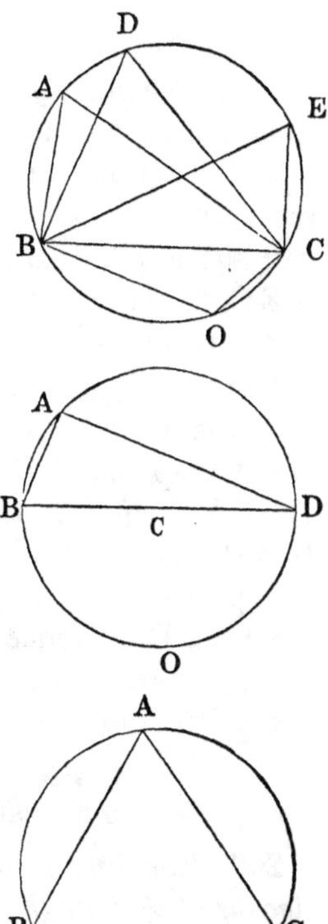

201. *Cor.* 1. All the angles, B A C, B D C, inscribed in the same segment, are equal; because they are all measured by the half of the same arc, B O C.

202. *Cor.* 2. Every angle, B A D, inscribed in a semicircle, is a right angle; because it is measured by half the semi-circumference, BOD; that is, by the fourth part of the whole circumference.

203. *Cor.* 3. Every angle, B A C, inscribed in a segment greater than a semicircle, is an acute angle; for it is measured by the half of the arc B O C, less than a semi-circumference.

And every angle, B O C, inscribed in a segment less than a semicircle, is an obtuse angle; for it is measured by half of the arc B A C, greater than a semi-circumference.

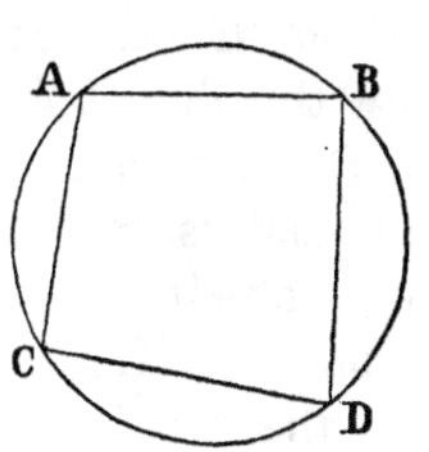

204. *Cor.* 4. The opposite angles, A and D, of an inscribed quadrilateral, A B D C, are together equal to two right angles; for the angle B A C is measured by half the arc B D C, and the angle B D C is measured by half the arc B A C; hence the two angles B A C, B D C, taken together, are measured by half the circumference; hence their sum is equal to two right angles.

Proposition XIX. — Theorem.

205. *The angle formed by the intersection of two chords is measured by half the sum of the two intercepted arcs.*

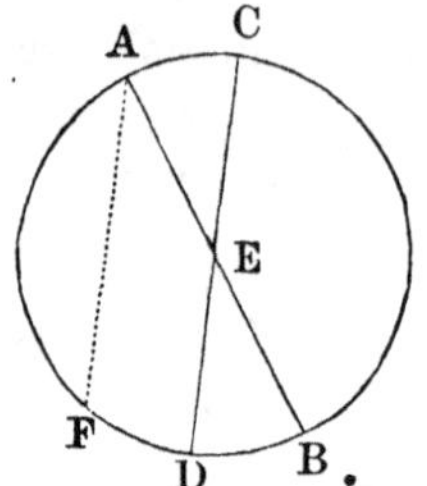

Let the two chords A B, C D intersect each other at the point E; then will the angle D E B, or its equal, A E C, be measured by half the sum of the two arcs D B and A C.

Draw A F parallel to D C; then will the arc F D be equal to the arc A C (Prop. XII.), and the angle F A B equal to the angle D E B (Prop. XXII. Bk. I.). But the angle F A B is measured by half the arc F D B (Prop. XVIII.); that is, by half the arc D B, plus half the arc F D. Hence, since F D is equal to A C, the angle D E B, or its equal angle A E C, is measured by half the sum of the intercepted arcs D B and A C

Proposition XX. — Theorem.

206. *The angle formed by a tangent and a chord is measured by half the intercepted arc.*

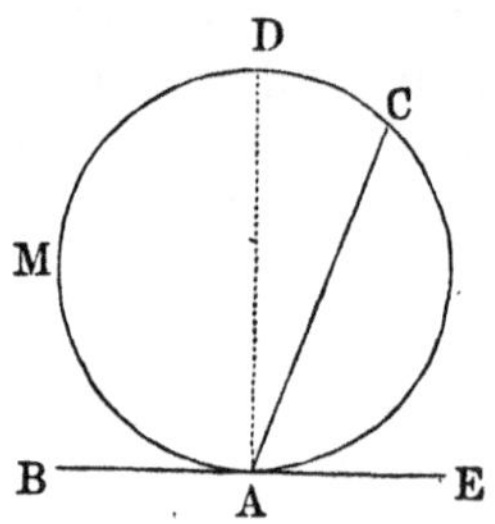

Let the tangent B E form, with the chord A C, the angle B A C; then B A C is measured by half the arc A M C.

From A, the point of contact, draw the diameter A D. The angle B A D is a right angle (Prop. X.), and is measured by half of the semi-circumference A M D (Prop. XVIII.); and the angle D A C is measured by half the arc D C; hence the sum of the angles B A D, D A C, or B A C, is measured by the half of A M D, plus the half of D C; or by half the whole arc A M D C.

In like manner, it may be shown that the angle C A E is measured by half the intercepted arc A C.

Proposition XXI. — Theorem.

207. *The angle formed by two secants is measured by half the difference of the two intercepted arcs.*

Let A B, A C be two secants forming the angle B A C; then will that angle be measured by half the difference of the two arcs B E C and D F.

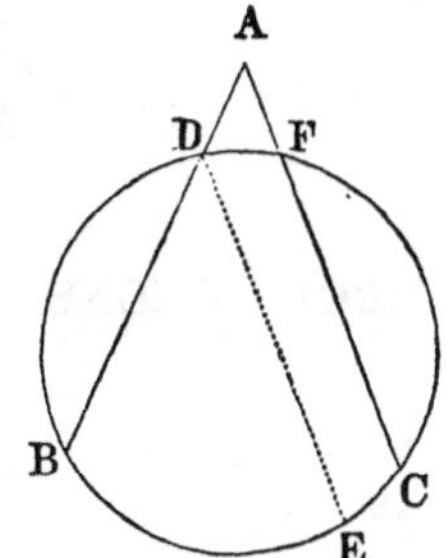

Draw D E parallel to A C; then will the arc E C be equal to the arc D F (Prop. XII.); and the angle B D E be equal to the angle B A C (Prop. XXII. Bk. I.). But the angle B D E is measured by half the arc B E (Prop. XVIII.); hence the equal angle B A C is also measured by half the arc B E; that is, by half the difference of the arcs B E C and E C, or, since E C is equal to D F, by half the difference of the intercepted arcs B E C and D F.

Proposition XXII. — Theorem.

208. *The angle formed by a secant and a tangent is measured by half the difference of the two intercepted arcs.*

Let the secant A B form, with the tangent A C, the angle B A C; then B A C is measured by half the difference of the two arcs B E F and F D.

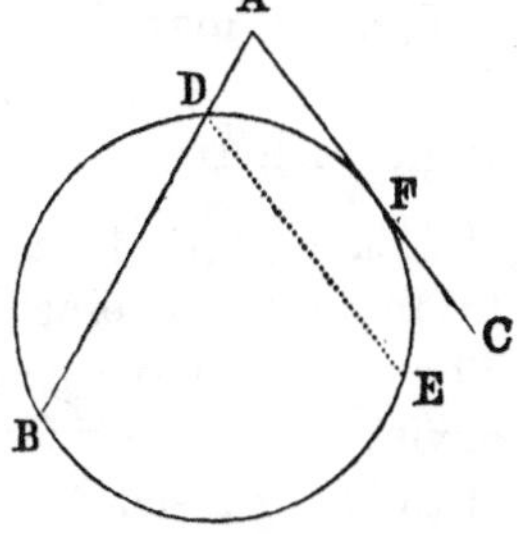

Draw D E parallel to A C; then will the arc E F be equal to the arc D F (Prop. XII.), and the angle B D E be equal to the angle B A C. But the angle B D E is measured by half of the arc B E (Prop. XVIII.); hence the equal angle B A C is also measured by half the arc B E; that is, by half the difference of the arcs B E F and E F, or, since E F is equal to D F, by half the difference of the intercepted arcs B E F and D F.

BOOK IV.

PROPORTIONS, AREAS, AND SIMILARITY OF FIGURES.

DEFINITIONS.

209. The AREA of a figure is its quantity of surface, and is expressed by the number of times which the surface contains some other area assumed as a unit of measure.

Figures have *equal* areas, when they contain the same unit of measure an equal number of times.

210. SIMILAR FIGURES are such as have the angles of the one equal to those of the other, each to each, and the sides containing the equal angles proportional.

211. EQUIVALENT FIGURES are such as have equal areas.

Figures may be equivalent which are not similar. Thus a circle may be equivalent to a square, and a triangle to a rectangle.

212. EQUAL FIGURES are such as, when applied the one to the other, coincide throughout (Art. 34, Ax. 14). Thus circles having equal radii are equal; and triangles having the three sides of the one equal to the three sides of the other, each to each, are also equal.

Equal figures are always similar; but similar figures may be very unequal.

213. In different circles, SIMILAR ARCS, SEGMENTS, or SECTORS are such as correspond to equal angles at the centres of the circles.

Thus, if the angles A and E are equal, the arc B C will be similar to the arc FG; the segment BDC to the segment F H G, and the sector A B C to the sector E F G.

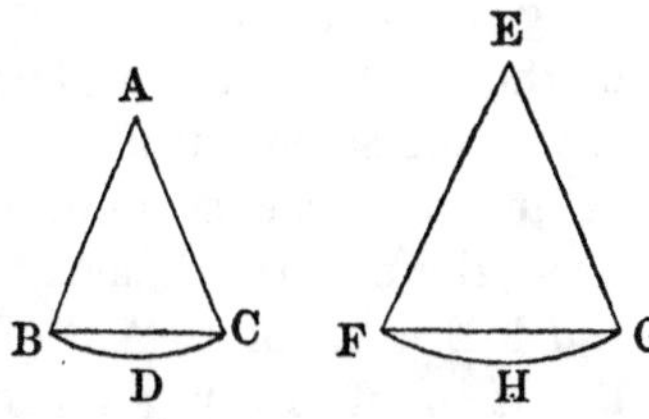

214. The ALTITUDE OF A TRIANGLE is the perpendicular, which measures the distance of any one of its vertices from the opposite side taken as a base; as the perpendicular A D let fall on the base B C in the triangle A B C.

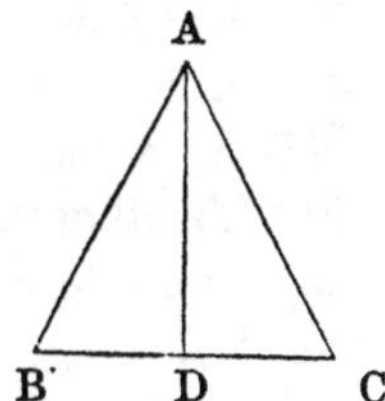

215. The ALTITUDE OF A PARALLELOGRAM is the perpendicular which measures the distance between its opposite sides taken as bases; as the perpendicular E F measuring the distance between the opposite sides, A B, D C, of the parallelogram A B C D.

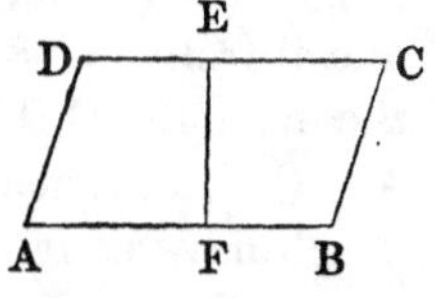

216. The ALTITUDE OF A TRAPEZOID is the perpendicular distance between its parallel sides; as the distance measured by the perpendicular E F between the parallel sides, A B, D C, of the trapezoid A B C D.

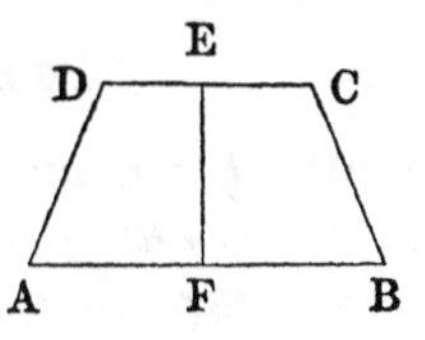

PROPOSITION I. — THEOREM.

217. *Parallelograms which have equal bases and equal altitudes are equivalent.*

Let A B C D, A B E F be two parallelograms having equal bases and equal altitudes; then these parallelograms are equivalent.

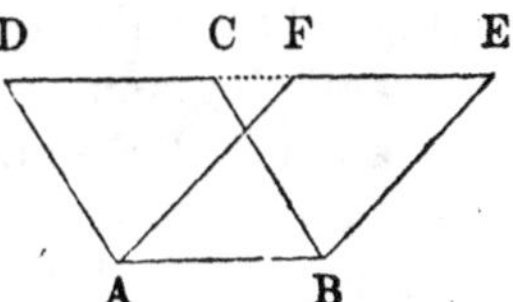

Let the base of the one parallelogram be placed on that of the other, so that A B shall be the common base. Now, since the two parallelograms are of the same altitude, their upper bases, D C, F E, will be in the same straight line, D C E F, parallel to A B. From the nature of parallelograms D C is equal to A B, and F E is equal to A B (Prop. XXXI. Bk. I.); therefore D C is equal to F E (Art. 34, Ax. 1); hence, if D C and F E be taken away from the same line, D E, the remainders C E and D F will be equal (Art. 34, Ax. 3). But A D is equal to B C and A F to B E (Prop. XXXI. Bk. I.); therefore the triangles D A F, C B E, are mutually equilateral, and consequently equal (Prop. XVIII. Bk. I.).

If from the quadrilateral A B E D, we take away the triangle A D F, there will remain the parallelogram A B E F; and if from the same quadrilateral A B E D, we take away the triangle C B E, there will remain the parallelogram A B C D. Hence the parallelograms A B C D, A B E F, which have equal bases and equal altitude, are equivalent.

218. *Cor.* Any parallelogram is equivalent to a rectangle having the same base and altitude.

Proposition II. — Theorem.

219. *If a triangle and a parallelogram have the same base and altitude, the triangle is equivalent to half the parallelogram.*

Let A B E be a triangle, and A B C D a parallelogram having the same base, A B, and the same altitude; then will the triangle be equivalent to half the parallelogram.

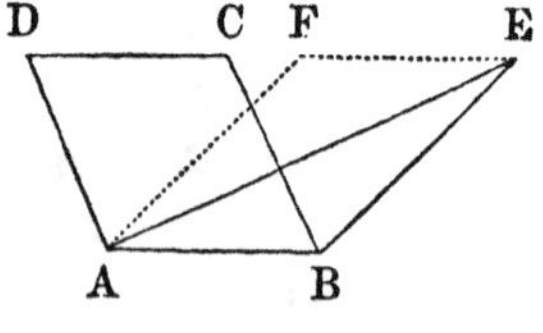

Draw A F, F E so as to form the parallelogram A B E F. Then the parallelograms A B C D, A B E F, having the same base and altitude, are equivalent (Prop. I.). But the triangle A B E is half the parallelogram A B E F (Prop. XXXI. Cor. 1, Bk. I.); hence the triangle A B E is equivalent to half the parallelogram A B C D (Art. 34, Ax. 7).

220. *Cor.* 1. Any triangle is equivalent to half a rectangle having the same base and altitude, or to a rectangle either having the same base and half of the same altitude, or having the same altitude and half of the same base.

221. *Cor.* 2. All triangles which have equal bases and altitudes are equivalent.

Proposition III.—Theorem.

222. *Two rectangles having equal altitudes are to each other as their bases.*

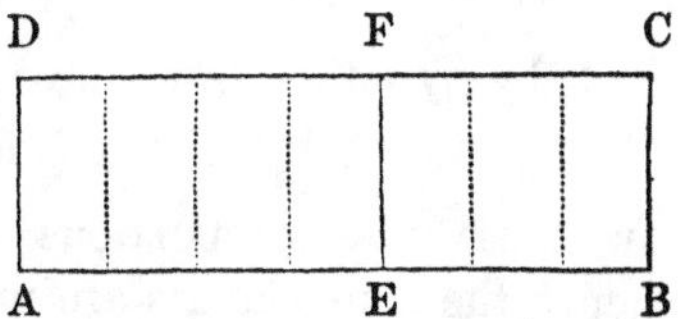

Let A B C D, A E F D be two rectangles having the common altitude A D; they are to each other as their bases A B, A E.

First. Suppose that the bases A B, A E are commensurable, and are to each other, for example, as the numbers 7 and 4. If A B is divided into seven equal parts, A E will contain four of those parts. At each point of division draw lines perpendicular to the base; seven rectangles will thus be formed, all equal to each other, since they have equal bases and the same altitude (Prop. I.). The rectangle A B C D will contain seven partial rectangles, while A E F D will contain four; hence the rectangle A B C D is to A E F D as 7 is to 4, or as A B is to A E. The same reasoning may be applied, whatever be the numbers expressing the ratio of the bases; hence, whatever be that ratio, when its terms are commensurable, we shall have

A B C D : A E F D : : A B : A E.

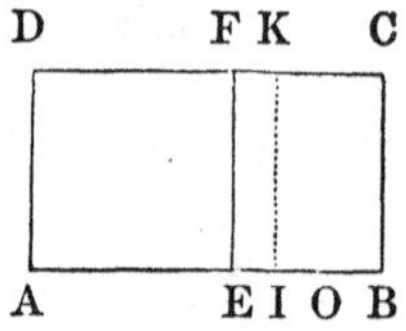

Second. Suppose that the bases A B, A E are incommensurable; we shall still have

A B C D : A E F D : : A B : A E.

For, if this proportion be not true, the first three terms remaining the same, the fourth term must be either greater or less than A E. Suppose it to be greater, and that we have

A B C D : A E F D : : A B : A O.

Conceive A B divided into equal parts, each of which is less than E O. There will be at least one point of division, I, between E and O. Through this point, I, draw the perpendicular I K; then the bases A B, A I will be commensurable, and we shall have

A B C D : A I K D : : A B : A I.

But, by hypothesis, we have

A B C D : A E F D : : A B : A O.

In these two proportions the antecedents are equal; hence the consequents are proportional (Prop. X. Cor. 2, Bk. II.), and we have

A I K D : A E F D : : A I : A O.

But A O is greater than A I; therefore, if this proportion is correct, the rectangle A E F D must be greater than the rectangle A I K D (Art. 125); on the contrary, however, it is less (Art. 34, Ax. 8); therefore the proportion is impossible. Hence, A B C D cannot be to A E F D as A B is to a line greater than A E.

In the same manner, it may be shown that the fourth term of the proportion cannot be less than A E; therefore it must be equal to A E. Hence, any two rectangles A B C D, A E F D, having equal altitudes, are to each other as their bases A B, A E.

Proposition IV.—Theorem.

223. *Any two rectangles are to each other as the products of their bases multiplied by their altitudes.*

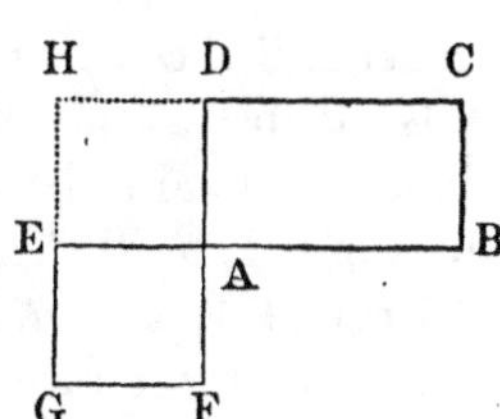

Let A B C D, A E G F be two rectangles; then will A B C D be to A E G F as A B multiplied by A D is to A E multiplied by A F. Having placed the two rectangles so that the angles at A are vertical, produce the sides G E, C D till they meet in H. The two rectangles A B C D, A E H D, having the same altitude, A D, are to each other as their bases, A B, A E. In like manner the two rectangles A E H D, A E G F, having the same altitude, A E, are to each other as their bases, A D, A F. Hence we have the two proportions,

A B C D : A E H D : : A B : A E,
A E H D : A E G F : : A D : A F.

Multiplying the corresponding terms of these proportions together (Prop. XIII. Bk. II.), and omitting the factor A E H D, which is common to both the antecedent and the consequent (Prop. IX. Bk. II.), we shall have

A B C D : A E G F : : A B × A D : A E × A F.

224. *Scholium.* Hence, we may assume as the measure of a rectangle, the product of its base by its altitude, provided we understand by this product the product of two numbers, one of which represents the number of linear units contained in the base, the other the number of linear units contained in the altitude.

The product of two lines is often used to designate their *rectangle;* but the term *square* is used to designate the product of a number multiplied by itself.

PROPOSITION V. — THEOREM.

225. *The area of any parallelogram is equal to the product of its base by its altitude.*

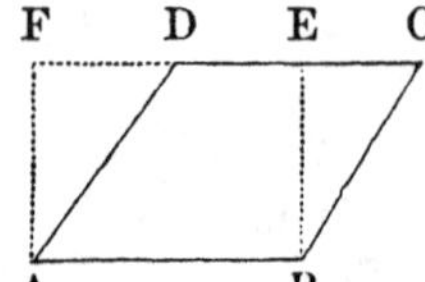

Let A B C D be any parallelogram, A B its base, and B E its altitude; then will its area be equal to the product of A B by B E.

Draw B E and A F perpendicular to A B, and produce C D to F. Then the parallelogram A B C D is equivalent to the rectangle A B E F, which has the same base, A B, and the same altitude, B E (Prop. I. Cor.). But the rectangle A B E F is measured by A B $\times$ B E (Prop. IV. Sch.); therefore A B $\times$ B E is equal to the area of the parallelogram A B C D.

226. *Cor.* Parallelograms having equal bases are to each other as their altitudes, and parallelograms having equal altitudes are to each other as their bases; and, in general, parallelograms are to each other as the products of their bases by their altitudes.

PROPOSITION VI. — THEOREM.

227. *The area of any triangle is equal to the product of its base by half its altitude*

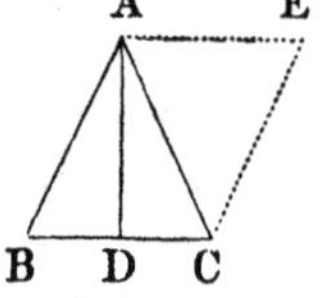

Let A B C be any triangle, B C its base, and A D its altitude; then its area will be equal to the product of B C by half of A D.

Draw A E and C E so as to form the parallelogram A B C E; then the triangle A B C is half the parallelogram A B C E, which has the same base B C, and the same altitude A D (Prop. II.); but the area of the parallelogram is equal to B C $\times$ A D (Prop. V.); hence the area of the triangle must be $\frac{1}{2}$ B C $\times$ A D, or B C $\times$ $\frac{1}{2}$ A D.

228. *Cor.* Triangles of equal altitudes are to each other as their bases, and triangles of equal bases are to each other as their altitudes; and, in general, triangles are to each other as the products of their bases and altitudes.

PROPOSITION VII. — THEOREM.

229. *The area of any trapezoid is equal to the product of its altitude by half the sum of its parallel sides.*

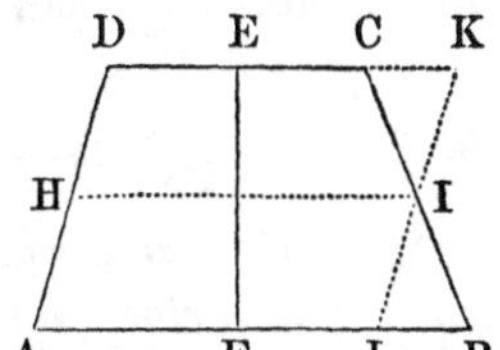

Let A B C D be a trapezoid, E F its altitude, and A B, C D its parallel sides; then its area will be equal to the product of E F by half the sum of A B and C D.

Through I, the middle point of the side B C, draw K L parallel to A D; and produce D C till it meet K L. In the triangles I B L, I C K, we have the sides I B, I C equal, by construction; the vertical angles L I B, C I K are equal (Prop. IV. Bk. I.); and, since C K and B L are parallel, the alternate angles I B L, I C K are also equal (Prop. XXII. Bk. I.); therefore the triangles I B L, I C K are equal (Prop. VI. Bk. I.); hence the trapezoid A B C D is equivalent to the parallelogram A D K L, and is measured by the product of E F by A L (Prop. V.).

But we have A L equal D K; and since the triangles I B L and K C I are equal, the sides B L and C K are equal; therefore the sum of A B and C D is equal to the sum of A L and D K, or twice A L. Hence A L is half the sum of the bases A B, C D; hence the area of the trapezoid A B, C D is equal to the product of the altitude E F by half the sum of the parallel sides A B, C D.

Cor. If through I, the middle point of B C, the line I H be drawn parallel to the base A B, the point H will also be the middle point of A D. For, since the figure A H I L is a parallelogram, as is likewise D H I K, their opposite sides being parallel, we have A H equal to I L, and D H equal to I K. But since the triangles B I L, C I K are equal, we have I L equal to I K; hence A H is equal to D H.

Now, the line H I is equal to A L, which has been shown to be equal to half the sum of A B and C D; therefore the area of the trapezoid is equal to the product of E F by H I. Hence, the area of a trapezoid is equal to the product of its altitude by the line connecting the middle points of the sides which are not parallel.

Proposition VIII. — Theorem.

230. *If a straight line be divided into two parts, the square described on the whole line is equivalent to the sum of the squares described on the parts, together with twice the rectangle contained by the parts.*

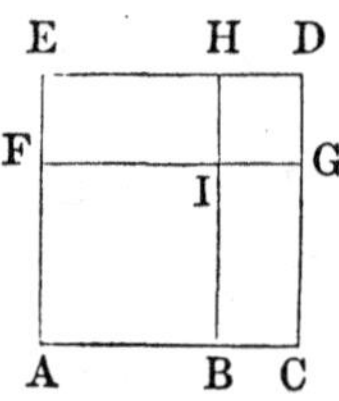

Let A C be a straight line, divided into two parts, A B, B C, at the point B; then the square described on A C is equivalent to the sum of the squares described on the parts A B, B C, together with twice the rectangle contained by A B, B C; that is,

$$\overline{AC}^2 = \overline{AB}^2 + \overline{BC}^2 + 2\,AB \times BC.$$

On A C describe the square A C D E; take A F equal to A B; draw F G parallel to A C, and B H parallel to A E.

The square A C D E is divided into four parts; the first, A B I F, is the square described on A B, since A F was taken equal to A B. The second, I G D H, is the square described upon B C; for, since A C is equal to A E, and A B is equal to A F, A C minus A B is equal to A E minus A F, which gives B C equal to E F. But I G is equal to B C, and D G to E F, since the lines are parallels; therefore I G D H is equal to the square described on B C.

These two parts being taken from the whole square, there remain two rectangles B C G I, E F I H, each of which is measured by A B × B C ; hence the square on the whole line A C is equivalent to the squares on the parts A B, BC, together with twice the rectangle of the parts.

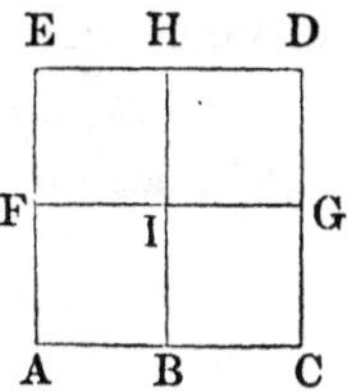

231. *Cor.* The square described on the whole line A C is equivalent to four times the square described on the half A B.

232. *Scholium.* This proposition is equivalent to the algebraical formula,

$$(a + b)^2 = a^2 + 2\,a\,b + b^2.$$

Proposition IX. — Theorem.

233. *The square described on the difference of two straight lines is equivalent to the sum of the squares described on the two lines, diminished by twice the rectangle contained by the lines.*

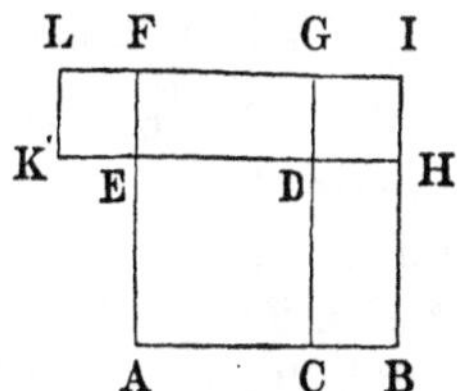

Let A B and B C be two lines, and A C their difference ; then will the square described on A C be equivalent to the sum of the squares described on A B, B C, diminished by twice the rectangle A B, B C ; that is,

$$(AB - BC)^2 \text{ or } \overline{AC}^2 = \overline{AB}^2 + \overline{BC}^2 - 2\ AB \times BC.$$

On A B describe the square A B I F ; take A E equal to A C ; draw C G parallel to B I, H K parallel to A B, and complete the square E F L K.

Since A F is equal to A B, and A E to A C, E F is equal to B C, and L F to G I ; therefore L G is equal to F I ; hence the two rectangles C B I G, G L K D are each measured by A B $\times$ B C. Take these rectangles from the whole figure A B I L K E, which is equivalent to $\mathrm{AB}^2 + \mathrm{BC}^2$, and there will evidently remain the square A C D E; hence the square on A C is equivalent to the sum of the squares on A B, B C, diminished by twice the rectangle contained by A B, B C.

234. *Scholium.* This proposition is equivalent to the algebraical formula,

$$(a - b)^2 = a^2 - 2\,a\,b + b^2.$$

PROPOSITION X. — THEOREM.

235. *The rectangle contained by the sum and difference of two straight lines is equivalent to the difference of the squares of these lines.*

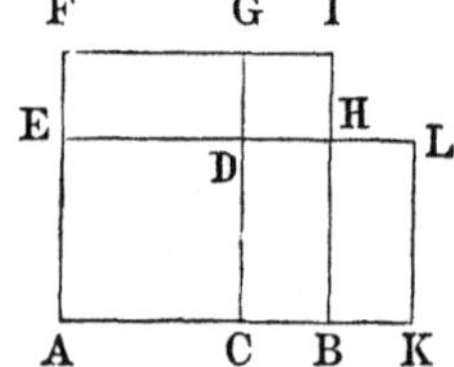

Let A B, B C be two lines; then will the rectangle contained by the sum and difference of A B, B C, be equivalent to the difference of the squares of A B, B C; that is,

$$(\mathrm{AB} + \mathrm{BC}) \times (\mathrm{AB} - \mathrm{BC}) = \overline{\mathrm{AB}}^2 - \overline{\mathrm{BC}}^2.$$

On A B describe the square A B I F, and on A C the square A C D E; produce C D to G; and produce A B until B K is equal to B C, and complete the rectangle A K L E.

The base A K of the rectangle is the sum of the two lines A B, B C; and its altitude A E is the difference of the same lines; therefore the rectangle A K L E is that contained by the sum and the difference of the lines A B, B C. But this rectangle is composed of the two parts A B H E and B H L K; and the part B H L K is equal to the rectangle E D G F, since B H is equal to D E, and B K to E F. Hence the rectangle A K L E is equivalent to A B H E plus E D G F, which is equivalent to the difference between the square A B I F described on A B, and D H I G described on B C; hence

$$(AB + BC) \times (AB - BC) = \overline{AB}^2 - \overline{BC}^2.$$

236. *Scholium.* This proposition is equivalent to the algebraical formula,

$$(a + b) \times (a - b) = a^2 - b^2.$$

PROPOSITION XI. — THEOREM.

237. *The square described on the hypothenuse of a right-angled triangle is equivalent to the sum of the squares described on the other two sides.*

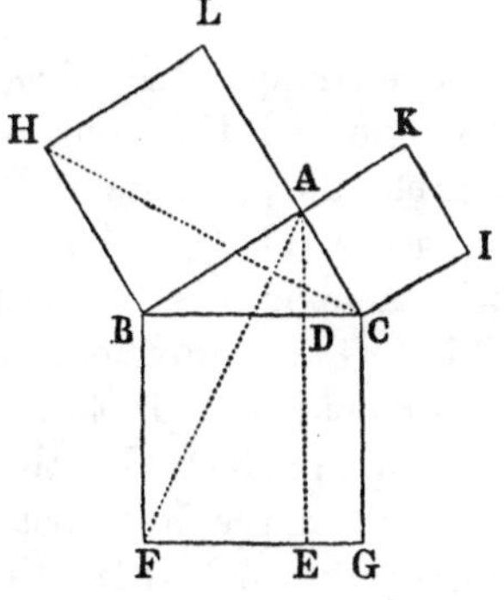

Let A B C be a right-angled triangle, having the right angle at A; then the square described on the hypothenuse B C will be equivalent to the sum of the squares on the sides B A, A C.

On B C describe the square B C G F, and on A B, A C the squares A B H L, A C I K; and through A draw A E parallel to B F or C G, and join A F, H C.

The angle A B F is composed of the angle A B C, together with the right angle C B F; the angle C B H is composed of the same angle A B C together with the right angle A B H; therefore the angle A B F is equal to the angle H B C. But we have A B equal to B H, being sides of the same square; and B F equal to B C, for the same reason; therefore the triangles A B F, H B C have two sides and the included angle of the one equal to two sides and the included angle of the other; hence they are themselves equal (Prop. V. Bk. I.).

But the triangle A B F is equivalent to half the rectangle B D E F, since they have the same base B F, and the same altitude B D (Prop. II. Cor. 1). The triangle H B C is, in like manner, equivalent to half the square A B H L; for the angles B A C, B A L being both right, A C and A L form one and the same straight line parallel to H B (Prop. II. Bk. I.); and consequently the triangle and the square have the same altitude A B (Prop. XXV. Bk. I.); and they also have the same base B H; hence the triangle is equivalent to half the square (Prop. II.).

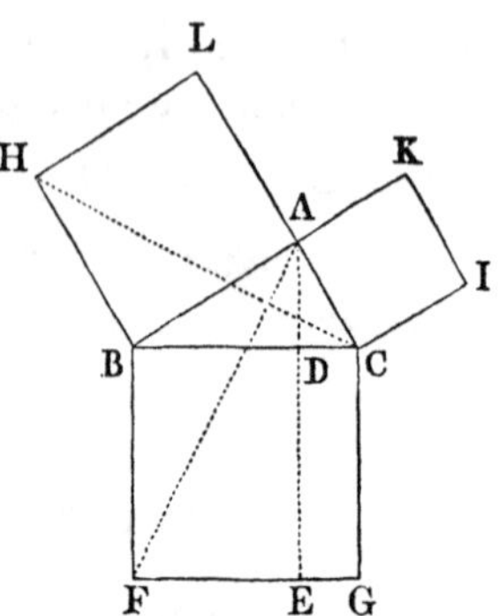

The triangle A B F has already been proved equal to the triangle H B C; hence the rectangle B D E F, which is double the triangle A B F, must be equivalent to the square A B H L, which is double the triangle H B C. In the same manner it may be proved that the rectangle C D E G is equivalent to the square A C I K. But the two rectangles B D E F, C D E G, taken together, compose the square B C G F; therefore the square B C G F, described on the hypothenuse, is equivalent to the sum of the squares A B H L, A C I K, described on the two other sides; that is,

$$\overline{BC}^2 \text{ is equivalent to } \overline{AB}^2 + \overline{AC}^2.$$

238. *Cor.* 1. *The square of either of the sides which form the right angle of a right-angled triangle is equivalent to the square of the hypothenuse diminished by the square of the other side;* thus,

$$\overline{AB}^2 \text{ is equivalent to } \overline{BC}^2 - \overline{AC}^2.$$

239. *Cor.* 2. *The square of the hypothenuse is to the square of either of the other sides, as the hypothenuse is to the part of the hypothenuse cut off, adjacent to that side,*

by the perpendicular let fall from the vertex of the right angle. For, on account of the common altitude B F, the square BCGF is to the rectangle BDEF as the base BC is to the base BD (Prop. III.); now, the square ABHL has been proved to be equivalent to the rectangle BDEF; therefore we have,

$$\overline{BC}^2 : \overline{AB}^2 : : BC : BD.$$

In like manner, we have,

$$\overline{BC}^2 : \overline{AC}^2 : : BC : CD.$$

240. *Cor.* 3. *If a perpendicular be drawn from the vertex of the right angle to the hypothenuse, the squares of the sides about the right angle will be to each other as the adjacent segments of the hypothenuse.* For the rectangles BDEF, DCGE, having the same altitude, are to each other as their bases, B D, C D (Prop. III.). But these rectangles are equivalent to the squares A B H L, A C I K; therefore we have,

$$\overline{AB}^2 : \overline{AC}^2 : : BD : DC.$$

241. *Cor.* 4. *The square described on the diagonal of a square is equivalent to double the square described on a side.* For let A B C D be a square, and A C its diagonal; the triangle A B C being right-angled and isosceles, we have,

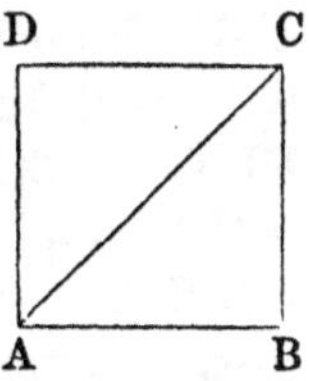

$$\overline{AC}^2 = \overline{AB}^2 + \overline{BC}^2 = 2\,\overline{AB}^2 = 2 \times ABCD.$$

242. *Cor.* 5. Since $\overline{AC}^2$ is equal to $2\,\overline{AB}^2$, we have

$$\overline{AC}^2 : \overline{AB}^2 : : 2 : 1;$$

and, extracting the square root, we have

$$AC : AB : : \sqrt{2} : 1;$$

hence, *the diagonal of a square is incommensurable with a side.*

243. NOTE.—The proposition may also be demonstrated as follows: —

Let A B C be a right-angled triangle, having the right angle at A; then the square described on the hypothenuse B C will be equivalent to the sum of the squares on the sides B A, A C.

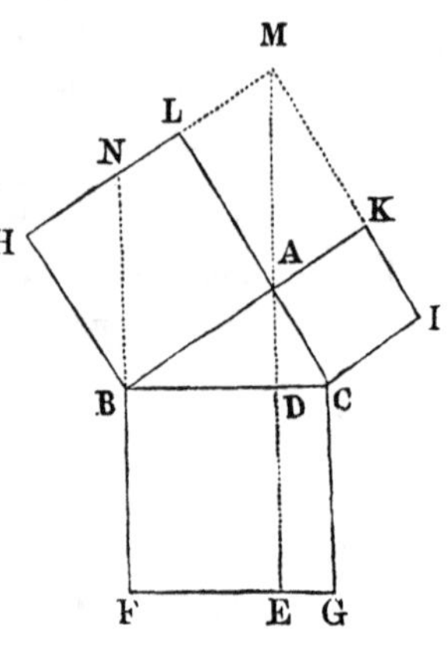

On B C describe the square B C G F, and on A B, A C the squares A B H L, A C I K; produce F B to N, H L and I K to M; and through A draw E D A parallel to F B N, and meeting the prolongation of H L in M.

Then, since the angles H B A, N B C are both right angles, if the common angle N B A be taken from each of these equals, there will remain the equal angles H B N, A B C; and, consequently, since the triangles H B N, A B C are both right-angled, and have also the sides B H, B A equal, their hypothenuses B N, B C are equal (Prop. VI. Cor., Bk. I.). But B C is equal to B F; therefore B N is equal to B F; hence the parallelograms B A M N, B D E F, of which the common altitude is B D, have equal bases; therefore the two parallelograms are equivalent (Prop. I.). But the parallelogram B A M N is equivalent to the square A B H L, since they have the same base B A, and the same altitude A L; hence the parallelogram B D E F is also equivalent to the square A B H L. In like manner it may be shown that the rectangle D C G E is equivalent to the square A C I K; hence the two rectangles together, that is, the square B C G F, are equivalent to the sum of the squares A B H L, A C I K.

PROPOSITION XII. — THEOREM.

244. *In any triangle, the square of the side opposite an acute angle is less than the sum of the squares of the base and the other side, by twice the rectangle contained by the base and the distance from the vertex of the acute angle to the perpendicular let fall from the vertex of the opposite angle on the base, or on the base produced.*

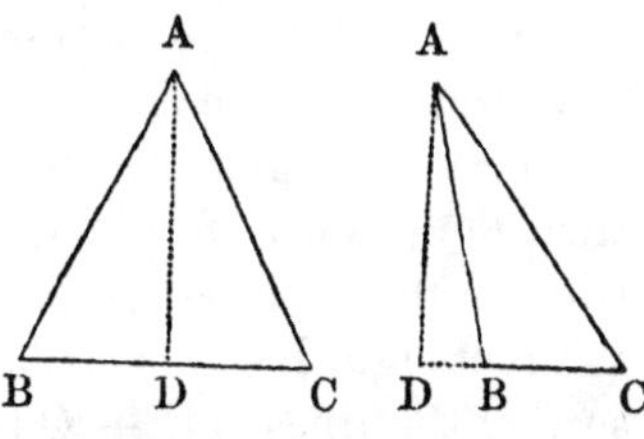

Let A B C be any triangle, C one of its acute angles, and A D the perpendicular let fall on the base B C, or on B C produced; then, in either case, will the square of A B be less than the sum of the squares of A C, B C, by twice the rectangle B C $\times$ C D.

First. When the perpendicular falls within the triangle A B C, we have B D $=$ B C $-$ C D; and consequently, $\overline{BD}^2 = \overline{BC}^2 + \overline{CD}^2 - 2\ BC \times CD$ (Prop. IX.). By adding $\overline{AD}^2$ to each of these equals, we have

$$\overline{BD}^2 + \overline{AD}^2 = \overline{BC}^2 + \overline{CD}^2 + \overline{AD}^2 - 2\ BC \times CD.$$

But the two right-angled triangles A D B, A D C give

$$\overline{AB}^2 = \overline{BD}^2 + \overline{AD}^2, \text{ and } \overline{AC}^2 = \overline{CD}^2 + \overline{AD}^2$$

(Prop. XI.); therefore,

$$\overline{AB}^2 = \overline{BC}^2 + \overline{AC}^2 - 2\ BC \times CD.$$

Secondly. When the perpendicular A D falls without the triangle A B C, we have B D $=$ C D $-$ B C; and consequently, $\overline{BD}^2 = \overline{CD}^2 + \overline{BC}^2 - 2\ CD \times BC$. By adding $\overline{AD}^2$ to each of these equals, we find, as before,

$$\overline{AB}^2 = \overline{BC}^2 + \overline{AC}^2 - 2\ BC \times CD.$$

PROPOSITION XIII. — THEOREM.

245. *In any obtuse-angled triangle, the square of the side opposite the obtuse angle is equivalent to the sum of the squares of the two other sides plus twice the rectangle contained by the one of those sides into the distance from the vertex of the obtuse angle to the perpendicular let fall from the vertex of the opposite angle to that side produced.*

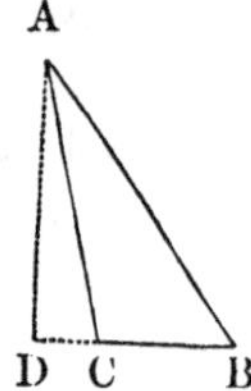

Let A C B be an obtuse-angled triangle, having the obtuse angle at C, and let A D be perpendicular to the base B C produced; then the square of A B is greater than the sum of the squares of B C, A C, by twice the rectangle B C × C D. Since B D is the sum of the lines B C + C D, we have

$$\overline{BD}^2 = BC^2 + \overline{CD}^2 + 2\,BC \times CD$$

(Prop. VIII.). By adding $\overline{AD}^2$ to each of these equals, we have

$$\overline{BD}^2 + \overline{AD}^2 = \overline{BC}^2 + \overline{CD}^2 + \overline{AD}^2 + 2\,BC \times CD.$$

But the two right-angled triangles A D B, A D C give

$$\overline{AB}^2 = BD^2 + \overline{AD}^2, \quad \text{and} \quad \overline{AC}^2 = \overline{CD}^2 + \overline{AD}^2$$

(Prop. XI.); therefore,

$$\overline{AB}^2 = \overline{BC}^2 + \overline{AC}^2 + 2\,BC \times CD.$$

246. *Scholium.* The right-angled triangle is the only one in which the sum of the squares of two sides is equivalent to the square of the third; for if the angle contained by the two sides is acute, the sum of their squares will be greater than the square of the opposite side; if obtuse, it will be less.

PROPOSITION XIV. — THEOREM.

247. *In any triangle, if a straight line be drawn from the vertex to the middle point of the base, the sum of the*

squares of the other two sides is equivalent to twice the square of the bisecting line, together with twice the square of half the base.

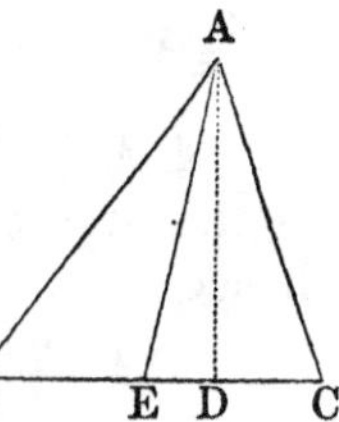

In any triangle A B C, draw the line A E from the vertex A to the middle of the base B C; then the sum of the squares of the two sides, A B, A C, is equivalent to twice the square of A E together with twice the square of B E.

On B C let fall the perpendicular A D; then, in the triangle A B E,

$$\overline{AB}^2 = \overline{AE}^2 + \overline{EB}^2 + 2\,EB \times ED$$

(Prop. XIII.), and, in triangle A E C,

$$\overline{AC}^2 = \overline{AE}^2 + \overline{EC}^2 - 2\,EC \times ED$$

(Prop. XII.). Hence, by adding the corresponding sides together, observing that since E B and E C are equal, $\overline{EB}^2$ is equal to $\overline{EC}^2$, and $EB \times ED$ to $EC \times ED$, we have

$$\overline{AB}^2 + \overline{AC}^2 = 2\,\overline{AE}^2 + 2\,\overline{EB}^2.$$

Proposition XV. — Theorem.

248. *In any parallelogram the sum of the squares of the four sides is equivalent to the sum of the squares of the two diagonals.*

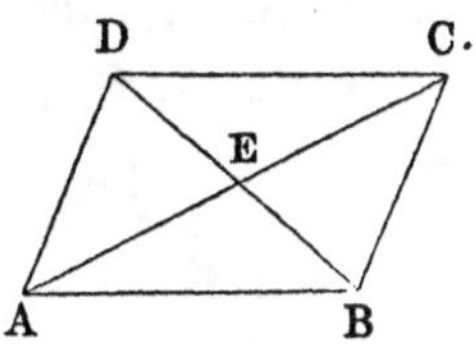

Let A B C D be any parallelogram, the diagonals of which are A C, B D; then the sum of the squares of A B, B C, C D, D A is equivalent to the sum of the squares of A C, B D.

For the diagonals A C, B D bisect each other (Prop. XXXIV. Bk. I.); hence, in the triangle A B C, $\overline{AB}^2 + \overline{BC}^2 = 2\,\overline{AE}^2 + 2\,\overline{BE}^2$ (Prop. XIV.); also, in the triangle A D C,

$$\overline{AD}^2 + \overline{DC}^2 = 2\,\overline{AE}^2 + 2\,\overline{DE}^2.$$

Hence, by adding the corresponding sides together, and observing that, since B E and D E are equal, $\overline{BE}^2$ and $\overline{DE}^2$ must also be equal, we shall have,

$$\overline{AB}^2 + \overline{BC}^2 + \overline{AD}^2 + \overline{DC}^2 = 4\,\overline{AE}^2 + 4\,\overline{DE}^2.$$

But 4 $\overline{AE}^2$ is the square of 2 A E, or of A C, and 4 $\overline{DE}^2$ is the square of 2 D E, or of B D (Prop. VIII. Cor.); hence,

$$\overline{BA}^2 + \overline{BC}^2 + \overline{CD}^2 + \overline{AD}^2 = \overline{AC}^2 + \overline{BD}^2.$$

Proposition XVI. — Theorem.

249. *In any quadrilateral the sum of the squares of the sides is equivalent to the sum of the squares of the diagonals, plus four times the square of the straight line that joins the middle points of the diagonals.*

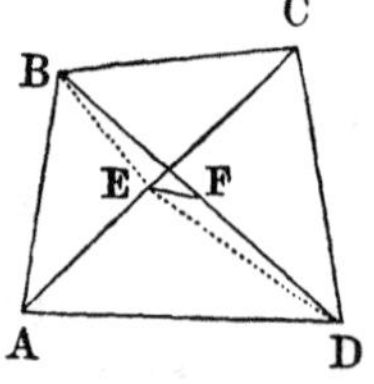

Let A B C D be any quadrilateral, the diagonals of which are A C, D B, and E F a straight line joining their middle points, E, F; then the sum of the squares of A B, B C, C D, A D is equivalent to $\overline{AC}^2 + \overline{BD}^2 + 4\,\overline{EF}^2$.

Join E B and E D; then in the triangle A B C,

$$\overline{AB}^2 + \overline{BC}^2 = 2\,\overline{AE}^2 + 2\,\overline{BE}^2$$

(Prop. XIV.), and in the triangle A D C,

$$\overline{AD}^2 + \overline{CD}^2 = 2\,\overline{AE}^2 + 2\,\overline{DE}^2.$$

Hence, by adding the corresponding sides, we have

$$\overline{AB}^2 + \overline{BC}^2 + \overline{AD}^2 + \overline{CD}^2 = 4\,\overline{AE}^2 + 2\,\overline{BE}^2 + 2\,\overline{DE}^2.$$

But 4 $\overline{AE}^2$ is equivalent to $\overline{AC}^2$ (Prop. VIII. Cor.), and 2 $\overline{BE}^2$ + 2 $\overline{DE}^2$ is equivalent to 4 $\overline{BF}^2$ + 4 $\overline{EF}^2$ (Prop. XIV.); hence,

$$\overline{AB}^2 + \overline{BC}^2 + \overline{AD}^2 + \overline{CD}^2 = \overline{AC}^2 + \overline{BD}^2 + 4\,\overline{EF}^2.$$

250. *Cor.* If the quadrilateral is a parallelogram, the points E and F will coincide; then the proposition will be the same as Prop. XV.

251. *Scholium.* Proposition XV. is only a particular case of this proposition.

Proposition XVII. — Theorem.

252. *If a straight line be drawn in a triangle parallel to one of the sides, it will divide the other two sides proportionally.*

Let ABC be a triangle, and DE a straight line drawn within it parallel to the side BC; then will

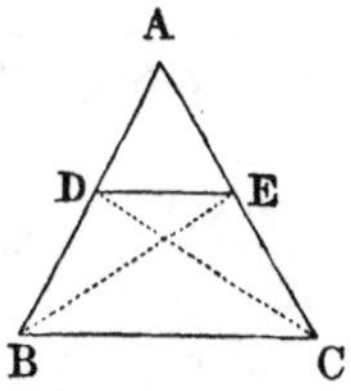

AD : DB : : AE : EC.

A

D E

B C

Join BE and DC; then the two triangles BDE, DEC have the same base, DE; they have also the same altitude, since the vertices B and C lie in a line parallel to the base; therefore the triangles are equivalent (Prop. II. Cor. 2).

The triangles ADE, BDE, having their bases in the same line AB, and having the common vertex E, have the same altitude, and therefore are to each other as their bases (Prop. VI. Cor.); hence

ADE : BDE : : AD : DB.

The triangles ADE, DEC, whose common vertex is D, have also the same altitude, and therefore are to each other as their bases; hence

ADE : DEC : : AE : EC.

But the triangles BDE, DEC have been shown to be equivalent; therefore, on account of the common ratio in the two proportions (Prop. X. Bk. II.),

AD : DB : : AE : EC.

253. *Cor.* 1. Hence, by composition (Prop. VII. Bk.

II.), we have A D + D B : A D : : A E + E C : A E, or A B : A D : : A C : A E; also, A B : B D : : A C : E C.

254. *Cor.* 2. If two or more straight lines be drawn in a triangle parallel to one of the sides, they will divide the other two sides proportionally.

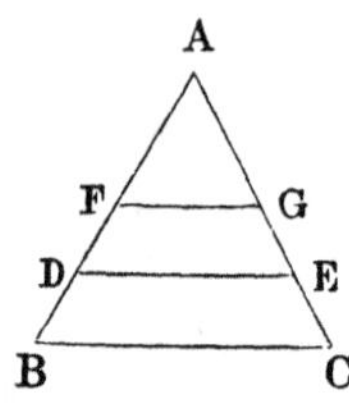

For, in the triangle A B C, since D E is parallel to B C, by the theorem, A D : D B : : A E : E C; and, in the triangle A D E, since F G is parallel to D E, by the preceding corollary, A D : F D : : A E : G E. Hence, since the antecedents are the same in the two proportions (Prop. X. Cor. 2, Bk. II.), F D : D B : : G E : E C.

PROPOSITION XVIII. — THEOREM.

255. *If a straight line divides two sides of a triangle proportionally, the line is parallel to the other side of the triangle.*

Let A B C be a triangle, and D E a straight line drawn in it dividing the sides A B, A C, so that A D : D B : : A E : E C; then will the line D E be parallel to the side B C.

Join B E and D C; then the triangles A D E, B D E, having their bases in the same straight line A B, and having a common vertex, E, are to each other as their bases A D, D B (Prop. VI. Cor.); that is,

A D E : B D E : : A D : D B.

Also, the triangles A D E, D E C, having the common vertex D, and their bases in the same line, are to each other as these bases, A E, E C; that is,

A D E : D E C : : A E : E C.

But, by hypothesis, A D : D B : : A E : E C; hence (Prop. X. Bk. II.),

A D E : B D E : : A D E : D E C;

that is, B D E, D E C have the same ratio to A D E; therefore the triangles B D E, D E C have the same area, and consequently are equivalent (Art. 211). Since these triangles have the same base, D E, their altitudes are equal (Prop. VI. Cor.); hence the line B C, in which their vertices are, must be parallel to D E.

PROPOSITION XIX. — THEOREM.

256. *The straight line bisecting any angle of a triangle divides the opposite side into parts, which are proportional to the adjacent sides.*

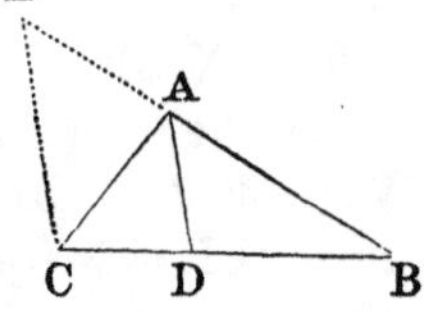

In any triangle, A B C, let the angle B A C be bisected by the straight line A D; then will

B D : D C : : A B : A C.

Through the point C draw C E parallel to A D, meeting B A produced in E. Then, since the two parallels A D, E C are met by the straight line A C, the alternate angles D A C, A C E are equal (Prop. XXII. Bk. I.); and the same parallels being met by the straight line B E, the opposite exterior and interior angles B A D, A E C are also equal (Prop. XXII. Bk. I.). But, by hypothesis, the angles D A C, B A D are equal; consequently the angle A C E is equal to the angle A E C; hence the triangle A C E is isosceles, and the side A E is equal to the side A C (Prop. VIII. Bk. I.). Again, since A D, in the triangle E B C, is parallel to E C, we have B D : D C : : A B : A E (Prop. XVII.), and, substituting A C in place of its equal A E,

B D : D C : : A B : A C.

PROPOSITION XX. — THEOREM.

257. *If a straight line drawn from the vertex of any angle of a triangle divides the opposite side into parts which are proportional to the adjacent sides, the line bisects the angle.*

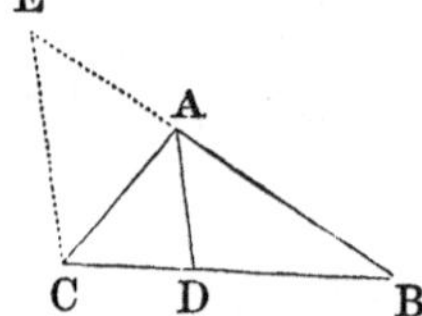

Let the straight line A D, drawn from the vertex of the angle B A C, in the triangle A B C, divide the opposite side B C, so that B D : D C : : A B : A C; then will the line A D bisect the angle B A C.

Through the point C draw C E parallel to A D, meeting B A produced in E. Then, by hypothesis, B D : D C : : A B : A C; and since A D is parallel to E C, B D : D C : : A B : A E (Prop. XVII.); then A B : A C : : A B : A E (Prop. X. Bk. II.); consequently A C is equal to A E; hence the angle A E C is equal to the angle A C E (Prop. VII. Bk. I.). But, since C E and A D are parallels, the angle A E C is equal to the opposite exterior angle B A D, and the angle A C E is equal to the alternate angle D A C (Prop. XXII. Bk. I.); hence the angles B A D, D A C are equal, and consequently the straight line A D bisects the angle B A C.

PROPOSITION XXI. — THEOREM.

258. *If the exterior angle formed by producing one of the sides of any triangle be bisected by a straight line which meets the base produced, the distances from the extremities of the base to the point where the bisecting line meets the base produced, will be to each other as the other two sides of the triangle.*

Let the exterior angle C A E, formed by producing the side B A of the triangle A B C, be bisected by the straight line A D, which meets the side B C produced in D, then will

B D : D C : : A B : A C.

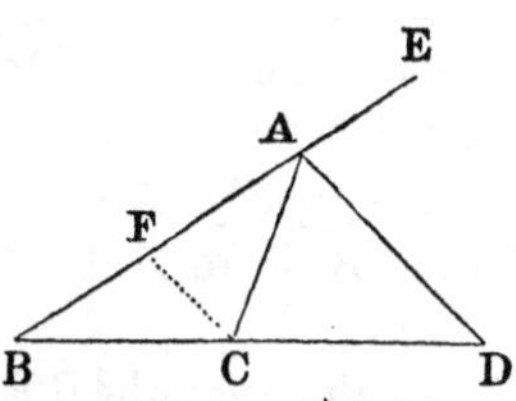

Through C draw C F parallel to A D; then the angle A C F is equal to the alternate angle C A D, and the exterior angle D A E is equal to the interior and opposite angle C F A (Prop. XXII. Bk. I.). But, by hypothesis, the angles C A D, D A E are equal; consequently the angle A C F is equal to the angle C F A; hence the triangle A C F is isosceles, and the side A C is equal to the side A F (Prop. VIII. Bk. I.). Again, since A D is parallel to F C, B D : D C : : B A : A F (Prop. XVII. Cor. 1), and substituting A C in the place of its equal A F, we have

B D : D C : : B A : A C.

Proposition XXII. — Theorem.

259. *Equiangular triangles have their homologous sides proportional, and are similar.*

Let the two triangles A B C, D C E be equiangular; the angle B A C being equal to the angle C D E, the angle A B C to the angle D C E, and the angle A C B to the angle D E C, then the homologous sides will be proportional, and we shall have

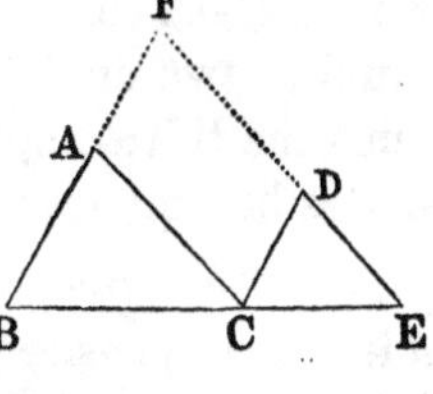

B C : C E : : A B : C D : : A C : D E.

For, let the two triangles be placed so that two homologous sides, B C, C E, may join each other, and be in the same straight line; and produce the sides B A, E D till they meet in F.

Since B C E is a straight line, and the angle B C A is equal to the angle C E D, A C is parallel to F E (Prop. XXI. Bk. I.); also, since the angle A B C is equal to the angle D C E, the line B F is parallel to the line C D. Hence the figure A C D F is a parallelogram; and, consequently, A F is equal to C D, and A C to F D (Prop. XXXI. Bk. I.).

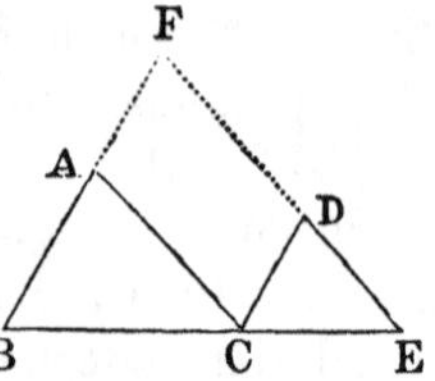

In the triangle B E F, since the line A C is parallel to the side F E, we have B C : C E : : B A : A F (Prop. XVII.); or, substituting C D for its equal, A F,

B C : C E : : B A : C D.

Again, C D is parallel to B F; therefore, B C : C E : : F D : D E; or, substituting A C for its equal F D,

B C : C E : : A C : D E.

And, since both these proportions contain the same ratio B C : C E, we have (Prop. X. Bk. II.)

A C : D E : : B A : C D.

Hence, the equiangular triangles B A C, C D E have their homologous sides proportional; and consequently the two triangles are similar (Art. 210).

260. *Cor.* Two triangles having two angles of the one equal to two angles of the other, each to each, are similar; since the third angles will also be equal, and the two triangles be equiangular.

261. *Scholium.* In similar triangles, the homologous sides are opposite to the equal angles; thus the angle A C B being equal to D E C, the side A B is homologous to D C; in like manner, A C and D E are homologous.

Proposition XXIII. — Theorem.

262. *Triangles which have their homologous sides proportional, are equiangular and similar.*

Let the two triangles A B C, D E F have their sides proportional, so that we have B C : E F : : A B : D E : : A C : D F;

then will the triangles have their angles equal; namely, the angle A equal to the angle D, the angle B to the angle E, and the angle C to the angle F.

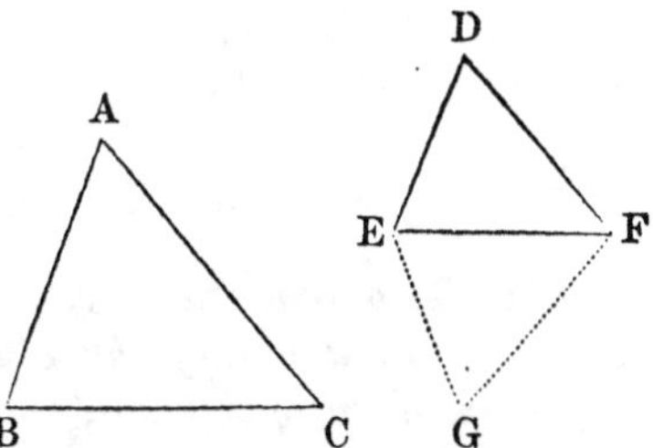

At the point E, in the straight line EF, make the angle FEG equal to the angle B, and at the point F, the angle EFG equal the angle C; the third angle G will be equal to the third angle A (Prop. XXVIII. Cor. 2, Bk. I.); and the two triangles ABC, EFG will be equiangular. Therefore, by the last theorem, we have

$$BC : EF :: AB : EG;$$

but, by hypothesis, we have

$$BC : EF :: AB : DE;$$

hence, EG is equal to DE.

By the same theorem, we also have

$$BC : EF :: AC : FG;$$

and, by hypothesis,

$$BC : EF :: AC : DF;$$

hence FG is equal to DF. Hence, the triangles EGF, DEF, having their three sides equal, each to each, are themselves equal (Prop. XVIII. Bk. I.). But, by construction, the triangle EGF is equiangular with the triangle ABC; hence the triangles DEF, ABC are also equiangular and similar.

263. *Scholium.* The two preceding propositions, together with that relating to the square of the hypothenuse (Art. 237), are the most important and fertile in results of any in Geometry. They are almost sufficient of themselves for all applications to subsequent reasoning, and for the

solution of all problems; since the general properties of triangles include, by implication, those of all figures.

PROPOSITION XXIV. — THEOREM.

264. *Two triangles, which have an angle of the one equal to an angle of the other, and the sides containing these angles proportional, are similar.*

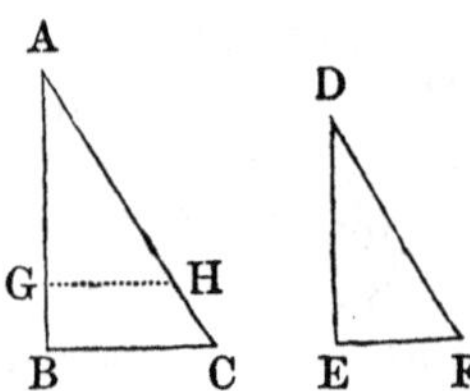

Let the two triangles A B C, D E F have the angle A equal to the angle D, and the sides containing these angles proportional, so that A B : D E : : A C : D F; then the triangles are similar.

Take A G equal D E, and draw G H parallel to B C. The angle A G H will be equal to the angle A B C (Prop. XXII. Bk. I.); and the triangles A G H, A B C will be equiangular; hence we shall have

A B : A G : : A C : A H.

But, by hypothesis,

A B : D E : : A C : D F;

and, by construction, A G is equal to D E; hence A H is equal to D F. Therefore the two triangles A G H, D E F, having two sides and the included angle of the one equal to two sides and the included angle of the other, each to each, are themselves equal (Prop. V. Bk. I.). But the triangle A G H is similar to A B C; therefore D E F is also similar to A B C.

PROPOSITION XXV. — THEOREM.

265. *Two triangles, which have their sides, taken two and two, either parallel or perpendicular to each other, are similar.*

Let the two triangles A B C, D E F have the side A B parallel to the side D E, B C parallel to E F, and A C parallel to D F; these triangles will then be similar.

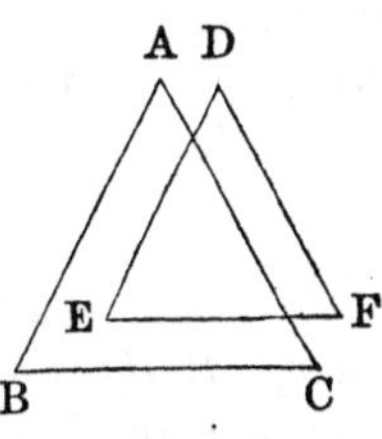

For, since the side A B is parallel to the side D E, and B C to E F, the angle A B C is equal to the angle D E F (Prop. XXVI. Bk. I.). Also, since A C is parallel to D F, the angle A C B is equal to the angle D F E, and the angle B A C to E D F; therefore the triangles A B C, D E F are equiangular; hence they are similar (Prop. XXII.).

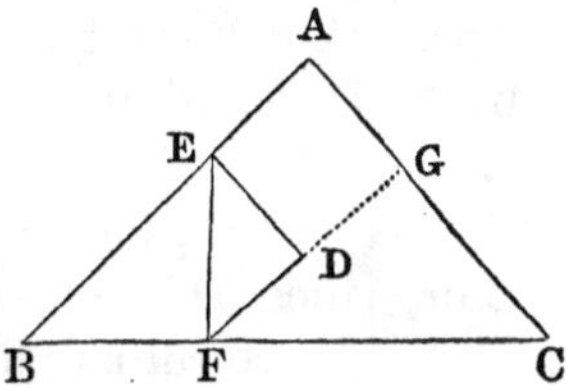

Again, let the two triangles A B C, D E F have the side D E perpendicular to the side A B, D F perpendicular to A C, and E F perpendicular to B C; these triangles are similar.

Produce F D till it meets A C at G; then the angles D G A, D E A of the quadrilateral A E D G are two right angles; and since all the four angles are together equal to four right angles (Prop. XXIX. Cor. 1, Bk. I.), the remaining two angles, E D G, E A G, are together equal to two right angles. But the two angles E D G, E D F are also together equal to two right angles (Prop. I. Bk. I.); hence the angle E D F is equal to E A G or B A C.

The two angles, G F C, G C F, in the right-angled triangle F G C, are together equal to a right angle (Prop. XXVIII. Cor. 5, Bk. I.), and the two angles G F C, G F E are together equal to the right angle E F C (Art. 34, Ax. 9); therefore G F E is equal to G C F, or D F E to B C A. Therefore the triangles A B C, D E F have two angles of the one equal to two angles of the other, each to each; hence they are similar (Prop. XXII. Cor.).

266. *Scholium.* When the two triangles have their sides parallel, the parallel sides are homologous; and when they have them perpendicular, the perpendicular sides are

homologous. Thus, D E is homologous with A B, D F with A C, and E F with B C.

Proposition XXVI. — Theorem.

267. *In any triangle, if a line be drawn parallel to the base, all lines drawn from the vertex will divide the parallel and the base proportionally.*

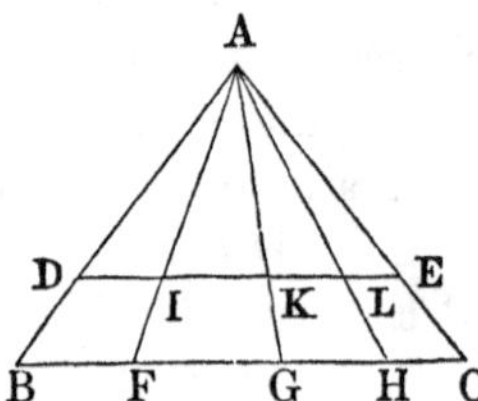

In the triangle B A C, let D E be drawn parallel to the base B C; then will the lines A F, A G, A H, drawn from the vertex, divide the parallel D E, and the base B C, so that

D I : B F : : I K : F G : : K L : G H.

For, since D I is parallel to B F, the triangles A D I and A B F are equiangular; and we have (Prop. XXII.),

D I : B F : : A I : A F;

and since I K is parallel to F G, we have in like manner,

A I : A F : : I K : F G;

and, since these two propositions contain the same ratio, A I : A F, we shall have (Prop. X. Cor. 1, Bk. II.),

D I : B F : : I K : F G.

In the same manner, it may be shown that

I K : F G : : K L : G H : : L E : H C.

Therefore the line D E is divided at the points I, K, L, as the base B C is, at the points F, G, H.

268. *Cor.* If B C were divided into equal parts at the points F, G, H, the parallel D E would also be divided into equal parts at the points I, K, L.

Proposition XXVII. — Theorem.

269. *In a right-angled triangle, if a perpendicular is drawn from the vertex of the right angle to the hypothe-*

nuse, the triangle will be divided into two triangles similar to the given triangle and to each other.

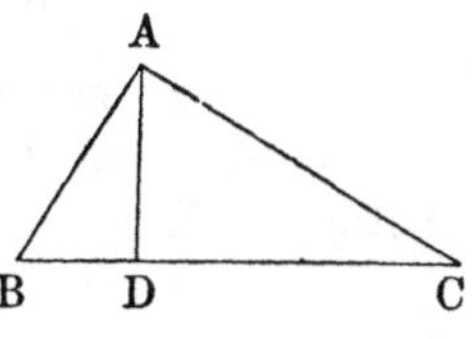

In the right-angled triangle A B C, from the vertex of the right angle B A C, let A D be drawn perpendicular to the hypothenuse B C; then the triangles B A D, D A C will be similar to the triangle A B C, and to each other.

For the triangles B A D, B A C have the common angle B, the right angle B D A equal to the right angle B A C, and therefore the third angle, B A D, of the one, equal to the third angle, C, of the other (Prop. XXVIII. Cor. 2, Bk. I.); hence these two triangles are equiangular, and consequently are similar (Prop. XXII.). In the same manner it may be shown that the triangles D A C and B A C are equiangular and similar. The triangles B A D and D A C, being each similar to the triangle B A C, are similar to each other.

270. *Cor.* 1. Each of the sides containing the right angle is a mean proportional between the hypothenuse and the part of it which is cut off adjacent to that side by the perpendicular from the vertex of the right angle.

For, the triangles B A D, B A C being similar, their homologous sides are proportional; hence

B D : B A : : B A : B C;

and, the triangles D A C, B A C being also similar,

D C : A C : : A C : B C;

hence each of the sides A B, A C is a mean proportional between the hypothenuse and the part cut off adjacent to that side.

271. *Cor.* 2. The perpendicular from the vertex of the right angle to the hypothenuse is a mean proportional between the two parts into which it divides the hypothenuse.

For, since the triangles A B D, A D C are similar, by comparing their homologous sides we have

B D : A D : : A D : D C;

hence, the perpendicular A D is a mean proportional between the parts D B, D C into which it divides the hypothenuse B C.

Proposition XXVIII. — Theorem.

272. *Two triangles, having an angle in each equal, are to each other as the rectangles of the sides which contain the equal angles.*

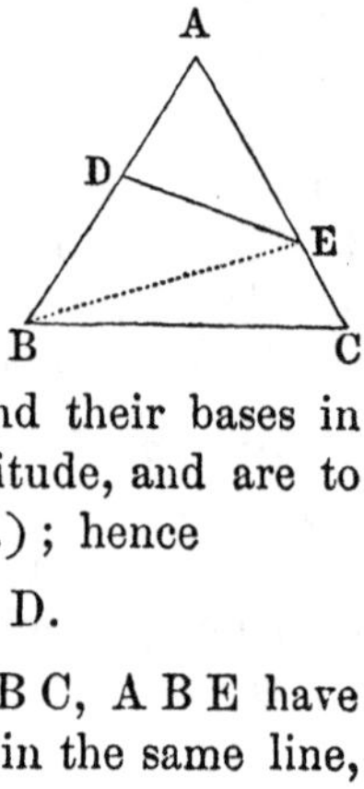

Let the two triangles A B C, A D E have the angle A in common; then will the triangle A B C be to the triangle A D E as A B × A C to A D × A E.

Join B E; then the triangles A B E, A D E, having the common vertex E, and their bases in the same line, A B, have the same altitude, and are to each other as their bases (Prop. VI. Cor.); hence

A B E : A D E : : A B : A D.

In like manner, since the triangles A B C, A B E have the common vertex B, and their bases in the same line, A C, we have

A B C : A B E : : A C : A E.

By multiplying together the corresponding terms of these proportions, and omitting the common term A B E, we have (Prop. XIII. Bk. II.),

A B C : A D E : : A B × A C : A D × A E.

273. *Cor.* If the rectangles of the sides containing the equal angles were equivalent, the triangles would be equivalent.

PROPOSITION XXIX. — THEOREM.

274. *Similar triangles are to each other as the squares described on their homologous sides.*

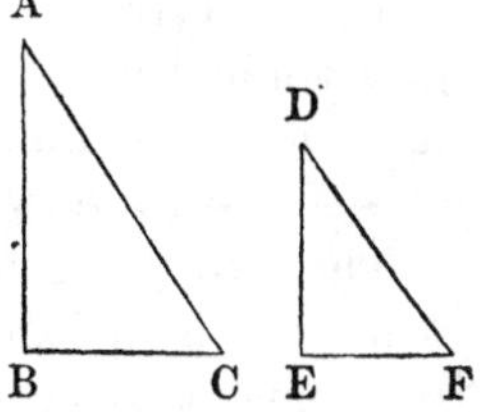

Let A B C, D E F be two similar triangles, and let A C, D F be homologous sides; then the triangle A B C will be to the triangle D E F as the square on A C is to the square on D F.

For, the triangles being similar, they have their homologous sides proportional (Art. 210); therefore

$$AB : DE :: AC : DF;$$

and multiplying the terms of this proportion by the corresponding terms of the identical proportion,

$$AC : DF :: AC : DF,$$

we have (Prop. XIII. Bk. II.),

$$AB \times AC : DE \times DF :: \overline{AC}^2 : \overline{DF}^2.$$

But, by reason of the equal angles A and D, the triangle ABC is to the triangle DEF as AB × AC is to DE × DF (Prop. XXVIII.); consequently (Prop. X. Bk. II.),

$$ABC : DEF :: \overline{AC}^2 : \overline{DF}^2.$$

Therefore, the two similar triangles A B C, D E F are to each other as the squares described on the homologous sides A C, D F, or as the squares described on any other two homologous sides.

PROPOSITION XXX. — THEOREM.

275. *Similar polygons may be divided into the same number of triangles similar each to each, and similarly situated.*

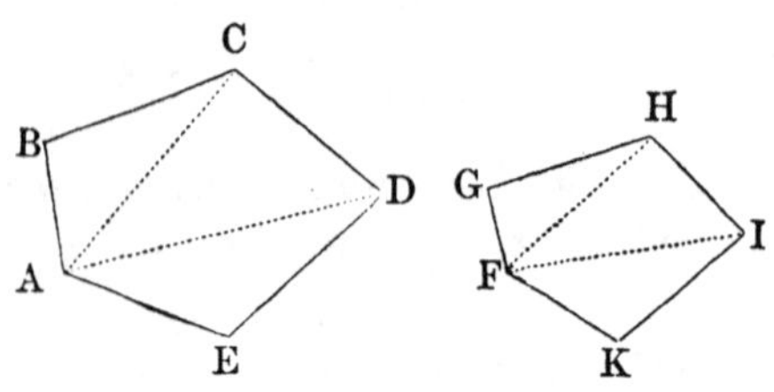

Let A B C D E, F G H I K be two similar polygons; they may be divided into the same number of triangles similar each to each, and similarly situated. From the homologous angles A and F, draw the diagonals A C, A D and F H, F I.

The two polygons being similar, the angles B and G, which are homologous, must be equal, and the sides A B, B C must also be proportional to F G, G H (Art. 210); that is, A B : F G : : B C : G H. Therefore the triangles A B C, F G H have an angle of the one equal to the angle of the other, and the sides containing these angles proportional; hence they are similar (Prop. XXIV.); consequently the angle B C A is equal to the angle G H F. These equal angles being taken from the equal angles B C D, G H I, the remaining angles A C D, F H I will be equal (Art. 34, Ax. 3). But, since the triangles A B C, F G H are similar, we have

A C : F H : : B C : G H;

and, since the polygons are similar (Art. 210),

B C : G H : : C D : H I;

hence (Prop. X. Cor. 1, Bk. II.),

A C : F H : : C D : H I.

But the terms of the last proportion are the sides about the equal angles A C D, F H I; hence the triangles A C D, F H I are similar (Prop. XXIV.). In the same manner, it may be shown that the corresponding triangles A D E, F I K are similar; hence the similar polygons may be divided into the same number of triangles similar each to each, and similarly situated.

276. *Cor. Conversely, if two polygons are composed*

of the same number of similar triangles, and similarly situated, the two polygons are similar.

For the similarity of the corresponding triangles give the angles A B C equal to F G H, B C A equal to G H F, and A C D equal to F H I; hence, B C D equal to G H I, likewise C D E equal to H I K, &c. Moreover, we have

A B : F G : : B C : G H : : A C : F H : : C D : H I, &c.;

therefore the two polygons have their angles equal and their sides proportional; hence they are similar.

Proposition XXXI. — Theorem.

277. *The perimeters of similar polygons are to each other as their homologous sides; and their areas are to each other as the squares described on these sides.*

Let A B C D E, F G H I K be two similar polygons; then their perimeters are to each other as their homologous sides

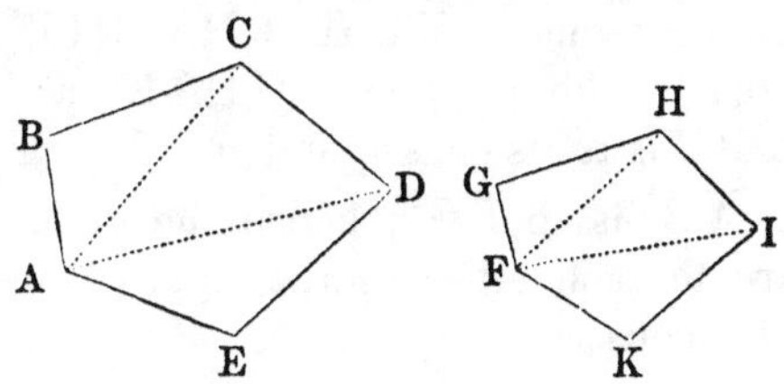

A B and F G, B C and G H, &c.; and their areas are to each other as $\overline{AB}^2$ is to $\overline{FG}^2$, $\overline{BC}^2$ to $\overline{GH}^2$, &c.

First. Since the two polygons are similar, we have

A B : F G : : B C : G H : : C D : H I, &c.

Now the sum of the antecedents A B, B C, C D, &c., which compose the perimeter of the first polygon, is to the sum of the consequents F G, G H, H I, &c., which compose the perimeter of the second polygon, as any one antecedent is to its consequent (Prop. XI. Bk. II.); therefore, as any two homologous sides are to each other, or as A B is to F G.

Secondly. From the homologous angles A and F, draw

the diagonals A C, A D and F H, F I. Then, since the triangles A B C, F G H are similar, the triangle

$$ABC : FGH :: \overline{AC}^2 : \overline{FH}^2$$

(Prop. XXIX.); and, since the triangles A C D, F H I are similar, the triangle $ACD : FHI :: \overline{AC}^2 : \overline{FH}^2$. But the ratio $\overline{AC}^2 : \overline{FH}^2$ is common to both of the proportions; therefore (Prop. X. Bk. II.),

$$ABC : FGH :: ACD : FHI.$$

By the same mode of reasoning, it may be proved that

$$ACD : FHI :: ADE : FIK,$$

and so on, if there were more triangles. Therefore the sum of the antecedents A B C, A C D, A D E, which compose the area of the polygon A B C D E, is to the sum of the consequents F G H, F H I, F I K, which compose the area of the polygon F G H I K, as any one antecedent A B C is to its consequent F G H (Prop. XI. Bk. II.), or as $\overline{AB}^2$ is to $\overline{FG}^2$; hence the areas of similar polygons are to each other as the squares described on their homologous sides.

278. *Cor.* 1. The perimeters of similar polygons are also to each other as their corresponding diagonals.

279. *Cor.* 2. The areas of similar polygons are to each other as the squares described on their corresponding diagonals.

PROPOSITION XXXII.—THEOREM.

280. *A chord in a circle is a mean proportional between the diameter and the part of the diameter cut off between one extremity of the chord and a perpendicular drawn from the other extremity to the diameter.*

Let A B be a chord in a circle, B C a diameter drawn from one extremity of A B, and A D a perpendicular drawn from the other extremity to B C; then

$$BD : AB :: AB : BC.$$

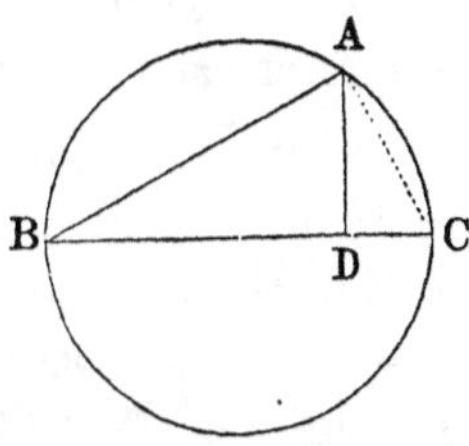

Join A C; then the triangle A B C, described in a semicircle, is right-angled at A (Prop. XVIII. Cor. 2, Bk. III.); and the triangle B A D is similar to the triangle B A C (Prop. XXVII.); hence, we have (Prop. XXVII. Cor. 1),

$$BD : AB :: AB : BC;$$

therefore the chord A B is a mean proportional between the diameter B C, and the part, B D, cut off between the extremity of the chord and the perpendicular from the other extremity.

281. *Cor.* If from any point, A, in the circumference of a circle, a perpendicular, A D, be drawn to the diameter B C, the perpendicular will be a mean proportional between the parts B D, D C into which it divides the diameter.

For, joining A B and A C, we have the triangle A B C, right-angled at A, and the triangles B A D, D A C similar to it and to each other (Prop. XXVII.); therefore (Prop. XXVII. Cor. 2),

$$BD : AD :: AD : DC,$$

or, what amounts to the same thing (Prop. III. Bk. II.),

$$BD \times DC = \overline{AD}^2.$$

Scholium. A part of a straight line cut off by another is called a *segment* of the line. Thus B D, D C are segments of the diameter B C.

Proposition XXXIII. — Theorem.

282. *If two chords in a circle intersect each other, the segments of the one are reciprocally proportional to the segments of the other.*

Let A B, C D be two chords, which intersect each other at E; then will

A E : D E : : E C : E B.

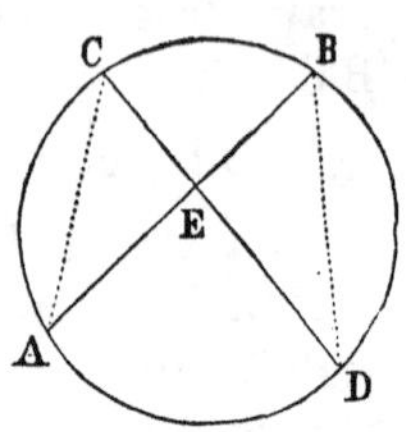

Join A C and B D. In the triangles A E C, B E D, the angles at E are equal being vertical angles (Prop. IV. Bk. I.); the angle A is equal to the angle D, being measured by half the same arc, B C (Prop. XVIII. Cor. 1, Bk. III.); for the same reason, the angle C is equal to the angle B; the triangles are therefore similar (Prop. XXII.), and their homologous sides give the proportion,

A E : D E : : E C : E B.

283. *Cor.* Hence, A E × E B = D E × E C; therefore the rectangle of the two segments of the one chord is equal to the rectangle of the two segments of the other.

Proposition XXXIV. — Theorem.

284. *If from the same point without a circle two secants be drawn, terminating in the concave arc, the whole secants will be reciprocally proportional to their external segments.*

Let E B, E C be two secants drawn from the point E without a circle, and terminating in the concave arc at the points B and C; then will

E B : E C : : E D : E A.

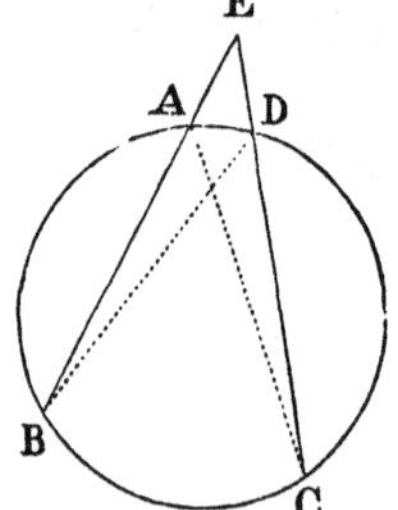

For, joining A C, B D, the triangles A E C, B E D have the angle E common; and the angles B and C, being measured by half the same arc, A D, are equal (Prop. XVIII. Cor. 1, Bk. III.); these triangles are therefore similar (Prop. XXII. Cor.), and their homologous sides give the proportion,

E B : E C : : E D : E A.

285. *Cor.* Hence, $EB \times EA = EC \times ED$; therefore the rectangle contained by the whole of one secant and its external segment is equivalent to the rectangle contained by the whole of the other secant and its external segment.

PROPOSITION XXXV. — THEOREM.

286. *If from a point without a circle there be drawn a tangent terminating in the circumference, and a secant terminating in the concave arc, the tangent will be a mean proportional between the whole secant and its external segment.*

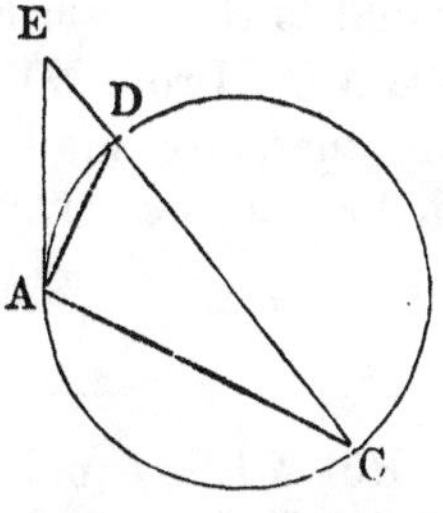

From the point E let the tangent E A, and the secant E C, be drawn; then will E C : E A : : E A : E D.

For, joining A D and A C, the triangles E A D, E A C have the angle E common; also, the angle E A D formed by a tangent and a chord has for its measure half the arc A D (Prop. XX. Bk. III.), and the angle C has the same measure; therefore the angle E A D is equal to the angle C; hence the two triangles are similar (Prop. XXII. Cor.), and give the proportion,

E C : E A : : E A : E D.

287. *Cor.* Hence, $\overline{EA}^2 = EC \times ED$; therefore the square of the tangent is equivalent to the rectangle contained by the whole secant and its external segment.

PROPOSITION XXXVI. — THEOREM.

288. *If any angle of a triangle is bisected by a line terminating in the opposite side, the rectangle of the other two sides is equivalent to the square of the bisecting line plus the rectangle of the segments of the third side.*

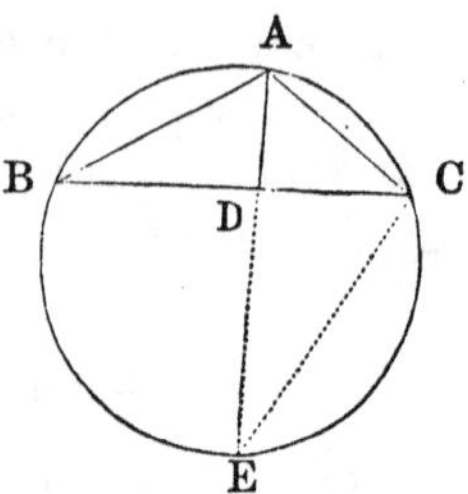

Let the triangle A B C have the angle BAC bisected by the straight line A D terminating in the opposite side B C; then the rectangle B A × A C is equivalent to the square of A D plus the rectangle B D × D C. Describe a circle through the three points A, B, C; produce A D till A meets the circumference at E, and join C E.

The triangles B A D, E A C have, by hypothesis, the angle B A D equal to the angle E A C; also the angle B equal to the angle E, being measured by half of the same arc A C (Prop. XVIII. Cor. 1, Bk. III.); these triangles are therefore similar (Prop. XXII. Cor.), and their homologous sides give the proportion,

$$BA : AE :: AD : AC;$$

hence, $$BA \times AC = AE \times AD.$$

But A E is equal to A D + D E, and multiplying each of these equals by A D, we have,

$$AE \times AD = \overline{AD}^2 + AD \times DE;$$

now, A D × D E is equivalent to B D × D C (Prop. XXXIII. Cor.); hence

$$BA \times AC = \overline{AD}^2 + BD \times DC.$$

Proposition XXXVII. — Theorem.

289. *The rectangle contained by any two sides of a triangle is equivalent to the rectangle contained by the diameter of the circumscribed circle and the perpendicular drawn to the third side from the vertex of the opposite angle.*

In any triangle A B C, let A D be drawn perpendicular to B C; and let E C be the diameter of the circle circumscribed about the triangle; then will A B × A C be equivalent to A D × C E.

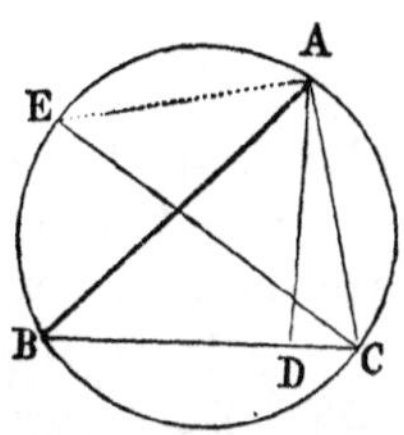

For, joining A E, the angle E A C is a right angle, being inscribed in a semicircle (Prop. XVIII. Cor. 2, Bk. III.); and the angles B and E are equal, being measured by half of the same arc, A C (Prop. XVIII. Cor. 1, Bk. III.); hence the two right-angled triangles are similar (Prop. XXII. Cor.), and give the proportion A B : C E : : A D : A C; hence

$$AB \times AC = CE \times AD.$$

290. *Cor.* If these equals be multiplied by B C, we shall have

$$AB \times AC \times BC = CE \times AD \times BC.$$

But A D × B C is double the area of the triangle (Prop. VI.); therefore the product of the three sides of a triangle is equal to its area multiplied by twice the diameter of the circumscribed circle.

Proposition XXXVIII. — Theorem.

291. *The rectangle contained by the diagonals of a quadrilateral inscribed in a circle is equivalent to the sum of the two rectangles of the opposite sides.*

Let A B C D be any quadrilateral inscribed in a circle, and A C, B D its diagonals; then the rectangle A C × B D is equivalent to the sum of the two rectangles A B × C D, A D × B C.

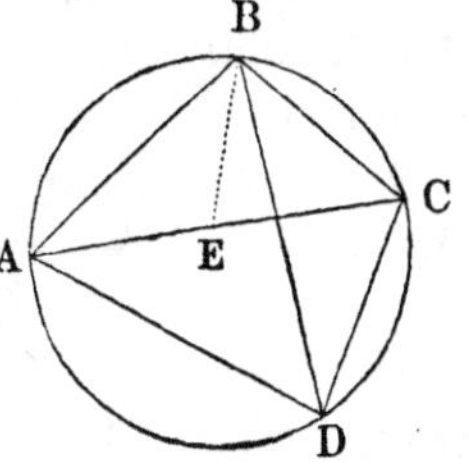

For, draw B E, making the angle A B E equal to the angle C B D; to each of these equals add the angle E B D, and we shall have the angle A B D equal to the angle E B C; and the angle ADB is equal to the angle BCE, being in the same segment (Prop. XVIII. Cor. 1, Bk. III.); therefore the triangles ABD, BCE are similar; hence the proportion,

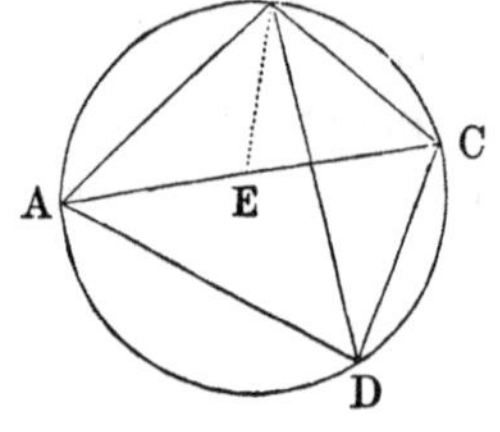

$$AD : BD :: CE : BC;$$

and, consequently,

$$AD \times BC = BD \times CE.$$

Again, since the angle ABE is equal to the angle CBD, and the angle BAE is equal to the angle BDC, being in the same segment (Prop. XVIII. Cor. 1, Bk. III.). the triangles ABE, BCD are similar; hence,

$$AB : AE :: BD : CD;$$

and consequently,

$$AB \times CD = AE \times BD.$$

By adding the corresponding terms of the two equations obtained, and observing that

$$BD \times AE + BD \times CE = BD\,(AE + CE) = BD \times AC,$$

we have

$$BD \times AC = AB \times CD + AD \times BC.$$

Proposition XXXIX.—Theorem.

292. *The diagonal of a square is incommensurable with its side.*

Let ABCD be any square, and AC its diagonal; then AC is incommensurable with the side AB.

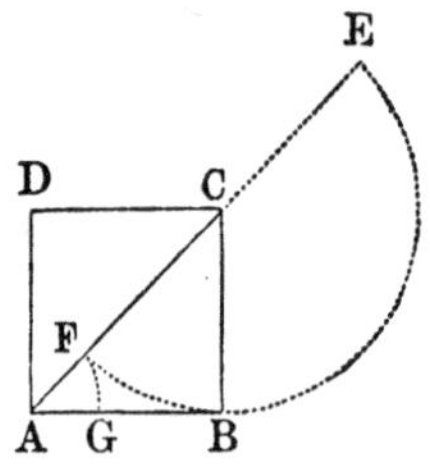

To find a common measure, if there be one, we must apply AB, or its equal CB, to CA, as often as it can be done. In order to do this, from the point C as a center, with a radius CB, describe the semicircle FBE, and produce AC to E. It is evident that CB is contained once in AC, with a remainder A F, which remainder must be compared with B C, or its equal, A B.

The angle A B C being a right angle, A B is a tangent to the circumference, and A E is a secant drawn from the same point, so that (Prop. XXXV.)

$$AF : AB :: AB : AE.$$

Hence, in comparing A F with A B, the equal ratio of A B to A E may be substituted; but A B or its equal C F is contained twice in A E, with a remainder A F; which remainder must again be compared with A B.

Thus, the operation again consists in comparing A F with A B, and may be reduced in the same manner to the comparison of A B, or its equal C F, with A E; which will result, as before, in leaving a remainder A F; hence, it is evident that the process will never terminate; consequently the diagonal of a square is incommensurable with its side.

293. *Scholium.* The impossibility of finding numbers to express the exact ratio of the diagonal to the side of a square has now been proved; but, by means of the continued fraction which is equal to that ratio, an approximation may be made to it, sufficiently near for every practical purpose.

BOOK V.

PROBLEMS RELATING TO THE PRECEDING BOOKS.

PROBLEM I.

294. *To bisect a given straight line, or to divide it into two equal parts.*

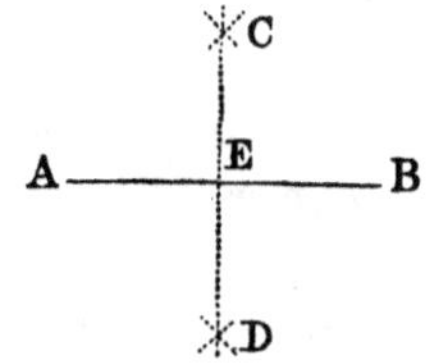

Let A B be a straight line, which it is required to bisect.

From the point A as a center, with a radius greater than the half of A B, describe an arc of a circle; and from the point B as a center, with the same radius, describe another arc, cutting the former in the points C and D. Through C and D draw the straight line C D; it will bisect A B in the point E.

For the two points C and D, being each equally distant from the extremities A and B, must both lie in the perpendicular raised from the middle point of A B (Prop. XV. Cor., Bk. I.). Therefore the line C D must divide the line A B into two equal parts at the point E.

PROBLEM II.

295. *From a given point, without a straight line, to draw a perpendicular to that line.*

Let A B be the straight line, and let C be a given point without the line.

From the point C as a center, and with a radius sufficiently great, describe an arc cutting the line A B in two points, A and B; then, from the points A and B as centers, with a radius greater than half of A B, describe two arcs cutting each other in D, and draw the straight line C D; it will be the perpendicular required.

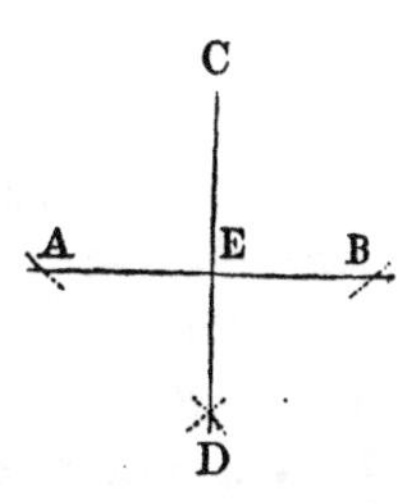

For, the two points C and D are each equally distant from the points A and B; hence, the line C D is a perpendicular passing through the middle of A B (Prop. XV. Cor., Bk. I.).

Problem III.

296. *At a given point in a straight line to erect a perpendicular to that line.*

Let A B be the straight line, and let D be a given point in it.

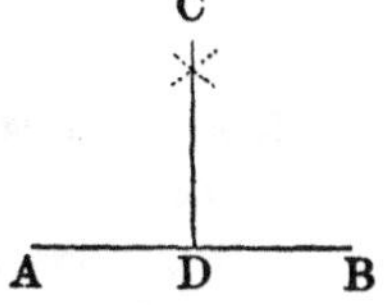

In the straight line A B, take the points A and B at equal distances from D; then from the points A and B as centers, with a radius greater than A D, describe two arcs cutting each other at C; through C and D draw the straight line C D; it will be the perpendicular required.

For the point C, being equally distant from A and B, must be in a line perpendicular to the middle of A B (Prop. XV. Cor., Bk. I.); hence C D has been drawn perpendicular to A B at the point D.

297. *Scholium.* The same construction serves for making a right angle, A D C, at a given point, D, on a given straight line, A B.

Problem IV.

298. *To erect a perpendicular at the end of a given straight line.*

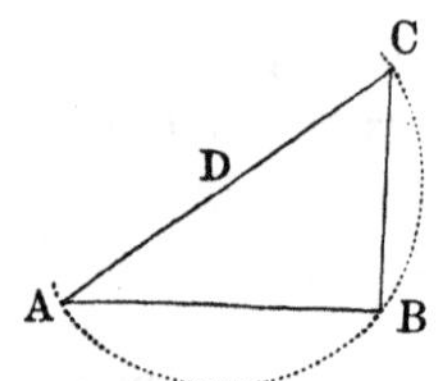

Let A B be the straight line, and B the end of it at which a perpendicular is to be erected.

From any point, D, taken without the line A B, with a radius equal to the distance D B, describe an arc cutting the line A B at the points A and B; through the point A, and the center D, draw the diameter A C. Then through C, where the diameter meets the arc, draw the straight line C B, and it will be the perpendicular required.

For the angle A B C, being inscribed in a semicircle, is a right angle (Prop. XVIII. Cor. 2, Bk. III.).

Problem V.

299. *At a point in a given straight line to make an angle equal to a given angle.*

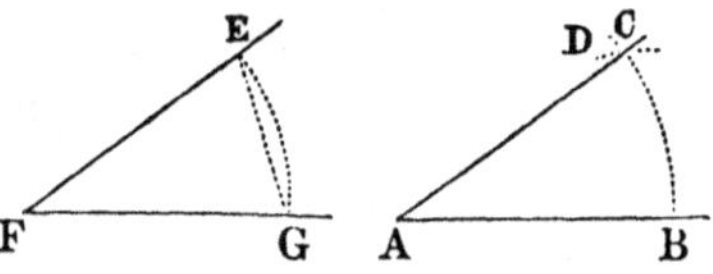

Let A be the given point, A B the given line, and E F G the given angle.

From the point F as a center, with any radius, describe an arc, G E, terminating in the sides of the angle; from the point A as a centre, with the same radius, describe the indefinite arc B D. Draw the chord G E; then from B as a centre, with a radius equal to G E, describe an arc cutting the arc B D in C. Draw A C, and the angle C A B will be equal to the given angle E F G.

For the two arcs, B C and G E, have equal radii and equal chords; therefore they are equal (Prop. III. Bk.

III.) ; hence the angles C A B, E F G, measured by these arcs, are also equal (Prop. V. Bk. III.).

Problem VI.

300. *To bisect a given arc, or a given angle.*

First. Let A D B be the given arc which it is required to bisect.

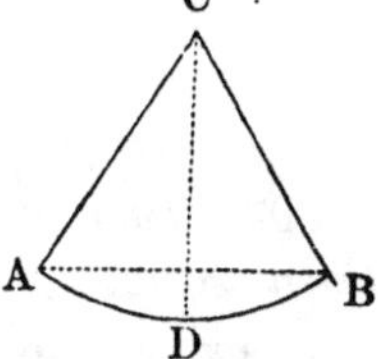

Draw the chord A B ; from the centre C draw the line C D perpendicular to A B (Prob. III.) ; it will bisect the arc A D B in the point D.

For C D being a radius perpendicular to a chord A B, must bisect the arc A D B which is subtended by that chord (Prop. VI. Bk. III.).

Secondly. Let A C B be the angle which it is required to bisect. From C as a center, with any radius, describe the arc A D B ; bisect this arc, as in the first case, by drawing the line C D ; and this line will also bisect the angle A C B.

For the angles A C D, B C D are equal, being measured by the equal arcs A D, D B (Prop. V. Bk. III.).

301. *Scholium.* By the same construction, we may bisect each of the halves A D, D B ; and thus, by successive subdivisions, a given angle or a given arc may be divided into four equal parts, into eight, into sixteen, &c.

Problem VII.

302. *Through a given point, to draw a straight line parallel to a given straight line.*

Let A be the given point, and C D the given straight line.

From A draw a straight line, A E, to any point, E, in C D. Then draw A B, making the angle E A B equal to the angle A E C (Prob. V.); and A B is parallel to C D.

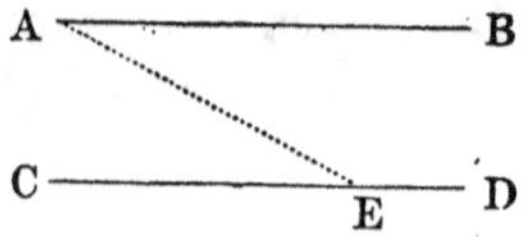

For the alternate angles E A B, A E C, made by the straight line A E meeting the two straight lines A B, C D, being equal, the lines A B and C D must be parallel (Prop. XX. Bk. I.).

Problem VIII.

303. *Two angles of a triangle being given, to find the third angle.*

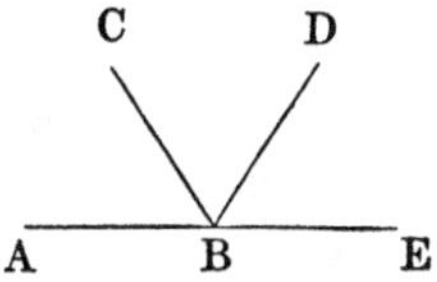

Draw the indefinite straight line A B E. At any point, B, make the angle A B C equal to one of the given angles (Prob. V.), and the angle C B D equal to the other given angle; then the angle D B E will be the third angle required.

For these three angles are together equal to two right angles (Prop. I. Cor. 2, Bk. I.), as are also the three angles of every triangle (Prop. XXVIII. Bk. I.); and two of the angles at B having been made equal to two angles of the triangle, the remaining angle D B E must be equal to the third angle.

Problem IX.

304. *Two sides of a triangle and the included angle being given, to construct the triangle.*

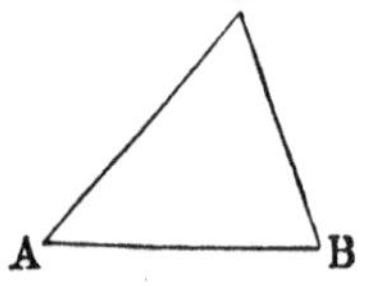

Draw the straight line A B equal to one of the two given sides. At the point A make an angle, C A B, equal to the given angle (Prob. V.); and take A C equal to the other given side. Join B C; and the triangle A B C will be the one required (Prop. V. Bk. I.).

PROBLEM X.

305. *One side and two angles of a triangle being given, to construct the triangle.*

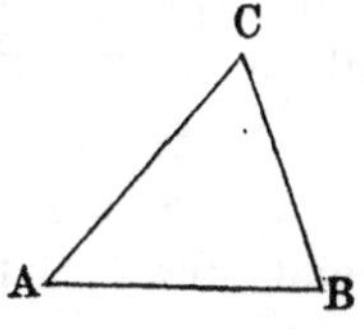

The two given angles will either be both adjacent to the given side, or one adjacent and the other opposite. In the latter case, find the third angle (Prob. VIII.); and the two angles adjacent to the given side will then be known.

In the former case, draw the straight line A B equal to the given side; at the point A, make an angle, B A C, equal to one of the adjacent angles, and at B an angle, A B C, equal to the other. Then the two sides A C, B C will meet, and form with A B the triangle required (Prop. VI. Bk. I.)

PROBLEM XI.

306. *Two sides of a triangle and an angle opposite one of them being given, to construct the triangle.*

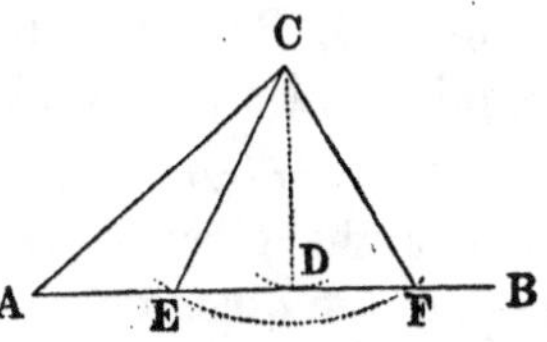

Draw the indefinite straight line A B. At the point A make an angle B A C equal to the given angle, and make A C equal to that side which is adjacent to the given angle. Then from C, as a center, with a radius equal to the other side, describe an arc, which must either touch the line A B in D, or cut it in the points E and F, otherwise a triangle could not be formed.

When the arc touches A B, a straight line drawn from C to the point of contact, D, will be perpendicular to A B (Prop. XI. Bk. III.), and the right-angled triangle C A D will be the triangle required.

When the arc cuts A B in two points, E and F, lying

on the same side of the point A, draw the straight lines C E, C F; and each of the two triangles C A E, C A F will satisfy the conditions of the problem. If, however, the two points E and F should lie on different sides of the point A, only one of the triangles, as C A F, will satisfy all the conditions; hence that will be the triangle required.

307. *Scholium.* The problem would be impossible, if the side opposite the given angle were less than the perpendicular let fall from the point C on the straight line AB.

Problem XII.

308. *The three sides of a triangle being given, to construct the triangle.*

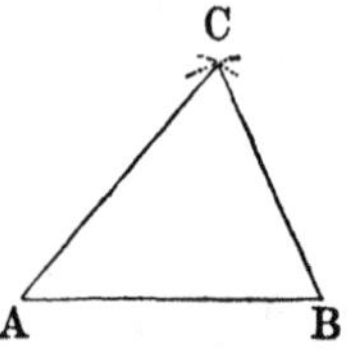

Draw the straight line A B equal to one of the given sides; from the point A as a center, with a radius equal to either of the other two sides, describe an arc; from the point B, with a radius equal to the third side, describe another arc cutting the former in the point C; draw the straight lines A C, B C; and the triangle A B C will be the one required (Prop. XVIII. Bk. I.).

309. *Scholium.* The problem would be impossible, if one of the given sides were equal to or greater than the sum of the other two.

Problem XIII.

310. *Two adjacent sides of a parallelogram and the included angle being given, to construct the parallelogram.*

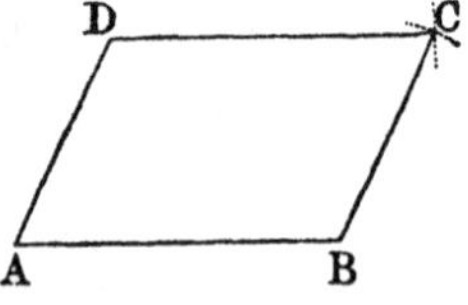

Draw the straight line A B equal to one of the given sides. At the point A make an angle, B A D, equal to the given angle, and take A D equal to the other given side. From the point D, with a radius equal to A B, describe an arc; and from the point B as a center, with a radius equal to A D, describe another arc cutting the former in the point C. Draw the straight lines C D, C B; and the parallelogram A B C D will be the one required.

For the opposite sides are equal, by construction; hence the figure is a parallelogram (Prop. XXXII. Bk. I.); and it is formed with the given sides and the given angle.

311. *Cor.* If the given angle is a right angle, the figure will be a rectangle; and if the adjacent sides are also equal, the figure will be a square.

Problem XIV.

312. *A circumference, or an arc, being given, to find the center of the circle.*

Take any three points, A, B, C, on the given circumference, or arc. Draw the chords A B, B C, and bisect them by the perpendiculars D E and F E (Prob. I.); the point E, in which these perpendiculars meet, is the center required.

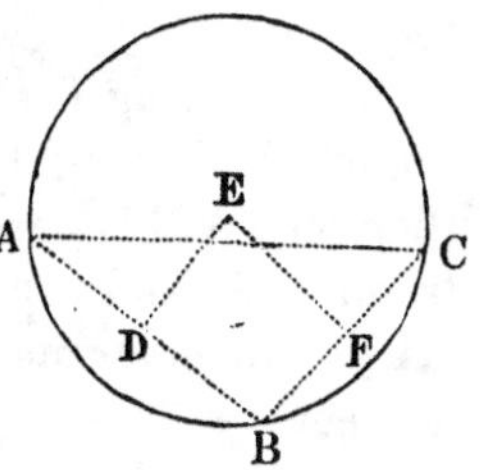

For the perpendiculars D E, F E must both pass through the center (Prop. VI. Cor. 2, Bk. III.), and E being the only point through which they both pass, E must be the center.

313. *Scholium.* By the same construction, a circumference may be made to pass through three given points, A, B, C, not in the same straight line; and also a circumference described in which a given triangle, A B C, shall be inscribed.

Problem XV.

314. *Through a given point to draw a tangent to a given circle.*

First. Let the given point A be in the circumference.

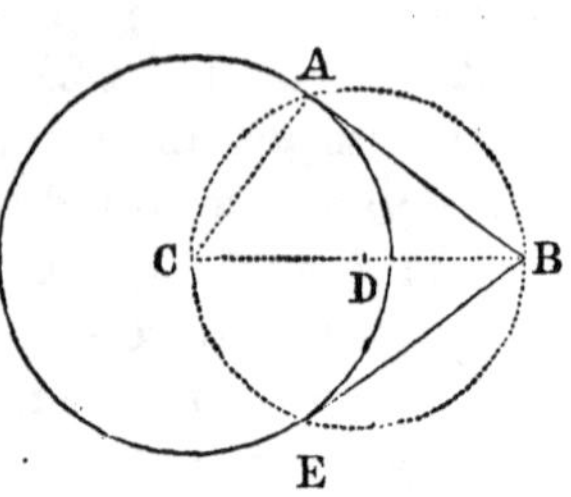

Find the center of the circle, C (Prob. XIV.); draw the radius C A; through the point A draw A B perpendicular to C A (Prob. IV.); and A B will be the tangent required (Prop. X. Bk. III.).

Secondly. Let the given point B be without the circumference.

Join the point B and the center C by the straight line B C; bisect B C in D; and from D as a center, with a radius equal to C D or D B, describe a circumference intersecting the given circumference in the points A and E. Draw A B and E B, and each will be a tangent as required.

For, drawing C A, the angle C A B, being inscribed in a semicircle, is a right angle (Prop. XVIII. Cor. 2, Bk. III.); therefore A B is perpendicular to the radius C A at its extremity, A, and consequently is a tangent (Prop. X. Bk. III.). In like manner it may be shown that E B is a tangent.

Problem XVI.

315. *On a given straight line to construct a segment of a circle that shall contain an angle equal to a given angle.*

Let A B be the given straight line. Through the point B draw the straight line B D, making the angle A B D equal to the given angle; draw B E perpendicular to B D; bisect A B, and from F erect the perpendicular F E. From the point E, where these perpendiculars meet, as a center, with the distance E B

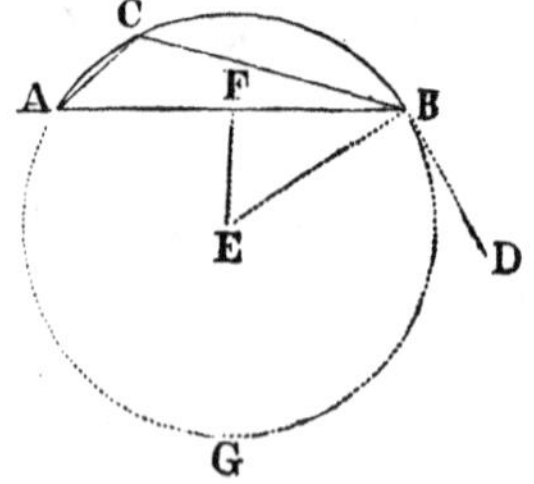

or E A, describe a circumference, and A C B will be the segment required.

For, since B D is a perpendicular at the extremity of the radius E B, it is a tangent (Prop. X. Bk. III.); and the angle A B D is measured by half the arc A G B (Prop. XX. Bk. III.). Also, the angle A C B, being an inscribed angle, is measured by half the arc A G B; therefore the angle A C B is equal to the angle A B D. But, by construction, the angle A B D is equal to the given angle; hence the segment A C B contains an angle equal to the given angle.

316. *Scholium.* If the given angle were acute, the center must lie within the segment (Prop. XVIII. Cor. 3, Bk. III.); and if it were right, the center must be in the middle of the line A B, and the required segment would be a semicircle.

Problem XVII.

317. *To inscribe a circle in any given triangle.*

Bisect any two of the angles, as A and B, by the straight lines A E and B E, meeting in the point E (Prob. VI.). From the point E let fall the perpendiculars E D, E F, E G (Prob. II.) on the three sides of the triangle; these perpendiculars will all be equal.

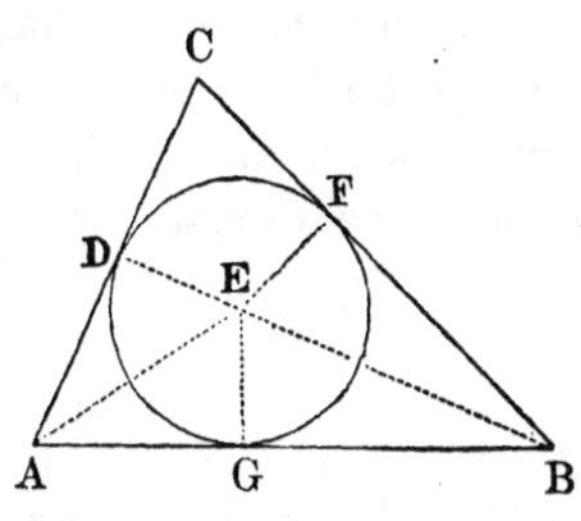

For, by construction, we have the angle D A E equal to the angle E A G, and the right angle A D E equal to the right angle A G E; hence the third angle A E D is equal to the third angle A E G. Moreover, A E is common to the two triangles A E D, A E G; hence the triangles themselves are equal, and E D is equal to E G. In the same manner it may be shown that the two triangles B E F,

B E G are equal; therefore E F is equal to E G; hence the three perpendiculars E D, E F, E G are all equal, and if, from the point E as a center, with the radius E D, a circle be described, it must pass through the points F and G.

318. *Scholium.* The three lines which bisect the angles of a triangle all meet in the center of the inscribed circle.

Problem XVIII.

319. *To inscribe a circle in a given square.*

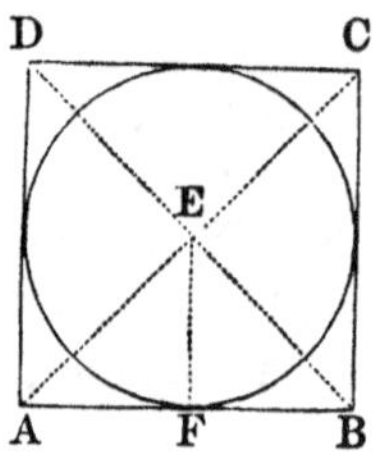

Draw the diagonals A C, D B, and from the point E, where the diagonals mutually bisect each other (Prop. XXXIV. Bk. I.), draw the straight line E F perpendicular to a side of the square. From E as a center, with a radius equal to E F, describe a circle, and it will touch each side of the square.

For the square is divided by the diagonals into four equal isosceles triangles; hence, the perpendicular, from the vertex E to the base, is the same in each triangle; therefore the circumference described from the center E, with the radius E F, passes through the extremities of each perpendicular; consequently, the sides of the square are tangents to the circle (Prop. X. Bk. III.).

Problem XIX.

320. *To find the side of a square which shall be equivalent to the sum of two given squares.*

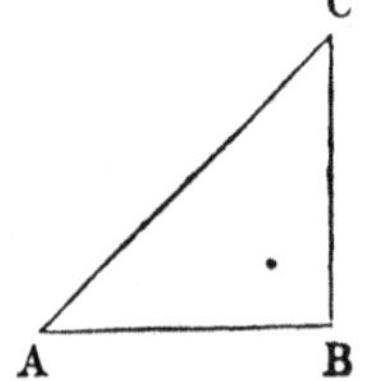

Draw the two straight lines A B, B C perpendicular to each other, taking A B equal to a side of one of the given squares, and B C equal to a side of the other. Join A C; this will be the side of the square required.

For, the triangle A B C being right-angled, the square that can be described upon the hypothenuse A C is equivalent to the sum of the squares that can be described upon the sides A B and B C (Prop. XI. Bk. IV.).

321. *Scholium.* A square may thus be found equivalent to the sum of any number of squares; for the construction which reduces two of them to one, will reduce three of them to two, and these two to one.

Problem XX.

322. *To find the side of a square which shall be equivalent to the difference of two given squares.*

Draw the two straight lines A B, A C perpendicular to each other, making A C equal to the side of the less square. Then from C as a center, with a radius equal to the side of the other square, describe an arc intersecting A B in the point B, and A B will be the side of the required square.

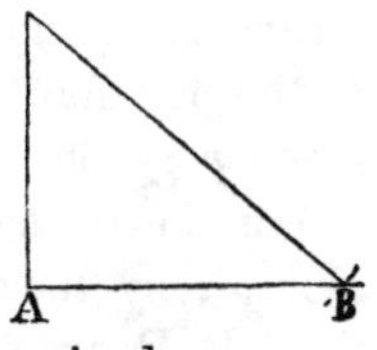

For, join B C, and the square that can be described upon A B is equivalent to the difference of the squares that can be described on B C and A C (Prop. XI. Cor. 1, Bk. IV.).

Problem XXI.

323. *To construct a rectangle that shall be equivalent to a given triangle.*

Let A B C be the given triangle.

Draw the indefinite straight line C D parallel to the base A B; bisect A B by the perpendicular E F, and make E G equal to F B. Then, by drawing G B, the rectangle E F B G is equal to the triangle A B C.

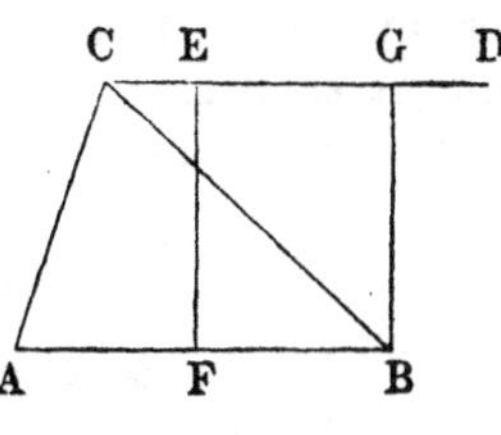

For the rectangle E F B G has the same altitude, E F, as the triangle A B C, and half its base (Prop. II. Cor. 1, Bk. IV.).

PROBLEM XXII.

324. *To construct a triangle that shall be equivalent to a given polygon.*

Let A B C D E be the given polygon.

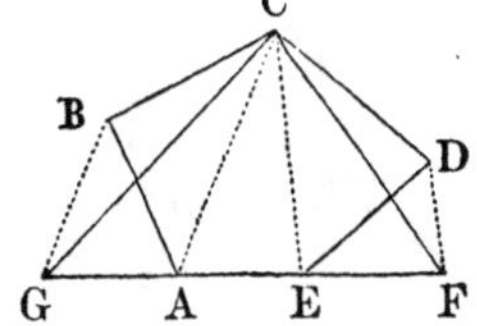

Draw the diagonal C E, cutting off the triangle C D E; through the point D draw D F parallel to C E, and meeting A E produced in F. Draw C F; and the polygon A B C D E will be equivalent to the polygon A B C F, which has one side less than the given polygon.

For the triangles C D E, C F E have the base C E common; they have also the same altitude, since their vertices, D, F, are situated in a line, D F, parallel to the base; these triangles are therefore equivalent (Prop. II. Cor. 2, Bk. IV.). Add to each of them the figure A B C E, and the polygon A B C D E will be equivalent to the polygon A B C F.

In like manner, the triangle C G A may be substituted for the equivalent triangle A B C, and thus the pentagon A B C D E will be changed into an equivalent triangle G C F.

The same process may be applied to every other polygon; for, by successively diminishing the number of its sides, one at each step of the process, the equivalent triangle will at last be found.

PROBLEM XXIII.

325. *To divide a given straight line into any number of equal parts.*

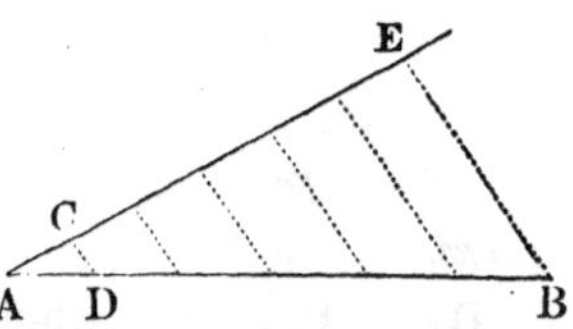

Let A B be the given straight line proposed to be divided into any number of equal parts; for example, six.

Through the extremity A draw the indefinite straight line A E, making any angle with A B. Take A C of any convenient length, and apply it six times upon A E. Join the last point of division, E, and the extremity B by the straight line E B; and through the point C draw C D parallel to E B; then A D will be the sixth part of the line A B, and, being applied six times to A B, divides it into six equal parts.

For, since C D is parallel to E B, in the triangle A B E, we have the proportion (Prop. XVII. Bk. IV.),

A D : A B : : A C : A E.

But A C is the sixth part of A E; hence A D is the sixth part of A B.

Problem XXIV.

326. *To divide a given straight line into parts that shall be proportional to other given lines.*

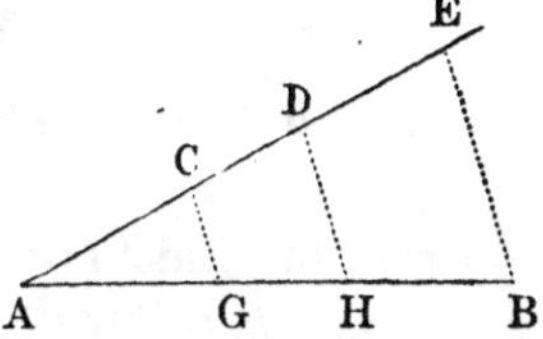

Let A B be the given straight line proposed to be divided into parts proportional to the given lines A C, C D, D E.

Through the point A draw the indefinite straight line A E, making any angle with A B. On A E lay off A C, C D, and D E. Join the points E and B by the straight line E B, and through the points C and D draw C G and D H parallel to E B; and the line A B will be divided into parts proportional to the given lines.

For, since C G and D H are each parallel to E B, we have the proportion (Prop. XVII. Cor. 2, Bk. IV.),

A C : A G : : C D : G H : : D E : H B.

PROBLEM XXV.

327. *To find a fourth proportional to three given straight lines.*

Draw the two indefinite straight lines A B, A E, forming any angle with each other.

On A B make A D equal to the first of the proposed lines, and A B equal to the second; and on A E make A E equal to the third. Join B E; and through the point D draw D C parallel to B E, and A C will be the fourth proportional required.

For, since D C is parallel to B E, we have the proportion (Prop. XVII. Cor. 1, Bk. IV.),

A B : A D : : A E : A C.

328. *Cor.* A third proportional to two given lines, A and B, may be found in the same manner, for it will be the same as a fourth proportional to the three lines, A, B, and B.

PROBLEM XXVI.

329. *To find a mean proportional between two given straight lines.*

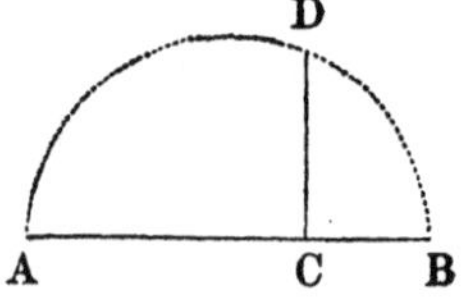

Draw the indefinite straight line A B. On A B take A C equal to the first of the given lines, and C B equal to the second. On A B, as a diameter, describe a semicircle, and at the point C draw the perpendicular C D, meeting the semi-circumference in D; C D will be the mean proportional required.

For the perpendicular C D, drawn from a point in the circumference to a point in the diameter, is a mean proportional between the two segments of the diameter A C, C B (Prop. XXXII. Cor., Bk. IV.); and these segments are equal to the given lines.

Problem XXVII.

330. *To divide a given straight line into two such parts, that the greater part shall be a mean proportional between the whole line and the other part.*

Let A B be the given straight line.

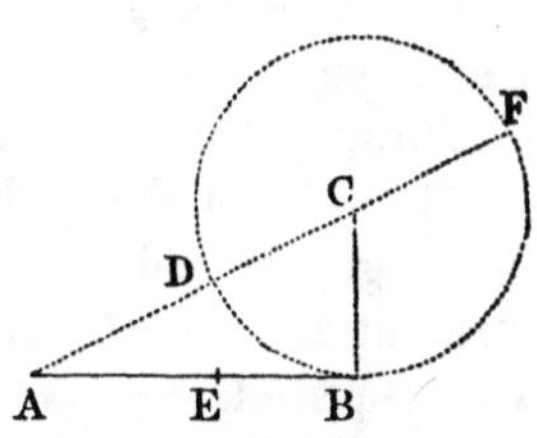

At the extremity, B, of the line A B, erect the perpendicular B C, equal to the half of A B. From the point C as a center, with the radius C B, describe a circle. Draw A C cutting the circumference in D; and take A E equal to A D. The line A B will be divided at the point E in the manner required; that is,

$$AB : AE :: AE : EB.$$

For A B, being perpendicular to the radius at its extremity, is a tangent (Prop. X. Bk. III.); and if A C be produced till it again meets the circumference, in F, we shall have (Prop. XXXV. Bk. IV.),

$$AF : AB :: AB : AD;$$

hence, by division (Prop. VIII. Bk. II.),

$$AF - AB : AB :: AB - AD : AD.$$

But, since the radius is the half of A B, the diameter D F is equal to A B, and consequently A F — A B is equal to A D, which is equal to A E; also, since A E is equal to A D, we have A B — A D equal to E B; hence,

$$AE : AB :: EB : AD, \text{ or } AE;$$

and, by inversion (Prop. V. Bk. II.),

$$AB : AE :: AE : EB.$$

331. *Scholium.* This sort of division of the line A B is called division in *extreme and mean ratio.*

PROBLEM XXVIII.

332. *Through a given point in a given angle, to draw a straight line, which shall have the parts included between that point and the sides of the angle equal to each other.*

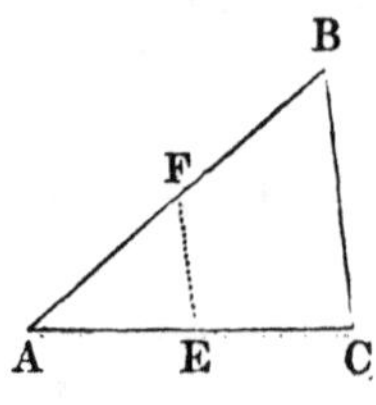

Let E be the given point, and A B C the given angle.

Through the point E draw E F parallel to B C, make A F equal to B F. Through the points A and E draw the straight line A E C, and it will be the line required.

For, E F being parallel to B C, we have (Prop. XVII. Bk. IV.),

$$AF : FB :: AE : EC;$$

but A F is equal to F B; therefore A E is equal to E C.

PROBLEM XXIX.

333. *On a given straight line to construct a rectangle that shall be equivalent to a given rectangle.*

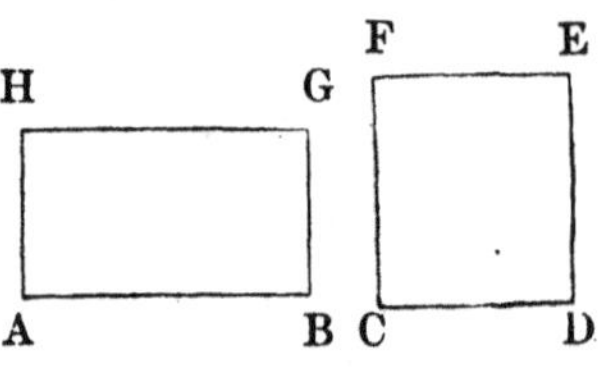

Let A B be the given straight line, and C D E F the given rectangle.

Find a fourth proportional to the three straight lines A B, C D, D E (Prob. XXV.); and let B G be that fourth proportional. The rectangle constructed on A B and B G will be equivalent to the rectangle C D E F.

For, since A B : C D : : D E : B G, it follows (Prop. I. Bk. II.) that

$$AB \times BG = CD \times DE;$$

hence, the rectangle A B G H, which is constructed on the line A B, is equivalent to the rectangle C D E F.

PROBLEM XXX.

334. *To construct a square that shall be equivalent to a given parallelogram, or to a given triangle.*

First. Let A B C D be the given parallelogram, A B its base, and D E its altitude.

Find a mean proportional between A B and D E (Prob. XXVI.); and the square constructed on that proportional will be equivalent to the parallelogram A B C D.

For, denoting the mean proportional by $x\,y$, we have, by construction,

$$\text{A B} : xy :: xy : \text{D E};$$

therefore,

$$\overline{xy}^2 = \text{A B} \times \text{D E};$$

but A B $\times$ D E is the measure of the parallelogram, and $\overline{x\,y}^2$ that of the square; hence they are equivalent.

Secondly. Let A B C be the given triangle, B C its base, and A D its altitude.

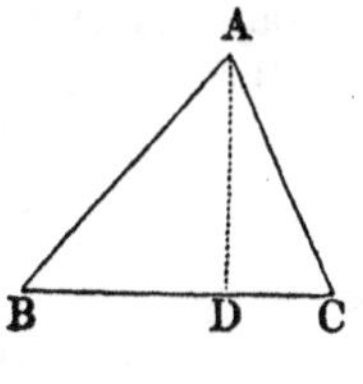

Find a mean proportional between B C and the half of A D, and let $x\,y$ denote that proportional; the square constructed on $x\,y$ will be equivalent to the triangle A B C.

For since, by construction,

$$\text{B C} : xy :: xy : \tfrac{1}{2}\,\text{A D},$$

it follows that

$$\overline{xy}^2 = \text{B C} \times \tfrac{1}{2}\,\text{A D};$$

hence the square constructed on $x\,y$ is equivalent to the triangle A B C.

PROBLEM XXXI.

335. *To construct a rectangle equivalent to a given square, and having the sum of its adjacent sides equal to a given line.*

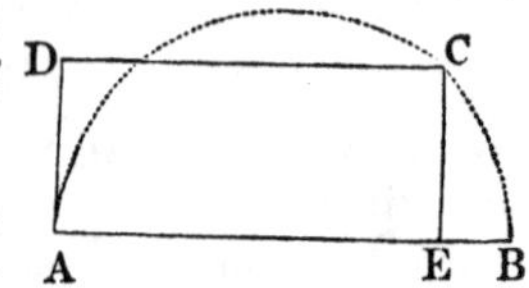

Let the straight line A B be equal to the sum of the adjacent sides of the required rectangle.

Upon A B as a diameter describe a semicircle; at the point A, draw A D perpendicular to A B, making A D equal to the side of the given square; then draw the line D C parallel to the diameter A B. From the point C, where the parallel meets the circumference, draw C E perpendicular to the diameter; A E and E B will be the sides of the rectangle required.

For their sum is equal to A B; and their rectangle A E $\times$ E B is equivalent to the square of C E, or to the square of A D (Prop. XXXII. Cor., Bk. IV.); hence, this rectangle is equivalent to the given square.

336. *Scholium.* The problem is impossible, when the distance A D is greater than the half the given line A B, for then the line D C will not meet the circumference.

PROBLEM XXXII.

337. *To construct a rectangle that shall be equivalent to a given square, and the difference of whose adjacent sides shall be equal to a given line.*

Let the straight line A B be equal to the difference of the adjacent sides of the required rectangle.

Upon A B as a diameter, describe a circle. At the extremity of the diameter, draw the tangent A D, making it equal to the side of the given square.

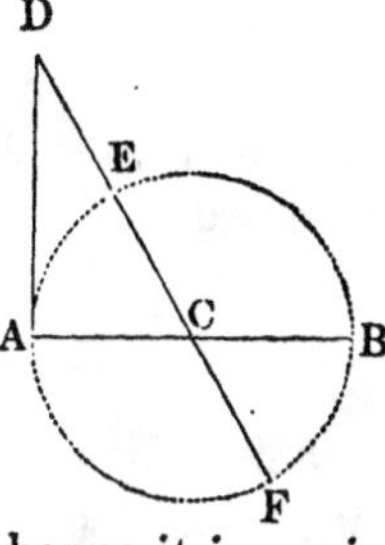

Through the point D and the centre C draw the secant D C F, intersecting the circumference in E; then D E and D F will be the adjacent sides of the rectangle required.

For the difference of these lines is equal to the diameter E F or A B; and the rectangle D E $\times$ D F is equal to $\overline{AD}^2$ (Prop. XXXV. Cor., Bk. IV.); hence it is equivalent to the given square.

Problem XXXIII.

338. *To construct a square that shall be to a given square as one given line is to another given line.*

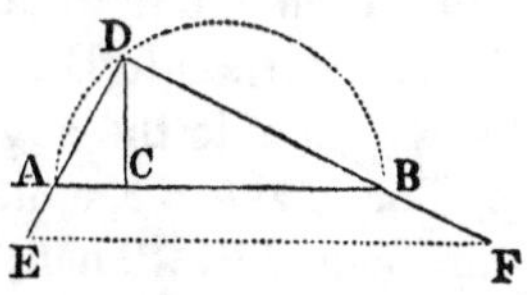

Draw the indefinite line A B, on which take A C equal to one of the given lines, and C B equal to the other. Upon A B as a diameter, describe a semicircle, and at the point C draw the perpendicular C D, meeting the circumference in D. Through the points A and B draw the straight lines D E, D F, making the former equal to the side of the given square; and through the point E draw E F parallel to A B; D F will be the side of the square required.

For, since E F is parallel to A B,

$$DE : DF :: DA : DB;$$

consequently (Prop. XV. Bk. II.),

$$\overline{DE}^2 : \overline{DF}^2 :: \overline{DA}^2 : \overline{DB}^2.$$

But in the right-angled triangle A D B the square of A D is to the square of D B as the segment A C is to the segment C B (Prop. XI. Cor. 3, Bk. IV.); hence,

$$\overline{DE}^2 : \overline{DF}^2 :: AC : CB.$$

But, by construction, D E is equal to the side of the given square; also, A C is equal to one of the given lines, and C B to the other; hence, the given square is to that constructed on D F as the one given line is to the other.

PROBLEM XXXIV.

339. *Upon a given base to construct an isosceles triangle, having each of the angles at the base double the vertical angle.*

Let A B be the given base.

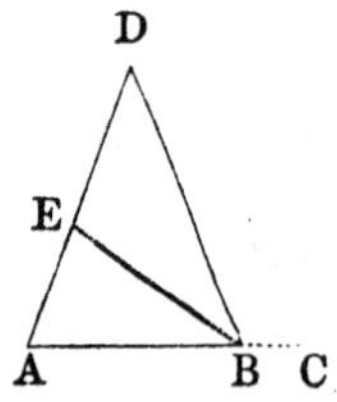

Produce A B to some point C till the rectangle A C × B C shall be equivalent to the square of A B (Prob. XXXII.); then, with the base A B and sides each equal to A C, construct the isosceles triangle D A B, and the angle A will double the angle D.

For, make D E equal to A B, or make A E equal to B C, and join E B. Then, by construction,

$$AD : AB :: AB : AE;$$

for A E is equal to B C; consequently the triangles D A B, B A E have a common angle, A, contained by proportional sides; hence they are similar (Prop. XXIV. Bk. IV.); therefore these triangles are both isosceles, for D A B is isosceles by construction, so that A B is equal to E B; but A B is equal to D E; consequently D E is equal to E B, and therefore the angle D is equal to the angle E B D; hence the exterior angle A E B is equal to double the angle D, but the angle A is equal to the angle A E B; therefore the angle A is double the angle D.

PROBLEM XXXV.

340. *Upon a given straight line to construct a polygon similar to a given polygon.*

Let A B C D E be the given polygon, and F G the given straight line.

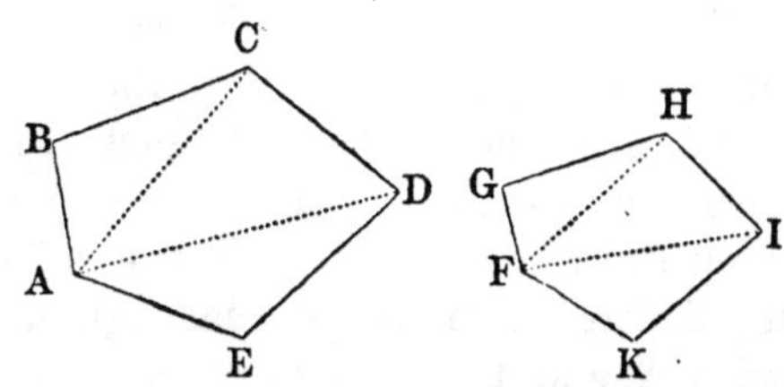

Draw the diagonals A C, A D. At the point F in the straight line F G, make the angle G F H equal to the angle B A C; and at the point G make the angle F G H equal to the angle A B C. The lines F H, G H will cut each other in H, and F G H will be a triangle similar to A B C. In the same manner, upon F H, homologous to A C, construct the triangle F I H similar to A D C; and upon F I, homologous to A D, construct the triangle F I K similar to A D E. The polygon F G H I K will be similar to A B C D E, as required.

For these two polygons are composed of the same number of triangles, similar each to each, and similarly situated (Prop. XXX. Cor., Bk. IV.).

Problem XXXVI.

341. *Two similar polygons being given, to construct a similar polygon, which shall be equivalent to their sum or their difference.*

Let A and B be two homologous sides of the given polygons.

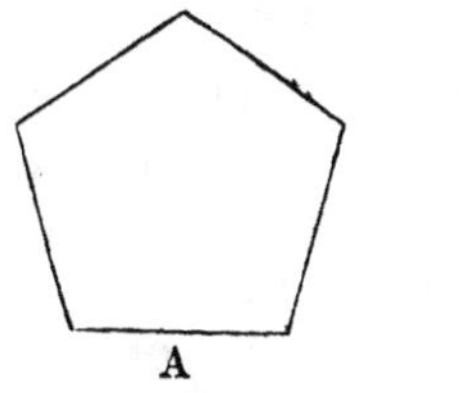

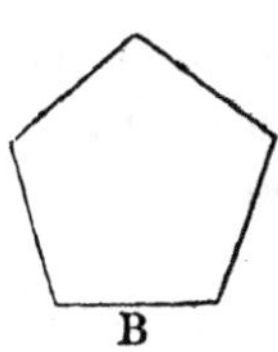

Find a square equal to the sum or to the difference of the squares described upon A and B; let x be the side of that square; then will x in the polygon required be the side which is homologous to the sides A and B in the given polygons. The polygon itself may then be constructed on x, by the last problem.

For similar figures are to each other as the squares of their homologous sides; but the square of the side x is equal to the sum or the difference of the squares described upon the homologous sides A and B; therefore the figure described upon the side x is equivalent to the sum or to the difference of the similar figures described upon the sides A and B.

Problem XXXVII.

342. *To construct a polygon similar to a given polygon, and which shall have to it a given ratio.*

Let A be a side of the given polygon.

Find the side B of a square, which is to the square on A in the given ratio of the polygons (Prob. XXXIII.).

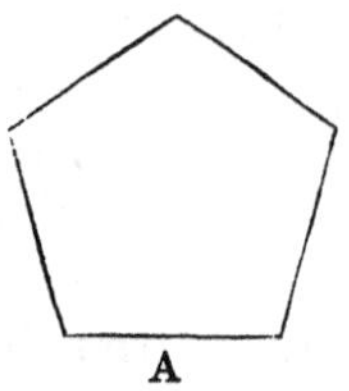

Upon B construct a polygon similar to the given polygon (Prob. XXXV.), and B will be the polygon required.

For the similar polygons constructed upon A and B have the same ratio to each other as the squares constructed upon A and B (Prop. XXXI. Bk. IV.).

Problem XXXVIII.

343. *To construct a polygon similar to a given polygon,* P, *and which shall be equivalent to another polygon,* Q.

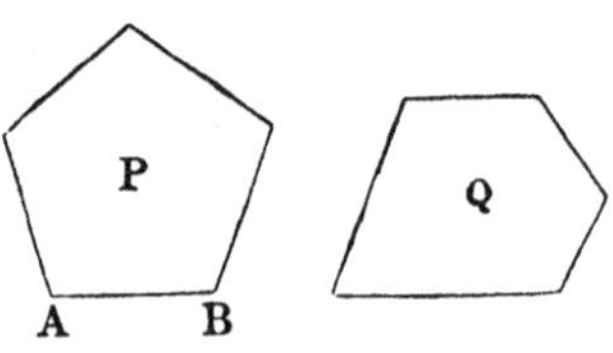

Find M, the side of a square, equivalent to the polygon P, and N, the side of a square equivalent to the polygon Q. Let x be a fourth proportional to the three given lines M, N, A B; upon the side x, homologous to A B, describe a polygon similar to the polygon P (Prob. XXXV.); it will also be equivalent to the polygon Q.

For, representing the polygon described upon the side x by y, we have

$$P : y :: \overline{AB}^2 : x^2;$$

but, by construction,

$$AB : x :: M : N, \quad \text{or} \quad \overline{AB}^2 : x^2 :: M^2 : N^2;$$

hence,

$$P : y :: M^2 : N^2.$$

But, by construction also, M^2 is equivalent to P, and N^2 is equivalent to Q; therefore,

$$P : y :: P : Q;$$

consequently y is equal to Q; hence the polygon y is similar to the polygon P, and equivalent to the polygon Q.

BOOK VI.

REGULAR POLYGONS, AND THE AREA OF THE CIRCLE.

DEFINITIONS.

344. A REGULAR POLYGON is one which is both equilateral and equiangular.

345. Regular polygons may have any number of sides: the equilateral triangle is one of three sides; the square is one of four.

PROPOSITION I.—THEOREM.

346. *Regular polygons of the same number of sides are similar figures.*

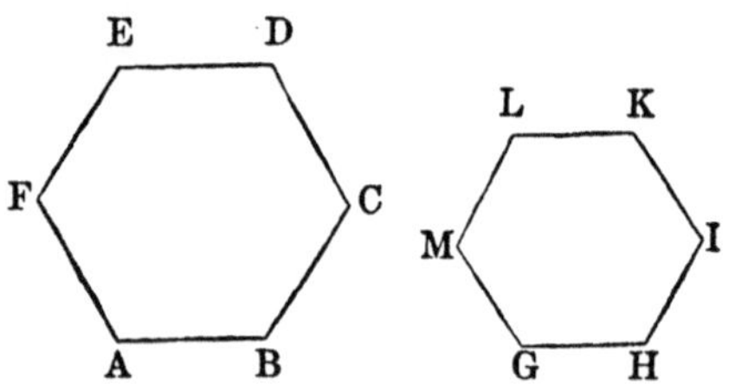

Let ABCDEF, GHIKLM, be two regular polygons of the same number of sides; then these polygons are similar.

For, since the two polygons have the same number of sides, they have the same number of angles; and the sum of all the angles is the same in the one as in the other (Prop. XXIX. Bk. I.). Also, since the polygons are equiangular, each of the angles A, B, C, &c. is equal to each of the angles G, H, I, &c.; hence the two polygons are mutually equiangular.

Again; the polygons being regular, the sides A B, B C, C D, &c. are equal to each other; so likewise are the sides G H, H I, I K, &c. Hence,

A B : G H : : B C : H I : : C D : I K, &c.

Therefore the two polygons have their angles equal, and their homologous sides proportional; hence they are similar (Art. 210).

347. *Cor.* The perimeters of two regular polygons of the same number of sides, are to each other as their homologous sides, and their areas are to each other as the squares of those sides (Prop. XXXI. Bk. IV.).

348. *Scholium.* The angle of a regular polygon is determined by the number of its sides (Prop. XXIX. Bk. I.).

Proposition II. — Theorem.

349. *A circle may be circumscribed about, and another inscribed in, any regular polygon.*

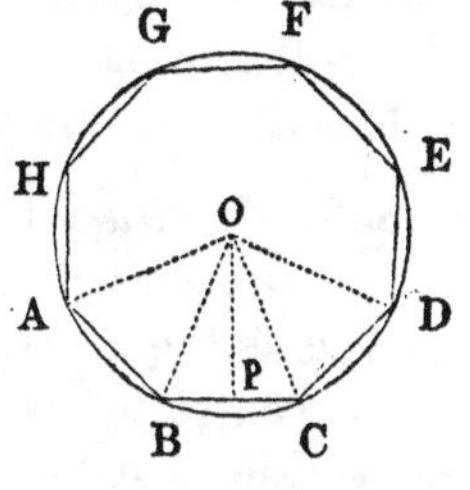

Let A B C D E F G H be any regular polygon; then a circle may be circumscribed about, and another inscribed in it.

Describe a circle whose circumference shall pass through the three points A, B, C, the center being O; let fall the perpendicular O P from O to the middle point of the side B C; and draw the straight lines O A, O B, O C, O D.

Now, if the quadrilateral O P C D be placed upon the quadrilateral O P B A, they will coincide; for the side O P is common, and the angle O P C is equal to the angle O P B, each being a right angle; consequently the side P C will fall upon its equal, P B, and the point C on B. Moreover, from the nature of the polygon, the angle P C D is equal to the angle P B A; therefore C D will take the direction B A, and C D being equal to B A, the point D will fall upon A, and the two quadrilaterals will coincide throughout. Therefore O D is equal to A O, and the circumference which passes through the three points A, B, C, will also pass through the point D. By the same mode of reasoning, it may be shown that the circle which passes through the three vertices B, C, D, will also pass through the vertex E, and so on. Hence, the circumference which passes through the three points A, B, C, passes through the vertices of all the angles of the polygon, and is circumscribed about the polygon (Art. 166).

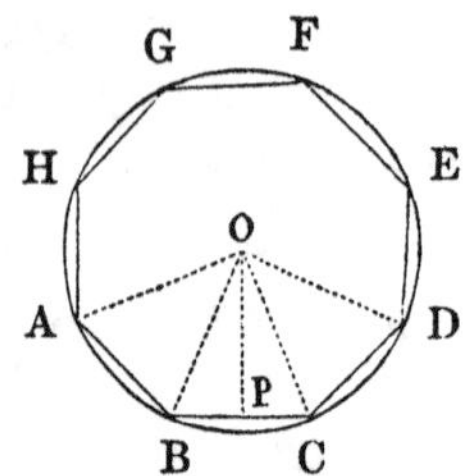

Again, with respect to this circumference, all the sides, A B, B C, C D, &c., of the polygon are equal chords; consequently they are equally distant from the centre (Prop. VIII. Bk. III.). Hence, if from the point O, as a centre, and with the radius O P, a circle be described, the circumference will touch the side B C, and all the other sides of the polygon, each at its middle point, and the circle will be inscribed in the polygon (Art. 168).

350. *Scholium* 1. The point O, the common center of the circumscribed and inscribed circles, may also be regarded as the centre of the polygon. The angle formed at the centre by two radii drawn to the extremities of the same side is called *the angle at the center;* and the perpendicular from the center to a side is called the *apothegm* of the polygon.

Since all the chords A B, B C, C D, &c. are equal, all the angles at the center must likewise be equal; therefore the value of each may be found by dividing four right angles by the number of sides of the polygon.

351. *Scholium* 2. To inscribe a regular polygon of any number of sides in a given circle, it is only necessary to

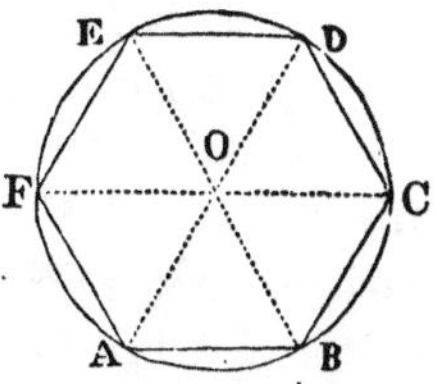

divide the circumference into as many equal parts as the polygon has sides; for the arcs being equal, the chords A B, B C, C D, &c. are also equal (Prop. III. Bk. III.); hence likewise the triangles A O B, B O C, C O D, &c. must be equal, since their sides are equal each to each (Prop. XVIII. Bk. I.); therefore all the angles A B C, B C D, C D E, &c. are equal; hence the figure A B C D E F is a regular polygon.

Proposition III. — Theorem.

352. *If from a common center a circle can be circumscribed about, and another circle inscribed within, a polygon, that polygon is regular.*

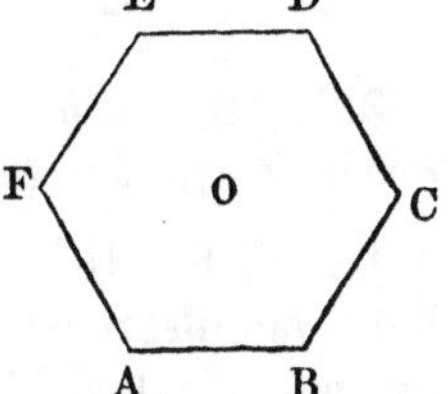

Suppose that from the point O, as a center, circles can be circumscribed about, and inscribed in, the polygon A B C D E F; then that polygon is regular.

For, supposing it to be described, the inner one will touch all the sides of the polygon; therefore these sides are equally distant from its center; and consequently, being chords of the outer circle, they are equal; therefore they include equal angles (Prop. XVIII. Cor. 1, Bk. III.). Hence the polygon is at once equilateral and equiangular; consequently it is regular (Art. 344).

Proposition IV. — Problem.

353. *To inscribe a square in a given circle.*

Draw two diameters, A C, B D, intersecting each other at right angles; join their extremities, A, B, C, D, and the figure A B C D will be a square.

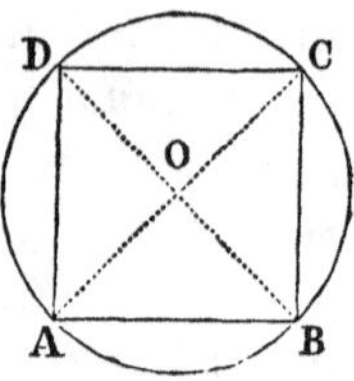

For, the angles A O B, B O C, &c. being equal, the chords A B, B C, &c. are also equal (Prop. III. Bk. III.); and the angles A B C, B C D, &c., being inscribed in semicircles, are right angles (Prop. XVIII. Cor. 2, Bk. III.). Hence A B C D is a square, and it is inscribed in the circle A B C D.

354. *Cor.* Since the triangle A O B is right-angled and isosceles, we have (Prop. XI. Cor. 5, Bk. IV.),

$$AB : AO :: \sqrt{2} : 1;$$

hence, *the side of the inscribed square is to the radius as the square root of 2 is to unity.*

Proposition V. — Theorem.

355. *The side of a regular hexagon inscribed in a circle is equal to the radius of the circle.*

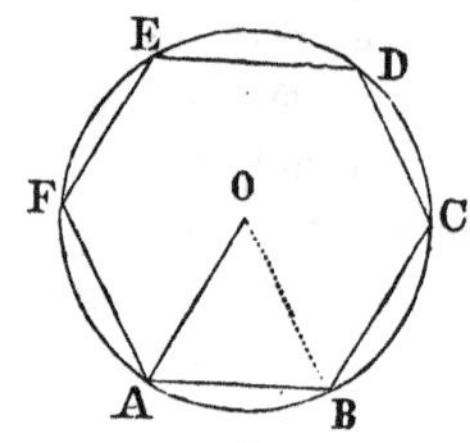

Let A B C D E F be a regular hexagon inscribed in a circle, the center of which is O; then any side, as B C, will be equal to the radius O A.

Join B O; and the angle at the centre, A O B, is one sixth of four right angles (Prop. II. Sch. 1), or one third of two right angles; therefore the two other angles, O A B, O B A, of the same triangle, are together equal to two thirds of two right angles (Prop. XXVIII. Bk. I.). But A O and B O being equal, the angles O A B, O B A are also equal (Prop. VII. Bk. I.); consequently, each is one third of two right angles. Hence the triangle A O B is equiangular; therefore A B, the side of the regular hexagon, is equal to A O, the radius of the circle (Prop. VIII. Cor. Bk. I.).

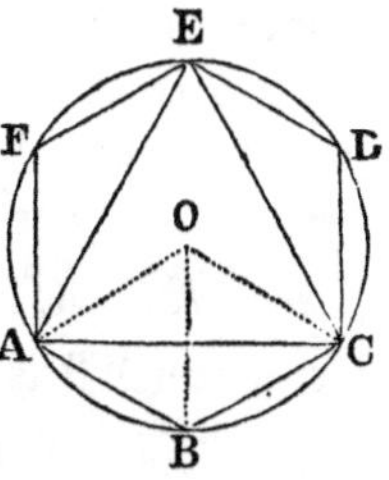

356. *Cor.* 1. To inscribe a regular hexagon in a given circle, apply the radius, A O, of the circle six times, as a chord to the circumference. Hence, beginning at any point A, and applying A O six times as a chord to the circumference, we are brought round to the point of beginning, and the inscribed figure A B C D E F, thus formed, is a regular hexagon.

357. *Cor.* 2. By joining the alternate angles of the inscribed regular hexagon by the straight lines A C, C E, E A, the figure A C E, thus inscribed in the circle, will be an equilateral triangle, since its sides subtend equal arcs, A B C, C D E, E F A, on the circumference (Prop. III. Bk. III.).

358. *Cor.* 3. Join O A, O C, and the figure A B C O is a rhombus, for each side is equal to the radius. Hence, the sum of the squares of the diagonals A C, O B is equivalent to the sum of the squares of the sides (Prop. XV. Bk. IV.); or to four times the square of the radius O B; that is, $\overline{AC}^2 + \overline{OB}^2$ is equivalent to 4 $\overline{AB}^2$, or 4 $\overline{OB}^2$; and taking away $\overline{OB}^2$ from both, there remains $\overline{AC}^2$ equivalent to 3 $\overline{OB}^2$; hence

$$\overline{AC}^2 : OB^2 :: 3 : 1, \quad \text{or} \quad AC : OB :: \sqrt{3} : 1;$$

hence, *the side of the inscribed equilateral triangle is to the radius as the square root of 3 is to unity.*

Proposition VI. — Problem.

359. *To inscribe a regular decagon in a given circle.*

Divide the radius, O A, of the given circle, in extreme and mean ratio, at the point M (Prob. XXVII. Bk. V.).

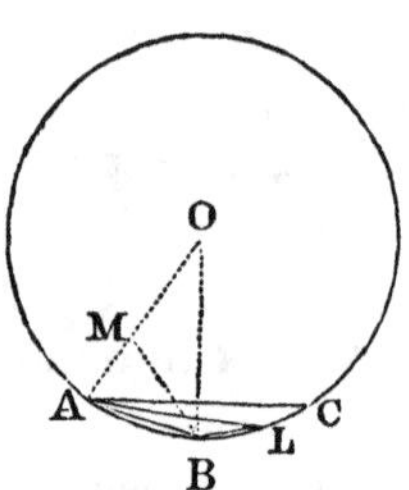

Take the chord A B equal to O M, and A B will be the side of a regular decagon inscribed in the circle. For we have by construction,

A O : O M : : O M : A M;

or, since A B is equal to O M,

A O : A B : : A B : A M.

Draw M B and B O; and the triangles A B O, A M B have a common angle, A, included between proportional sides; hence the two triangles are similar (Prop. XXIV. Bk. IV.). Now, the triangle O A B being isosceles, A M B must also be isosceles, and A B is equal to B M; but A B is equal to O M, consequently M B is equal to M O; hence the triangle M B O is isosceles.

Again, the angle A M B, being exterior to the isosceles triangle B M O, is double the interior angle O (Prop. XXVII. Bk. I.). But the angle A M B is equal to the angle M A B; hence the triangle O A B is such, that each of the angles at the base, O A B, O B A, is double the angle O, at its vertex. Hence the three angles of the triangle are together equal to five times the angle O, which consequently is a fifth part of two right angles, or the tenth part of four right angles; therefore the arc A B is the tenth part of the circumference, and the chord A B is the side of an inscribed regular decagon.

360. *Cor.* 1. By joining the vertices of the alternate angles A, C, &c. of the regular decagon, a regular pentagon may be inscribed. Hence, the chord A C is the side of an inscribed regular pentagon.

361. *Cor.* 2. A B being the side of the inscribed regular decagon, let A L be the side of an inscribed regular hexagon (Prop. V. Cor. 1). Join B L; then B L will be the side of an inscribed regular pentedecagon, or regular polygon of fifteen sides. For A B cuts off an arc equal to a tenth part of the circumference; and A L subtends an

arc equal to a sixth of the circumference; therefore B L, the difference of these arcs, is a fifteenth part of the circumference; and since equal arcs are subtended by equal chords, it follows that the chord B L may be applied exactly fifteen times around the circumference, thus forming a regular pentedecagon.

362. *Scholium.* If the arcs subtended by the sides of any inscribed regular polygon be severally bisected, the chords of those semi-arcs will form another inscribed polygon of double the number of sides. Thus, from having an inscribed square, there may be inscribed in succession polygons of 8, 16, 32, 64, &c. sides; from the hexagon may be formed polygons of 12, 24, 48, 96, &c. sides; from the decagon, polygons of 20, 40, 80, &c. sides; and from the pentedecagon, polygons of 30, 60, 120, &c. sides.

NOTE. — For a long time the polygons above noticed were supposed to include all that could be inscribed in a circle. In the year 1801, M. Gauss, of Göttingen, made known the curious discovery that the circumference of a circle could be divided into any number of equal parts capable of being expressed by the formula $2^n + 1$, provided it be a prime number. Now, the number 3 is the simplest of this kind, it being the value of the above formula when the exponent n is 1; the next prime number is 5, and this is contained in the formula. But the polygons of 3 and of 5 sides have already been inscribed. The next prime number expressed by the formula is 17, so that it is possible to inscribe a regular polygon of 17 sides in a circle. The investigations, however, which establish this geometrical fact involve considerations of a nature that do not enter into the elements of Geometry.

PROPOSITION VII. — PROBLEM.

363. *A regular inscribed polygon being given, to circumscribe a similar polygon about the same circle.*

Let A B C D E F be a regular polygon inscribed in a circle whose centre is O.

Through M, the middle point of the arc A B, draw the tangent, G H; also draw tangents at the middle points of the arcs B C, C D, &c.; these tangents are parallel to the chords A B, B C, C D, &c. (Prop. XI. Bk. III., and Prop. VI. Cor. 1, Bk. III.), and by their intersections form the regular circumscribed polygon G H I, &c. similar to the one inscribed.

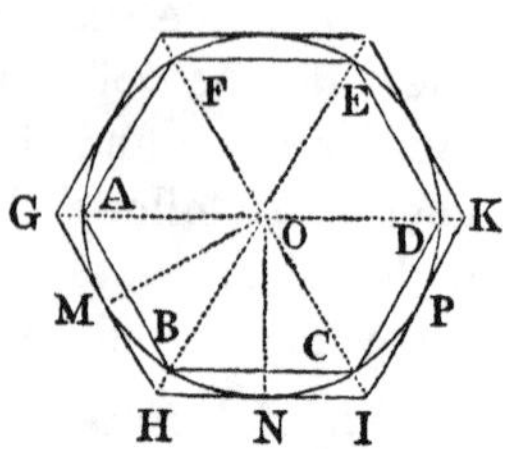

Since M is the middle point of the arc A B, and N the middle point of the equal arc B C, the arcs B M, B N are halves of equal arcs, and therefore are equal; that is, the vertex, B, of the inscribed polygon is at the middle point of the arc M N. Draw O H; the line O H will pass through the point B. For, the right-angled triangles O M H, O N H, having the common hypothenuse O H, and the side O M equal to O N, must be equal (Prop. XIX. Bk. I.), and consequently the angle M O H is equal to H O N, wherefore the line O H passes through the middle point, B, of the arc M N. In like manner, it may be shown that the line O I passes through the middle point, C, of the arc N P; and so with the other vertices.

Since G H is parallel to A B, and H I to B C, the angle G H I is equal to the angle A B C (Prop. XXVI. Bk. I.); in like manner, H I K is equal to B C D; and so with the other angles; hence, the angles of the circumscribed polygon are equal to those of the inscribed polygon. And, further, by reason of these same parallels, we have

$$GH : AB :: OH : OB, \text{ and } HI : BC :: OH : OB;$$

therefore (Prop. X. Bk. II.),

$$GH : AB :: HI : BC.$$

But A B is equal to B C, therefore G H is equal to H I. For the same reason, H I is equal to I K, &c.; consequently, the sides of the circumscribed polygon are all equal; hence this polygon is regular, and similar to the inscribed one.

364. *Cor.* 1. Conversely, if the circumscribed polygon G H I K, &c. is given, and it is required, by means of it, to construct a similar inscribed polygon, draw the straight lines O G, O H, &c. from the vertices of the angles G, H, I, &c. of the given polygon to the center; the lines will meet the circumference in the points A, B, C, &c. Join these points by the chords A B, B C, &c., which will form the inscribed polygon. Or simply join the points of contact, M, N, P, &c., by chords, M N, N P, &c., which likewise would form an inscribed polygon similar to the circumscribed one.

365. *Cor.* 2. Hence, we may circumscribe about a circle any regular polygon similar to an inscribed one, and conversely.

366. *Cor.* 3. It has been shown that N H and H M are equal; therefore the sum of N H and H M, which is equal to the sum of H M and M G, is equal to H G, one of the equal sides of the polygon.

367. *Scholium.* From having a circumscribed regular polygon, another having double the number of sides may be readily constructed, by drawing tangents to the points of bisection of the arcs, intercepted by the sides of the proposed polygon, limiting these tangents by those sides. In like manner other circumscribed polygons may be formed; but it is plain that each of the polygons so formed will be less than the preceding polygon, being entirely comprehended in it.

Proposition VIII. — Theorem.

368. *The area of a regular polygon is equivalent to the product of its perimeter by half of the radius of the inscribed circle.*

Let A B C D E F be a regular polygon, and O the centre of the inscribed circle.

From O let the straight lines O A, O B, &c. be drawn to

the vertices of all the angles of the polygon, and the polygon will be divided into as many equal triangles as it has sides; and let the radii O M, O N, &c. of the inscribed circle be drawn to the centres of the sides of the polygon, or to the points of tangency M, N, &c., and these radii are perpendicular to the sides respectively (Prop. XI. Bk. III.); therefore the radius of the circle is equal to the altitude of the several triangles.

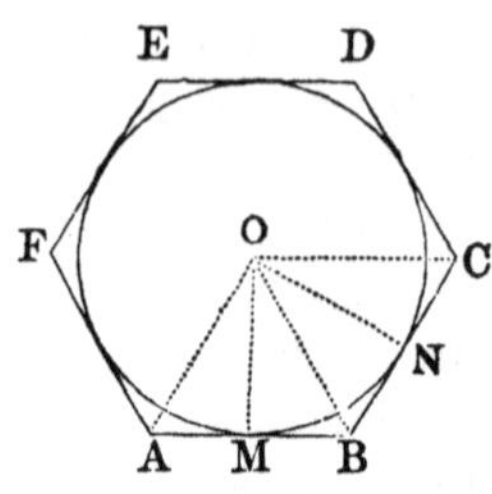

Now, the triangle A O B is measured by the product of A B by half of O M (Prop. VI. Bk. IV.); the triangle O B C by the product of B C by half of O N. But O M is equal to O N; hence the two triangles taken together are measured by the sum of A B and B C by half of O M. In like manner the measure of the other triangles may be found; hence, the sum of all the triangles, or the whole polygon, is equal to the sum of the bases A B, B C, &c., or the perimeter of the polygon, multiplied by half of O M, or half the radius of the inscribed circle.

Proposition IX. — Theorem.

369. *The perimeters of two regular polygons, having the same number of sides, are to each other as the radii of the circumscribed circles, and, also, as the radii of the inscribed circles; and their areas are to each other as the squares of those radii.*

Let A B be a side of one polygon, O the center, and consequently O A the radius of the circumscribed circle, and O M, perpendicular to A B, the radius of the inscribed circle. Let G H be a side of the other polygon, C the center, C G and C N the radii of the circumscribed and the inscribed circles.

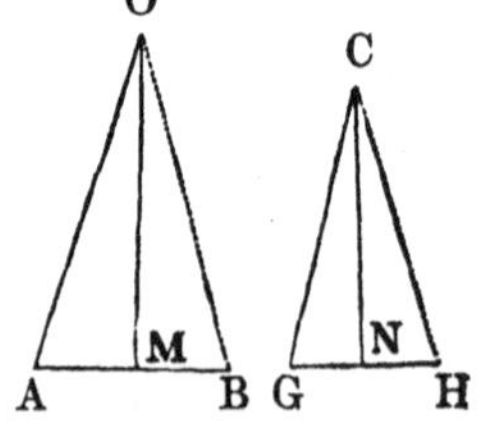

The perimeters of the two polygons are to each other as the sides A B and G H (Prop. XXXI. Bk. IV.), but the angles A and G are equal, being each half of the angle of the polygon; so also are the angles B and H; hence, drawing O B and C H, the isosceles triangles A B O, G H C are similar, as are likewise the right-angled triangles A M O, G N C; hence

A B : G H : : A O : G C : : M O : N C.

Hence, the perimeters of the polygons are to each other as the radii A O, G C of the circumscribed circles, and, also, as the radii M O, N C of the inscribed circles.

The surfaces of these polygons are to each other as the squares of the homologous sides A B, G H (Prop. XXXI. Bk. IV.); they are therefore to each other as the squares of A O, G C, the radii of the circumscribed circles, or as the squares of O M, C N, the radii of the inscribed circles.

Proposition X. — Problem.

370. *The surface of a regular inscribed polygon, and that of a similar circumscribed polygon, being given; to find the surfaces of regular inscribed and circumscribed polygons having double the number of sides.*

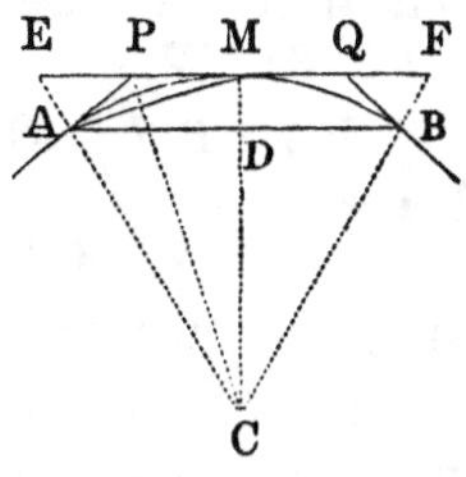

Let A B be a side of the given inscribed polygon; E F, parallel to A B, a side of the circumscribed polygon, and C the centre of the circle. Draw the chord A M, and the tangents A P, B Q; then A M will be a side of the inscribed polygon, having twice the number of sides; and P Q, the double of P M, will be a side of the similar circumscribed polygon.

Let A, then, be the surface of the inscribed polygon whose side is A B, B that of the similar circumscribed polygon; A′ the surface of the polygon whose side is A M,

B′ that of the similar circumscribed polygon: A and B are given; we have to find A′ and B′.

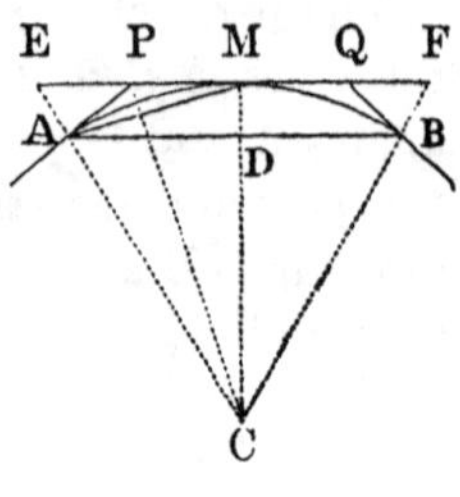

First. The triangles A C D, A C M, whose common vertex is A, are to each other as their bases C D, C M (Prop. VI. Cor., Bk. IV.); they are likewise as the polygons A and A′; hence

$$A : A' :: CD : CM.$$

Again, the triangles C A M, C M E, whose common vertex is M, are to each other as their bases C A, C E; they are likewise to each other as the polygons A′ and B; hence

$$A' : B :: CA : CE.$$

But, since A D and M E are parallel, we have,

$$CD : CM :: CA : CE;$$

hence

$$A : A' :: A' : B;$$

hence, *the polygon A′ is a mean proportional between the two given polygons.*

Secondly. The altitude C M being common, the triangle C P M is to the triangle C P E as P M is to P E; but since C P bisects the angle M C E, we have (Prop. XIX. Bk. IV.),

$$PM : PE :: CM : CE :: CD : CA :: A : A';$$

hence

$$CPM : CPE :: A : A';$$

and, consequently,

$$CPM : CPM + CPE \text{ or } CME :: A : A + A'.$$

But C M P A or 2 C M P and C M E are to each other as the polygons B′ and B; hence

$$B' : B :: 2\,A : A + A';$$

which gives

$$B' = \frac{2\,A \times B}{A + A'};$$

or, *the polygon B′ is equal to the quotient of twice the product of the given polygons divided by the sum of the inscribed polygons.*

Thus, by means of the polygons A and B, it is easy to find the polygons A′ and B′, which have double the number of sides.

Proposition XI. — Theorem.

371. *A circle being given, two similar polygons can always be formed, the one circumscribed about the circle, the other inscribed in it, which shall differ from each other by less than any assignable surface.*

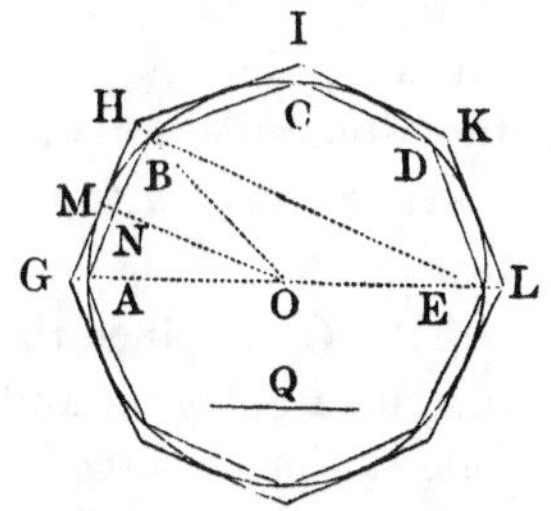

Let Q be the side of a square less than the given surface.

Bisect A C, a fourth part of the circumference, and then bisect the half of this fourth, and so proceed until an arc is found whose chord A B is less than Q. As this arc must be an exact part of the circumference, if we apply the chords A B, B C, &c., each equal to A B, the last will terminate at A, and there will be inscribed in the circle a regular polygon, A B C D E, &c. Next describe about the circle a similar polygon, G H I K L, &c. (Prop. VII.); and the difference of these two polygons will be less than the square of Q.

Find the center, O; from the points G and H draw the straight lines G O, H O, and they will pass through the points A and B (Prop. VII.). Draw also O M to the point of tangency, M; and it will bisect A B in N, and be perpendicular to it (Prop. VI. Cor. 1, Bk. III.). Produce A O to E, and draw B E.

Let P represent the circumscribed polygon, and *p* the inscribed polygon. Then, since these polygons are similar, they are as the squares of the homologous sides G H,

A B (Prop. XXXI. Bk. IV.); but the triangles G O H, A O B are similar (Prop. XXIV. Bk. IV.); hence they are to each other as the squares of the homologous sides O G and O A (Prop. XXIX. Bk. IV.); therefore

$$P : p : : \overline{OG}^2 : \overline{OA}^2 \text{ or } \overline{OM}^2.$$

Again, the triangles O G M, E A B, having their sides respectively parallel, are similar; therefore

$$P : p : : \overline{OG}^2 : \overline{OM}^2 : : \overline{AE}^2 : \overline{BE}^2;$$

and, by division,

$$P : P - p : : \overline{AE}^2 : \overline{AE}^2 - \overline{EB}^2 \text{ or } \overline{AB}^2.$$

But P is less than the square described on the diameter A E; therefore P — p is less than the square described on A B, that is, less than the given square Q. Hence, the difference between the circumscribed and inscribed polygons may always be made less than any given surface.

372. *Cor.* Since the circle is obviously greater than any inscribed polygon, and less than any circumscribed one, it follows that *a polygon may be inscribed or circumscribed, which will differ from the circle by less than any assignable magnitude.*

Proposition XII. — Problem.

373. *To find the approximate area of a circle whose radius is unity.*

Let the radius of the circle be 1, and let the first inscribed and circumscribed polygons be squares; the side of the inscribed square will be $\sqrt{2}$ (Prop. IV. Cor.), and that of the circumscribed square will be equal to the diameter 2. Hence the surface of the inscribed square is 2, and that of the circumscribed square is 4. Let, therefore A = 2, and B = 4. Now it has been proved, in Proposition X., that the surface of the inscribed octagon, or, as it has been represented, A′, is a mean proportional between the two squares A and B, so that $A' = \sqrt{8} =$ 2.8284271; and it has also been proved, in the same proposition, that the circumscribed octagon, represented by B', $= \frac{2\,A \times B}{A + A'}$; so that $B' = \frac{16}{2 + \sqrt{8}} = 3.3137085$. The inscribed and the circumscribed octagons being thus determined, we can easily, by means of them, determine the polygons having twice the number of sides. We have only in this case to put $A = 2.8284271$, $B = 3.3137085$; and we shall find $A' = \sqrt{A \times B} = 3.0614674$, and $B' = \frac{2\,A \times B}{A + A'} = 3.1825979$.

In like manner may be determined the area of polygons of sixteen sides, and thence the area of polygons of thirty-two sides, and so on till we arrive at an inscribed and a circumscribed polygon differing so little from each other, and consequently from the circle, that the difference shall be less than any assignable magnitude (Prop. XI. Cor.).

The subjoined table exhibits the area, or numerical expression for the surface, of these polygons, carried on till they agree as far as the seventh place of decimals.

Number of sides.	Inscribed Polygons.	Circumscribed Polygons.
4	2.0000000	4.0000000
8	2.8284271	3.3137085
16	3.0614674	3.1825979
32	3.1214451	3.1517249
64	3.1365485	3.1441148
128	3.1403311	3.1422236
256	3.1412772	3.1417504
512	3.1415138	3.1416321
1024	3.1415729	3.1416025
2048	3.1415877	3.1415951
4096	3.1415914	3.1415933
8192	3.1415923	3.1415928
16384	3.1415925	3.1415927
32768	3.1415926	3.1415926

It appears, therefore, that the inscribed and circumscribed polygons of 32768 sides differ so little from each other that the numerical value of each, as far as seven places of decimals, is absolutely the same; as the circle is between the two, it cannot, strictly speaking, differ from either so much as they do from each other; so that the number 3.1415926 expresses the area of a circle whose radius is 1, correctly, as far as seven places of decimals.

Some doubt may exist, perhaps, about the last decimal figure, owing to errors proceeding from the parts omitted; but the calculation has been carried on with an additional figure, that the final result here given might be absolutely correct even to the last decimal place.

374. *Cor.* Since the inscribed and circumscribed polygons are regular, and have the same number of sides, they are similar (Prop. I.); therefore, by increasing the number of the sides, the corresponding polygons formed will approach to an equality with the circle. Now if, by continual bisections, the polygons formed shall have their number of sides indefinitely great, each side will become indefinitely small, and the inscribed and circumscribed polygons will ultimately coincide with each other. But when they coincide with each other, they must each coincide with the circle, since no part of an inscribed polygon can be without the circle, nor can any part of a circumscribed one be within it; hence, *the perimeters of the polygons must coincide with the circumference of the circle, and be equal to it.*

375. *Scholium.* Every circle, therefore, may be regarded as a polygon of an infinite number of sides.

Note. — This new definition of the circle, if it does not appear at first view to be very strict, has at least the advantage of introducing more simplicity and precision into demonstrations. (*Cours de Géométrie Élémentaire*, par Vincent et Bourdon.)

PROPOSITION XIII. — THEOREM.

376. *The circumferences of circles are to each other as their radii, and their areas are to each other as the squares of their radii.*

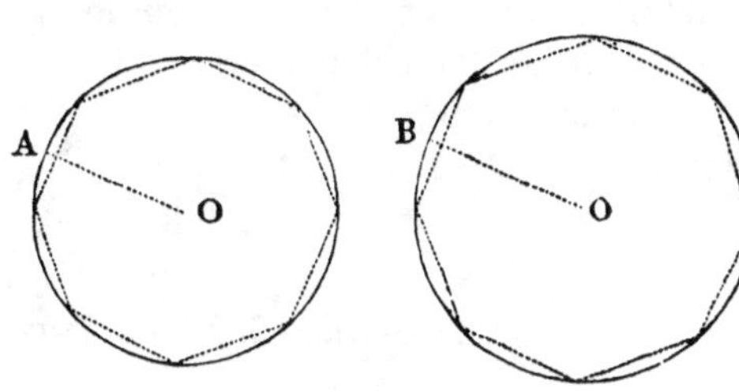

Let C denote the circumference of one of the circles, R its radius O A, A its area; and let C′ denote the circumference of the other circle, r its radius O B, A′ its area; then will

$$C : C' :: R : r,$$

and

$$A : A' :: R^2 : r^2.$$

Inscribe within the given circles two regular polygons of the same number of sides; and, whatever be the number of sides, the perimeters of the polygons will be to each other as the radii O A and O B (Prop. IX.). Now, conceive the arcs subtending the sides of the polygon to be continually bisected, forming other inscribed polygons, until polygons are formed of an indefinite number of sides, and therefore having perimeters coinciding with the circumference of the circumscribed circles (Prop. XII. Cor.); and we shall have

$$C : C' :: R : r.$$

Again, the areas of the inscribed polygons are to each other as $\overline{OA}^2$ to $\overline{OB}^2$ (Prop. IX.). But when the number of sides of the polygons is indefinitely increased, the areas of the polygons become equal to the areas of the circles; hence we shall have

$$A : A' :: R^2 : r^2.$$

377. *Cor.* 1. The circumferences of circles are to each other as twice their radii, or as their diameters.

For, multiplying the terms of the second ratio in the first proportion by 2, we have

$$C : C' :: 2R : 2r.$$

378. *Cor.* 2. The areas of circles are to each other as the squares of their diameters.

For, multiplying the second ratio of the second proportion by 4, or 2 squared, we have

$$A : A' :: 4R^2 : 4r^2.$$

Proposition XIV. — Theorem.

379. *Similar arcs are to each other as their radii; and similar sectors are to each other as the squares of their radii.*

Let A B, D E be similar arcs; A C B, D O E, similar sectors; and denote the radii C A and O D by R and r; then will

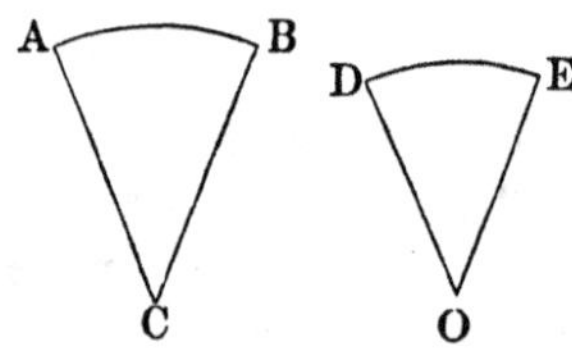

$$AB : DE :: R : r,$$

and $$ACB : DOE :: R^2 : r^2.$$

For, since the arcs are similar, the angle C is equal to the angle O (Art. 213). But the angle C is to four right angles as the arc A B is to the whole circumference described with the radius C A (Prop. XVII. Sch. 2, Bk. III.); and the angle O is to four right angles as the arc D E is to the circumference described with the radius O D. Hence, the arcs A B, D E are to each other as the circumferences of which they form a part. But these circumferences are to each other as their radii, C A, O D (Prop. XIII.); therefore

$$Arc\ AB : Arc\ DE :: R : r.$$

By like reasoning, the sectors A C B, D O E are to each

other as the whole circles of which they are a part; and these are as the squares of their radii (Prop. XIII.); therefore

$$Sector\ ACB : Sector\ DOE :: R^2 : r^2.$$

PROPOSITION XV. — THEOREM.

380. *The area of a circle is equal to the product of the circumference by half the radius.*

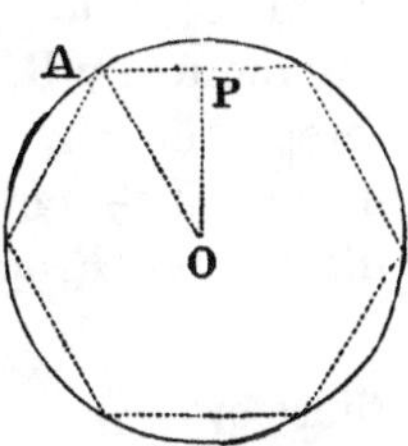

Let C denote the circumference of the circle, whose center is O, R its radius OA, and A its area; then will

$$A = C \times \tfrac{1}{2} R.$$

For, inscribe in the circle any regular polygon, and from the center draw OP perpendicular to one of the sides. The area of the polygon, whatever be the number of sides, will be equal to its perimeter multiplied by half of OP (Prop. VIII.). Conceive the arcs subtending the sides of the polygon to be continually bisected, until a polygon is formed having an indefinite number of sides; its perimeter will be equal to the circumference of the circle (Prop. XII. Cor.), and OP be equal to the radius OA; therefore the area of the polygon is equal to that of the circle; hence

$$A = C \times \tfrac{1}{2} R.$$

381. *Cor.* 1. The area of a sector is equal to the product of its arc by half of its radius.

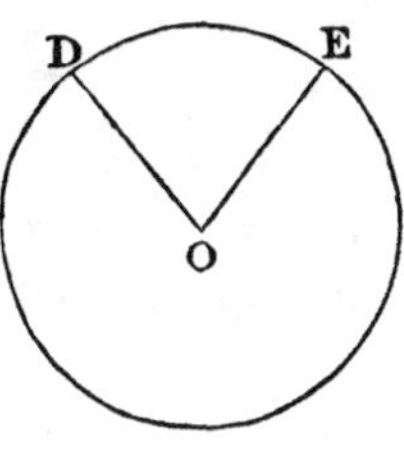

For, let C denote the circumference of the circle of which the sector DOE is a part, R its radius OD, and A its area; then we shall have (Prop. XVII. Sch. 2, Bk. III.),

$$Sector\ DOE : A :: Arc\ DE : C;$$

hence, since equimultiples of two magnitudes have the same ratio as the magnitudes themselves (Prop. IX. Bk. II.),

$$\textit{Sector}\ \mathrm{DOE} : \mathrm{A} :: \textit{Arc}\ \mathrm{DE} \times \tfrac{1}{2}\mathrm{R} : \mathrm{C} \times \tfrac{1}{2}\mathrm{R}.$$

But A, or the area of the whole circle, is equal to $C \times \frac{1}{2} R$; hence, the area of the sector D O E is equal to the arc $DE \times \frac{1}{2} R$.

382. *Cor.* 2. Let the circumference of the circle whose diameter is unity be denoted by π (which is called *pi*), the radius by R, and the diameter by D; and the circumference of any other circle by C, and its area by A. Then, since circumferences are to each other as their diameters (Prop. XIII. Cor. 1), we shall have,

$$C : D :: \pi : 1;$$

therefore

$$C = D \times \pi = 2\,R \times \pi.$$

Multiplying both numbers of this equation by $\frac{1}{2}$ R, we have

$$C \times \tfrac{1}{2} R = R^2 \times \pi, \quad \text{or} \quad A = R^2 \times \pi;$$

that is, *the area of a circle is equal to the product of the square of its radius by the constant number* π.

383. *Cor.* 3. The circumference of every circle is equal to the product of its diameter, or twice its radius, by the constant number π.

384. *Cor.* 4. The constant number π denotes the ratio of the circumference of any circle to its diameter; for $\frac{C}{D} = \pi$.

385. *Scholium* 1. The exact numerical value of the ratio denoted by π can be only approximately expressed. The approximate value found by Proposition XII. is 3.1415926; but, for most practical purposes, it is sufficiently accurate to take $\pi = 3.1416$. The symbol π is the first letter of the Greek word *περίμετρον*, *perimetron*, which signifies *circumference*.

386. *Scholium* 2. The QUADRATURE OF THE CIRCLE is the problem which requires the finding of a square equivalent in area to a circle having a given radius. Now, it has just been proved that a circle is equivalent to the rectangle contained by its circumference and half its radius; and this rectangle may be changed into a square, by finding a mean proportional between its length and its breadth (Prob. XXVI. Bk. V.). To square the circle, therefore, is to find the circumference when the radius is given; and for effecting this, it is enough to know the ratio of the circumference to its radius, or its diameter.

But this ratio has never been determined except approximately; but the approximation has been carried so far, that a knowledge of the exact ratio would afford no real advantage whatever beyond that of the approximate ratio. Professor Rutherford extended the approximation to 208 places of decimals, and Dr. Clausen to 250 places. The value of π, as developed to 208 places of decimals, is
3.14159265358979323846264338327950288419716939937
51058209749445923078164062862089986280348253427 17
06798214808651328230664709384460955058223172535 94
08128484737813920386338302157473996008259312591 29
40183280651744.

Such an approximation is evidently equivalent to perfect correctness; the root of an imperfect power is in no case more accurately known.

PROPOSITION XVI. — PROBLEM.

387. *To divide a circle into any number of equal parts by means of concentric circles.*

Let it be proposed to divide the circle, whose center is O, into a certain number of equal parts, — three for instance, — by means of concentric circles.

Draw the radius A O; divide A O into three equal parts, A B, B C, C O. Upon A O describe a semi-circumference, and draw the perpendiculars, B E, C D, meeting that semi-circumference in the points E, D. Join O E, O D, and with these lines as radii from the center, O, describe circles; these circles will divide the given circle into the required number of equal parts.

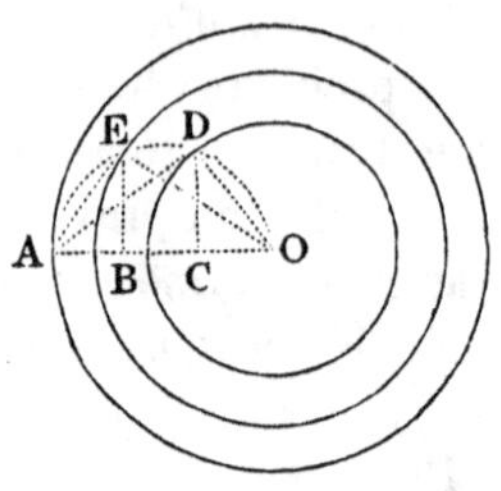

For join A E, A D; then the angle A D O, being in a semicircle, is a right angle (Prop. XVIII. Cor. 2, Bk. III.); hence the triangles D A O, D C O are similar, and consequently are to each other as the squares of their homologous sides; that is,

$$DAO : DCO :: \overline{OA}^2 : \overline{OD}^2;$$

but

$$DAO : DCO :: OA : OC;$$

hence

$$\overline{OA}^2 : \overline{OD}^2 :: OA : OC;$$

consequently, since circles are to each other as the squares of their radii (Prop. XIII.), it follows that the circle whose radius is O A, is to that whose radius is O D, as O A to O C; that is to say, the latter is one third of the former.

In the same manner, by means of the right-angled triangles E A O, E B O, it may be proved that the circle whose radius is O E, is two thirds that whose radius is O A. Hence, the smaller circle and the two surrounding *annular* spaces are all equal.

NOTE. — This useful problem was first solved by Dr. Hutton, the justly distinguished English mathematician.

BOOK VII.

PLANES. — DIEDRAL AND POLYEDRAL ANGLES.

DEFINITIONS.

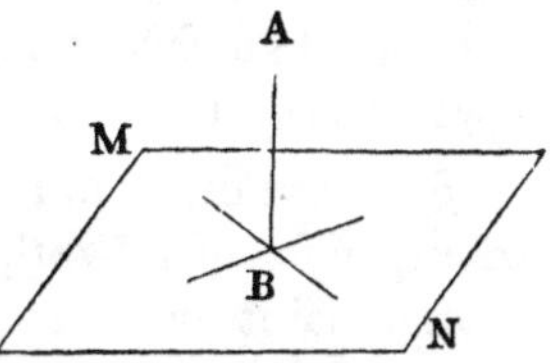

388. A STRAIGHT line is *perpendicular to a plane*, when it is perpendicular to every straight line which it meets in that plane.

Conversely, the plane, in the same case, is *perpendicular to the line.*

The *foot* of the perpendicular is the point in which it meets the plane.

Thus the straight line A B is perpendicular to the plane M N; the plane M N is perpendicular to the straight line A B; and B is the foot of the perpendicular A B.

389. A line is *parallel to a plane* when it cannot meet the plane, however far both of them may be produced.

Conversely, the plane, in the same case, is parallel to the line.

390. Two *planes are parallel to each other*, when they cannot meet, however far both of them may be produced.

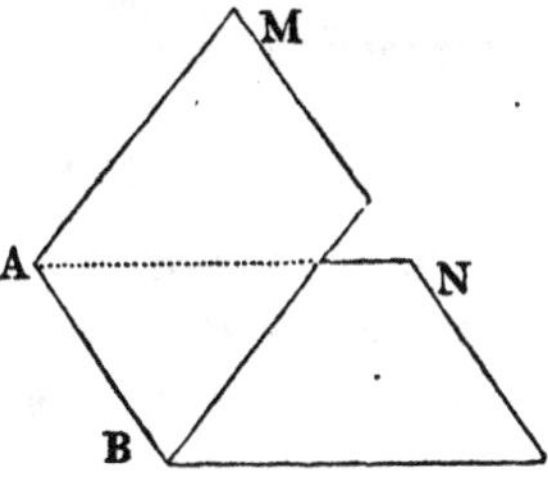

391. A DIEDRAL ANGLE is an angle formed by the intersection of two planes, and is measured by the inclination of two straight lines drawn from any point in the line of intersection, perpendicular to that line, one being drawn in each plane.

The line of common section is called the *edge*, and the two planes are called the faces, of the diedral angle.

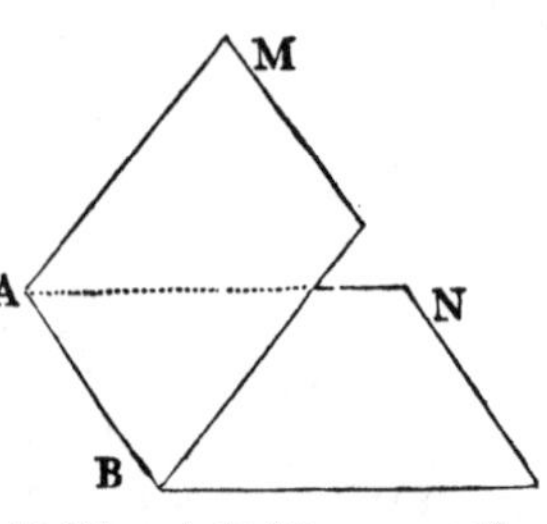

Thus the two planes A B M, A B N, whose line of intersection is A B, form a diedral angle, of which the line A B is the edge, and the planes A B M, A B N are the faces.

392. A diedral angle may be acute, right, or obtuse.

If the two faces are perpendicular to each other, the angle is right.

393. A POLYEDRAL ANGLE is an angle formed by the meeting at one point of more than two plane angles, which are not in the same plane.

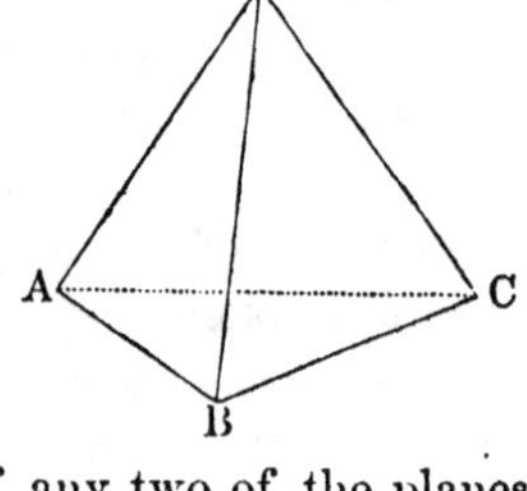

The common point of meeting of the planes is called the *vertex*, each of the plane angles a *face*, and the line of common section of any two of the planes an *edge* of the polyedral angle.

Thus the three plane angles A S B, B S C, C S A form a polyedral angle, whose vertex is S, whose faces are the plane angles, and whose edges are the sides, A S, B S, C S, of the same angles.

394. A polyedral angle formed by three faces is called a *triedral* angle; by four faces, a *tetraedral;* by five faces, a *pentaedral*, &c.

PROPOSITION I. — THEOREM.

395. *A straight line cannot be partly in a plane, and partly out of it.*

For, by the definition of a plane (Art. 10), a straight

line which has two points in common with a plane lies wholly in that plane.

396. *Scholium.* To determine whether a surface is a plane, apply a straight line in different directions to that surface, and ascertain whether the line throughout its whole extent touches the surface.

PROPOSITION II. — THEOREM.

397. *Two straight lines which intersect each other lie in the same plane and determine its position.*

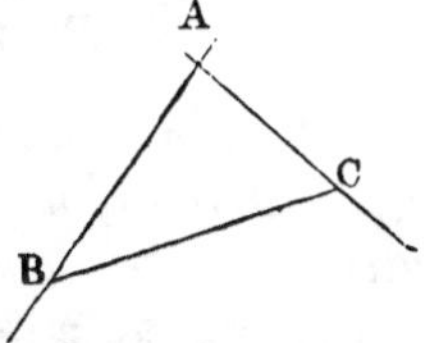

Let A B, A C be two straight lines which intersect each other in A; then these lines will be in the same plane.

Conceive a plane to pass through A B, and to be turned about A B, until it pass through the point C; then, the two points A and C being in this plane, the line A C lies wholly in it (Art. 10). Hence, the position of the plane is determined by the condition of its containing the two straight lines A B, A C.

398. *Cor.* 1. A triangle, A B C, or three points, A, B, C, not in a straight line, determine the position of a plane.

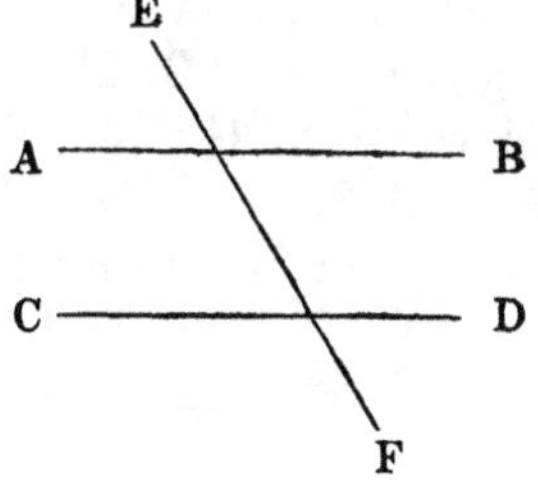

399. *Cor.* 2. Hence, also, two parallels, A B, C D, determine the position of a plane; for, drawing the secant E F, the plane of the two straight lines A B, E F is that of the parallels A B, C D.

PROPOSITION III. — THEOREM.

400. *If two planes cut each other, their common section is a straight line.*

Let the two planes A B, C D cut each other, and let E, F be two points in their common section. Draw the straight line E F. Now, since the points E and F are in the plane A B, and also in the plane C D, the straight line E F, joining E and F, must be wholly in each plane, or is common to both of them. Therefore, the common section of the two planes A B, C D is a straight line.

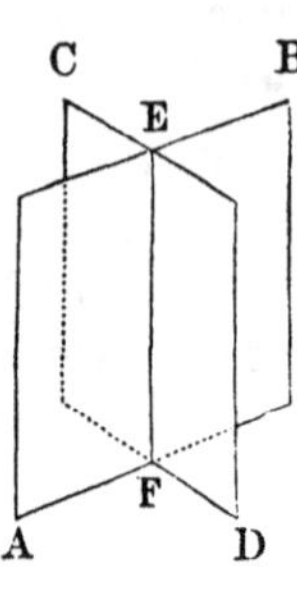

PROPOSITION IV. — THEOREM.

401. *If a straight line is perpendicular to each of two straight lines, at their point of intersection, it is perpendicular to the plane in which the two lines lie.*

Let the straight line A B be perpendicular to each of the straight lines C D, E F, at B, the point of their intersection, and M N the plane in which the lines C D, E F lie; then will A B be perpendicular to the plane M N.

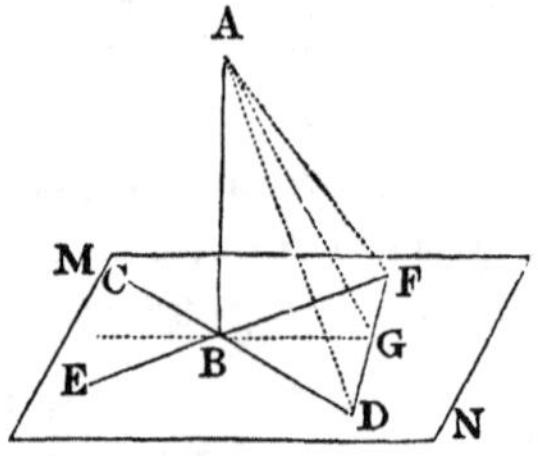

Through the point B draw any straight line, B G, in the plane M N; and through any point G draw D G F, meeting the lines C D, E F in such a manner that D G shall be equal to G F (Prob. XXVIII. Bk. V.). Join A D, A G, A F.

The line D F being divided into two equal parts at the point G, the triangle D B F gives (Prop. XIV. Bk. IV.)

$$\overline{BF}^2 + \overline{BD}^2 = 2\,\overline{BG}^2 + 2\,\overline{GF}^2.$$

The triangle D A F, in like manner, gives

$$\overline{AF}^2 + \overline{AD}^2 = 2\,\overline{AG}^2 + 2\,\overline{GF}^2.$$

Subtracting the first equation from the second, and observing that the triangles A B F, A B D, each being right-angled at B, give

$$\overline{AF}^2 - \overline{BF}^2 = \overline{AB}^2, \quad \text{and} \quad \overline{AD}^2 - \overline{BD}^2 = \overline{AB}^2,$$

we shall have

$$\overline{AB}^2 + \overline{AB}^2 = 2\,\overline{AG}^2 - 2\,\overline{BG}^2.$$

Therefore, by taking the halves of both members, we have

$$\overline{AB}^2 = \overline{AG}^2 - \overline{BG}^2, \quad \text{or} \quad \overline{AG}^2 = \overline{AB}^2 + \overline{BG}^2;$$

hence, the triangle A B G is right-angled at B, and the side A B is perpendicular to B G.

In the same manner, it may be shown that A B is perpendicular to any other straight line in the plane M N, which it may meet at B; therefore A B is perpendicular to the plane M N (Art. 388).

402. *Scholium.* Thus it is evident, not only that a straight line may be perpendicular to all the straight lines which pass through its foot, in a plane, but it always must be so whenever it is perpendicular to two straight lines drawn in the plane; which shows the accuracy of the first definition (Art. 388).

403. *Cor.* 1. The perpendicular A B is shorter than any oblique line A G; therefore it measures the shortest distance from the point A to the plane M N.

404. *Cor.* 2. From any given point, B, in a plane, only one perpendicular to that plane can be drawn. For if there could be two, conceive a plane to pass through them, intersecting the plane M N in B G; the two perpendiculars would then be perpendicular to the straight line B G at the same point, and in the same plane, which is impossible (Prop. XIII. Cor., Bk. I.).

It is also impossible to let fall from a given point out of a plane two perpendiculars to that plane. For, suppose A B, A G to be two such perpendiculars, then the triangle A B G will have two right angles, A B G, A G B, which is impossible (Prop. XXVIII. Cor. 3, Bk. I.).

PROPOSITION V. — THEOREM.

405. *Oblique lines drawn from a point to a plane at equal distances from a perpendicular drawn from the same point to it, are equal; and of two oblique lines unequally distant from the perpendicular, the more remote is the longer.*

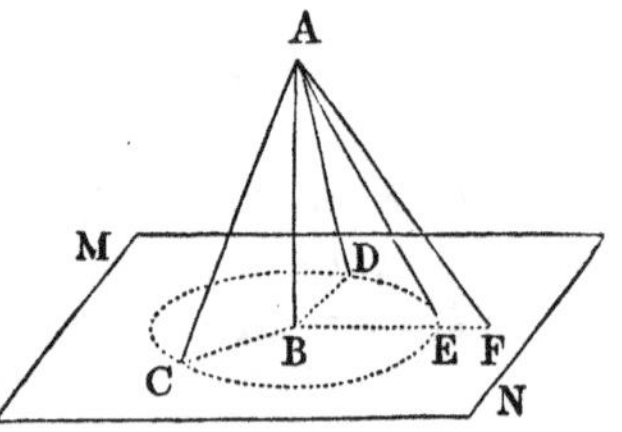

Let A B be perpendicular to the plane M N; and A C, A D, A E be oblique lines, from the point A, meeting the plane at equal distances, B C, B D, B E, from the perpendicular; and A F a line meeting the plane more remote from the perpendicular; then will A C, A D, A E be equal to each other, and A F be longer than A C.

For, the angles A B C, A B D, A B E being right angles, and the distances B C, B D, B E being equal to each other, the triangles A B C, A B D, A B E have in each an equal angle contained by equal sides; consequently they are equal (Prop. V. Bk. I.); therefore, the hypothenuses, or the oblique lines A C, A D, A E, are equal to each other.

In like manner, since the distance B F is greater than B C, or its equal B E, the oblique line A F must be greater than A E, or its equal A C (Prop. XIV. Bk. I.).

406. *Cor.* All the equal oblique lines A C, A D, A E, &c. terminate in the circumference of a circle, C D E, described from B, the foot of the perpendicular, as a center; therefore, a point, A, being given out of a plane, the point B, at which the perpendicular let fall from it would meet that plane, may be found by taking upon the plane three points, C, D, E, equally distant from the point A, and then finding the center of the circle which passes through these points; this centre will be the point B required.

407. *Scholium.* The angle A C B is called *the inclination of the oblique line* A C *to the plane* M N; which inclination is evidently equal with respect to all such lines, A C, A D, A E, as are equally distant from the perpendicular; for all the triangles A C B, A D B, A E B, &c. are equal to each other.

Proposition VI. — Theorem.

408. *If from the foot of a perpendicular a straight line be drawn at right angles to any straight line of the plane, and a straight line be drawn from the point of intersection to any point of the perpendicular, this last line will be perpendicular to the line of the plane.*

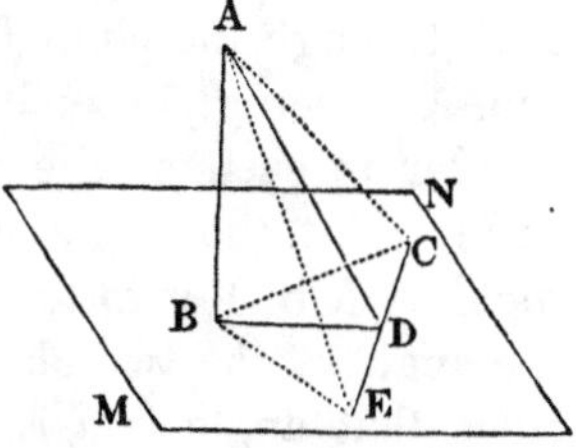

Let A B be perpendicular to the plane M N, and B D a straight line drawn through B, cutting at right angles the straight line C E in the plane; draw the straight line A D from the point of intersection, D, to any point, A, in the perpendicular A B; and A D will be perpendicular to C E.

For, take D E equal to D C, and join B E, B C, A E, A C. Since D E is equal to D C, the two right-angled triangles B D E, B D C are equal, and the oblique line B E is equal to B C (Prop. V. Bk. I.); and since B E is equal to B C, the oblique line A E is equal to A C (Prop. V. Bk. I.); therefore the line A D has two of its points, A and D, equally distant from the extremities E and C; hence, A D is a perpendicular to E C, at its middle point, D (Prop. XV. Cor., Bk. I.).

409. *Cor.* It is also evident that C E is perpendicular to the plane of the triangle A B D, since C E is perpendicular at the same time to the two straight lines A D and B D (Prop. IV.).

Proposition VII. — Theorem.

410. *If a straight line is perpendicular to a plane, every plane which passes through that line is also perpendicular to the plane.*

Let A B be a straight line perpendicular to the plane M N; then will any plane, A C, passing through A B, be perpendicular to M N.

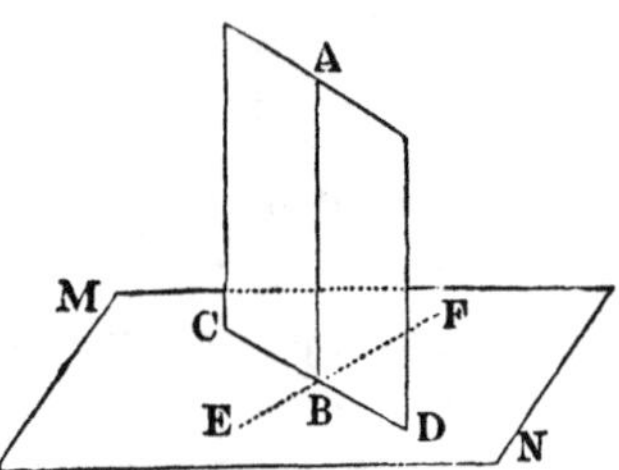

For, let C D be the intersection of the planes A C, M N; in the plane M N draw E F, through the point B, perpendicular to C D; then the line A B, being perpendicular to the plane M N, is perpendicular to each of the two straight lines C D, E F (Art. 388). But the angle A B E, formed by the two perpendiculars A B, E F to their common section, C D, measures the angle of the two planes A C, M N (Art. 391); hence, since that angle is a right angle, the two planes are perpendicular to each other.

411. *Cor.* When three straight lines, as A B, C D, E F, are perpendicular to each other, each of those lines is perpendicular to the plane of the other two, and the three planes are perpendicular to each other.

Proposition VIII. — Theorem.

412. *If two planes are perpendicular to each other, a straight line drawn in one of them, perpendicular to their common section, will be perpendicular to the other plane.*

Let A C, M N be two planes perpendicular to each other, and let the straight line A B be drawn in the plane A C perpendicular to the common section C D; then will A B be perpendicular to the plane M N.

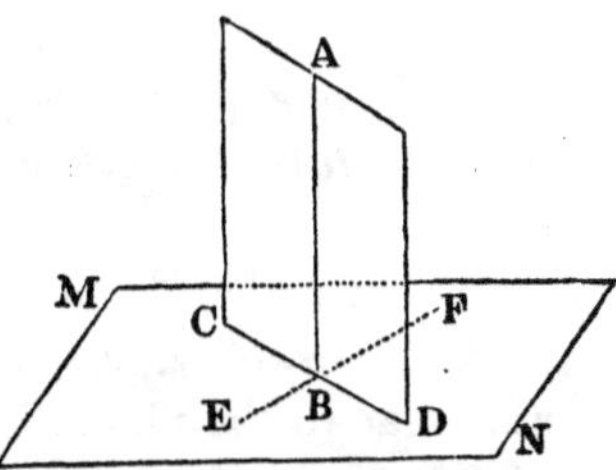

For, in the plane M N, draw E F, through the point B, perpendicular to C D; then, since the planes A C, M N are perpendicular, the angle A B E is a right angle (Art. 391); therefore the line A B is perpendicular to the two straight lines C D, E F, at the point of their intersection; hence it is perpendicular to their plane, M N (Prop. IV.).

413. *Cor.* If the plane A C is perpendicular to the plane M N, and if at a point B of the common section we erect a perpendicular to the plane M N, that perpendicular will be in the plane A C. For, if not, there may be drawn in the plane A C a line, A B, perpendicular to the common section C D, which would be at the same time perpendicular to the plane M N. Hence, at the same point B there would be two perpendiculars to the plane M N, which is impossible (Prop. IV. Cor. 2).

Proposition IX. — Theorem.

414. *If two planes which cut each other are perpendicular to a third plane, their common section is perpendicular to the same plane.*

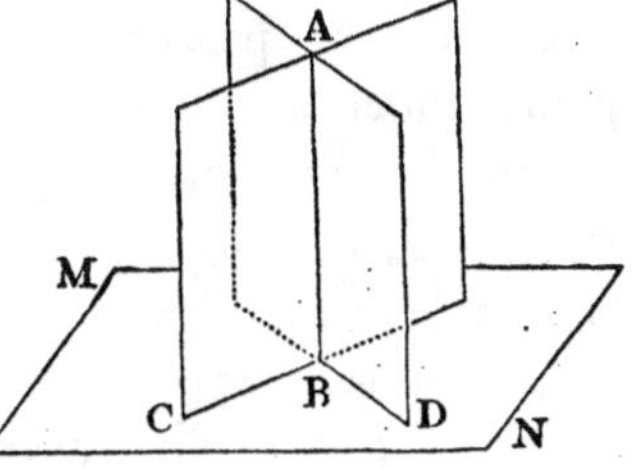

Let the two planes C A, D A, which cut each other in the straight line A B, be each perpendicular to the plane M N; then will their common section A B be perpendicular to M N.

For, at the point B, erect a perpendicular to the plane M N; that perpendicular must be at once in the plane C A and in the plane D A (Prop. VIII. Cor.); hence, it is their common section, A B.

PROPOSITION X.—THEOREM.

415. *If one of two parallel straight lines is perpendicular to a plane, the other is also perpendicular to the same plane.*

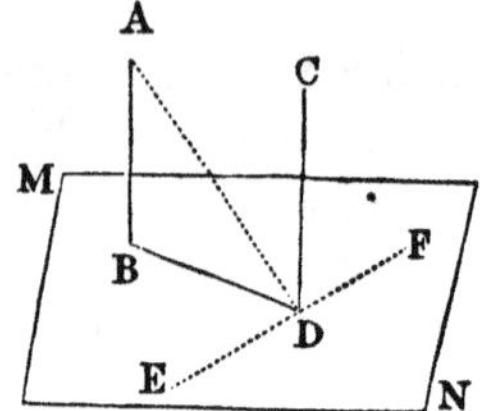

Let A B, C D be two parallel straight lines, of which A B is perpendicular to the plane M N; then will C D also be perpendicular to it.

For, pass a plane through the parallels A B, C D, cutting the plane M N in the straight line B D. In the plane M N draw the straight line E F, at right angles with B D; and join A D.

Now, E F is perpendicular to the plane A B D C (Prop. VI. Cor.); therefore the angle C D E is a right angle; but the angle C D B is also a right angle, since A B is perpendicular to B D, and C D parallel to A B (Prop. XXII. Cor., Bk. I.); therefore the line C D is perpendicular to the two straight lines E F, B D; hence it is perpendicular to their plane, M N (Prop. IV.).

416. *Cor.* 1. Conversely, if the straight lines A B, C D are perpendicular to the same plane, M N, they must be parallel. For, if they be not so, draw, through the point D, a line parallel to A B; this parallel will be perpendicular to the plane M N; hence, through the same point D more than one perpendicular may be erected to the same plane, which is impossible (Prop. IV. Cor. 2).

417. *Cor.* 2. Two lines, A and B, parallel to a third, C, are parallel to each other; for, conceive a plane perpendicular to the line C; the lines A and B, being parallel to C, will be perpendicular to the same plane; hence, by the preceding corollary, they will be parallel to each other.

The three lines are supposed to be not in the same plane; otherwise the proposition would be already demonstrated (Prop. XXIV. Bk. I.).

PROPOSITION XI. — THEOREM.

418. *If a straight line without a plane is parallel to a line within the plane, it is parallel to the plane.*

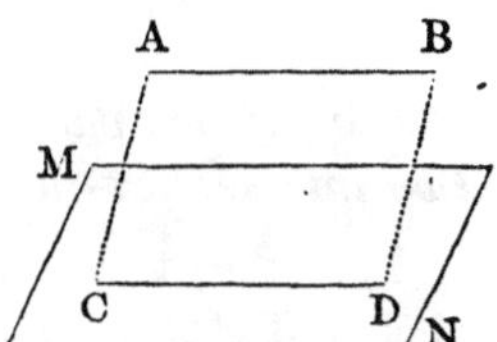

Let the straight line A B, without the plane M N, be parallel to the line C D in that plane; then will A B be parallel to the plane M N.

Conceive a plane A B C D to pass through the parallels A B, C D. Now, if the line A B, which lies in the plane A B C D, could meet the plane M N, it could only be in some point of the line C D, the common section of the two planes; but the line A B cannot meet C D, since they are parallel (Art. 17); therefore it will not meet the plane M N; hence it is parallel to that plane (Art. 389).

PROPOSITION XII. — THEOREM.

419. *If two planes are perpendicular to the same straight line, they are parallel to each other.*

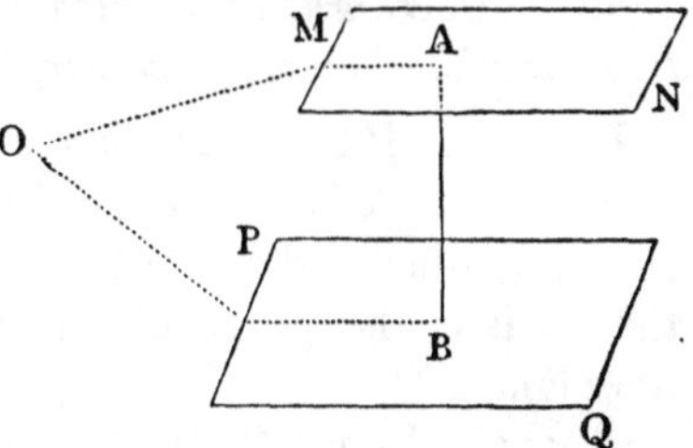

Let the planes M N, P Q, be each perpendicular to the straight line A B; then will they be parallel to each other.

For, if they can meet, on being produced, let O be one of their common points; and join O A, O B. The line A B, which is perpendicular to the plane M N, is perpendicular to the straight line O A, drawn through its foot in that plane (Art. 388). For the same reason, A B is perpendicular to B O. Therefore O A and O B are two perpendiculars let fall from the same point, O, upon the same straight line, A B, which is impossible (Prop. XIII. Bk. I.).

Therefore, the planes M N, P Q cannot meet on being produced; hence they are parallel to each other.

Proposition XIII. — Theorem.

420. *If two parallel planes are cut by a third plane, the two intersections are parallel.*

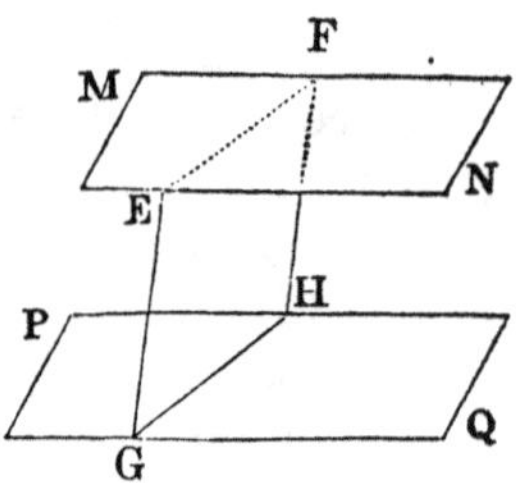

Let the two parallel planes MN and P Q be cut by the plane E F G H, and let their intersections with it be E F, G H; then E F is parallel to G H.

For, if the lines E F, G H, lying in the same plane, were not parallel, they would meet each other on being produced; therefore the planes M N, P Q, in which those lines are situated, would also meet, which is impossible, since these planes are parallel.

Proposition XIV. — Theorem.

421. *A straight line which is perpendicular to one of two parallel planes, is also perpendicular to the other plane.*

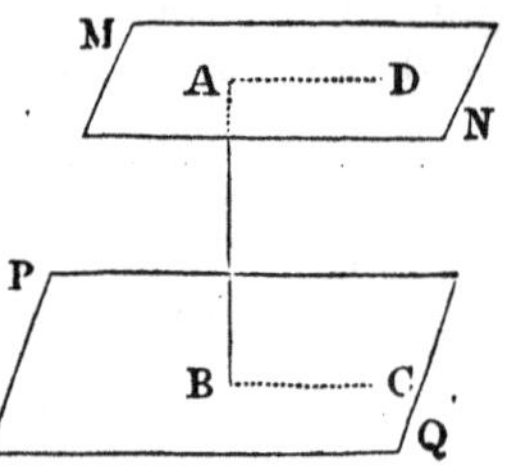

Let M N, P Q be two parallel planes, and A B a straight line perpendicular to the plane M N; then A B is also perpendicular to the plane P Q.

Draw any line, B C, in the plane P Q; and through the lines A B, B C, conceive a plane, A B C, to pass, intersecting the plane M N in A D; the intersection A D will be parallel to B C (Prop. XIII.). But the line A B, being perpendicular to the plane M N, is perpendicular to the straight line A D; consequently it will be perpendicular to its parallel B C (Prop. XXII. Cor., Bk. I.).

Hence the line A B, being perpendicular to any line, B C, drawn through its foot in the plane P Q, is consequently perpendicular to the plane P Q (Art. 388).

PROPOSITION XV. — THEOREM.

422. *Parallel straight lines included between two parallel planes are equal.*

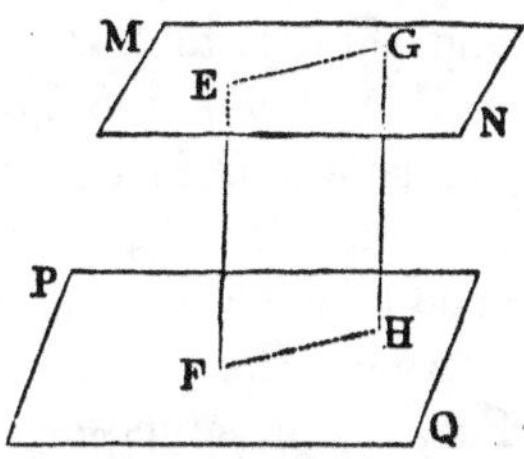

Let E F, G H be two parallel straight planes, included between two parallel planes, M N, P Q; then E F and G H are equal.

For, through the parallels E F, G H conceive the plane E F G H to pass, intersecting the parallel planes in E G, F H. The intersections E G, F H are parallel to each other (Prop. XIII.); and E F, G H are also parallel; consequently the figure E F G H is a parallelogram; hence E F is equal to G H (Prop. XXXI. Bk. I.).

423. *Cor. Two parallel planes are everywhere equidistant.* For, if E F, G H are perpendicular to the two planes M N, P Q, they will be parallel to each other (Prop. X. Cor. 1); and consequently equal.

PROPOSITION XVI. — THEOREM.

424. *If two angles not in the same plane have their sides parallel and lying in the same direction, these angles will be equal, and their planes will be parallel.*

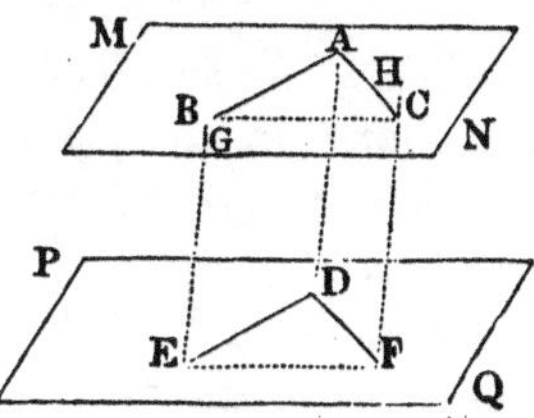

Let B A C, E D F be two triangles, lying in different planes, M N and P Q, having their sides parallel and lying in the same direction; then the angles BAC, EDF will be equal, and their planes, M N, P Q, be parallel.

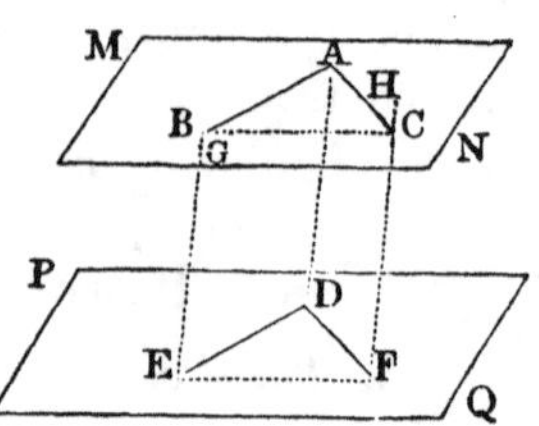

For, take A B equal to E D, and A C equal to D F; and join B C, E F, B E, A D, C F. Since A B is equal and parallel to E D, the figure A B E D is a parallelogram (Prop. XXXIII. Bk. I.); therefore A D is equal and parallel to B E. For a similar reason, C F is equal and parallel to A D; hence, also, B E is equal and parallel to C F; hence the figure B C F E is a parallelogram, and the side B C is equal and parallel to E F; therefore the triangles B A C, E D F have their sides equal, each to each; hence the angle B A C is equal to the angle E D F.

Again, the plane B A C is parallel to the plane E D F. For, if not, suppose a plane to pass through the point A, parallel to E D F, meeting the lines B E, C F, in points different from B and C, for instance G and H. Then the three lines G E, A D, H F will be equal (Prop. XV.). But the three lines B E, A D, C F are already known to be equal; hence B E is equal to G E, and H F is equal to C F, which is absurd; hence the plane B A C is parallel to the plane E D F.

425. *Cor.* If two parallel planes M N, P Q, are met by two other planes, A B E D, A C F D, the angles B A C, E D F, formed by the intersections of the parallel planes, are equal; for the intersection A B is parallel to E D, and A C to D F (Prop. XIII.); therefore the angle B A C is equal to the angle E D F.

Proposition XVII. — Theorem.

426. *If three straight lines not in the same plane are equal and parallel, the triangles formed by joining the extremities of these lines will be equal, and their planes will be parallel.*

Let B E, A D, C F be three equal and parallel straight lines, not in the same plane, and let B A C, E D F be two

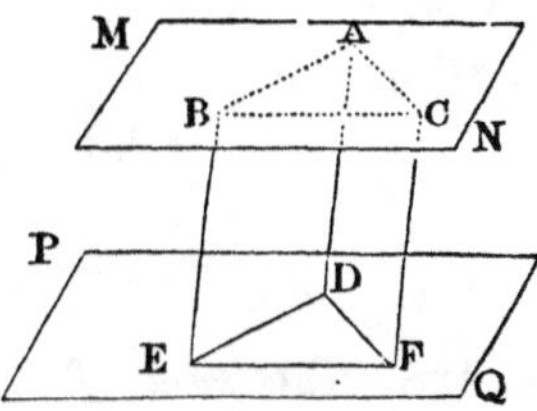

triangles formed by joining the extremities of these lines; then will these triangles be equal, and their planes parallel.

For, since B E is equal and parallel to A D, the figure A B E D is a parallelogram; hence, the side A B is equal and parallel to D E (Prop. XXXIII. Bk. I.). For a like reason, the sides B C, E F are equal and parallel; so also are A C, D F; hence, the two triangles B A C, E D F, having their sides equal, are themselves equal (Prop. XVIII. Bk. I.); consequently, as shown in the last proposition, their planes are parallel.

Proposition XVIII. — Theorem.

427. *If two straight lines are cut by three parallel planes, they will be divided proportionally.*

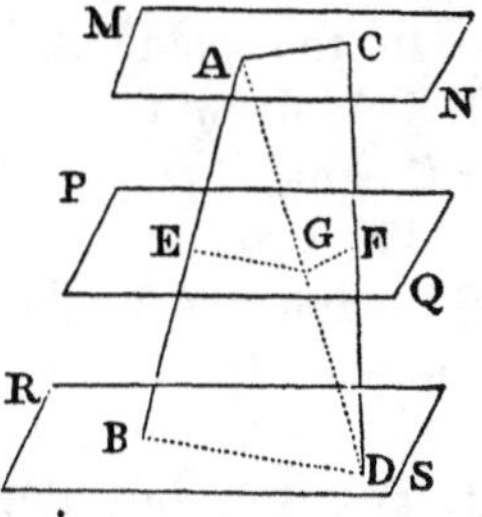

Let the straight line A B meet the parallel planes, M N, P Q, R S, at the points A, E, B; and the straight line C D meet the same planes at the points C, F, D; then will

A E : E B : : C F : F D.

Draw the line A D, meeting the plane P Q in G, and draw A C, E G, B D. Then the two parallel planes P Q, R S, being cut by the plane A B D, the intersections E G, B D are parallel (Prop. XIII.); and, in the triangle A B D, we have (Prop. XVII. Bk. IV.),

A E : E B : : A G : G D.

In like manner, the intersections A C, G F being parallel, in the triangle A D C, we have

A G : G D : : C F : F D;

hence, since the ratio A G : G D is common to both proportions, we have

A E : E B : : C F : F D.

Proposition XIX. — Theorem.

428. *The sum of any two of the plane angles which form a triedral angle is greater than the third.*

The proposition requires demonstration only when the plane angle, which is compared to the sum of the other two, is greater than either of them.

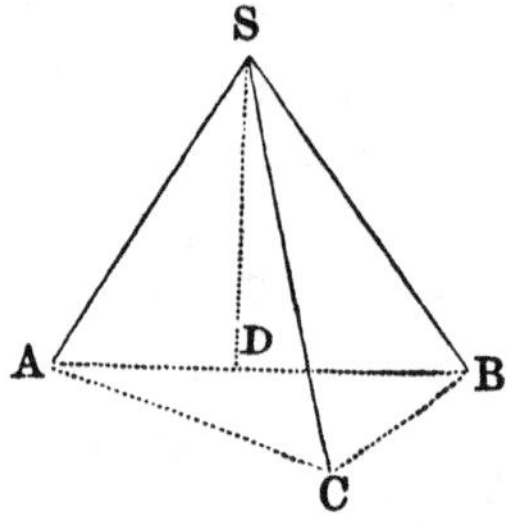

Let the triedral angle whose vertex is S be formed by the three plane angles A S B, A S C, B S C; and suppose the angle A S B to be greater than either of the other two; then the angle A S B is less than the sum of the angles A S C, B S C.

In the plane A S B make the angle B S D equal to B S C; draw the straight line A D B at pleasure; make S C equal S D, and draw A C, B C.

The two sides B S, S D are equal to the two sides B S, S C, and the angle B S D is equal to the angle B S C; therefore the triangles B S D, B S C are equal (Prop. V. Bk. I.); hence the side B D is equal to the side B C. But A B is less than the sum of A C and B C; taking B D from the one side, and from the other its equal, B C, there remains A D less than A C. The two sides A S, S D of the triangle A S D, are equal to the two sides A S, S C, of the triangle A S C, and the third side A D is less than the third side A C; hence the angle A S D is less than the angle A S C (Prop. XVII. Bk. I.). Adding B S D to one, and its equal, B S C, to the other, we shall have the sum of A S D, B S D, or A S B, less than the sum of A S C, B S C.

Proposition XX. — Theorem.

429. *The sum of the plane angles which form any polyedral angle is less than four right angles.*

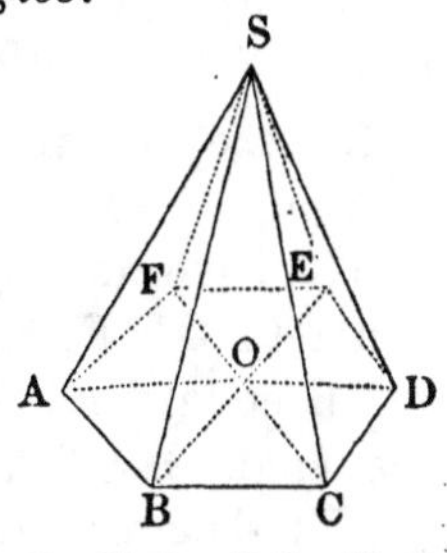

Let the polyedral angles whose vertex is S be formed by any number of plane angles, A S B, B S C, C S D, &c.; the sum of all these plane angles is less than four right angles.

Let the planes forming the polyedral angle be cut by any plane, A B C D E F. From any point, O, in this plane, draw the straight lines A O, B O, C O, D O, E O, F O. The sum of the angles of the triangles A S B, B S C, &c. formed about the vertex S, is equal to the sum of the angles of an equal number of triangles A O B, B O C, &c. formed about the point O. But at the point B the sum of the angles A B O, O B C, equal to A B C, is less than the sum of the angles A B S, S B C (Prop. XIX.); in the same manner, at the point C we have the sum of B C O, O C D less than the sum of B C S, S C D; and so with all the angles at the points D, E, &c. Hence, the sum of all the angles at the bases of the triangles whose vertex is O, is less than the sum of all the angles at the bases of the triangles whose vertex is S; therefore, to make up the deficiency, the sum of the angles formed about the point O is greater than the sum of the angles formed about the point S. But the sum of the angles about the point O is equal to four right angles (Prop. IV. Cor. 2, Bk. I.); therefore the sum of the angles about S must be less than four right angles.

430. *Scholium.* This demonstration supposes that the polyedral angle is convex; that is, that no one of the faces would, on being produced, cut the polyedral angle; if it were otherwise, the sum of the plane angles would no longer be limited, and might be of any magnitude.

PROPOSITION XXI. — THEOREM.

431. *If two triedral angles are formed by plane angles which are equal each to each, the planes of the equal angles will be equally inclined to each other.*

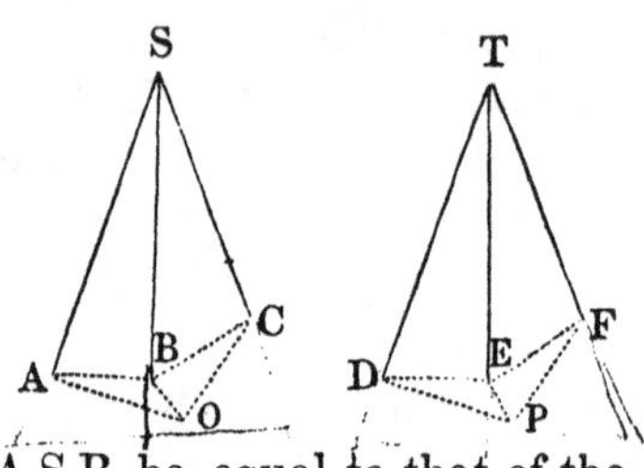

Let the two triedral angles whose vertexes are S and T, have the angle ASC equal to D T F, the angle A S B equal to D T E, and the angle B S C equal to E T F; then will the inclination of the planes A S C, A S B be equal to that of the planes D T F, D T E.

For, take S B at pleasure; draw B O perpendicular to the plane A S C; from the point O, at which the perpendicular meets the plane, draw O A, O C, perpendicular to S A, S C; and join A B, B C. Next, take T E equal S B; draw E P perpendicular to the plane D T E; from the point P draw P D, P F, perpendicular respectively to T D, T F; and join D E, E F.

The triangle S A B is right-angled at A, and the triangle T D E at D; and since the angle A S B is equal to D T E, we have S B A equal to T E D. Also, S B is equal to T E; therefore the triangle S A B is equal to T D E; hence S A is equal to T D, and A B is equal to D E.

In like manner it may be shown that S C is equal to T F, and B C is equal to E F. We can now show that the quadrilateral A S C O is equal to the quadrilateral D T F P; for, place the angle A S C upon its equal D T F; since S A is equal to T D, and S C is equal to T F, the point A will fall on D, and the point C on F; and, at the same time, A O, which is perpendicular to S A, will fall on D P, which is perpendicular to T D, and, in like manner, C O on F P; wherefore the point O will fall on the point P, and A O will be equal to D P.

But the triangles A O B, D P E are right-angled at O and P; the hypotenuse A B is equal to D E, and the side A O is equal to D P; hence the two triangles are equal (Prop. XIX. Bk. I.); and, consequently, the angle O A B is equal to the angle P D E. The angle O A B is the inclination of the two planes A S B, A S C; and the angle P D E is that of the two planes D T E, D T F; hence, those two inclinations are equal to each other.

432. *Scholium* 1. It must, however, be observed, that the angle A of the right-angled triangle O A B is properly the inclination of the two planes A S B, A S C only when the perpendicular B O falls on the same side of S A with S C; for if it fell on the other side, the angle of the two planes would be obtuse, and joined to the angle A of the triangle O A B it would make two right angles. But, in the same case, the angle of the two planes D T E, D T F would also be obtuse, and joined to the angle D of the triangle D P E it would make two right angles; and the angle A being thus always equal to the angle D, it would follow in the same manner that the inclination of the two planes A S B, A S C must be equal to that of the two planes D T E, D T F.

433. *Scholium* 2. If two triedral angles are formed by three plane angles respectively equal to each other, and if at the same time the equal or homologous angles are *similarly situated*, the two angles are equal. For, by the proposition, the planes which contain the equal angles of the triedral angles are equally inclined to each other.

434. *Scholium* 3. When the equal plane angles forming the two triedral angles are *not similarly situated*, these angles are equal in all their constituent parts, but, not admitting of superposition, are said to be *equal by symmetry*, and are called *symmetrical angles*.

BOOK VIII.

POLYEDRONS.

DEFINITIONS.

435. A POLYEDRON is a solid, or volume, bounded by planes.

The bounding planes are called the *faces* of the polyedron; and the lines of intersection of the faces are called the *edges* of the polyedron.

436. A PRISM is a polyedron having two of its faces equal and parallel polygons, and the other faces parallelograms.

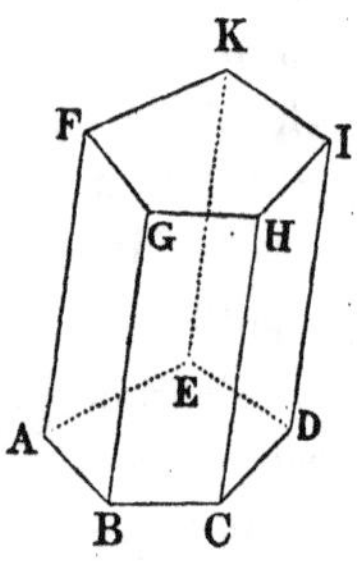

The equal and parallel polygons are called the *bases* of the prism, and the parallelograms its *lateral* faces. The lateral faces taken together constitute the *lateral* or *convex surface* of the prism.

Thus the polyedron A B C D E – K is a prism, having for its bases the equal and parallel polygons A B C D E, F G H I K, and for its lateral faces the parallelograms A B G F, B C H G, &c.

The *principal edges* of a prism are those which join the corresponding angles of the bases; as A F, B G, &c.

437. The altitude of a prism is a perpendicular drawn from any point in one base to the plane of the other.

438. A RIGHT PRISM is one whose principal edges are perpendicular to the planes of its bases. Each of the

edges is then equal to the altitude of the prism. Every other prism is *oblique*, and has each edge greater than the altitude.

439. A prism is *triangular*, *quadrangular*, *pentangular*, *hexangular*, &c., according as its base is a triangle, a quadrilateral, a pentagon, a hexagon, &c.

440. A PARALLELOPIPEDON is a prism whose bases are parallelograms; as the prism A B C D – H.

The parallelopipedon is *rectangular* when all its faces are rectangles; as the parallelopipedon A B C D – H.

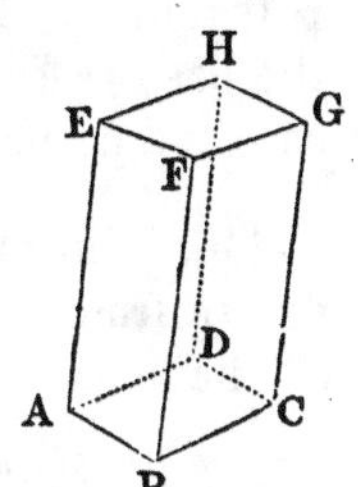

441. A CUBE, or REGULAR HEXAEDRON, is a rectangular parallelopipedon having all its faces equal squares; as the parallelopipedon A B C D – H.

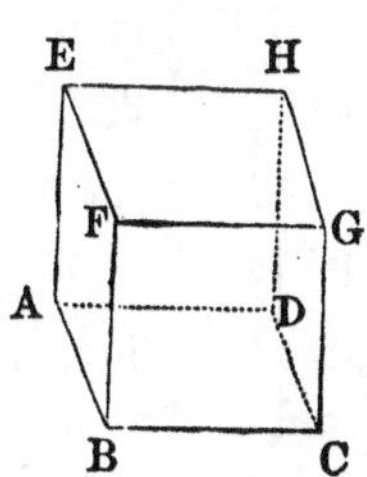

442. A PYRAMID is a polyedron of which one of the faces is any polygon, and all the others are triangles meeting at a common point.

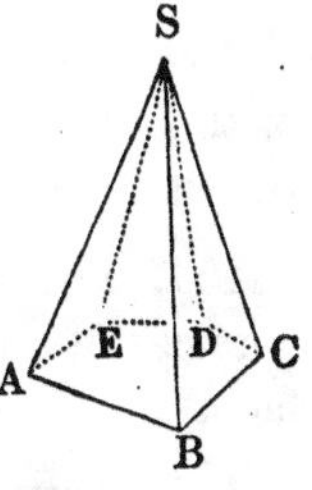

The polygon is called the *base* of the pyramid, the triangles its *lateral faces*, and the point at which the triangles meet its *vertex*. The lateral faces taken together constitute the *lateral* or *convex surface* of the pyramid.

Thus the polyedron A B C D E – S is a pyramid, having for its base the polygon A B C D E, for its lateral faces the triangles A S B, B S C, C S D, &c., and for its vertex the point S.

443. The ALTITUDE of a pyramid is a perpendicular drawn from the vertex to the plane of the base.

444. A pyramid is *triangular*, *quadrangular*, &c., according as its base is a triangle, a quadrilateral, &c.

445. A RIGHT PYRAMID is one whose base is a regular polygon, and the perpendicular drawn from the vertex to the base passes through the centre of the base. In this case the perpendicular is called the *axis* of the pyramid.

446. The SLANT HEIGHT of a right pyramid is a line drawn from the vertex to the middle of one of the sides of the base.

447. A FRUSTUM of a pyramid is the part of the pyramid included between the base and a plane cutting the pyramid parallel to the base.

448. The ALTITUDE of the frustum of a pyramid is the perpendicular distance between its parallel bases.

449. The SLANT HEIGHT of a frustum of a right pyramid is that part of the slant height of the pyramid which is intercepted between the bases of the frustum.

450. The AXIS of the frustum of a pyramid is that part of the axis of the pyramid which is intercepted between the bases of the frustum.

451. The DIAGONAL of a polyedron is a line joining the vertices of any two of its angles which are not in the same face.

452. SIMILAR POLYEDRONS are those which are bounded by the same number of similar faces, and have their polyedral angles respectively equal.

453. A REGULAR POLYEDRON is one whose faces are all equal and regular polygons, and whose polyedral angles are all equal to each other.

PROPOSITION I.—THEOREM.

454. *The convex surface of a right prism is equal to the perimeter of its base multiplied by its altitude.*

Let ABCDE-K be a right prism; then will its convex surface be equal to the perimeter of its base,

$$AB + BC + CD + DE + EA,$$

multiplied by its altitude AF.

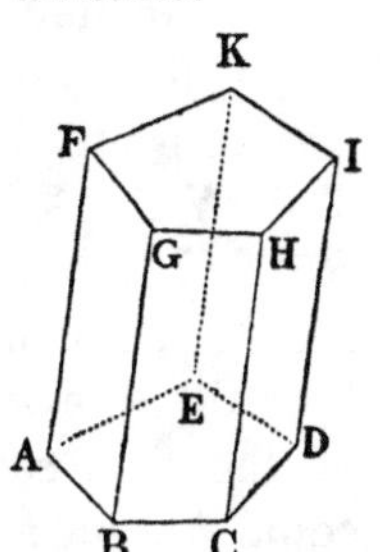

For, the convex surface of the prism is equal to the sum of the parallelograms AG, BH, CI, DK, EF (Art. 436). Now, the area of each of those parallelograms is equal to its base, AB, BC, CD, &c., multiplied by its altitude, AF, BG, CH, &c. (Prop. V. Bk. IV.). But the altitudes AF, BG, CH, &c. are each equal to AF, the altitude of the prism. Hence, the area of these parallelograms, or the convex surface of the prism, is equal to

$$(AB + BC + CD + DE + EA) \times AF;$$

or the product of the perimeter of the prism by its altitude.

455. *Cor.* If two right prisms have the same altitude, their convex surfaces are to each other as the perimeters of their bases.

PROPOSITION II.—THEOREM.

456. *In every prism, the sections formed by parallel planes are equal polygons.*

Let the prism ABCDE-K be intersected by the parallel planes NP, SV; then are the sections NOPQR, STVXY equal polygons.

For the sides ST, NO are parallel, being the intersections of two parallel planes with a third plane ABGF

(Prop. XIII. Bk. VII.); these same sides S T, N O, are included between the parallels N S, O T, which are sides of the prism; hence N O is equal to S T. For like reasons, the sides O P, P Q, Q R, &c. of the section N O P Q R, are respectively equal to the sides T V, V X, X Y, &c. of the section S T V X Y; and since the equal sides are at the same time parallel, it follows that the angles N O P, O P Q, &c. of the first section are respectively equal to the angles S T V, T V X of the second (Prop. XVI. Bk. VII.). Hence, the two sections N O P Q R, S T V X Y, are equal polygons.

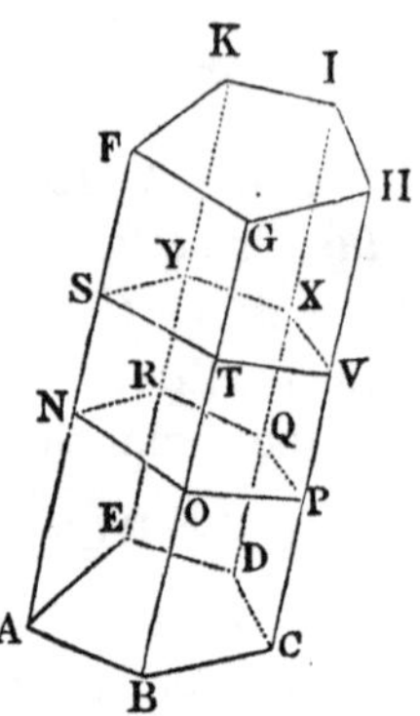

457. *Cor.* Every section made in a prism parallel to its base, is equal to that base.

PROPOSITION III. — THEOREM.

458. *Two prisms are equal, when the three faces which form a triedral angle in the one are equal to those which form a triedral angle in the other, each to each, and are similarly situated.*

Let the two prisms A B C D E - K and L M O P Q - Y have the faces which form the triedral angle B equal to the faces which form the triedral angle M; that is, the base A B C D E equal to the base L M N O P Q, the parallelogram A B G F equal to the parallelogram L M S R, and the parallelogram B C H G equal to M O T S; then the two prisms are equal.

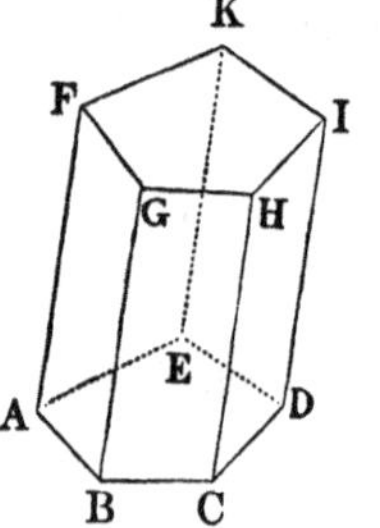

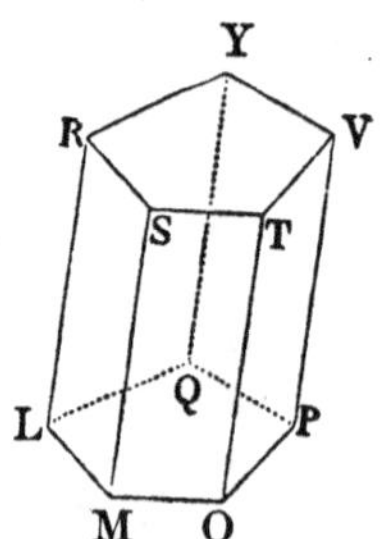

For, apply the base A B C D E to the equal base LMOPQ; then, the triedral angles B and M, being equal, will coincide, since the plane angles which form these triedral angles are equal each to each, and similarly situated (Prop. XXI. Sch. 2, Bk. VII.); hence the edge B G will fall on its equal M S, and the face B H will coincide with its equal MT, and the face BF with its equal MR. But the upper bases are equal to their corresponding lower bases (Art. 436); therefore the bases F G H I K, R S T V Y are equal; hence they coincide with each other. Therefore H I coincides with T V, IK with V Y, and KF with Y R; and consequently the lateral faces coincide. Hence the two prisms coincide throughout, and are equal.

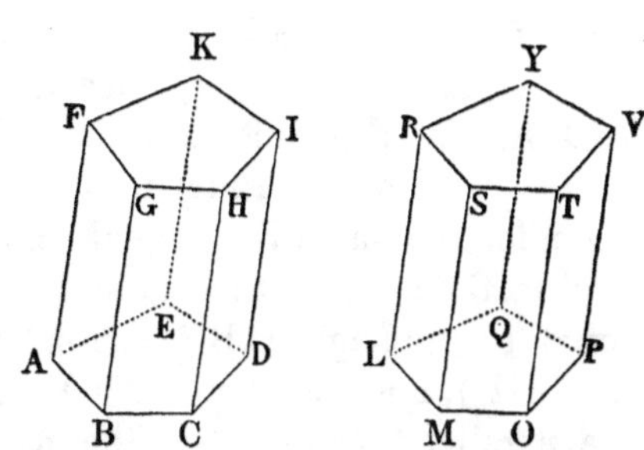

459. *Cor.* Two right prisms, which have equal bases and equal altitudes, are equal.

For, since the side AB is equal to LM, and the altitude B G to M S, the rectangle A B G F is equal to the rectangle L M S R; so, also, the rectangle B G H C is equal to M S T O; and thus the three faces which form the triedral angle B, are equal to the three faces which form the triedral angle M. Hence the two prisms are equal.

Proposition IV. — Theorem.

460. *In every parallelopipedon the opposite faces are equal and parallel.*

Let A B C D – H be a parallelopipedon; then its opposite faces are equal and parallel.

The bases A B C D, E F G H are equal and parallel (Art. 436), and it remains only to be shown that the same is true of any two opposite lateral faces, as B C G F, A D H E. Now, since the base A B C D is a parallelogram, the side A D is equal and parallel to B C. For a similar reason, A E is equal and parallel to B F; hence the angle D A E is equal to the angle C B F (Prop. XVI. Bk. VII.), and the planes D A E, C B F are parallel; hence, also, the parallelogram B C G F is equal to the parallelogram A D H E. In the same way, it may be shown that the opposite faces A B F E, D C G H are equal and parallel.

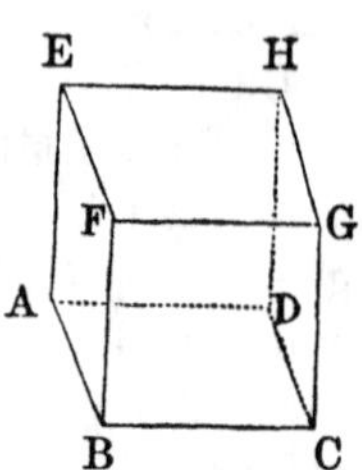

461. *Cor.* Any two opposite faces of a parallelopipedon may be assumed as its bases, since any face and the one opposite to it are equal and parallel.

Proposition V. — Theorem.

462. *The diagonals of every parallelopipedon bisect each other.*

Let A B C D – H be a parallelopipedon; then its diagonals, as B H, D F, will bisect each other.

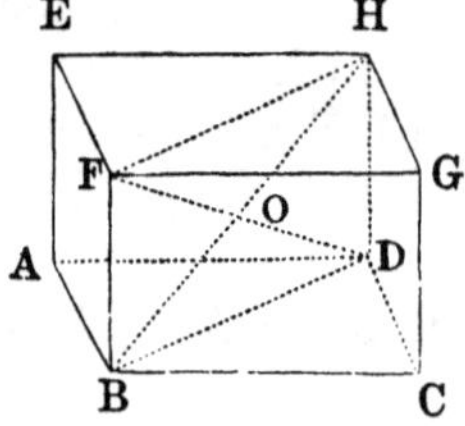

For, since B F is equal and parallel to D H, the figure B F H D is a parallelogram; hence the diagonals B H, D F bisect each other at the point O (Prop. XXXIV. Bk. I.). In the same manner it may be shown that the two diagonals A G and C E bisect each other at the point O; hence the several diagonals bisect each other.

463. *Scholium.* The point at which the diagonals mutually bisect each other may be regarded as the centre of the parallelopipedon.

Proposition VI. — Theorem.

464. *Any parallelopipedon may be divided into two equivalent triangular prisms by a plane passing through its opposite diagonal edges.*

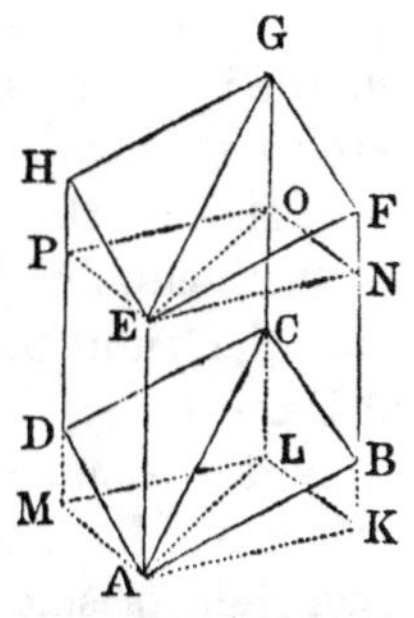

Let any parallelopipedon, A B C D–H, be divided into two prisms, A B C – G, A D C – G, by a plane, A C G E, passing through opposite diagonal edges; then will the two prisms be equivalent.

Through the vertices A and E, draw the planes A K L M, E N O P, perpendicular to the edge A E, and meeting B F, C G, D H, the three other edges of the parallelopipedon, in the points K, L, M, and in N, O, P. The sections A K L M, E N O P are equal, since they are formed by planes perpendicular to the same straight lines, and hence parallel (Prop. II.). They are parallelograms, since the two opposite sides of the same section, A K, L M, are the intersections of two parallel planes, A B F E, D C G H, by the same plane, A K L M (Prop. XIII. Bk. VII.).

For a like reason, the figure A M P E is a parallelogram; so, also, are A K N E, K L O N, L M P O, the other lateral faces of the solid A K L M – P; consequently, this solid is a prism (Art. 436); and this prism is right, since the edge A E is perpendicular to the plane of its base. This right prism is divided by the plane A L O E into the two right prisms A K L – O, A M L – O, which, having equal bases, A K L, A M L, and the same altitude, A E, are equal (Prop. III. Cor.).

Now, since A E H D, A E P M are parallelograms, the sides D H, M P, being each equal to A E, are equal to each other; and taking away the common part, D P, there remains D M equal to H P. In the same manner it may be shown that C L is equal to G O.

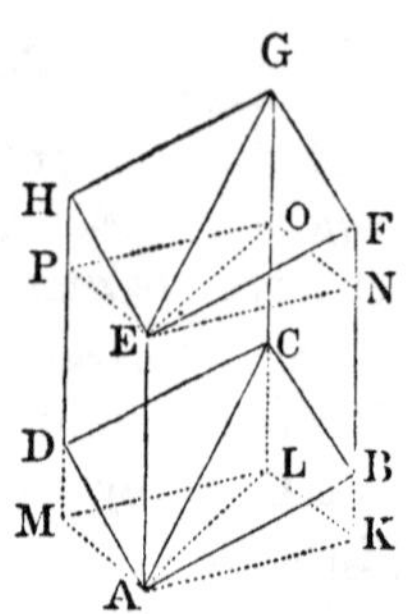

Conceive now E P O, the base of the solid E P O – G, to be applied to its equal A M L, the point P falling upon M, and the point O upon L; the edges G O, H P will coincide with their equals C L, D M, since they are all perpendicular to the same plane, A K L M. Hence the two solids coincide throughout, and are therefore equal. To each of these equals add the solid A D C – P, and the right prism A M L – O is equivalent to the prism A D C – G.

In the same manner, it may be proved that the right prism A K L – O is equivalent to the prism A B C – G. The two right prisms A K L – O, A M L – O being equal, it follows that two triangular prisms, A B C – G, A D C – G, are equivalent to each other.

465. *Cor.* Every triangular prism is half of a parallelopipedon having the same triedral angle, with the same edges.

Proposition VII. — Theorem.

466. ***Two parallelopipedons, having a common lower base, and their upper bases in the same plane and between the same parallels, are equivalent to each other.***

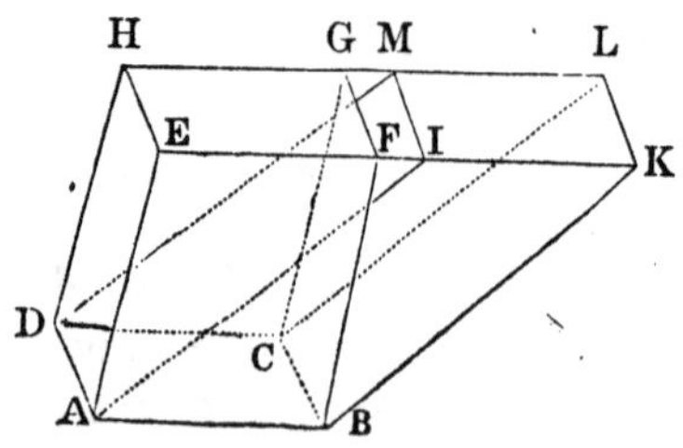

Let the two parallelopipedons A G, A L have the common base ABCD, and their upper bases, E F G H, I K L M, in the same plane, and between the same parallels, E K, H L; then the parallelopipedons will be equivalent.

There may be three cases, according as E I is greater or less than, or equal to, E F; but the demonstration is the same for each.

Since A E is parallel to B F, and H E to G F, the plane angle A E I is equal to B F K, H E I to G F K, and H E A to G F B. Of these six plane angles, the three first form the polyedral angle E, the three last the polyedral angle F; consequently, since these plane angles are equal each to each, and similarly situated, the polyedral angles, E, F, must be equal. Now conceive the prism A E I – M to be applied to the prism B F K – L; the base A E I, being placed upon the base B F K, will coincide with it, since they are equal; and, since the polyedral angle E is equal to the polyedral angle F, the side E H will fall upon its equal, F G. But the base A E I and its edge E H determine the prism A E I – M, as the base B F K and its edge F G determine the prism B F K – L (Prop. III.); hence the two prisms coincide throughout, and therefore are equal to each other.

Take away, now, from the whole solid A E L C, the prism A E I – M, and there will remain the parallelopipedon A L; and take away from the same solid A L the prism B F K – L, and there will remain the parallelopipedon A G; hence the two parallelopipedons A L, A G are equivalent.

PROPOSITION VIII. — THEOREM.

467. *Two parallelopipedons having the same base and the same altitude are equivalent.*

Let the two parallelopipedons A G, A L have the common base A B C D, and the same altitude; then will the two parallelopipedons be equivalent.

For, the upper bases E F G H, I K L M being in the same plane, produce the edges E F, H G, L K, I M, till by their intersections they form the parallelogram N O P Q; this parallelogram is equal to either of the bases I L, E G, and is between the same parallels; hence N O P Q is equal to the common base A B C D, and is parallel to it.

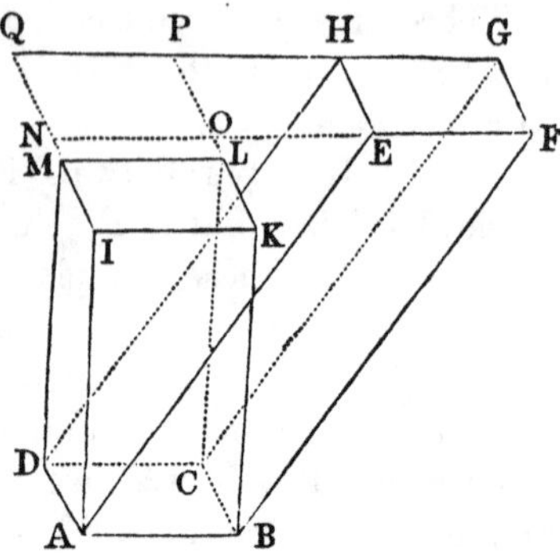

Now, if a third parallelopipedon be conceived, which, with the same lower base A B C D, has for its upper base NOPQ, this third parallelopipedon will be equivalent to the parallelopipedon A G, since the lower base is the same, and the upper bases lie in the same plane and between the same parallels, G Q, F N (Prop. VII.).

For the same reason, this third parallelopipedon will also be equivalent to the parallelopipedon A L; hence the two parallelopipedons A G, A L, which have the same base and the same altitude, are equivalent.

Proposition IX. — Theorem.

468. *Any oblique parallelopipedon is equivalent to a rectangular parallelopipedon having the same altitude and an equivalent base.*

Let A G be any parallelopipedon; then A G will be equivalent to a rectangular parallelopipedon having the same altitude and an equivalent base.

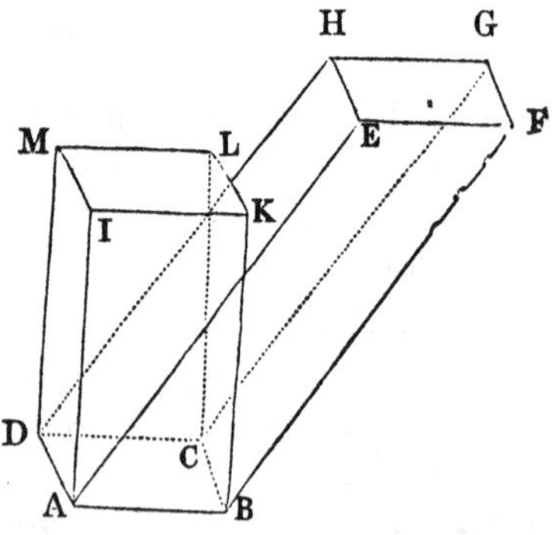

From the points A, B, C, D, draw A I, B K, C L, D M, perpendicular to the lower base, and equal in altitude to A G; there will thus be formed the parallelopipedon A L, equivalent to A G (Prop. VIII.), and having its lateral faces, A K, B L, &c., rectangular. Now, if the base A B C D is a rectangle, A L will be a rectangular parallelopipedon equivalent to A G.

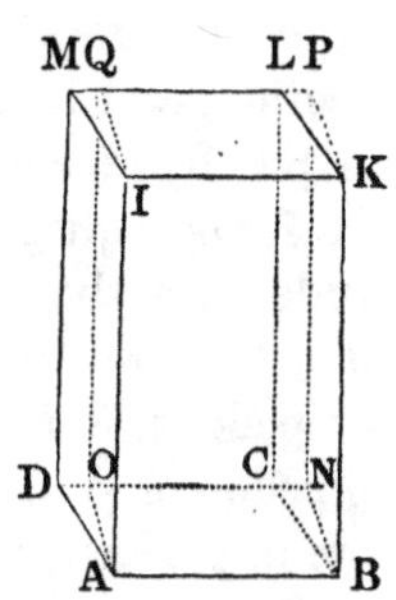

But if A B C D is not a rectangle, draw A O, B N, each perpendicular to C D; also O Q, N P, each perpendicular to the base; then we shall have a rectangular parallelopipedon A B N O – Q. For, by construction, the bases A B N O, I K P Q are rectangles; so, also, are the lateral faces, the edges A I, O Q, &c. being perpendicular to the plane of the base; therefore the solid A P is a rectangular parallelopipedon. But the two parallelopipedons A P, A L may be considered as having the same base, A B K I, and the same altitude, A O; hence they are equivalent. Hence the parallelopipedon A G, which was shown to be equivalent to the parallelopipedon A L, is also equivalent to the rectangular parallelopipedon A P, having the same altitude, A I, and a base, A B N O, equivalent to the base A B C D.

Proposition X.—Theorem.

469. *Two rectangular parallelopipedons, which have the same base, are to each other as their altitudes.*

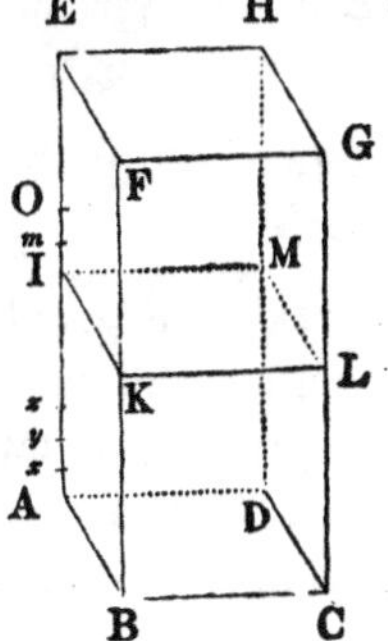

Let the two parallelopipedons A G, A L have the same base, A B C D; then they are to each other as their altitudes, A E, A I.

First. Suppose the altitudes A E, A I are to each other as two whole numbers; for example, as 15 is to 8. Divide A E into 15 equal parts, of which A I will contain 8. Through x, y, z, &c., the points of division, conceive planes to

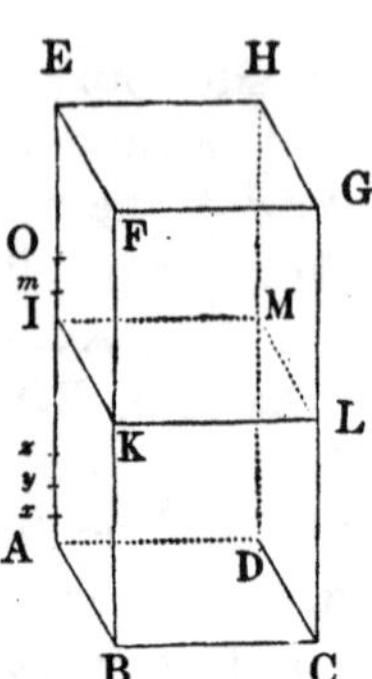

pass parallel to the common base. These planes will divide the solid A G into 15 small parallelopipedons, all equal to each other, having equal bases and equal altitudes; equal bases, since every section, as I K L M, parallel to the base A B C D, is equal to that base (Prop. II.), and equal altitudes, since the altitudes are the equal divisions A x, x y, y z, &c. But of those 15 equal parallelopipedons, 8 are contained in A L; hence the parallelopipedon A G is to the parallelopipedon A L as 15 is to 8, or, in general, as the altitude A E is to the altitude A I.

Secondly. If the ratio of A E to A I cannot be exactly expressed by numbers, we shall still have the proportion,

Solid A G : *Solid* A L : : A E : A I.

For, if this proportion is not correct, suppose we have

Solid A G : *Solid* A L : : A E : A O greater than A I.

Divide A E into equal parts, each of which shall be less than I O; there will be at least one point of division, m, between I and O. Let P represent the parallelopipedon, whose base is A B C D, and altitude A m; since the altitudes A E, A m are to each other as two whole numbers, we shall have

Solid A G : P : : A E : A m.

But, by hypothesis, we have

Solid A G : *Solid* A L : : A E : A O;

hence (Prop. X. Cor. 2, Bk. II.),

Solid A L : P : : A O : A m.

But A O is greater than A m; hence, if the proportion is correct, the parallelopipedon A L must be greater than P. On the contrary, however, it is less; consequently the solid A G cannot be to the solid A L as the line A E is to a line greater than A I.

By the same mode of reasoning, it may be shown that the fourth term of the proportion cannot be less than A I; therefore it must be equal to A I. Hence rectangular parallelopipedons, having the same base, are to each other as their altitudes.

PROPOSITION XI. — THEOREM.

470. *Two rectangular parallelopipedons, having the same altitude, are to each other as their bases.*

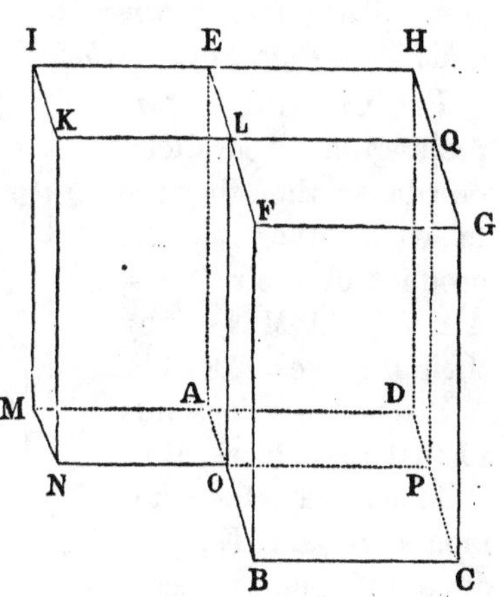

Let the two rectangular parallelopipedons A G, A K have the same altitude, A E; then they are to each other as their bases.

Place the two solids so that their faces, B E, O E, may have the common angle B A E; produce the plane O N K L till it meets the plane D C G H in P Q; we shall thus have a third parallelopipedon, A Q, which may be compared with each of the parallelopipedons A G, A K. The two solids, A G, A Q, having the same base, A E H D, are to each other as their altitudes A B, A O (Prop. X.); in like manner, the two solids A Q, A K, having the same base, A O L E, are to each other as their altitudes A D, A M. Hence we have the two proportions,

Solid A G : *Solid* A Q : : A B : A O,

Solid A Q : *Solid* A K : : A D : A M.

Multiplying together the corresponding terms of these

proportions, and omitting, in the result, the common factor *Solid* A Q, we shall have,

Solid A G : *Solid* A K : : A B × A D : A O × A M.

But A B × A D measures the base A B C D (Prop. IV. Sch., Bk. IV.); and A O × A M measures the base A M N O; hence two rectangular parallelopipedons of the same altitude are to each other as their bases.

PROPOSITION XII.—THEOREM.

471. *Any two rectangular parallelopipedons are to each other as the product of their bases by their altitudes.*

Let A G, A Z be two rectangular parallelopipedons; then they are to each other as the product of their bases, A B C D, A M N O, by their altitudes, A E, A X.

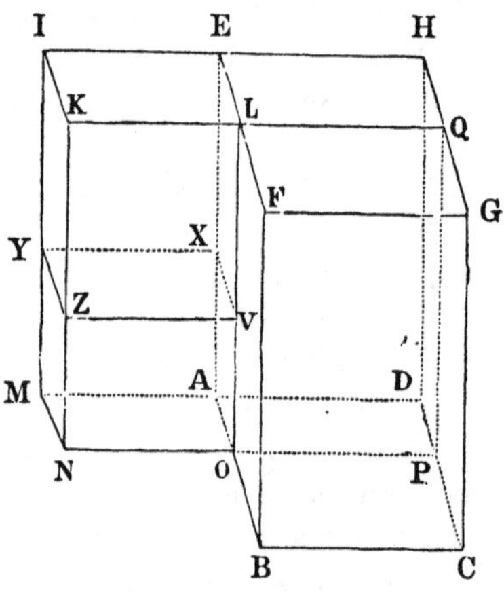

Place the two solids so that their faces, B E, O X, may have the common angle B A E; produce the planes necessary for completing the third parallelopipedon, A K, having the same altitude with the parallelopipedon A G. By the last proposition, we shall have

Solid A G : *Solid* A K : : A B C D : A M N O.

But the two parallelopipedons A K, A Z, having the same base, A M N O, are to each other as their altitudes, A E, A X (Prop. X.); hence we have

Solid A K : *Solid* A Z : : A E : A X.

Multiplying together the corresponding terms of these

proportions, and omitting, in the result, the common factor *Solid* A K, we shall have

Solid A G : *Solid* A Z : : A B C D $\times$ A E : A M N O $\times$ A X.

Hence, any two rectangular parallelopipedons are to each other as the products of their bases by their altitudes.

472. *Scholium* 1. We are consequently authorized to assume, as the measure of a rectangular parallelopipedon, the product of its base by its altitude; in other words, *the product of its three dimensions.* But by the product of two or more lines is always meant the product of the numbers which represent them; those numbers themselves being determined by the particular linear unit, which may be assumed as the standard. It is necessary, therefore, in comparing magnitudes, that the measuring unit be the same for each of the magnitudes compared.

473. *Scholium* 2. The measured magnitude of a solid, or volume, is called its *volume*, *solidity*, or *solid contents.* We assume as the *unit of volume*, or *solidity*, the cube, each of whose edges is the linear unit, and each of whose faces is the unit of surface.

Proposition XIII. — Theorem.

474. *The solid contents of a parallelopipedon, and of any other prism, are equal to the product of its base by its altitude.*

First. Any parallelopipedon is equivalent to a rectangular parallelopipedon having the same altitude and an equivalent base (Prop. IX.). But the solid contents of a rectangular parallelopipedon are equal to the product of its base by its altitude; therefore the solid contents of any parallelopipedon are equal to the product of its base by its altitude.

Second. Any triangular prism is half of a parallelopipedon, so constructed as to have the same altitude, and a base twice as great (Prop. VI.). But the solid contents of the parallelopipedon are equal to the product of its base by its altitude; hence, that of the triangular prism is also equal to the product of its base, or half that of the parallelopipedon, by its altitude.

Third. Any prism may be divided into as many triangular prisms of the same altitude, as there are triangles in the polygon taken for a base. But the solid contents of each triangular prism are equal to the product of its base by its altitude; and, since the altitude is the same in each, it follows that the sum of all these prisms is equal to the sum of all the triangles taken as bases multiplied by the common altitude.

Hence the solid contents of any prism are equal to the product of its base by its altitude.

475. *Cor.* When any two prisms have the same altitude, the products of the bases by the altitudes will be as the bases (Prop. IX. Bk. II.); hence, *prisms of the same altitude are to each other as their bases.* For a like reason, *prisms of the same base are to each other as their altitudes.*

Proposition XIV. — Theorem.

476. *Similar prisms are to each other as the cubes of their homologous edges.*

Let ABC–E, FHI–M be two similar prisms; these prisms are to each other as the cubes of their homologous edges, AB and FH.

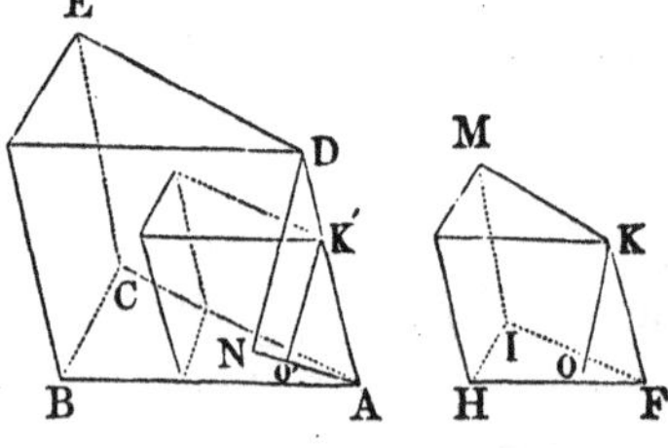

For, from D and K, homologous angles of the two prisms, draw the perpendiculars DN, KO, to the bases ABC, FHI. Take AK′ equal to FK, and join AN.

Draw K′ O′ perpendicular to A N in the plane A N D, and K′ O will be perpendicular to the plane A B C, and equal to K O, the altitude of the prism F H I – M. For, conceive the triedral angles A and F to be applied the one to the other; the planes containing them, and therefore the perpendiculars K′ O′, K O, will coincide.

Now, since the bases A B C, F H I are similar, we have (Prop. XXIX. Bk. IV.),

$$\textit{Base}\ ABC : \textit{Base}\ FHI :: \overline{AB}^2 : \overline{FH}^2;$$

and, because of the similar triangles D A N, K F O, and of the similar parallelograms D B, K H, we have

$$DN : KO :: DA : KF :: AB : FH.$$

Hence, multiplying together the corresponding terms of these proportions, we have

$$\textit{Base}\ ABC \times DN : \textit{Base}\ FHI \times KO : \overline{AB}^3 : \overline{FH}^3.$$

But the product of the base by the altitude is equal to the solidity of a prism (Prop. XIII.); hence

$$\textit{Prism}\ ABC - E : \textit{Prism}\ FHI - M :: \overline{AB}^3 : \overline{FH}^3.$$

Proposition XV. — Theorem.

477. *The convex surface of a right pyramid is equal to the perimeter of its base, multiplied by half the slant height.*

Let A B C D E – S be a right pyramid, and S M its slant height; then the convex surface is equal to the perimeter A B + B C + C D + D E + E A multiplied by ½ S M.

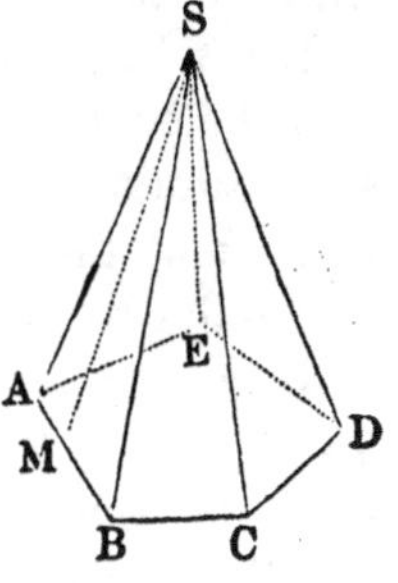

The triangles S A B, S B C, S C D, &c. are all equal; for the sides A B, B C, C D, &c. are equal (Art. 445), and the sides S A, S B, S C, &c., being oblique lines meeting the base at equal distances from a perpendicular let fall from the vertex S to the center of the base, are also equal (Prop. V. Bk. VII.). Hence, these triangles are all equal (Prop. XVIII. Bk. I.); and the altitude of each is equal to the slant height S M. But the area of a triangle is equal to the product of its base multiplied by half its altitude (Prop. VI. Bk. IV.). Hence, the areas of the triangles S A B, S B C, S C D, &c. are equal to the sum of the bases A B, B C, C D, &c. multiplied by half the common altitude, S M; that is, the convex surface of the pyramid is equal to the perimeter of the base multiplied by half the slant height.

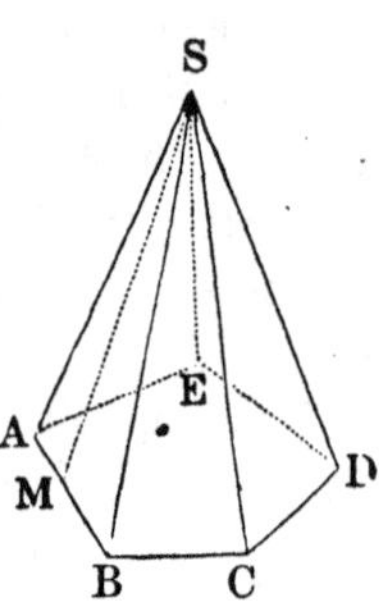

478. *Cor.* The lateral faces of a right pyramid are equal isosceles triangles, having for their bases the sides of the base of the pyramid.

PROPOSITION XVI.—THEOREM.

479. *If a pyramid be cut by a plane parallel to its base,—*

1*st.* *The edges and the altitude will be divided proportionally.*

2*d.* *The section will be a polygon similar to the base.*

Let the pyramid A B C D E – S, whose altitude is S O, be cut by a plane, G H I K L, parallel to its base; then will the edges S A, S B, S C, &c., with the altitude S O, be divided proportionally; and the section G H I K L will be similar to the base A B C D E.

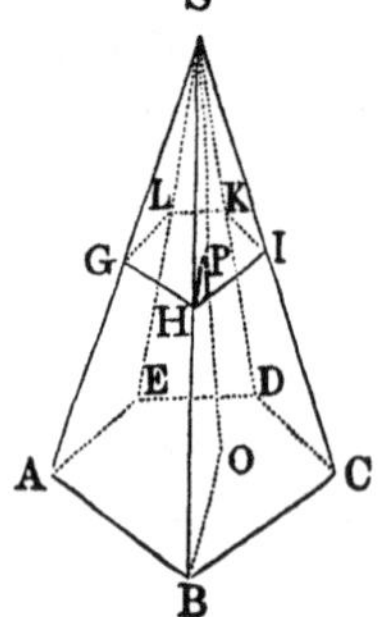

First. Since the planes A B C, G H I are parallel, their intersections A B, G H, by the third plane S A B, are parallel (Prop. XIII. Bk. VII.); hence the triangles S A B, S G H are similar (Prop. XXV. Bk. IV.), and we have

S A : S G : : S B : S H.

For the same reason, we have

S B : S H : : S C : S I;

and so on. Hence all the edges, S A, S B, S C, &c., are cut proportionally in G, H, I, &c. The altitude S O is likewise cut in the same proportion, at the point P; for B O and H P are parallel; therefore we have

S O : S P : : S B : S H.

Secondly. Since G H is parallel to A B, H I to B C, I K to C D, &c. the angle G H I is equal to A B C, the angle H I K to B C D, and so on (Prop. XVI. Bk. VII.). Also, by reason of the similar triangles S A B, S G H, we have

A B : G H : : S B : S H;

and by reason of the similar triangles S B C, S H I, we have

S B : S H : : B C : H I;

hence, on account of the common ratio S B : S H,

A B : G H : : B C : H I.

For a like reason, we have

B C : H I : : C D : I K,

and so on. Hence the polygons A B C D E, G H I K L have their angles equal, each to each, and their homologous sides proportional; hence they are similar.

480. *Cor.* 1. *If two pyramids have the same altitude, and their bases in the same plane, their sections made by a plane parallel to the plane of their bases are to each other as their bases.*

Let A B C D E – S, M N O – S be two pyramids, having the same altitude, and their bases in the same plane; and let G H I K L, P Q R be sections made by a plane parallel to the plane of their bases; then these sections are to each other as the bases A B C D E, M N O.

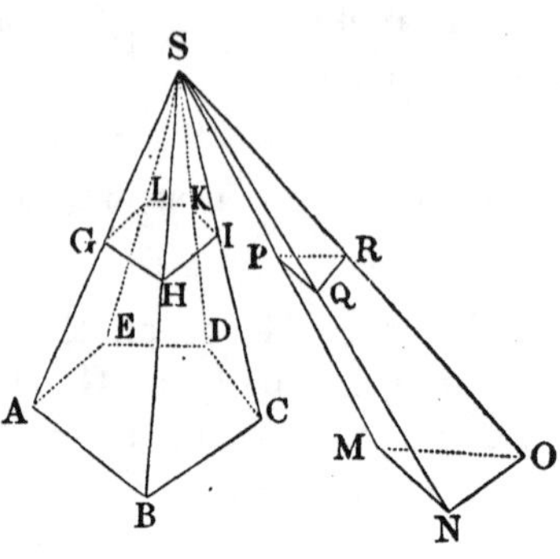

For, the two polygons A B C D E, G H I K L being similar, their surfaces are as the squares of the homologous sides A B, G H (Prop. XXXI. Bk. IV.). But

$$AB : GH :: SA : SG.$$

Hence,

$$ABCDE : GHIKL :: \overline{SA}^2 : \overline{SG}^2.$$

For the same reason,

$$MNO : PQR :: \overline{SM}^2 : \overline{SP}^2.$$

But since G H I K L and P Q R are in the same plane, we have also (Prop. XVIII. Bk. VII.),

$$SA : SG :: SM : SP;$$

hence,

$$ABCDE : GHIKL :: MNO : PQR;$$

therefore the sections G H I K L, P Q R are to each other as the bases A B C D E, M N O.

481. *Cor.* 2. If the bases A B C D E, M N O are equivalent, any sections, G H I K L, P Q R, made at equal distances from those bases, are likewise equivalent.

Proposition XVII. — Theorem.

482. *The convex surface of a frustum of a right pyramid is equal to half the sum of the perimeters of its two bases, multiplied by its slant height.*

Let A B C D E – L be the frustum of a right pyramid, and M N its slant height; then the convex surface is equal to the sum of the perimeters of the two bases A B C D E, G H I K L, multiplied by half of M N.

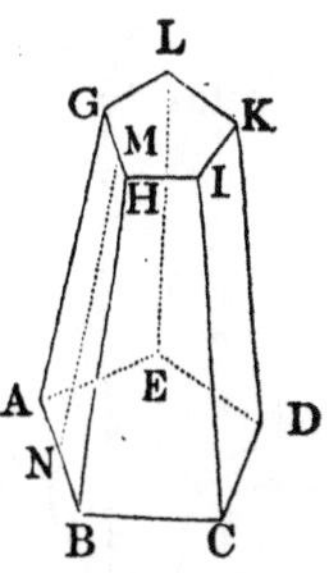

For the upper base G H I K L is similar to the base A B C D E (Prop. XVI.), and A B C D E is a regular polygon (Art. 445); hence the sides G H, H I, I K, K L, and L G are all equal to each other. The angles G A B, A B H, H B C, &c. are equal (Prop. XV. Cor.), and the edges A G, B H, C I, &c. are also equal (Prop. XVI.); therefore the faces A H, B I, C K, &c. are all equal trapezoids (Art. 28), having a common altitude, M N, the slant height of the frustum. But the area of either trapezoid, as A H, is equal to $\frac{1}{2}$ (A B + G H) × M N (Prop. VII. Bk. IV.); hence the areas of all the trapezoids, or the convex surface of frustum, are equal to half the sum of the perimeters of the two bases multiplied by the slant height.

Proposition XVIII. — Theorem.

483. *Triangular pyramids, having equivalent bases and the same altitude, are equivalent.*

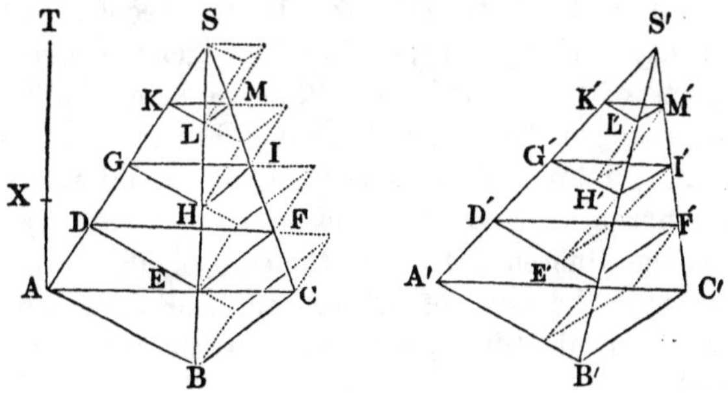

Let A B C – S, A′ B′ C′ – S′ be two triangular pyramids, having equivalent bases, A B C, A′ B′ C′, situated in the same plane; and let them have the same altitude, A T; then these pyramids are equivalent.

For, if the two pyramids are not equivalent, let A′ B′ C′ – S′ be the smaller, and suppose A X to be the altitude of a prism, which, having A B C for its base, is equal to their difference.

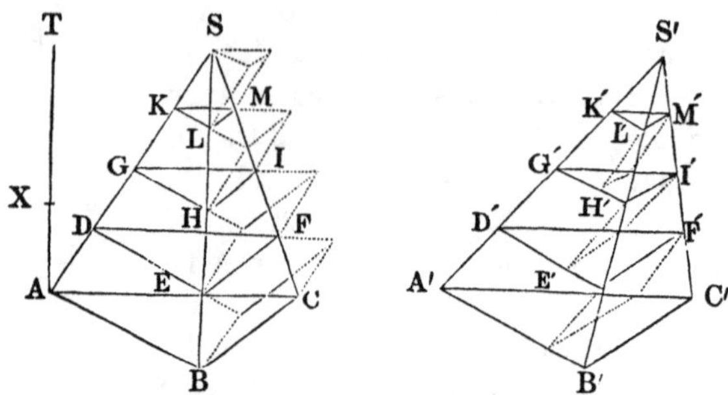

Divide the altitude A T into equal parts, each less than A X; through each point of division pass a plane parallel to the plane of the base, thus forming corresponding sections in the two pyramids, equivalent each to each, namely, D E F to D′ E′ F′, G H I to G′ H′ I′, &c.

Upon the triangles A B C, D E F, G H I, &c., taken as bases, construct exterior prisms, having for edges the parts A D, D G, G K, &c. of the edge S A; in like manner, on the bases D′ E′ F′, G′ H′ I′, &c. in the second pyramid, construct interior prisms, having for edges the corresponding parts of S′ A′. It is plain that the sum of all the exterior prisms of the pyramid A B C – S is greater than this pyramid; and also that the sum of all the interior prisms of the pyramid A′ B′ C′ – S′ is less than this pyramid. Hence, the difference between the sum of all the exterior prisms and the sum of all the interior ones, must be greater than the difference between the two pyramids themselves.

Now, beginning with the bases A B C, A′ B′ C′, the second exterior prism, D E F – G, is equivalent to the first interior prism, D′ E′ F′ – A′, since they have equal altitudes, and their bases, D E F, D′ E′ F′, are equivalent. For a like reason, the third exterior prism, G H I – K, and the second interior prism, G′ H′ I′ – D′, are equivalent; and so on to the last in each series. Hence, all the exterior prisms of the pyramid A B C – S, excepting the first prism, A B C – D, have equivalent corresponding ones in the interior prisms of the pyramid A B C′ – S′. Therefore the prism A B C – D is the difference between the sum of all the exterior prisms of the pyramid A B C – S, and the sum of the interior prisms of the pyramid A′ B′ C′ – S′. But the difference between these two sets of prisms has been proved to be greater than that of the two pyramids, which latter difference we supposed to be equal to the prism A B C – X. Hence, the prism A B C – D must be greater than the prism A B C – X, which is impossible, since they have the same base, A B C, and the altitude of the first is less than A X, the altitude of the second. Hence, the supposed inequality between the two pyramids cannot exist; therefore the two pyramids A B C – S, A′ B′ C′ – S′, having the same altitude and equivalent bases, are themselves equivalent.

PROPOSITION XIX.—THEOREM.

484. *Every triangular pyramid is a third part of a triangular prism having the same base and the same altitude.*

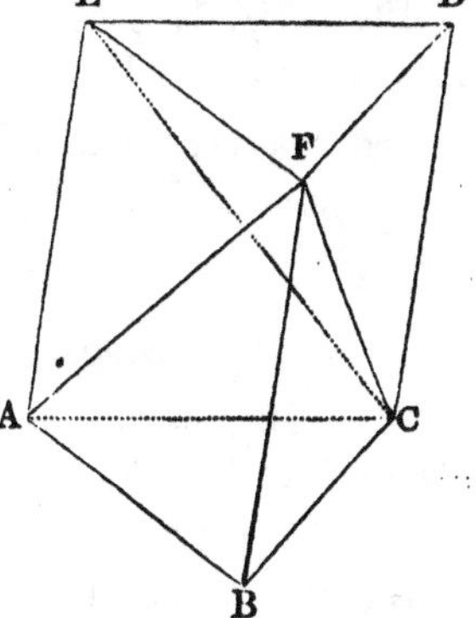

Let A B C – F be a triangular pyramid, and A B C – D E F a triangular prism of the same base and the same altitude; then the pyramid is one third of the prism.

Cut off the pyramid A B C – F from the prism, by the plane F A C; there will remain the solid A C D E – F, which may be considered as a quadrangular pyramid, whose vertex is F, and whose base is the parallelogram A C D E. Draw the

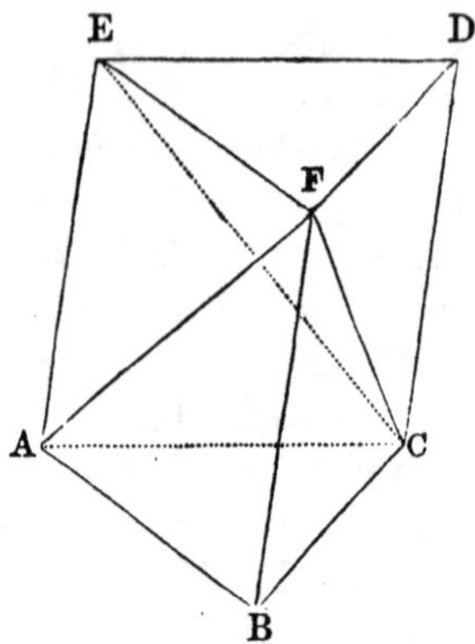

diagonal C E, and pass the plane F C E, which will cut the quadrangular pyramid into two triangular ones, ACE–F, EDC–F. These two triangular pyramids have for their common altitude the perpendicular let fall from F on the plane A C D E; they have equal bases, since the triangles A C E, C D E are halves of the same parallelogram; hence the two pyramids A C E – F, C D E – F are equivalent (Prop. XVIII.). But the pyramid C D E – F and the pyramid A B C – F have equal bases, A B C, D E F; they have also the same altitude, namely, the distance between the parallel planes A B C, D E F; hence the two pyramids are equivalent. Now, the pyramid C D E – F has been proved equivalent to A C E – F; hence the three pyramids A B C – F, C D E – F, A C E – F, which compose the whole prism A B C – D E F, are all equivalent; therefore, either pyramid, as A B C – F, is the third part of the prism, which has the same base and the same altitude.

485. *Cor.* 1. Every triangular prism may be divided into three equivalent triangular pyramids.

486. *Cor.* 2. The solidity of a triangular pyramid is equal to a third part of the product of its base by its altitude.

PROPOSITION XX. — THEOREM.

487. *The solidity of every pyramid is equal to the product of its base by one third of its altitude.*

Let A B C D E – S be any pyramid, whose base is A B C D E, and altitude S O; then its solidity is equal to A B C D E × ⅓ S O.

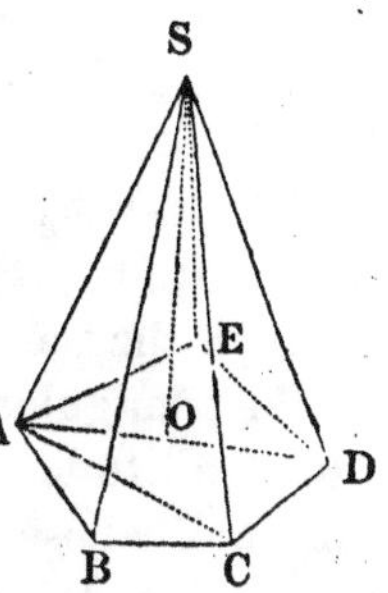

Draw the diagonals A C, A D, and pass the planes S A C, S A D through these diagonals and the vertex S; the polygonal pyramid A B C D E – S will be divided into several triangular pyramids, all having the same altitude, S O. But each of these pyramids is measured by the product of its base, B A C, C A D, D A E, by a third part of its altitude, S O (Prop. XIX. Cor. 2); hence, the sum of these triangular pyramids, or the polygonal pyramid A B C D E – S, will be measured by the sum of the triangles B A C, C A D, D A E, or the polygon A B C D E, multiplied by one third of S O; hence, every pyramid is measured by the product of its base by one third of its altitude.

488. *Cor.* 1. Every pyramid is the third part of the prism which has the same base and the same altitude.

489. *Cor.* 2. Pyramids having the same altitude are to each other as their bases.

490. *Cor.* 3. Pyramids having the same base, or equivalent bases, are to each other as their altitudes.

491. *Cor.* 4. Pyramids are to each other as the products of their bases by their altitudes.

492. *Scholium.* The solidity of any polyedron may be found by dividing it into pyramids, by passing planes through its vertices.

PROPOSITION XXI. — THEOREM.

493. *A frustum of a pyramid is equivalent to the sum of three pyramids, having for their common altitude the altitude of the frustum, and whose bases are the two bases of the frustum and a mean proportional between them.*

First. Let A B C – D E F be the frustum of a pyramid, whose base is a triangle. Pass a plane through the points

A, E, C; it cuts off the triangular pyramid A B C – E, whose altitude is that of the frustum, and whose base, A B C, is the lower base of the frustum. Pass another plane through the points D, E, C; it cuts off the triangular pyramid D E F – C, whose altitude is that of the frustum, and whose base, D E F, is the upper base of the frustum.

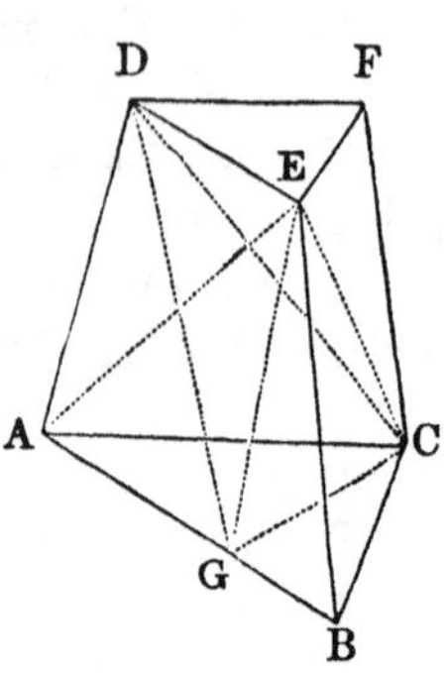

There now remains of the frustum the pyramid A C D – E. Draw E G parallel to A D; join C G and D G. Then, since E G is parallel to A D, it is parallel to the plane A C D (Prop. XI. Bk. VII.); and the pyramid A C D – E is equivalent to the pyramid A C D – G, since they have the same base, A C D, and their vertices, E and G, lie in the same straight line parallel to the common base. But the pyramid A C D – G is the same as the pyramid A G C – D, whose altitude is that of the frustum, and whose base, A G C, as will be proved, is a mean proportional between the bases A B C and D E F.

The two triangles A G C, D E F have the angles A and D equal to each other (Prop. XVI. Bk. VII.); hence we have (Prop. XXVIII. Bk. IV.),

$$AGC : DEF :: AG \times AC : DE \times DF;$$

but since A G is equal to D E,

$$AGC : DEF :: AC : DF.$$

We have, also (Prop. VI. Cor., Bk. IV.),

$$ABC : AGC :: AB : AG \text{ or } DE.$$

But the similar triangles A B C, D E F give

$$AB : DE :: AC : DF;$$

hence (Prop. X. Bk. II.),

$$ABC : AGC :: AGC : DEF;$$

that is, the base A G C is a mean proportional between the bases A B C, D E F of the frustum.

Secondly. Let G H I K L – M N O P Q be the frustum of a pyramid, whose base is any polygon.

Let A B C – S be a triangular pyramid having the same altitude, and an equivalent base, with any polygonal pyramid, G H I K L – T; these pyramids are equivalent (Prop. XX. Cor. 3.)

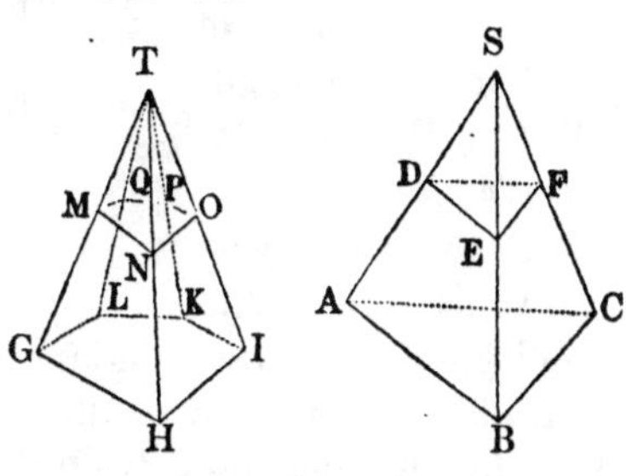

The bases of the two pyramids may be regarded as situated in the same plane, in which case the plane MNOPQ produced will form in the triangular pyramid a section, D E F, at the same distance above the common plane of the bases; and therefore the section D E F will be to the section M N O P Q as the base A B C is to the base G H I K L (Prop. XVI. Cor. 1); and since the bases are equivalent, the sections will be so likewise. Hence, the pyramids M N O P Q – T, D E F – S, having the same altitude and equivalent bases, are equivalent. For the same reason, the entire pyramids G H I K L – T, A B C – S are equivalent; consequently, the frustums G H I K L – M N O P Q, A B C – D E F, are equivalent. But the frustum A B C – D E F has been shown to be equivalent to the sum of three pyramids having for their common altitude the altitude of the frustum, and whose bases are the two bases of the frustum, and a mean proportional between them. Hence the proposition is true of the frustum of any pyramid.

Proposition XXII. — Theorem.

494. *Similar pyramids are to each other as the cubes of their homologous edges.*

Let A B C – S and D E F – S be two similar pyramids; these pyramids are to each other as the cubes of their homologous edges A B and D E, or B C and E F, &c.

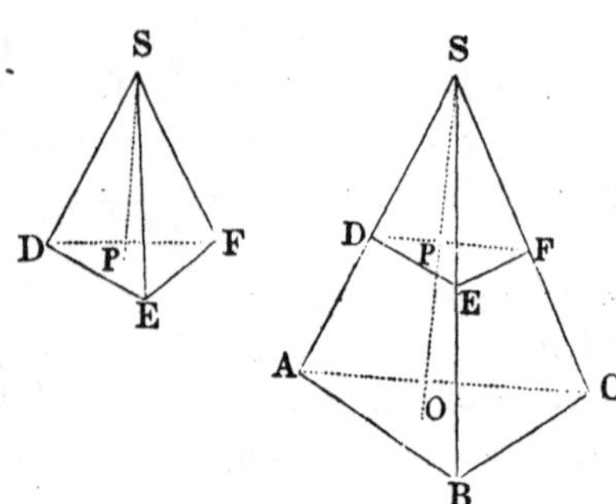

For, the two pyramids being similar, the homologous polyedral angles at the vertices are equal (Art. 452); hence the smaller pyramid may be so applied to the larger, that the polyedral angle S shall be common to both.

In that case, the bases A B C, D E F will be parallel; for, since the homologous faces are similar, the angle S D E is equal to S A B, and S E F to S B C; hence the plane A B C is parallel to the plane D E F (Prop. XVI. Bk. VII.). Then let S O be drawn from the vertex S perpendicular to the plane A B C, and let P be the point where this perpendicular meets the plane D E F. From what has already been shown (Prop. XVI.), we shall have

$$SO : SP :: SA : SD :: AB : DE;$$

and consequently,

$$\tfrac{1}{3} SO : \tfrac{1}{3} SP :: AB : DE.$$

But the bases A B C, D E F are similar; hence (Prop. XXIX. Bk. IV.),

$$ABC : DEF :: \overline{AB}^2 : \overline{DE}^2.$$

Multiplying together the corresponding terms of these two proportions, we have

$$ABC \times \tfrac{1}{3} SO : DEF \times \tfrac{1}{3} SP :: \overline{AB}^3 : \overline{DE}^3.$$

Now, $ABC \times \frac{1}{3} SO$ represents the solidity of the pyramid A B C – S, and $DEF \times \frac{1}{3} SP$ that of the pyramid D E F – S (Prop. XX.); hence two similar pyramids are to each other as the cubes of their homologous edges.

PROPOSITION XXIII. — THEOREM.

495. *There can be no more than five regular polyedrons.*

For, since regular polyedrons have equal regular polygons for their faces, and all their polyedral angles equal, there can be but few regular polyedrons.

First. If the faces are equilateral triangles, polyedrons may be formed of them, having each polyedral angle contained by *three* of these triangles, forming a solid bounded by four equal equilateral triangles; or by *four*, forming a solid bounded by eight equal equilateral triangles; or by *five*, forming a solid bounded by twenty equal equilateral triangles. No others can be formed with equilateral triangles. For six of these angles are equal to four right angles, and cannot form a polyedral angle (Prop. XX. Bk. VII.).

Secondly. If the faces are squares, their angles may be arranged by threes, forming a solid bounded by six equal squares. Four angles of a square are equal to four right angles, and cannot form a polyedral angle.

Thirdly. If the faces are regular pentagons, their angles may be arranged by threes, forming a solid bounded by twelve equal and regular pentagons.

We can proceed no farther. Three angles of a regular hexagon are equal to four right angles; three of a heptagon are greater. Hence, there can be formed no more than five regular polyedrons, — three with equilateral triangles, one with squares, and one with pentagons.

496. *Scholium.* The regular polyedron bounded by four equilateral triangles is called a TETRAEDRON; the one bounded by eight is called an OCTAEDRON; the one bounded by twenty is called an ICOSAEDRON. The regular polyedron bounded by six equal squares is called a HEXAEDRON, or CUBE; and the one bounded by twelve equal and regular pentagons is called a DODECAEDRON.

BOOK IX.

THE SPHERE, AND ITS PROPERTIES.

DEFINITIONS.

497. A SPHERE is a solid, or volume, bounded by a curved surface, all points of which are equally distant from a point within, called the center.

The sphere may be conceived to be formed by the revolution of a semicircle, D A E, about its diameter, D E, which remains fixed.

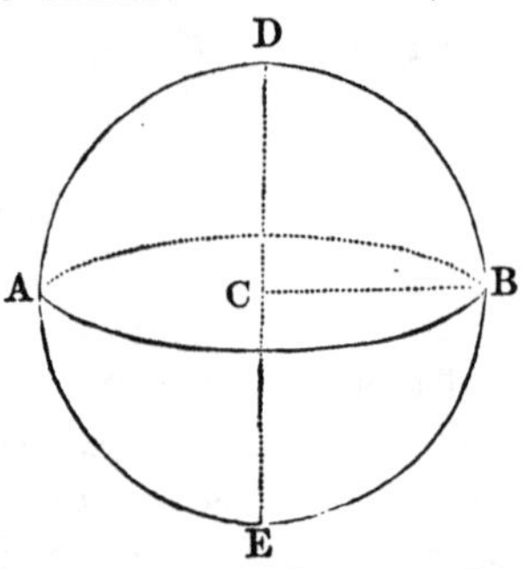

498. The RADIUS of a sphere is a straight line drawn from the center to any point in surface, as the line C B.

The DIAMETER, or AXIS, of a sphere is a line passing through the center, and terminated both ways by the surface, as the line D E.

Hence, all the radii of a sphere are equal; and all the diameters are equal, and each is double the radius.

499. A CIRCLE, it will be shown, is a section of a sphere.

A GREAT CIRCLE of the sphere is a section made by a plane passing through the center, and having the center of the sphere for its center; as the section A B, whose center is C.

500. A SMALL CIRCLE of the sphere is any section made by a plane not passing through the center.

501. The POLE of a circle of the sphere is a point in the

surface equally distant from every point in the circumference of the circle.

502. It will be shown (Prop. V.) that every circle, great or small, has two poles.

503. A PLANE is TANGENT to a sphere, when it meets the sphere in but one point, however far it may be produced.

504. A SPHERICAL ANGLE is the difference in the direction of two arcs of great circles of the sphere; as A E D, formed by the arcs E A, D E.

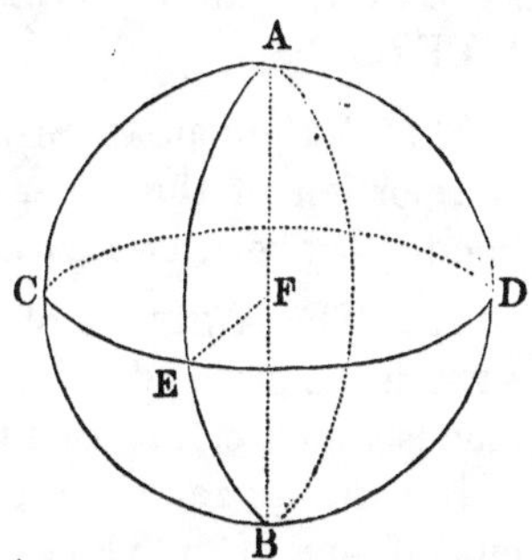

It is the same as the angle resulting from passing two planes through those arcs; as the angle formed on the edge EF, by the planes EAF, EDF.

505. A SPHERICAL TRIANGLE is a portion of the surface of a sphere bounded by three arcs of great circles, each arc being less than a semi-circumference; as A E D.

These arcs are named the *sides* of the triangle; and the angles which their planes form with each other are the *angles* of the triangle.

506. A spherical triangle takes the name of *right-angled*, *isosceles*, *equilateral*, in the same cases as a plane triangle.

507. A SPHERICAL POLYGON is a portion of the surface of a sphere bounded by several arcs of great circles.

508. A LUNE is a portion of the surface of a sphere comprehended between semi-circumferences of two great circles; as A I G B D F.

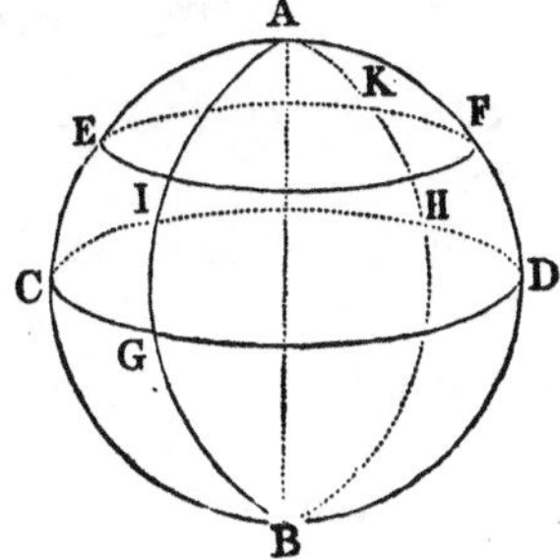

509. A SPHERICAL WEDGE, or UNGULA, is that portion of a sphere comprehended between

two great semicircles having a common diameter.

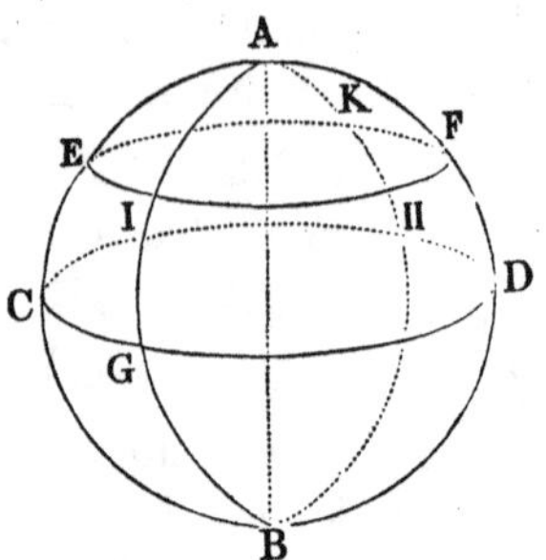

510. A ZONE is a portion of the surface of a sphere cut off by a plane, or comprehended between two parallel planes; as EIFK-A, or CGDH-EIFK.

511. A SPHERICAL SEGMENT is a portion of the sphere cut off by a plane, or comprehended between two parallel planes.

512. The ALTITUDE of a ZONE or of a SPHERICAL SEGMENT is the perpendicular distance between the two parallel planes which comprehend the zone or segment.

In case the zone or segment is a portion of the sphere cut off, one of the planes is a tangent to the sphere.

513. A SPHERICAL SECTOR is a solid described by the revolution of a circular sector, in the same manner as the semicircle of which it is a part, by revolving round its diameter, describes a sphere.

514. A SPHERICAL PYRAMID is a portion of the sphere comprehended between the planes of a polyedral angle whose vertex is the center.

The *base* of the pyramid is the spherical polygon intercepted by the same planes.

PROPOSITION I.—THEOREM.

515. *Every section of a sphere made by a plane is a circle.*

Let A B E be a section made by a plane in the sphere whose center is C. From the centre, C, draw C D perpendicular to the plane A B E; and draw the lines C A, C B, C E, to different points of the curve A B E, which bounds the section.

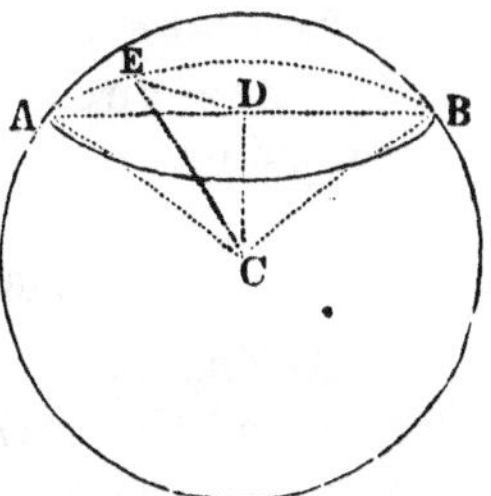

The oblique lines C A, C B, C E are equal, being radii of the sphere; therefore they are equally distant from the perpendicular, C D (Prop. V. Cor., Bk. VII.). Hence, the lines D A, D B, D E, and, in like manner, all the lines drawn from D to the boundary of the section, are equal; and therefore the section A B E is a circle whose center is D.

516. *Cor.* 1. If the section passes through the center of the sphere, its radius will be the radius of the sphere; hence all great circles are equal.

517. *Cor.* 2. Two great circles always bisect each other. For, since the two circles have the same center, their common intersection, passing through the center, must be a common diameter bisecting both circles.

518. *Cor.* 3. Every great circle divides the sphere and its surface into two equal parts. For if the two hemispheres were separated, and afterwards placed on the common base, with their convexities turned the same way, the two surfaces would exactly coincide.

519. *Cor.* 4. The center of a small circle, and that of the sphere, are in a straight line perpendicular to the plane of the small circle.

520. *Cor.* 5. Small circles are less according to their distance from the center; for, the greater the distance C D, the smaller the chord A B, the diameter of the small circle A B E.

521. *Cor.* 6. The arc of a great circle may be made to pass through any two points on the surface of a sphere; for the two given points and the center of the sphere determine the position of a plane. If, however, the two given points be the extremities of a diameter, these two points

and the center would be in a straight line, and any number of great circles may be made to pass through the two given points.

Proposition II. — Theorem.

522. *Any one side of a spherical triangle is less than the sum of the other two.*

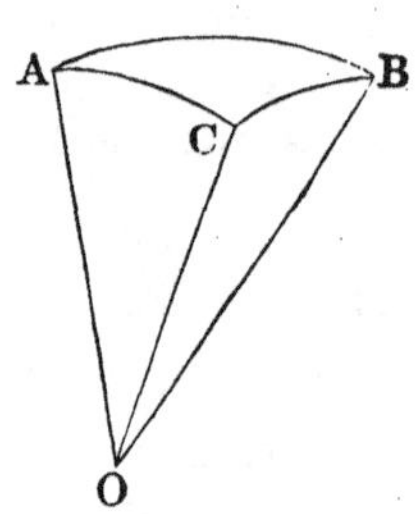

Let A B C be any spherical triangle; then any side, as A B, is less than the sum of the other two sides, A C, B C.

For, draw the radii O A, O B, O C, and the plane angles A O B, A O C, C O B will form a triedral angle, O. The angles A O B, A O C, C O B will be measured by A B, A C, B C, the side of the spherical triangle. But each of the three plane angles forming a triedral angle is less than the sum of the other two (Prop. XIX. Bk. VII.). Hence, any side of a spherical triangle is less than the sum of the other two.

Proposition III. — Theorem.

523. *The shortest path from one point to another, on the surface of a sphere, is the arc of the great circle which joins the two given points.*

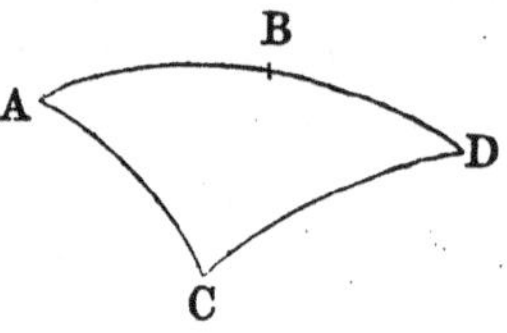

Let A B D be the arc of the great circle which joins the points A and D; then the line A B D is the shortest path from A to D on the surface of the sphere.

For, if possible, let the shortest path on the surface from A to D pass through the point C, out of the arc of the great circle A B D. Draw A C, D C, arcs of great circles, and take D B equal to D C. Then in the spherical triangle A B D C the side A B D is less than the sum of the sides A C, D C (Prop. II.); and subtracting the equal D B and D C, there will remain A B less than A C.

Now, the shortest path, on the surface, from D to C, whether it is the arc D C, or any other line, is equal to the shortest path from D to B; for, revolving D C about the diameter which passes through D, the point C may be brought into the position of the point B, and the shortest path from D to C be made to coincide with the shortest path from D to B. But, by hypothesis, the shortest path from A to D passes through C; consequently, the shortest path on the surface from A to C cannot be greater than that from A to B.

Now, since A B has been proved to be less than A C, the shortest path from A to C must be greater than that from A to B; but this has just been shown to be impossible. Hence, no point of the shortest path from A to D can lie out of the arc A B D; consequently, this arc of a great circle is itself the shortest path between its extremities.

524. *Cor.* The distance between any two points of surface, on the surface of a sphere, is measured by the arc of a great circle joining the two points.

PROPOSITION IV. — THEOREM.

525. ***The sum of all the sides of any spherical polygon is less than the circumference of a great circle.***

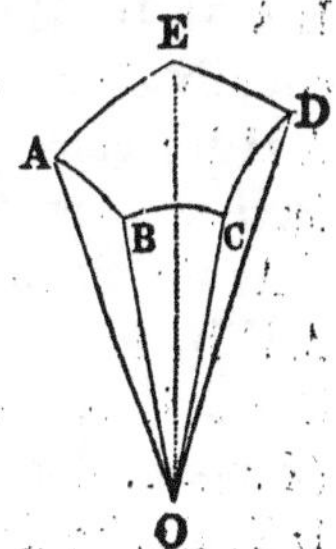

Let A B C D E be a spherical polygon; then the sum of the sides A B, B C, C D, &c. is less than the circumference of a great circle.

For, from O, the center of the sphere, draw the radii O A, O B, O C, &c., and the plane angles A O B, B O C, C O B, &c. will form a polyedral angle at O. Now, the sum of the plane angles which form a polyedral angle is less than four right angles (Prop. XX. Bk. VII.). Hence, the sum of the arcs A B, B C, C D, &c., which measure these angles, and bound the spherical polygon, is less than the circumference of a great circle.

526. *Cor.* The sum of the three sides of a spherical triangle is less than the circumference of a great circle, since a triangle is a polygon of three sides.

PROPOSITION V. — THEOREM.

527. *The extremities of a diameter of a sphere are the poles of all circles of the sphere whose planes are perpendicular to that diameter.*

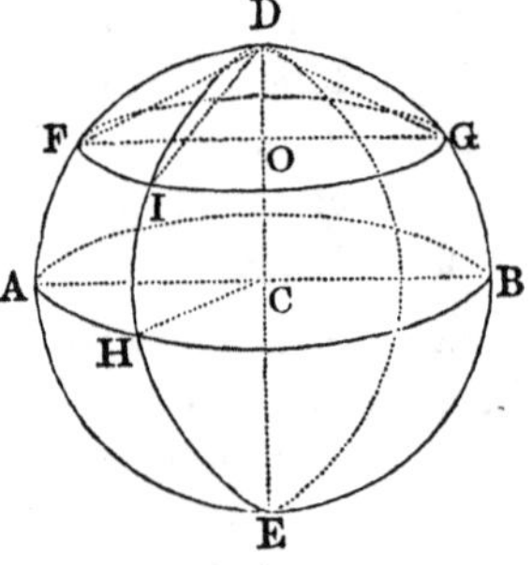

Let D E be a diameter perpendicular to A H B, a great circle of a sphere, and also to the small circle F I G; then D and E, the extremities of this diameter, are the poles of these two circles.

For, since D E is perpendicular to the plane A H B, it is perpendicular to all the straight lines, A C, H C, B C, &c., drawn through its foot in this plane; hence, all the arcs D A, D H, D B, &c. are quarters of the circumference. So, likewise, are all the arcs E A, E H, E B, &c.; hence the points D and E are each equally distant from all the points of the circumference, A H B; consequently D and E are poles of that circumference (Art. 501).

Again, since the radius D C is perpendicular to the plane A H B, it is perpendicular to the parallel plane F I G; hence it passes through O, the center of the circle F I G (Prop. I. Cor. 4). Hence, if the oblique lines D F, D I, D G, &c. be drawn, these lines will be equally distant from the perpendicular D O, and will themselves be equal (Prop. V. Bk. VII.). But the chords being equal, the arcs are equal; hence the point D is a pole of the small circle F I G; and, for like reasons, the point E is the other pole.

528. *Cor.* 1. Every arc of a great circle, D H, drawn from a point in the arc of a great circle, A H B, to its pole, is a quarter of the circumference, and is called a quadrant. This quadrant makes a right angle with the arc A H. For, the line D C being perpendicular to the plane A H C, every plane D H C passing through the line D C is perpendicular to the plane A H C (Prop. VII. Bk. VII.); hence the angle of those planes, or the angle A H D, is a right angle (Art. 506).

529. *Cor.* 2. To find the pole of a given arc, A H, draw the indefinite arc H D perpendicular to A H, and take H D equal to a quadrant; the point D will be one of the poles of the arc A H D; or at each of the two points A and H, draw the arcs A D and H D perpendicular to A H; the point of their intersection, D, will be the pole required.

530. *Cor.* 3. Conversely, if the distance of the point D from each of the points A and H is equal to a quadrant, the point D will be the pole of the arc A H; and the angles D A H, A H D will be right.

For, let C be the center of the sphere, and draw the radii C A, C D, C H. Since the angles A C D, H C D are right, the line C D is perpendicular to the two straight lines C A, C H; hence it is perpendicular to their plane (Prop. IV. Bk. VII.). Hence the point D is the pole of the arc A H; and consequently the angles D A H, A H D are right angles.

531. *Scholium.* A circle may be described on the surface of a sphere with the same facility as on a plane surface. For instance, by turning the arc D F, or any other line extending to the same distance, round the point D the

extremity, F, will describe the small circle F I G; and by turning the quadrant D F A round the point D, its extremity, A, will describe the great circle A H B.

Proposition VI. — Theorem.

532. *A plane perpendicular to a radius, at its termination in the surface, is tangent to the sphere.*

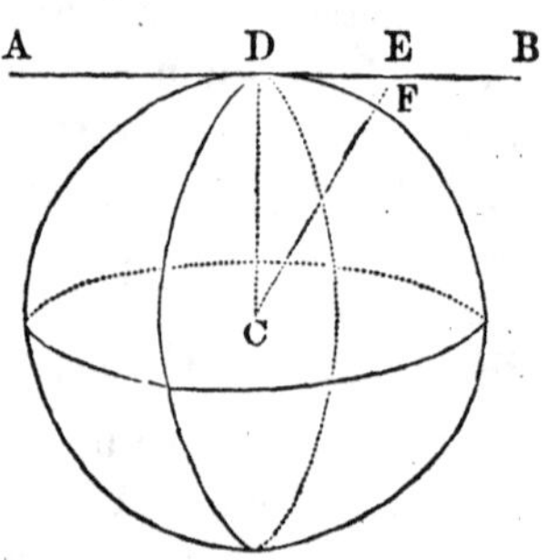

Let A D B be a plane perpendicular to a radius, C D, at its termination, D; then the plane A D B is a tangent to the sphere.

For, draw from the center, C, any other straight line, C E, to the plane, A D B. Then, since C D is perpendicular to the plane, it is shorter than the oblique line C E; hence the radius C F is shorter than C E; consequently the point E is without the sphere. The same may be shown of any other point in the plane A D B, except the point D; hence the plane can meet the sphere in but one point, and therefore is a tangent to the sphere (Art. 503).

533. *Scholium.* In the same manner, it may be proved that two spheres are tangent to each other, when the distance between their centers is equal to the sum or the difference of their radii; in which case the centers and the point of contact lie in the same straight line.

Proposition VII. — Theorem.

534. *The angle formed by two arcs of great circles is equal to the angle formed by the tangents of those arcs at the point of their intersection, and is measured by the arc of a great circle described from its vertex as a pole, and intercepted between its sides, produced if necessary.*

Let B A C be an angle formed by the two arcs A B, A C; then will it be equal to the angle E A F, formed by the tangents A E, A F, and it is measured by B C, the arc of a great circle described from the vertex A as a pole.

For the tangent A E, drawn in the plane of the arc A B, is perpendicular to the radius A O (Prop. X. Bk. III.); and the tangent A F, drawn in the plane of the arc A C, is perpendicular to the same radius A O. Hence the angle E A F is equal to the angle of the planes A O B, A O C (Art. 391); which is that of the arcs A B, A C.

Also, if the arcs A B, A C are both quadrants, the lines O B, O C will be perpendicular to A O, and the angle B O C will be equal to the angle of the planes A O B, A O C; hence the arc B C is the measure of the angle of these planes, or the measure of the angle C A B.

535. *Cor.* 1. The angles of spherical triangles may be compared together, by means of the arcs of great circles described from their vertices as poles, and included between their sides; hence it is easy to make an angle of this kind equal to a given angle.

536. *Cor.* 2. Vertical angles, such as A O C and B O D, are equal; for each of them is equal to the angle formed by the two planes A O B, C O D.

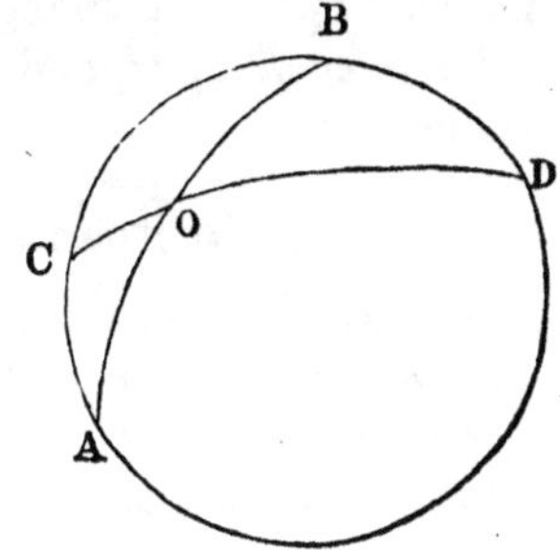

It is also evident that the two adjacent angles, A O C, C O B, taken together, are equal to two right angles.

Proposition VIII. — Theorem.

537. *If from the vertices of any spherical triangle, as poles, arcs of great circles are described, a second triangle is formed, whose vertices will be poles to the sides of the first triangle.*

Let A B C be any spherical triangle; and from the vertices, A, B, C, as poles, let the arcs E F, F D, D E be described, and a second triangle, D E F, is formed, whose vertices, D, E, F, will be poles to the sides of the triangle A B C.

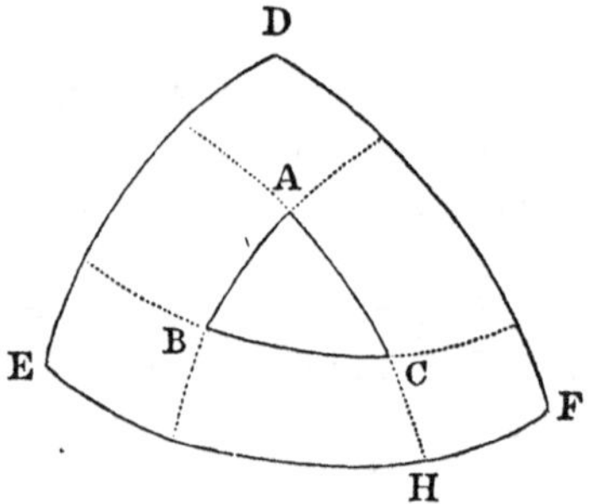

For, the point A being the pole of the arc E F, the distance A E is a quadrant; the point C being the pole of the arc D E, the distance C E is also a quadrant; hence the point E is at the distance of a quadrant from each of the points A and C; hence it is the pole of the arc A C (Prop. V. Cor. 3). In like manner, it may be shown that D is the pole of the arc B C, and F that of the arc A B.

538. *Scholium.* Hence the triangle A B C may be described by means of D E F, as D E F may be by means of A B C. Spherical triangles thus described are said to be *polar to each other*, and are called *polar* or *supplemental* triangles.

Proposition IX. — Theorem.

539. *Each of the angles of a spherical triangle is measured by a semi-circumference minus the side lying opposite to it in the polar triangle.*

Let A B C be a spherical triangle, and D E F a triangle polar to it; then each of the angles of A B C is measured by a semi-circumference minus the side lying opposite to it in D E F.

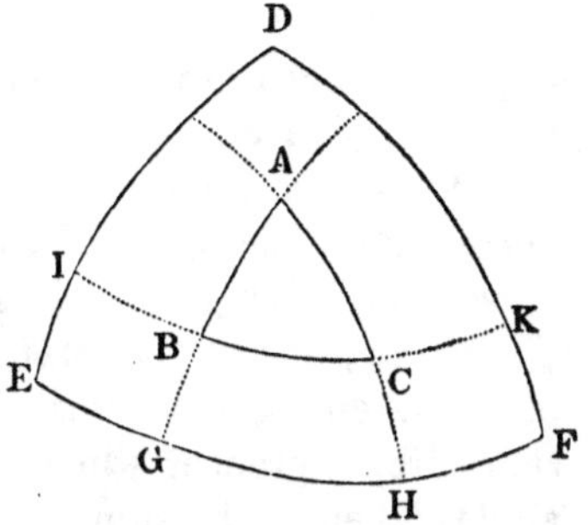

For, produce the sides A B, A C, if necessary, till they meet E F in G and H. The point A being the pole of the arc G H, the angle A will be measured by that arc (Prop. VII.). But, E being the pole of A H, the arc E H is a quadrant; and F being the pole of A G, F G is a quadrant. Hence, E H and G F together are equal to a semi-circumference. Now, the sum of E H and G F is equal to the sum of E F and G H; hence the arc G H, which measures the angle A, is equal to a semi-circumference minus the side E F. In like manner, the angle B will be measured by a semi-circumference minus D F; and the angle C by a semi-circumference minus D E.

540. *Cor.* This property must be reciprocal in the two triangles, since they are polar to each other. The angle D, for example, of the triangle D E F, is measured by the arc I K; but the sum of I K and B C is equal to the sum of I C and B K, which is equal to a semi-circumference; hence the arc I K, the measure of D, is equal to a semi-circumference minus B C. In like manner, it may be shown that E is measured by a semi-circumference minus A C, and F by a semi-circumference minus A B.

Proposition X.—Theorem.

541. *The sum of the angles in any spherical triangles is less than six right angles, and greater than two.*

First. Every angle of a spherical triangle is less than two right angles; hence, the sum of the three is less than six right angles.

Secondly. The measure of each angle of a spherical triangle is equal to the semi-circumference minus the corresponding side of the polar triangle (Prop. IX.); hence, the sum of the three is measured by three semi-circumferences minus the sum of the sides of the polar triangle. Now, this latter sum is less than a circumference (Prop. IV. Cor.); therefore, taking it away from three semi-circumferences, the remainder will be greater than one semi-circumference, which is the measure of two right angles; hence, the sum of the three angles of a spherical triangle is greater than two right angles.

542. *Cor*. 1. The sum of the angles of a spherical triangle is not constant, like that of the angles of a rectilineal triangle. It varies between two right angles and six, without ever arriving at either of these limits. Two given angles, therefore, do not serve to determine the third.

543. *Cor*. 2. A spherical triangle may have two, or even three right angles, or obtuse angles.

544. *Scholium.* If a spherical triangle has two right angles, it is said to be *bi-rectangular;* and if it has three right angles, it is said to be *tri-rectangular*, or *quadrantal.* The quadrantal triangle is evidently contained eight times in the surface of the sphere.

Proposition XI. — Theorem.

545. *If around the vertices of any two angles of a given spherical triangle, as poles, the circumferences of two circles be described, which shall pass through the third angle of the triangle, and then if through the other point in which these circumferences intersect, and the vertices of the first two angles of the triangles, arcs of two great circles be drawn, the triangle thus formed will have all its parts equal to those of the given triangle, each to each.*

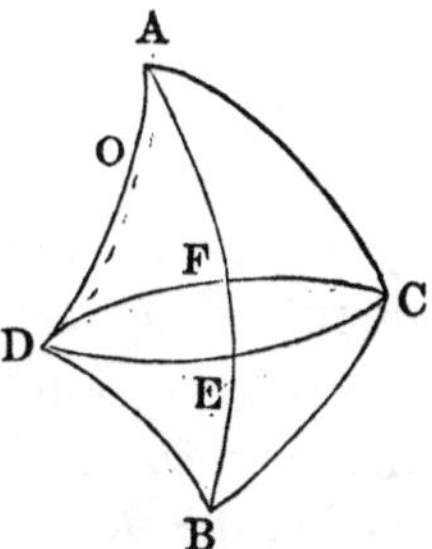

Let A B C be the given spherical triangle, and C E D, D F C arcs described about the vertices of any two of its angles, A and B, as poles; then will the triangle A D B have all its parts equal to those of A B C.

For, by construction, the side A D is equal to A C, D B is equal to B C, and A B is common; hence the two triangles have their sides equal, each to each. We are now to show that the angles opposite these equal sides are also equal.

If the center of the sphere is supposed to be at O, a triedral angle may be conceived as formed at O by the three plane angles A O B, A O C, B O C; also, another triedral angle may be conceived as formed by the three plane angles A O B, A O D, B O D. Now, since the sides of the triangle A B C are equal to those of the triangle A D B, the plane angles forming the one of these triedral angles are equal to the plane angles forming the other, each to each. Therefore the planes, in which the equal angles lie, are equally inclined to each other (Prop. XXI. Bk. VII.); hence, all the angles of the spherical triangle D A B are respectively equal to those of the triangle C A B; namely, D A B is equal to B A C, D B A to A B C, and A D B to A C B; hence, the sides and angles of the triangle A D B are equal to the sides and the angles of the triangle A C B, each to each.

546. *Scholium.* The equality of these triangles is not, however, an absolute equality, or one of superposition; for it would be impossible to apply them to each other exactly, unless they were isosceles. The equality here meant is that by *symmetry;* therefore the triangles A C B, A D B are termed *symmetrical triangles.*

Proposition XII.—Theorem.

547. *If two triangles on the same sphere, or on equal spheres, are mutually equilateral, they are mutually equiangular; and their equal angles are opposite to equal sides.*

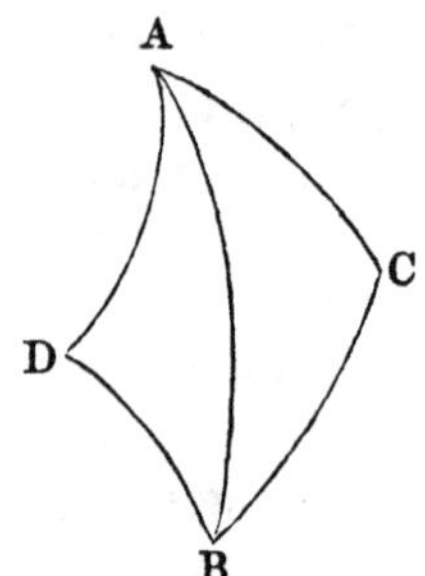

Let A B C, A B D be two triangles on the same sphere, or on equal spheres, having the sides of the one respectively equal to those of the other; then the angles opposite to the equal sides, in the two triangles, are equal.

For, with three given sides, A B, A C, B C, there can be constructed only two triangles, A C B, A B D, and these triangles will be equal, each to each, in the magnitude of all their parts (Prop. XI.). Hence, these two triangles, which are mutually equilateral, must be either absolutely equal, or equal by *symmetry;* in either case they are mutually equiangular, and the equal angles lie opposite to equal sides.

Proposition XIII.—Theorem.

548. *If two triangles on the same sphere, or on equal spheres, are mutually equiangular, they are mutually equilateral.*

Let A and B be the two given triangles; P and Q, their polar triangles.

Since the angles are equal in the triangles A and B, the sides will be equal in the polar triangles P and Q (Prop. IX.). But since the triangles P and Q are mutually equilateral, they must also be mutually equiangular (Prop. XII.); and, the angles being equal in the triangles P and Q, it follows that the sides are equal in their polar triangles A and B. Hence, the triangles A and B, which are mutually equiangular, are at the same time mutually equilateral.

PROPOSITION XIV. — THEOREM.

549. *If two triangles on the same sphere, or on equal spheres, have two sides and the included angle in the one equal to two sides and the included angle in the other, each to each, the two triangles are equal in all their parts.*

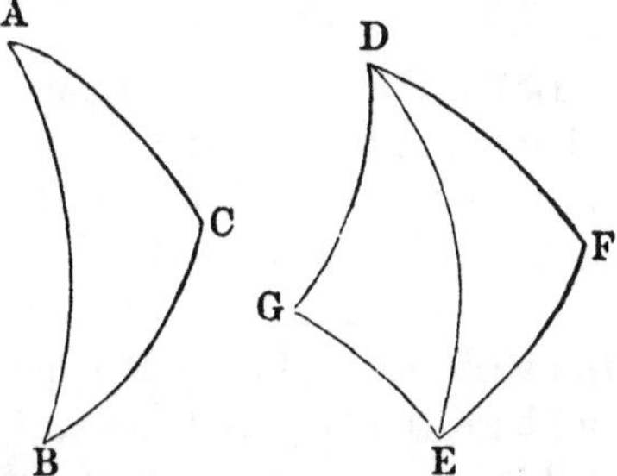

In the two triangles A B C, D E F, let the side A B be equal to the side D E, the side A C to the side D F; and the angle B A C to the angle E D F; then the triangles will be equal in all their parts.

Let the triangle D E G be symmetrical with the triangle D E F (Prop. XI. Sch.), having the side E G equal to E F, the side G D equal to F D, and the side E D common, and consequently the angles of the one equal to those of the other (Prop. XII.).

Now, the triangle A B C may be applied to the triangle D E F, or to D E G symmetrical with D E F, just as two rectilineal triangles are applied to each other, when they have an equal angle included between equal sides. Hence, all the parts of the triangle A B C will be equal to all the parts of the triangle D E F, each to each; that is, besides the three parts equal by hypothesis, we shall have the side B C equal to E F, the angle A B C equal to D E F, and the angle A C B equal to D F E.

550. *Cor.* If two triangles, A B C, D E F, on the same sphere, or on equal spheres, have two angles and the included side in the one equal to two angles and the included side in the other, each to each, the two triangles are equal in all their parts.

For one of these triangles, or the triangle symmetrical with it, may be applied to the other, as is done in the corresponding case of rectilineal triangles.

Proposition XV. — Theorem.

551. *In every isosceles spherical triangle, the angles opposite the equal sides are equal; and, conversely, if two angles of a spherical triangle are equal, the triangle is isosceles.*

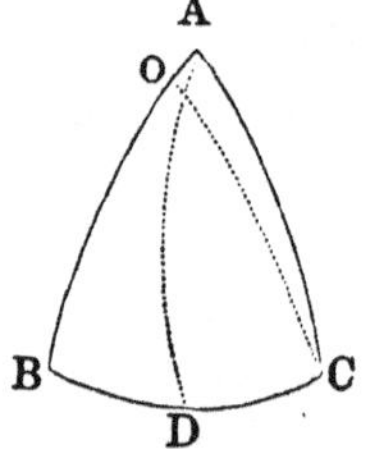

Let A B C be an isosceles spherical triangle, in which the side A B is equal to the side A C; then will the angle B be equal to the angle C.

For, if the arc A D be drawn from the vertex A to the middle point, D, of the base, the two triangles A B D, A C D will have all the sides of the one respectively equal to the corresponding sides of the other, namely, A D common, B D equal to D C, and A B equal to A C; hence their angles must be equal; consequently, the angles B and C are equal.

Conversely. Let the angles B and C be equal; then will the side A C be equal to A B.

For, if A C and A B are not equal, let A B be the greater of the two; take B O equal to A C, and draw O C. The two sides B O, B C in the triangle B O C are equal to the two sides A B, B C in the triangle B A C; the angle O B C, contained by the first two, is equal to A C B, contained by the second two. Hence, the two triangles B O C, B A C have all their other parts equal (Prop. XIV. Cor.); hence the angle O C B is equal to A B C. But, by hypothesis, the angle A B C is equal to A C B; hence we have O C B equal to A C B, which is impossible; therefore A B cannot be unequal to A C; consequently the sides A B, A C, opposite the equal angles B and C, are equal.

552. *Cor.* The angle B A D is equal to D A C, and the angle B D A is equal to A D C; the last two are therefore right angles; hence the arc drawn from the vertex of an isosceles spherical triangle to the middle of the base, is perpendicular to the base, and bisects the vertical angle.

PROPOSITION XVI. — THEOREM.

553. *In a spherical triangle, the greater side is opposite the greater angle; and, conversely, the greater angle is opposite the greater side.*

In the triangle A B C, let the angle A be greater than B; then will the side B C, opposite to A, be greater than A C, opposite to B.

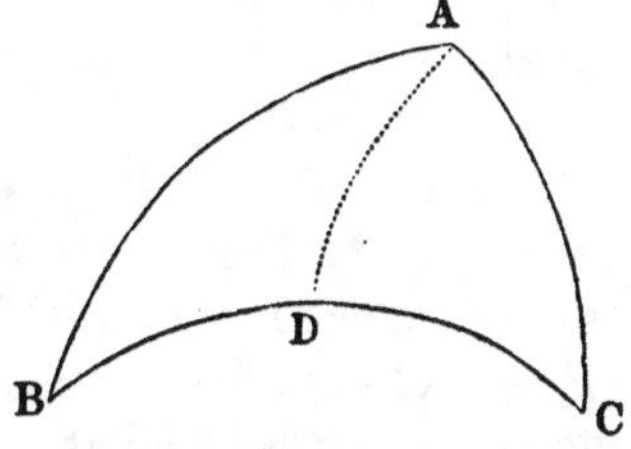

Take the angle B A D equal to the angle B; then, in the triangle A B D, we shall have the side A D equal to D B (Prop. XV.). But the sum of A D plus D C is greater than A C; hence, putting D B in the place of A D, we shall have the sum of D B plus D C, or B C, greater than A C.

Conversely. Let the side B C be greater than A C; then the angle B A C will be greater than A B C. For, if B A C were equal to A B C, we should have B C equal to A C; and if B A C were less than A B C, we should then have, as has just been shown, B C less than A C. Both of these results are contrary to the hypothesis; hence the angle B A C is greater than A B C.

PROPOSITION XVII. — THEOREM.

554. *If two triangles on the same sphere, or on equal spheres, are mutually equilateral, they are equivalent.*

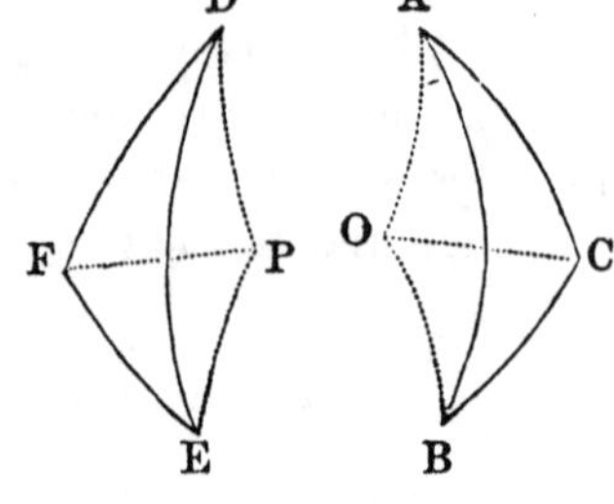

Let A B C, D E F be two triangles, having the three sides of the one equal to the three sides of the other, each to each, namely, A B to D E, A C to D F, and C B to E F; then their triangles will be equivalent.

Let O be the pole of the small circle passing through the three points A, B, C; draw the arcs O A, O B, O C, and they will all be equal (Prop. V. Sch.). At the point F make the angle D F P equal to A C O; make the arc F P equal to C O; and draw D P, E P.

The sides D F, F P are equal to the sides A C, C O, and the angle D F P is equal to the angle A C O; hence the two triangles D F P, A C O are equal in all their parts (Prop. XIV.); hence the side D P is equal to A O, and the angle D P F is equal to A O C.

In the triangles D F E, A B C, the angles D F E, A C B, opposite to the equal sides D E, A B, are equal (Prop. XII.). Taking away the equal angles D F P, A C O, there will remain the angle P F E, equal to O C B. The sides P F, F E are equal to the sides O C, C B; hence the two triangles F P E, C O B are equal in all their parts (Prop. XIV.); hence the side PE is equal to O B, and the angle F P E is equal to C O B.

Now, the triangles D F P, A C O, which have the sides equal, each to each, are at the same time isosceles, and may be applied the one to the other. For, having placed O A upon its equal P D, the side O C will fall on its equal P F, and thus the two triangles will coincide; consequently they are equal, and the surface D P F is equal to A O C. For a like reason, the surface F P E is equal to C O B, and the surface D P E is equal to A O B; hence we have

$$AOC + COB - AOB = DPF + FPE - DPE,$$

or, $$ABC = DEF.$$

Hence the two triangles A B C, D E F are equivalent.

555. *Cor.* 1. If two triangles on the same sphere, or on equal spheres, are mutually equiangular, they are equivalent. For in that case the triangles will be mutually equilateral.

556. *Cor.* 2. Hence, also, if two triangles on the same sphere, or on equal spheres, have two sides and the included angle, or have two angles and the included side, in the one equal to those in the other, the two triangles are equivalent.

557. *Scholium.* The poles O and P might lie within the triangles A B C, D E F; in which case it would be requisite to add the three triangles D P F, F P E, D P E together, to form the triangle D E F; and in like manner to add the three triangles A O C, C O B, A O B together, to form the triangle A B C; in all other respects the demonstration would be the same.

Proposition XVIII. — Theorem.

558. *The area of a lune is to the surface of the sphere as the angle of the lune is to four right angles, or as the arc which measures that angle is to the circumference.*

Let A C B D be a lune upon a sphere whose diameter is A B; then will the area of the lune be to the surface of the sphere as the angle D O C to four right angles, or as the arc D C to the circumference of a great circle.

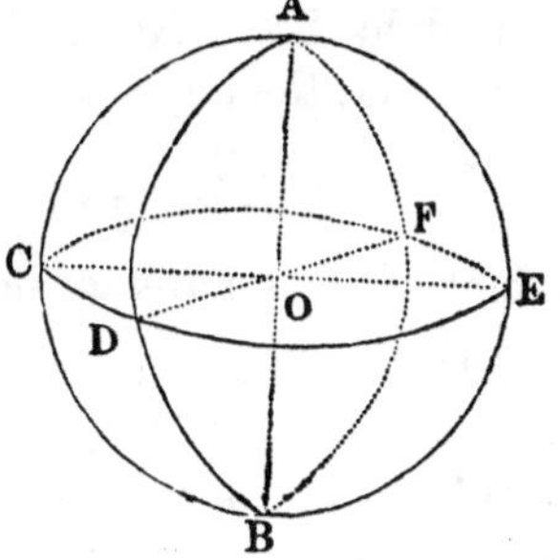

For, suppose the arc C D to be to the circumference C D E F in the ratio of two whole numbers, as 5 to 48, for example.

Then, if the circumference C D E F be divided into 48 equal parts, C D will contain 5 of them; and if the pole A be joined with the several points of division by as many quadrants, we shall have 48 triangles on the surface of the hemisphere ACDEF, all equal, since all their parts are equal. Hence, the whole sphere must contain 96 of these triangles, and the lune A C B D 10 of them; consequently, the lune is to the sphere as 10 is to 96, or as 5 to 48; that is, as the arc C D is to the circumference.

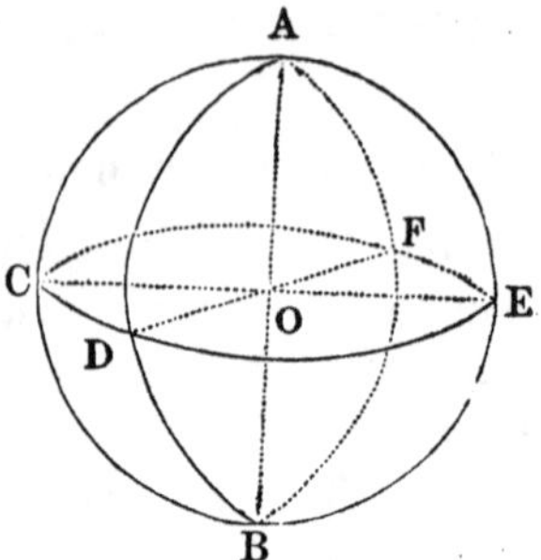

If the arc C D is not commensurable with the circumference, it may still be shown, by a mode of reasoning exemplified in Prop. XVI. Bk. III., that the lune is to the sphere as C D is to the circumference.

559. *Cor.* 1. Two lunes on the same sphere, or on equal spheres, are to each other as the angles included between their planes.

560. *Cor.* 2. It has been shown that the whole surface of the sphere is equal to eight quadrantal triangles (Prop. X. Sch.). Hence, if the area of a quadrantal triangle be represented by T, the surface of the sphere will be represented by 8 T. Now, if the right angle be assumed as unity, and the angle of the lune be represented by A, we have,

$$\text{Area of the lune} : 8\,T :: A : 4,$$

which gives the area of lune equal to $2\,A \times T$.

561. *Cor.* 3. The spherical ungula included by the planes A C B, A D B, is to the whole sphere as the angle D O C is to four right angles. For, the lunes being equal, the spherical ungulas will also be equal; hence, two spherical ungulas on the same sphere, or on equal spheres,

are to each other as the angles included between their planes.

PROPOSITION XIX.—THEOREM.

562. *If two great circles intersect each other on the surface of a hemisphere, the sum of the opposite triangles thus formed is equivalent to a lune, whose angle is equal to the angle formed by the circles.*

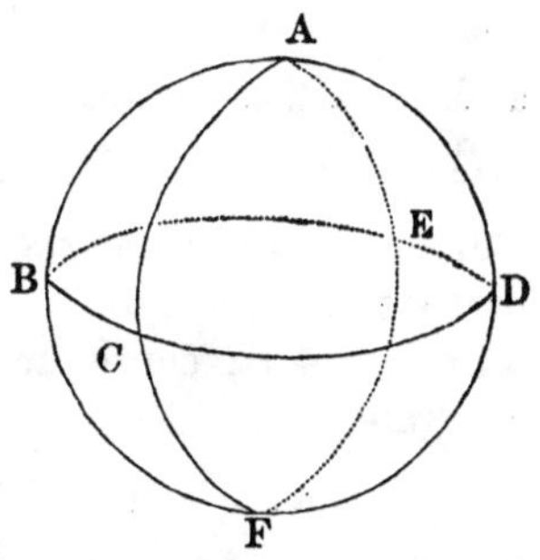

Let the great circles B A D, C A E intersect on the surface of a hemisphere, A B C D E; then will the sum of the opposite triangles, B A C, D A E, be equal to a lune whose angle is D A E.

For, produce the arcs A D, A E till they meet in F; and the arcs B A D, A D F will each be a semi-circumference. Now, if we take away A D from both, we shall have D F equal to B A. For a like reason, we have E F equal to C A. D E is equal to B C. Hence, the two triangles B A C, D E F are mutually equilateral; therefore they are equivalent (Prop. XVII.). But the sum of the triangles D E F, D A E is equivalent to the lune A D F E, whose angle is D A E.

PROPOSITION XX.—THEOREM.

563. *The area of a spherical triangle is equal to the excess of the sum of its three angles above two right angles, multiplied by the quadrantal triangle.*

Let A B C be a spherical triangle; its area is equal to the excess of the sum of its angles, A, B, C, above two right angles multiplied by the quadrantal triangle.

For produce the sides of the triangle A B C till they

meet the great circle DEFGHI, drawn without the triangle. The two triangles ADE, AGH are together equivalent to the lune whose angle is A (Prop. XIX.), and whose area is expressed by $2A \times T$ (Prop. XVIII. Cor. 2). Hence we have

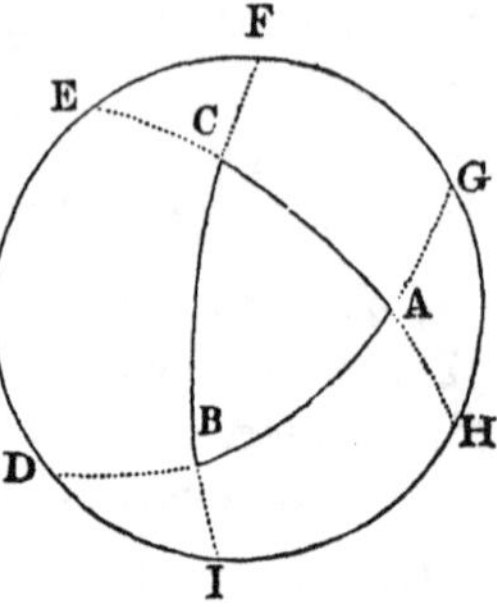

$$ADE + AGH = 2A \times T;$$

and, for a like reason,

$$BGF + BID = 2B \times T, \text{ and } CIH + CFE = 2C \times T.$$

But the sum of these six triangles exceeds the hemisphere by twice the triangle ABC; and the hemisphere is represented by $4T$; consequently, twice the triangle ABC is equivalent to

$$2A \times T + 2B \times T + 2C \times T - 4T;$$

therefore, once the triangle ABC is equivalent to

$$(A + B + C - 2) \times T.$$

Hence the area of a spherical triangle is equal to the excess of the sum of its three angles above two right angles multiplied by the quadrantal triangle.

564. *Cor.* If the sum of the three angles of a spherical triangle is equal to three right angles, its area is equal to the quadrantal triangle, or to an eighth part of the surface of the sphere; if the sum is equal to four right angles, the area of the triangle is equal to two quadrantal triangles, or to a fourth part of the surface of the sphere, &c.

PROPOSITION XXI. — THEOREM.

565. *The area of a spherical polygon is equal to the excess of the sum of all its angles above two right angles taken as many times as the polygon has sides, less two, multiplied by the quadrantal triangle.*

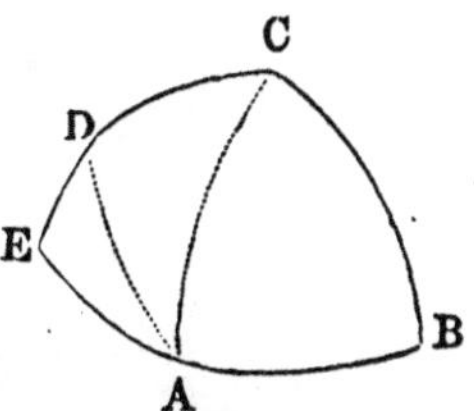

Let A B C D E be any spherical polygon. From one of the vertices, A, draw the arcs A C, A D to the opposite vertices; the polygon will be divided into as many spherical triangles as it has sides less two. But the area of each of these triangles is equal to the excess of the sum of its three angles above two right angles multiplied by the quadrantal triangle (Prop. XX.); and the sum of the angles in all the triangles is evidently the same as that of all the angles in the polygon; hence the area of the polygon A B C D E is equal to the excess of the sum of all its angles above two right angles taken as many times as the polygon has sides, less two, multiplied by the quadrantal triangle.

566. *Cor.* If the sum of all the angles of a spherical polygon be denoted by S, the number of sides by n, the quadrantal triangle by T, and the right angle be regarded as *unity*, the area of the polygon will be expressed by

$$\overline{S - 2(n-2)} \times T = (S - 2n + 4) \times T.$$

BOOK X.

THE THREE ROUND BODIES.

DEFINITIONS.

567. A CYLINDER is a solid, which may be described by the revolution of a rectangle turning about one of its sides, which remains immovable; as the solid described by the rectangle A B C D revolving about its side A B.

The BASES of the cylinder are the circles described by the sides, A C, B D, of the revolving rectangle, which are adjacent to the immovable side, A B.

The AXIS of the cylinder is the straight line joining the centres of its two bases; as the immovable line A B.

The CONVEX SURFACE of the cylinder is described by the side C D of the rectangle, opposite to the axis A B.

568. A CONE is a solid which may be described by the revolution of a right-angled triangle turning about one of its perpendicular sides, which remains immovable; as the solid described by the right-angled triangle A B C revolving about its perpendicular side A B.

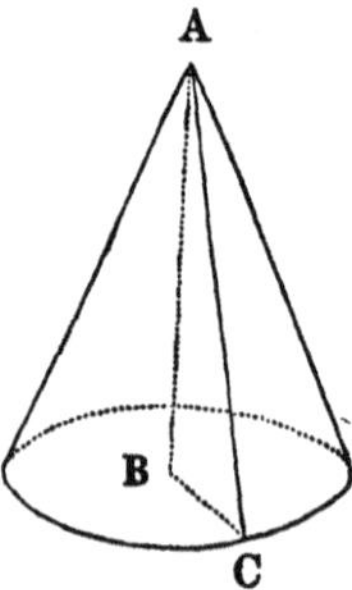

The BASE of the cone is the circle described by the revolution of the side B C, which is perpendicular to the immovable side.

The CONVEX SURFACE of a cone is described by the hypothenuse, A C, of the revolving triangle.

The VERTEX of the cone is the point A, where the hypothenuse meets the immovable side.

The AXIS of the cone is the straight line joining the vertex to the centre of the base ; as the line A B.

The ALTITUDE of a cone is a line drawn from the vertex perpendicular to the base; and is the same as the axis, A B.

The SLANT HEIGHT, or SIDE, of a cone, is a straight line drawn from the vertex to the circumference of the base ; as the line A C.

569. The FRUSTUM of a cone is the part of a cone included between the base and a plane parallel to the base ; as the solid C D – F.

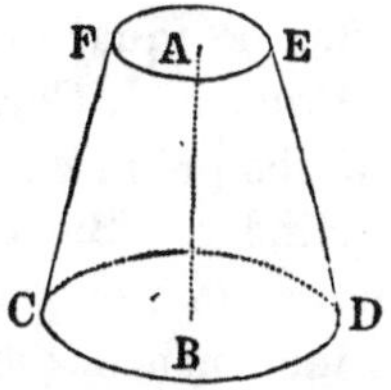

The AXIS, or ALTITUDE, of the frustum, is the perpendicular line A B included between the two bases; and the SLANT HEIGHT, or SIDE, is that portion of the slant height of the cone which lies between the bases ; as F C.

570. SIMILAR CYLINDERS, or CONES, are those whose axes are to each other as the radii, or diameters, of their bases.

571. The sphere, cylinder, and cone are termed the THREE ROUND BODIES of elementary Geometry.

PROPOSITION I. — THEOREM.

572. *The convex surface of a cylinder is equal to the circumference of its base multiplied by its altitude.*

Let A B C D E F – G be a cylinder, whose circumference is the circle A B C D E F, and whose altitude is the line A G; then its convex surface is equal to A B C D E F multiplied by A G.

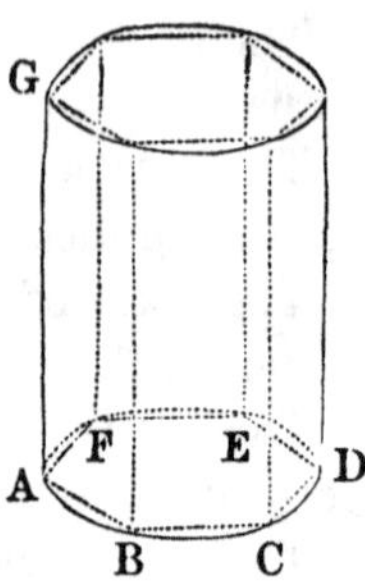

In the base of the cylinder inscribe any regular polygon, A B C D E F, and on this polygon construct a right prism of the same altitude with the cylinder. The prism will be inscribed in the convex surface of the cylinder. The convex surface of this prism is equal to the perimeter of its base multiplied by its altitude, A G (Prop. I. Bk. VIII.).

Conceive now the arcs subtending the sides of the polygon to be continually bisected, until a polygon is formed having an indefinite number of sides; its perimeter will then be equal to the circumference of the circle ABCDEF (Prop. XII. Cor., Bk. VI.); and thus the convex surface of the prism will coincide with the convex surface of the cylinder. But the convex surface of the prism is always equal to the perimeter of its base multiplied by its altitude; hence, the convex surface of the cylinder is equal to the circumference of its base multiplied by its altitude.

573. *Cor.* 1. If two cylinders have the same altitude, their convex surfaces are to each other as the circumferences of their bases.

574. *Cor.* 2. If H represent the altitude of a cylinder, and R the radius of its base, then we shall have the circumference of the base represented by $2\,R \times \pi$ (Prop. XV. Cor. 3, Bk. VI.), and the convex surface of the cylinder by $2\,R \times \pi \times H$.

Proposition II. — Theorem.

575. *The solid contents of a cylinder are equal to the product of its base by its altitude.*

Let A B C D E F - G be a cylinder whose base is the circle A B C D E F, and whose altitude is the line A G; then its solid contents are equal to the product of A B C D E F by A G.

In the base of the cylinder inscribe any regular polygon, A B C D E F, and on this polygon construct a right prism of the same altitude with the cylinder. The prism will be inscribed in the convex surface of the cylinder. The solid contents of this prism are equal to the product of its base by its altitude (Prop. XIII. Bk. VIII.).

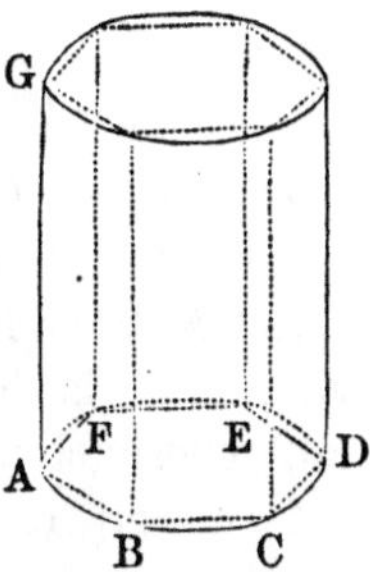

Conceive now the number of the sides of the polygon to be indefinitely increased, until its perimeter coincides with the circumference of the circle A B C D E F (Prop. XII. Cor., Bk. VI.), and the solid contents of the prism will equal those of the cylinder. But the solid contents of the prism will still be equal to the product of its base by its altitude; hence the solid contents of the cylinder are equal to the product of its base by its altitude.

576. *Cor.* 1. Cylinders of the same altitude are to each other as their bases; and cylinders of equal bases are to each other as their altitudes.

577. *Cor.* 2. Similar cylinders are to each other as the cubes of their altitudes, or as the cubes of the diameters of their bases. For the bases are as the squares of their radii (Prop. XIII. Bk. VI.), and the cylinders being similar, the radii of their bases are to each other as their altitudes (Art. 570); therefore the bases are as the squares of the altitudes; hence, the products of the bases by the altitudes, or the cylinders themselves, are as the cubes of the altitudes.

578. *Cor.* 3. If the altitude of a cylinder be represented by H, and the area of its base by $R^2 \times \pi$ (Prop. XV. Cor. 2, Bk. VI.), the solid contents of the cylinder will be represented by $R^2 \times \pi \times H$.

PROPOSITION III. — THEOREM.

579. *The convex surface of a cone is equal to the circumference of the base multiplied by half the slant height.*

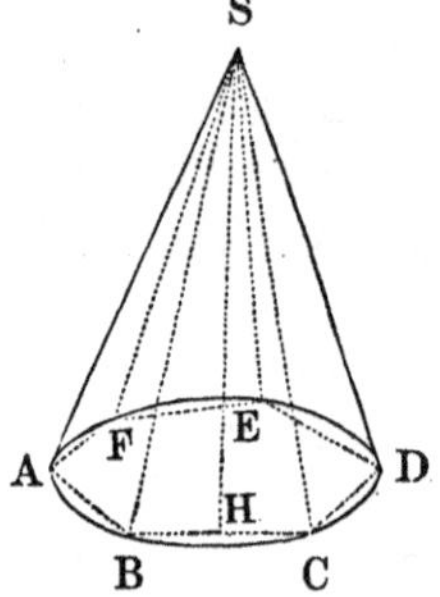

Let A B C D E F–S be a cone whose base is the circle A B C D E F, and whose slant height is the line S A; then its convex surface is equal to A B C D E F multiplied by $\frac{1}{2}$ S A.

In the base of the cone inscribe any regular polygon, A B C D E F, and on this polygon construct a regular pyramid having the same vertex, S, with the cone. Then a right pyramid will be inscribed in the cone.

From S draw S H perpendicular to B C, a side of the polygon. The convex surface of the pyramid is equal to the perimeter of its base, multiplied by half its slant height, S H (Prop. XV. Bk. VIII.). Conceive now the arcs subtending the sides of the polygon to be continually bisected, until a polygon is formed having an indefinite number of sides; its perimeter will equal the circumference of the circle A B C D E F; its slant height, S H, will equal that of the cone, and its convex surface coincide with the convex surface of the cone. But the convex surface of every right pyramid is equal to the perimeter of its base, multiplied by half the slant height; hence the convex surface of the cone is equal to the circumference of its base multiplied by half its slant height.

580. *Cor.* If S A represent the slant height of a cone, and R the radius of the base, then, since the circumference of the base is represented by $2\,R \times \pi$ (Prop. XV. Cor. 3, Bk. VI.), the convex surface of the cone will be represented by $2\,R \times \pi \times \frac{1}{2}\,S\,A$, equal to $\pi \times R \times S\,A$.

Proposition IV. — Theorem.

581. *The convex surface of a frustum of a cone is equal to half the sum of the circumference of the two bases multiplied by its slant height.*

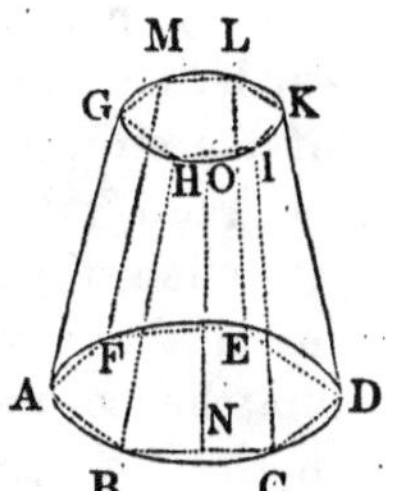

Let A B C D E F – M be the frustum of a cone, and A G its slant height; then the convex surface is equal to half the sum of the circumferences of the two bases A B C D E F, G H I K L M, multiplied by A G.

For, inscribe in the bases of the frustum two regular polygons of the same number of sides, having their sides parallel, each to each. Draw the straight lines A G, B H, C I, &c., joining the vertices of the corresponding angles, and these lines will be the edges of the frustum of a pyramid inscribed in the frustum of the cone. The convex surface of the frustum of the pyramid is equal to half the sum of the perimeters of the two bases multiplied by its slant height, O N (Prop. XVII. Bk. VIII.).

Conceive now the number of sides of the inscribed polygons to be indefinitely increased; the perimeters of the polygons will then coincide with the circumferences of the circles A B C D E F, G H I K L M; and the slant height, O N, of the frustum of the pyramid, will equal the slant height, A G, of the frustum of the cone; and the surfaces of the two frustums will coincide.

But the convex surface of every frustum of a right pyramid is equal to half the sum of the perimeters of its two bases, multiplied by its slant height; hence, the convex surface of the frustum of the cone is equal to half the sum of the circumference of its two bases multiplied by half its slant height.

582. *Cor.* Through R, the middle point of the side K D,

draw the diameter R S T, parallel to the diameter A Q D, and the straight lines R U, K V, parallel to the axis P Q. Then, since D R is equal to R K, D U is equal to U V (Prop. XVII. Cor. 2, Bk. IV.); hence, the radius S R is equal to half the sum of the radii Q D, P K.

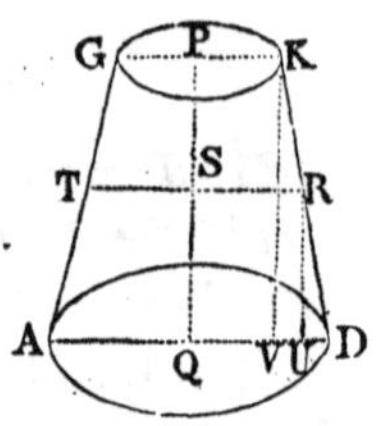

But the circumferences of circles being to each other as their radii (Prop. XIII. Bk. VI.), the circumference of the section of which S R is the radius is equal to half the sum of the circumferences of which Q D, P K are the radii; hence, the convex surface of a frustum of a cone is equal to the slant height multiplied by the circumference of a section at equal distances between the two bases.

Proposition V. — Theorem.

583. *The solidity of a cone is equal to the product of its base by one third of its altitude.*

Let A B C D E F - S be a cone, whose base is A B C D E F, and altitude S H; then its solidity is equal to A B C D E F × $\frac{1}{3}$ S H.

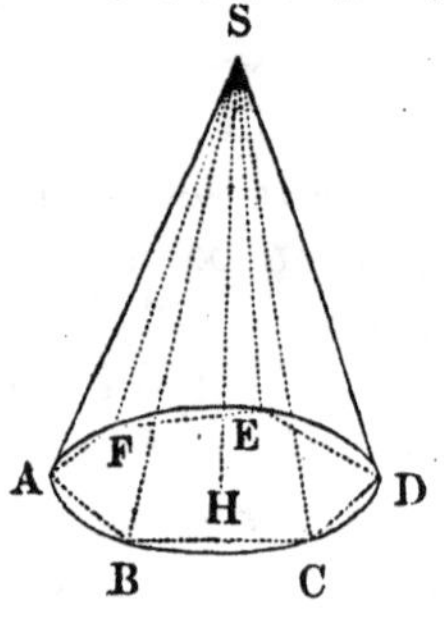

In the base of the cone inscribe any regular polygon, A B C D E F, and on this polygon construct a regular pyramid, having the same vertex, S, with the cone. Then a right pyramid will be inscribed in the cone; and its solidity will be equal to the product of its base by one third of its altitude (Prop. XX. Bk. VIII.).

Conceive, now, the number of sides of the polygon to be indefinitely increased, and its perimeter will become equal to the circumference of the cone, and the pyramid will exactly coincide with the cone. But the solidity of every right pyramid is equal to the product of the base by one third of its altitude; hence, the solidity of a cone is equal to the product of its base by one third of its altitude.

584. *Cor.* 1. A cone is the third of a cylinder having the same base and the same altitude; hence it follows, —

1. That cones of equal altitudes are to each other as their bases;

2. That cones of equal bases are to each other as their altitudes;

3. That similar cones are as the cubes of the diameters of their bases, or as the cubes of their altitudes.

585. *Cor.* 2. If the altitude of a cone be represented by H, and the radius of its base by R, the solidity of the cone will be represented by

$$R^2 \times \pi \times \tfrac{1}{3} H, \quad \text{or} \quad \tfrac{1}{3} \pi \times R^2 \times H.$$

PROPOSITION VI. — THEOREM.

586. *The solidity of the frustum of a cone is equivalent to the sum of three cones, having for their common altitude the altitude of the frustum, and whose bases are the two bases of the frustum, and a mean proportional between them.*

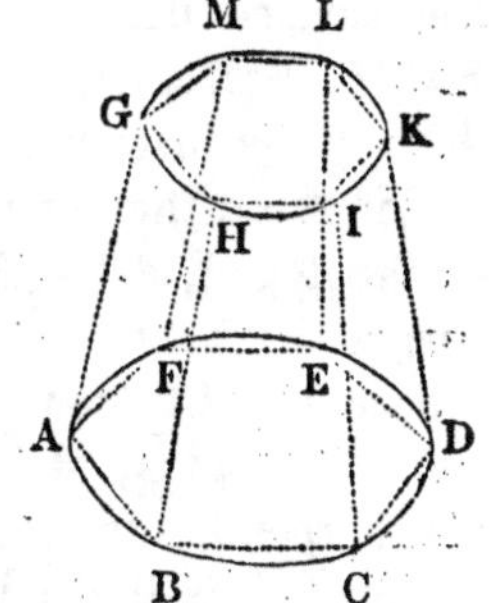

Let A B C D E F – M be the frustum of a cone; then will its solidity be equivalent to the sum of three cones having the same altitude as the frustum, and whose bases are the two bases of the frustum, and a mean proportional between them.

For, inscribe in the two bases of the frustum two regular polygons having the same number of sides, and having their sides parallel, each to each. Let the vertices of the corresponding angles be joined by the straight lines B H, C I, &c., and there is inscribed in the frustum of the cone the frustum of a regular pyramid. The solidity of the frustum of this pyramid is equivalent to the sum of three pyramids, having for their common altitude the altitude of the frustum, and whose bases are the two bases of the frustum, and a mean proportional between them.

Conceive now the number of the sides of the polygons to be indefinitely increased; and the bases of the frustum of the pyramid will equal the bases of the frustum of the cone; and the two frustums will coincide. Hence the frustum of a cone is equivalent to the sum of three cones, having for their common altitude the altitude of the frustum, and whose bases are the two bases of the frustum, and a mean proportional between them.

Proposition VII. — Theorem.

587. *If any regular semi-polygon be revolved about a line passing through the center and the vertices of opposite angles, the surface described will be equal to the product of its axis by the circumference of its inscribed circle.*

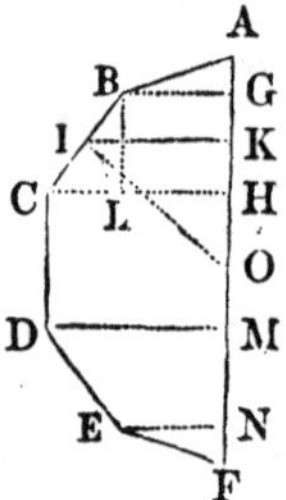

Let the regular semi-polygon ABCDEF be revolved about AF as an axis; then the surface described by the sides AB, BC, CD, &c. will equal the product of AF by the inscribed circle.

For, from the vertices B, C, D, E of the semi-polygon, draw BG, CH, DM, EN, perpendicular to the axis AF; and from the center, O, draw OI perpendicular to one of the sides; also draw IK perpendicular to AF, and BL perpendicular to CH.

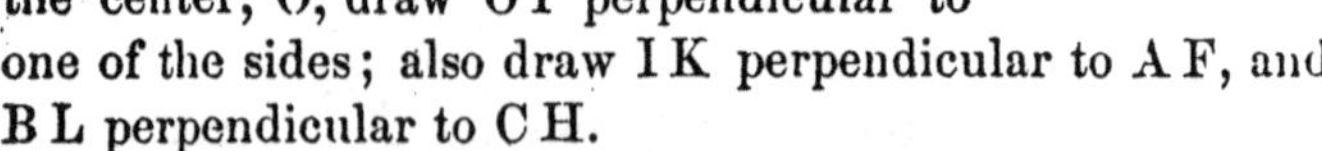

Now OI is the radius of the inscribed circle (Prop. II. Bk. VI.); and the surface described by the revolution of a side, BC, of a regular polygon, is equal to BC multiplied by the circumference, IK (Prop. IV. Cor.).

The two triangles O I K, B C L, having their sides perpendicular to each other, are similar (Prop. XXV. Bk. IV.); therefore,

B C : B L or G H : : O I : I K : : *Circ.* O I : *Circ.* I K.

Hence (Prop. I. Bk. II.),

$$\text{B C} \times \textit{Circ.}\ \text{I K} = \text{G H} \times \textit{Circ.}\ \text{O I};$$

that is, the surface described by B C is equal to the product of the altitude G H by the circumference of the inscribed circle. The same may be shown of each of the other sides; hence, the surface described by all the sides taken together is equal to the product of the sum of the altitudes A G, G H, H M, M N, N F, by the circ. O I, or to the product of the axis A F by the circ. O I.

Proposition VIII. — Theorem.

588. *The surface of a sphere is equal to the product of its diameter by the circumference of a great circle.*

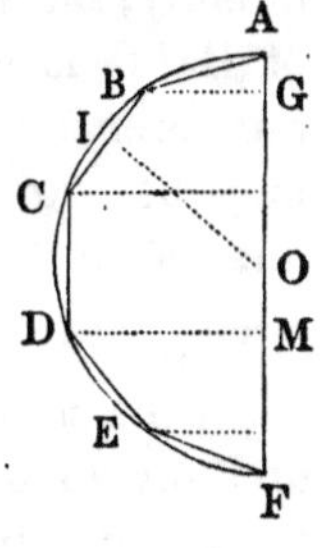

Let A B C D E F be a semicircle in which is inscribed any regular semi-polygon; from the center, O, draw O I perpendicular to one of the sides.

If now the semicircle and the semi-polygon be revolved about the axis A F, the surface described by the semicircle will be the surface of a sphere (Art. 497), and that described by the semi-polygon will be equal to the product of its axis, A F, by the circumference, O I (Prop. VII.); and the same is true, whatever be the number of sides of the polygon.

Conceive the number of sides of the semi-polygon to be made, by continual bisections, indefinitely great; then its perimeter will coincide with the semi-circumference A B C D E F, and the perpendicular O I will be equal to the radius O A; hence, the surface of the sphere is equal to the product of the diameter by the circumference of a great circle.

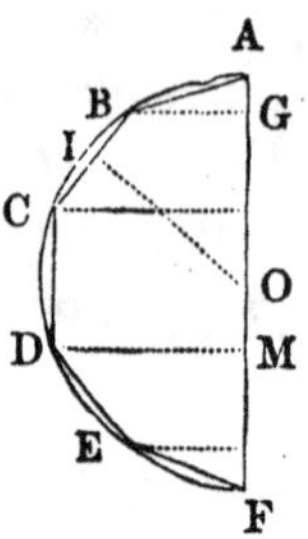

589. *Cor.* 1. *The surface of a sphere is equal to the area of four of its great circles.*

For the area of a circle is equal to the product of the circumference by half the radius, or one fourth of the diameter (Prop. XV. Bk. VI.).

590. *Cor.* 2. *The surface of a zone or segment is equal to the product of its altitude by the circumference of a great circle.*

For the surface described by the sides B C, C D of the inscribed polygon is equal to the product of the altitude G M by the circumference of the inscribed circle O I. If, now, the number of the sides of an inscribed polygon be indefinitely increased, its perimeter will equal the circle, and B C, C D will coincide with the arc B C D; consequently, the surface of the zone described by the revolution of B C D is equal to the product of its altitude by the circumference of a great circle. In like manner, the same may be proved true of a segment, or a zone having but one base.

591. *Cor.* 3. The surfaces of two zones, or segments upon the same sphere, are to each other as their altitudes; and any zone or segment is to the surface of the sphere as the altitude of that zone or segment is to the diameter.

592. *Cor.* 4. If the radius of a sphere is represented by R, and its diameter by D, its surface will be represented by

$$4\pi \times R^2, \quad \text{or} \quad \pi \times D^2.$$

593. *Cor.* 5. Hence, the surfaces of spheres are to each other as the squares of their radii or diameters.

594. *Cor.* 6. If the altitude of a zone or segment is

represented by H, the surface of a zone or segment will be represented by

$$2\pi \times R \times H, \quad \text{or} \quad \pi \times D \times H.$$

PROPOSITION IX. — THEOREM.

595. *The solidity of a sphere is equal to the product of its surface by one third of its radius.*

For a sphere may be regarded as composed of an indefinite number of pyramids, each having for its base a part of the surface of the sphere, and for its vertex the center of the sphere; consequently, all these pyramids have the radius of the sphere as their common altitude.

Now, the solidity of every pyramid is equal to the product of its base by one third of its altitude (Prop. XX. Bk. VIII.); hence, the sum of the solidities of these pyramids is equal to the product of the sum of their bases by one third of their common altitude. But the sum of their bases is the surface of the sphere, and their common altitude its radius; consequently, the solidity of the sphere is equal to the product of its surface by one third of its radius.

596. *Cor.* 1. *The solidity of a spherical pyramid or sector is equal to the product of the polygon or zone which forms its base, by one third of the radius.*

For the polygon or zone forming the base of the spherical pyramid or sector may be regarded as composed of an indefinite number of planes, each serving as a base to a pyramid, having for its vertex the centre of the sphere.

597. *Cor.* 2. Spherical pyramids, or sectors of the same sphere or of equal spheres, are to each other as their bases.

598. *Cor.* 3. A spherical pyramid or sector is to the sphere of which it is a part, as its base is to the surface of the sphere.

599. *Cor.* 4. Hence, spherical sectors upon the same

sphere are to each other as the altitudes of the zones forming their bases (Prop. VIII. Cor. 3); and any spherical sector is to the sphere as the altitude of the zone forming its base is to the diameter of the sphere.

600. *Cor.* 5. If the radius of a sphere is represented by R, its diameter by D, and its surface by S, its solidity will be represented by

$$S \times \tfrac{1}{3} R = 4 \pi \times R^2 \times \tfrac{1}{3} R = \tfrac{4}{3} \pi \times R^3 \text{ or } \tfrac{1}{6} \pi \times D^3.$$

601. *Cor* 6. Hence, the solidities of spheres are to each other as the cubes of their radii.

602. *Cor.* 7. If the altitude of the zone which forms the base of a sector be represented by H, the solidity of the sector will be represented by

$$2 \pi \times R \times H \times \tfrac{1}{3} R = \tfrac{2}{3} \pi \times R^2 \times H.$$

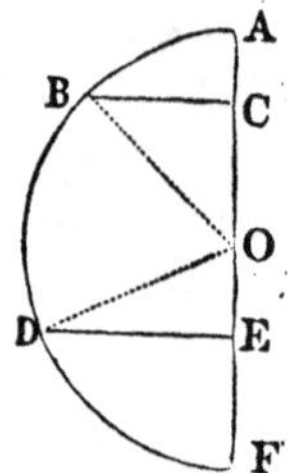

603. *Scholium.* The solidity of the spherical segment less than a hemisphere, and of one base, formed by the revolution of a portion, A B C, of a semicircle about the radius O A, is equivalent to the solidity of the spherical sector formed by A O B, less the solidity of the cone formed by O B C.

The solidity of the spherical segment greater than a hemisphere, and of one base, formed by the revolution of A D E, is equivalent to the solidity of the spherical sector formed by A O D, plus the solidity of the cone formed by O D E.

The solidity of the spherical segment of two bases formed by the revolution of C B D E about the axis A F, is equivalent to the solidity of the segment formed by A D E, less the solidity of the segment formed by A B C.

Proposition X.—Theorem.

604. *The surface of a sphere is equivalent to the convex surface of the circumscribed cylinder, and is two thirds*

of the whole surface of the cylinder; also, the solidity of the sphere is two thirds of that of the circumscribed cylinder.

Let ABFI be a great circle of the sphere; DEGH the circumscribed square; then, if the semicircle ABF and the semi-square ADEF be revolved about the diameter AF, the semicircle will describe a sphere, and the semi-square a cylinder circumscribing the sphere.

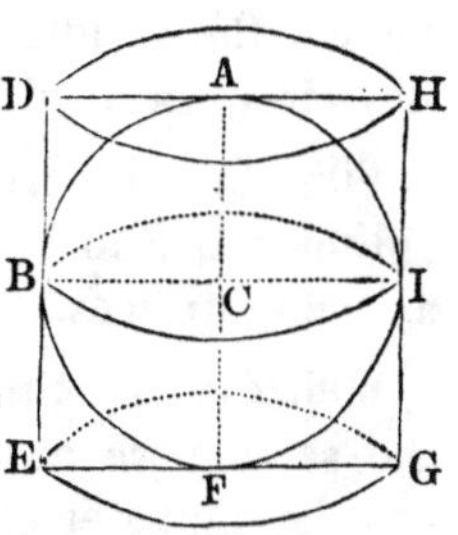

The convex surface of the cylinder is equal to the circumference of its base multiplied by its altitude (Prop. I.). But the base of the cylinder is equal to the great circle of the sphere, its diameter EG being equal to the diameter BI, and the altitude DE is equal to the diameter AF; hence, the convex surface of the cylinder is equal to the circumference of the great circle multiplied by its diameter. This measure is the same as that of the surface of the sphere (Prop. VIII.); hence, the surface of the sphere is equal to the convex surface of the circumscribed cylinder.

But the surface of the sphere is equal to four great circles of the sphere (Prop. VIII. Cor. 1); hence, the convex surface of the cylinder is also equal to four great circles; and adding the two bases, each equal to a great circle, the whole surface of the circumscribed cylinder is equal to six great circles of the sphere; hence, the surface of the sphere is $\frac{4}{6}$ or $\frac{2}{3}$ of the whole surface of the circumscribed sphere.

In the next place, since the base of the circumscribed cylinder is equal to a great circle of the sphere, and its altitude to the diameter, the solidity of the cylinder is equal to a great circle multiplied by its diameter (Prop. II.). But the solidity of the sphere is equal to its surface, or four great circles, multiplied by one third of its radius (Prop. IX.), which is the same as one great circle multiplied by $\frac{4}{3}$ of the radius, or by $\frac{2}{3}$ of the diameter; hence, the solidity of the sphere is equal to $\frac{2}{3}$ of that of the circumscribed cylinder.

605. *Cor.* 1. Hence the sphere is to the circumscribed cylinder as 2 to 3; and their solidities are to each other as their surfaces.

606. *Cor.* 2. Since a cone is one third of a cylinder of the same base and altitude (Prop. V. Cor. 1), if a cone has the diameter of its base and its altitude each equal to the diameter of a given sphere, the solidities of the cone and sphere are to each other as 1 to 2; and the solidities of the cone, sphere, and circumscribing cylinder are to each other, respectively, as 1, 2, and 3.

BOOK XI.

APPLICATIONS OF GEOMETRY TO THE MENSURATION OF PLANE FIGURES.

DEFINITIONS.

607. MENSURATION OF PLANE FIGURES is the process of determining the areas of plane surfaces.

608. The AREA of a figure, or its quantity of surface, is determined by the number of times the given surface contains some other area, assumed as the unit of measure.

609. The MEASURING UNIT assumed for a given surface is called the *superficial* unit, and is usually a *square*, taking its name from the *linear* unit forming its side; as a square whose side is 1 inch, 1 foot, 1 yard, &c.

Some superficial units, however, have no corresponding linear unit; as the rood, acre, &c.

610. TABLE OF LINEAR MEASURES.

12	Inches	make	1 Foot.
3	Feet	"	1 Yard.
$5\frac{1}{2}$	Yards	"	1 Rod or Pole.
40	Rods	"	1 Furlong.
8	Furlongs	"	1 Mile.

Also,

$7\frac{92}{100}$	Inches	"	1 Link.
25	Links	"	1 Rod or Pole.
100	Links	"	1 Chain.
10	Chains	"	1 Furlong.
8	Furlongs	"	1 Mile.

NOTE.—For other linear measures, see National Arithmetic, Art. 133, 134, 136.

611. TABLE OF SURFACE MEASURES.

144	Square Inches	make	1 Square Foot.
9	Square Feet	"	1 Square Yard.
$30\frac{1}{4}$	Square Yards	"	1 Square Rod or Pole.
40	Square Rods	"	1 Rood.
4	Roods	"	1 Acre.
640	Acres	"	1 Square Mile.

Also,

625	Square Links	"	1 Square Rod.
16	Square Rods	"	1 Square Chain.
10	Square Chains	"	1 Acre.

612. Since an acre is equal to 10 chains, or 100,000 links, square chains may be readily reduced to acres by pointing off one decimal place from the right, and square links by pointing off five decimal places from the right.

PROBLEM I.

613. To find the area of a PARALLELOGRAM.

Multiply the base by the altitude, and the product will be the area (Prop. V. Bk. IV.).

EXAMPLES.

D C

A B

1. What is the area of a square, A B C D, whose side is 25 feet?

$25 \times 25 = 625$ feet, Ans.

2. What is the area of a square field whose side is 35.25 chains? Ans. 124 A. 1 R. 1 P.

3. How many square feet of boards are required to lay a floor 21 ft. 6 in. square?

4. Required the area of a square farm, whose side is 3,525 links.

D C

A B

5. What is the area of the rectangle A B C D, whose length, A B, is 56 feet, and whose width, A D, is 37 feet?

$56 \times 37 = 2,072$ feet, Ans.

6. How many square feet in a plank, of a rectangular form, which is 18 feet long and 1 foot 6 inches wide?

7. How many acres in a rectangular garden, whose sides are 326 and 153 feet? Ans. 1 A. 23 P. $6\frac{1}{4}$ yd.

8. A rectangular court 68 ft. 3 in. long, by 56 ft. 8 in. broad, is to be paved with stones of a rectangular form, each 2 ft. 3 in. by 10 in.; how many stones will be required? Ans. $2{,}062\frac{2}{3}$ stones.

9. Required the area of the rhomboid A B C D, of which the side A B is 354 feet, and the perpendicular distance, E F, between A B and the opposite side C D, is 192 feet.

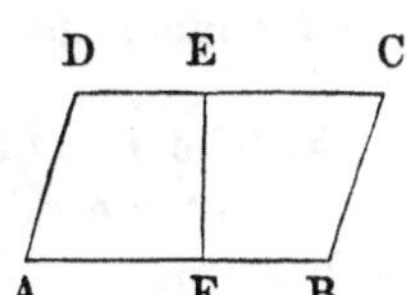

$$354 \times 192 = 67{,}968 \text{ feet, Ans.}$$

10. How many square feet in a flower-plat, in the form of a rhombus, whose side is 12 feet, and the perpendicular distance between two opposite sides of which is 8 feet?

11. How many acres in a rhomboidal field, of which the sides are 1,234 and 762 links, and the perpendicular distance between the longer sides of which is 658 links? Ans. 8 A. 19 P. 4 yd. $6\frac{1}{4}$ ft.

Problem II.

614. The area of a SQUARE being given, to find the side.

Extract the square root of the area.

Scholium. This and the two following problems are the converse of Prob. I.

Examples.

1. What is the side of a square containing 625 square feet?

$$\sqrt{625} = 25 \text{ feet, the side required.}$$

2. The area of a square farm is 124 A. 1 R. 1 P.; how many links in length is its side?

3. A certain corn-field in the form of a square contains

15 A. 2 R. 20 P. If the corn is planted on the margin, 4 hills to a rod in length, how many hills are there on the margin of the field? Ans. 800 hills.

PROBLEM III.

615. The area of a RECTANGLE and either of its sides being given, to find the other side.

Divide the area by the given side, and the quotient will be the other side.

EXAMPLES.

1. The area of a rectangle is 2,072 feet, and the length of one of the sides is 56 feet; what is the length of the other side?

$$2072 \div 56 = 37 \text{ feet, the side required.}$$

2. How long must a rectangular board be, which is 15 inches in width, to contain 11 square feet?

3. A rectangular piece of land containing 6 acres is 120 rods long; what is its width? Ans. 8 rods.

4. The area of a rectangular farm is 266 A. 3 R. 8 P., and the breadth 46 chains; what is the length? Ans. 58 chains.

PROBLEM IV.

616. The area of a RHOMBOID or RHOMBUS and the length of the base being given, to find the altitude; or the area and the altitude being given, to find the base.

Divide the area by the length of the base, and the quotient will be the altitude; or divide the area by the altitude, and the quotient will be the length of the base.

EXAMPLES.

1. The area of a rhomboid is 67,968 square feet, and the length of the side taken as its base 354 feet; what is the altitude?

$$67{,}968 \div 354 = 192 \text{ feet, the altitude required.}$$

2. The area of a piece of land in the form of a rhombus

is 69,452 square feet, and the perpendicular distance between two of its opposite sides is 194 feet; required the length of one of the equal sides. Ans. 358 ft.

3. On a base 12 feet in length it is required to find the altitude of a rhomboid containing 968 square feet.

4. The area of a rhomboidal-shaped park is 1 A. 3 R. 34 P. $5\frac{1}{4}$ yd.; and the perpendicular distance between the two shorter sides is 96 yards; required the length of each of these sides? Ans. 18 rods.

PROBLEM V.

617. The diagonal of a SQUARE being given, to find the area.

Divide the square of the diagonal by 2, and the quotient will be the area. (Prop. XI. Cor. 4, Bk. IV.)

EXAMPLES.

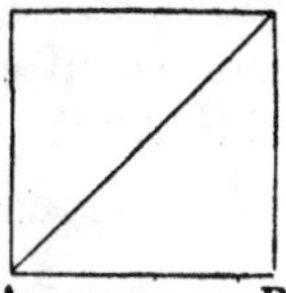

1. The diagonal, A C, of the square A B C D, is 30 feet; what is the area?

$30^2 = 900$; $900 \div 2 = 450$ square feet, [the area required.

D C A B

2. The diagonal of a square field is 45 chains; how many acres does it contain?

3. The distance across a public square diagonally is 27 rods; what is the area of the square?

PROBLEM VI.

618. The area of a SQUARE being given, to find the diagonal.

Extract the square root of double the area.

Scholium. This problem is the converse of the last.

EXAMPLES.

1. The area of a square is 450 square feet; what is its diagonal?

$450 \times 2 = 900$; $\sqrt{900} = 30$ feet, the diagonal required.

2. The area of a public square is 4 A. 2 R. 9 P.; what is the distance across it diagonally?

3. The area of a square farm is 57.8 acres; what is the diagonal in chains? Ans. 34 chains.

PROBLEM VII.

619. The sides of a RECTANGLE being given, to cut off a given area by a line parallel to either side.

Divide the given area by the side which is to retain its length or width, and the quotient will be the length or width of the part to be cut off. (Prop. IV. Sch., Bk. IV.)

EXAMPLES.

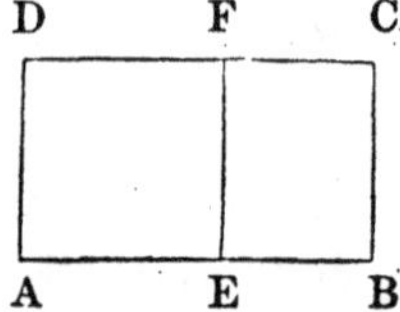

1. If the sides of a rectangle, ABCD, are 25 and 14 feet, how wide an area, EBCF, to contain 154 square feet, can be cut off by a line parallel to the side AD?

$$154 \div 14 = 11 \text{ feet, the width required.}$$

2. A farmer has a field 16 rods square, and wishes to cut off from one side a rectangular lot containing exactly one acre; what must be the width of the lot?

3. A carpenter sawed off, from the end of a rectangular plank, in a line parallel to its width, 5 square feet. From the remainder he then sawed off, in a line parallel to the length, 8 square feet. Required the dimensions of the part still remaining, provided the original dimensions of the plank were 20 feet by 15 inches.

Ans. 16 feet by 9 inches.

4. The length of a certain rectangular lot is 64 rods, and its width 50 rods; how far from the longer side must a parallel line be drawn to cut off an area of 4 acres, and how far from the shorter side of the remaining portion to cut off 5 acres and 2 roods? How many acres will remain after the two portions are cut off?

PROBLEM VIII.

620. To find the area of a TRIANGLE, the base and altitude being given.

Multiply the base by half the altitude (Prop. VI. Bk. IV.).

621. *Scholium.* The same result can be obtained by multiplying the altitude by half the base, or by multiplying together the base and altitude and taking half the product.

EXAMPLES.

1. Required the area of the triangle A B C, whose base, B C, is 210, and altitude, A D, is 190 feet.

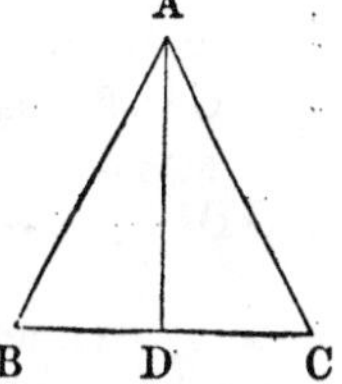

$210 \times \frac{190}{2} = 19{,}950$ square feet, the area required.

2. A piece of land is in the form of a right-angled triangle, having the sides about the right angle, the one 254 and the other 136 yards; required the area in acres.

Ans. 3 A. 2 R. 10 P. 29½ yd.

3. Required the number of square feet in a triangular board whose base is 27 inches and altitude 27 feet.

4. What is the area of a triangle whose base is 15.75 chains, and the altitude 10.22 chains?

5. What is the area of a triangular field whose base is 97 rods, and the perpendicular distance from the base to the opposite angle 40 rods? Ans. 12 A. 20 P.

PROBLEM IX.

622. To find the area of a TRIANGLE, the three sides being given.

From half the sum of the three sides subtract each

side; multiply the half sum and the three remainders together, and the square root of the product will be the area required.

For, let A B C be a triangle whose three sides, A B, B C, A C, are given, but not the altitude C D, and let the side B C be represented by a, A C by b, and A B by c.

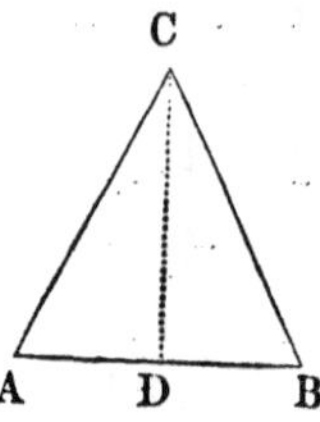

Now, since A is an acute angle of the triangle A B C, we have (Prop. XII. Bk. IV.),

$$a^2 = b^2 + c^2 - 2c \times \mathrm{AD}, \quad \text{or} \quad \mathrm{AD} = \frac{b^2 + c^2 - a^2}{2c}.$$

Hence, in the right-angled triangle A D C, we have (Prop. XI. Cor. 1, Bk. IV.),

$$\mathrm{CD}^2 = b^2 - \frac{(b^2 + c^2 - a^2)^2}{4c^2} = \frac{4b^2c^2 - (b^2 + c^2 - a^2)^2}{4c^2};$$

and, by extracting the square root,

$$\mathrm{CD} = \frac{\sqrt{4b^2c^2 - (b^2 + c^2 - a^2)^2}}{2c}.$$

But the area of the triangle A B C is equivalent to the product of c by half of C D (Prob. VIII.); hence

$$\mathrm{ABC} = \tfrac{1}{4}\sqrt{4b^2c^2 - (b^2 + c^2 - a^2)^2}.$$

The expression $4b^2c^2 - (b^2 + c^2 - a^2)^2$, being the difference of two squares, can be decomposed into

$$(2bc + b^2 + c^2 - a^2) \times (2bc - b^2 - c^2 + a^2).$$

Now, the first of these factors may be transformed to $(b + c)^2 - a^2$, and consequently may be resolved into $(b + c + a) \times (b + c - a)$; and the second is the same thing as $a^2 - (b - c)^2$, which is equal to $(a + b - c) \times (a - b + c)$. We have then

$$4b^2c^2 - (b^2 + c^2 - a^2)^2 = (a + b + c) \times (b + c - a) \times (a + c - b) \times (a + b - c).$$

Let S represent half the sum of the three sides of the triangle; then

$$a + b + c = 2\,S; \quad b + c - a = 2\,(S - a);$$
$$a + c - b = 2\,(S - b); \quad a + b - c = 2\,(S - c);$$

hence

$$ABC = \tfrac{1}{4}\sqrt{16\,S\,(S - a) \times (S - b) \times (S - c)},$$

which, being reduced, gives as the area of the triangle, as given above,

$$\sqrt{S\,(S - a) \times (S - b) \times (S - c)}.$$

EXAMPLES.

1. What is the area of a triangle, ABC, whose sides, AB, BC, CA, are 40, 30, and 50 feet?

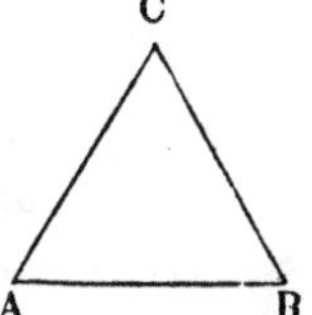

$\overline{30 + 40 + 50} \div 2 = 60$, half the sum of the three sides.
$60 - 30 = 30$, first remainder.
$60 - 40 = 20$, second remainder.
$60 - 50 = 10$, third remainder.

$60 \times 30 \times 20 \times 10 = 360{,}000$; $\sqrt{360{,}000} = 600$, square feet, the area required.

2. How many square feet in a triangular floor, whose sides are 15, 16, and 21 feet?

3. Required the area of a triangular field whose sides are 834, 658, and 423 links.
Ans. 1 A. 1 R. 20 P. 4 yd. 1.6 ft.

4. Required the area of an equilateral triangle, of which each side is 15 yards.

5. What is the area of a garden in the form of a parallelogram, whose sides are 432 and 263 feet, and a diagonal 342 feet? Ans. 2 A. 10 P. 11.46 yd.

6. Required the area of an isosceles triangle, whose base is 25 and each of its equal sides 40 rods.

7. What is the area of a rhomboidal field, whose sides are 57 and 83 rods, and the diagonal 127 rods?
Ans. 22 A. 3 R. 21 P. 26 yd. 5 ft.

PROBLEM X.

623. Any two sides of a RIGHT-ANGLED TRIANGLE being given, to find the third side.

To the square of the base add the square of the perpendicular; and the square root of the sum will give the hypothenuse (Prop. XI. Bk. IV.).

From the square of the hypothenuse subtract the square of the given side, and the square root of the difference will be the side required (Prop. XI. Cor. 1, Bk. IV.).

EXAMPLES.

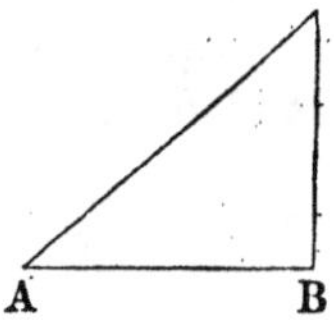

1. The base, AB, of the triangle ABC is 48 feet, and the perpendicular, BC, 36 feet; what is the hypothenuse?

$48^2 + 36^2 = 3600$; $\sqrt{3600} = 60$ feet, [the hypothenuse required.

C

A B

2. The hypothenuse of a triangle is 53 feet, and the perpendicular 28 feet; what is the base?

3. Two ships sail from the same port, one due west 50 miles, and the other due south 120 miles; how far are they apart? Ans. 130 miles.

4. A rectangular common is 25 rods long and 20 rods wide; what is the distance across it diagonally?

5. If a house is 40 feet long and 25 feet wide, with a pyramidal-shaped roof 10 feet in height, how long is a rafter which reaches from the vertex of the roof to a corner of the building?

6. There is a park in the form of a square containing 10 acres; how many rods less is the distance from the centre to each corner, than the length of the side of the square? Ans. 11.716 rods.

PROBLEM XI.

624. The sum of the hypothenuse and perpendicular

and the base of a RIGHT-ANGLED TRIANGLE being given, to find the hypothenuse and the perpendicular.

To the square of the sum add the square of the base, and divide the amount by twice the sum of the hypothenuse and perpendicular, and the quotient will be the hypothenuse.

From the sum of the hypothenuse and perpendicular subtract the hypothenuse, and the remainder will be the perpendicular.

625. *Scholium.* This problem may be regarded as equivalent to the sum of two numbers and the difference of their squares being given, to find the numbers (National Arithmetic, Art. 553).

NOTE. — The learner should be required to give a geometrical demonstration of the problem, as an exercise in the application of principles.

EXAMPLES.

1. The sum of the hypothenuse and the perpendicular of a right-angled triangle is 160 feet, and the base 80 feet; required the hypothenuse and the perpendicular.

Ans. Hypothenuse, 100 ft.; perpendicular, 60 ft.

$$160^2 + 80^2 = 32,000; \ 32,000 \div (160 \times 2) = 100;$$
$$160 - 100 = 60.$$

2. Two ships leave the same anchorage; the one, sailing due north, enters a port 50 miles from the place of departure, and the other, sailing due east, also enters a port, but by sailing thence in a direct course enters the port of the first; now, allowing that the second passed over, in all, 90 miles, how far apart are the two ports?

3. A tree 100 feet high, standing perpendicularly on a horizontal plane, was broken by the wind, so that, as it fell, while the part broken off remained in contact with the upright portion, the top reached the ground 40 feet from the foot of the tree; what is the length of each part?

Ans. The part broken off, 58 ft.; the upright, 42 ft.

PROBLEM XII.

626. The area and the base of a TRIANGLE being given, to find the altitude; or the area and altitude being given, to find the base.

Divide double the area by the base, and the quotient will be the altitude; or divide double the area by the altitude, and the quotient will be the base.

627. *Scholium.* This problem is the converse of Prob. VIII.

EXAMPLES.

1. The area of a triangle is 1300 square feet, and the base 65 feet; what is the altitude?

$1300 \times 2 = 2600$; $2600 \div 65 = 40$ ft., altitude required.

2. The area of a right-angled triangle is 17,272 yards, of which one of the sides about the right angle is 136 yards; required the other perpendicular side.

3. The area of a triangle is 46.25 chains, and the altitude 5.2 chains; what is the base?

4. A triangular field contains 30 A. 3 R. 27 P.; one of its sides is 97 rods; required the perpendicular distance from the opposite angle to that side. Ans. 102 rods.

PROBLEM XIII.

628. To find the area of a TRAPEZOID.

Multiply half the sum of its parallel sides by its altitude (Prop. VII. Bk. IV.).

EXAMPLES.

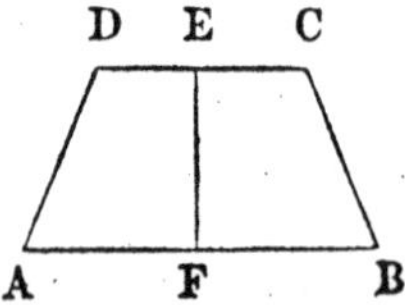

1. What is the area of the trapezoid A B C D, whose parallel sides, A B, D C, are 32 and 24 feet, and the altitude, E F, 20 feet?

$32 + 24 = 56$; $56 \div 2 = 28$; $28 \times 20 = 560$ sq. ft., [the area required.

2. How many square feet in a board in the form of a trapezoid, whose width at one end is 2 feet 3 inches, and at the other 1 foot 6 inches, the length being 16 feet?

3. Required the area of a garden in the form of a trapezoid, whose parallel sides are 786 and 473 links, and the perpendicular distance between them 986 links.

Ans. 6 A. 33 P. 3 yd.

4. How many acres in a quadrilateral field, having two parallel sides 83 and 101 rods in length, and which are distant from each other 60 rods?

Problem XIV.

629. To find the area of a REGULAR POLYGON, the perimeter and apothegm being given.

Multiply the perimeter by half the apothegm, and the product will be the area (Prop. VIII. Bk. VI.).

630. *Scholium.* This is in effect resolving the polygon into as many equal triangles as it has sides, by drawing lines from the center to all the angles, then finding their areas, and taking their sum.

Examples.

1. Required the area of a regular hexagon, A B C D E F, whose sides, A B, B C, &c. are each 15 yards, and the apothegm, O M, 13 yards.

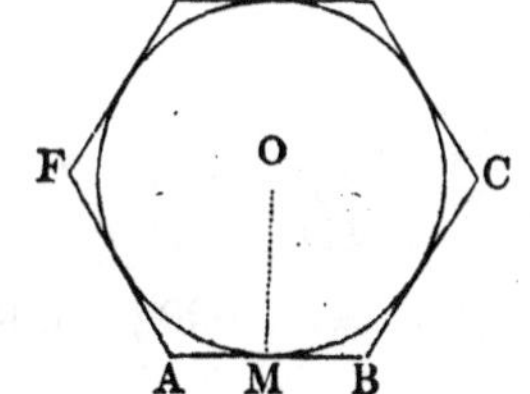

$15 \times 6 = 90$; $90 \div \frac{13}{2} = 585$ yd., [the area required.

2. What is the area of a regular pentagon, whose sides are each 25 feet, and the perpendicular from the center to a side 17.205 feet?

3. A park is laid out in the form of a regular heptagon, whose sides are each 19.263 chains; and the perpendicular

distance from the center to each of the sides is 20 chains. How many acres does it contain?

Ans. 134 A. 3 R. 14 P.

Problem XV.

631. To find the area of a REGULAR POLYGON, its side or perimeter being given.

Multiply the square of the side of the polygon by the area of a similar polygon whose side is unity or 1 (Prop. XXXI. Bk. IV.).

632. A Table of Regular Polygons whose Side is 1.

NAMES.	AREAS.	NAMES.	AREAS.
Triangle,	0.4330127	Octagon,	4.8284271
Square,	1.0000000	Nonagon,	6.1818242
Pentagon,	1.7204774	Decagon,	7.6942088
Hexagon,	2.5980762	Undecagon,	9.3656399
Heptagon,	3.6339124	Dodecagon,	11.1961524

The apothegm of any regular polygon whose side is 1 being ascertained, its area is computed readily, by Prob. XIV.

Examples.

1. Required the area of an equilateral triangle, whose side is 100 feet.

$100^2 = 10{,}000$; $10{,}000 \times 0.4330127 = 4330.127$ square [feet, the area required.

2. What is the area of a regular pentagon, whose side is 37 yards?

3. How many acres in a field in the form of a regular undecagon, whose side is 27 yards?

Ans. 1 A. 1 R. 25 P. 21 yd. 2.7 ft.

4. What is the area of an octagonal floor, whose side is 15 ft. 6 in.?

5. How many acres in a regular nonagon, whose perimeter is 2286 feet? Ans. 9 A. 24 P. 28 yd.

PROBLEM XVI.

633. To find the side of any REGULAR POLYGON, its area being given.

Divide the given area by the area of a similar polygon whose side is 1, *and the square root of the quotient will be the side required.*

634. *Scholium.* This problem is the converse of Prob. XV.

EXAMPLES.

1. The area of an equilateral triangle is 4330.127 square feet; what is its side?

$4330.127 \div .4330127 = 10{,}000$; $\sqrt{10{,}000} = 100$ feet, [the side required.

2. The area of a regular hexagon is 1039.23 feet; what is its side?

3. The area of a regular decagon is 7 P. 18 yd. 5 ft. 128.55 in.; what is its side? Ans. 16 ft. 5 in.

PROBLEM XVII.

635. To find the area of an IRREGULAR POLYGON.

Divide the polygon into triangles, or triangles and trapezoids, and find the areas of each of them separately; the sum of these areas will be the area required.

636. *Scholium.* When the irregular polygon is a quadrilateral, the area may be found by multiplying together the diagonal and half the sum of the perpendiculars drawn from it to the opposite angles.

EXAMPLES.

1. Required the area of the irregular pentagon A B C D E, of which the diagonal A C is 20 feet, and A D 36 feet; and the perpendicular distance from the angle B to A C is 8 feet, from C to A D 12 feet, and from E to A D 6 feet.

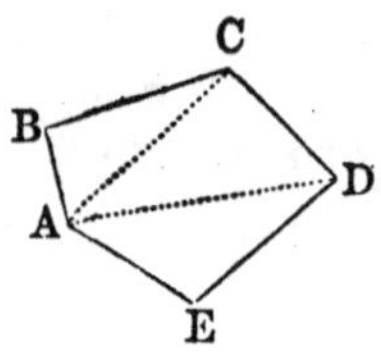

$20 \times \frac{8}{2} = 80$; $36 \times \frac{12}{2} = 216$; $36 \times \frac{6}{2} = 108$;
$80 + 216 + 108 = 504$ sq. ft., the area required.

2. What is the area of a trapezium, whose diagonal is 42 feet, and the two perpendiculars from the diagonal to the opposite angles are 16 and 18 feet?

3. In an irregular hexagon, A B C D E F, are given the sides A B 536, B C 498, C D 620, D E 580, E F 398, and A F 492 links, and the diagonals A C 918, C E 1048, and A E 652 links; required the area.

Ans. 6 A. 2 R. 9 P. 23 yd. 8.4 ft.

4. In measuring along one side, AB, of a quadrangular field, A B C D, that side and the perpendiculars let fall on it from two opposite corners measured as follows: A B 1110, A E 110, A F 745, D E 352, C F 595 links. What is the area of the field? Ans. 4 A. 1 R. 5 P. 24 yd.

5. In a four-sided rectilineal field, A B C D, on account of obstructions, there could be taken only the following measures: the two sides B C 265 and A D 220 yards, the diagonal A C 378, and the two distances of the perpendiculars from the ends of the diagonal, namely, A E 100, and C F 70 yards. Required the area in acres.

PROBLEM XVIII.

637. To find the circumference of a CIRCLE, when the diameter is given, or the diameter when the circumference is given.

Multiply the diameter by 3.1416, *and the product will be the circumference; or, divide the circumference by*

3.1416, *and the quotient will be the diameter* (Prop. XV. Cor. 3, Bk. VI.).

638. *Scholium.* The diameter may also be found by multiplying the circumference by .31831, the reciprocal of 3.1416.

EXAMPLES.

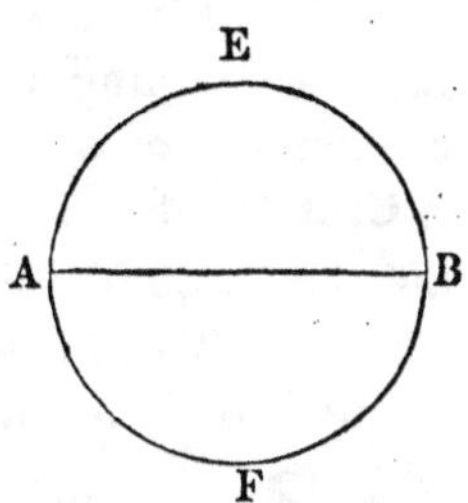

1. The diameter, A B, of the circle A E B F is 100 feet; what is its circumference?

100 × 3.1416 = 314.16 feet, the [circumference required.

2. Required the circumference of a circle whose diameter is 628 links. Ans. 1 fur. 38 rd. 5 yd. 1.56 in.

3. If the diameter of the earth is 7912 miles, what is its circumference?

4. Required the diameter of a circular pond whose circumference is 928 rods.

Ans. 7 fur. 15 rd. 2 yd. 5.55 in.

5. The circumference of a circular garden is 1043 feet; what is its radius? Ans. 10 rd. 1 ft.

PROBLEM XIX.

639. To find the length of an arc of a circle containing any number of degrees, the radius or diameter being given.

Multiply the number of degrees in the given arc by 0.01745, *and the product by the radius of the circle.*

For, when the diameter of a circle is 1, the circumference is 3.1416 (Prop. XV. Sch. 1, Bk. VI.); hence, when the radius is 1, the circumference is 6.2832; which, divided by 360, the number of degrees into which every circle is supposed to be divided, gives 0.01745, the length of the arc of 1 degree, when the radius is 1.

640. *Scholium.* Each of the 360 degrees of a circle,

marked thus, 360°, is divided into 60 minutes, marked thus, 60′, and each minute into 60 seconds, marked thus, 60″ (National Arithmetic, Art. 143).

EXAMPLES.

1. What is the length of an arc, A D, containing 60° 30′ on the circumference of a circle whose radius, A C, is 100 feet?

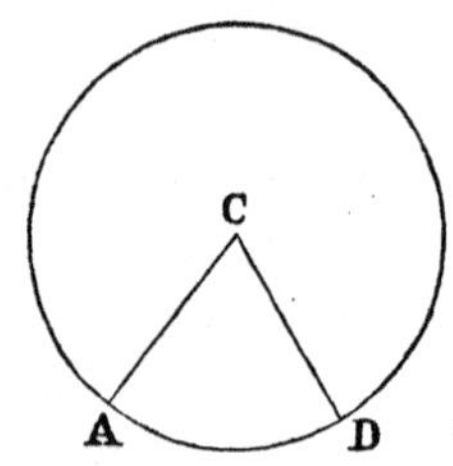

60° 30′ = 60.5°; 60.5 × 0.01745 = 1.055725; 1.055725 × 100 = 105.5725 ft., arc required.

2. Required the length of an arc of 31° 15′, the radius being 12 yards.

3. Required the length of an arc of 12° 10′, the diameter being 20 feet. Ans. 2.1231 feet.

4. What is the length of an arc of 57° 17′ 44½″, the radius being 25 feet? Ans. 25 feet.

PROBLEM XX.

641. To find the area of a circle.

Multiply the circumference by half the radius (Prop. XV. Bk. VI.); *or, multiply the square of the radius by* 3.1416 (Prop. XV. Cor. 2, Bk VI.).

642. *Scholium.* Multiplying the circumference by half the radius is the same as multiplying the circumference and diameter together, and taking one fourth of the product. Now, denoting the circumference by c, and the diameter by d, since $c = 3.1416 \times d$ (Prob. XVIII.), we have $(d \times 3.1416 \times d) \div 4 = d^2 \times 0.7854 =$ the area of a circle. Again, since $d = c \div 3.1416$ (Prob. XVIII.), we have $c \div 3.1416 \times c \div 4 = c^2 \div 12.5664$, which is, by taking the reciprocal of 12.5664, equal to $c^2 \times 0.07958$ = the area of the circle. Hence the area of the circle may also be found by *multiplying the square of the diam-*

eter by 0.7854; *or by multiplying the square of the circumference by* 0.07958.

EXAMPLES.

1. The circumference of a circle is 314.16 feet, and its radius 50 feet; what is its area?

$314.16 \times \frac{50}{2} = 7854$ feet, the area required.

2. If the circumference of a circle is 355 feet, and its diameter 113 feet, what is the area?

3. What is the area of a circular garden, whose radius is 281½ links? Ans. 2 A. 1 R. 38 rd. 9 yd. 5 ft.

4. A horse is tethered in a meadow by a cord 39.25075 yards long; over how much ground can he graze?

5. Required the area of a semicircle, the diameter of the whole circle being 751 feet.

Ans. 5 A. 13 P. 16 yd.

PROBLEM XXI.

643. To find the DIAMETER OR CIRCUMFERENCE, the area being given.

Divide the area by 0.7854, *and the square root of the quotient will be the diameter; or, divide the area by* 0.07958, *and the square root of the quotient will be the circumference.*

644. *Scholium.* This problem is the converse of Prob. XX.

EXAMPLES.

1. The area of a circle is 314.16 feet; what is the diameter?

$314.16 \div 0.7854 = 400$; $\sqrt{400} = 20$ feet, the diameter [required.

2. What must be the length of a cord to be used as a radius in describing a circle which shall contain exactly 1 acre?

3. The area of a circular pond is 6 A. 1 R. 27 P. 18.2 yd.; what is the circumference? Ans. 625 yd.

4. The area of a circle is 7856 feet; what is the circumference?

5. The length of a rectangular garden is 32, and its width 18 rods; required the diameter of a circular garden having the same area. Ans. 27 rd. 1 ft. 4 in.

Problem XXII.

645. To find the area of a SECTOR of a circle.

Multiply the arc of the sector by half of its radius (Prop. XV. Cor. 1, Bk. VI.); *or,*

As 360° *are to the degrees in the arc of the sector, so is the area of the circle to the area of the sector.*

Examples.

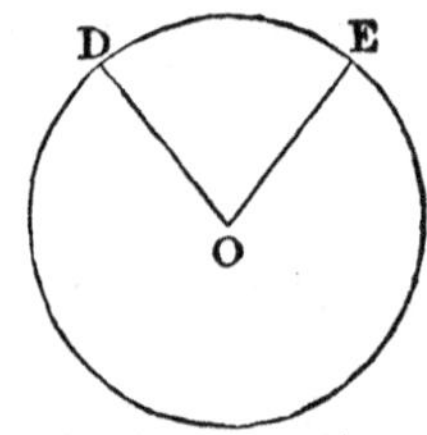

1. Required the area of a sector, D E, whose arc is 80 feet, and its radius, O E, 70 feet.

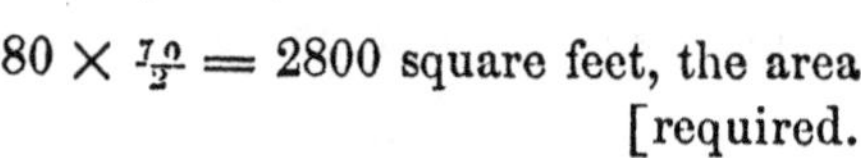

$80 \times \frac{70}{2} = 2800$ square feet, the area [required.

2. Required the area of a sector, of which the arc is 90 and the radius 112 yards.

3. Required the area of a sector, of which the angle is 137° 20′, and the radius 456 links.

Ans. 2 A. 1 R. 38 P. 21.92 yd.

Problem XXIII.

646. To find the area of a SEGMENT of a circle.

Find the area of the sector having the same arc with the segment, and also the area of the triangle formed by the chord of the segment and the radii of the sector. Then, if the segment is less than a semicircle, take the difference of these areas; but if greater, take their sum.

647. *Scholium.* When the height of the segment and

the diameter of the circle are given, the area may be readily found by means of a table of segments, *by dividing the height by the diameter, and looking in the table for the quotient in the column of heights, and taking out, in the next column on the right hand, the corresponding area; which, multiplied by the square of the diameter, will give the area required.*

When the quotient cannot be exactly found in the table, proportions may be instituted so as to find the area between the next higher and the next lower, in the same ratio that the given height varies from the next higher and lower heights.

648. TABLE OF SEGMENTS.

Height.	Seg. Area.	Height.	Seg. Area.	Height.	Seg. Area.	Height.	Seg. Area.	Height.	Seg. Area.
.01	.00133	.11	.04701	.21	.11990	.31	.20738	.41	.30319
.02	.00375	.12	.05339	.22	.12811	.32	.21667	.42	.31304
.03	.00687	.13	.06000	.23	.13646	.33	.22603	.43	.32293
.04	.01054	.14	.06683	.24	.14494	.34	.23547	.44	.33284
.05	.01468	.15	.07387	.25	.15354	.35	.24498	.45	.34278
.06	.01924	.16	.08111	.26	.16226	.36	.25455	.46	.35274
.07	.02417	.17	.08853	.27	.17109	.37	.26418	.47	.36272
.08	.02944	.18	.09613	.28	.18002	.38	.27386	.48	.37270
.09	.03502	.19	.10390	.29	.18905	.39	.28359	.49	.38270
.10	.04088	.20	.11182	.30	.19817	.40	.29337	.50	.39270

The segments in the table are those of a circle whose diameter is 1, and the first column contains the corresponding heights divided by the diameter. The method of calculating the areas of segments from the elements in the table depends upon the principle that similar plane figures are to each other as the squares of their like linear dimensions.

EXAMPLES.

1. What is the area of the segment A B E, its arc A E B being 73.74°, its chord A B being 12 feet, and

the radius, C B, of the circle 10 feet ?

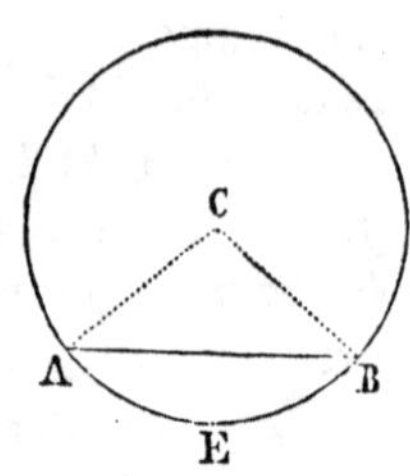

$0.7854 \times 20^2 = 314.16$, area of circle; then $360° : 73.74° :: 314.16 : 64.3504$, area of sector A E B C; and, by Problem IX., 48 is the area of the triangle A B C; $64.3504 - 48 = 16.3504$ feet, the area required.

2. Required the area of a segment whose height is 18, and the diameter of the circle 50 feet.

$18 \div 50 = .36$; to which the corresponding area in the table is .25455; $.25455 \times 50^2 = 636.375$, area required.

3. Required the area of a segment whose arc is 100°, chord 153.208 feet, and the diameter of the circle 200 feet.

4. What is the area of a segment whose height is 4 feet, and the radius 51 feet ? Ans. 106 feet.

5. Required the area of a segment, the arc being 160°, chord 196.9616 feet, and the radius of the circle 100 feet.

Problem XXIV.

649. To find the area of a CIRCULAR ZONE, or the space included between two parallel chords and their intercepted arcs.

From the area of the whole circle subtract the areas of the segments on the sides of the zone.

Examples.

1. What is the area of a zone whose chords are each 12 feet, subtending each an arc of 73.74°, when the radius of the circle is 10 feet ?

Area of the whole circle by Prob. XX. = 314.16; area of each segment by Prob. XXIII. = 16.3504; $16.3504 \times 2 = 32.7008$ = area of both segments; $314.16 - 32.7008 = 281.4592$, the area required.

2. What is the area of a circular zone whose longer chord is 20 yards, subtending an arc of 60°, and the shorter chord 14.66 yards, subtending an arc of 43°, the diameter of the circle being 40 yards?

3. A circle whose diameter is 20 feet is divided into three parts by two parallel chords; one of the segments cut off is 8 feet in height, and the other 6 feet; what is the area of the circular zone? Ans. 117.544 ft.

PROBLEM XXV.

650. To find the area of a CRESCENT.

Find the difference of the areas of the two segments formed by the arcs of the crescent and its chord.

EXAMPLES.

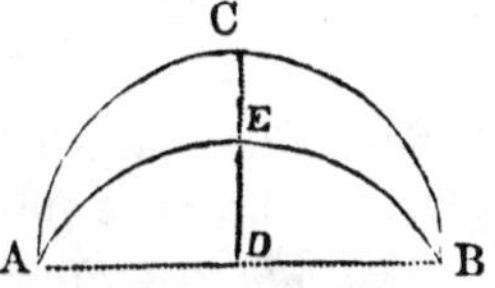

1. The arcs A C B, A E B, of circles having the same radius, 50 rods, intersecting, form the crescent A C B E; the height, D C, of the segment A C B is 60 rods, and the height, D E, of the segment A B E is 40 rods; what is the area of the crescent?

The area of the segment A C B, by Prob. XXIII., is 4920.3 rods, and that of the segment A B E is 2933.7 rods; $4920.3 - 2933.7 = 1986.6$ rods, the area of the crescent.

2. If the arc of a circle whose diameter is 24 yards intersects a circle whose diameter is 20 yards, forming a crescent, so that the height of the segment of the first circle is 5.072 yards, and that of the segment of the second circle is 8 yards, what is the area of the crescent?

PROBLEM XXVI.

651. To find the area of a CIRCULAR RING, or the space included between two concentric circles.

Find the areas of the two circles separately (Prob. XX.), *and take the difference of these areas; or sub-*

tract the square of the less diameter from the square of the greater, and multiply their difference by 0.7854 (Prob. XX. Sch.).

EXAMPLES.

1. Required the area of the ring formed by two circles whose diameters are 30 and 50 feet.

$50^2 - 30^2 = 1400$; $1400 \times 0.7854 = 1099.56$ sq. feet, [the area of the ring.

2. What is the area of a ring formed by two circles whose radii are 36 and 24 feet?

3. A circular park, 256 yards in diameter, has a carriage-way running around it 20 feet wide; what is the area of the carriage-way?

Ans. 1 A. 2 R. 26 P. 21.5 yd.

PROBLEM XXVII.

652. The diameter or circumference of a CIRCLE being given, to find the side of an EQUIVALENT SQUARE.

Multiply the diameter by 0.8862, *or the circumference by* 0.2821; *the product in either case will be the side of an equivalent square.*

For, since 0.7854 is the area of a circle whose diameter is 1 (Prob. XX. Sch.), the square root of 0.7854, which is 0.8862, is the side of a square which is equivalent to a circle whose diameter is 1. Now when the circumference is 1, the side of an equivalent square must have the same ratio to 0.8862 as the diameter 1 has to its circumference 3.1416 (Prop. XV. Cor. 4, Bk. VI.); and $0.8862 \div 3.1416$ gives 0.2821 as the side of the equivalent square when the circumference is 1.

EXAMPLES.

1. The diameter of a circle is 120 feet; what is the side of an equivalent square?

$120 \times 0.8862 = 106.344$ feet, the side required.

2. The circumference of a circle is 100 yards; what is the side of an equivalent square? Ans. 28.21 yd.

3. There is a circular floor 30 feet in diameter; what is the side of a square floor containing the same area?

4. If 500 feet is the circumference of a circular island, what is the side of a square of equal area?

Ans. 141.05 ft.

PROBLEM XXVIII.

653. The diameter or circumference of a CIRCLE being given, to find the side of the INSCRIBED SQUARE.

Multiply the diameter by 0.7071, *or the circumference by* 0.2251; *the product in either case will be the side of the inscribed square.*

For 0.7071 is the side of the inscribed square when the diameter of the circumscribed circle is 1, since the side of the inscribed square is to the radius of the circle as the square root of 2 to 1 (Prop. IV. Cor., Bk. VI.); consequently, the side is to the diameter, or twice the radius, as half the square root of 2 is to 1, and half the square root of 2 is 0.7071, approximately. Now, the ratio of the diameter of a circle to the side of its inscribed square being as 1 to 0.7071, and the ratio of the circumference of a circle to its diameter as 3.1416 to 1, the ratio of the inscribed square is to the circumference of the circle as 0.7071 to 3.1416; and 0.7071 ÷ 3.1416 gives 0.2251 as the side of the inscribed square when the circumference is 1.

EXAMPLES.

1. The diameter, A C, of a circle is 110 feet; what is the side, A B, of the inscribed square?

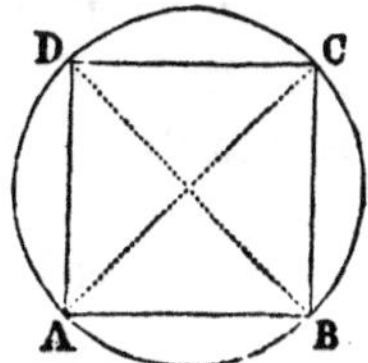

$110 \times 0.7071 = 77.781$ feet, the side required.

2. The circumference of a circle is 300 feet; what is the side of the inscribed square? Ans. 67.53 ft.

3. A log is 36 inches in diameter; of how many inches square can a stick be hewn from it?

4. There is a circular field 1000 rods in circuit; what is the side of the largest square that can be described in it? Ans. 225.10 rods.

PROBLEM XXIX.

654. The diameter or circumference of a CIRCLE being given, to find the side of an INSCRIBED EQUILATERAL TRIANGLE.

Multiply the diameter by 0.8660, *or the circumference by* 0.2757; *the product in either case will be the side of the inscribed equilateral triangle.*

For 0.8660 is the side of the inscribed equilateral triangle when the diameter of the circumscribed circle is 1, since the side of the inscribed equilateral triangle is to the radius of the circle as the square root of 3 is to 1 (Prop. V. Cor. 3, Bk. VI.); consequently, the side is to the diameter, or twice the radius, as half the square root of 3 is to 1, and half the square root of 3 is 0.8660, approximately. Also, since the ratio of the circumference of a circle to its diameter is as 3.1416 to 1, the side of the inscribed equilateral triangle, when the circumference is 1, equals $0.8660 \div 3.1416$, or 0.2757.

EXAMPLES.

1. Required the side of an equilateral triangle that may be inscribed in a circle 101 feet in diameter.

$101 \times 0.8660 = 87.4660$ feet, the side required.

2. Required the side of an equilateral triangle that may be inscribed in a circle 80 rods in circumference.

Ans. 22.05 rods.

3. Required the side of the largest equilateral triangular beam that can be hewn from a piece of round timber 36 inches in diameter.

4. Required the side of an equilateral triangle that can be inscribed in a circle 251.33 feet in circumference.

5. How much less is the area of an equilateral triangle that can be inscribed in a circle 100 feet in diameter, than the area of the circle itself? Ans. 4606.4 sq. ft.

THE ELLIPSE.

655. An ELLIPSE is a plane figure bounded by a curve, from any point of which the sum of the distances to two fixed points is equal to a straight line drawn through those two points, and terminated both ways by the curve.

Thus A D B C is an ellipse. The two fixed points G and H are called the *foci*. The longest diameter, A B, of the ellipse is called its *major* or *transverse axis*, and its shortest diameter, C D, is called its *minor* or *conjugate axis*.

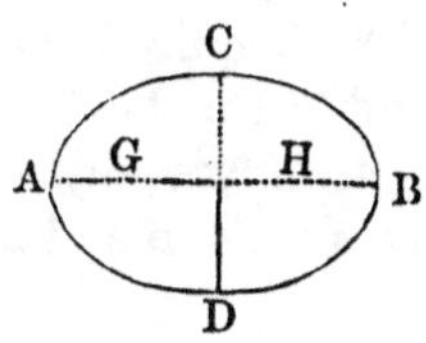

656. The AREA of an ellipse is a mean proportional between the areas of two circles whose diameters are the two axes of the ellipse.

This, however, can only be well demonstrated by means of Analytical Geometry, a branch of the mathematics with which the learner here is not supposed to be acquainted.

PROBLEM XXX.

657. To find the area of an ELLIPSE, the major and minor axes being given.

Multiply the axes together, and their product by 0.7854, *and the result will be the area.*

For $AB^2 \times 0.7854$ expresses the area of a circle whose diameter is A B, and $CD^2 \times 0.7854$ expresses the area of a circle whose diameter is C D; and the product of these two areas is equal to $AB^2 \times CD^2 \times 0.7854^2$, which is equal to the square of A B × C D × 0.7854 ; hence, A B × C D × 0.7854 is a mean proportional between the areas of the two circles whose diameters are A B and C D (Prop. IV. Bk. II.) ; consequently it measures the area of an ellipse whose axes are A B and C D (Art. 656).

EXAMPLES.

1. Required the area of an ellipse, of which the major axis is 60 feet, and the minor axis 40 feet.

$60 \times 40 \times 0.7854 = 1884.96$ sq. ft., the area required.

2. What is the area of an ellipse whose axes are 75 and 35 feet ?

3. Required the area of an ellipse whose axes are 526 and 354 inches. Ans. 112 yd. 7 ft. 84.62 in.

4. How many acres in an elliptical pond whose semi-axes are 436 and 254 feet ?

Ans. 7 A. 3 R. 37 P. 27 yd. 7 ft.

BOOK XII.

APPLICATIONS OF GEOMETRY TO THE MENSURATION OF SOLIDS.

DEFINITIONS.

658. MENSURATION OF SOLIDS, or VOLUMES, is the process of determining their contents.

The SUPERFICIAL CONTENTS of a body is its quantity of surface.

The SOLID CONTENTS of a body is its measured magnitude, volume, or solidity.

659. The UNIT OF VOLUME, or SOLIDITY, is a cube, whose faces are each a *superficial* unit of the surface of the body, and whose edges are each a *linear* unit of its linear dimensions.

660. TABLE OF SOLID MEASURES.

1728	Cubic	Inches	make	1 Cubic Foot
27	"	Feet	"	1 " Yard.
$4492\frac{1}{8}$	"	Feet	"	1 " Rod.
32,768,000	"	Rods	"	1 " Mile.
Also,				
231	"	Inches	"	1 Liquid Gallon.
$268\frac{4}{5}$	"	Inches	"	1 Dry Gallon.
$2150\frac{42}{100}$	"	Inches	"	1 Bushel.
128	"	Feet	"	1 Cord.

PROBLEM I.

661. To find the surface of a RIGHT PRISM.

Multiply the perimeter of the base by the altitude, and the product will be the CONVEX *surface* (Prop. I. Bk.

VIII.). *To this add the areas of the two bases, and the result will be the* ENTIRE *surface.*

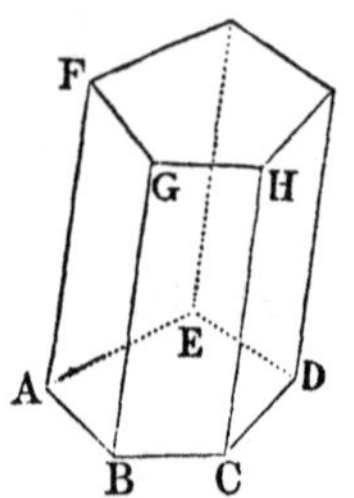

EXAMPLES.

1. Required the convex surface of a pentangular prism, having each side of its base, A B C D E, equal to 2 feet, and its altitude, A F, equal to 5 feet.

$2 \times 5 = 10$; $10 \times 5 = 50$ square feet,
[the convex surface required.

2. The altitude of a hexangular prism is 12 feet, two of its faces are each 2 feet wide, three are each $2\frac{1}{2}$ feet wide, and the remaining face is 9 inches wide; what is the convex surface of the prism?

3. Required the entire surface of a cube, the length of each edge being 25 feet.

4. Required, in square yards, the wall surface of a rectangular room, whose height is 20 feet, width 30 feet, and length 50 feet. Ans. $355\frac{5}{9}$ sq. yd.

PROBLEM II.

662. To find the solidity of a PRISM.

Multiply the area of its base by its altitude, and the product will be its solidity (Prop. XIII. Bk. VIII.).

EXAMPLES.

1. Required the solidity of a pentangular prism, having each side of its base equal to 2 feet, and its altitude equal to 5 feet.

$2^2 \times 1.72048 = 6.88192$; $6.88192 \times 5 = 34.40960$ cubic
[feet, the solidity required.

2. Required the solidity of a triangular prism, whose length is 10 feet, and the three sides of whose base are 3, 4, and 5 feet. Ans. 60.

3. A slab of marble is 8 feet long, 3 feet wide, and 6 inches thick; required its solidity.

4. There is a cistern in the form of a cube, whose edge is 10 feet; what is its capacity in liquid gallons?

Ans. 7480.519 gallons.

5. Required the solid contents of a quadrilateral prism, the length being 19 feet, the sides of the base 43, 54, 62, and 38, and the diagonal between the first and second sides, 70 inches. Ans. 306.047 cu. ft.

6. How many cords in a range of wood cut 4 feet long, the range being 4 feet 6 inches high and 160 feet long?

Problem III.

663. To find the surface of a RIGHT PYRAMID.

Multiply the perimeter of the base by half its slant height, and the product will be the CONVEX *surface* (Prop. XV. Bk. VIII.). *To this add the area of the base, and the result will be the* ENTIRE *surface.*

664. *Scholium.* The surface of an oblique pyramid is found by taking the sum of the areas of its several faces.

Examples.

1. Required the convex surface of a pentangular pyramid, A B C D E – S, each side of whose base, A B C D E, is 5 feet, and whose slant height, S M, is 20 feet.

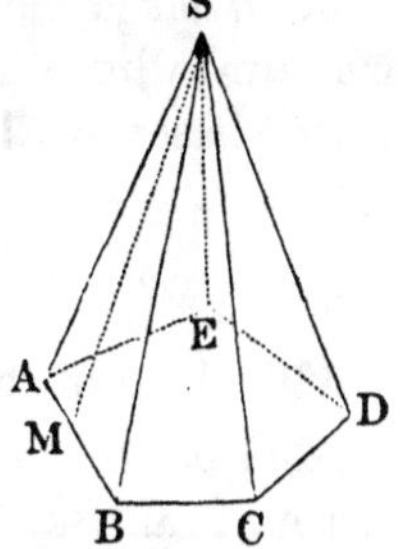

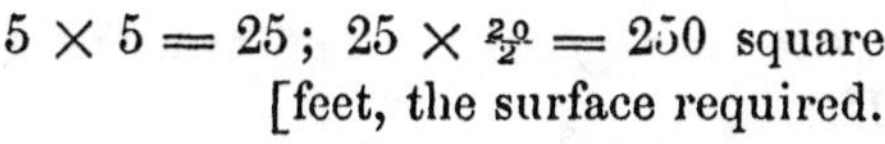

$5 \times 5 = 25$; $25 \times \frac{20}{2} = 250$ square [feet, the surface required.

2. What is the entire surface of a triangular pyramid, of which the slant height is 18 feet, and each side of the base 42 inches? Ans. 99.804 sq. ft.

3. Required the convex surface of a triangular pyramid, the slant height being 20 feet, and each side of the base 3 feet.

4. What is the entire surface of a quadrangular pyramid, the sides of the base being 40 and 30 inches, and the slant height upon the greater side 20.04, and upon the less side 20.07 feet? Ans. 125.308 ft.

PROBLEM IV.

665. To find the surface of a FRUSTUM OF A RIGHT PYRAMID.

Multiply half the sum of the perimeters of its two bases by its slant height, and the product will be the CONVEX *surface* (Prop. XVII. Bk. VIII.); *to this add the areas of the two bases, and the result will be the* ENTIRE *surface.*

EXAMPLES.

1. What is the entire surface of a rectangular frustum whose slant height is 12 feet, and the sides of whose bases are 5 and 2 feet?

$5 \times 4 = 20$; $2 \times 4 = 8$; $20 + 8 = 28$; $\frac{28}{2} \times 12 = 168$; $5^2 + 2^2 = 29$; $168 + 29 = 197$ sq. ft., area required.

2. Required the convex surface of a regular hexangular frustum, whose slant height is 16 feet, and the sides of whose bases are 2 feet 8 inches and 3 feet 4 inches.

3. What is the entire surface of a regular pentangular frustum, whose slant height is 11 feet, and the sides of whose bases are 18 and 34 inches?

Ans. 136.849 sq. ft.

PROBLEM V.

666. To find the solidity of a PYRAMID.

Multiply the area of its base by one third of its altitude (Prop. XX. Bk. VIII.).

EXAMPLES.

1. Required the solidity of a pentangular pyramid, A B C D E – S, each side of whose base, A B C D E, is 5 feet, and whose altitude, S O, is 15 feet.

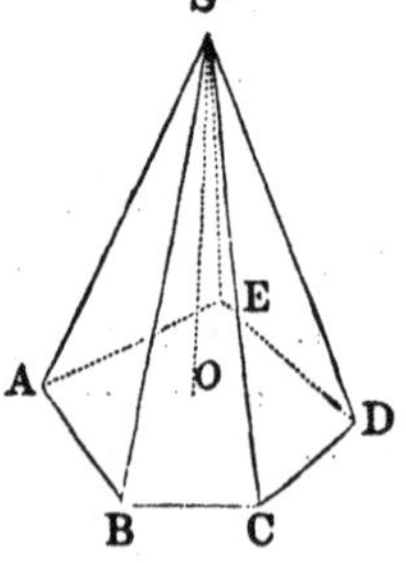

$5^2 \times 1.7205 = 43.0125$; $43.0125 \times \frac{15}{3} = 215.0575$ cu. ft., the solidity required.

2. What is the solidity of a hexangular pyramid, the altitude of which is 9 feet, and each side of the base 29 inches?

3. What is the solidity of a square pyramid, each side of whose base is 30 feet, and whose perpendicular height is 25 feet? Ans. 7500.

4. Required the solid contents of a triangular pyramid, the perpendicular height of which is 24 feet, and the sides of the base 34, 42, and 50 inches. Ans. 39.2354 cu. ft.

Problem VI.

667. To find the solidity of a FRUSTUM OF A PYRAMID.

Add together the areas of the two bases and a mean proportional between them, and multiply that sum by one third of the altitude of the frustum (Prop. XXI. Bk. VIII.).

Examples.

1. Required the solidity of the frustum of a quadrangular pyramid, the sides of whose bases are 3 feet and 2 feet, and whose altitude is 15 feet.

$3 \times 3 = 9$; $2 \times 2 = 4$; $\sqrt{9 \times 4} = 6$ (Prop. IV. Bk. II.);

$(9 + 4 + 6) \times \frac{15}{3} = 95$ cu. ft., solidity required.

2. How many cubic feet in a stick of timber in the form of a quadrangular frustum, the sides of whose bases are 15 inches and 6 inches, and whose altitude is 20 feet?

3. Required the solid contents of a pentangular frustum, whose altitude is 5 feet, each side of whose lower base is 18 inches, and each side of whose upper base is 6 inches. Ans. 9.319 cu. ft.

4. Required the solidity of the frustum of a triangular pyramid, the altitude of which is 14 feet, the sides of the lower base 21, 15, and 12, and those of the upper base 14, 10, and 8 feet. Ans. 868.752 cu. ft.

The Wedge.

668. A Wedge is a polyedron bounded by a rectangle, called the base of the wedge; by two trapezoids, called the sides, which meet in an edge parallel to the base; and by two triangles, called the ends of the wedge.

Thus A B C D − G H is a wedge, of which A B C D is the rectangular base; A B H G, D C H G, the trapezoidal sides, which meet in the edge GH; and ADG, B C H, the triangular ends.

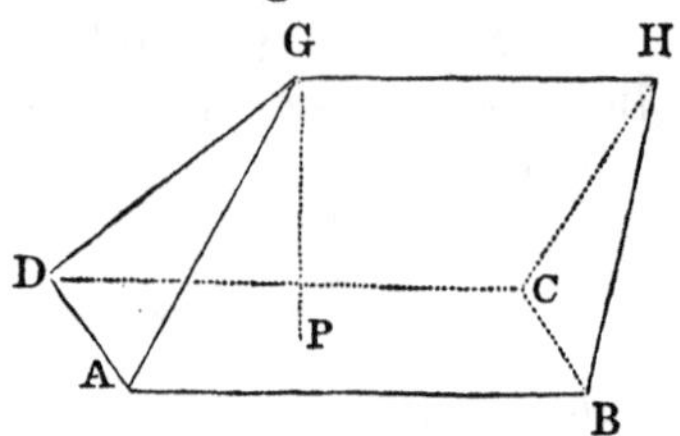

The *altitude* of a wedge is the perpendicular distance from its edge to the plane of its base; as G P.

Problem VII.

669. To find the solidity of a wedge.

Add the length of the edge to twice the length of the base; multiply the sum by one sixth of the product of the altitude of the wedge and the breadth of the base.

For, let L equal A B, the length of the base; l equal GH, the length of the edge; b equal B C, the breadth of the base; and h equal P G, the height of the wedge. Then $\text{L} - l =$ A B — G H = A M.

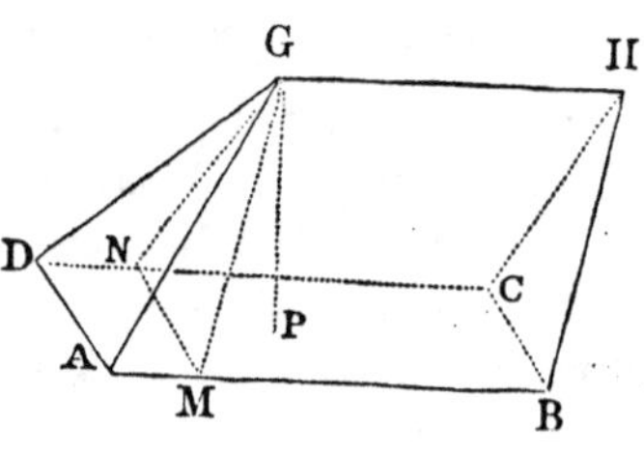

Now, if the length of the base and the edge be *equal*, the polyedron is equal to half a parallelopipedon having the same base and altitude (Prop. VI. Bk. VIII.), and its solidity will be equal to $\frac{1}{2}\, b\, l\, h$ (Prop. XIII. Bk. VIII.).

If the length of the base is *greater* than that of the edge, let a section, M N G, be made parallel to B C H.

This section will divide the whole wedge into the quadrangular pyramid A M N D – G, and the triangular prism B C H – G.

The solidity of A M N D – G is equal to $\frac{1}{3} b h \times (L - l)$ (Prob. V.); and the solidity of B C H – G is equal to $\frac{1}{2} b l h$; hence the solidity of the whole wedge is equal to

$$\frac{1}{2} b h l + \frac{1}{3} b h \times (L - l) = \frac{1}{6} b h \, 3 l + \frac{1}{6} b h \, 2 L - \frac{1}{6} b h \, 2 l = \frac{1}{6} b h \times (2 L + l).$$

But, if the length of the base is *less* than that of the edge, the solidity of the wedge will be equal to the prism less the pyramid; or to

$$\frac{1}{2} b h l - \frac{1}{3} b h \times (l - L) = \frac{1}{6} b h \, 3 l - \frac{1}{6} b h \, 2 l + \frac{1}{6} b h \, 2 L = \frac{1}{6} b h \times (2 L + l).$$

EXAMPLES.

1. Required the solidity of a wedge, the edge of which is 10 inches, the sides of the base 12 inches and 6 inches, and the altitude 14 inches.

$10 + (12 \times 2) = 34$; $34 \times \frac{14 \times 6}{6} = 476$ cu. in., the solidity required.

2. What is the solidity of a wedge, of which the edge is 24 inches, the sides of the base 36 inches and 9 inches, and the altitude 22 inches?

3. How many solid feet in a wedge, of which the sides of the base are 35 inches and 15 inches, the length of the edge 55 inches, and the altitude $17\frac{3}{20}$ inches?

Ans. 3 cu. ft. $175\frac{5}{8}$ cu. in.

RECTANGULAR PRISMOID.

670. A RECTANGULAR PRISMOID is a polyedron bounded by two rectangles, called the bases of the prismoid, and by four trapezoids called the lateral faces of the prismoid.

The *altitude* of a prismoid is the perpendicular distance between its bases.

Problem VIII.

671. To find the solidity of a RECTANGULAR PRISMOID.

Add the area of the two bases to four times the area of a parallel section at equal distances from the bases; multiply the sum by one sixth of the altitude.

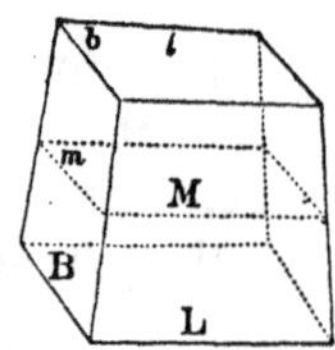

Let L and B be the length and breadth of the lower base, l and b the length and breadth of the upper base, M and m the length and breadth of the parallel section equidistant from the bases, and h the altitude of the prismoid.

If a plane be passed through the opposite edges L and l, the prismoid will be divided into two wedges, having for bases the bases of the prismoid, and for edges L and l.

The solidity of these wedges, which compose the prismoid, is (Prob. VII.),

$$\tfrac{1}{6}\,\mathrm{B}\,h \times (2\,\mathrm{L} + l) + \tfrac{1}{6}\,b\,h \times (2\,l + \mathrm{L}) = \tfrac{1}{6}\,h\,(2\,\mathrm{B}\,\mathrm{L} + \mathrm{B}\,l + 2\,b\,l + b\,\mathrm{L}).$$

But M being equally distant from L and l, $2\,\mathrm{M} = \mathrm{L} + l$, and $2\,m = \mathrm{B} + b$ (Prop. VII. Cor., Bk. IV.); consequently,

$$4\,\mathrm{M}\,m = (\mathrm{L} + l) \times (\mathrm{B} + b) = \mathrm{B}\,\mathrm{L} + \mathrm{B}\,l + b\,\mathrm{L} + b\,l.$$

Substituting $4\,\mathrm{M}\,m$ for its base, in the preceding equation, we have, as the expression of the solidity of a prismoid,

$$\tfrac{1}{6}\,h\,(\mathrm{B}\,\mathrm{L} + b\,l + 4\,\mathrm{M}\,m).$$

672. *Scholium.* This demonstration applies to prismoids of other forms. For, whatever be the form of the two bases, there may be inscribed in each such a number of small rectangles that the sum of them in each base shall differ less from that base than any assignable quantity; so that the sum of the rectangular prismoids that may be

constructed on these rectangles will differ from the given prismoid by less than any assignable quantity.

EXAMPLES.

1. Required the solidity of a prismoid, the larger base of which is 30 inches by 27 inches, the smaller base 24 inches by 18 inches, and the altitude 48 inches.

$30 \times 27 = 810$; $24 \times 18 = 432$; $\frac{30 + 24}{2} \times \frac{27 + 18}{2} \times 4$
$= 2430$; $(810 + 432 + 2430) \times \frac{48}{6} = 29{,}376$ cu. in.
$= 17$ cu. ft., the solidity required.

2. What is the solidity of a stick of timber, whose larger end is 24 inches by 20 inches, the smaller end 16 inches by 12 inches, and the length 18 feet?

3. What is the solidity of a block, whose ends are respectively 30 by 27 inches and 24 by 18 inches, and whose length is 36 inches?

4. What is the capacity in gallons of a cistern $47\frac{1}{4}$ inches deep, whose inside dimensions are, at the top $81\frac{1}{2}$ and 55 inches, and at the bottom 41 and $29\frac{1}{2}$ inches?

Ans. 546.929 gall.

PROBLEM IX.

673. To find the surface of a REGULAR POLYEDRON.

Multiply the area of one of the faces by the number of faces; or multiply the square of one of the edges of the polyedron by the surface of a similar polyedron whose edges are 1.

For, since the faces of a regular polyedron are all equal, it is evident that the area of one face multiplied by the number of faces will give the area of the whole surface. Also, since the surfaces of regular polyedrons of the same name are bounded by the same number of similar polygons (Prop. I. Bk. VI.), their surfaces are to each other as the squares of the edges of the polyedrons (Prop. I. Cor., Bk. VI.).

674. Table of Surfaces and Solidities of Polyedrons whose Edge is 1.

NAMES.	NO. OF FACES.	SURFACES.	SOLIDITIES.
Tetraedron,	4	1.7320508	0.1178511
Hexaedron,	6	6.0000000	1.0000000
Octaedron,	8	3.4641016	0.4714045
Dodecaedron,	12	20.6457288	7.6631189
Icosaedron,	20	8.6602540	2.1816950

The surfaces in the table are obtained by multiplying the area of one of the faces of the polyedron, as given in Art. 632, by the number of faces.

Examples.

1. What is the surface of an octaedron whose edge is 16 inches?

$16^2 \times 3.4641016 = 886.81$ sq. in., the area required.

2. Required the surface of an icosaedron whose edge is 20 inches.

3. Required the surface of a dodecaedron whose edge is 12 feet. Ans. 2972.985 sq. ft.

Problem X.

675. To find the solidity of a regular polyedron.

Multiply the surface by one third of the perpendicular distance from the center to one of the faces; or multiply the cube of one of the edges by the solidity of a similar polyedron whose edge is 1.

For any regular polyedron may be divided into as many equal pyramids as it has faces, the common vertex of the pyramids being the center of the polyedron; hence, the solidity of the polyedron must equal the product of the areas of all its faces by one third the perpendicular distance from the center to each face of the polyedron.

Also, since similar pyramids are to each other as the cubes of their homologous edges (Prop. XXII. Bk. VIII.), two polyedrons containing the same number of similar pyramids are to each other as the cubes of their edges; hence, the solidity of a polyedron whose edge is 1 (Art. 673), may be used to measure other similar polyedrons.

EXAMPLES.

1. Required the solidity of an octaedron whose edge is 16 inches.

$16^3 \times 0.4714045 = 1930.8728$ cu. in., solidity required.

2. What is the solidity of a tetraedron whose edge is 2 feet?

3. Required the solidity of an icosaedron whose edge is 15 inches. Ans. 7363.2206 cu. in.

PROBLEM XI.

676. To find the surface of a CYLINDER.

Multiply the circumference of its base by its altitude, and the product will be the CONVEX *surface* (Prop. I. Bk. X.). *To this add the areas of its two bases, and the result will be the* ENTIRE *surface.*

EXAMPLES.

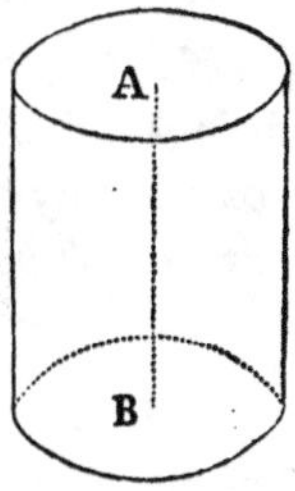

1. What is the entire surface of a cylinder, the altitude of which, A B, is 10 feet, and the circumference of the base 20 feet?

$10 \times 20 = 200$; $20^2 \times 0.07958 \times 2 = 63.264$; $200 + 63.264 = 263.264$ sq. ft., the surface required.

2. Required the convex surface of a cylinder whose altitude is 16 feet, and the circumference of whose base is 21 feet.

3. What is the entire surface of a cylinder whose altitude is 10 inches, and whose circumference is 4 feet?

4. How many times must a cylinder 5 feet 3 inches long, and 21 inches in diameter, revolve, to roll an acre?

Ans. 1509.18 times.

PROBLEM XII.

677. To find the solidity of a CYLINDER.

Multiply the area of the base by the altitude, and the product will be the solidity (Prop. II. Bk. X.).

EXAMPLES.

1. What is the solidity of a cylinder, whose altitude is 10 feet, and the circumference of whose base is 20 feet?

$20^2 \times 0.07958 \times 10 = 318.32$ cu. ft., solidity required.

2. Required the solidity of a cylindrical log, whose length is 9 feet, and the circumference of whose base is 6 feet.

Ans. 25.7831 cu. ft.

3. The Winchester bushel is a hollow cylinder $18\frac{1}{2}$ inches in diameter, and 8 inches deep; what is its capacity in cubic inches?

PROBLEM XIII.

678. To find the surface of a CONE.

Multiply the circumference of the base by half the slant height (Prob. III. Bk. X.), *and the product will be the convex surface. To this add the area of the base, and the result will be the entire surface.*

EXAMPLES.

1. What is the convex surface of a cone, whose slant height is 28 feet, and the circumference of whose base is 40 feet?

$40 \times \frac{28}{2} = 560$ sq. ft., the surface required.

2. Required the entire surface of a cone, whose slant height is 14 feet, and the circumference of whose base is 92 inches.

3. What is the surface of a cone, whose slant height is 9 feet, and the diameter of whose base is 36 inches?

4. How many yards of canvas are required for the covering of a conical tent, the slant height of which is 30 feet, and the circumference of the base 900 feet?

Ans. 1500 sq. yd.

PROBLEM XIV.

679. To find the surface of a FRUSTUM OF A CONE.

Multiply half the sum of the circumferences of its two bases by its slant height, and the product will be the convex surface (Prop. IV. Bk. X.). *To this add the area of its bases, and the result will be the entire surface.*

680. *Scholium.* The convex surface of a frustum of a cone may also be found *by multiplying the slant height* by the circumference of a section at equal distances between the two bases (Prop. IV. Cor., Bk. X.).

EXAMPLES.

1. Required the convex surface of a frustum of a cone, whose slant height is 20 feet, and the circumferences of whose bases are 30 feet and 40 feet.

$$\frac{30+40}{2} \times 20 = 700 \text{ sq. ft., the surface required.}$$

2. Required the surface of a frustum of a cone, the diameters of the bases being 43 inches and 23 inches, and the slant height 9 feet.

3. What is the convex surface of a frustum of a cone, of which a section equidistant from its two bases is 24 feet in circumference, the slant height of the frustum being 19 feet?

4. From a cone the circumference of whose base is 10 feet, and whose slant height is 30 feet, a cone has been cut off, whose slant height is 8 feet. What is the convex surface of the frustum? Ans. $139\frac{1}{3}$ sq. ft.

PROBLEM XV.

681. To find the solidity of a CONE.

Multiply the area of its base by one third of its altitude, and the product will be the solidity (Prop. V. Bk. X.).

EXAMPLES.

1. What is the solidity of a cone whose altitude is 42 feet, and the diameter of whose base is 10 feet?

$10^2 \times 0.7854 \times \frac{42}{3} = 1099.56$ cu. ft., solidity required.

2. Required the solidity of a cone whose altitude is 63 feet, and the radius of whose base is 12 feet 6 inches.

3. How many cubic feet in a conical stick of timber, whose length is 18 feet, the diameter at the larger end being 42 inches? Ans. 57.7269 cu. ft.

PROBLEM XVI.

682. To find the solidity of the FRUSTUM OF A CONE.

Add together the areas of the two bases and a mean proportional between them, and multiply that sum by one third of the altitude of the frustum; and the result will be the solidity required (Prop. VI. Bk. X.).

EXAMPLES.

1. What is the solidity of a frustum of a cone, C D E F, whose altitude, A B, is 21 feet, and the area of whose bases, F E, C D, are 80 square feet and 300 square feet?

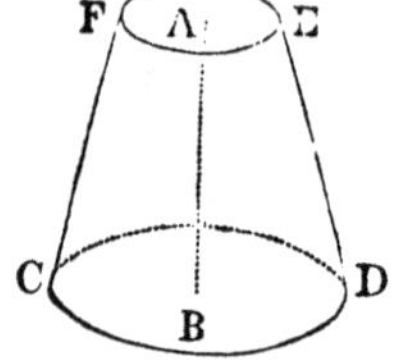

$(80 + 300 + \sqrt{80 \times 300}) \times \frac{21}{3} =$ 3732.96 cu. ft., solidity required.

2. Required the solidity of a frustum of a cone, the diameters of the bases being 38 and 27 inches, and the altitude 11 feet.

3. If a cask, which is two equal frustums of cones joined together at the larger bases, have its bung diameter 28

inches, the head diameter 20 inches, and length 40 inches, how many gallons of wine will it hold? Ans. 79.06.

PROBLEM XVII.

683. To find the surface of a SPHERE.

Multiply the diameter by the circumference of a great circle of the sphere (Prop. VIII. Bk. X.); *or multiply the area of one great circle of the sphere by* 4 (Prop. VIII. Cor 1, Bk. X.); *or multiply* 3.1416 *by the square of the diameter* (Prop. VIII. Cor. 4, Bk. X.).

EXAMPLES.

1. What is the surface of a sphere, whose diameter, ED, is 40 feet, and whose circumference, A E B D, is 125.664?

125.664 × 40 = 5026.56 sq. [ft., the surface required.

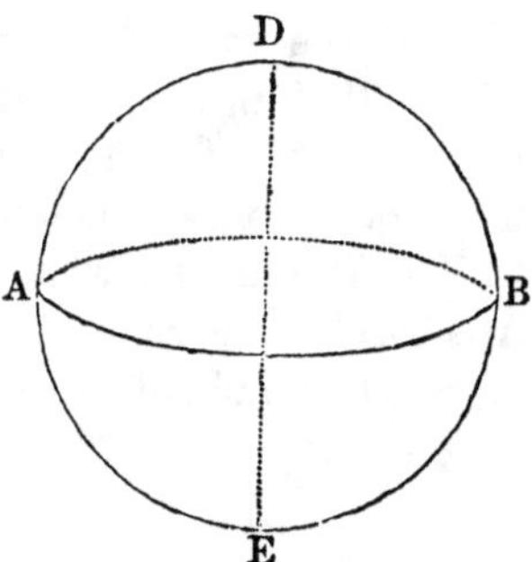

2. Required the surface of a sphere whose diameter is 30 inches.

3. What is the surface of a globe whose diameter is 7 feet and circumference 21.99 feet? Ans. 153.93.

4. How many square miles of surface has the earth, its diameter being 7912 miles?

PROBLEM XVIII.

684. To find the surface of a ZONE or SEGMENT OF A SPHERE.

Multiply the altitude of the zone or segment by the circumference of a great circle of the sphere (Prop. VIII. Cor. 2, Bk. X.); *or multiply the product of the diameter and altitude by* 3.1416 (Prop. VIII. Cor. 6, Bk. X.).

EXAMPLES.

1. What is the surface of a segment of a sphere, the altitude of the segment being 10 feet, and the diameter of the sphere 50 feet?

$50 \times 10 \times 3.1416 = 1570.80$ sq. ft., surface required.

2. The altitude of a segment of a sphere is 38 inches, and the circumference of the sphere is 25 feet; what is the surface of the segment?

3. Required the surface of a zone or segment, the diameter of the sphere being 72 feet, and the altitude of the zone 24 feet. Ans. 5428.6848 sq. ft.

4. If the earth be regarded as a perfect sphere whose axis is 7912 miles, and the part of the axis corresponding to each of the frigid zones is 327.192848, to each of the temperate zones 2053.468612, and to the torrid zone 3150.67708 miles; what is the surface of each zone?

Ans. Each frigid zone 8132797.39568; each temperate zone 51041592.99898; torrid zone 78314115.07768 miles.

PROBLEM XIX.

685. To find the solidity of a SPHERE.

Multiply the surface of the sphere by one third of its radius (Prop. IX. Bk. X.); *or multiply the cube of the diameter of the sphere by* 0.5236 (Prop. IX. Cor. 5, Bk. X.).

EXAMPLES.

1. What is the solidity of a sphere whose diameter is 40 inches?

$40^3 \times 0.5236 = 33510.4$ cu. in., the solidity required.

2. Required the solidity of a globe whose circumference is 60 inches.

3. What is the solidity of the moon in cubic miles, supposing it a perfect sphere with a diameter of 2160 miles?

4. Required the solidity of the earth, supposing it to be a perfect sphere, whose diameter is 7912 miles.

Ans. 259332805349.80493 cu. miles.

PROBLEM XX.

686. To find the surface of a SPHERICAL POLYGON.

From the sum of all the angles subtract the product of two right angles by the number of sides less two; divide the remainder by 90°, and multiply the quotient by one eighth of the surface of the sphere; and the result will be the surface of the spherical polygon (Prop. XX. Bk. IX.).

EXAMPLES.

1. Required the surface of a spherical polygon having five sides, described on a sphere whose diameter is 100 feet, the sum of the angles being 720 degrees.

$2 \times 90° \times (5 - 2) = 540°$; $(720° - 540°) \div 90° = 2$;
$100^2 \times 3.1416 = 31416$; $2 \times \frac{31416}{8} = 7854$ sq. ft., the surface required.

2. What is the surface of a triangle on a sphere whose diameter is 20 feet, the angles being 150°, 90°, and 54°?

PROBLEM XXI.

687. To find the solidity of a SPHERICAL PYRAMID or SECTOR.

Multiply the area of the polygon or zone which forms the base of the pyramid or sector by one third of the radius (Prop. IX. Cor. 1, Bk. X.); *or multiply the altitude of the base by the square of the radius, and that product by* 2.0944 (Prop. IX. Cor. 7, Bk. X.).

EXAMPLES.

1. Required the solidity of a spherical sector, A C B E, the altitude, E D, of the zone forming its base being 5 feet, and the radius, C B, of the sphere being 12 feet.

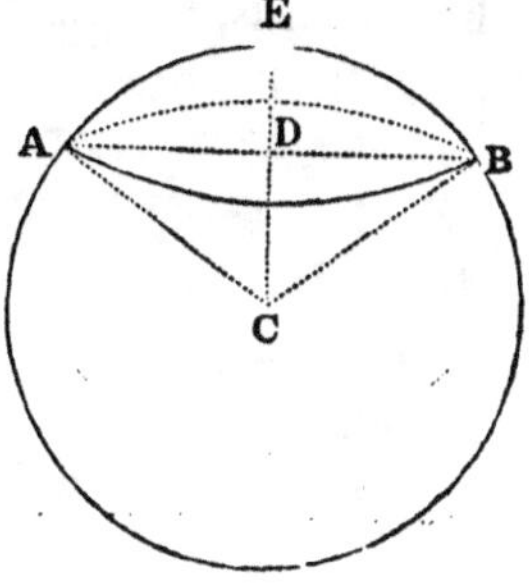

$5 \times 24 \times 3.1416 = 376.992$;
$376.992 \times \frac{12}{3} = 1507.968$ cu. ft., the solidity required.

2. What is the solidity of a spherical pyramid, the area of its base being 364 square feet, and the diameter of the sphere 60 feet?

3. Required the solidity of a spherical sector, whose base is a zone 16 inches in altitude, in a sphere 3 feet in diameter.

4. What is the solidity of a spherical sector, whose base is a zone 6 feet in altitude, in a sphere 18 feet in diameter? Ans. 1017.88 cu. ft.

Problem XXII.

688. To find the solidity of a SPHERICAL SEGMENT.

When the segment is LESS *than a hemisphere, from the solidity of the spherical* SECTOR *whose base is the zone of the segment, take the solidity of the cone whose vertex is the center of the sphere, and whose base is the circular base of the segment; but when the segment is* GREATER *than a hemisphere, take the sum of these solidities* (Prop. IX. Sch., Bk. X.).

689. *Scholium.* If the segment has two plane bases, its solidity may be found *by taking the difference of the two segments which lie on the same side of its two bases* (Prop. IX. Sch., Bk. X.).

Examples.

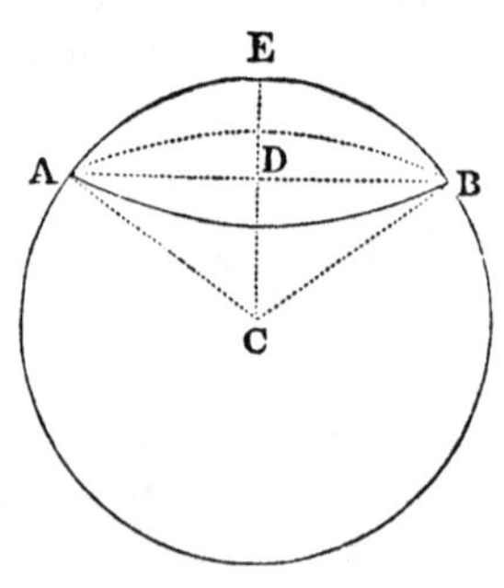

1. What is the solidity of a segment, A B E, whose altitude, E D, is 5 feet, cut from a sphere whose radius, C E, is 20 feet?

The altitude of the cone A B C is equal to C E — E D, or 20 — 5, which is equal to 15 feet; and the radius of its base is equal to $\sqrt{CA^2 - CD^2}$, or $\sqrt{20^2 - 15^2}$, which is equal to 13.23; consequently the diameter A B is equal to 26.46 feet; $5 \times 20^2 \times 2.0944 = 4188.8$

cubic feet, the solidity of the sector A C D E (Prob. XXI.); $26.46^2 \times 0.7854 \times \frac{15}{3} = 2946.99$ cubic feet, the solidity of the cone A B – C (Prob. XV.); $4188.8 - 2946.99 = 1241.81$ cubic feet, the solidity of the segment A B E required.

2. Required the solidity of a segment, whose altitude is 57 inches, the diameter of the sphere being 153 inches.

3. What is the solidity of a spherical segment, whose altitude is 13 feet, and the diameter of the sphere 33 feet 6 inches?

4. Required the solidity of the segments of the earth which are bounded severally by its five zones, the earth's diameter being 7912 miles, and the part of the diameter corresponding to each of the frigid zones being 327.19, to each temperate zone 2053.47, and to the torrid zone 3150.68.

Ans. Each frigid zone 1293793463.32, each temperate zone 55013912318.45, and the torrid zone 146717393786.26 cubic miles.

The Spheroid.

690. A SPHEROID is a solid which may be described by the revolution of an ellipse about one of its axes, which remains immovable.

An *oblate* spheroid is one described by the revolution of the ellipse about its *minor* or *conjugate* axis.

A *prolate* spheroid is one described by the revolution of the ellipse about its major or transverse axis.

Problem XXIII.

691. To find the solidity of a SPHEROID.

Multiply the square of the axis of revolution by the fixed axis, and that product by 0.5236.

A full demonstration of this, which is based upon the principle that a spheroid is two thirds of its circumscribing cylinder, would require a knowledge of Conic Sections, or of the Differential and Integral Calculi, with neither of which is the learner here supposed to be acquainted.

The relation, however, of the spheroid to its circumscribing cylinder, is that which the sphere sustains to its circumscribing cylinder (Prop. X. Bk. X.).

Now the area of the base of the cylinder is found by multiplying the square of the axis of revolution by 0.7854, and the solidity of the cylinder by multiplying that product by the fixed axis (Prop. II. Bk. X.). But the solidity of the spheroid is only two thirds of that of the cylinder; hence, to obtain the solidity of the former, instead of multiplying by 0.7854, we must use a factor only two thirds as large, which will be 0.5236.

Examples.

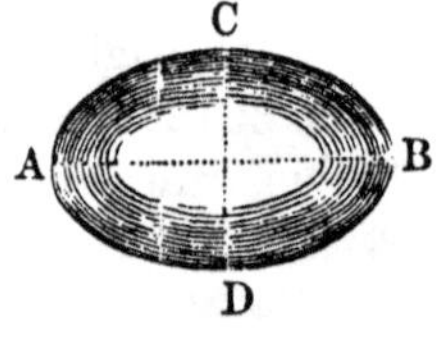

1. What is the solidity of the oblate spheroid A C B D, whose fixed axis, C D, is 30 inches, and the axis of revolution, A B, 40 inches.

$40^2 \times 30 \times 0.5236 = 25132.8$ cubic inches, the solidity required.

2. Required the solidity of a prolate spheroid, whose fixed axis is 50 feet, and the axis of revolution 36 feet.

3. What is the solidity of a prolate, and also of an oblate spheroid, the axes of each being 25 and 15 inches?

Ans. Prolate, 2945.25 cu. in.; oblate, 4908.75 cu. in.

4. What is the solidity of a prolate, and also of an oblate spheroid, the axes of each being 3 feet 6 inches and 2 feet 10 inches?

5. Required the solidity of the earth, its figure being that of an oblate spheroid whose axes are 7925.3 and 7898.9 miles. Ans. 259774584886.834 cubic miles.

BOOK XIII.

MISCELLANEOUS GEOMETRICAL EXERCISES.

1. If the opposite angles formed by four lines meeting at a point are equal, these lines form but two straight lines.

2. If the equal sides of an isosceles triangle are produced, the two exterior angles formed with the base will be equal.

3. The sum of any two sides of a triangle is greater than the third side.

4. If from any point within a triangle two straight lines are drawn to the extremities of either side, they will include a greater angle than that contained by the other two sides.

5. If two quadrilaterals have the four sides of the one equal to the four sides of the other, each to each, and the angle included by any two sides of the one equal to the angle contained by the corresponding sides of the other, the quadrilaterals are themselves equal.

6. The sum of the diagonals of a trapezium is less than the sum of any four lines which can be drawn to the four angles from any point within the figure, except from the intersection of the diagonals.

7. Lines joining the corresponding extremities of two equal and parallel straight lines, are themselves equal and parallel, and the figure formed is a parallelogram.

8. If, in the sides of a square, at equal distances from the four angles, points be taken, one in each side, the straight lines joining these points will form a square.

9. If one angle of a parallelogram is a right angle, all its angles are right angles.

10. Any straight line drawn through the middle point of a diagonal of a parallelogram to meet the sides, is bisected in that point, and likewise bisects the parallelogram.

11. If four magnitudes are proportionals, the first and second may be multiplied or divided by the same magnitude, and also the third and fourth by the same magnitude, and the resulting magnitudes will be proportionals.

12. If four magnitudes are proportionals, the first and third may be multiplied or divided by the same magnitude, and also the second and fourth by the same magnitude, and the resulting magnitudes will be proportionals.

13. If there be two sets of proportional magnitudes, the quotients of the corresponding terms will be proportionals.

14. If any two points be taken in the circumference of a circle, the straight line joining them will lie wholly within the circle.

15. The diameter is the longest straight line that can be inscribed in a circle.

16. If two straight lines intercept equal arcs of a circle, and do not cut each other within the circle, the lines will be parallel.

17. If a straight line be drawn to touch a circle, and be parallel to a chord, the point of contact will be the middle point of the arc cut off by that chord.

18. If two circles cut each other, and from either point of intersection diameters be drawn, the extremities of these diameters and the other point of intersection will be in the same straight line.

19. If one of the equal sides of an isosceles triangle be the diameter of a circle, the circumference of the circle will bisect the base of the triangle.

20. If the opposite angles of a quadrilateral be together equal to two right angles, a circle may be circumscribed about the quadrilateral.

21. Parallelograms which have two sides and the included angle equal in each, are themselves equal.

22. Equivalent triangles upon the same base, and upon the same side of it, are between the same parallels.

23. If the middle points of the sides of a trapezoid, which are not parallel, be joined by a straight line, that line will be parallel to each of the two parallel sides, and be equal to half their sum.

24. If, in opposite sides of a parallelogram, at equal distances from opposite angles, points be taken, one in each side, the straight line joining these points will bisect the parallelogram.

25. The perimeter of an isosceles triangle is greater than the perimeter of a rectangle, which is of the same altitude with, and equivalent to, the given triangle.

26. If the sides of the square described upon the hypothenuse of a right-angled triangle be produced to meet the sides (produced if necessary) of the squares described upon the other two sides of the triangle, the triangles thus formed will be similar to the given triangle, and two of them will be equal to it.

27. A square circumscribed about a given circle is double a square inscribed in the same circle.

28. If the sum of the squares of the four sides of a quadrilateral be equivalent to the sum of the squares of the two diagonals, the figure is a parallelogram.

29. Straight lines drawn from the vertices of a triangle, so as to bisect the opposite sides, bisect also the triangle.

30. The straight lines which bisect the three angles of a triangle meet in the same point.

31. The area of a triangle is equal to its perimeter multiplied by half the radius of the inscribed circle.

32. If the points of bisection of the sides of a given triangle be joined, the triangle so formed will be one fourth of the given triangle.

33. To describe a square upon a given straight line.

34. To find in a given straight line a point equally distant from two given points.

35. To construct a triangle, the base, one of the angles at the base, and the sum of the other two sides being given.

36. To trisect a right angle.

37. To divide a triangle into two parts by a line drawn parallel to a side, so that these parts shall be to each other as two given straight lines.

38. To divide a triangle into two parts by a line drawn perpendicular to the base, so that these parts shall be to each other as two given lines.

39. To divide a triangle into two parts by a line drawn from a given point in one of the sides, so that the parts shall be to each other as two given lines.

40. To divide a triangle into a square number of equal triangles, similar to each other and to the original triangle.

41. To trisect a given straight line.

42. To inscribe a square in a given right-angled isosceles triangle.

43. To inscribe a square in a given quadrant.

44. To describe a circle that shall pass through a given point, have a given radius, and touch a given straight line.

45. To describe a circle, the centre of which shall be in the perpendicular of a given right-angled triangle, and the circumference of which shall pass through the right angle and touch the hypothenuse.

46. To describe three circles of equal diameters which shall touch each other, and to describe another circle which shall touch the three circles.

47. If, on the diameter of a semicircle, two equal circles be described, and in the curvilinear space included by the three circumferences a circle be inscribed, its diameter will be to that of the equal circles in the ratio of two to three.

48. If two points be taken in the diameter of a circle,

equidistant from the centre, the sum of the squares of two lines drawn from these points to any point in the circumference will always be the same.

49. Given the vertical angle, and the radii of the inscribed and circumscribed circles, to construct the triangle.

50. If a diagonal cuts off three, five, or any odd number of sides from a regular polygon, the diagonal is parallel to one of the sides.

51. The area of a regular hexagon inscribed in a circle is double that of an equilateral triangle inscribed in the same circle.

52. The side of a square circumscribed about a circle is equal to the diagonal of a square inscribed in the same circle.

53. To describe a circle equal to half a given circle.

54. A regular duodecagon is equivalent to three fourths of the square constructed on the diameter of its circumscribed circle; or is equal to the square constructed on the side of the equilateral triangle inscribed in the same circle.

55. If semicircles be described on the sides of a right-angled triangle as diameters, the one described on the hypothenuse will be equal to the sum of the other two.

56. If on the sides of a triangle inscribed in a semicircle, semicircles be described, the two crescents thus formed will together equal the area of the triangle.

57. If the diameter of a semicircle be divided into any number of parts, and on them semicircles be described, their circumferences will together be equal to the circumference of the given semicircle.

58. To divide a circle into any number of parts, which shall all be equal in area and equal in perimeter, and not have the parts in the form of sectors.

59. To draw a straight line perpendicular to a plane, from a given point above the plane.

60. Two straight lines not in the same plane being

given in position, to draw a straight line which shall be perpendicular to them both.

61. The solidity of a triangular prism is equal to the product of the area of either of its rectangular sides as a base multiplied by half its altitude on that base.

62. All prisms of equal bases and altitudes are equal in solidity, whatever be the figure of their bases.

63. The convex surface of a regular pyramid exceeds the area of its base in the ratio that the slant height of the pyramid exceeds the radius of the circle inscribed in its base.

64. If from any point in the circumference of the base of a cylinder, a straight line be drawn perpendicular to the plane of the base, it will be wholly in the surface of the cylinder.

65. A cylinder and a parallelopipedon of equal bases and altitudes are equivalent to each other.

66. If two solids have the same height, and if their sections made at equal altitudes, by planes parallel to the bases, have always the same ratio which the bases have to one another, the solids have to one another the same ratio which their bases have.

67. The side of the largest cube that can be inscribed in a sphere, is equal to the square root of one third of the square of the diameter of the sphere.

68. To cut off just a square yard from a plank 14 feet 3 inches long, and of a uniform width, at what distance from the edge must a line be struck? Ans. $7\frac{11}{19}$ in.

69. How much carpeting a yard wide will be required to cover the floor of an octagonal hall, whose sides are 10 feet each?

70. The perambulator, or surveying-wheel, is so constructed as to turn just twice in the length of a rod; what is its diameter? Ans. 2.626 ft.

71. What is the excess of a floor 50 feet long by 30 broad, above two others, each of half its dimensions?

72. The four sides of a trapezium are 13, 13.4, 24, and 18 feet, and the first two contain a right angle. Required the area. Ans. 253.38 sq. ft.

73. If an equilateral triangle, whose area is equal to 10,000 square feet, be surrounded with a walk of uniform width, and equal to the area of the inscribed circle, what is the width of the walk? Ans. 11.701 ft.

74. A right-angled triangle has its base 16 rods, and its perpendicular 12 rods, and a triangle is cut off from it by a line parallel to its base, of which the area is 24 rods. Required the sides of that triangle. Ans. 8, 6, and 10 rods.

75. There is a circular pond whose area is 5028$\frac{4}{7}$ square feet, in the middle of which stood a pole 100 feet high; now, the pole having been broken off, it was observed that the top portion resting on the stump just reached the brink of the pond. What is the height of the piece left standing? Ans. 41.9968 ft.

76. The area of a square inscribed in a circle is 400 square feet; required the diagonal of a square circumscribed about the same circle.

77. The four sides of a field, whose diagonals are equal, are known to be 25, 35, 31, and 19 rods, in a successive order; what is the area of the field?

Ans. 4 A. 1 R. 38$\frac{1}{4}$ p.

78. The wheels of a chaise, each 4 feet high, in turning within a ring, moved so that the outer wheel made two turns while the inner made one, and their distance from one another was 5 feet; what were the circumferences of the tracks described by them?

Ans. Outer, 62.8318 ft.; inner, 31.4159 ft.

79. The girt of a vessel round the outside of the hoop is 22 inches, and the hoop is 1 inch thick; required the true girt of the vessel.

80. If one of the Egyptian pyramids is 490 feet high, having each slant side an equilateral triangle and the base a square, what is the area of the base?

Ans. 11 A. 3 rd. 223$\frac{1}{4}$ ft.

81. An ellipse is surrounded by a wall 14 inches thick; its axes are 840 links and 612 links; required the quantity of ground enclosed, and the quantity occupied by the wall.

Ans. 4 A. 6 rd. enclosed, and 1760.49 sq. ft., area occupied by the wall.

82. There is a meadow of 1 acre in the form of a square; what must be the length of the rope by which a horse, tied equidistant from each angle, can be permitted to graze over the entire meadow?

83. A gentleman has a rectangular garden, whose length is 100 feet and breadth 80 feet; what must be the uniform width of a walk half-way round the same, to take up just half the garden? Ans. 25.9688 ft.

84. Two trees, 100 feet asunder, are placed, the one at the distance of 100 feet, and the other 50 feet from a wall; what is the distance that a person must pass over in running from one tree to touch the wall, and then to the other tree, the lines of distance making equal angles with the wall? Ans. 173.205 ft.

85. There is a rectangular park 400 feet long and 300 feet broad, all round which, and close by the wall, is a border 10 feet broad; close by the border there is a walk, and also two others, crossing each other and the park at right angles, in the middle of the garden. The walks are all of one breadth, and their area takes up one tenth of the whole park; required the breadth of the walks.

Ans. 6.2375 ft.

86. A farmer borrowed a cubical pile of wood, which measured 6 feet every way, and repaid it by two cubical piles, of which the sides were 3 feet each; what part of the quantity borrowed has he returned?

87. A board is 10 feet long, 8 inches in breadth at the greater end, and 6 inches at the less; how much must be cut off from the less end to make a square foot?

Ans. 23.2493 in.

88. A piece of timber is 10 feet long, each side of the

greater base 9 inches, and each side of the less 6 inches; how much must be cut off from the less end to contain a solid foot? Ans. 3.39214 ft.

89. What must be the inside dimensions of a cubical box to hold 200 balls, each $2\frac{1}{2}$ inches in diameter?

90. Near my house I intend making a hexagonal or six-sided seat around a tree, for which I have procured a pine plank $16\frac{1}{2}$ feet long and 11 inches broad; what must be the inner and outer lengths of each side of the seat, that there may be the least loss in cutting up the plank?

Ans. 26.64915 in. inner, and 39.35085 in. outer length.

91. Required the capacity of a tub in the form of a frustum of a cone, of which the greatest diameter is 48 inches, the inside length of the staves 30 inches, and the diagonal between the farthest extremities of the diameters 50 inches. Ans. 165.34 gals.

92. The front of a house is of such a height, that, if the foot of a ladder of a certain length be placed at the distance of 12 feet from it, the top of the ladder will just reach to the top of the house; but if the foot of the ladder be placed 20 feet from the front, its top will fall 4 feet below the top of the house. Required the height of the house, and the length of the ladder.

Ans. 34 feet, the height of the building; 36.0555 feet, the length of the ladder.

93. A sugar-loaf in form of a cone is 20 inches high; it is required to divide it equally among three persons, by sections parallel to the base; what is the height of each part?

Ans. Upper 13.8672, next 3.6044, lowest 2.5284 in.

94. Within a rectangular court, whose length is four chains, and breadth three chains, there is a piece of water in the form of a trapezium, whose opposite angles are in a direct line with those of the court, and the respective distances of the angles of the one from those of the other are 20, 25, 40, and 45 yards, in a successive order; required the area of the water. Ans. 960 sq. yd.

95. What will the diameter of a sphere be, when its solidity and the area of its surface are expressed by the same numbers? Ans. 6.

96. There is a circular fortification, which occupies a quarter of an acre of ground, surrounded by a ditch coinciding with the circumference, 24 feet wide at bottom, 26 at top, and 12 deep; how much water will fill the ditch, if it slope equally on both sides? Ans. 135483.25 cu. ft.

97. A father, dying, left a square field containing 30 acres to be divided among his five sons, in such a manner that the oldest son may have 8 acres, the second 7, the third 6, the fourth 5, and the fifth 4 acres. Now, the division fences are to be so made that the oldest son's share shall be a narrow piece of equal breadth all around the field, leaving the remaining four shares in the form of a square; and in like manner for each of the other shares, leaving always the remainders in form of squares, one within another, till the share of the youngest be the innermost square of all, equal to 4 acres. Required a side of each of the enclosures.

Ans. 17.3205, 14.8324, 12.2474, 9.4868, and 6.3246 chains.

98. Required the dimensions of a cone, its solidity being 282 inches, and its slant height being to its base diameter as 5 to 4.

Ans. 9.796 in. the base diameter; 12.246 in. the slant height; and 11.223 in. the altitude.

99. A gentleman has a piece of ground in form of a square, the difference between whose side and diagonal is 10 rods. He would convert two thirds of the area into a garden of an octagonal form, but would have a fish-pond at the centre of the garden, in the form of an equilateral triangle, whose area must equal five square rods. Required the length of each side of the garden, and of each side of the pond.

Ans. 8.9707 rods, each side of the garden, and 3.398 rods, each side of the pond.

BOOK XIV.

APPLICATIONS OF ALGEBRA TO GEOMETRY.

692. WHEN it is proposed to solve a geometrical problem by aid of Algebra, draw a figure which shall represent the several parts or conditions of the problem, both known and required.

Represent the known parts by the first letters of the alphabet, and the required parts by the last letters.

Then, observing the geometrical relations that the parts of the figure have to each other, make as many independent equations as there are unknown quantities introduced, and the solution of these equations will determine the unknown quantities or required parts.

To form these equations, however, no definite rules can be given; but the best aids may be derived from experience, and a thorough knowledge of geometrical principles.

It should be the aim of the learner to effect the simplest solution possible of each problem.

PROBLEM I.

693. *In a right-angled triangle, having given the hypothenuse, and the sum of the other two sides, to determine these sides.*

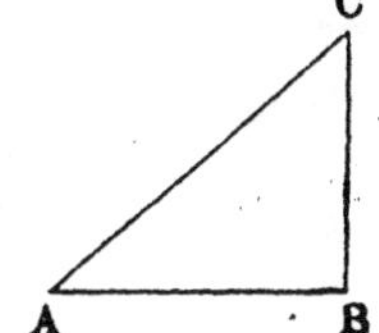

Let A B C be the triangle, right-angled at B. Put A C $= a$, the sum A B $+$ B C $= s$, A B $= x$, and B C $= y$.

Then, $x + y = s.$

and (Prop. XI. Bk. IV.),

$$x^2 + y^2 = a^2.$$

From the first equation, $x = s - y.$

Substitute in second equation this value of x,

$$s^2 - 2\,s\,y + 2\,y^2 = a^2.$$

Or, $2\,y^2 - 2\,s\,y = a^2 - s^2,$

Or, $y^2 - s\,y = \frac{1}{2}\,a^2 - \frac{1}{2}\,s^2.$

By completing the square,

$$y^2 - s\,y + \tfrac{1}{4}\,s^2 = \tfrac{1}{2}\,a^2 - \tfrac{1}{4}\,s^2,$$

Extracting sq. root, $y - \frac{1}{2}\,s = \pm\sqrt{\frac{1}{2}\,a^2 - \frac{1}{4}\,s^2},$

Or, $y = \frac{1}{2}\,s \pm \sqrt{\frac{1}{2}\,a^2 - \frac{1}{4}\,s^2}.$

If A C = 5, and the sum A B + B C = 7, $y = 4$ or 3, and $x = 3$ or 4.

PROBLEM II.

694. *Having given the base and perpendicular of a triangle, to find the side of an inscribed square.*

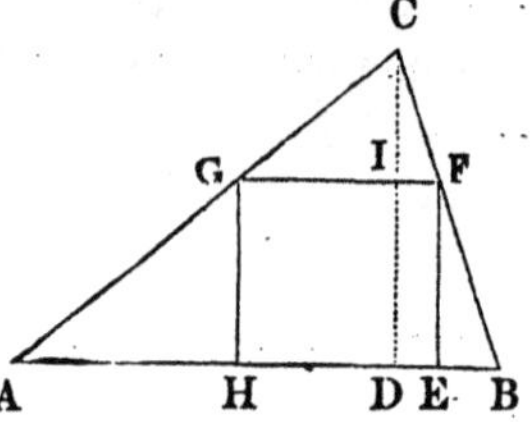

Let A B C be the triangle, and H E F G the inscribed square. Put A B $= b$, C D $= a$, and G F or G H = D I $= x$; then will C I = C D — D I = $a - x$.

Since the triangles A B C, G F C are similar,

$$AB : CD :: GF : CI,$$

or $b : a :: x : a - x.$

Hence, $ab - bx = ax,$

or, $x = \dfrac{ab}{a + b}.$

that is, *the side of the inscribed square is equal to the product of the base by the altitude, divided by their sum.*

PROBLEM III.

695. *Having given the lengths of two straight lines drawn from the acute angles of a right-angled triangle to the middle of the opposite sides, to determine those sides.*

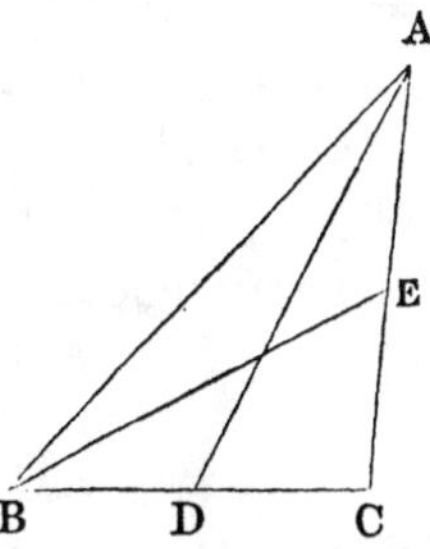

Let A B C be the given triangle, and A D, B E the given lines.

Put A D $= a$, B E $= b$, C D or $\frac{1}{2}$ C B $= x$, and C E or $\frac{1}{2}$ C A $= y$; then, since $CD^2 + CA^2 = AD^2$, and $CE^2 + CB^2 = BE^2$,

we have $$x^2 + 4\,y^2 = a^2,$$

and $$y^2 + 4\,x^2 = b^2.$$

By subtracting the second equation from four times the first,

$$15\,y^2 = 4\,a^2 - b^2,$$

or, $$y = \sqrt{\frac{4\,a^2 - b^2}{15}};$$

by subtracting the first equation from four times the second,

$$15\,x^2 = 4\,b^2 - a^2,$$

or, $$x = \sqrt{\frac{4\,b^2 - a^2}{15}};$$

which values of x and y are half the base and perpendiculars of the triangle.

PROBLEM IV.

696. *In an equilateral triangle, having given the lengths of the three perpendiculars drawn from a point within to the three sides, to determine these sides.*

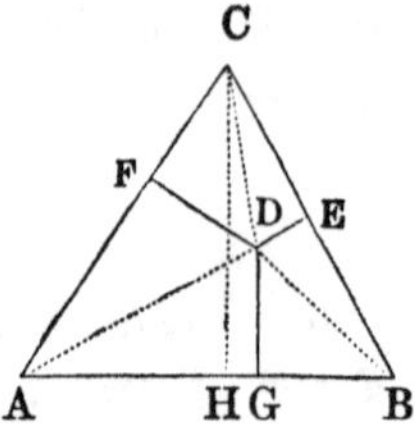

Let A B C be the equilateral triangle, and D E, D F, D G the given perpendiculars from the point D. Draw D A, D B, D C to the vertices of the three angles, and let fall the perpendicular, C H, on the base, A B.

Put D E $= a$, D F $= b$, D G $= c$, and A H or B H, half the side of the equilateral triangle, $= x$. Then A C or B C $= 2x$, and C H $= \sqrt{\text{AC}^2 - \text{AH}^2}$ $= \sqrt{4x^2 - x^2} = \sqrt{3x^2} = x\sqrt{3}$. Now, since the area of a triangle is equal to the product of half its base by its altitude (Prop. VI. Bk. IV.),

$$\text{The triangle ACB} = \tfrac{1}{2}\,\text{AB} \times \text{CH} = x \times x\sqrt{3} = x^2\sqrt{3}.$$
$$\text{ABD} = \tfrac{1}{2}\,\text{AB} \times \text{DG} = x \times c \quad = cx.$$
$$\text{BCD} = \tfrac{1}{2}\,\text{BC} \times \text{DE} = x \times a \quad = ax.$$
$$\text{ACD} = \tfrac{1}{2}\,\text{AC} \times \text{DF} = x \times b \quad = bx.$$

But the three triangles A B D, B C D, A C D are together equal to the triangle A C B.

Hence, $x^2\sqrt{3} = ax + bx + cx = x\,(a + b + c)$,

or, $x\sqrt{3} = a + b + c$;

or, $x = \dfrac{a + b + c}{\sqrt{3}}$.

Hence each side, or $2x = \dfrac{2\,(a + b + c)}{\sqrt{3}}$.

697. *Cor.* Since the perpendicular, C H, is equal to $x\sqrt{3}$, it is equal to $a + b + c$; that is, *the whole perpendicular of an equilateral triangle is equal to the sum of all the perpendiculars let fall from any point in the triangle to each of its sides.*

PROBLEM V.

698. *To determine the radii of three equal circles described within and tangent to a given circle, and also tangent to each other.*

Let AF be the radius of the given circle, and BE the radius of one of the equal circles described within it. Put $AF = a$, and $BE = x$; then each side of the equilateral triangle, BCD, formed by joining the centers of the required circles, will be represented by $2x$, and its altitude, CE, by $\sqrt{4x^2 - x^2}$, or $x\sqrt{3}$.

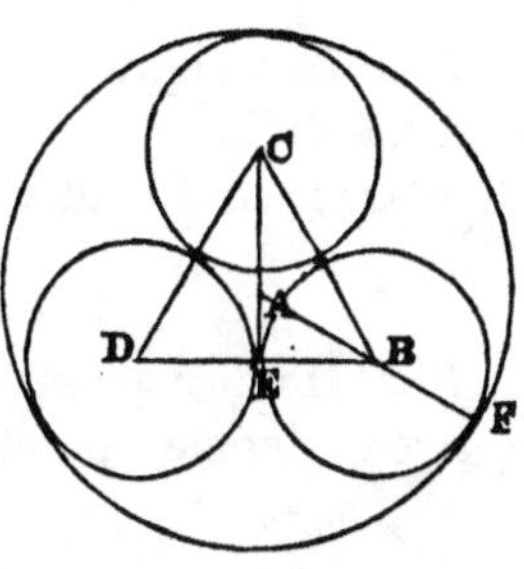

The triangles BCE, ABE are similar, since the angles BCE and ABE are equal, each being half as great as one of the angles of the equilateral triangle, and the angle BEC is common.

Hence, $\quad CE : BE :: BC : AB,$

or $\quad x\sqrt{3} : x :: 2x : AB,$

and $\quad AB = \dfrac{2x}{\sqrt{3}}.$

But $\quad AB + BF = AF;$

hence, $\quad \dfrac{2x}{\sqrt{3}} + x = a,$

or $\quad 2x + x\sqrt{3} = a\sqrt{3},$

or $\quad (2 + \sqrt{3})\,x = a\sqrt{3}.$

Hence, $\quad x = \dfrac{a\sqrt{3}}{2 + \sqrt{3}} = \dfrac{a}{2.1547} = a \times 0.4641.$

Problem VI.

699. In a right-angled triangle, having given the base, and the sum of the perpendicular and hypothenuse, to find these two sides.

Problem VII.

700. In a rectangle, having given the diagonal and perimeter, to find the sides.

PROBLEM VIII.

701. In a right-angled triangle, having given the base, and the difference between the hypothenuse and perpendicular, to find both these two sides.

PROBLEM IX.

702. Having given the area of a rectangle inscribed in a given triangle, to determine the sides of the rectangle.

PROBLEM X.

703. In a triangle, having given the ratio of the two sides, together with both the segments of the base, made by a perpendicular from the vertical angle, to determine the sides of the triangle.

PROBLEM XI.

704. In a triangle, having given the base, the sum of the other two sides, and the length of a line drawn from the vertical angle to the middle of the base, to find the sides of the triangle.

PROBLEM XII.

705. In a triangle, having given the two sides about the vertical angle together with the line bisecting that angle, and terminating in the base, to find the base.

PROBLEM XIII.

706. To determine a right-angled triangle, having given the perimeter and the radius of its inscribed circle.

PROBLEM XIV.

707. To determine a triangle, having given the base, the perpendicular, and the ratio of the two sides.

PROBLEM XV.

708. To determine a right-angled triangle, having given the hypothenuse, and the side of the inscribed square.

Problem XVI.

709. In a right-angled triangle, having given the perimeter, or sum of all the sides, and the perpendicular let fall from the right angle on the hypothenuse, to determine the triangle, that is, its sides.

Problem XVII.

710. To determine a right-angled triangle, having given the hypothenuse, and the difference of two lines drawn from the two acute angles to the centre of the inscribed circle.

Problem XVIII.

711. To determine a triangle, having given the base, the perpendicular, and the difference of the two other sides.

Problem XIX.

712. To determine a triangle, having given the lengths of three lines drawn from the three angles to the middle of the opposite sides.

Problem XX.

713. In a triangle, having given all the three sides, to find the radius of the inscribed circle.

Problem XXI.

714. To determine a right-angled triangle, having given the side of the inscribed square, and the radius of the inscribed circle.

Problem XXII.

715. To determine a triangle, having given the base, the perpendicular, and the rectangle of the two other sides.

Problem XXIII.

716. To determine a right-angled triangle, having given the hypothenuse, and the radius of the inscribed circle.

Problem XXIV.

717. To determine a right-angled triangle, having given the hypothenuse and the difference between a side and the radius of the inscribed circle.

Problem XXV.

718. To determine a triangle, having given the base, the line bisecting the vertical angle, and the diameter of the circumscribing circle.

Problem XXVI.

719. There are two stone pillars in a garden, whose perpendicular heights are 20 and 30 feet, and the distance between them 60 feet. A ladder is to be placed at a certain point in the line of distance, of such a length, that it may just reach the top of both the pillars. What is the length of the ladder, and how far from each pillar must it be placed?

Ans. 39.5899 feet, length of the ladder; $34\frac{1}{6}$ feet, distance of the foot of the ladder from the bottom of the lower pillar; and $25\frac{5}{6}$ feet, distance of the foot of the ladder from the bottom of the higher pillar.

Problem XXVII.

720. There is a cistern, the sum of the length and breadth of which is 84 inches, the diagonal of the top 60 inches, and the ratio of the breadth to the depth as 25 to 7. What are its dimensions, provided it has the form of a rectangular parallelopipedon?

Ans. Length 48 inches; width 36 inches; depth 10.08 inches.

PROBLEM XXVIII.

721. The three distances from an oak, growing in an open plain, to the three visible corners of a square field, lying at some distance, are known to be 78, 59.161, and 78 poles, in successive order. What are the dimensions of the field, and its area?

Ans. Side of the square 24 rd.; area 3 A. 2 R. 16 rd.

PROBLEM XXIX.

722. There is a house of three equal stories in height. Now a ladder being raised against it, at 20 feet distance from the foot of the building, reaches the top; whilst another ladder, 12 feet shorter, raised from the same point, reaches only to the top of the second story. What is the height of the building? Ans. 41.696 ft.

PROBLEM XXX.

723. The solidity of a cone is 2513.28 cubic inches, and the slant side of a frustum of it, whose solidity is 2474.01, is 19.5 inches. Required the dimensions of the cone.

Ans. Altitude 24 inches; base diameter 20 inches.

PROBLEM XXXI.

724. Within a rectangular garden containing just an acre of ground, I have a circular fountain, whose circumference is 40, 28, 52, and 60 yards distant from the four angles of the garden. From these dimensions, the length and breadth of the garden, and likewise the diameter of the fountain, are required.

Ans. Length 94.996 yds.; width 50.949 yds.; diameter of the fountain 20 yds.

PROBLEM XXXII.

725. There is a vessel in the form of a frustum of a cone, standing on its lesser base, whose solidity is 8.67 feet, the depth 21 inches, its greater base diameter to that

of the lesser as 7 to 5, into which a globe had accidentally been put, whose solidity was $2\frac{1}{2}$ times the measure of its surface. Required the diameters of the vessel and of the globe, and how many gallons of water would be requisite just to cover the latter within the former.

Ans. 35 and 25 inches, top and bottom diameters of the frustum; 15 inches, diameter of the globe; and 34.2 gallons, the water required.

Problem XXXIII.

726. Three trees, A, B, C, whose respective heights are 114, 110, and 98 feet, are standing on a horizontal plane, and the distance from A to B is 112, from B to C is 104, and from A to C is 120 feet. What is the distance from the top of each tree to a point in the plane which shall be equally distant from each? Ans. 126.634 ft.

Problem XXXIV.

727. A person possessed a rectangular meadow, the fences of which had been destroyed, and the only mark left was an oak-tree in the east corner; he however recollected the following particulars of the dimensions. It had once been resolved to divide the meadow into two parts by a hedge running diagonally; and he recollected that a segment of the diagonal intercepted by a perpendicular from one of the corners was 16 chains, and the same perpendicular, produced 2 chains, met the other side of the meadow. Now the owner has bequeathed it to four grandchildren, whose shares are to be bounded by the diagonal and perpendicular produced. What is the area of the meadow, and what are the several shares?

Ans. Area of the whole meadow, 16 acres; shares, 1 R. 24 rd.; 1 A. 2 R. 16 rd.; 6 A. 1 R. 24 rd.; 7 A. 2 R. 16 rd.

THE END

ELEMENTS

OF

PLANE AND SPHERICAL TRIGONOMETRY;

WITH

PRACTICAL APPLICATIONS.

TRIGONOMETRY.

BOOK I.

LOGARITHMS.

1. THE LOGARITHM of a number is the exponent of the power to which a given fixed number must be raised in order to produce the first number.

2. The BASE of the system is the fixed number.

3. The base, in the common system of logarithms, is 10. Hence, since

$10^0 =$	1,	0	is the logarithm of	1;
$10^1 =$	10,	1	" "	10;
$10^2 =$	100,	2	" "	100;
$10^3 =$	1,000,	3	" "	1,000;
$10^4 =$	10,000,	4	" "	10,000;
	&c.,		&c.	

It thus appears that, in the common system, the logarithm of every number between 1 and 10 is some number between 0 and 1; that is, a proper fraction. The logarithm of every number between 10 and 100 is some number between 1 and 2; that is, 1 plus a fraction. The logarithm of every number between 100 and 1,000 is some number between 2 and 3; that is, 2 plus a fraction; and so on.

4. By means of *negative* exponents the application of logarithms may be extended, in the common system, to numbers less than 1. Thus, since

$10^{-1} = 0.1,\quad -1$ is the logarithm of 0.1;
$10^{-2} = 0.01,\quad -2$ " " 0.01;
$10^{-3} = 0.001,\quad -3$ " " 0.001;
$10^{-4} = 0.0001,\quad -4$ " " 0.0001;
&c., &c.

From this it appears that the logarithm of every number between 1 and 0.1 is some number between 0 and —1; that is, —1 plus a fraction. The logarithm of every number between 0.1 and 0.01 is some number between —1 and —2; that is, —2 plus a fraction. The logarithm of every number between 0.01 and 0.001 is some number between —2 and —3; that is, —3 plus a fraction; and so on.

5. In the common system, as the logarithms of all numbers which are not exact powers of 10 are incommensurable with those numbers, their values can only be obtained approximately, and are expressed by decimals.

6. The *integral* part of any logarithm is called the CHARACTERISTIC, and the *decimal* part is sometimes called the MANTISSA.

7. *The characteristic of the logarithm of* ANY NUMBER GREATER THAN UNITY, *is one less than the number of integral figures in the given number.*

For it has been shown (Art. 3) that the logarithm of 1 is 0, of 10 is 1, of 100 is 2, of 1000 is 3, and so on.

8. *The characteristic of the logarithm of* ANY DECIMAL FRACTION *is a negative number, and is one more than the number of ciphers between the decimal point and the first significant figure.*

For it has been shown (Art. 4) that the logarithm of 0.1 is —1, of 0.01 is —2, of 0.001 is —3, and so on.

NOTE.—In general, whether the given number be integral, fractional, or mixed, *the characteristic of the logarithm of any number expressed decimally is the distance of the first, or left-hand, significant figure from the units' place, being positive when that figure is on the left of the units' place, and negative when on the right.*

GENERAL PROPERTIES OF LOGARITHMS.

9. *The logarithm of a* PRODUCT *is equal to the sum of the logarithms of its factors.*

For let M and N be any two numbers, x and y their respective logarithms, and a the base of the system. Then, by definition (Art. 1), we have

$$M = a^x, \quad N = a^y.$$

Multiplying equations, member by member, we have

$$MN = a^x a^y = a^{x+y}.$$

Therefore, $\log (M \times N) = x + y = \log M + \log N.$

10. *The logarithm of a* QUOTIENT *is equal to the logarithm of the dividend diminished by that of the divisor.*

For, by Art. 9, we have

$$M = a^x, \quad N = a^y.$$

Dividing the first equation by the second, member by member, we have

$$\frac{M}{N} = \frac{a^x}{a^y} = a^{x-y}.$$

Therefore, $\log \left(\frac{M}{N}\right) = x - y = \log M - \log N.$

11. *The logarithm of any* POWER *of a number is equal to the product of the logarithm of the number by the exponent of the power.*

For let m be any number, and take the equation (Art. 9)

$$M = a^x,$$

then, raising both sides to the mth power, we have

$$M^m = (a^x)^m = a^{xm}.$$

Therefore, $\log (M^m) = xm = (\log M) \times m.$

12. *The logarithm of the* ROOT *of any number is equal to the logarithm of the number divided by the index of the root.*

For, let n be any number, and take the equation (Art. 9)

$$M = a^x,$$

then, extracting the nth root of both sides, we have

$$\sqrt[n]{M} = \sqrt[n]{a^x} = a^{\frac{x}{n}}.$$

Therefore, $\log(\sqrt[n]{M}) = \frac{x}{n} = \frac{\log M}{n}$.

13. Hence, by means of logarithms, we can perform multiplication by addition, and division by subtraction; also, we can raise a number to any power by a single multiplication, and extract any root of a number by a single division.

14. *All numbers, integral, fractional, or mixed, having the same succession of significant figures, have logarithms with the same decimal part.*

For since the logarithm of 10 is 1, the product of any number by 10 will have a logarithm increased by 1; and, likewise, the quotient of any number divided by 10 will have a logarithm diminished by 1; and, 1 being an integer, the logarithms will differ only in their characteristics.

Thus, the logarithm	of	235	is	2.371068
"	"	2350	"	3.371068
"	"	23.5	"	1.371068
"	"	2.35	"	0.371068
"	"	.235	"	$\bar{1}.371068$
"	"	.0235	"	$\bar{2}.371068$

15. The negative sign placed over the characteristic indicates that it alone is negative, the decimal part being always positive.

TABLE OF LOGARITHMS.

16. A Table of Logarithms usually contains all the whole numbers between 1 and a given number, with their logarithms. The accompanying table contains the logarithms of all numbers from 1 up to 10,000, calculated to six places of decimals.

17. In the table, the characteristics of the logarithms of the first 100 numbers are inserted; but for all other numbers the decimal part only of the logarithms is given, while the characteristic is left to be supplied by inspection, according to the principles already furnished (Art. 7, 8).

18. The numbers are in the column headed N, and their logarithms, or the decimal parts of their logarithms, are opposite

on the same line. When the first two figures of the decimal are the same for several successive logarithms, they are not repeated for each, but, being used once, are then left to be supplied.

19. In the column headed D are the mean or average differences of the ten logarithms against which they are placed.

To find the Logarithm of any Number.

20. *When the given number is any integer of* ONE *or* TWO *figures.*

Look on the first page of the table, and opposite the given number will be found the logarithm with its characteristic. Thus,

the logarithm of 63 is 1.799341;
" " 98 " 1.991226.

21. *When the given number is any integer of* THREE FIGURES.

Look in the table for the given number, and opposite the same, in the column headed 0, will be found the decimal part of the logarithm, to which must be prefixed 2 as the characteristic (Art. 7). Thus,

the logarithm of 110 is 2.041393;
" " 817 " 2.912222.

22. *When the given number is any integer of* FOUR *figures, either with or without ciphers annexed.*

Find the first three figures of the given number in the column headed N, and, opposite to them, in the column headed by the fourth figure, will be found the decimal part of the logarithm; to which the characteristic, as determined by Art. 7, must be prefixed. Thus,

the logarithm of 4901 is 3.690285;
" " 9677 " 3.985741;
" " 31250 " 4.494850.

23. *When the given number is any integer of* FIVE *or* MORE *figures.*

Find the logarithm of the first four figures as in Art. 22,

regarding the others as ciphers annexed; then take, from the column headed D, the number on the same horizontal line with the decimal part of the logarithm, and multiply it by the remaining figures of the given number; reject from the right of the product thus obtained as many figures as there were in the multiplier, and add what is left to the decimal part of the logarithm already found; and the sum will be the required logarithm. Thus, if it be required to find the logarithm of 93192:

the logarithm of	93190	is	4.969369	Dif. from col. D,	47
			9.4		2
" "	93192	"	4.969378.		9.4

This process is based upon the supposition that the differences of logarithms are proportional to the differences of their corresponding numbers, which is not strictly correct, yet sufficiently exact for practical purposes.

When the figure or figures rejected from the right of the product, considered decimally, exceed in value .5, the right-hand figure of what is left to be added must be increased by 1, to insure greater accuracy in the result.

24. *When the given number is any* DECIMAL FRACTION, *or any mixed number expressed decimally.*

Find the decimal part of the logarithm of the number, as if it were an integer, and prefix the proper characteristic (Arts. 7 and 8). Thus,

the logarithm of 93.192 is 1.969378;
" " 4526.375 " 3.655751;
" " .0006801 " $\overline{4}$.832573.

25. *When the given number is any* COMMON FRACTION.

Reduce the given fraction to a decimal, and find its logarithm, as in Art. 24; or, since a fraction is an expression of division, subtract the logarithm of the denominator from the logarithm of the numerator, and the difference will be the logarithm of the fraction (Art. 10). Thus,

the logarithm of $\frac{3}{4}$, or .75, is $\overline{1}$.875061.

Or,

the logarithm of the numerator, 3, is 0.477121
" " " denominator, 4, " 0.602060

" " " fraction, $\frac{3}{4}$ " $\overline{1}.875061$

To find the Number corresponding to any Logarithm.

26. *When the given logarithm is* WITHIN *the limits of the table.*

Look in the column headed 0, for the first two or three figures of the logarithm, neglecting the characteristic, and, if *all* the figures of the logarithm are found in that column, the corresponding number will be on the same horizontal line, in the column headed N. If, however, the decimal part of the logarithm be not exactly found in the column headed 0, look for it in one of the nine following columns, and the first three figures of the corresponding number will be on the same horizontal line in the column headed N, and the fourth will be at the head of the column in which the logarithm was found.

Make the number correspond with the characteristic given, if necessary, by pointing off decimals or annexing ciphers (Arts. 7 and 8). Thus,

the number corresponding to the logarithm 3.146128 is 1400;
" " " 0.370143 " 2.345;
" " " $\overline{2}.907680$ " .08085.

27. *When the given logarithm is* NOT WITHIN *the limits of the table.*

From the decimal part of the given logarithm subtract the decimal part of that next less; annex to their difference two or more ciphers, and divide by the number, in the column headed D, opposite the decimal part taken from the table. Annex the result to the number corresponding to the lesser logarithm, and point off according to the characteristic, as before.

It sometimes happens, in dividing by the tabular difference, that there are not as many figures in the quotient as there are ciphers annexed to the dividend. In such a case, supply the deficiency, as in the division of decimals, by prefixing a cipher or ciphers to the quotient before annexing.

This process, like its converse (Art. 23), is based upon the supposition that the differences of logarithms are proportional to the differences of their corresponding numbers.

NOTE. The number corresponding to a given logarithm, when obtained by the use of a table calculated to six decimal places, is reliable only to the sixth figure, and sometimes that figure of an answer is not strictly correct.

Let it be required to find the number corresponding to the logarithm 2.633356.

The dec. part of the given log. is .633356
" " log. next less is .633266, correspon. num., 4298
Their difference is 90.00
Difference from column D is 101 $= 89$
Logarithm 2.633356 has for its corresponding number 429.889

The number corresponding to the logarithm 3.441049 is 2760.89
" " " " $\bar{2}$.497935 is .0314728
" " " " 2.436811 is 273.408

ARITHMETICAL COMPLEMENT.

28. The arithmetical complement of any logarithm is the difference between it and 10.

Thus, the arithmetical complement of the logarithm of 41, is $10 - \log 41 = 10 - 1.612784 = 8.387216$.

29. The arithmetical complement of a logarithm may be readily found, from the table, *by subtracting each figure of the logarithm from* 9, *excepting the last significant figure at the right, which must be taken from* 10; for this is equivalent to subtracting the logarithm from 10.

30. *The difference of two logarithms is equal to the sum of the logarithm to be diminished and the arithmetical complement of the other, less* 10.

For let a be any logarithm, and b a logarithm to be subtracted from it; then their difference will be $a - b$.

Now the arithmetical complement of b is $10 - b$; adding $10 - b$ to a, we have $a + 10 - b$; subtracting 10, we have

$$a+10-b-10=a-b;$$

the same result as before.

31. Hence, since an arithmetical complement added makes the result 10 too great, a corresponding allowance must be made in any operation in which arithmetical complements of logarithms are used.

Multiplication by Logarithms.

32. *Add the logarithms of the factors; and the sum will be the logarithm of their product* (Art. 9).

The term *sum*, here used, is to be understood in its *algebraic* signification. Therefore, since the characteristic alone of a logarithm is negative (Art. 15), whatever there is to be carried from the decimal part, in the operation, must either be added to a positive characteristic, or subtracted from one that is negative. Also, when the characteristics of the logarithms are not either all positive or all negative, the difference between their sums must be taken, and the sign of the greater prefixed.

Ex. 1. Multiply 120, 101, and .015 together.

Log 120	=	2.079181
" 101	=	2.004321
" .015	=	$\bar{2}$.176091
Product = 181.8		2.259593

Here, the $\bar{2}$ cancels a positive 2, so we have but 2 to set down.

2. Multiply 3.26 by .0085. Ans. .02771.
3. Multiply 6651 by 108. Ans. 718308.

Division by Logarithms.

33. *Subtract the logarithm of the divisor from the logarithm of the dividend, and the difference will be the logarithm of their quotient* (Art. 10). Or,

Add the arithmetical complement of the logarithm of the divisor to the logarithm of the dividend, and the sum, less 10, *will be the logarithm of the quotient* (Art. 31).

The term *difference*, here used, is to be understood in its *algebraic* signification. Therefore, the sign of the characteristic of the divisor must be changed; and then, if the characteristics of the divisor and dividend have the same sign, their sum must be taken, but when of different signs, their difference, with the sign of the greater, for the characteristic of the logarithm of the quotient. Also, if 1 is carried from the decimal part, it must be regarded as positive, and must be united with the characteristic of the divisor before it is changed.

Ex. 1. Divide 850 by .093.

FIRST OPERATION.		SECOND OPERATION.	
Log 850 =	2.929419	Log 850 =	2.929419
" .093 =	$\bar{2}$.968483	" .093 ar. co. =	11.031517
Quot. 9139.8	3.960936	Quot. 9139.8	3.960936

Here, in the first operation, 1 carried from the decimal part to the $\bar{2}$ changes it to $\bar{1}$, which being taken from 2, leaves 3 to set down; and, in the second operation, 10 is taken from the sum of the characteristics (Art. 31).

2. Divide 2625 by 125. Ans. 21.
3. Divide .02771 by .0085. Ans. 3.26.
4. Divide 117.1347 by 5.062. Ans. 23.14.
5. Find the 4th term of the proportion,

219 : 63.05 :: 378.

Log 378 =	2.577492
" 63.05 =	1.799685
" 219 ar. co. =	7.659556
4th term = 108.826	2.036733

6. Find the 4th term of the proportion, 720 : 196 :: 155.5. Ans. 42.33.

Involution by Logarithms.

34. *Multiply the logarithm of the given number by the exponent of the power to which the number is to be raised; and the product will be the logarithm of the required power* (Art. 11).

Since the exponent of any power is positive, a negative characteristic multiplied by it will give a negative result; but that which is to be carried from the decimal part will be positive; therefore, their difference will be the characteristic of the product.

Ex. 1. Required the square, or second power, of 31.

$$\begin{array}{lcr} \text{Log } 31 & = & 1.491362 \\ & & 2 \\ \hline \text{Ans. } 961 & & 2.982724 \end{array}$$

2. Required the cube, or third power, of .25.

$$\begin{array}{lcr} \text{Log } .25 & = & \bar{1}.397940 \\ & & 3 \\ \hline \text{Ans. } 0.015625 & & \bar{2}.193820 \end{array}$$

3. Required the tenth power of .64. Ans. .0115292.

Evolution by Logarithms.

35. *Divide the logarithm of the given number by the index of the root; and the quotient will be the logarithm of the required root* (Art. 12).

When the characteristic of the logarithm is negative, and does not contain the given divisor without a remainder, we may increase the characteristic by any number that will make it exactly divisible, provided we prefix an equal positive number to the decimal part of the logarithm.

Ex. 1. Required the square, or second root, of 1296.

$$\begin{array}{lcl} \text{Log } 1296 & = & 3.112605 \\ (\text{Log } 1296) \div 2 & = & 1.556303 \qquad \text{Ans. } 36. \end{array}$$

2. Required the cube, or third root, of .00048.

$$\begin{array}{lcl} \text{Log } .00048 & = & \bar{4}.681241 \\ (\text{Log } .00048) \div 3 & = & \bar{2}.893747 \quad \text{Ans. } .078297. \end{array}$$

Here, the negative characteristic $\bar{4}$ not being exactly divisible by 3, it is increased by 2 to make it so, and then the 2 borrowed is restored, by regarding 2 as prefixed to the decimal part.

3. Required the fourth root of .434296. Ans. .811794.

4. What is the tenth root of 2? Ans. 1.0718.

BOOK II.

PLANE TRIGONOMETRY.

DEFINITIONS AND ELEMENTARY PRINCIPLES.

36. TRIGONOMETRY is the science which treats of methods of computing angles and triangles.

37. PLANE TRIGONOMETRY treats of methods of computing plane angles and triangles.

38. The MAGNITUDE OF ANGLES is represented by numbers expressing how many times they contain a certain angle fixed upon as the *unit* of angular measure.

For this purpose a right angle is generally divided into 90 equal parts called *degrees*, each degree into 60 equal parts called *minutes*, each minute into 60 equal parts called *seconds*; then an angle is expressed by the number of degrees, minutes, seconds, and decimal parts of a second, which it contains.

39. Degrees, minutes, and seconds, are marked by the symbols $^\circ$, $'$, $''$; thus, to represent 16 degrees, 9 minutes, 23.5 seconds, we write $16^\circ\ 9'\ 23''.5$.

40. Since angles at the centre of a circle are to each other as the arcs of the circumference intercepted between their sides (Geom., Prop. XVII. Bk. III.), these arcs may be regarded as the measures of the angles, and the number of *units of arc* intercepted on the circumference may be used to express both the arc and the corresponding angle.

41. A *degree of arc* is $\frac{1}{360}$ of a circumference; a *minute*, $\frac{1}{60}$ of a degree; a *second*, $\frac{1}{60}$ of a minute; and these arcs subtend angles of a degree, a minute, and a second, respectively, at the centre.

42. For simplifying calculations, the radius employed in measuring angles, being constant, is taken at an assumed value of unity, as the *linear unit of measure.*

43. Since the value of the constant ratio of the circumference to the diameter of a circle, represented by π, is 3.14159 (Geom., Prop. XV. Sch. 1, Bk. VI.), if the radius of a circle is denoted by r, its circumference is $2\pi r$, where $\pi = 3.14159$. Hence, as r is taken as unity, any number of degrees may be expressed as a multiple or fractional part of π. Thus $360° = 2\pi$, $180° = \pi$, $90° = \frac{\pi}{2}$, and $30° = \frac{\pi}{6}$.

44. The COMPLEMENT OF AN ANGLE, or arc, is the remainder obtained by subtracting the angle or arc from 90°. Thus the complement of 45° is 45°, and the complement of 31° is 59°.

When an angle, or arc, is greater than 90°, its complement is negative. Thus the complement of 127° is — 37°.

Since the two acute angles of a right-angled triangle are together equal to a right angle, they are complements one of the other.

45. The SUPPLEMENT OF AN ANGLE, or arc, is the remainder obtained by subtracting the angle or arc from 180°. Thus the supplement of 110° is 70°.

When the angle is greater than 180°, its supplement is negative. Thus the supplement of 200° is — 20°.

Since the three angles of any triangle are together equal to two right angles, any one of them is a supplement of the sum of the other two.

TRIGONOMETRIC FUNCTIONS.

46. TRIGONOMETRIC FUNCTIONS are the quantities by which angles are subjected to computation.

These we shall consider, in accordance with the best modern authorities, as *ratios* formed by comparing the sides of a right-angled triangle, and thus capable of comparison one with another by means of their geometrical properties.

These ratios have received the special names of *sine, tangent, secant, cosine, cotangent, and cosecant.*

There are also sometimes employed the quantities termed *versed sine, coversed sine,* and *suversed sine.*

47. *The* SINE *of an angle is the ratio of the opposite side to the hypothenuse.*

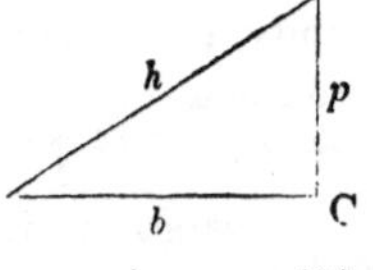

Thus, in any right-angled triangle, $A\ B\ C$, if the sides be denoted by p, b, h, we shall have,

$$\sin A = \frac{p}{h}, \quad \sin B = \frac{b}{h}. \qquad (1)$$

48. *The* TANGENT *of an angle is the ratio of the opposite side to the adjacent side.*

$$\text{Thus,} \qquad \tan A = \frac{p}{b}, \quad \tan B = \frac{b}{p}. \qquad (2)$$

49. *The* SECANT *of an angle is the ratio of the hypothenuse to the adjacent side.*

$$\text{Thus,} \qquad \sec A = \frac{h}{b}, \quad \sec B = \frac{h}{p}. \qquad (3)$$

50. *The* COSINE, COTANGENT, *and* COSECANT *of an angle are respectively the* SINE, TANGENT, *and* SECANT *of its complement.*

Hence, since the acute angles of a right-angled triangle are complements one of the other (Art. 44), we have, according to the definitions,

$$\left.\begin{array}{ll} \cos A = \sin B = \frac{b}{h}, & \cos B = \sin A = \frac{p}{h}; \\ \cot A = \tan B = \frac{b}{p}, & \cot B = \tan A = \frac{p}{b}; \\ \operatorname{cosec} A = \sec B = \frac{h}{p}, & \operatorname{cosec} B = \sec A = \frac{h}{b}. \end{array}\right\} \quad (4)$$

51. Since $\frac{h}{p}$ is the reciprocal of $\frac{p}{h}$, $\frac{b}{p}$ of $\frac{p}{b}$, and $\frac{b}{h}$ of $\frac{h}{b}$, we see that *the cosecant, cotangent, and cosine of an angle are respectively the reciprocals of the sine, tangent, and secant of the angle.* That is,

$$\left.\begin{array}{lll} \cos A = \frac{1}{\sec A}, & \cot A = \frac{1}{\tan A}, & \operatorname{cosec} A = \frac{1}{\sin A}; \\ \sin A = \frac{1}{\operatorname{cosec} A}, & \tan A = \frac{1}{\cot A}, & \sec A = \frac{1}{\cos A}; \\ \sin A \operatorname{cosec} A = 1, & \cos A \sec A = 1, & \tan A \cot A = 1. \end{array}\right\} \quad (5)$$

52. If the cosine of A be subtracted from unity, the remainder is called the *versed sine* of A; if the sine of A be subtracted from unity, the remainder is called the *coversed sine* of A; and if the cosine of A be added to unity, the sum is called the *suversed sine* of A. Hence,

$$\left.\begin{array}{r}\text{vers } A = 1 - \cos A, \quad \text{covers } A = 1 - \sin A, \\ \text{suvers } A = 1 + \cos A.\end{array}\right\} \quad (6)$$

53. *The values of trigonometric ratios remain the same so long as the angle continues the same.*

Let BAC be any angle; in AB take any point, B, and draw BC perpendicular to AC; also take any other point, B', and draw $B'C'$ perpendicular to AC. Then, since the triangles ABC, $AB'C'$ are similar, their sides have to one another the same ratio (Geom., Art. 210), and therefore sin A, tan A, &c. will have the same values, whether ABC or $AB'C'$ be the triangle by the sides of which they are expressed. It is also evident that their values would change with a change of the angle. Hence,

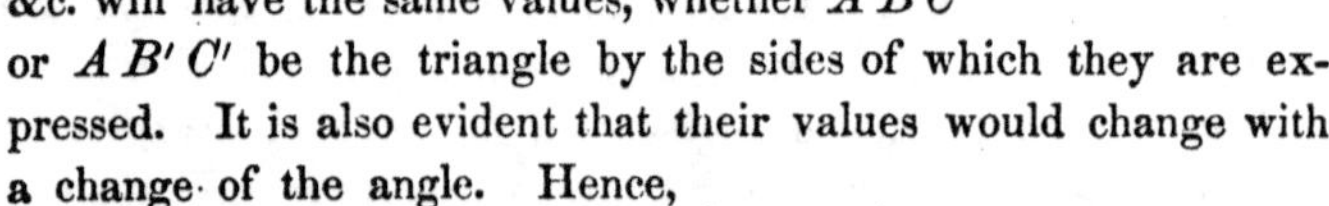

The trigonometric ratios determine the angles, and conversely; that is, any determinate values being given for the one, determinate values can be found for the other.

54. The terms sine, tangent, secant, &c., were formerly * considered to be *functions of an arc*, and denoted certain *trigonometric lines.*

Thus, let O be the centre of any circle, AA'' its diameter, and AB any arc; draw the radius OA' at right angles to AA'', and draw tangents to the circle at the points A and A'; produce OB to meet the first tangent in T and the second tangent in T'; draw BD perpendicular to OA, and BD' perpendicular to OA'. Then, by the old definitions, the *lines* of the figure are considered to

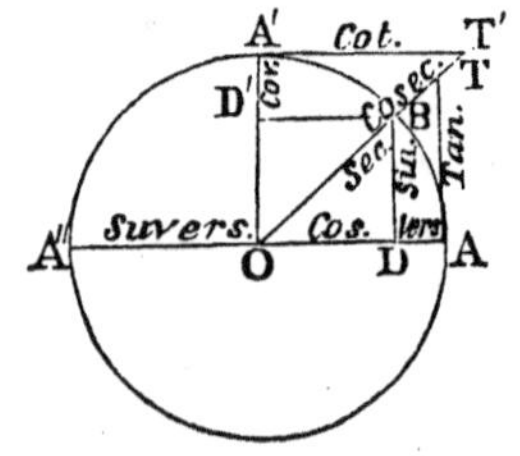

* "The modern method has now completely superseded the ancient method in English works." — *Todhunter's Trigonometry*, p. 49.

be the functions of the arc $A B$. $B D$ is the *sine* of the arc $A B$, $O D$ its *cosine*, $A T$ its *tangent*, $A' T'$ its *cotangent*, $O T$ its *secant*, $O T'$ its *cosecant*, $A D$ its *versed sine*, $A' D'$ its *coversed sine*, and $A'' D$ its *suversed sine*. Also the line joining A and B is the *chord* of the arc $A B$.

That is, in the circle whose radius is unity ;—

The SINE *of an arc, or of the angle measured by that arc, is the perpendicular let fall from one extremity of the arc, upon the diameter passing through the other extremity.*

The COSINE *is the distance from the centre to the foot of the sine.*

The trigonometric TANGENT *is that part of the tangent touching one extremity of the arc, which is intercepted between that extremity and the radius produced passing through the other extremity.*

The SECANT *is that part of the radius produced which is intercepted between the centre and the tangent.*

The VERSED SINE *is that part of the diameter intercepted between the foot of the sine and the origin of the arc.*

The COTANGENT, COSECANT, *and* COVERSED SINE *are tangent, secant, and versed sine, respectively, of the complement of an arc or angle.* The cosine is also equal to the sine of the complement, as $O D = D' B$.

The SUVERSED SINE *is that part of the diameter which remains after taking away the versed sine,* or it is the versed sine of the supplement.

55. If the radius of the circle be *unity*, the numerical value of the sine and other trigonometric functions is the same in both the old and new systems, for

$$\sin A O B = \frac{B D}{O B}, \qquad \sin A B = B D.$$

But $O B$ is the radius of the circle, and denoting it by r, we have

$$\sin A B = \sin A O B \times r, \qquad \sin A O B = \frac{\sin A B}{r};$$

and making radius $= 1$, we have

$$\sin A B = \sin A O B. \tag{7}$$

In like manner it may be shown, that similar results hold for all the other trigonometric functions. Hence any formula expressed in the old system may be immediately converted into a formula expressed in the new system, by supposing the radius of the circle to be equal to unity.

56. The sine, cosine, tangent, and cotangent constitute the *primary class* of trigonometric ratios, as they are by far most frequently used; and the others form a subordinate class, the employment of which is occasionally attended with convenience. They are collected, for more ready reference, in the following

TABLE.

1.	$\sin A = \frac{p}{h}$	1.	$\sin A = \frac{1}{\operatorname{cosec} A}$
2.	$\cos A = \frac{b}{h}$	2.	$\cos A = \frac{1}{\sec A}$
3.	$\tan A = \frac{p}{b}$	3.	$\tan A = \frac{1}{\cot A}$
4.	$\cot A = \frac{b}{p}$	4.	$\cot A = \frac{1}{\tan A}$
5.	$\sec A = \frac{h}{b}$	5.	$\sec A = \frac{1}{\cos A}$
6.	$\operatorname{cosec} A = \frac{h}{p}$	6.	$\operatorname{cosec} A = \frac{1}{\sin A}$
7.	$\operatorname{vers} A = 1 - \frac{b}{h}$	7.	$\operatorname{vers} A = 1 - \cos A$
8.	$\operatorname{covers} A = 1 - \frac{p}{h}$	8.	$\operatorname{covers} A = 1 - \sin A$
9.	$\operatorname{suvers} A = 1 + \frac{b}{h}$	9.	$\operatorname{suvers} A = 1 + \cos A$

Other Relations between Trigonometric Functions of the same Angle.

57. *To find the* cosine *of an angle by means of its sine.*

From the right-angled triangle ABC (Geom., Prop. XI. Bk. IV.) we have

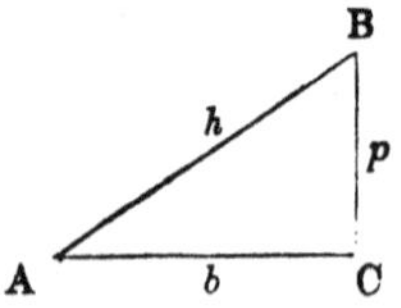

$$p^2 + b^2 = h^2.$$

Dividing both sides of the equation by h^2

A B C h p b

gives $$\frac{p^2}{h^2}+\frac{b^2}{h^2}=1;$$

or, by definition (Art. 47, 50),

$$\sin^2 A+\cos^2 A=1; \tag{8}$$

therefore $$\cos^2 A=1-\sin^2 A, \tag{9}$$

and $$\cos A=\sqrt{1-\sin^2 A}; \tag{10}$$

in which "$\sin^2 A$" denotes "the square of the sine of A."

58. *To find the* SINE *of an angle by means of its cosine.*

Since, by (8), $\sin^2 A+\cos^2 A=1$,

$$\sin^2 A=1-\cos^2 A, \tag{11}$$

and $$\sin A=\sqrt{1-\cos^2 A}. \tag{12}$$

59. *To find the* TANGENT *and* COTANGENT *of an angle by means of the sine and cosine.*

By (2) we have

$$\tan A=\frac{p}{b}, \qquad \text{and} \qquad \frac{\sin A}{\cos A}=\frac{p}{h}\div\frac{b}{h}=\frac{p}{b};$$

therefore $$\tan A=\frac{\sin A}{\cos A}. \tag{13}$$

Then, by Art. 51, $$\operatorname{cotan} A=\frac{\cos A}{\sin A}. \tag{14}$$

60. *To find the* SECANT *and* COSECANT *of an angle by means of the tangent.*

From the right-angled triangle ABC we have

$$h^2=b^2+p^2.$$

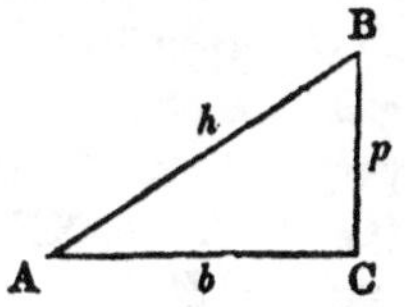

Dividing both sides of the equation by b^2, gives

$$\frac{h^2}{b^2}=1+\frac{p^2}{b^2};$$

or, by definitions (Art. 48, 49),

$$\sec^2 A=1+\tan^2 A. \tag{15}$$

Again, since
$$h^2 = p^2 + b^2,$$
$$\frac{h^2}{p^2} = 1 + \frac{b^2}{p^2};$$
or, by definitions (Art. 50),
$$\text{cosec}^2 A = 1 + \cot^2 A. \qquad (16)$$

61. In general, any one of the six trigonometric ratios of an angle being given, the relations expressed by the foregoing formulæ will enable us to find the value of all the rest. These are termed the *elementary formulæ*, and are collected in the following

TABLE.

1. $\sin^2 A + \cos^2 A = 1.$	
2. $\sin^2 A = 1 - \cos^2 A.$	3. $\cos^2 A = 1 - \sin^2 A.$
4. $\tan A = \dfrac{\sin A}{\cos A}.$	5. $\cot A = \dfrac{\cos A}{\sin A}.$
6. $\sec^2 A = 1 + \tan^2 A.$	7. $\text{cosec}^2 A = 1 + \cot^2 A.$

Relations between Trigonometric Functions of Different Angles.

62. *To find the* SINE *and* COSINE *of the* SUM *of two angles by means of their sines and cosines.*

Let the two angles be COD, DOE. In the line OE take any point, E, draw EF perpendicular to OC, and ED perpendicular to OD. Draw DG perpendicular to EF, and DC perpendicular to OC. The triangles GED and COD have their sides perpendicular, hence they are similar (Geom., Prop. XXV. Bk. IV.), and the angles DEG and COD are equal.

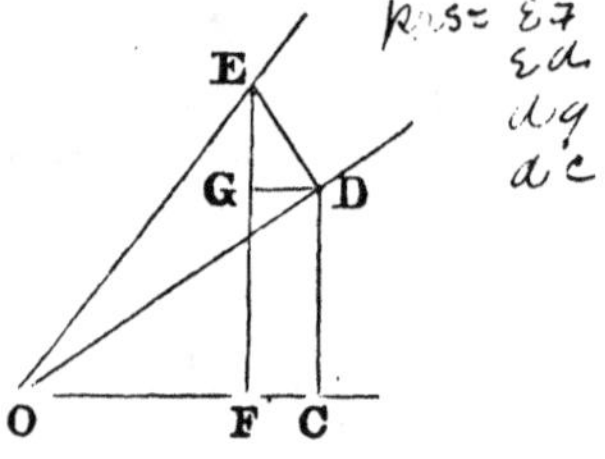

Let $a = COD = DEG$, and $b = DOE$.

Then
$$a + b = COE,$$
and
$$\sin(a + b) = \frac{EF}{OE} = \frac{GF + EG}{OE} = \frac{DC}{OE} + \frac{EG}{OE};$$

or, substituting for $\frac{DC}{OE}$ the ratios of which it is formed,

$$\frac{DC}{OD} \times \frac{OD}{OE} = \sin a \cos b,$$

and in like manner, for $\frac{EG}{OE}$,

$$\frac{EG}{ED} \times \frac{ED}{OE} = \cos a \sin b,$$

we have $\quad \sin(a+b) = \sin a \cos b + \cos a \sin b. \qquad (17)$

Again, $\cos(a+b) = \frac{OF}{OE} = \frac{OC - CF}{OE} = \frac{OC}{OE} - \frac{DG}{OE}$;

or, substituting for $\frac{OC}{OE}$ the ratios of which it is formed,

$$\frac{OC}{OD} \times \frac{OD}{OE} = \cos a \cos b,$$

and in like manner, for $\frac{DG}{OE}$,

$$\frac{DG}{DE} \times \frac{DE}{OE} = \sin a \sin b,$$

we have $\quad \cos(a+b) = \cos a \cos b - \sin a \sin b. \qquad (18)$

63. *To find the* SINE *and* COSINE *of the* DIFFERENCE *of two angles by means of their sines and cosines.*

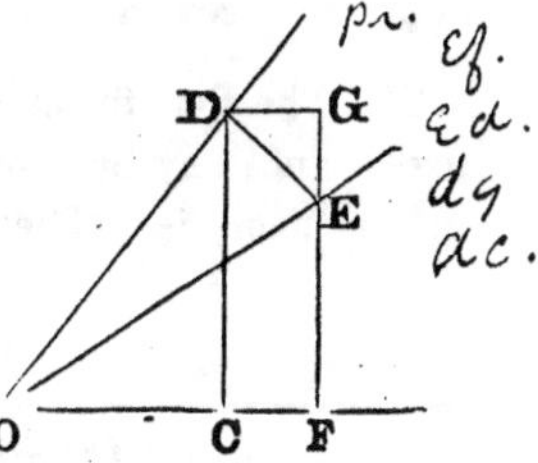

Let the two angles be FOD, DOE. In the line OE take any point, E, draw EF perpendicular to OF, and ED perpendicular to OD. Draw DG perpendicular to FE produced, and DC perpendicular to OF. The triangles GED and COD have their sides perpendicular, hence they are similar (Geom., Prop. XXV. Bk. IV.), and the angles DEG and COD are equal.

Let $a = COD = DEG$, and $b = DOE$.

Then $\quad a - b = FOE,$

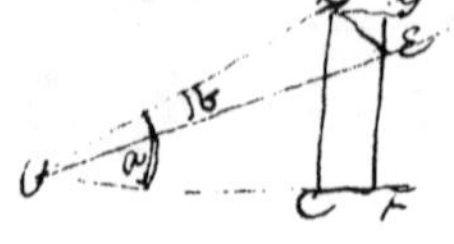

and $\sin(a-b) = \frac{EF}{OE} = \frac{GF-GE}{OE} = \frac{DC}{OE} - \frac{GE}{OE}$;

or, substituting for $\frac{DC}{OE}$ the ratios of which it is formed,

$$\frac{DC}{OD} \times \frac{OD}{OE} = \sin a \cos b,$$

and in like manner, for $\frac{GE}{OE}$,

$$\frac{GE}{ED} \times \frac{ED}{OE} = \cos a \sin b,$$

we have $\sin(a-b) = \sin a \cos b - \cos a \sin b.$ (19)

Again, $\cos(a-b) = \frac{OF}{OE} = \frac{OC+CF}{OE} = \frac{OC}{OE} + \frac{DG}{OE}$;

or, substituting for $\frac{OC}{OE}$ the ratios of which it is formed,

$$\frac{OC}{OD} \times \frac{OD}{OE} = \cos a \cos b,$$

and in like manner, for $\frac{DG}{OE}$,

$$\frac{DG}{ED} \times \frac{ED}{OE} = \sin a \sin b,$$

we have $\cos(a-b) = \cos a \cos b + \sin a \sin b.$ (20)

64. The four formulæ last established apply to arcs as well as angles, and may be considered the *fundamental formulæ* of subsequent analysis. They are brought together in the following

TABLE.

1. $\sin(a+b) = \sin a \cos b + \cos a \sin b.$
2. $\cos(a+b) = \cos a \cos b - \sin a \sin b.$
3. $\sin(a-b) = \sin a \cos b - \cos a \sin b.$
4. $\cos(a-b) = \cos a \cos b + \sin a \sin b.$

SIGNS OF THE TRIGONOMETRIC FUNCTIONS.

65. If on any line, straight or curved, different distances be measured from a fixed point of origin, the distances which have contrary situations may by convention be introduced into our calculations, by affecting the quantities representing their magnitudes by contrary signs.

Let O be a fixed point in any line, $A A''$, and suppose we have to determine the situations of other points in this line with respect to O. The position of any point in the line will be known if we know the distance of the point from O, and also know on which side of O the point lies. Now it is found convenient to adopt the following *convention:* distances measured in one direction from O along the line will be denoted by *positive* quantities, and distances measured in the contrary direction from O will be denoted by *negative* quantities.

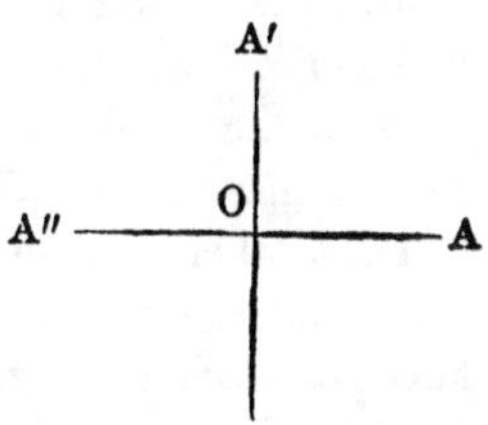

Thus, for example, suppose that distances measured from O towards the *right* are denoted by *positive* numbers, and let A be a point, the distance of which from O is denoted by 2 or $+2$; then if A'' be a point situated just as far to the *left* of O as A is to the *right*, the distance of A'' from O will be denoted by -2.

In like manner, if distances originating in $A A''$, and taken along $O A'$, or only parallel to $O A'$, when measured *upwards* be denoted by *positive* quantities, on being measured *downwards* they will be denoted by *negative* quantities.

66. A similar convention may conveniently be adopted with respect to angles.

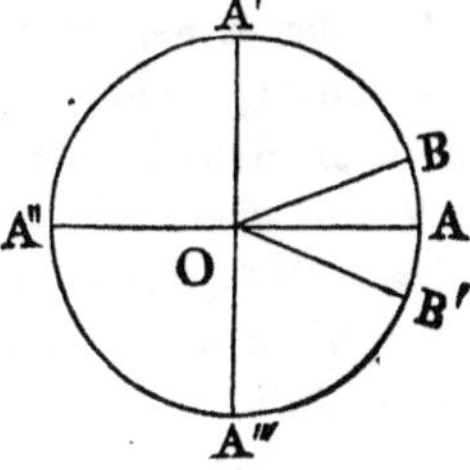

Let any line, $O B$, revolve from the position $O A$, in one direction round O, forming the angle $B O A$, and let this angle be denoted by a *positive* quantity; then, if the line $O B$ revolve, from the position $O\,A$, round O in the contrary direction, forming the angle $B'\,O\,A$, this angle may be denoted by a *negative* quantity.

Thus, for example, if each of the angles $A\,O\,B$ and $A\,O\,B'$ is two ninths of a right angle, and we denote the former by $20°$ or $+20°$, the latter may be denoted by $-20°$.

The direction of the positive distances is quite indifferent; but, being once fixed, the negative distances must lie in the contrary direction.

67. The representation of angles as the measure of *the revolution of a line*, turning in a plane about one of its own points, leads to the consideration of angles, not only greater than two right angles, but of all possible magnitudes.

Thus, when the line $O\,B$, starting from the initial position $O\,A$, has passed A'', or made more than half a revolution, we have described an angular magnitude of more than $180°$; and when it has passed on to A, we have an angular magnitude of $360°$. If it now continues to revolve in the same direction till it arrives again at B, we have an angular magnitude of $360° + 20° = 380°$, and thus we may conceive of angles of all magnitudes. In like manner negative angles of all magnitudes may be formed by the describing line $O\,B$ revolving from $O\,A$, but in a contrary direction.

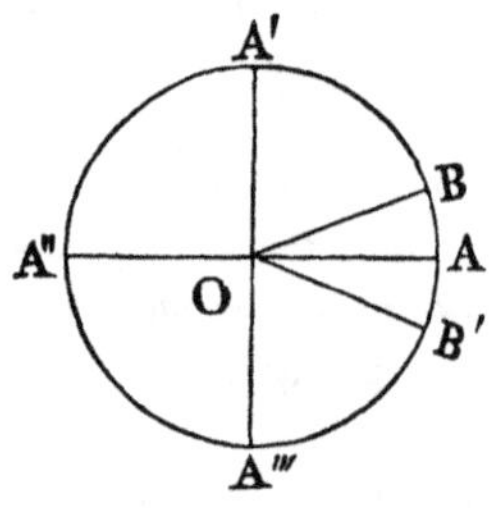

68. The algebraic signs of the trigonometric functions can be readily fixed in the mind by being represented geometrically. Thus,

Let the extremity of a revolving line, starting from the initial position $O\,A$, describe the positive arc $A\,B$ less than $90°$, $A\,B'$ between $90°$ and $180°$, $A\,A'B''$ between $180°$ and $270°$, and $A\,A'A''B'''$ between $270°$ and $360°$. Then, according to the definitions of Art. 54, $B\,D$, $B'D'$,

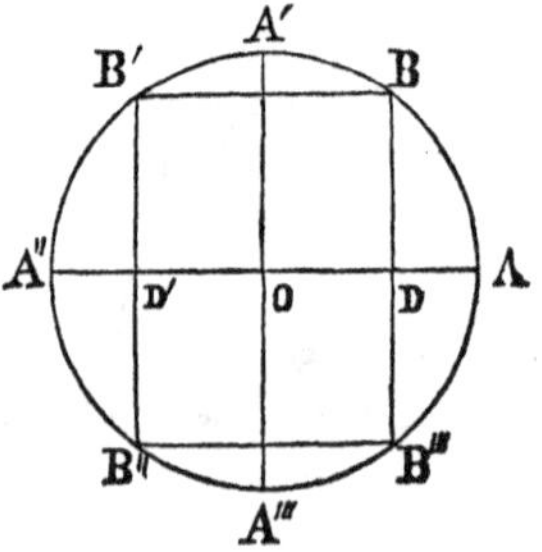

$B''D'$, and $B'''D$ are the sines, and OD and OD' are the cosines, of the angles measured by the arcs terminating in each of the four quadrants.

As all the functions of an angle less than 90° are considered positive, their direction will fix the signs for other quadrants.

It will be seen (Art. 65) that the sines are *above* the diameter AA'', and *positive*, in the first and second quadrants, but *below*, and *negative*, in the third and fourth quadrants.

Also (Art. 65), the cosines are to the *right* of the diameter $A'A'''$, and *positive*, in the first and fourth quadrants, but to the *left*, and *negative*, in the second and third quadrants.

As $\tan A = \frac{\sin A}{\cos A}$ (13), the tangent must be *positive* when the sine and cosine have the *same sign*, and *negative* when they have *unlike signs*. Hence the tangents are *positive* in the first and third quadrants, and *negative* in the second and fourth quadrants, a result which may also be obtained by noticing whether the tangents must run *above* or *below* the origin A, to meet the secant.

The *cotangent* of any angle or arc always has the same algebraic sign as its *tangent*, the *secant* the same as the *cosine*, and the *cosecant* the same as the *sine*; for they are reciprocals (Art. 51).

The versed sine, coversed sine, and suversed sine, since they are referred to the origins of their arcs, A, A', and A'', as fixed points, instead of the centre O, can have but one direction, and therefore are always *positive*.

By comparing the sine $B'''D$ and the cosine OD of the negative arc AB''' (Art. 66) with those of the equal positive arc AB, it will be seen that the cosines are identical, and consequently the secants are equal; but the sines, and, consequently, the tangents, cotangents, and cosecants, have *unlike* algebraic signs. The functions of the arc AB''', terminating in the first negative quadrant, are the same as those of the arc $AA'A''B'''$, terminating in the fourth positive quadrant. The second negative and third positive, the third negative and second positive, and the fourth negative and first positive quadrants likewise have functions with the *same* algebraic signs.

69. From the results above obtained is formed the following

TABLE.

Positive Quadrant.	Sine.	Cosine.	Tangent,	Cotan't	Secant.	Cosecant.	Negative Quadrant.
First.	+	+	+	+	+	+	Fourth.
Second.	+	—	—	—	—	+	Third.
Third.	—	—	+	+	—	—	Second.
Fourth.	—	+	—	—	+	—	First.

Values of the Trigonometric Functions of certain Angles.

70. The definitions of the trigonometric functions already given (Art. 46–50) apply directly only to angles not exceeding a right angle. But by means of the formulæ which have been deduced from them we may now extend the definitions so as to render them applicable to angles of any magnitude.

71. *To find the* SINE, *&c. of* 30° and of 60°.

Let ABC be an equilateral triangle, then each of its angles equals one third of two right angles, or 60°. Draw BD perpendicular to AC, then the angle ABD is equal to $\frac{1}{2}ABC$, AD is equal to DC, and $AD = \frac{1}{2}BC = \frac{1}{2}AB$.

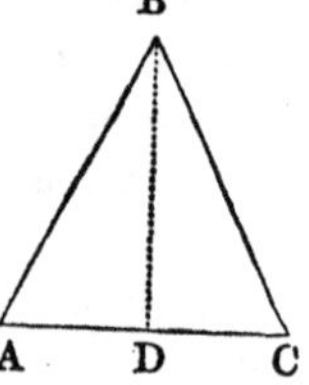

Therefore,

$$\sin ABD = \frac{AD}{AB} = \frac{\frac{1}{2}AB}{AB} = \frac{1}{2};$$

or, since 30° and 60° are complements the one of the other,

$$\sin 30° = \cos 60° = \tfrac{1}{2}, \tag{21}$$

whence by (10)

$$\cos 30° = \sin 60° = \sqrt{1 - \tfrac{1}{4}} = \tfrac{1}{2}\sqrt{3}. \tag{22}$$

Then, by (13) and (5),

$$\tan 30° = \cot 60° = \frac{\frac{1}{2}}{\frac{1}{2}\sqrt{3}} = \frac{1}{\sqrt{3}} = \frac{1}{3}\sqrt{3}, \tag{23}$$

$$\cot\ 30° = \tan\ 60° = \frac{\sqrt{3}}{1} = \sqrt{3}, \quad (24)$$

$$\sec\ 30° = \operatorname{cosec} 60° = \frac{1}{\frac{1}{2}\sqrt{3}} = \frac{2}{\sqrt{3}} = \frac{2}{3}\sqrt{3}, \quad (25)$$

$$\operatorname{cosec} 30° = \sec\ 60° = \frac{1}{\frac{1}{2}} = 2. \quad (26)$$

72. *To find the* SINE, *&c. of* 45°.

Since 45° is the complement of 45°,

$$\sin\ 45° = \cos\ 45°.$$

Then making $A = 45°$ in (8), we have

$$\sin^2 45° + \cos^2 45° = 2\sin^2 45° = 2\cos^2 45° = 1,$$

or

$$\sin^2 45° = \cos^2 45° = \tfrac{1}{2},$$

$$\sin\ 45° = \cos\ 45° = \sqrt{\tfrac{1}{2}} = \tfrac{1}{2}\sqrt{2}. \quad (27)$$

Hence by (13) and (5),

$$\tan\ 45° = \cot\ 45° = \frac{\frac{1}{2}\sqrt{2}}{\frac{1}{2}\sqrt{2}} = 1, \quad (28)$$

$$\sec\ 45° = \operatorname{cosec} 45° = \frac{1}{\frac{1}{2}\sqrt{2}} = \sqrt{2}. \quad (29)$$

73. *To find the* SINE, *&c. of* 0° *and of* 90°.

Since 0° and 90° are complements the one of the other,

$$\sin\ 0° = \cos\ 90°.$$

Then making $a = b$ in (19) and (20), we have

$$\sin\ 0° = \cos\ 90° = \sin a \cos a - \cos a \sin a = 0, \quad (30)$$

$$\cos\ 0° = \sin\ 90° = \cos a \cos a + \sin a \sin a,$$

or by (8), $\cos\ 0° = \sin\ 90° = \cos^2 a + \sin^2 a = 1.$ (31)

Hence by (13) and (5),

$$\tan\ 0° = \cot\ 90° = \tfrac{0}{1} = 0, \quad (32)$$

$$\cot\ 0° = \tan\ 90° = \tfrac{1}{0} = \infty, \quad (33)$$

$$\sec\ 0° = \operatorname{cosec} 90° = \tfrac{1}{1} = 1, \quad (34)$$

$$\operatorname{cosec} 0° = \sec\ 90° = \tfrac{1}{0} = \infty. \quad (35)$$

74. *To find the* SINE, *&c. of* 180°.

Let $a = b = 90°$ in (17) and (18); then, by means of (30) and (31), we have

$$\sin 180° = 1 \times 0 + 0 \times 1 = 0, \qquad (36)$$

$$\cos 180° = 0 \times 0 - 1 \times 1 = -1. \qquad (37)$$

Hence, by (13) and (5),

$$\tan 180° = \frac{0}{-1} = 0, \qquad \cot 180° = \frac{1}{0} = \infty, \qquad (38)$$

$$\sec 180° = \frac{1}{-1} = -1, \qquad \text{cosec } 180° = \frac{1}{0} = \infty. \qquad (39)$$

75. *To find the* SINE, *&c. of* 270°.

Let $a = 180°$ and $b = 90°$ in (17) and (18), and we have

$$\sin 270° = 0 \times 0 + (-1) \times 1 = -1, \qquad (40)$$

$$\cos 270° = (-1) \times 0 - 0 \times 1 = 0. \qquad (41)$$

Hence, by (13) and (5),

$$\tan 270° = \frac{-1}{0} = \infty, \qquad \cot 270° = \frac{0}{-1} = 0, \qquad (42)$$

$$\sec 270° = \frac{1}{0} = \infty, \qquad \text{cosec } 270° = \frac{1}{-1} = -1. \qquad (43)$$

76. *To find the* SINE, *&c. of* 360°.

Let $a = b = 180°$ in (17) and (18), and we have

$$\sin 360° = 0 \times (-1) + (-1) \times 0 = 0, \qquad (44)$$

$$\cos 360° = (-1) \times (-1) - 0 \times 0 = 1. \qquad (45)$$

But these values for the sine and cosine of 360° are the same as those for the sine and cosine of 0°. Hence,

All the trigonometric functions of 360° *are the same as those for* 0°.

77. *To find the* SINE, *&c. of the supplement of an angle.*

Let $a = 180°$ in (19) and (20); then, by means of (36) and (37), we have

$$\sin (180° - b) = \sin b, \quad \cos (180° - b) = -\cos b \qquad (46)$$

whence, by (13) and (5),

$$\tan (180° - b) = \frac{\sin b}{-\cos b} = -\tan b, \qquad (47)$$

$$\cot (180° - b) = \frac{1}{-\tan b} = -\cot b, \qquad (48)$$

$$\sec (180° - b) = \frac{1}{-\cos b} = -\sec b, \qquad (49)$$

$$\text{cosec} (180° - b) = \frac{1}{\sin b} = \text{cosec } b; \qquad (50)$$

that is, *the sine and cosecant of the supplement of an angle are the same as those of the angle itself; and the cosine, tangent, cotangent, and secant are the negatives of those of the angle.*

78. It follows from the preceding article, that *the sine and cosecant of an obtuse angle are positive, while its cosine, tangent, cotangent, and secant are negative,* as has before been shown geometrically (Art. 68, 69).

79. *To find the* SINE, *&c. of a negative angle.*

Let $a = 0°$ in (19) and (20); then, by means of (30), (31), (13), and (5), we have

$$\sin (-b) = -\sin b, \qquad \cos (-b) = \cos b, \qquad (51)$$

$$\tan (-b) = -\tan b, \qquad \cot (-b) = -\cot b, \qquad (52)$$

$$\sec (-b) = \sec b, \qquad \text{cosec} (-b) = -\text{cosec } b; \qquad (53)$$

that is, *the cosine and secant of the negative of an angle are the same as those of the angle itself; and the sine, tangent, cotangent, and cosecant of the negative of an angle are the negatives of those of the angle.* These results correspond with those obtained geometrically (Art. 68).

80. *To find the* SINE, *&c. of an angle which exceeds* 180°.

Let $a = 180°$ in (17) and (18); then, by means of (36) and (37), we have

$$\sin (180° + b) = -\sin b, \qquad \cos (180° + b) = -\cos b, \qquad (54)$$

$$\tan (180° + b) = \tan b, \qquad \cot (180° + b) = \cot b, \qquad (55)$$

$$\sec (180° + b) = -\sec b, \qquad \text{cosec} (180° + b) = -\text{cosec } b; \qquad (56)$$

that is, *the tangent and cotangent of an angle which exceeds* 180° *are equal to those of its excess above* 180°; *and the sine, cosine, secant, and cosecant of this angle are the negatives of those of its excess.*

81. It follows from the preceding article, that *the tangent and cotangent of an angle which exceeds* 180° *and is less than* 270° *are positive; while its sine, cosine, secant, and cosecant are negative.*

Also, by considering b greater than 90° (Art. 78), that *the cosine and secant of an angle which exceeds* 270° *and is less than* 360° *are positive; while its sine, tangent, cotangent, and cosecant are negative.* (See Art. 68, 69.)

82. *To find the* SINE, *&c. of an angle which exceeds* 360°.

Let $a = 360°$ in (17) and (18); then, by means of (44) and (45), we have

$$\sin(360° + b) = \sin b, \quad \cos(360° + b) = \cos b; \quad (57)$$

that is, *all the trigonometric functions of an angle which exceeds* 360° *are the same as those of the excess above* 360°, *so that* 360° *may be suppressed as often as it can be, so far as the function of the angle is concerned.*

83. The trigonometric functions of any angle whatever can now be readily expressed in those of an angle not exceeding 90°. Thus,

1. The trigonometric functions of any *negative* angle can be made to depend upon those of the corresponding *positive* angle (Art. 79).

2. Any angle exceeding 360°, as far as the trigonometric functions are concerned, may be replaced by an angle less than 360° (Art. 82).

3. Any angle exceeding 180° can in like manner be replaced by an angle less than 180° (Art. 80).

4. The trigonometric functions of any angle exceeding 90° may be made to depend upon those of an angle less than 90° (Art 77, 78).

For example,

$\sin 600° = \sin (360° + 240°) = \sin 240° = \sin (180° + 60°)$
$= -\sin 60°,$

$\tan (-1000°) = -\tan 1000° = -\tan (720° + 280°) =$
$-\tan 280° = -\tan (180° + 100°) = -\tan 100° =$
$-\tan (180° - 80°) = \tan 80°.$

84. It will be seen from the preceding articles that the sine and cosine may have any value between -1 and $+1$; the tangent and cotangent, any value between $-\infty$ and $+\infty$; the secant and cosecant, any value between $-\infty$ and -1 and between $+1$ and $+\infty$. It might also be shown that the versed sine, coversed sine, and suversed sine may have any value between 0 and 2.

It will also be found that no trigonometric function changes its sign except when it passes through the value zero or the value infinity.

85. The values of the functions of 0°, 90°, 180°, 270°, and 360° can be readily recalled, by being represented geometrically, according to the definitions of Art. 54. Thus,

$\sin 0° = 0$, $\cos 0° = OA = R = 1$,
$\tan 0° = 0$, and $\sec 0° = OA = 1$;
$\sin 90° = OA' = 1$, $\cos 90° = 0$;
$\sin 180° = 0$, $\cos 180° = OA'' = -1$;
$\sin 270° = OA''' = -1$, $\cos 270° = 0$.

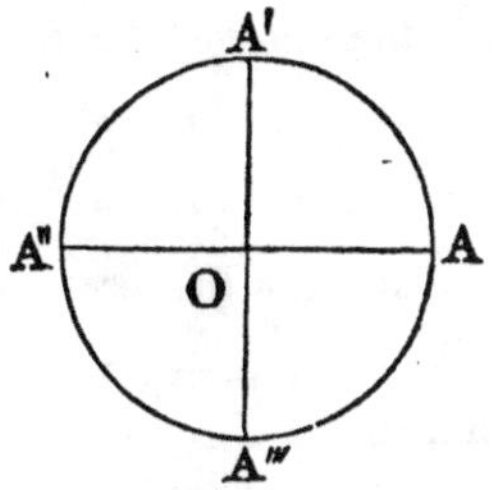

The tangent for either 90° or 270° would be a line drawn through A parallel to the secant, which would be $A'A'''$ prolonged, and as they are each to be limited by their mutual intersection, they must both be infinite.

The cotangent of either 0° or 180° would be an infinite line drawn through A', and parallel to the cosecant, which would be AA'' infinitely prolonged.

$\text{vers } 0° = 0$, $\text{vers } 90° = \text{vers } 270° = AO = 1$, $\text{vers } 180° = AA'' = 2$; $\text{covers } 0° = \text{covers } 180° = A'O = 1$, $\text{covers } 90° = 0$, $\text{covers } 270° = A'A''' = 2$; $\text{suvers } 0° = A''A = 2$, $\text{suvers } 90° = \text{suvers } 270° = A''O = 1$, $\text{suvers } 180° = 0$.

TABLE.

Degrees.	Sine.	Cosine.	Tangent.	Cotangent.	Secant.	Cosecant.
0	0	+1	0	∞	+1	∞
90	+1	0	∞	0	∞	+1
180	0	—1	0	∞	—1	∞
270	—1	0	∞	0	∞	—1
360	0	+1	0	∞	+1	∞

GENERAL FORMULÆ.

86. From the four fundamental formulæ (Art. 64), a large number of other formulæ of general utility may be deduced.

87. *To find expressions for the products of sines and cosines, and for their sums and differences.*

The sum and difference of equations (17) and (19) are

$$\sin(a+b)+\sin(a-b)=2\sin a\cos b, \qquad (58)$$

$$\sin(a+b)-\sin(a-b)=2\cos a\sin b; \qquad (59)$$

and the sum and difference of (18) and (20) are

$$\cos(a+b)+\cos(a-b)=2\cos a\cos b, \qquad (60)$$

$$\cos(a+b)-\cos(a-b)=-2\sin a\sin b. \qquad (61)$$

Now, if in the formulæ we let

$$a+b=A, \text{ and } a-b=B,$$

that is,

$$a=\tfrac{1}{2}(A+B), \text{ and } b=\tfrac{1}{2}(A-B),$$

we shall have,

$$\sin A+\sin B=2\sin\tfrac{1}{2}(A+B)\cos\tfrac{1}{2}(A-B), \qquad (62)$$

$$\sin A-\sin B=2\cos\tfrac{1}{2}(A+B)\sin\tfrac{1}{2}(A-B), \qquad (63)$$

$$\cos A+\cos B=2\cos\tfrac{1}{2}(A+B)\cos\tfrac{1}{2}(A-B), \qquad (64)$$

$$\cos B-\cos A=2\sin\tfrac{1}{2}(A+B)\sin\tfrac{1}{2}(A-B), \qquad (65)$$

in which A and B represent any two angles, and consequently admit of every possible value. These formulæ are of frequent application, especially in calculations effected by logarithms; (58), (59), (60), and (61) serve to transform a product to a sum or difference, and (62), (63), (64), and (65) serve to transform a sum or difference to a product.

88. Dividing formula (62) by (63), we have

$$\frac{\sin A + \sin B}{\sin A - \sin B} = \frac{\sin \frac{1}{2}(A+B) \cos \frac{1}{2}(A-B)}{\cos \frac{1}{2}(A+B) \sin \frac{1}{2}(A-B)},$$

which, by means of (13) and (5), becomes

$$\frac{\sin A + \sin B}{\sin A - \sin B} = \tan \tfrac{1}{2}(A+B) \cot \tfrac{1}{2}(A-B),$$

or,

$$\frac{\sin A + \sin B}{\sin A - \sin B} = \frac{\tan \frac{1}{2}(A+B)}{\tan \frac{1}{2}(A-B)}, \qquad (66)$$

and by (14),

$$\frac{\sin A + \sin B}{\sin A - \sin B} = \frac{\cot \frac{1}{2}(A-B)}{\cot \frac{1}{2}(A+B)}; \qquad (67)$$

that is,

The sum of the sines of two angles is to their difference as the tangent of half the sum of the angles is to the tangent of half their difference, or as the cotangent of half their difference is to the cotangent of half their sum.

89. By means of (62), (63), (64), and (13), we obtain,

$$\frac{\sin A + \sin B}{\cos A + \cos B} = \frac{2 \sin \frac{1}{2}(A+B) \cos \frac{1}{2}(A-B)}{2 \cos \frac{1}{2}(A+B) \cos \frac{1}{2}(A-B)} = \tan \tfrac{1}{2}(A+B), \quad (68)$$

$$\frac{\sin A - \sin B}{\cos A + \cos B} = \frac{2 \cos \frac{1}{2}(A+B) \sin \frac{1}{2}(A-B)}{2 \cos \frac{1}{2}(A+B) \cos \frac{1}{2}(A-B)} = \tan \tfrac{1}{2}(A-B), \quad (69)$$

that is,

The sum of the sines of two angles divided by the sum of their cosines is equal to the tangent of half the sum of the angles; and

The difference of the sines of two angles divided by the sum of their cosines is equal to the tangent of half the difference of the angles.

90. *To find the tangent and cotangent of the sum of two angles by means of their tangents.*

Let A and B be the two angles; then, by (13),

$$\tan(A+B) = \frac{\sin(A+B)}{\cos(A+B)};$$

or, substituting for sin $(A+B)$, cos $(A+B)$, their values from (17) and (18),

$$\tan(A+B)=\frac{\sin A\cos B+\cos A\sin B}{\cos A\cos B-\sin A\sin B}.$$

Dividing all the terms of the numerator and denominator by $\cos A\cos B$, we have

$$\tan(A+B)=\frac{\frac{\sin A}{\cos A}+\frac{\sin B}{\cos B}}{1-\frac{\sin A}{\cos A}\times\frac{\sin B}{\cos B}},$$

or, by (13),

$$\tan(A+B)=\frac{\tan A+\tan B}{1-\tan A\tan B}, \qquad (70)$$

and, by (5),

$$\cot(A+B)=\frac{1-\tan A\tan B}{\tan A+\tan B}. \qquad (71)$$

91. *To find the tangent and cotangent of the difference of two angles by means of their tangents.*

By (13),

$$\tan(A-B)=\frac{\sin(A-B)}{\cos(A-B)},$$

then, in like manner as in Art. 90, we have,

$$\tan(A-B)=\frac{\tan A-\tan B}{1+\tan A\tan B}, \qquad (72)$$

and

$$\cot(A-B)=\frac{1+\tan A\tan B}{\tan A-\tan B}. \qquad (73)$$

92. *To find the* SINE, *&c. of double an angle, by means of the functions of the angle itself.*

In the expression for sin $(A+B)$ and cos $(A+B)$, let $B=A$,

then $\sin 2A=\sin A\cos A+\sin A\cos A$,

or, $$\sin 2A=2\sin A\cos A; \qquad (74)$$

and $\cos 2A=\cos A\cos A-\sin A\sin A$,

or, $$\cos 2A=\cos^2 A-\sin^2 A. \qquad (75)$$

Substituting in the latter, first the value of $\cos^2 A$ and then the value of $\sin^2 A$, from (9) and (11), we have

$$\cos 2A = 1 - 2\sin^2 A, \tag{76}$$

$$\cos 2A = 2\cos^2 A - 1. \tag{77}$$

By means of (70) and (71), we have

$$\tan 2A = \frac{2\tan A}{1 - \tan^2 A}, \tag{78}$$

$$\cot 2A = \frac{1 - \tan^2 A}{2\tan A}. \tag{79}$$

93. *To find the* SINE, *&c. of half an angle by means of the sine or cosine of the angle itself.*

Let $\frac{1}{2}A = A$ in (76) and (77), and transpose; then

$$2\sin^2 \tfrac{1}{2}A = 1 - \cos A, \tag{80}$$

$$2\cos^2 \tfrac{1}{2}A = 1 + \cos A; \tag{81}$$

whence

$$\sin \tfrac{1}{2}A = \sqrt{\frac{1 - \cos A}{2}}, \quad \cos \tfrac{1}{2}A = \sqrt{\frac{1 + \cos A}{2}}, \tag{82}$$

$$\tan \tfrac{1}{2}A = \frac{\sin \frac{1}{2}A}{\cos \frac{1}{2}A} = \sqrt{\frac{1 - \cos A}{1 + \cos A}}. \tag{83}$$

By multiplying both numerator and denominator by $\sqrt{1 - \cos A}$, or by $\sqrt{1 + \cos A}$, we obtain (12),

$$\tan \tfrac{1}{2}A = \frac{1 - \cos A}{\sin A} = \frac{\sin A}{1 + \cos A}. \tag{84}$$

NATURAL SINES AND COSINES.

94. NATURAL SINES, COSINES, &c. are the values of the sines, cosines, &c. expressed in natural numbers.

95. A table containing these values is called a table of natural sines and cosines.

96. The semi-circumference of a circle whose radius is 1 is equal to 3.1415926 nearly (Geom., Prop. XV. Sch. 2, Bk. VI.),

and this divided by 10800, the number of minutes in 180°, will give .0002908882 for the arc of 1′, which may be taken also for the sine of an angle of 1′.

By means of formula (10),

$$\cos 1' = \sqrt{1 - \sin^2 1'} = .9999999577.$$

Then by transposition of formulæ (58) and (60),

$$\sin(a+b) = 2 \sin a \cos b - \sin(a-b),$$
$$\cos(a+b) = 2 \cos a \cos b - \cos(a-b),$$

in which, making b equal to 1′, and a, in succession, equal 1′, 2′, 3′, &c., we obtain for the sines,

$$\sin 2' = 2 \sin 1' \cos 1' - \sin 0' = .0005817764,$$
$$\sin 3' = 2 \sin 2' \cos 1' - \sin 1' = .0008726646,$$
$$\sin 4' = 2 \sin 3' \cos 1' - \sin 2' = .0011635526,$$

&c., &c.,

and for the cosines,

$$\cos 2' = 2 \cos 1' \cos 1' - \cos 0' = .9999998308,$$
$$\cos 3' = 2 \cos 2' \cos 1' - \cos 1' = .9999996193,$$
$$\cos 4' = 2 \cos 3' \cos 1' - \cos 2' = .9999993232,$$

&c., &c.,

thus obtaining the sines and cosines up to 45°.

The tangents may readily be found by dividing the sines by the cosines (13); and the secants, cotangents, and cosecants by dividing 1 by the cosines, tangents, and sines, respectively (Art. 51).

97. The sines, tangents, and secants of angles greater than 45° are respectively the cosines, cotangents, and cosecants of their complements, which are less than 45°; and, by their definitions, cosines, cotangents, and cosecants are the sines, tangents, and secants of complements (Art. 50). Thus,

$$\sin 46° = \cos(90° - 46°) = \cos 44°, \quad \tan 51° = \cot 39°,$$
$$\cos 50° = \sin 40, \quad \cot 88° = \tan 2°.$$

Tables, therefore, do not go beyond 45°; or, rather, are so arranged that each number answers as a function of both an angle less than 45° and its complement greater than 45°.

TABLE OF LOGARITHMIC SINES, COSINES, &c.

98. A TABLE of LOGARITHMIC SINES, COSINES, &c. contains the logarithms of the numbers expressing the natural sines, cosines, &c.

99. Since the sines and cosines are never greater than 1, and tangents likewise, when under 45°, their logarithms properly have *negative* characteristics. But to avoid the inconvenience of these, the characteristics are, by common consent, increased by 10. Thus the characteristic 9 is used in the place of —1, 8 in place of —2, &c.

The radius, therefore, of the logarithmic sines, cosines, &c. is, as arbitrarily assumed, 10^{10}, or 10,000,000,000.

100. In the accompanying table the degrees are given at the top and bottom of the page, and the minutes in the columns at the sides designated by M.

The column headed D contains the increase or decrease for 1 second. This is obtained by taking one sixtieth of the difference between the logarithmic sine, cosine, &c. of an angle or arc, and that next exceeding it by 1 minute. The result is placed against the lesser angle or arc.

TO FIND THE LOGARITHMIC SINE, &C. OF ANY ANGLE OR ARC.

101. If the angle or arc is less than 45°, look for the degrees at the *top* of the table, and for the minutes on the *left;* then, opposite to the minutes, on the same horizontal line, and in the column headed *Sine*, will be found the logarithmic sine; in the column headed *Cosine* will be found the logarithmic cosine, &c. Thus,

the logarithmic sine of 19° 23′ is 9.520990,
" " cosine of 31° 47′ " 9.929442,
" " tangent of 43° 5′ " 9.970922.

102. If the angle or arc is between 45° and 90°, look for the degrees at the *bottom* of the table, and for the minutes on the *right*; then, opposite to the minutes, and in the column designated at the bottom *Sine*, will be found the logarithmic sine; in the column designated at the bottom *Cosine* will be found the logarithmic cosine, &c. Thus,

the logarithmic sine of 80° 11′ is 9.993594,
" " cosine of 65° 59′ " 9.609597,
" " cotangent of 73° 35′ " 9.469280.

103. If the angle or arc is between 90° and 180°, subtract it from 180°, and take the logarithmic sine, &c. of the remainder. Thus,

the logarithmic sine of 112° is the logarithmic sine of 68°.
" " tangent of 98° " " tangent of 82°.

104. If the angle or arc is expressed in degrees, minutes, and seconds, find the logarithmic sine, &c. of the degrees and minutes as before; then multiply the number opposite, in the column headed D, by the seconds, and *add* the product to the number first found, for sines and tangents, but *subtract* it for cosines and cotangents.

Thus, if the logarithmic sine of 30° 25′ 42″ is required,

The logarithmic sine of 30° 25′ is		9.704395
Tabular difference,	3.59	
Number of seconds,	42	
Product,	150.78	150.78
Logarithmic sine of 30° 25′ 42″ is		9.704546

It is customary to omit the decimal figures at the right, but to increase the last figure retained, by 1, when the figure at the left of those omitted is 5 or greater than 5.

105. The secants and cosecants are not included in the table, since they may be readily derived from the cosines and sines.

By (5), $\sec A \cos A = 1$, and $\log \sec A + \log \cos A = 0$; but as log sec and log cos are each increased by 10 (Art. 99), the second member of the equation must be increased by 20, that is, logarithmic secant = 20 — logarithmic cosine.

In like manner,

logarithmic cosecant = 20 — logarithmic sine.

Hence, to find the logarithmic *secant*, subtract the logarithmic cosine from 20; and to find the logarithmic *cosecant*, subtract the logarithmic sine from 20. Thus,

The logarithmic secant of 65° 59′ is 10.390403
" " cosecant of 30° 25′ 42″ " 10.295454.

To find the Angle or Arc corresponding to any Logarithmic Sine, &c.

106. Look in the column designated by the same name with the given logarithm for the sine, &c. which is *nearest* to the given one, and if the name be at the *head* of the column, take the degrees at the *top* of the table, and the minutes on the *left*; but if the name be at the *foot* of the column, take the degrees at the *bottom*, and the minutes on the *right*. Thus,

The angle or arc corresponding to the logarithmic sine 9.681443 is 28° 42′.

The angle or arc corresponding to the logarithmic tan 9.984079 is 43° 57′.

The angle or arc corresponding to the logarithmic cos 9.731603 is 57° 23′.

107. If the given logarithmic sine, &c. is not found exactly, or very nearly, then, to find the *seconds*, subtract from the given logarithm that next less in the table, to the remainder annex two ciphers, divide the result by the number in the column headed D, and the quotient will be the number of seconds to be *added* to the degrees and minutes of the lesser logarithm for sines and tangents, or to be *subtracted* for cosines and cotangents.

Thus, to find the angle or arc corresponding to the logarithmic sine 9.938070.

Given log sine,	9.938070	
Next less,	9.938040	corresponding angle, 60° 7′
Diff. from column D,	1.21)30.00	25″
The log sine 9.938070 has for its cor. angle or arc,		60° 7′ 25″

The angle or arc corresponding to the logarithmic tangent 9.497200 is 17° 26′ 33″.

The angle or arc corresponding to the logarithmic cosine 9.792477 is 51° 40′ 30″.

EXAMPLES.

1. Required the logarithmic sine of 28° 42′. Ans. 9.681443.
2. Required the logarithmic cosine of 59° 33′ 47″. Ans. 9.704657.
3. Required the logarithmic cotangent of 127° 2′. Ans. 9.877640.
4. Required the logarithmic sine of 81° 20′. Ans. 9.995013.
5. Required the logarithmic secant of 51° 40′ 30″. Ans. 10.207523.
6. Required the logarithmic tangent of 74° 21′ 20″. Ans. 10.552778.
7. Required the logarithmic cosecant of 102° 24′ 41″. Ans. 10.010270.
8. Required the logarithmic tangent of 1° 59′ 51″.8. Ans. 8.542587.
9. Required the angle of the logarithmic sine 9.999969. Ans. 89° 19′.
10. Required the arc of the logarithmic tangent 9.645270. Ans. 23° 50′ 17″.
11. Required the angle of the logarithmic cosine 9.598075. Ans. 66° 39′.
12. Required the angle of the logarithmic cotangent 10.301470. Ans. 26° 32′ 31″.
13. Required the arc of the logarithmic sine 9.893410. Ans. 51° 28′ 40″.
14. Required the angle of the logarithmic cosine 9.421157. Ans. 105° 17′ 29″.
15. Required the arc of the logarithmic tangent 9.692125. Ans. 26° 12′ 20″.
16. Required the angle of the logarithmic cotangent 9.421901. Ans. 75° 12′ 6″.

BOOK III.

SOLUTION OF PLANE TRIANGLES.

108. THE SOLUTION OF TRIANGLES is the process by which, when the values of a sufficient number of their elements are given, the values of the remaining elements are computed.

The *elements* of every triangle are the three sides and the three angles. Three of these elements must be given, one of which must be a side, in order to solve a plane triangle.

The solution of plane triangles depends upon the following

FUNDAMENTAL PROPOSITIONS.

109. *In a right-angled triangle, the side opposite to an acute angle is equal to the product of the hypothenuse into the sine of the angle; and the side adjacent to an acute angle is equal to the product of the hypothenuse into the cosine of the angle.*

Let $A B C$ be a triangle having a right angle at C; then, by (1),

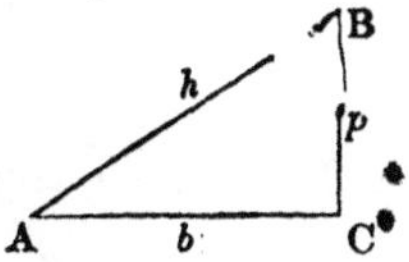

$$\sin A = \frac{p}{h}, \qquad \sin B = \frac{b}{h};$$

therefore $\qquad p = h \sin A, \qquad b = h \sin B. \qquad (85)$

Again, by (4), $\qquad \cos A = \frac{b}{h}, \qquad \cos B = \frac{p}{h};$

therefore $\qquad b = h \cos A, \qquad p = h \cos B. \qquad (86)$

110. *In a right-angled triangle, the side opposite to an acute angle is equal to the product of the other side into the tangent of the angle; and the side adjacent to an acute angle is equal to the product of the other side into the cotangent of the angle.*

For, by (2), $\tan A = \frac{p}{b}$, $\tan B = \frac{b}{p}$,

therefore $p = b \tan A$, $b = p \tan B$. (87)

Again, by (4), $\cot A = \frac{b}{p}$, $\cot B = \frac{p}{b}$,

therefore $b = p \cot A$, $p = b \cot B$. (88)

111. *In any plane triangle, the sides are proportional to the sines of the opposite angles.*

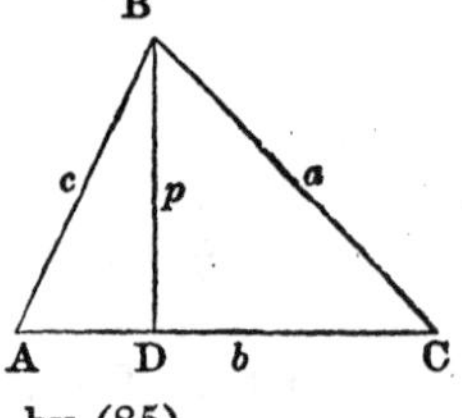

Let $A B C$ be any triangle, in which the sides opposite the angles A, B, C, respectively, are denoted by a, b, and c. From one of the angles, as B, draw BD perpendicular to the opposite side $A C$, and denote the line $B D$ by p. Then the right-angled triangles, CBD, $A B D$, give, by (85),

$$p = a \sin C, \qquad p = c \sin A;$$

whence, $a \sin C = c \sin A$,

which gives the proportion

$$a : c :: \sin A : \sin C. \tag{89}$$

In like manner it may be proved that

$$a : b :: \sin A : \sin B, \tag{90}$$

$$c : b :: \sin C : \sin B, \tag{91}$$

and these three proportions give

$$a : b : c :: \sin A : \sin B : \sin C, \tag{92}$$

which may also be written

$$\frac{a}{\sin A} = \frac{b}{\sin B} = \frac{c}{\sin C}. \tag{93}$$

The angle C was *acute*, but had it been *obtuse*, or a right angle, the results would have been the same. The proposition, therefore, applies in every case.

112. *In any plane triangle, the sum of any two sides is to their difference as the tangent of half the sum of the opposite angles is to the tangent of half their difference.*

For, by (90), $a : b :: \sin A : \sin B$;

whence (Geom., Prop. XII. Bk. II.),

$$a + b : a - b :: \sin A + \sin B : \sin A - \sin B,$$

which may also be written,

$$\frac{a+b}{a-b} = \frac{\sin A + \sin B}{\sin A - \sin B}.$$

But, by formula (66),

$$\frac{\sin A + \sin B}{\sin A - \sin B} = \frac{\tan \frac{1}{2}(A+B)}{\tan \frac{1}{2}(A-B)};$$

therefore,
$$\frac{a+b}{a-b} = \frac{\tan \frac{1}{2}(A+B)}{\tan \frac{1}{2}(A-B)}, \qquad (94)$$

or, as it may be written,

$$a + b : a - b :: \tan \tfrac{1}{2}(A+B) : \tan \tfrac{1}{2}(A-B). \qquad (95)$$

113. *In any triangle, the square of any side is equal to the sum of the squares of the two other sides, diminished by twice the rectangle of these sides multiplied by the cosine of the included angle.*

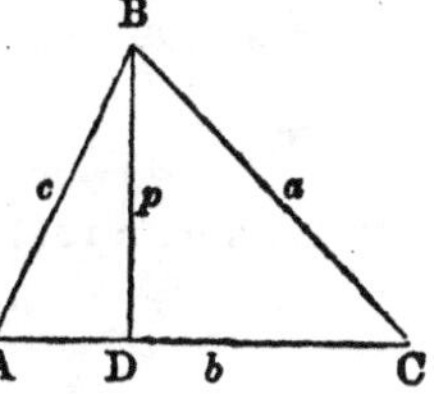

Let ABC be any plane triangle, in which the sides opposite the angles A, B, C, respectively, are denoted by a, b, c. Draw BD from one of the angles, B, perpendicular to the opposite side, AC. Then, if A is acute, we have by Geometry (Prop. XII. Bk. IV.),

$$a^2 = b^2 + c^2 - 2\,b\,AD;$$

but from the right-angled triangle ABD, by (86), we have

$$AD = c \cos A;$$

therefore,
$$a^2 = b^2 + c^2 - 2\,bc \cos A. \qquad (96)$$

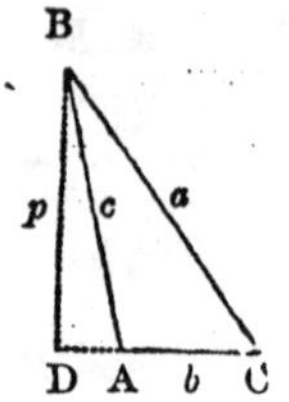

When the angle A is obtuse, the point D will fall on the other side of A, and we have by Geometry (Prop. XIII. Bk. IV.),

$$a^2 = b^2 + c^2 + 2\,b\,AD.$$

B

p c a

D A b C

But since BAD is now the supplement of BAC, by Art. 77 we have

$$AD = c \cos BAD = -c \cos BAC = -c \cos A.$$

Substituting this value of AD, we have as before,

$$a^2 = b^2 + c^2 - 2\,bc \cos A.$$

When A is a right angle and a the hypothenuse, $\cos A$ is zero (30), and (96) becomes

$$a^2 = b^2 + c^2,$$

and thus the formula (96) is true, whatever the angle A may be.

In like manner we have

$$b^2 = a^2 + c^2 - 2\,ac \cos B, \quad (97)$$

$$c^2 = a^2 + b^2 - 2\,ab \cos C. \quad (98)$$

114. *The cosine of any angle of a plane triangle is equal to the fraction whose numerator is the sum of the squares of the containing sides, diminished by the square of the opposite side, and whose denominator is twice the product of the containing sides.*

For, by (96), $a^2 = b^2 + c^2 - 2\,bc \cos A$,

whence, $$\cos A = \frac{b^2 + c^2 - a^2}{2\,bc}. \quad (99)$$

Similarly, from (97) and (98), we have

$$\cos B = \frac{a^2 + c^2 - b^2}{2\,ac}, \quad \cos C = \frac{a^2 + b^2 - c^2}{2\,ab}. \quad (100)$$

115. By these formulæ the angles of a triangle can be found when the sides are given, but they cannot be conveniently applied in computation by logarithms.

We then subtract both members of formula (99) from 1, and obtain

$$1 - \cos A = 1 - \frac{b^2 + c^2 - a^2}{2\,bc},$$

and, substituting for $1 - \cos A$ its value, $2 \sin^2 \frac{1}{2} A$, by (80), we have

$$2 \sin^2 \tfrac{1}{2} A = 1 - \frac{b^2 + c^2 - a^2}{2\,b\,c} = \frac{a^2 - (b - c)^2}{2\,b\,c}$$

$$= \frac{(a + b - c)\ (a - b + c)}{2\,bc};$$

whence, $$\sin^2 \tfrac{1}{2} A = \frac{(a + b - c)\ (a - b + c)}{4\,bc}. \qquad (101)$$

Let now $2\,s = a + b + c$, so that s is half the sum of the sides of the triangle; then

$$a + b - c = 2\,(s - c), \quad a - b + c = 2\,(s - b).$$

Substituting these values in the preceding equation, and reducing, we have

$$\sin \tfrac{1}{2} A = \sqrt{\frac{(s - b)\ (s - c)}{b\ c}}. \qquad (102)$$

In like manner we may obtain

$$\sin \tfrac{1}{2} B = \sqrt{\frac{(s - a)\ (s - c)}{a\ c}}, \qquad (103)$$

$$\sin \tfrac{1}{2} C = \sqrt{\frac{(s - a)\ (s - b)}{a\ b}}. \qquad (104)$$

That is,

The sine of half of any angle in a plane triangle is equal to the square root of half the sum of the three sides less one of the adjacent sides, into half the sum less the other adjacent side, divided by the rectangle of the two adjacent sides.

116. If 1 be added to both sides of (99), then, substituting for $1 + \cos A$ its value, $2 \cos^2 \frac{1}{2} A$, by (81), we have

$$2 \cos^2 \tfrac{1}{2} A = 1 + \frac{b^2 + c^2 - a^2}{2\,b\,c} = \frac{(b + c)^2 - a^2}{2\,b\,c}$$

$$= \frac{(b + c + a)\ (b + c - a)}{2\,b\,c};$$

whence, $$\cos^2 \tfrac{1}{2} A = \frac{(b + c + a)\ (b + c - a)}{4\,b\,c}. \qquad (105)$$

Let now $s =$ half the sum of the sides of the triangle, as in Art. 115; then,

$$b + c + a = 2\,s, \quad b + c - a = 2\,(s - a).$$

Substituting these values in the preceding equation, we have

$$\cos \tfrac{1}{2} A = \sqrt{\frac{s\,(s - a)}{b\,c}}. \qquad (106)$$

Similarly,

$$\cos \tfrac{1}{2} B = \sqrt{\frac{s\,(s - b)}{a\,c}}, \qquad (107)$$

$$\cos \tfrac{1}{2} C = \sqrt{\frac{s\,(s - c)}{a\,b}}. \qquad (108)$$

That is,

The cosine of half of any angle of a plane triangle is equal to the square root of half the sum of the three sides, into half the sum less the side opposite the angle, divided by the rectangle of the two adjacent sides.

117. Dividing (102) by (106), (103) by (107), and (104) by (108), we have, by (13),

$$\tan \tfrac{1}{2} A = \sqrt{\frac{(s - b)\,(s - c)}{s\,(s - a)}}; \qquad (109)$$

$$\tan \tfrac{1}{2} B = \sqrt{\frac{(s - a)\,(s - c)}{s\,(s - b)}}; \qquad (110)$$

$$\tan \tfrac{1}{2} C = \sqrt{\frac{(s - a)\,(s - b)}{s\,(s - c)}}. \qquad (111)$$

That is,

The tangent of half of any angle of a plane triangle is equal to the square root of half the sum of the three sides, less one of the adjacent sides, into half the sum less the other adjacent side, divided by half the sum, into half the sum less the side opposite the angle.

SOLUTION OF RIGHT-ANGLED TRIANGLES.

118. In a right-angled triangle, the side opposite to the right angle is called the *hypothenuse;* that adjacent to the right angle, and upon which the triangle is supposed to stand, is called the

base ; and the other side adjacent to the right angle, the ***perpendicular.*** The base and perpendicular have been termed the sides about the right angle. Of the acute angles, that adjacent to the base has been termed the angle at the base, and the other the angle at the perpendicular.

Thus, let $A\,B\,C$ be any right-angled triangle, with the right angle at C, then h represents the hypothenuse, b the base, p the perpendicular, A the acute angle at the base, and B the acute angle at the perpendicular.

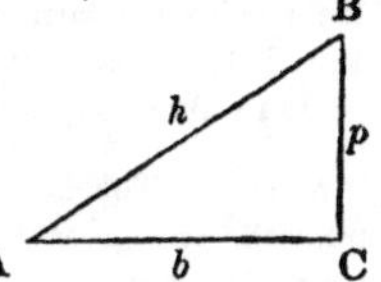

119. In order to solve the triangle, two elements other than the right angle must be given, one of them being a side. Hence there will be four cases in which there may be given, respectively,

I. The hypothenuse and an acute angle.
II. A side about the right angle and an acute angle.
III. The hypothenuse and a side about the right angle.
IV. The two sides about the right angle.

Case I.

120. ***Given the hypothenuse and an acute angle.***

Let there be given, in the right-angled triangle $A\,B\,C$, the hypothenuse h and the acute angle A; to find the angle B, the perpendicular p, and the base b.

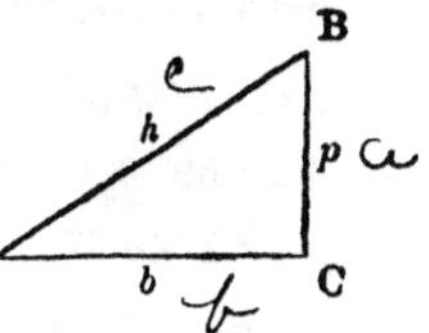

To find B. The angle B is the complement of A (Art. 44); hence,

$$B = 90^\circ - A.$$

To find p and b. By (85) and (86) we have

$$p = h \sin A = h \cos B,$$

$$b = h \cos A = h \sin B;$$

or, by logarithms,

$$\log p = \log h + \log \sin A = \log h + \log \cos B, \quad (112)$$

$$\log b = \log h + \log \cos A = \log h + \log \sin B. \quad (113)$$

That is,

The logarithm of either side about the right angle is equal to the logarithm of the hypothenuse, plus the logarithmic sine of the opposite angle, or plus the logarithmic cosine of the adjacent angle.

NOTE 1. As the logarithmic sine and cosine are increased by 10 (Art. 99), the resulting logarithm will be so much too great, and must be diminished by 10. This increase by 10 will affect the work wherever the logarithms of trigonometric functions are used.

NOTE 2. The last figure of an answer may occasionally be found to differ from the one given in this work, when it has been obtained by the use of different formulæ or tables. The results are not, however, generally carried so far as to admit of such a difference. When two methods of solving give different results, that is inserted which is most accurate, whether obtained by the usual method or not.

EXAMPLES.

1. Given the hypothenuse of a right-angled triangle equal to 1785.395 feet, and the angle at the base equal to 59° 37′ 42″; to solve the triangle.

Solution. The angle at the perpendicular $= 90° - 59° 37' 42'' = 30° 22' 18''$. Let, now, $h = 1785.395$ feet and $A = 59° 37' 42''$, and we have, by (112) and (113),

$h = 1785.395$	log 3.251734		log 3.251734
$A = 59° 37' 42''$	log sin 9.935892		log cos 9.703813
$p = 1540.37$	log 3.187626	$b = 902.708$	log 2.955547

Ans. Angle at the perpendicular, 30° 22′ 18″; perpendicular, 1540.37 feet; base, 902.708 feet.

2. Given the hypothenuse of a right-angled triangle equal to 25 yards, and one of the acute angles equal to 54° 30′; to solve the triangle.

3. Given the hypothenuse of a right-angled triangle equal to 173.2 feet, and one of the acute angles equal to 37° 2′ 43″; required the other parts.

Ans. Angle, 52° 57′ 17″; sides, 104.34 feet and 138.24 feet.

CASE II.

121. *Given a side about the right angle, and an acute angle.*

Let there be given (Fig. Art. 120) the side b and the angle A; to solve the triangle.

To find B. The angle B is the complement of A; hence,

$$B = 90° - A.$$

To find p. By (87) and (88), we have

$$p = b \tan A = b \cot B;$$

or, by logarithms,

$$\log p = \log b + \log \tan A = \log b + \log \cot B. \quad (114)$$

To find h. By means of (113), we obtain

$$\log h = \log b - \log \cos A = \log b - \log \sin B. \quad (115)$$

Given the side p and the angle A; to solve the triangle.

To find B. We have, as before, the angle B, the complement of A, or $B = 90° - A$.

To find b. By (87) and (88), we have

$$b = p \cot A = p \tan B;$$

or, by logarithms,

$$\log b = \log p + \log \cot A = \log p + \log \tan B. \quad (116)$$

To find h. By means of (112), we obtain

$$\log h = \log p - \log \sin A = \log p - \log \cos B. \quad (117)$$

That is,

The logarithm of either side about the right angle is equal to the logarithm of the other, plus the logarithmic tangent of the angle opposite, or plus the logarithmic cotangent of the angle adjacent to the former.

The logarithm of the hypothenuse is equal to the logarithm of either side about the right angle, minus the logarithmic sine of the angle opposite, or minus the logarithmic cosine of the angle adjacent to the side.

EXAMPLES.

1. Given the side b of a right-angled triangle equal to 902.708 feet, and the acute angle A equal to $59° 37' 42''$; to solve the triangle.

Solution. The angle $B = 90° - 59° 37' 42'' = 30° 22' 18''$. By (114) and (115), we have

$b = 902.708$	log 2.955547		log 2.955547
$A = 59° 37' 42''$	log tan 10.232078		ar. co. log cos 0.296187
$p = 1540.37$	log 3.187625	$h = 1785.395$	log 3.251734

Ans. Angle B, $30° 22' 18''$; perpendicular, 1540.37 feet; hypothenuse, 1785.395 feet.

2. Given one of the sides about the right angle of a right-angled triangle equal to 14.52 rods, and the opposite angle equal to $35° 30'$; to solve the triangle.

3. Given the perpendicular of a right-angled triangle equal to 3555.4 yards, and the angle at the perpendicular equal to $33° 30' 47''$; to solve the triangle.

Ans. Angle at the base, $56° 29' 13''$; base, 2354.4 yards; hypothenuse, 4264.3 yards.

CASE III.

122. *Given the hypothenuse and a side about the right angle.*

Let there be given (Fig. Art. 120) the hypothenuse h and the side p; to solve the triangle.

To find A and B. By (1) and (4), we have

$$\sin A = \cos B = \frac{p}{h};$$

or, by logarithms,

$$\log \sin A = \log \cos B = \log p - \log h. \qquad (118)$$

To find b. By (85) and (86), we have

$$b = h \cos A = h \sin B;$$

or, by logarithms,

$$\log b = \log h + \log \cos A = \log h + \log \sin B. \qquad (119)$$

Also, by Geometry (Prop. XI. Bk. IV.), we have

$$h^2 = p^2 + b^2; \qquad (120).$$

whence, $b^2 = h^2 - p^2 = (h+p)\,(h-p),$

$$b = \sqrt{(h+p)\,(h-p)};$$

or, by logarithms,

$$\log b = \tfrac{1}{2}\log(h+p) + \tfrac{1}{2}\log(h-p). \qquad (121)$$

That is,

The logarithmic sine of one of the acute angles, or the logarithmic cosine of the other, is equal to the logarithm of the side opposite the former angle, minus the logarithm of the hypothenuse.

The logarithm of either side about the right angle is equal to the logarithm of the hypothenuse, plus the logarithmic cosine of the angle adjacent, or plus the logarithmic sine of the angle opposite.

EXAMPLES.

1. Given the hypothenuse of a right-angled triangle equal to 1785.395 feet, and the perpendicular equal to 1540.37; to find the other parts.

Solution. By (118) and (119), we have

$p = 1540.37$	log	3.187626		
$h = 1785.395$	ar. co. log	6.748266		log 3.251734
$A = 59°\ 37'\ 42''$	log sin	9.935892	log cos A	9.703813
$B = 30°\ 22'\ 18''$	log cos			
			$b = 902.708$	log 2.955547

Ans. Base, 902.708 feet; angle at the base, 59° 37′ 42″; angle at the perpendicular, 30° 22′ 18″.

2. Given the hypothenuse of a right-angled triangle equal to 73 feet, and one of the sides equal to 55 feet; to solve the triangle.

3. Given the hypothenuse of a right-angled triangle equal to 643.7 rods, and the base equal to 473.8; to find the perpendicular and the two acute angles.

Ans. Perpendicular, 435.73 rods; acute angles, 42° 36′ 12″ 47° 23′ 48″.

Case IV.

123. *Given the two sides about the right angle.*

Let there be given (Fig. Art. 120) the sides p and b; to solve the triangle.

To find A and B. By (2) and (4), we have

$$\tan A = \cot B = \frac{p}{b};$$

or by logarithms,

$$\log \tan A = \log \cot B = \log p - \log b. \qquad (122)$$

To find h. By (1), we have

$$\sin A = \frac{p}{h}, \quad \text{whence } h = \frac{p}{\sin A}; \qquad (123)$$

or, by logarithms,

$$\log h = \log p - \log \sin A; \qquad (124)$$

Also, by (120),

$$h^2 = p^2 + b^2, \text{ whence } h = \sqrt{p^2 + b^2}. \qquad (125)$$

That is,

The logarithmic tangent of one of the acute angles, or the logarithmic cotangent of the other, is equal to the logarithm of the side opposite the former angle, minus the logarithm of the side adjacent.

The logarithm of the hypothenuse is equal to the logarithm of either side, minus the logarithmic sine of the angle opposite the side.

EXAMPLES.

1. Given of a right-angled triangle the side p equal to 1540.37 feet, and the side b equal to 902.708 feet; to solve the triangle.

Solution. By (122) and (124), we have

$p = 1540.37$	log 3.187626			log 3.187626
$b = 902.708$	ar. co. log 7.044453			
$A = 59°\ 37'\ 42''$	log tan	10.232079	ar. co. log sin A	0.064108
$B = 80°\ 22'\ 18''$	log cot		$h = 1785.395$	log 3.251734

Ans. Hypothenuse, 1785.395 feet; acute angles, 59° 37′ 42″, 30° 22′ 18″.

2. Given the perpendicular of a right-angled triangle equal to 65 feet, and the base equal to 72 feet; to find the hypothenuse and the two acute angles.

3. Given the perpendicular of a right-angled triangle equal to 2.269 rods, and the base equal to 126.9 rods; required the hypothenuse and the two acute angles.

Ans. Hypothenuse, 126.92 rods; acute angles, 1° 1′ 28″, 88° 58′ 32″.

SOLUTION OF OBLIQUE-ANGLED TRIANGLES.

124. Since there must be given three elements, one of which is a side (Art. 108), there will be four cases, the data in them being, respectively,

I. One side and any two angles.
II. Two sides and an angle opposite one of them.
III. Two sides and the included angle.
IV. The three sides.

CASE I.

125. *Given one side and two angles.*

Let there be given in the triangle ABC, the side a, and the two angles A and B; to solve the triangle.

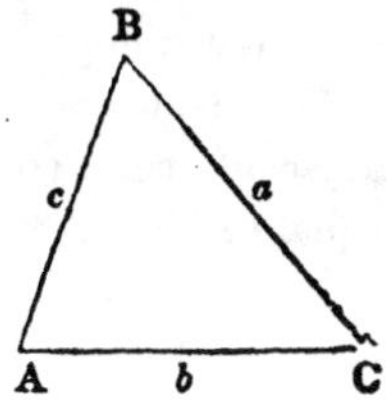

To find C. Since the sum of the three angles must be 180°, we have

$$C = 180° - (A + B).$$

To find b and c. By (90) and (89), we have

$$a : b :: \sin A : \sin B,$$

$$a : c :: \sin A : \sin C;$$

whence,
$$b = \frac{a \sin B}{\sin A}, \qquad c = \frac{a \sin C}{\sin A}, \qquad (126)$$

or, by logarithms,

$$\log b = \log a + \log \sin B - \log \sin A, \qquad (127)$$

$$\log c = \log a + \log \sin C - \log \sin A. \qquad (128)$$

That is,

The logarithm of the required side is equal to the logarithm of the given side, plus the logarithmic sine of the angle opposite the required side, minus the logarithmic sine of the angle opposite the given side.

EXAMPLES.

1. Given of a triangle the side a equal to 9459.31 feet, the angle A equal to $71° 3' 34''$, and the angle B equal to $53° 26'$; to find the sides b, c, and the angle C.

Solution. $C = 180° - (71° 3' 34'' + 53° 26') = 55° 30' 26''$.

Then, by (127) and (128), we have

$a = 9459.31$	log 3.975859		log 3.975859
$A = 71° 3' 34''$	ar.co.log sin 0.024176		ar. co. log sin 0.024176
$B = 53° 26'$	log sin 9.904804		
$C = 55° 30' 26''$			log sin 9.916032
$b = 8032.28$	log 3.904839	$c = 8242.64$	log 3.916067

Ans. Angle C, $55° 30' 26''$; side b, 8032.28 feet; side c, 8242.64 feet.

2. Given one side of a triangle equal to 110 rods, the opposite angle equal to $50° 5'$, and an adjacent angle equal to $33° 55'$; to solve the triangle.

3. Given one side of a triangle equal to 654 feet, one of the adjacent angles equal to $41° 0' 39''$, and the other adjacent angle equal to $55° 34' 8''$; to find the other parts.

Ans. Angle, $83° 25' 13''$; sides, 432 feet, 543 feet.

CASE II.

126. *Given two sides and an angle opposite one of them.*

Let there be given in any triangle, ABC, the two sides a, b, and the angle A opposite to one of them; to solve the triangle.

To find B. By (90), we have

$$a : b :: \sin A : \sin B,$$

whence,

$$\sin B = \frac{b \sin A}{a}, \tag{129}$$

or, by logarithms,

$$\log \sin B = \log b + \log \sin A - \log a. \qquad (130)$$

That is,

The logarithmic sine of a required angle whose opposite side is given, is equal to the logarithm of that side, plus the logarithmic sine of the given angle, minus the logarithm of its opposite side.

To find C. We have $C = 180° - (A + B)$.

To find c. By (128), after C is found, we have

$$\log c = \log a + \log \sin C - \log \sin A.$$

127. Whenever the given angle is acute, and the side opposite to it is less than the side adjacent to it, there may be formed, as shown in Geometry (Prob. XI. Bk. V.), two triangles, each satisfying the given conditions, and, therefore, there will be two solutions. Thus (Fig. Art. 126) with two given sides a, b, equal respectively to $C B$ and $A C$, and the given acute angle A opposite the less side $C B$, there may always be formed two triangles, $A B C$, $A B' C$, which have A, a, b in common, and the angles $A B C$, $A B' C$ supplements of each other. In one of them, therefore, the required angle is acute, and in the other it is obtuse.

When the given angle is obtuse, the required angle must of necessity be acute, since a triangle can have but one obtuse angle.

When the given angle is acute, and its opposite side is greater than the side opposite to the required angle, that must also be acute, since the greater angle must be opposite the greater side.

When the side opposite the given angle is exactly a perpendicular let fall from C on $A B$, the required angle is a right angle.

If the side opposite the given angle be less than the perpendicular, the solution is impossible, since there will be no triangle with the given parts.

When two values are admissible for B, in case of ambiguity, two corresponding values will exist for C and c.

EXAMPLES.

1. Given of any triangle $A\,B\,C$, the side b equal to 216 yards, the side a equal to 117 yards, and the angle opposite the side a equal to 22° 37′; to solve the triangle.

Solution. By (130), we have

$a = 117$	ar. co. log sin 7.931814
$b = 216$	log 2.334454
$A = 22°\ 37'$	log sin 9.584968
$B = 45°\ 13'\ 55''$ or $134°\ 46'\ 5''$	log sin 9.851236
$A + B = 67°\ 50\ 55''$ or $157°\ 23'\ 5''$	

$$C = 180° - 67°\ 50'\ 55'' = 112°\ 9'\ 5'', \text{ or}$$
$$C = 180° - 157°\ 23'\ 5'' = 22°\ 36'\ 55''.$$

Then, by (128), we have

$a = 117$	log 2.068186		log 2.068186
$C = 112°\ 9'\ 5''$	log sin 9.966700	or $= 22°\ 36'\ 55''$	log sin 9.584943
$A = 22° 37'$	ar. co. log sin 0.415032		ar. co. log sin 0.415032
$c = 281.785$	log 2.449918	or $= 116.99$	log 2.068161

Ans. Angle B, 45° 13′ 55″, or 134° 46′ 5″; angle C, 112° 9′ 5″, or 22° 36′ 55″; side c, 281.785 yd., or 116.99 yd.

2. Given two sides of a triangle equal to 9459.31 feet and 8032.28 feet, and the angle opposite the first side equal to 71° 3′ 34″; to find the other parts.

Solution.

$a = 9459.31$	ar. co. log 6.024141	log 3.975859
$b = 8032.28$	log 3.904839	
$A = 71°\ 3'\ 34''$	log sin 9.975824	ar. co. log sin 0.024176
$B = 53°\ 26'$	log sin 9.904804	
$C = 180° - 124°\ 29'\ 34'' = 55°\ 30'\ 26''$		log sin 9.916032
	$c = 8242.64$	log 3.916067

Ans. Side, 8242.64 feet; angles, 53° 26′, 55° 30′ 26″.

3. Given two sides of a triangle equal to 80 rods and 142.6

rods, and the angle opposite the second side equal to 96°; to solve the triangle.

4. Given in a triangle $A B C$, the side a equal to 32.1098 rods, the side b equal to 125.701 rods, and the angle A equal to 14° 48′; to solve the triangle.

Ans. Angle B, 90°; angle C, 75° 12′; side c, 121.531 rods.

5. Given two sides of a triangle equal to 1540.37 feet and 760.9 feet, and the angle opposite the second equal to 30° 22′ 8″; to find the other side and angles. Ans. Impossible.

Case III.

128. *Given two sides and the included angle.*

Let there be given in the triangle $A B C$ the sides a and b and the included angle C, to solve the triangle.

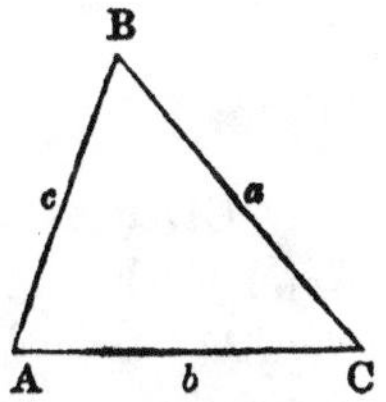

To find A and B, we have

$$A + B = 180° - C,$$

and

$$\tfrac{1}{2}(A + B) = 90° - \tfrac{1}{2}C = \text{complement of } \tfrac{1}{2}C;$$

whence,

$$\tan \tfrac{1}{2}(A + B) = \cot \tfrac{1}{2}C. \qquad (131)$$

Then, the half difference of A and B is found by means of (95), which gives

$$a + b : a - b :: \tan \tfrac{1}{2}(A + B) : \tan \tfrac{1}{2}(A - B);$$

whence,

$$\tan \tfrac{1}{2}(A - B) = \frac{a-b}{a+b} \tan \tfrac{1}{2}(A + B) = \frac{a-b}{a+b} \cot \tfrac{1}{2}C, \quad (132)$$

or, by logarithms,

$$\log \tan \tfrac{1}{2}(A-B) = \log (a-b) - \log (a+b) + \log \tan \tfrac{1}{2}(A+B)$$
$$= \log (a - b) - \log (a + b) + \log \cot \tfrac{1}{2}C. \qquad (133)$$

That is,

The logarithmic tangent of half the difference of the two required angles is equal to the logarithm of the difference of the given sides, minus the logarithm of their sum, plus the logarithmic tangent of half the sum of the required angles, or plus the logarithmic cotangent of half the given angle.

Since $\frac{1}{2}(A+B)$ is known, when $\frac{1}{2}(A-B)$ is found, we have

$$A = \tfrac{1}{2}(A+B) + \tfrac{1}{2}(A-B),$$

$$B = \tfrac{1}{2}(A+B) - \tfrac{1}{2}(A-B).$$

That is,

The GREATER *of the two required angles is equal to half their sum, plus half their difference; and the* SMALLER *angle is equal to half their sum, minus half their difference.*

To find c. By (128), we have

$$\log c = \log a + \log \sin C - \log \sin A.$$

EXAMPLES.

1. Given of any triangle ABC, the side a equal to 9459.31 feet, the side b equal to 8032.28 feet, and the included angle C equal to 55° 30′ 26″; to find the side c and the angles A and B.

Solution. $A + B = 180° - C = 124° 29' 34''$, and $\frac{1}{2}(A+B) = 62° 14' 47''$. Then, by (133),

$a + b =$	17491.59	ar. co. log	5.757170
$a - b =$	1427.03	log	3.154433
$\frac{1}{2}(A+B) =$	62° 14′ 47″	log tan	10.278844
$\frac{1}{2}(A-B) =$	8° 48′ 47″	log tan	9.190447
$B =$	53° 26′		
$A =$	71° 3′ 34″	ar. co. log sin	0.024176
$C =$	55° 30′ 26″	log sin	9.916032
$a =$	9459.31	log	3.975859
$c =$	8242.64	log	3.916067

Ans. Side c, 8242.64 ft.; angle A, 71° 3′ 34″; angle B, 53° 26′.

2. Given two sides of a triangle equal to 142.6 feet and 110 feet, and the included angle equal to 33° 55′; to solve the triangle.

3. Given the two sides of a triangle equal to 153 rods and 137 rods, and the included angle equal to 40° 33′ 12″; to find the other parts.

Ans. Side, 101.615 feet; angles, 78° 13′ 1″ and 61° 13′ 47″.

CASE IV.

129. *Given the three sides.*

Let there be given (Fig. Art. 128) the three sides a, b, and c; to solve the triangle.

To find A, B, and C. By (102), (103), and (104), we have

$$\sin \tfrac{1}{2} A = \sqrt{\frac{(s-b)(s-c)}{bc}},$$

$$\sin \tfrac{1}{2} B = \sqrt{\frac{(s-a)(s-c)}{ac}},$$

$$\sin \tfrac{1}{2} C = \sqrt{\frac{(s-a)(s-b)}{ab}};$$

or, by logarithms,

$$\log \sin \tfrac{1}{2} A = \frac{\log (s-b) + \log (s-c) - \log b - \log c}{2}, \quad (134)$$

$$\log \sin \tfrac{1}{2} B = \frac{\log (s-a) + \log (s-c) - \log a - \log c}{2}, \quad (135)$$

$$\log \sin \tfrac{1}{2} C = \frac{\log (s-a) + \log (s-b) - \log a - \log b}{2}. \quad (136)$$

That is,

The logarithmic sine of half of any angle of a triangle is equal to the logarithm of the difference between half the sum of the sides and one of the adjacent sides, plus the logarithm of the difference between half the sum and the other adjacent side, minus the logarithms of those two sides, divided by 2.

130. A, B, and C can also be determined by formulæ (106), (107), and (108) for the cosine of half an angle, and by formulæ (109), (110), and (111) for the tangent of half an angle.

When the half angle is less than 45°, the table will determine it from its sine with greater precision than from the cosine, and *vice versa* when the half angle is greater than 45°.

The method by the tangent of half the angle is precise, and requires the use of but four logarithms.

NOTE. This case may also be solved by drawing a perpendicular from the vertex to the base of the triangle, thus dividing it into two right-angled triangles, of which the hypothenuses are known, and the sum of whose bases is the base of the original triangle. Let s and s' represent CD and DA (Fig. Art. 113), then (Geom., Prop. XI. Bk. IV.),

$$p^2 = c^2 - s'^2 = a^2 - s^2, \quad \text{or,} \quad s^2 - s'^2 = a^2 - c^2,$$

whence, $(s + s')(s - s') = (a + c)(a - c)$.

Substituting b for $s + s'$, $\quad s - s' = \frac{(a + c)(a - c)}{b}$,

a form to which logarithms can be readily applied.

Knowing $s + s'$ and $s - s'$, s and s' can at once be found, and thence the angles A, C, and B, by Art. 122.

EXAMPLES.

1. Given of any triangle ABC, the side a equal to 216 yards, the side b equal to 217 yards, and the side c equal to 235 yards; to find the angles A, B, and C.

Solution. By (134), (135), and (136) we have

$a = 216$		ar.co.log 7.665546	ar.co.log 7.665546
$b = 217$	ar.co.log 7.663540		ar.co.log 7.663540
$c = 235$	ar.co.log 7.628932	ar.co.log 7.628932	
$s - a = 118$		log 2.071882	log 2.071882
$s - b = 117$	log 2.068186		log 2.068186
$s - c = 99$	log 1.995635	log 1.995635	
	2) 19.356293	2) 19.361995	2) 19.469154
log sines	9.678147	9.680998	9.734577

$\frac{1}{2}A = 28° 27' 47''$; $\frac{1}{2}B = 28° 40' 4''.4$; $\frac{1}{2}C = 32° 52' 8''.6$.
Ans. $A = 56° 55' 34''$; $B = 57° 20' 8''.8$; $C = 65° 44' 17''.2$.

2. Given the three sides of a triangle equal to 432, 543, and 654; to solve the triangle by means of the cosine.

3. Given the three sides of a triangle equal to 95.12, 162.34, and 98; to solve the triangle by means of the tangent.

Ans. The angles, 32° 14′ 53″; 114° 24′ 9″; 33° 20′ 58″.

BOOK IV.

PRACTICAL APPLICATIONS.

DETERMINATION OF HEIGHTS AND DISTANCES.

131. A HORIZONTAL PLANE is one which is parallel to the horizon.

A VERTICAL PLANE is one which is perpendicular to a horizontal plane.

A HORIZONTAL LINE is one which is parallel to the horizon.

A VERTICAL LINE is one which is perpendicular to a horizontal plane.

132. A HORIZONTAL ANGLE is one the plane of whose sides is horizontal.

A VERTICAL ANGLE is one the plane of whose sides is vertical.

An ANGLE OF ELEVATION is a vertical angle having one side horizontal and the inclined side above it; as the angle CAB.

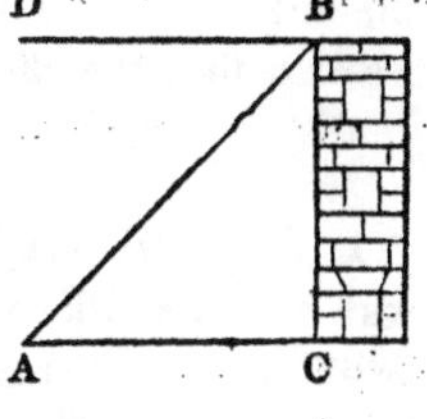

An ANGLE OF DEPRESSION is a vertical angle having one side horizontal and the inclined side under it; as the angle DBA.

133. *To determine the height of a vertical object standing on a horizontal plane.*

Let B be the top of the object, and let it be required to find its height BC.

Measure from the foot of the object, in the horizontal plane, any convenient distance, as $A\,C$, as a base line, and at A observe the angle of elevation $C\,A\,B$. Then, in the right-angled triangle $A\,B\,C$, we have known the side $A\,C$ and the acute angle A; therefore we can determine the height $B\,C$ by Art. 121.

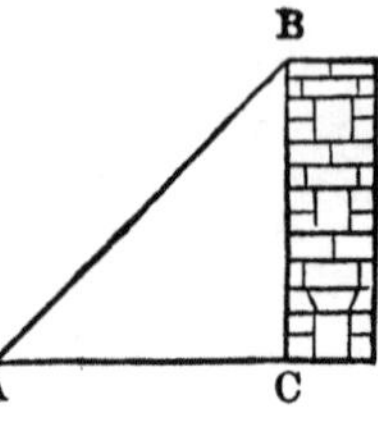

EXAMPLES.

1. Standing on the edge of a moat 40 feet wide, I observe that the wall of a fort upon the opposite brink subtends an angle at the point of observation of 36° 52′ 12″; required the height of the wall. Ans. 30 feet.

2. The angle of elevation of the top of a flag-staff, measured on a horizontal plane, at a distance of 89 feet from the foot of the staff, is 41° 29′; what is the height of the staff?

134. *To find the distance of a vertical object, its height being given.*

Let $B\,C$ be the object whose height is given, and let it be required to find the distance $A\,C$.

Measure the angle of elevation $C\,A\,B$, or the angle of depression $D\,B\,A$, which is equal to $C\,A\,B$. Then, in the right-angled triangle $A\,B\,C$, we have known the side $B\,C$ and the angles; therefore we can find the distance $A\,C$ by Art. 121.

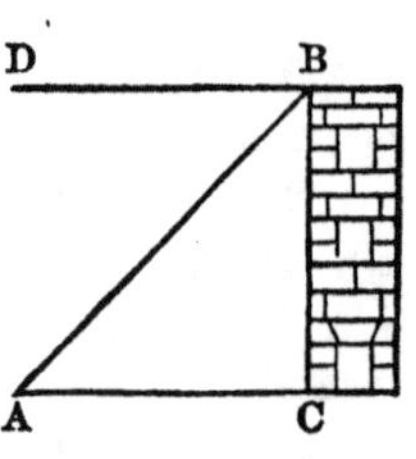

EXAMPLES.

1. A tree 91 feet in height stands on the same horizontal plane with a dial, at which the angle of elevation subtended by the tree is 32° 22′; required the distance of the dial from the foot of the tree. Ans. 143.6 feet.

2. From the top of a house whose height is 30 feet, I observe that the angle of depression of an object standing on the same horizontal plane with the house is 36° 52′ 12″; required the

distance of the object from the base of the house, and also the length of the line that will just connect the object with the top of the house.

135. *To find the distance of an inaccessible point on a horizontal plane.* a : c :: Sin A : Sin C.

Let C be the point inaccessible from A and B, and let it be required to find its distance from each of those points.

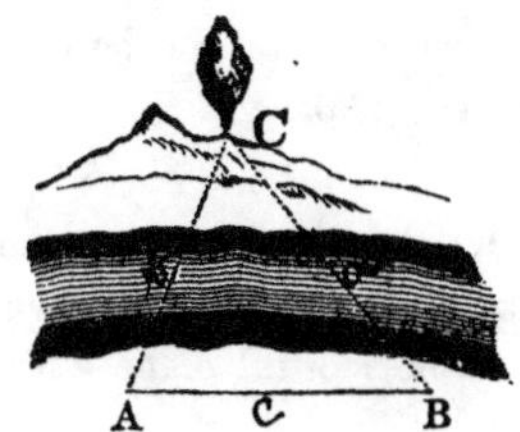

Measure as a horizontal base line the distance between A and B, and observe the horizontal angles CAB and CBA. Then, in the triangle ABC, there will be known the side AB and the angles; therefore the sides AC and BC can be found by Art. 125.

EXAMPLES.

1. Wanting to know the distances of two objects from a tree, inaccessible by reason of an intervening river, I measured the distance in a straight line between the two objects, and found it to be 772.45 feet; I also found the horizontal angles formed by the extremities of the straight line with the tree to be 80° 58′ 4″ and 43° 33′ 44″. Required the distances of the objects from the tree. Ans. The one, 926.01 feet; the other, 646.16 feet.

2. Two ships are engaged in cannonading a fort by the seaside; the ships are 131.89 rods apart, and the two angles at the ends of the straight line connecting the ships, formed by that line and lines drawn to the fort, are 18° 52′ 13″ and 152° 11′ 42″. Required the distance of each ship from the fort.

136. *To find the height of an inaccessible object above a horizontal plane.* c : b :: Sin C : Sin B.

First Method. Let B be the top of the object, and let it be required to find the height BC.

Measure a horizontal base line, AC', of any convenient length, directly toward the object, and observe the angles of elevation at A and C'. Then, in the triangle ABC', since

$BC'A$ is the supplement of $CC'B$, we have known the side AC' and all the angles; therefore we can find the side AB by Art. 125. Then, in the right-angled triangle ABC, we have known the hypothenuse AB and the angles; therefore we can find the height BC by Art. 120.

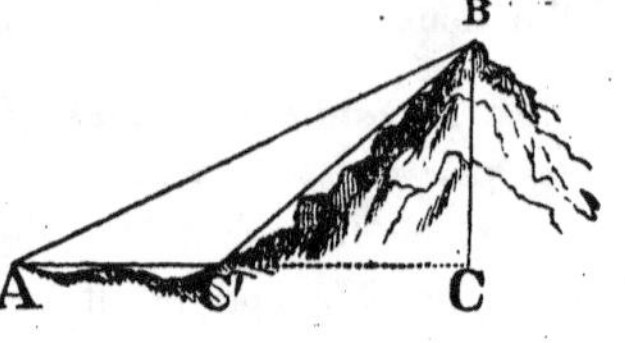

EXAMPLES.

1. Required the altitude of a hill whose angle of elevation, taken at the foot of it, was 55° 54′, and 300 feet back, on the same horizontal plane with the foot, the angle was 33° 20′.

Ans. 355.71 feet.

2. Two observers at sea, 800 yards apart, noticed at the same instant a meteor bearing due east from each; to the one its angle of elevation was 57°, and to the other the same angle was 31° 28′. Required the altitude of the meteor above the horizontal plane of the ships.

Second Method. Let B be the top of the object, and let it be required to find the height BC. Now, suppose it is not convenient to measure a horizontal base line directly toward the object, and we measure it in *any* direction, AB', also measuring the angles CAB' and $CB'A$. Then, in the horizontal triangle $AB'C$, we know the side AB' and all the angles; therefore the side AC can be found by Art. 125. Then, also, by observing the angle of elevation CAB, we shall, in the right-angled triangle ABC, know the side AC and all the angles; therefore the height BC can be found by Art. 121.

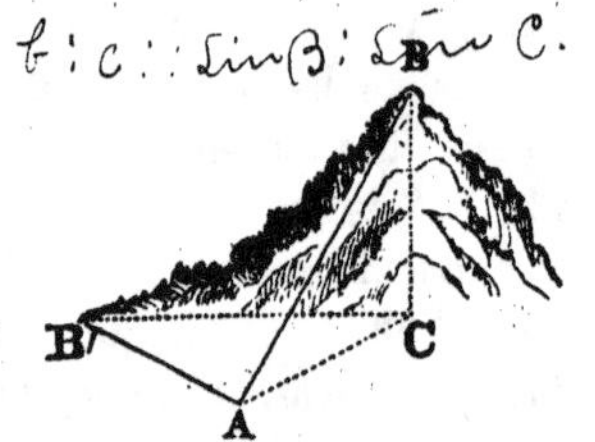

EXAMPLE.

1. A person on one side of a river observed an eagle's nest on an inaccessible mountain-crag on the opposite side, and being desirous of ascertaining its height above the level of the river, he measured along the shore a straight line 110 yards in length, and

found the horizontal angles of its extremities with the object to be 33° 55′ and 96°, and also the angle of elevation at the latter to be 45°. Required the height of the nest above the water.

Ans. 240 feet.

137. *To find the distance between two objects separated by an impassable barrier.*

Let A and B be two objects separated by an impassable barrier, and let it be required to find the distance, AB, between them.

Take any point, C, from which A and B are both visible and accessible. Measure CA and CB, and also note the angle ACB. Then, since in the triangle ABC the two sides CA and CB, with their included angle, are known, the distance AB can be found by Art. 128.

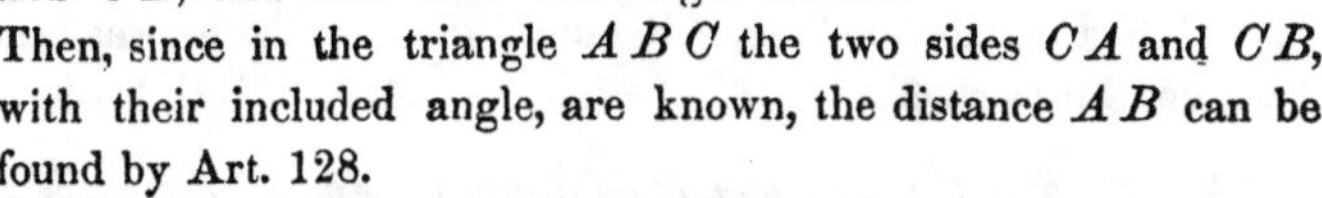

EXAMPLES.

1. Two bounds of a lot have between them an impassable morass, and, wishing to find their distance apart, I have taken their distances from a third point, which could be seen from each. These distances are 124.75 and 171.41 rods, and the angle at that point subtended by the bounds is 99° 25′. How far are the bounds apart? Ans. 227.91 rods.

2. The distance between two trees cannot be directly measured, in consequence of an intervening obstacle, but within sight of each is a third tree, and their distances from this are known to be 274.65 and 396.11 yards, and the angle at that point subtended by the two trees is 8° 56′ 5″. Required the distance between the two trees.

138. *To find the distance between two inaccessible objects.*

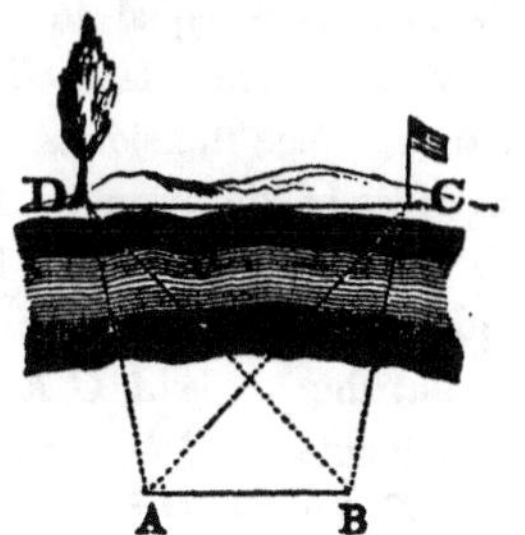

Let C and D be the objects, and A and B two accessible points, from which both the objects are visible. Measure the base line $A\ B$, and observe the angles $D\ A\ B$, $D\ B\ A$, $C\ A\ B$, and $C\ B\ A$. Then, in the triangle DAB, since we have the side AB and all the angles, we can find the side BD by Art. 125. In the triangle ABC we have the side AB and all the angles, hence we can find BC. Then, BD and BC being found, we have in the triangle BCD the sides BD and BC, with their included angle; therefore we can find the distance CD by Art. 128.

EXAMPLE.

1. Wanting to ascertain the distance between a tree, D, and a flagstaff, C, on the opposite side of a river from me, I measured along the shore, on the horizontal plane with the objects, a base line, AB, of 110 yards. At A, the angle DAB equals 96°, and CAB equals 29° 56′; at B, the angle DBA equals 33° 55′, and CBA equals 133° 50′. Required the distance between the tree and the flagstaff. Ans. 261.81 yards.

139. *To find the distances from a given point, of three objects whose distances from each other are known.*

Let it be required to find the distances from D, a given point, of three objects, A, B, and C, whose distances from each other are known.

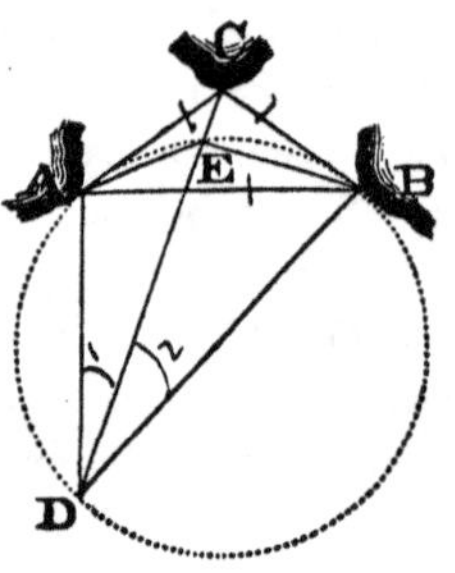

Observe the angles ADC and BDC. Describe a circle about the triangle ADB, and draw AE and EB; then the angle ABE is equal to the angle ADE, since both are measured by half of the same arc AE (Geom., Prop. XVIII. Bk. III.); also the angle BAE is equal to the angle BDE, for a like reason. Now, in the triangle AEB, the side AB and all the angles are known, hence the side AE may be found by Art. 125. Again, the sides of the triangle ABC being given, we may find the angle BAC by Art. 129; then, in the triangle AEC, there will be known the two sides AC, AE, and the included angle CAE, so that the angle ACE may be found by Art. 128. Then, in the triangle ACD, we shall know the side AC and the angles ACD and ADC; therefore we can find the distance AD

by Art. 125, and thence the other two distances, $C D$ and $B D$.

EXAMPLE.

1. On approaching a harbor, at the point D, I observed three headlands, A, B, and C. Now it appeared from a chart that the distance from A to B was 800 yards, from A to C 600 yards, and from B to C 400 yards; the angle $A D C$ I found by observation to be $33° 45'$, and the angle $B D C$ to be $22° 30'$. What was the distance of each of the headlands from me?

Ans. A, 710.19 yards; B, 934.29 yards; C, 1042.52 yards.

DETERMINATION OF AREAS.

140. The AREA of any figure, or its quantity of surface, is determined by the number of times the given surface contains some other area, assumed as the unit of measure, as a square *inch*, a square *foot*, &c.

The areas of *parallelograms*, *triangles*, *trapezoids*, &c. can be determined by direct application of the principles of Geometry; but sometimes it is convenient to determine areas, especially of triangles, by means of their lines and angles, which requires the aid of Trigonometry.

141. *To find the area of a triangle by means of two of its sides and the included angle.*

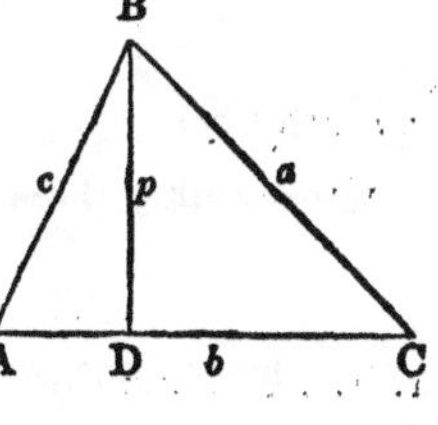

Let $A B C$ be any plane triangle, in which are given the sides b and c and the included angle A, to find the area of the triangle. Draw the perpendicular, p, from B to the opposite side, $A C$; then, since the area of the triangle is equal to half the product of its base by its altitude (Geom., Prop VI. Bk. IV.),

$$\text{area of } A B C = \tfrac{1}{2} b p. \qquad (137)$$

But, by (85), $$p = c \sin A;$$

whence, $$\text{area } A B C = \tfrac{1}{2} b c \sin A, \qquad (138)$$

or, by logarithms,

$$\log \text{area } A\,B\,C = \log \tfrac{1}{2}\,b + \log c + \log \sin A. \qquad (139)$$

That is,

The logarithm of the area of a triangle is equal to the logarithm of half of either side, plus the logarithm of either of the other sides, plus the logarithmic sine of their included angle.

EXAMPLE.

1. Required the area of a triangle which has two of its sides equal to 105 and 85 feet, and the included angle equal to 28° 5′.

Ans. 2100 sq. ft.

142. In like manner, the area of any *parallelogram* may be found, when two of its adjacent sides and the included angle are known; for the diagonal divides a parallelogram into two equal triangles (Geom., Prop. XXXI. Cor. 1, Bk. I.).

EXAMPLE.

1. What is the area of a piece of ground, in the form of a parallelogram, which has two adjacent sides equal, respectively, to 120 and 212 rods, and their included angle equal to 85° 30′?

143. *To find the area of a triangle by means of a side and the angles.*

In the triangle $A\,B\,C$ (Fig. Art. 141), let the side c and the angles be given, to find the area of the triangle. By means of Art. 111 we have

$$b = \frac{c \sin B}{\sin C}; \qquad (140)$$

and by (85)

$$p = c \sin A.$$

Substituting these values in (137), we obtain

$$\text{area of } A\,B\,C = \frac{c^2 \sin A \sin B}{2 \sin C}, \qquad (141)$$

or, by logarithms,

$$\log 2 \text{ area} ABC = 2 \log c + \log \sin A + \log \sin B - \log \sin C. \qquad (142)$$

That is,

The logarithm of double the area of a triangle is equal to twice the logarithm of either side, plus the logarithmic sines of its adjacent angles, minus the logarithmic sine of its opposite angle.

EXAMPLES.

1. A triangular lot has a side equal to 45 rods, and the adjacent angles equal to 70° and 69° 40′; required the area of the lot. Ans. 1378.41 sq. rods.

2. Given of a triangular field $A B C$, the angle A equal to 31° 27′, the angle B equal to 101° 31′, and the included side $A B$ equal to 30 rods; required the area of the field.

144. *To find the area of a triangle by means of its three sides.*

Let $A B C$ (Fig. Art. 141) be the given triangle. Then, by (138),

$$\text{area of } A B C = \tfrac{1}{2} b c \sin A;$$

but, by taking twice the product of the values of $\sin \frac{1}{2} A$ and $\cos \frac{1}{2} A$, in (102) and (106), we have, by (74),

$$\sin A = \frac{2}{b c} \sqrt{s (s - a) (s - b) (s - c)}, \qquad (143)$$

in which s denotes half the sum of the sides of the triangle.

Substituting in the preceding equation this value of $\sin A$, we obtain

$$\text{area of } A B C = \tfrac{1}{2} b c \times \frac{2}{b c} \sqrt{s (s - a) (s - b) (s - c)};$$

whence, $\text{area of } A B C = \sqrt{s (s - a) (s - b) (s - c)}; \qquad (144)$

or, by logarithms,

$$\log \text{area } ABC = \frac{\log s + \log (s - a) + \log (s - b) + \log (s - c)}{2}. \qquad (145)$$

That is,

The logarithm of the area of a triangle is equal to half the sum of the logarithm of half the sum of the sides and the logarithms of the remainders obtained by taking each side separately from half the sum of the sides.

EXAMPLES.

1. Given the three sides of a triangle equal to 30, 40, and 60 rods, respectively; required the area of the triangle.

Ans. 533.27 sq. rods.

2. A certain fort is in the form of an equilateral triangle, whose sides are each 600 feet; required the area occupied by the fort.

MISCELLANEOUS PROBLEMS.

1. The angle of elevation of a vertical tower is observed to be 30°, at the end of a horizontal base line of 100 yards, measured from its foot. Required the height of the tower.

2. A rope-dancer wishes to ascend a steeple 100 feet high, by means of a rope 196 feet long. If he can do so, find at what inclination he must be able to walk up the rope.

3. From the summit of a pier which rises 100 feet above the margin of a river, the angle of depression of the opposite margin was found to be 33° 16′. Required the width of the river.

4. If the distance of the moon from the earth be taken at 238500 miles, and the angle subtended by the semidiameter of the moon be 15′ 33″.5 at that distance, what is the moon's diameter? Ans. 2158 miles.

5. A point of land was observed by a ship at sea to bear east by south, that is, 11° 15′ S. of E.; and after sailing northeast 12 miles, it was found to bear southeast by east, that is, 33° 45′ S. of E. Required the distance of the headland from the ship at the last observation. Ans. 26.07 miles.

6. From the top of Mont Blanc, 3 miles high, the angle of depression of the remotest visible point of the earth's surface is 2° 13′ 27″. Required the diameter of the earth, supposing it to be a perfect sphere; and, also, the utmost distance from which the mountain is visible.

Ans. Diameter, 7958 miles; distance, 154.5 miles.

7. A side of the base of a square pyramid is 200 feet, and each edge is 150 feet; required the slope of each face.

Ans. 26° 34′, nearly.

8. I have a meadow in the form of a parallelogram, whose two adjacent sides are 20 rods and 18 rods, including an angle of 78° 9′; the same has been divided into two equal lots by a fence running diagonally. Required the area of each lot.

Ans. 176.16 square rods.

9. A traveler wishing to know the distance and height of a mountain-top over which he had to pass, took the angle of its

elevation at two stations, in a direct line towards it, the one 3 miles, or 5280 yards, nearer the mountain than the other, and found the angles to be 2° 45′ and 3° 20′. Required the horizontal distance of the mountain-top from the nearer station, and its height. Ans. Distance, 24840 yards; height, 1447 yards.

10. From the top of a light-house the angle of depression of a ship at anchor was observed to be 4° 52′, from the bottom of the light-house the angle was 4° 2′. Required the horizontal distance of the vessel, and the height of the hill on which the light-house is placed, the height of the light-house being 60 feet.

Ans. Horizontal distance, 4100.4 feet; height, 289.12 feet.

11. When a tower 150 feet high throws a shadow 75 feet long upon the horizontal plane on which the tower stands, what is the sun's altitude (Art. 189)? Ans. 63° 26′ 6″.

12. The sides of a triangle are equal to 3 and 12, respectively, and the included angle is 30°; find the hypothenuse of an equal right-angled isosceles triangle. Ans. 6.

13. From a window near the bottom of a house, which seemed to be on a level with the bottom of a steeple, I took the angle of elevation of the top of the steeple, equal to 40°; then from another window, 18 feet directly above the former, the like angle was 37° 30′. Required the height and distance of the steeple.

Ans. Height, 210.4 feet; distance, 250.8 feet.

14. Two pulleys, whose diameters are 6 inches and 4 feet 3 inches, respectively, are placed at a distance of 3 feet 6 inches from centre to centre. What must be the length of a belt which shall connect them, by passing around their circumferences, without crossing? Ans. 15 feet 5.9 inches.

15. A tower is surrounded by a circular moat. At noon on a certain day, the shadow of the top of the flag-staff is observed to project 45 feet beyond the edge of the moat. When the sun is due west, on the same day, the shadow projects 120 feet beyond the moat. The distance between the extremities of the shadows is 375 feet. The angle of elevation of the top of the flag-staff from any point of the edge of the moat is 60°. Find the height of the tower, and the altitude of the sun at noon.

Ans. 311.77 feet; 54° 10′ 57″.

BOOK V.

SPHERICAL TRIGONOMETRY.

DEFINITIONS.

145. Spherical Trigonometry treats of methods of computing spherical triangles.

146. A spherical triangle is a portion of the surface of a sphere bounded by three arcs of a great circle, each of which is less than a semi-circumference.

The three planes in which the arcs lie form a polyedral angle at the centre of the sphere.

The angles of a spherical triangle are the diedral angles made by the plane faces which form the polyedral angle.

147. The sides and angles of spherical triangles are usually both expressed in degrees, minutes, &c.

The circumference, however, is sometimes supposed to be divided into 24 equal parts, called *hours;* each hour into 60 equal parts, called *minutes of time;* each minute into 60 equal parts, called *seconds of time.* Then a side is expressed by the number of hours, minutes, seconds, and decimal parts of a second, which it contains.

Hours, minutes, and seconds are denoted by *h.*, *m.*, and *s.* Thus, 3h. 35m. 5.8s.

RELATIONS BETWEEN THE SIDES AND ANGLES OF SPHERICAL TRIANGLES.

148. *In any spherical triangle, the sines of the sides are proportional to the sines of the opposite angles.*

Let $A B C$ be any spherical triangle; A, B, and C the angles opposite to its sides a, b, and c, respectively; and O the centre of the sphere.

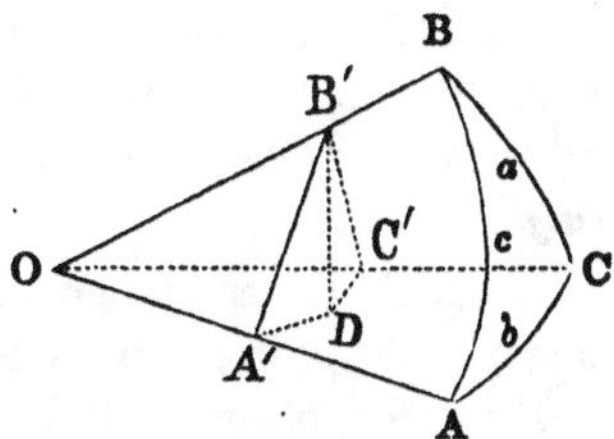

Take any point B' in $O B$, and draw $B' D$ perpendicular to the plane $A O C$; from D draw $D A'$, $D C'$, perpendicular to $O A$, $O C$, respectively; join $B' A'$, $B' C'$.

$B' C' O$ is a right angle (Geom., Prop. VI. Bk. VII.); therefore,

$$B' C' = O B' \sin B' O C' = O B' \sin a,$$

and

$$B' D = B' C' \sin B' C' D = B' C' \sin C = O B' \sin a \sin C.$$

In like manner,

$$B' D = O B' \sin c \sin A;$$

and, by the two preceding equations,

$$O B' \sin a \sin C = O B' \sin c \sin A,$$

whence,

$$\frac{\sin a}{\sin c} = \frac{\sin A}{\sin C}; \quad (146)$$

or, in the form of a proportion,

$$\sin a : \sin c :: \sin A : \sin C. \quad (147)$$

In a similar way it may be proved that

$$\sin a : \sin b :: \sin A : \sin B, \quad (148)$$

$$\sin c : \sin b :: \sin C : \sin B. \quad (149)$$

The figure supposes a, c, B, C, &c. each less than 90°, but the relation stated may be shown to hold when the figure is modified to meet any case whatever. For instance, if C alone is greater than 90°, the point D will fall beyond $O C$, instead of between $O C$ and $O A$; then, $B' C' D$ will be the supplement of C, and thus, since the sine of an angle and its supplement are the same, the sine of $B' C' D$ is still equal to the sine of C.

149. *In any spherical triangle, the cosine of any side is equal to the product of the cosines of the other two sides, plus the product of the sines of those two sides into the cosine of their included angle.*

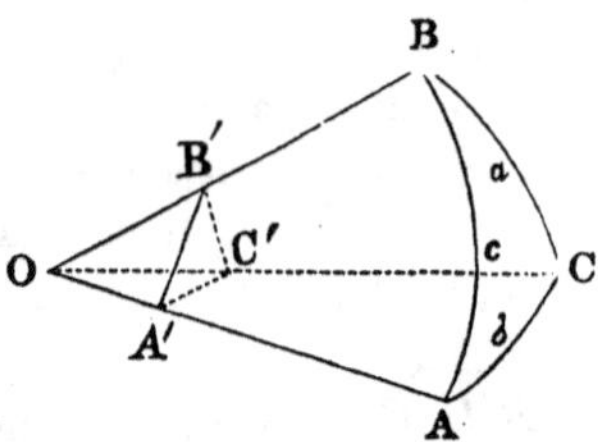

Let ABC be any spherical triangle, O the centre of the sphere.

Draw the plane $B'A'C'$ perpendicular to OA. Then the angle $B'A'C'$ is equal to the angle A, the angle $B'OC'$ measures the side a, and in the triangles $A'B'C'$, $OB'C'$ we have, by Art. 113,

$$\overline{B'C'}^2 = \overline{A'B'}^2 + \overline{A'C'}^2 - 2\,A'B' \times A'C' \cos A,$$

$$\overline{B'C'}^2 = \overline{OB'}^2 + \overline{OC'}^2 - 2\,OB' \times OC' \cos a.$$

Subtracting the first equation from the second, observing that $\overline{OB'}^2 - \overline{A'B'}^2$ and $\overline{OC'}^2 - \overline{A'C'}^2$ are each equal to $\overline{OA'}^2$, since the triangles $OA'B'$, $OA'C'$ are right-angled at A', we have

$$0 = 2\,\overline{OA'}^2 + 2\,A'B' \times A'C' \cos A - 2\,OB' \times OC' \cos a;$$

therefore, $$\cos a = \frac{OA' \times OA'}{OB' \times OC'} + \frac{A'B' \times A'C'}{OB' \times OC'} \cos A.$$

Substituting the functions derived from the triangles $OA'B'$, $OA'C'$, we have

$$\cos a = \cos b \cos c + \sin b \sin c \cos A. \tag{150}$$

In like manner may be deduced

$$\cos b = \cos c \cos a + \sin c \sin a \cos B, \tag{151}$$

$$\cos c = \cos a \cos b + \sin a \sin b \cos C. \tag{152}$$

The preceding construction supposes the sides b and c, which contain the angle A, to be both less than 90°, but the formulæ obtained may be shown to be applicable in all cases.

150. *In any spherical triangle, the cosine of any angle is equal to the product of the sines of the other two angles into the cosine of their included side, minus the product of the cosines of those two angles.*

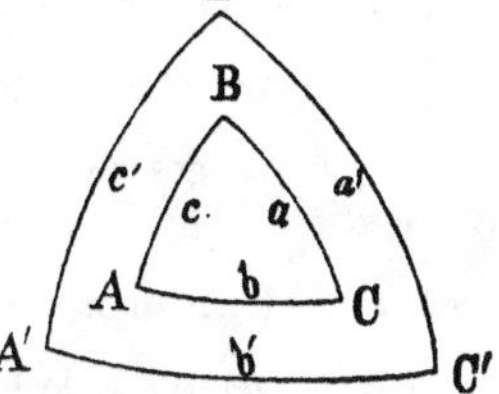

Let $A'B'C'$ be the polar triangle of $A\,B\,C$; denote its angles by A', B', and C', and its sides by a', b', and c'. Then (Geom., Prop. IX. Bk. IX.),

$$A' = 180° - a, \quad B' = 180° - b, \quad C' = 180° - c;$$

$$a' = 180° - A, \quad b' = 180° - B, \quad c' = 180° - C.$$

Applying (150) to $A'B'C'$, we have

$$\cos a' = \cos b' \cos c' + \sin b' \sin c' \cos A';$$

or, by (46), $-\cos A = \cos B \cos C - \sin B \sin C \cos a;$

whence, $$\cos A = \sin B \sin C \cos a - \cos B \cos C. \quad (153)$$

In like manner may be deduced

$$\cos B = \sin C \sin A \cos b - \cos C \cos A, \quad (154)$$

$$\cos C = \sin A \sin B \cos c - \cos A \cos B. \quad (155)$$

151. *In any spherical triangle, the cotangent of one side into the sine of another side is equal to the cotangent of the angle opposite the first side into the sine of the included angle, plus the cosine of the second side into the cosine of the included angle.*

By (150) and (152) we have

$$\cos a = \cos b \cos c + \sin b \sin c \cos A,$$

$$\cos c = \cos a \cos b + \sin a \sin b \cos C;$$

and by means of (147),

$$\sin c = \sin a \frac{\sin C}{\sin A}.$$

Substituting these values of $\cos c$ and $\sin c$ in the first equation, we obtain

$$\cos a = (\cos a \cos b + \sin a \sin b \cos C) \cos b + \frac{\sin a \sin b \cos A \sin C}{\sin A};$$

or,

$$\cos a = \cos a \cos^2 b + \sin a \sin b \cos b \cos C + \sin a \sin b \cot A \sin C.$$

Therefore, transposing $\cos a \cos^2 b$, and observing that, by (11),

$$\cos a - \cos a \cos^2 b = \cos a \sin^2 b,$$

we have

$$\cos a \sin^2 b = \sin a \sin b \cot A \sin C + \sin a \sin b \cos b \cos C,$$

and dividing the whole by $\sin a \sin b$, we obtain

$$\cot a \sin b = \cot A \sin C + \cos b \cos C. \qquad (156)$$

152. By interchanging the letters in (156), we obtain

$$\cot a \sin c = \cot A \sin B + \cos c \cos B, \qquad (157)$$

$$\cot b \sin a = \cot B \sin C + \cos a \cos C, \qquad (158)$$

$$\cot b \sin c = \cot B \sin A + \cos c \cos A, \qquad (159)$$

$$\cot c \sin a = \cot C \sin B + \cos a \cos B, \qquad (160)$$

$$\cot c \sin b = \cot C \sin A + \cos b \cos A. \qquad (161)$$

153. The formulæ developed in the preceding articles are general, and apply to every case of spherical triangles, but require some transformations to render them more convenient for logarithmic computations.

The formulæ (150), (151), and (152) of Art. 149 are considered the *fundamental formulæ* of spherical trigonometry, since from them all its other formulæ may be deduced.

154. *To express the sine, cosine, and tangent of half an angle of a triangle as functions of the sides.*

By means of (150) we have

$$\cos A = \frac{\cos a - \cos b \cos c}{\sin b \sin c}, \qquad (162)$$

but this formula is not suited to logarithmic computation.

We then subtract each member of the equation from 1, and obtain (Art. 63),

$$1 - \cos A = 1 - \frac{\cos a - \cos b \cos c}{\sin b \sin c} = \frac{\cos (b - c) - \cos a}{\sin b \sin c}.$$

Substituting for $1 - \cos A$ its value, $2 \sin^2 \frac{1}{2} A$ (80), we obtain

$$2 \sin^2 \tfrac{1}{2} A = \frac{\cos (b - c) - \cos a}{\sin b \sin c}.$$

Now if, in (65), we make $A = a$, and $B = b - c$,

$\frac{1}{2}(A + B) = \frac{1}{2}(a + b - c), \quad \frac{1}{2}(A - B) = \frac{1}{2}(a - b + c),$

then,

$\cos (b - c) - \cos a = 2 \sin \frac{1}{2}(a + b - c) \sin \frac{1}{2}(a - b + c),$

which, substituted in the preceding equation, gives

$$\sin^2 \tfrac{1}{2} A = \frac{\sin \frac{1}{2}(a - b + c) \sin \frac{1}{2}(a + b - c)}{\sin b \sin c}. \qquad (163)$$

Let, now, s = half the sum of the sides of the triangle; then,

$$a + b - c = 2(s - c), \quad a - b + c = 2(s - b).$$

Substituting these values in the last equation, and reducing, we have

$$\sin \tfrac{1}{2} A = \sqrt{\frac{\sin (s - b) \sin (s - c)}{\sin b \sin c}}. \qquad (164)$$

Similarly,

$$\sin \tfrac{1}{2} B = \sqrt{\frac{\sin (s - c) \sin (s - a)}{\sin c \sin a}}, \qquad (165)$$

$$\sin \tfrac{1}{2} C = \sqrt{\frac{\sin (s - a) \sin (s - b)}{\sin a \sin b}}. \qquad (166)$$

Adding each member of equation (162) to 1, and observing that $1 + \cos A = 2 \cos^2 \frac{1}{2} A$ (81), by means of (65), we have

$$\cos^2 \tfrac{1}{2} A = \frac{\sin \frac{1}{2}(a + b + c) \sin \frac{1}{2}(b + c - a)}{\sin b \sin c}.$$

Introducing $s = \frac{1}{2}(a + b + c)$, and reducing, we have

$$\cos \tfrac{1}{2} A = \sqrt{\frac{\sin s \sin (s - a)}{\sin b \sin c}}. \qquad (167)$$

Similarly,

$$\cos \tfrac{1}{2} B = \sqrt{\frac{\sin s \sin (s - b)}{\sin c \sin a}}, \qquad (168)$$

$$\cos \tfrac{1}{2} C = \sqrt{\frac{\sin s \sin (s - c)}{\sin a \sin b}}. \qquad (169)$$

Again, dividing (164), (165), and (166) by (167), (168), and (169), respectively, we obtain

$$\tan \tfrac{1}{2} A = \sqrt{\frac{\sin (s-b) \sin (s-c)}{\sin s \sin (s-a)}}, \tag{170}$$

$$\tan \tfrac{1}{2} B = \sqrt{\frac{\sin (s-c) \sin (s-a)}{\sin s \sin (s-b)}}, \tag{171}$$

$$\tan \tfrac{1}{2} C = \sqrt{\frac{\sin (s-a) \sin (s-b)}{\sin s \sin (s-c)}}. \tag{172}$$

155. *To express the sine, cosine, and tangent of half a side of a triangle as functions of the angles.*

By means of (153) we have

$$\cos a = \frac{\cos A + \cos B \cos C}{\sin B \sin C}. \tag{173}$$

Whence,

$$1 - \cos a = 1 - \frac{\cos A + \cos B \cos C}{\sin B \sin C} = -\frac{\cos A + \cos (B + C)}{\sin B \sin C},$$

and

$$\sin^2 \tfrac{1}{2} a = - \frac{\cos \frac{1}{2} (A + B + C) \cos \frac{1}{2} (B + C - A)}{\sin B \sin C}. \tag{174}$$

Making $\frac{1}{2}(A + B + C) = S$, substituting, and reducing, we have

$$\sin \tfrac{1}{2} a = \sqrt{\frac{-\cos S \cos (S - A)}{\sin B \sin C}}.$$

Also,

$$\left.\begin{aligned} \sin \tfrac{1}{2} b &= \sqrt{\frac{-\cos S \cos (S - B)}{\sin C \sin A}}, \\ \sin \tfrac{1}{2} c &= \sqrt{\frac{-\cos S \cos (S - C)}{\sin A \sin B}}. \end{aligned}\right\} \tag{175}$$

In like manner, we obtain

$$\left.\begin{aligned} \cos \tfrac{1}{2} a &= \sqrt{\frac{\cos (S - B) \cos (S - C)}{\sin B \sin C}}, \\ \cos \tfrac{1}{2} b &= \sqrt{\frac{\cos (S - C) \cos (S - A)}{\sin C \sin A}}, \\ \cos \tfrac{1}{2} c &= \sqrt{\frac{\cos (S - A) \cos (S - B)}{\sin A \sin B}}. \end{aligned}\right\} \tag{176}$$

Hence,

$$\left.\begin{aligned}\tan \tfrac{1}{2} a &= \sqrt{\frac{-\cos S \cos (S-A)}{\cos (S-B) \cos (S-C)}}, \\ \tan \tfrac{1}{2} b &= \sqrt{\frac{-\cos S \cos (S-B)}{\cos (S-C) \cos (S-A)}}, \\ \tan \tfrac{1}{2} c &= \sqrt{\frac{-\cos S \cos (S-C)}{\cos (S-A) \cos (S-B)}}.\end{aligned}\right\} \qquad (177)$$

Since S is always greater than 90° and less than 270° (Geom., Prop. X. Bk. IX.), $\cos S$ is always negative, and therefore $-\cos S$ in the numerators of the first and third of the above sets of formulæ is essentially positive.

156. *To prove Napier's Analogies.*

Let $$m = \frac{\sin A}{\sin a} = \frac{\sin B}{\sin b};$$

then, $$\sin A = m \sin a, \qquad \sin B = m \sin b,$$

$$\sin A + \sin B = m (\sin a + \sin b), \qquad (178)$$

$$\sin A - \sin B = m (\sin a - \sin b). \qquad (179)$$

By (153) and (154) we have

$$\cos A + \cos B \cos C = \sin B \sin C \cos a = m \sin C \cos a \sin b,$$

$$\cos B + \cos A \cos C = \sin A \sin C \cos b = m \sin C \sin a \cos b.$$

Adding these equations, factoring, and reducing by (17),

$$(\cos A + \cos B)(1 + \cos C) = m \sin C \sin (a + b). \qquad (180)$$

Dividing (178) by (180), and multiplying by $\sin C$,

$$\frac{\sin A + \sin B}{\cos A + \cos B} \times \frac{\sin C}{1 + \cos C} = \frac{\sin a + \sin b}{\sin (a + b)}. \qquad (181)$$

Now, by means of (62), (63), and (74), we obtain

$$\frac{\sin a + \sin b}{\sin (a + b)} = \frac{\cos \frac{1}{2}(a - b)}{\cos \frac{1}{2}(a + b)}, \qquad (182)$$

and
$$\frac{\sin a - \sin b}{\sin (a + b)} = \frac{\sin \frac{1}{2}(a - b)}{\sin \frac{1}{2}(a + b)}. \qquad (183)$$

Substituting in (181) the value of each expression, from (68), (84), and (182),

$$\tan \tfrac{1}{2}(A + B) \times \tan \tfrac{1}{2} C = \frac{\cos \frac{1}{2}(a - b)}{\cos \frac{1}{2}(a + b)},$$

or,

$$\frac{\cos \frac{1}{2}(a + b)}{\cos \frac{1}{2}(a - b)} = \frac{\cot \frac{1}{2} C}{\tan \frac{1}{2}(A + B)}. \qquad (184)$$

In like manner, from (179) and (180),

$$\frac{\sin A - \sin B}{\cos A + \cos B} \times \frac{\sin C}{1 + \cos C} = \frac{\sin a - \sin b}{\sin (a + b)},$$

whence, by (69), (84), and (183),

$$\tan \tfrac{1}{2}(A - B) \times \tan \tfrac{1}{2} C = \frac{\sin \frac{1}{2}(a - b)}{\sin \frac{1}{2}(a + b)},$$

or,

$$\frac{\sin \frac{1}{2}(a + b)}{\sin \frac{1}{2}(a - b)} = \frac{\cot \frac{1}{2} C}{\tan \frac{1}{2}(A - B)}. \qquad (185)$$

Formulæ (184) and (185) may be thus expressed:

$$\cos \tfrac{1}{2}(a + b) : \cos \tfrac{1}{2}(a - b) :: \cot \tfrac{1}{2} C : \tan \tfrac{1}{2}(A + B), \quad (186)$$

$$\sin \tfrac{1}{2}(a + b) : \sin \tfrac{1}{2}(a - b) :: \cot \tfrac{1}{2} C : \tan \tfrac{1}{2}(A - B). \quad (187)$$

That is,

The cosine of half the sum of two sides of a spherical triangle is to the cosine of half their difference as the cotangent of half the included angle is to the tangent of half the sum of the other two angles.

The sine of half the sum of two sides of a spherical triangle is to the sine of half their difference as the cotangent of half the included angle is to the tangent of half the difference of the other two angles.

By applying (186) and (187) to the polar triangle, Art. 150, we obtain

$$\cos \tfrac{1}{2} (A + B) : \cos \tfrac{1}{2} (A - B) :: \tan \tfrac{1}{2} c : \tan \tfrac{1}{2} (a + b), \quad (188)$$

$$\sin \tfrac{1}{2} (A + B) : \sin \tfrac{1}{2} (A - B) :: \tan \tfrac{1}{2} c : \tan \tfrac{1}{2} (a - b). \quad (189)$$

That is,

The cosine of half the sum of two angles of a spherical triangle is to the cosine of half their difference as the tangent of half the included side is to the tangent of half the sum of the other two sides.

The sine of half the sum of two angles of a spherical triangle is to the sine of half their difference as the tangent of half the included side is to the tangent of half the difference of the other two sides.

The above four proportions are called, from their inventor, *Napier's Analogies.*

RELATIONS BETWEEN THE SIDES AND ANGLES OF RIGHT-ANGLED SPHERICAL TRIANGLES.

157. *The sine of either oblique angle is equal to the sine of the opposite side, divided by the sine of the hypothenuse.*

Let $A\,B\,C$ be any spherical triangle, right-angled at C.

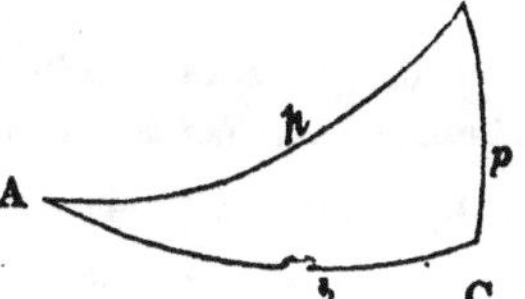

By means of (146) we have

$$\sin A = \frac{\sin p}{\sin h} \sin C;$$

but, as $C = 90°$, $\sin C = 1$, and

$$\sin A = \frac{\sin p}{\sin h}. \quad (190)$$

In like manner,

$$\sin B = \frac{\sin b}{\sin h}. \quad (191)$$

158. *The cosine of either oblique angle is equal to the tangent of the adjacent side, divided by the tangent of the hypothenuse.*

By means of (161) we have

$$\cot h \sin b = \cot C \sin A + \cos b \cos A\,;$$

but, if $C = 90°$, then $\cot C = 0$, and

$$\cot h \sin b = \cos b \cos A,$$

or, $$\cos A = \frac{\cot h \sin b}{\cos b} = \cot h \tan b;$$

whence, $$\cos A = \frac{\tan b}{\tan h}. \qquad (192)$$

Also, by means of (160),

$$\cos B = \frac{\tan p}{\tan h}. \qquad (193)$$

159. *The tangent of either oblique angle is equal to the tangent of the opposite side, divided by the sine of the adjacent side.*

By means of (156) we have

$$\cot p \sin b = \cot A \sin C + \cos b \cos C;$$

but, by making $C = 90°$, $\sin C = 1$, $\cos C = 0$, and

$$\cot A = \cot p \sin b = \frac{\sin b}{\tan p},$$

or, $$\tan A = \frac{\tan p}{\sin b}. \qquad (194)$$

Also, by means of (158),

$$\tan B = \frac{\tan b}{\sin p}. \qquad (195)$$

160. *The sine of either oblique angle is equal to the cosine of the other, divided by the cosine of its opposite side.*

By means of (154) we have

$$\cos B = \sin A \sin C \cos b - \cos A \cos C,$$

which, by making $C = 90°$, becomes

$$\cos B = \cos b \sin A,$$

whence, $$\sin A = \frac{\cos B}{\cos b}. \qquad (196)$$

In like manner, by means of (153),

$$\sin B = \frac{\cos A}{\cos p}. \qquad (197)$$

161. *The cosine of the hypothenuse is equal to the product of the cosines of the other two sides.*

By means of (152) we have

$$\cos h = \cos p \cos b + \sin p \sin b \cos C,$$

which, by making $C = 90°$, becomes

$$\cos h = \cos p \cos b. \qquad (198)$$

162. *The cosine of the hypothenuse is equal to the product of the cotangents of the two oblique angles.*

By means of (155) we have

$$\cos C = \sin A \sin B \cos h - \cos A \cos B,$$

which, by making $C = 90°$, becomes

$$\sin A \sin B \cos h = \cos A \cos B,$$

or,

$$\cos h = \frac{\cos A \cos B}{\sin A \sin B} = \cot A \cot B. \qquad (199)$$

163. The preceding formulæ may readily be remembered from their similarity to the corresponding ones for plane triangles; and, for convenience of reference, they are brought together in the following

TABLE.

1.	$\sin A = \frac{\sin p}{\sin h}.$	2.	$\sin B = \frac{\sin b}{\sin h}.$
3.	$\cos A = \frac{\tan b}{\tan h}.$	4.	$\cos B = \frac{\tan p}{\tan h}.$
5.	$\tan A = \frac{\tan p}{\sin b}.$	6.	$\tan B = \frac{\tan b}{\sin p}.$
7.	$\sin A = \frac{\cos B}{\cos b}.$	8.	$\sin B = \frac{\cos A}{\cos p}.$
9.	$\cos h = \cos p \cos b.$	10.	$\cos h = \cot A \cot B.$

SOLUTION OF RIGHT-ANGLED SPHERICAL TRIANGLES.

164. The solution of spherical triangles is the process by which, when the values of a sufficient number of their six elements are given, we calculate the values of the remaining elements.

In order to solve a right-angled spherical triangle, two of its elements, other than the right angle, must be given.

165. The formulæ requisite for the solution of right-angled spherical triangles are readily furnished by means of the relations demonstrated in the foregoing articles. Thus,

$$\sin A = \frac{\sin p}{\sin h} \quad \text{gives} \quad \sin p = \sin A \sin h, \qquad (200)$$

$$\sin B = \frac{\sin b}{\sin h} \quad " \quad \sin b = \sin B \sin h, \qquad (201)$$

$$\cos A = \frac{\tan b}{\tan h} \quad " \quad \cos A = \cot h \tan b, \qquad (202)$$

$$\cos B = \frac{\tan p}{\tan h} \quad " \quad \cos B = \cot h \tan p, \qquad (203)$$

$$\tan B = \frac{\tan b}{\sin p} \quad " \quad \sin p = \cot B \tan b, \qquad (204)$$

$$\tan A = \frac{\tan p}{\sin b} \quad " \quad \sin b = \cot A \tan p, \qquad (205)$$

$$\sin B = \frac{\cos A}{\cos p} \quad " \quad \cos A = \sin B \cos p, \qquad (206)$$

$$\sin A = \frac{\cos B}{\cos b} \quad " \quad \cos B = \sin A \cos b, \qquad (207)$$

which, with equations (198) and (199),

$$\cos h = \cos p \cos b, \qquad \cos h = \cot A \cot B,$$

enable us to determine every case of right-angled spherical triangles. For every one of these ten equations is a distinct combination, involving three of the five quantities, p, b, h, A, B; and five quantities, taken three at a time, can be combined only in ten different ways.

Napier's Circular Parts.

166. If, in any right-angled spherical triangle, the right angle be left out of consideration, the two sides adjacent to the right angle, and the complements of the hypothenuse and of the two other angles, are called the five *circular parts* of the triangle.

Thus, in the spherical triangle $A B C$, right-angled at C, the circular parts are p, b, and the complements of h, A, and B.

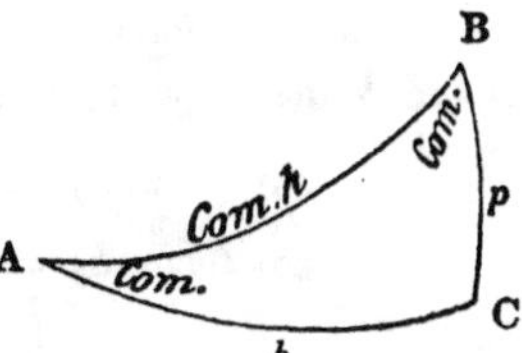

167. When any one of the five parts is taken for the *middle part*, the two adjacent to it, one on either side, are called the *adjacent parts*, and the other two parts are called the *opposite parts*. Then, whatever be the middle part, we have as

THE RULES OF NAPIER.

I. *The sine of the middle part is equal to the product of the tangents of the adjacent parts.*

II. *The sine of the middle part is equal to the product of the cosines of the opposite parts.*

168. Napier's rules may be proved by showing that they agree with the results already established, Art. 165. Thus,

1. Let b be taken for the middle part; then p and the complement of A will be the adjacent parts, and the complements of B and h will be the opposite parts, and by the rules we have

$$\sin b = \tan (\text{com. } A) \tan p,$$

$$\sin b = \cos (\text{com. } B) \cos (\text{com. } h);$$

whence, by Art. 50,

$$\sin b = \cot A \tan p, \quad \sin b = \sin B \sin h$$

which agree with (205) and (201).

In like manner, if p be taken as the middle part,

$$\sin p = \tan (\text{com. } B) \tan b,$$

$$\sin p = \cos (\text{com. } A) \cos (\text{com. } h);$$

whence,

$$\sin p = \cot B \tan b, \quad \sin p = \sin A \sin h,$$

which agree with (204) and (200).

2. Let the complement of h be taken as the middle part;

then the complements of A and B will be the adjacent parts, p and b the opposite parts, and we have

$$\sin(\text{com. } h) = \tan(\text{com. } A) \tan(\text{com. } B),$$

$$\sin(\text{com. } h) = \cos p \cos b;$$

whence,

$$\cos h = \cot A \cot B, \quad \cos h = \cos p \cos b,$$

which agree with (199) and (198).

3. Let the complement of A be taken as the middle part; then b and the complement of h will be the adjacent parts, p and the complement of B the opposite parts, and we have

$$\sin(\text{com. } A) = \tan(\text{com. } h) \tan b,$$

$$\sin(\text{com. } A) = \cos(\text{com. } B) \cos p;$$

whence,

$$\cos A = \cot h \tan b, \quad \cos A = \sin B \cos p,$$

which agree with (202) and (206).

In like manner,

$$\sin(\text{com. } B) = \tan(\text{com. } h) \tan p,$$

$$\sin(\text{com. } B) = \cos(\text{com. } A) \cos b;$$

whence,

$$\cos B = \cot h \tan p, \quad \cos B = \sin A \cos b,$$

which agree with (203) and (207).

169. Any element of a spherical triangle is less than 180° (Geom., Art. 505, 539). Two parts are said to be of the *same species* when they are in the same quadrant, that is, when they are both less, or both greater, than 90°; and of *different species* when one terminates in the first and the other in the second quadrant.

170. In order to determine whether a part sought is less or greater than 90°, the algebraic signs of the terms should be observed, according to Art. 68 or 78. When, however, the part sought is determined by its sine, since the sines in both the first and second quadrants are positive, there will be two solutions,

unless the ambiguity be removed by one of the following rules:—

1. *In any right-angled spherical triangle, an oblique angle and its opposite side are always of the same species.*

For, by (205), $\sin b = \cot A \ \tan p$,

in which, since $\sin b$ is always positive, $\cot A$ and $\tan p$ must always have the same sign, that is, A and p must be of the same species.

2. *When the two sides about the right angle are of the same species, the hypothenuse is less than* 90°, *but when they are of different species, the hypothenuse is greater than* 90°.

For, by (198), $\cos h = \cos p \ \cos b$,

in which, if $\cos p$ and $\cos b$ have the same signs, $\cos h$ will be positive, but if they have unlike signs, $\cos h$ will be negative.

171. In the solution of right-angled spherical triangles, there will be six cases to consider, in which there may be given, respectively,

I. The hypothenuse and an oblique angle.
II. The hypothenuse and one side.
III. One side and its adjacent oblique angle.
IV. One side and its opposite oblique angle.
V. The two sides about the right angle.
VI. The two oblique angles.

Case I.

172. *Given the hypothenuse and an oblique angle.*

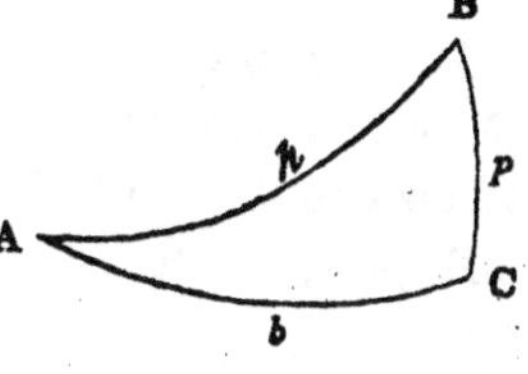

Let there be given in the right-angled spherical triangle ABC, the hypothenuse h and the oblique angle A; to solve the triangle.

To find p. Make p the middle part, and we have, by Napier's rules, or by (200),

$$\sin p = \sin A \ \sin h,$$

or, by logarithms,

$$\log \sin p = \log \sin A + \log \sin h. \qquad (208)$$

To find b. Make the complement of A the middle part, and we have, by Napier's rules, or by (202),

$$\cos A = \cot h \ \tan b;$$

whence, $$\tan b = \tan h \ \cos A, \qquad (209)$$

or, by logarithms,

$$\log \tan b = \log \tan h + \log \cos A. \qquad (210)$$

To find B. Make the complement of h the middle part, and we have, by Napier's rules, or by (199),

$$\cos h = \cot A \ \cot B;$$

whence, $$\cot B = \cos h \ \tan A, \qquad (211)$$

or, by logarithms,

$$\log \cot B = \log \cos h + \log \tan A. \qquad (212)$$

Thus, b and B, by observing the algebraic signs, are determined without ambiguity; and p, though determined by its sine, is not ambiguous, since it must be of the same species as A (Art. 170).

EXAMPLES.

1. Given in a right-angled spherical triangle $A B C$, right-angled at C, the hypothenuse h equal to 105° 34′, and the angle A equal to 80° 40′; to solve the triangle.

Solution.

By (208),	By (210),	By (212),
h, log sin + 9.983770	log tan — 10.555053	log cos — 9.428717
A, log sin + 9.994212	log cos + 9.209992	log tan + 10.784220
p, log sin + 9.977982	b, log tan — 9.765045	B, log cot — 10.212937

Hence, $p = 71° 54′ 33″$, $b = 149° 47′ 37″$, $B = 148° 30′ 54″$.

2. Given in the spherical triangle $A B C$, right-angled at C,

the hypothenuse h equal to 70° 23′ 42″, and the angle A equal to 66° 20′ 40″; to find the other parts.

Ans. p, 59° 38′ 26″; b, 48° 24′ 15″; B, 52° 32′ 55″.

CASE II.

173. *Given the hypothenuse and one side.*

Let there be given (Fig. Art. 172) the hypothenuse h and the side p; to solve the triangle.

To find A. Make p the middle part, and we have, by Napier's rules, or by (200),

$$\sin p = \sin A \sin h;$$

whence,
$$\sin A = \frac{\sin p}{\sin h}, \tag{213}$$

or, by logarithms,

$$\log \sin A = \log \sin p - \log \sin h. \tag{214}$$

To find B. Make the complement of B the middle part, and we have, by Napier's rules, or by (203),

$$\cos B = \cot h \tan p,$$

or, by logarithms,

$$\log \cos B = \log \cot h + \log \tan p. \tag{215}$$

To find b. Make the complement of h the middle part, and we have, by Napier's rules, or by (198),

$$\cos h = \cos p \cos b;$$

whence,
$$\cos b = \frac{\cos h}{\cos p}, \tag{216}$$

or, by logarithms,

$$\log \cos b = \log \cos h - \log \cos p. \tag{217}$$

Here, as in the preceding article, b and B are determined without ambiguity, for there is only one angle less than 180° corresponding to a given cosine; and A must be of the same species as p.

EXAMPLES.

1. Given in a right-angled spherical triangle $A\ B\ C$, the hypothenuse h equal to $91°\ 42'$, and the side p equal to $95°\ 22'\ 30''$; to solve the triangle.

Ans. A, $95°\ 6'$; B, $71°\ 36'\ 45''$; b, $71°\ 32'\ 12''$.

2. Given in a right-angled spherical triangle, the hypothenuse equal to $70°\ 23'$ and a side equal to $48°\ 24'$; to solve the triangle.

Case III.

174. *Given one side and its adjacent oblique angle.*

Let there be given (Fig. Art. 172) the side b and the angle A; to solve the triangle.

To find B. Make the complement of B the middle part, and we have, by Napier's rules, or by (207),

$$\cos B = \sin A\ \cos b,$$

or, by logarithms,

$$\log \cos B = \log \sin A + \log \cos b. \qquad (218)$$

To find p. Make b the middle part, and we have, by Napier's rules, or by (205),

$$\sin b = \cot A\ \tan p;$$

whence,

$$\tan p = \tan A\ \sin b, \qquad (219)$$

or, by logarithms,

$$\log \tan p = \log \tan A + \log \sin b. \qquad (220)$$

To find h. Make the complement of A the middle part, and we have, by Napier's rules, or by (202),

$$\cos A = \cot h\ \tan b;$$

whence,

$$\cot h = \cos A \cot b, \qquad (221)$$

or, by logarithms,

$$\log \cot h = \log \cos A + \log \cot b. \qquad (222)$$

EXAMPLES.

1. Given in a spherical triangle $A B C$, right-angled at C, the side b equal to 29° 46′ 8″, and the angle A equal to 137° 24′ 21″; to solve the triangle.

Ans. B, 54° 1′ 16″; p, 155° 27′ 54″; h, 142° 9′ 13″.

2. Given in a spherical triangle $A B C$, right-angled at C, the side p equal to 149° 47′ 23″, and the angle B equal to 80° 40′; to find the other parts.

Case IV.

175. *Given one side and its opposite oblique angle.*

Let there be given in a spherical triangle $A B C$, right-angled at C, the side p and the opposite angle A; to solve the triangle.

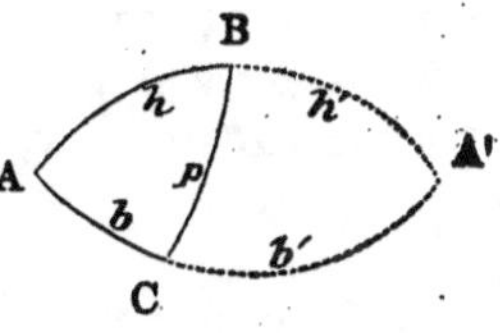

To find h. Make p the middle part, and we have, by Napier's rules, or by (200),

$$\sin p = \sin A \sin h;$$

whence,

$$\sin h = \frac{\sin p}{\sin A}, \tag{223}$$

or, by logarithms,

$$\log \sin h = \log \sin p - \log \sin A. \tag{224}$$

To find b. Make b the middle part, and we have, by Napier's rules, or by (205),

$$\sin b = \cot A \tan p,$$

or, by logarithms,

$$\log \sin b = \log \cot A + \log \tan p. \tag{225}$$

To find B. Make the complement of A the middle part, and we have, by Napier's rules, or by (206),

$$\cos A = \sin B \cos p;$$

whence,

$$\sin B = \frac{\cos A}{\cos p}, \tag{226}$$

or, by logarithms,

$$\log \sin B = \log \cos A - \log \cos p. \tag{227}$$

Here, since all the unknown parts are determined by their sines, and since there are always two angles less than 180° corresponding to a given sine, h, b, and B may be taken either acute or obtuse; hence there may be two solutions.

For, produce $A\,B$ and $A\,C$ till they meet in A', then we have a second triangle, $A'\,B\,C$, which satisfies the given conditions, for it has a right angle at C, the given side p, and A' equal to A, the given angle. But h', b', and B, the other parts of the second triangle, are respectively the supplements of h, b, and B of the first triangle.

When, however, p is given equal to A, we have h, b, and B, each equal to 90°, and the triangle $A'B\,C$ is equal to the triangle $A\,B\,C$ (Geom., Prop. XII. Bk. IX).

When p and A are both equal to 90°, h is also equal to 90°, and b and B are equal, but indeterminate.

EXAMPLES.

1. Given in a spherical triangle $A\,B\,C$, right-angled at C, the side p equal to 36° 31′, and the angle A equal to 37° 25′; to solve the triangle.

Ans. h, 78° 20′, or 101° 40′; b, 75° 26′, or 104° 34′; B, 81° 12′, or 98° 48′, when carried only to minutes.

2. Given in a spherical triangle $A\,B\,C$, right-angled at C, the side b equal to 79° 30′, and the angle B equal to 89° 35′; to solve the triangle.

Case V.

176. *Given the two sides about the right angle.*

Let there be given (Fig. Art. 172) the sides p and b; to solve the triangle.

To find h. Make the complement of h the middle part, and we have, by Napier's rules, or by (198),

$$\cos h = \cos p \, \cos b,$$

or, by logarithms,

$$\log \cos h = \log \cos p + \log \cos b. \qquad (228)$$

To find A. Make b the middle part, and we have, by Napier's rules, or by (205),

$$\sin b = \cot A \tan p;$$

whence,
$$\cot A = \cot p \sin b, \quad (229)$$
or, by logarithms,

$$\log \cot A = \log \cot p + \log \sin b. \quad (230)$$

To find B. Make p the middle part, and we have, by Napier's rules, or by (204),

$$\sin p = \cot B \tan b;$$

whence
$$\cot B = \sin p \cot b, \quad (231)$$
or, by logarithms,

$$\log \cot B = \log \sin p + \log \cot b. \quad (232)$$

These formulæ determine h, A, and B without ambiguity.

EXAMPLES.

1. In a spherical triangle $A\,B\,C$ are given the sides about the right angle, p equal to 48° 24′ 15″, and b equal to 59° 38′ 27″; to solve the triangle.

Ans. h, 70° 23′ 42″; A, 52° 32′ 55″; B, 66° 20′ 40″.

2. Given in a right-angled spherical triangle, the side p equal to 95° 22′ 30″, and the side b equal to 71° 32′ 14″; to find the other parts.

Case VI.

177. *Given the two oblique angles.*

Let there be given (Fig. Art. 172) the angles A and B; to solve the triangle.

To find h. Make the complement of h the middle part, and we have, by Napier's rules, or by (199),

$$\cos h = \cot A \cot B,$$

or, by logarithms,

$$\log \cos h = \log \cot A + \log \cot B. \quad (233)$$

To find p. Make the complement of A the middle part, and we have, by Napier's rules, or by (206),

9

$$\cos A = \sin B \cos p;$$

whence,
$$\cos p = \frac{\cos A}{\sin B}, \tag{234}$$
or, by logarithms,
$$\log \cos p = \log \cos A - \log \sin B. \tag{235}$$

To find b. Make the complement of B the middle part, and we have, by Napier's rules, or by (207),

$$\cos B = \sin A \cos b;$$

whence,
$$\cos b = \frac{\cos B}{\sin A}, \tag{236}$$
or, by logarithms,
$$\log \cos b = \log \cos B - \log \sin A. \tag{237}$$

Here h, p, and b are determined without ambiguity.

EXAMPLES.

1. In a right-angled spherical triangle ABC are given the two oblique angles, A equal to $44° 50'$, and B equal to $65° 49' 53''$; to solve the triangle.

Ans. h, $63° 10' 4''$; p, $38° 59' 11''$; b, $54° 30'$.

2. Given, in a right-angled spherical triangle, the two oblique angles, A equal to $125° 30'$, and B equal to $80° 40'$; to find the other parts.

Quadrantal Triangles.

178. A QUADRANTAL TRIANGLE is a spherical triangle having one of its sides quadrantal, or equal to 90°.

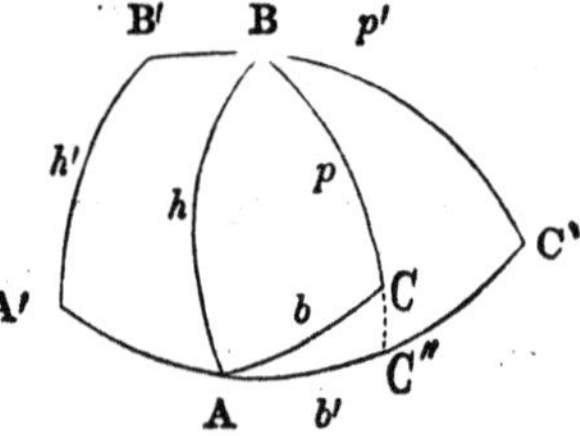

Quadrantal triangles may be solved in the same manner as right-angled spherical triangles, by means of the polar triangle.

Let ABC be a quadrantal triangle, and $A'B'C'$ denote a triangle polar to it; then, by Art. 150, we have

$$A' = 180° - p, \quad B' = 180° - b, \quad C' = 180° - h;$$
$$p' = 180° - A, \quad b' = 180° - B, \quad h' = 180° - C.$$

Now, if the side h be taken equal to 90°, its corresponding polar angle C' will also equal 90°; hence the polar triangle will be right-angled, and can be solved by application of the preceding formulæ for right-angled spherical triangles, and thus the required parts of the quadrantal triangle may be determined.

A triangle, one of whose sides is a quadrant, may also be solved by laying off a quadrant on one of the other sides, prolonged if necessary, and connecting this last point with the other extremity of the original quadrant by the arc of a great circle, thus making the original quadrantal triangle either the difference or the sum of a bi-quadrantal and a right-angled spherical triangle. Solving the latter solves the original triangle. Thus, AC'' measures B, $CAC'' = 90° - A$, $CC'' = 90° - p$, $ACC'' = 180° - C$, and solving the triangle ACC'' also solves the triangle ABC.

EXAMPLES.

1. Let there be given, in a quadrantal triangle ABC, the side h equal to 90°, the angle A equal to 54° 43′, and the angle B equal to 42° 12′; to find the other parts.

By taking the supplements of the given parts, we have in the polar triangle,

$$p' = 125° 17', \qquad b' = 137° 48',$$

whence A', B', and h' are determined as in Art. 176, and the supplements of these give the required parts of the quadrantal triangle. Ans. p, 64° 34′ 40″; b, 48° 0′ 16″; C, 115° 20′ 5″.

2. Given two sides of a quadrantal triangle equal to 72° 53′ and 51° 4′, to find the angle opposite to the quadrantal side.

Ans. 104° 24′ 21″.

SOLUTION OF OBLIQUE-ANGLED SPHERICAL TRIANGLES.

179. In the solution of oblique-angled spherical triangles, it is sometimes found convenient, especially in removing an ambiguity, to refer to one or more of the following propositions, of which the first four have been demonstrated in Book IX. of the Geometry.

I. *Any side of a spherical triangle is less than the sum of the other two.*

II. *The sum of the sides is less than* 360°.

III. *The sum of the angles is greater than* 180°.

IV. *The greater side is opposite the greater angle, and conversely.*

V. *Any angle is greater than the difference between* 180° *and the sum of the other two angles.*

VI. *A side which differs more from* 90° *than another side, is of the same species as its opposite angle.*

For, by (150), we have

$$\cos a = \cos b \cos c + \sin b \sin c \cos A;$$

whence,

$$\cos A = \frac{\cos a - \cos b \cos c}{\sin b \sin c},$$

in which the denominator is always positive.

Then, if a differs more from 90° than b or than c, $\cos a$ is numerically greater than $\cos b$, or than $\cos c$, and we have

$$\cos a > \cos b \cos c,$$

hence, the sign of the numerator, and consequently the sign of $\cos A$, is the same as that of $\cos a$, that is, A and a are in the same quadrant.

VII. *An angle which differs more from* 90° *than another angle, is of the same species as its opposite side.*

For, by (153), we have

$$\cos A = \sin B \sin C \cos a - \cos B \cos C;$$

whence,

$$\cos a = \frac{\cos A + \cos B \cos C}{\sin B \sin C},$$

in which, if A differs more from 90° than B, or than C, $\cos A$ is numerically greater than $\cos B$, or than $\cos C$, and the sign of $\cos a$ is the same as that of $\cos A$, that is, a and A are in the same quadrant.

VIII. *When the sum of two sides is greater than, equal to, or less than* 180°, *the sum of the two opposite angles is the same.*

For, by means of (188),

$$\tan \tfrac{1}{2}(a+b) \cos \tfrac{1}{2}(A+B) = \tan \tfrac{1}{2} c \cos \tfrac{1}{2}(A-B),$$

in which the second member is always positive, since $\frac{1}{2}c$ and $\frac{1}{2}(A-B)$ are each less than 90°, so that the factors of the first member, $\tan \frac{1}{2}(a+b)$ and $\cos \frac{1}{2}(A+B)$ must have the same sign. Therefore, $\frac{1}{2}(a+b)$ and $\frac{1}{2}(A+B)$ are of the same species.

180. In the solution of oblique-angled spherical triangles, there are six cases, the data in them being, respectively,

I. Two sides and an angle opposite one of them.
II. Two angles and a side opposite one of them.
III. Two sides and the included angle.
IV. Two angles and the included side.
V. The three sides.
VI. The three angles.

Case I.

181. *Given two sides and an angle opposite one of them.*

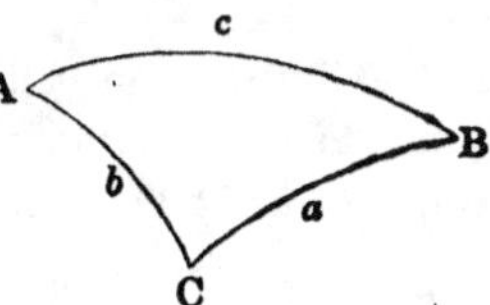

Let there be given, in the oblique-angled spherical triangle ABC, the sides a and b, and the angle A; to solve the triangle.

To find B. We have, from (148),

$$\sin B = \frac{\sin b}{\sin a} \sin A,$$

or, by logarithms,

$$\log \sin B = \log \sin b - \log \sin a + \log \sin A. \quad (238)$$

To find C and c. We have, by Napier's analogies, (186) and (188),

$$\cot \tfrac{1}{2} C = \frac{\cos \frac{1}{2}(a+b)}{\cos \frac{1}{2}(a-b)} \tan \tfrac{1}{2}(A+B),$$

$$\tan \tfrac{1}{2} c = \frac{\cos \frac{1}{2}(A+B)}{\cos \frac{1}{2}(A-B)} \tan \tfrac{1}{2}(a+b);$$

or, by logarithms,

$$\log \cot \tfrac{1}{2} C = \log \cos \tfrac{1}{2}(a+b) - \log \cos \tfrac{1}{2}(a-b) + \log \tan \tfrac{1}{2}(A+B), \quad (239)$$

$$\log \tan \tfrac{1}{2} c = \log \cos \tfrac{1}{2}(A+B) - \log \cos \tfrac{1}{2}(A-B) + \log \tan \tfrac{1}{2}(a+b), \quad (240)$$

which determine $\frac{1}{2} C$ and $\frac{1}{2} c$, and thence C and c.

In this case, since B is found from its sine, it will sometimes admit of two values, the one supplementary to the other. When B has two values, C and c must each have two corresponding values. Whether both values of B are admissible must be determined by one of the propositions of Art. 179.

Thus (Prop. VI.), if b differs more from 90° than a, B must be of the same species as b, and there can be but one solution; but if b differs less from 90° than a, there may be two solutions.

Or (Prop. VIII.), if only one of the supplementary values of B makes $\frac{1}{2}(A+B)$ of the same species as $\frac{1}{2}(a+b)$, there can be but one solution; but if both values of B fulfil that condition, there will be two solutions.

EXAMPLES.

1. Given, in an oblique-angled spherical triangle, the side a equal to 63° 50′, the side b equal to 80° 19′, and the angle A equal to 51° 30′; to solve the triangle.

Solution. By (238) we have

$a = 63° 50'$	ar. co. log sin	0.046958
$b = 80° 19'$	log sin	9.993768
$A = 51° 30'$	log sin	9.893544
$B = 59° 15' 57''$, or $120° 44' 3''$	log sin	9.934270

As b differs less from 90° than a, both values of B are admissible, and we have $\frac{1}{2}(b-a) = 8° 14' 30''$, $\frac{1}{2}(a+b) = 72° 4' 30''$, $\frac{1}{2}(A+B) = 55° 22' 58''$ or $86° 7' 2''$, and $\frac{1}{2}(B-A) = 3° 52' 58''$ or $34° 37' 2''$. The cosines of $\frac{1}{2}(b-a)$ and $\frac{1}{2}(B-A)$ are the same as those of $\frac{1}{2}(a-b)$ and $\frac{1}{2}(A-B)$, respectively, by Art. 79. Hence, by (239) and (240),

$\frac{1}{2}(b-a)$	ar. co. log cos + 0.004508		ar. co. log cos + 0.004508
$\frac{1}{2}(a+b)$	log cos + 9.488229		log cos + 9.488229
$\frac{1}{2}(A+B)$	log tan + 10.160964	or	log tan + 11.168314
$\frac{1}{2}C$	log cot + 9.653701	or	log cot + 10.661051

$$\tfrac{1}{2}C = 65^\circ\ 44'\ 53'' \text{ or } 12^\circ\ 18'\ 42'',$$
$$C = 131^\circ\ 29'\ 46'' \text{ or } 24^\circ\ 37'\ 24''.$$

$\frac{1}{2}(B-A)$	ar. co. log cos + 0.000998	or	ar. co. log cos + 0.084618
$\frac{1}{2}(A+B)$	log cos + 9.754418	or	log cos + 8.830687
$\frac{1}{2}(a+b)$	log tan + 10.490161		log tan + 10.490161
$\frac{1}{2}c$	log tan + 10.245577	or	log tan + 9.405466

$$\tfrac{1}{2}c = 60^\circ\ 23'\ 57'' \text{ or } 14^\circ\ 16'\ 18'',$$
$$c = 120^\circ\ 47'\ 54'' \text{ or } 28^\circ\ 32'\ 36''.$$

2. Given, in an oblique-angled spherical triangle, two sides equal to 99° 40′ 48″ and 64° 23′ 15″, and an angle opposite to the first of these equal to 95° 38′ 4″; to find the other side and angles.

Ans. Side, 100° 49′ 30″; angles, 65° 33′ 10″ and 97° 26′ 30″.

Case II.

182. *Given two angles and a side opposite one of them.*

Let there be given, in the oblique-angled spherical triangle $A\,B\,C$ (Fig. Art. 181), the angles A and B, and the side a; to solve the triangle.

To find b. We have, from (148),

$$\sin b = \frac{\sin B}{\sin A} \sin a,$$

or, by logarithms,

$$\log \sin b = \log \sin B - \log \sin A + \log \sin a. \quad (241)$$

To find C and c. We use equations (239) and (240), as in the last article.

This case is exactly analogous to Case I., and gives rise to the same ambiguities, as may be shown by passing to the polar triangle.

If B differs more from 90° than A, b must be of the same species as B, and there can be but one solution; but if B differs less from 90° than A, there may be two solutions. (Prop. VII. Art. 179.)

Or, if only one of the supplementary values of b makes $\frac{1}{2}(a+b)$ of the same species as $\frac{1}{2}(A+B)$, there can be but one solution; but if both values of b fulfil that condition, there will be two solutions. (Prop. VIII. Art. 179.)

EXAMPLES.

1. Given, in an oblique-angled spherical triangle, the angle A equal to 135°, the angle B equal to 60°, and the side a equal to 155°; to find the other parts.

Ans. C, 98° 3′ 4″ or 16° 57′ 1″; b, 31° 10′ 17″ or 148° 49′ 43″; c, 143° 42′ 57″ or 10° 2′ 6″.

2. Given, in an oblique-angled spherical triangle, two angles equal to 97° 26′ 30″ and 65° 33′ 10″, and the side opposite to the first equal to 100° 49′ 30″; to find the other parts.

Case III.

183. *Given two sides and the included angle.*

Let there be given, in the oblique-angled spherical triangle ABC (Fig. Art. 181), the sides a and b, and the included angle C; to solve the triangle.

To find A and B. By means of Napier's analogies (186) and (187), we have

$$\tan \tfrac{1}{2}(A+B) = \frac{\cos \frac{1}{2}(a-b)}{\cos \frac{1}{2}(a+b)} \cot \tfrac{1}{2} C,$$

$$\tan \tfrac{1}{2}(A-B) = \frac{\sin \frac{1}{2}(a-b)}{\sin \frac{1}{2}(a+b)} \cot \tfrac{1}{2} C;$$

or, by logarithms,

$$\log \tan \tfrac{1}{2}(A+B) = \log \cos \tfrac{1}{2}(a-b) - \log \cos \tfrac{1}{2}(a+b) + \log \cot \tfrac{1}{2} C, \qquad (242)$$

$$\log \tan \tfrac{1}{2}(A-B) = \log \sin \tfrac{1}{2}(a-b) - \log \sin \tfrac{1}{2}(a+b) + \log \cot \tfrac{1}{2} C, \qquad (243)$$

which determine $\frac{1}{2}(A+B)$ and $\frac{1}{2}(A-B)$. The sum of these values gives A, and the second subtracted from the first gives B.

To find c. We use equation (240), as in the first two cases. The value of c might also be obtained by (147) or (149); but as it is thus determined from its sine, it would be necessary to remove the ambiguity by means of the principles contained in Art. 179.

As A, B, and c may all be found by means of tangents, there can be but one value for each. It will be observed that $\frac{1}{2}(A+B)$ must always be of the same species as $\frac{1}{2}(a+b)$. (Prop. VIII. Art. 179.)

EXAMPLES.

1. Given, in an oblique-angled spherical triangle $A\,B\,C$, the side a equal to 70°, the side b equal to 38° 30′, and the included angle C equal to 31° 34′ 26″; to solve the triangle.

Solution.

$\frac{1}{2}(a+b) = 54° \; 15'$, $\frac{1}{2}(a-b) = 15° \; 45'$, and $\frac{1}{2}C = 15° \; 47' \; 13''$; then,

By (242),			By (243),	
$\frac{1}{2}(a+b)$	ar. co. log cos +	0.233402	ar. co. log sin +	0.090672
$\frac{1}{2}(a-b)$	log cos +	9.983381	log sin +	9.433675
$\frac{1}{2}C$	log cot +	10.548635	log cot +	10.548635
$\frac{1}{2}(A+B)$	log tan +	10.765418	$\frac{1}{2}(A-B)$ log tan +	10.072982

$\frac{1}{2}(A+B) = 80° \; 15' \; 41''$ $\qquad$ $\frac{1}{2}(A-B) = 49° \; 47' \; 30''$

$A = 130° \; 3' \; 11''$ $\qquad$ $B = 30° \; 28' \; 11''$

By (240),

$\frac{1}{2}(A-B)$	$= 49° \; 47' \; 30''$	ar. co. log cos +	0.190058
$\frac{1}{2}(A+B)$	$= 80° \; 15' \; 41''$	log cos +	9.228282
$\frac{1}{2}(a+b)$	$= 54° \; 15'$	log tan +	10.142730
$\frac{1}{2}c$	$= 20°$	log tan +	9.561070

Ans. Angle A, 130° 3′ 11″; angle B, 30° 28′ 11″; side c, 40°.

2. Given, in an oblique-angled spherical triangle, an angle equal to 48° 36′, and the two adjacent sides equal to 112° 22′ 58½″ and 89° 16′ 53½″; to find the other parts.

CASE IV.

184. *Given two angles and the included side.*

Let there be given, in the oblique-angled spherical triangle ABC (Fig. Art. 181), the angles A and B, and the included side c; to solve the triangle.

To find a and b. By means of Napier's analogies (188) and (189), we have

$$\tan \tfrac{1}{2}(a+b) = \frac{\cos \tfrac{1}{2}(A-B)}{\cos \tfrac{1}{2}(A+B)} \tan \tfrac{1}{2} c,$$

$$\tan \tfrac{1}{2}(a-b) = \frac{\sin \tfrac{1}{2}(A-B)}{\sin \tfrac{1}{2}(A+B)} \tan \tfrac{1}{2} c;$$

or, by logarithms,

$$\log \tan \tfrac{1}{2}(a+b) = \log \cos \tfrac{1}{2}(A-B) - \log \cos \tfrac{1}{2}(A+B) + \log \tan \tfrac{1}{2} c, \qquad (244)$$

$$\log \tan \tfrac{1}{2}(a-b) = \log \sin \tfrac{1}{2}(A-B) - \log \sin \tfrac{1}{2}(A+B) + \log \tan \tfrac{1}{2} c, \qquad (245)$$

which determine $\frac{1}{2}(a+b)$ and $\frac{1}{2}(a-b)$, and thence a and b.

To find C. We use equation (239), as in the first two cases; but (147) or (149) may be employed, as in the last case.

This case is analogous to Case III., and gives rise to no ambiguity.

EXAMPLES.

1. Given, in an oblique-angled spherical triangle ABC, the angles A and B equal to 119° 15′ and 70° 39′, and the side c equal to 52° 39′ 4″; to solve the triangle.

Ans. Sides a and b, 112° 22′ 58½″ and 89° 16′ 53½″; angle C, 48° 36′.

2. In an oblique-angled spherical triangle, given two angles equal to 130° 3′ 11″ and 31° 34′ 26″, and the included side equal to 38° 30′; to find the other parts.

CASE V.

185. *Given the three sides.*

Let there be given, in the oblique-angled spherical triangle ABC (Fig. Art. 181), the sides a, b, and c; to solve the triangle.

To find A, B, and C, we have, by (164), (165), and (166),

$$\sin \tfrac{1}{2} A = \sqrt{\frac{\sin (s-b) \sin (s-c)}{\sin b \sin c}},$$

$$\sin \tfrac{1}{2} B = \sqrt{\frac{\sin (s-c) \sin (s-a)}{\sin c \sin a}},$$

$$\sin \tfrac{1}{2} C = \sqrt{\frac{\sin (s-a) \sin (s-b)}{\sin a \sin b}};$$

or, by logarithms,

$$\log \sin \tfrac{1}{2} A = \frac{\log \sin (s-b) + \log \sin (s-c) - \log \sin b - \log \sin c}{2}, \quad (246)$$

$$\log \sin \tfrac{1}{2} B = \frac{\log \sin (s-c) + \log \sin (s-a) - \log \sin c - \log \sin a}{2}, \quad (247)$$

$$\log \sin \tfrac{1}{2} C = \frac{\log \sin (s-a) + \log \sin (s-b) - \log \sin a - \log \sin b}{2}. \quad (248)$$

A, B, and C can also be determined by formulæ (167), (168), and (169) for the cosine of half an angle, and by formulæ (170), (171), and (172) for the tangent of half an angle.

Since the half-angles must be less than 90°, there is no ambiguity in determining the angles by any of these formulæ.

EXAMPLES.

1. Given, in an oblique-angled spherical triangle, the side a equal to 70°, the side b equal to 38°, and the side c equal to 40°; to find the angles.

Solution.

$$s = 74°, \quad s - a = 4°, \quad s - b = 36°, \quad s - c = 34°.$$

	By (246),	By (247),	By (248),
$s-b$,	log sin 9.769219		log sin 9.769219
$s-c$,	log sin 9.747562	log sin 9.747562	
$s-a$,		log sin 8.843585	log sin 8.843585
b,	ar.co.log sin 0.210658		ar.co.log sin 0.210658
c,	ar.co.log sin 0.191933	ar.co.log sin 0.191933	
a,		ar.co.log sin 0.027014	ar.co.log sin 0.027014
	2) 19.919372	2) 18.810094	2) 18.850476
	$\tfrac{1}{2} A$, log sin 9.959686	$\tfrac{1}{2} B$, log sin 9.405047	$\tfrac{1}{2} C$, log sin 9.425238

$\frac{1}{2}A = 65° 41' 33''.7$ $\frac{1}{2}B = 14° 43' 18''$ $\frac{1}{2}C = 15° 26' 21''.7$

Ans. A, 131° 23′ 7″; B, 29° 26′ 36″; C, 30° 52′ 43″.

2. Given, in an oblique-angled spherical triangle, the sides equal to 112° 22′ 59″, 89° 16′ 53″, and 52° 39′ 4″; to solve the triangle.

Case VI.

186. *Given the three angles.*

Let there be given, in the oblique-angled spherical triangle ABC (Fig. Art. 181), the angles A, B, and C; to solve the triangle.

To find a, b, and c, we have, by (175),

$$\sin \tfrac{1}{2} a = \sqrt{\frac{-\cos S \cos (S-A)}{\sin B \sin C}},$$

$$\sin \tfrac{1}{2} b = \sqrt{\frac{-\cos S \cos (S-B)}{\sin C \sin A}},$$

$$\sin \tfrac{1}{2} c = \sqrt{\frac{-\cos S \cos (S-C)}{\sin A \sin B}};$$

or, by logarithms,

$$\log \sin \tfrac{1}{2} a = \frac{\log \cos S + \log \cos (S-A) - \log \sin B - \log \sin C}{2}, \quad (249)$$

$$\log \sin \tfrac{1}{2} b = \frac{\log \cos S + \log \cos (S-B) - \log \sin C - \log \sin A}{2}, \quad (250)$$

$$\log \sin \tfrac{1}{2} c = \frac{\log \cos S + \log \cos (S-C) - \log \sin A - \log \sin B}{2}. \quad (251)$$

a, b, and c can also be determined by formulæ (176) for the cosine of half an angle, and by formulæ (177) for the tangent of half an angle.

Here a, b, and c are determined without ambiguity.

EXAMPLES.

1. Given, in an oblique-angled spherical triangle, the angle A equal to 120° 43′ 37″, the angle B equal to 109° 55′ 42″, and the angle C equal to 116° 38′ 33″; to find the sides.

Ans. a, 115° 13′ 26″; b, 98° 21′ 39″; c, 109° 50′ 20″.

2. Given the angles in an oblique-angled spherical triangle equal to 131° 23′ 7″, 29° 26′ 36″, and 30° 52′ 43″; to solve the triangle.

BOOK VI.

APPLICATIONS OF SPHERICAL TRIGONOMETRY TO ASTRONOMY AND GEOGRAPHY.

187. The CELESTIAL SPHERE is the spherical concave surrounding the earth, in which all the heavenly bodies appear to be situated.

188. The ZENITH is that pole of the horizon which is directly overhead.

189. The ALTITUDE of a heavenly body is its distance above the horizon, measured on the arc of a great circle passing through that body and the zenith.

190. The DECLINATION of a heavenly body is its distance north or south of the celestial equator, measured on a meridian.

191. *The altitude of the celestial pole is equal to the latitude of the place where the observer is located.*

For the distance from the zenith to the celestial equator is the latitude of the place, and the distance from the zenith to the pole is its complement; but the distance from the zenith to the pole is also the complement of the altitude of the pole; hence the latitude of the place and the altitude of the pole are equal.

192. *To find the time of the* RISING AND SETTING OF THE SUN *at any place, the sun's declination and the latitude of the place being given.*

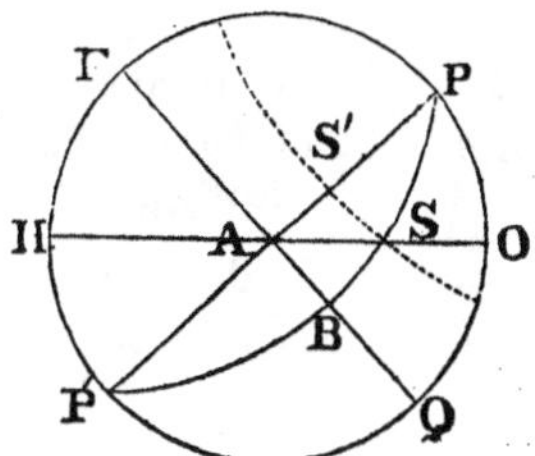

Let P represent the celestial north pole, $E\,A\,Q$ the celestial equator, $H\,A\,O$ the rational horizon, S the place of the sun's rising, S' the position of the sun at 6 o'clock, PEP' the meridian of the given place, PBP' the meridian passing through S, and PAP' the meridian 90° distant from PEP', passing through S'.

From the time of the sun's rising to 6 o'clock, it will pass over SS, the arc of a small circle, corresponding to BA, the arc of a great circle. The length of BA, expressed in time (Art. 147), will then give the amount to be taken from or added to 6 o'clock, to give the time of the sun's rising or setting.

BS is the sun's declination, PO is the latitude of the place (Art. 191), and QO, which measures the angle BAS, is its complement; hence, in the right-angled spherical triangle ABS, there are known the side BS and the angle BAS, from which, by Art. 175,

$$\sin BA = \tan BS \cot BAS,$$

or, log sin BA = log tan sun's decl. + log tan lat. of place.

After reducing the arc BA to time, at the rate of 15° to an hour, or 4m. to a degree, it must be added to 6 o'clock for the time of the sun's setting, and subtracted for its rising, when the declination and latitude are both north or both south; but subtracted for its setting and added for its rising, when one is north and the other south.

The preceding reasoning rests upon the assumption that the sun's declination does not change between sunrise and sunset, which, although not strictly true, is accurate enough for our present purpose. The time obtained is *apparent time*, and a correction must be applied if we wish to find mean time, or that indicated by the clock. Another correction is necessary for refraction. Neither of these corrections has, however, been applied to the answers that follow.

EXAMPLES.

1. Required the time of the sun's rising and setting in Edinburgh, latitude 55° 57′ N., when the sun's declination is 23° 28′ N.

Ans. Rises, 3h. 20m. 7s.; sets, 8h. 39m. 53s.

2. What is the time of the sun's rising and setting in latitude 60° 3′ N., when the sun's declination is 23° 28′ S.?

Ans. Rises, 9h. 15m. 33s.; sets, 2h. 44m. 27s.

3. Required the time of the sun's rising and setting in places whose latitude is 48° S., when the sun's declination is 15° S.

193. *To find the* HOUR OF THE DAY *at any place, the latitude of the place and the sun's declination and altitude being given.*

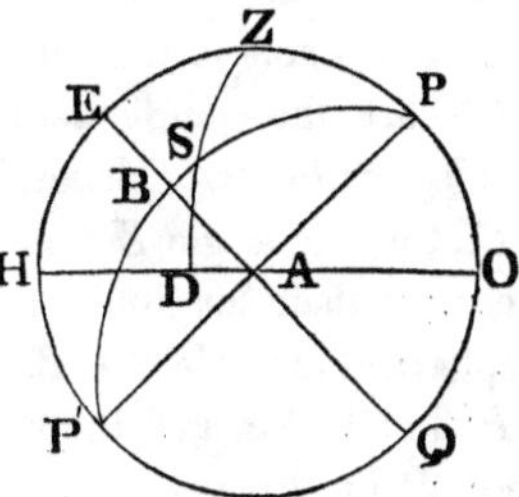

Let Z represent the zenith, and $Z D$ an arc of a great circle drawn through the zenith and the sun's place, S; $P B P'$, a meridian drawn through the sun's place, &c., as in the last article.

As before, the arc $A B$, added to or subtracted from 6 o'clock, will give the time when the sun is at S; but it will be more convenient to use its complement, $E B$, which is the time before or after 12 o'clock.

$E Z$ is the latitude of the place, and $P Z$ is its complement; $B S$ is the sun's declination, and $P S$ is its complement; $S D$ is the altitude of the sun, and $Z S$ is its complement; hence, in the spherical triangle $Z P S$, the three sides are known, and the angle $Z P S$, or the arc $E B$, may be found by Art. 185.

If either the sun's declination, or the latitude of the place, is south, it must be considered negative in taking its complement, unless the south pole is taken as a vertex of the triangle, when north will be negative.

EXAMPLES.

1. Required the apparent time of day in the morning, at a place in latitude 39° 54′ N., the sun's declination being 17° 29′ N., and its corrected altitude 15° 54′.

Ans. 6h. 25m. 30s. A. M.

2. In latitude 36° 39′ S., when the sun's declination was 9° 27′ N., its corrected altitude was observed, in the afternoon, to be 10° 40′; what was the apparent solar time?

Ans. 4h. 36m. 10s. P. M.

3. Required the apparent time of day in Boston, latitude 42° 21′ N., when the sun's declination is 20° S., and its corrected altitude 15° 15′, the sun being east of the meridian.

194. *To find the* SHORTEST DISTANCE *between two places on the earth's surface, and the* BEARING *of one from the other, their latitudes and longitudes being given.*

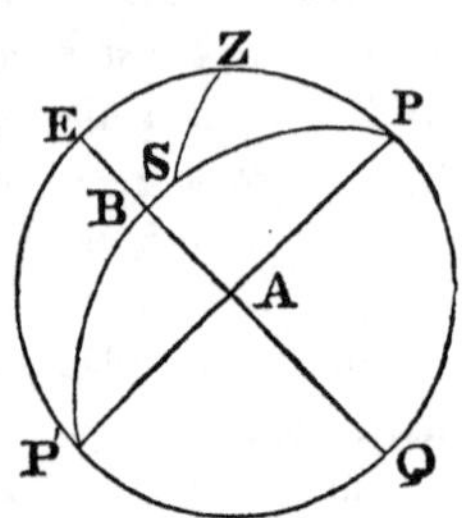

Let Z and S represent the two points on the earth's surface, and P the north pole of the earth. PZ and PS are the complements of the latitudes of the two places, and the arc EB, or the angle ZPS, is the difference of their longitudes; hence, in the spherical triangle SPZ, the two sides PZ and PS, and their included angle P, are known, from which the side ZS, and the angles ZSP and SZP may be found by Art. 183.

The distance ZS can easily be reduced to miles by allowing 69.16 statute miles, or 60 nautical miles, to a degree. The answers which follow are given in statute miles.

If one place is south and the other north of the equator, the south latitude must be considered negative in taking its complement.

EXAMPLES.

1. What is the distance and bearing of Jerusalem, lat. 31° 47′ N., long. 35° 20′ E., from London, lat. 51° 30′ N., long. 6′ W.?

Ans. Distance, 2248 miles; bearing, S. 66° 31′ E.

2. Required the distance and bearing of Cape Horn, lat. 55° 58′ S., long. 67° 21′ W., from London.

Ans. Distance, 8363 miles; bearing, S. 36° 59′ W.

3. Required the distance and bearing of Quito, lat. 0°, long. 78° 45′ W., from San Francisco, lat. 37° 49′ N., long. 122° 14′ W.

A

TABLE

OF LOGARITHMIC

SINES, COSINES, TANGENTS, AND COTANGENTS,

FOR EVERY

DEGREE AND MINUTE OF THE

QUADRANT.

0°

M.	Sine.	D.	Cosine.	D.	Tang.	D.	Cotang.	
0	— ∞		10.000000		— ∞		∞	60
1	6.463726	5017.17	.000000	.00	6.463726	5017.17	3.536274	59
2	.764756	2934.85	.000000	.00	.764756	2934.85	.235244	58
3	.940847	2082.31	.000000	.00	.940847	2082.31	.059153	57
4	7.065786	1615.17	.000000	.00	7.065786	1615.17	2.934214	56
5	.162696	1319.68	.000000	.00	.162696	1319.68	.837304	55
6	.241877	1115.78	9.999999	.01	.241878	1115 78	.758122	54
7	.308824	966.53	.999999	.01	.308825	996.53	.691175	53
8	.366816	852.54	.999999	.01	.366817	852.54	.633183	52
9	.417968	762.63	.999999	.01	.417970	762.63	.582030	51
10	.463725	689.88	.999998	.01	.463727	689.88	.536273	50
11	7.505118	629.81	9.999998	.01	7.505120	629.81	2.494880	49
12	.542906	579.37	.999997	.01	.542909	579.38	.457091	48
13	.577668	536.41	.999997	.01	.577672	536.42	.422328	47
14	.609853	499.38	.999996	.01	.609857	499.39	.390143	46
15	.639816	467.14	.999996	.01	.639820	467.15	.360180	45
16	.667845	438.81	.999995	.01	.667849	438.82	.332151	44
17	.694173	413.72	.999995	.01	.694179	413.73	.305821	43
18	.718997	391.35	.999994	.01	.719004	391.36	.280997	42
19	.742477	371.27	.999993	.01	.742484	371.28	.257516	41
20	.764754	353.15	.999993	.01	.764761	353 17	.235239	40
21	7.785943	336.72	9.999992	.01	7 785951	336.73	2.214049	39
22	.806146	321.75	.999991	.01	.806155	321.76	.193845	38
23	.825451	308.05	.999990	.01	.825460	308.06	.174540	37
24	.843934	295.47	.999989	.02	.843944	295.49	.156056	36
25	.861662	283.88	.999988	.02	.861674	283.90	.138326	35
26	.878695	273.17	.999988	.02	.878708	273.18	.121292	34
27	.895085	263.23	.999987	.02	.895099	263.25	.104901	33
28	.910879	253.99	.999986	.02	.910894	254.01	.089106	32
29	.926119	245.38	.999985	.02	.926134	245.40	.073866	31
30	.940842	237.33	.999983	.02	.940858	237.35	.059142	30
31	7.955082	229.80	9.999982	.02	7.955100	229.81	2.044900	29
32	.968870	222.73	.999981	.02	.968889	222.75	.031111	28
33	.982233	216.08	.999980	.02	.982253	216 10	.017747	27
34	.995198	209.81	.999979	.02	.995219	209.83	.004781	26
35	8.007787	203.90	.999977	.02	8.007809	203.92	1.992191	25
36	.020021	198.31	.999976	.02	.020045	198.33	.979955	24
37	.031919	193.02	.999975	.02	.031945	193.05	.968055	23
38	.043501	188.01	.999973	.02	.043527	188.03	.956473	22
39	.054781	183.25	.999972	.02	.054809	183.27	.945191	21
40	.065776	178.72	.999971	.02	.065806	178.74	.934194	20
41	8.076500	174.41	9.999969	.02	8.076531	174.44	1.923469	19
42	.086965	170.31	.999968	.02	.086997	170.34	.913003	18
43	.097183	166 39	.999966	.02	.097217	166.42	.902783	17
44	.107167	162.65	.999964	.03	.107202	162.68	.892797	16
45	.116926	159.08	.999963	.03	.116963	159.10	.883037	15
46	.126471	155.66	.999961	.03	.126510	155.68	.873490	14
47	.135810	152.38	.999959	.03	.135851	152.41	.864149	13
48	.144953	149.24	.999958	.03	.144996	149.27	.855004	12
49	.153907	146.22	.999956	.03	.153952	146.27	.846048	11
50	.162681	143.33	.999954	.03	.162727	143.36	.837273	10
51	8.171280	140.54	9.999952	.03	8.171328	140.57	1.828672	9
52	.179713	137.86	.999950	.03	.179763	137.90	.820237	8
53	.187985	135.29	.999948	.03	.188036	135.32	.811964	7
54	.196102	132.80	.999946	.03	.196156	132.84	.803844	6
55	.204070	130.41	.999944	.03	.204126	130.44	.795874	5
56	.211895	128.10	.999942	.04	.211953	128.14	.788047	4
57	.219581	125.87	.999940	.04	.219641	125.90	.780359	3
58	.227134	123.72	.999938	.04	.227195	123.76	.772805	2
59	.234557	121.64	.999936	.04	.234621	121.68	.765379	1
60	.241855		.999934		.241921		.758079	0
	Cosine.	D.	Sine.	D	Cotang.	D.	Tang.	M.

89°

1°

M.	Sine.	D.	Cosine.	D.	Tang.	D.	Cotang.	
0	8.241855	119.63	9.999934	.04	8.241921	119.67	1.758079	60
1	.249033	117.68	.999932	.04	.249102	117.72	.750898	59
2	.256094	115.80	.999929	.04	.256165	115.84	.743835	58
3	.263042	113.98	.999927	.04	.263115	114.02	.736885	57
4	.269881	112.21	.999925	.04	.269956	112.25	.730044	56
5	.276614	110.50	.999922	.04	.276691	110.54	.723309	55
6	.283243	108.83	.999920	.04	.283323	108.87	.716677	54
7	.289773	107.21	.999918	.04	.289856	107.26	.710144	53
8	.296207	105.65	.999915	.04	.296292	105.70	.703708	52
9	.302546	104.13	.999913	.04	.302634	104.18	.697366	51
10	.308794	102.66	.999910	.04	.308884	102.70	.691116	50
11	8.314904	101.22	9.999907	.04	8.315046	101.26	1.684954	49
12	.321027	99.82	.999905	.04	.321122	99.87	.678878	48
13	.327016	98.47	.999902	.04	.327114	98.51	.672886	47
14	.332924	97.14	.999899	.05	.333025	97.19	.666975	46
15	.338753	95.86	.999897	.05	.338856	95.90	.661144	45
16	.344504	94.60	.999894	.05	.344610	94.65	.655390	44
17	.350181	93.38	.999891	.05	.350289	93.43	.649711	43
18	.355783	92.19	.999888	.05	.355895	92.24	.644105	42
19	.361315	91.03	.999885	.05	.361430	91.08	.638570	41
20	.366777	89.90	.999882	.05	.366895	89.95	.633105	40
21	8.372171	88.80	9.999879	.05	8.372292	88.85	1.627708	39
22	.377499	87.72	.999876	.05	.377622	87.77	.622378	38
23	.382762	86.67	.999873	.05	.382889	86.72	.617111	37
24	.387962	85.64	.999870	.05	.388092	85.70	.611908	36
25	.393101	84.64	.999867	.05	.393234	84.70	.606766	35
26	.398179	83 66	.999864	.05	.398315	83.71	.601685	34
27	.403199	82.71	.999861	05	.403338	82.76	.596662	33
28	.408161	81.77	.999858	.05	.408304	81.82	.591696	32
29	.413068	80.86	.999854	.05	.413213	80.91	.586787	31
30	.417919	79.96	.999851	.06	.418068	80.02	.581932	30
31	8.422717	79.09	9.999848	.06	8.422869	79.14	1.577131	29
32	.427462	78.23	.999844	.06	.427618	78.30	.572382	28
33	.432156	77.40	.999841	.06	432315	77.45	.567685	27
34	.436800	76.57	.999838	.06	.436962	76.63	.563038	26
35	.441394	75.77	.999834	.06	.441560	75.83	.558440	25
36	.445941	74.99	.999831	.06	.446110	75.05	.553890	24
37	.450440	74.22	.999827	.06	.450613	74.28	.549387	23
38	.454893	73.46	.999823	.06	.455070	73.52	.544930	22
39	.459301	72.73	.999820	.06	.459481	72.79	.540519	21
40	.463665	72.00	.999816	.06	.463849	72.06	.536151	20
41	8.467985	71.29	9.999812	.06	8.468172	71.35	1.531828	19
42	.472263	70.60	.999809	.06	.472454	70.66	.527546	18
43	.476498	69.91	.999805	.06	.476693	69.98	.523307	17
44	.480693	69.24	.999801	.06	.480892	69.31	.519108	16
45	.484848	68.59	.999797	.07	.485050	68 65	.514950	15
46	.488963	67 94	.999793	.07	.489170	68.01	.510830	14
47	.493040	67.31	.999790	.07	.493250	67.38	.506750	13
48	.497078	66.69	.999786	.07	.497293	66.76	.502707	12
49	.501080	66.08	.999782	.07	.501298	66.15	.498702	11
50	.505045	65.48	.999778	.07	.505267	65.55	.494733	10
51	8.508974	64.89	9.999774	.07	8.509200	64.96	1.490800	9
52	.512867	64.31	.999769	.07	.513098	64.39	.486902	8
53	.516726	63.75	.999765	.07	.516961	63.82	.483039	7
54	.520551	63.19	.999761	.07	.520790	63.26	.479210	6
55	.524343	62.64	.999757	.07	.524586	62.72	.475414	5
56	.528102	62.11	.999753	.07	.528349	62.18	.471651	4
57	.531828	61.58	.999748	.07	.532080	61.65	.467920	3
58	.535523	61.06	.999744	.07	.535779	61.13	.464221	2
59	.539186	60.55	.999740	.07	.539447	60.62	.460553	1
60	.542819		.999735		.543084		.456916	0
	Cosine.	D	Sine.	D.	Cotang.	D.	Tang.	M.

2°

M	Sine.	D	Cosine.	D.	Tang.	D.	Cotang.	
0	8.542819		9.999735		8.543084		1.456916	60
1	.546422	60.04	.999731	.07	.546691	60.12	.453309	59
2	.549995	59.55	.999726	.07	.550268	59.62	.449732	58
3	.553539	59.06	.999722	.07	.553817	59.14	.446183	57
4	.557054	58.58	.999717	.08	.557336	58.66	.442664	56
5	.560540	58.11	.999713	.08	.560828	58.19	.439172	55
6	.563999	57.65	.999708	.08	.564291	57.73	.435709	54
7	.567431	57.19	.999704	.08	.567727	57.27	.432273	53
8	.570836	56.74	.999699	.08	.571137	56.82	.428863	52
9	.574214	56.30	.999694	.08	.574520	56.38	.425480	51
10	.577566	55 87	.999689	.08	.577877	55.95	.422123	50
11	8.580892	55.44	9.999685	.08	8.581208	55.52	1.418792	49
12	.584193	55.02	.999680	.08	.584514	55.10	.415486	48
13	.587469	54.60	.999675	.08	.587795	54.68	.412205	47
14	.590721	54.19	.999670	.08	.591051	54.27	.408949	46
15	.593948	53.79	.999665	.08	.594283	53.87	.405717	45
16	.597152	53.39	.999660	.08	.597492	53.47	.402508	44
17	.600332	53.00	.999655	.08	.600677	53.08	.399323	43
18	.603489	52.61	.999650	.08	.603839	52.70	.396161	42
19	.606623	52.23	.999645	.08	.606978	52.32	.393022	41
20	.609734	51.86	.999640	.09	.610094	51.94	.389906	40
21	8.612823	51.49	9.999635	.09	8.613189	51.58	1.386811	39
22	.615891	51.12	.999629	.09	.616262	51.21	.383738	38
23	.618937	50.76	.999624	.09	.619313	50.85	.380687	37
24	.621962	50.41	.999619	.09	.622343	50.50	.377657	36
25	.624965	50.06	.999614	.09	.625352	50.15	.374648	35
26	.627948	49.72	.999608	.09	.628340	49.81	.371660	34
27	.630911	49.38	.999603	.09	.631308	49.47	.368692	33
28	.633854	49 04	.999597	.09	.634256	49.13	.365744	32
29	.636776	48.71	.999592	.09	.637184	48.80	.362816	31
30	.639680	48.39	.999586	.09	.640093	48.48	.359907	30
31	8.642563	48.06	9.999581	.09	8 642982	48.16	1.357018	29
32	.645428	47.75	.999575	.09	.645853	47.84	.354147	28
33	.648274	47.43	.999570	.09	.648704	47.53	.351296	27
34	.651102	47.12	.999564	.09	.651537	47.22	.348463	26
35	.653911	46.82	.999558	.10	.654352	46.91	.345648	25
36	.656702	46.52	.999553	.10	·657149	46.61	.342851	24
37	.659475	46.22	.999547	.10	.659928	46.31	.340072	23
38	.662230	45.92	.999541	.10	.662689	46.02	.337311	22
39	.664968	45.63	.099535	.10	.665433	45.73	.334567	21
40	.667689	45.35	.999529	.10	.668160	45.44	.331840	20
41	8.670393	45.06	9.999524	.10	8.670870	45.16	1 329130	19
42	.673080	44.79	.999518	.10	·673563	44.88	.326437	18
43	.675751	44.51	.999512	.10	.676239	44.61	.323761	17
44	.678405	44.24	.999506	.10	.678900	44.34	.321100	16
45	.681043	43.97	.999500	.10	.681544	44.07	.318456	15
46	.683665	43.70	.999493	.10	.684172	43.80	.315828	14
47	.686272	43.44	.999487	.10	.686784	43.54	.313216	13
48	.688863	43.18	.999481	.10	.689381	43.28	.310619	12
49	.691438	42.92	.999475	.10	.691963	43.03	.308037	11
50	.693998	42.67	.999469	.10	.694529	42.77	.305471	10
51	8.696543	42.42	9.999463	.10	8 697081	42.52	1.302919	9
52	.699073	42 17	.999456	.11	.699617	42.28	.300383	8
53	.701589	41.92	.999450	.11	.702139	42.03	.297861	7
54	.704090	41.68	.999443	.11	.704646	41.79	.295354	6
55	.706577	41.44	.999437	.11	.707140	41.55	.292860	5
56	.709049	41.21	.999431	.11	.709618	41.32	.290382	4
57	.711507	40.97	.999424	.11	.712083	41.08	.287917	3
58	.713952	40.74	.999418	.11	.714534	40.85	.285465	2
59	.716383	40.51	.999411	.11	.716972	40.62	.283028	1
60	.718800	40.29	.999404	.11	719396	40.40	.280604	0
	Cosine.	D.	Sine.	D.	Cotang.	D.	Tang.	M.

87°

3°

M.	Sine.	D.	Cosine.	D.	Tang.	D.	Cotang.	
0	8.718800	40.06	9.999404	.11	8.719396	40.17	1.280604	60
1	.721204	39.84	.999398	.11	.721806	39.95	.278194	59
2	.723595	39.62	.999391	.11	.724204	39.74	.275796	58
3	.725972	39.41	.999384	.11	.726588	39.52	.273412	57
4	.728337	39.19	.999378	.11	.728959	39.30	.271041	56
5	.730688	38.98	.999371	.11	.731317	39.09	.268683	55
6	.733027	38.77	.999364	.12	.733663	38.89	.266337	54
7	.735354	38.57	.999357	.12	.735996	38.68	.264004	53
8	.737667	38.36	.999350	.12	.738317	38.48	.261683	52
9	.739969	38.16	.999343	.12	.740626	38.27	.259374	51
10	.742259	37.96	.999336	.12	.742922	38.07	.257078	50
11	8.744536	37.76	9.999329	.12	8.745207	37.87	1.254793	49
12	.746802	37.56	.999322	.12	.747479	37.68	.252521	48
13	.749055	37.37	.999315	.12	.749740	37.49	.250260	47
14	.751297	37.17	.999308	.12	.751989	37.29	.248011	46
15	.753528	36.98	.999301	.12	.754227	37.10	.245773	45
16	.755747	36.79	.999294	.12	.756453	36.92	.243547	44
17	.757955	36.61	.999286	.12	.758668	36.73	.241332	43
18	.760151	36.42	.999279	.12	.760872	36.55	.239128	42
19	.762337	36.24	.999272	.12	.763065	36.36	.236935	41
20	.764511	36.06	.999265	.12	.765246	36.18	.234754	40
21	8.766675	35.88	9.999257	.12	8.767417	36.00	1.232583	39
22	.768828	35.70	.999250	.13	.769578	35.83	.230422	38
23	.770970	35.53	.999242	.13	.771727	35.65	.228273	37
24	.773101	35.35	.999235	.13	.773866	35.48	.226134	36
25	.775223	35.18	.999227	.13	.775995	35.31	.224005	35
26	.777333	35.01	.999220	.13	.778114	35.14	.221886	34
27	.779434	34.84	.999212	.13	.780222	34.97	.219778	33
28	.781524	34.67	.999205	.13	.782320	34.80	.217680	32
29	.783605	34.51	.999197	.13	.784408	34.64	.215592	31
30	.785675	34.34	.999189	.13	.786486	34.47	.213514	30
31	8.787736	34.18	9.999181	.13	8.788554	34.31	1.211446	29
32	.789787	34.02	.999174	.13	.790613	34.14	.209387	28
33	.791828	33.86	.999166	.13	792662	33.99	.207338	27
34	.793859	33.70	.999158	.13	.794701	33.83	.205299	26
35	.795881	33.54	.999150	.13	.796731	33.68	.203269	25
36	.797894	33.39	.999142	.13	.798752	33.52	.201248	24
37	.799897	33.23	.999134	.13	.800763	33.37	.199237	23
38	.801892	33.08	.999126	.13	.802765	33.22	.197235	22
39	.803876	32.93	.999118	.13	.804758	33.07	.195242	21
40	.805852	32.78	.999110	.13	.806742	32.92	.193258	20
41	8.807819	32.63	9.999102	.13	8.808717	32.77	1.191288	19
42	.809777	32.49	.999094	.14	.810683	32.62	.189317	18
43	.811726	32.34	.099086	.14	.812641	32.48	.187359	17
44	.813667	32.19	.999077	.14	.814589	32.33	.185411	16
45	.815599	32.05	.999069	.14	.816529	32.19	.183471	15
46	.817522	31.91	.999061	.14	.818461	32.05	.181539	14
47	.819436	31.77	.999053	.14	.820384	31.91	.179616	13
48	.821343	31.63	.999044	.14	.822298	31.77	.177702	12
49	.823240	31.49	.999036	.14	.824205	31.63	.175795	11
50	825130	31.35	.999027	.14	.826103	31.50	.173897	10
51	8.827011	31.22	9.999019	.14	8.827992	31.36	1.172008	9
52	.828884	31.08	.999010	.14	.829874	31.23	.170126	8
53	.830749	30.95	.999002	.14	.831748	31.10	.168252	7
54	.832607	30.82	.998993	.14	.883613	30.96	.166387	6
55	.834456	30.69	.998984	.14	.835471	30.83	.164529	5
56	.836297	30.56	.998976	.14	.887321	30.70	.162679	4
57	838130	30.43	.998967	.15	.839163	30.57	.160837	3
58	.839956	30.30	.998958	.15	.840998	30.45	.159002	2
59	.841774	30.17	.998950	.15	.842825	30.32	.157175	1
60	.843585		.998941		.844644		.155356	0
	Cosine	D.	Sine.	D.	Cotang.	D.	Tang.	M

86°

4°

M	Sine.	D	Cosine.	D.	Tang.	D.	Cotang.	
0	8.843585	30.05	9.998941	.15	8.844644	30.19	1.155356	60
1	.845387	29.92	.998932	.15	.846455	30.07	.153545	59
2	.847183	29.80	.998923	.15	.848260	29.95	.151740	58
3	.848971	29.67	.998914	.15	.850057	29.82	.149943	57
4	.850751	29.55	.998905	.15	.851846	29.70	.148154	56
5	.852525	29.43	.998896	.15	.853628	29.58	.146372	55
6	.854291	29.31	.998887	.15	.855403	29.46	.144597	54
7	.856049	29.19	.998878	.15	.857171	29.35	.142829	53
8	.857801	29.07	.998869	.15	.858932	29.23	.141068	52
9	.859546	28.96	.998860	.15	.860686	29.11	.139314	51
10	.861283	28.84	.998851	.15	.862433	29.00	.137567	50
11	8.863014	28.73	9.998841	.15	8.864173	28.88	1.135827	49
12	.864738	28.61	.998832	.15	.865906	28.77	.134094	48
13	.866455	28.50	.998823	.16	.867632	28.66	.132368	47
14	.868165	28.39	.998813	.16	.869351	28.54	.130649	46
15	.869868	28.28	.998804	.16	.871064	28.43	.128936	45
16	.871565	28.17	.998795	.16	.872770	28.32	.127230	44
17	.873255	28.06	.998785	.16	.874469	28.21	.125531	43
18	.874938	27.95	.998776	.16	.876162	28.11	.123838	42
19	.376615	27.83	.998766	.16	.877849	28.00	.122151	41
20	.878285	27.73	998757	.16	.879529	27.89	.120471	40
21	8.879949	27.63	9.998747	.16	8.881202	27.79	1.118798	39
22	.881607	27.52	.998738	.16	.882869	27.68	.117131	38
23	.883258	27.42	.998728	.16	.884530	27.58	.115470	37
24	.884903	27.31	.998718	.16	.886185	27.47	.113815	36
25	.886542	27.21	.998708	.16	.887833	27.37	.112167	35
26	.888174	27.11	.998699	.16	.889476	27.27	.110524	34
27	.889801	27.00	.998689	.16	.891112	27.17	.108888	33
28	.891421	26.90	.998679	.16	.892742	27.07	.107258	32
29	.893035	26.80	.998669	.17	.894366	26.97	.105634	31
30	.894643	26.70	.998659	.17	.895984	26.87	.104016	30
31	8.896246	26.60	9.998649	.17	8.897596	26.77	1.102404	29
32	.897842	26.51	.998639	.17	.899203	26.67	.100797	28
33	.899432	26.41	.998629	.17	.900803	26.58	.099197	27
34	.901017	26.31	.998619	.17	.902398	26.48	.097602	26
35	.902596	26.22	.998609	.17	.903987	26.38	.096013	25
36	.904169	26.12	.998599	.17	.905570	26.29	.094430	24
37	.905736	26.03	.998589	.17	.907147	26.20	.092853	23
38	.907297	25.93	.998578	.17	.908719	26.10	.091281	22
39	.908853	25.84	.998568	.17	.910285	26.01	.089715	21
40	.910404	25.75	.998558	.17	.911846	25.92	.088154	20
41	8.911949	25.66	9.998548	.17	8.913401	25.83	1.086599	19
42	.913488	25.56	.998537	.17	.914951	25.74	.085049	18
43	.915022	25.47	.998527	.17	.916495	25.65	.083505	17
44	.916550	25.38	.998516	.18	.918034	25.56	.081966	16
45	.918073	25.29	.998506	.18	.919568	25.47	.080432	15
46	.919591	25.20	.998495	.18	.921096	25.38	.078904	14
47	.921103	25.12	.998485	.18	.922619	25.30	.077381	13
48	.922610	25.03	.998474	.18	.924136	25.21	.075864	12
49	.924112	24.94	.998464	.18	.925649	25.12	.074351	11
50	.925609	24.86	998453	.18	.927156	25.03	072844	10
51	8.927100	24.77	9.998442	.18	8.928658	24.95	1.071342	9
52	.928587	24.69	.998431	.18	.930155	24.86	.069845	8
53	.930068	24.60	.998421	.18	.931647	24.78	.068353	7
54	.931544	24.52	.998410	.18	.933134	24.70	.066866	6
55	.933015	24.43	.998399	.18	.934616	24.61	.065384	5
56	.934481	24.35	.998388	.18	.936093	24.53	.063907	4
57	.935942	24.27	.998377	.18	.937565	24.45	.062435	3
58	.937398	24.19	.998366	.18	.939032	24.37	.060968	2
59	.938850	24.11	.998355	.18	.940494	24.29	.059506	1
60	.940296		.998344		.941952		.058048	0
	Cosine.	D.	Sine.	D.	Cotang.	D.	Tang.	M.

85°

5°

M.	Sine.	D.	Cosine.	D.	Tang.	D.	Cotang.	
0	8.940296	24.03	9.998344	.19	8.941952	24.21	1.058048	60
1	.941738	23.94	.998333	.19	.943404	24.13	.056596	59
2	.943174	23.87	.998322	.19	.944852	24.05	.055148	58
3	.944606	23.79	.998311	.19	.946295	23.97	.053705	57
4	.946034	23.71	.998300	.19	.947734	23.90	.052266	56
5	.947456	23.63	.998289	.19	.949168	23.82	.050832	55
6	.948874	23.55	.998277	.19	.950597	23.74	.049403	54
7	.950287	23.48	.998266	.19	.952021	23.66	.047979	53
8	.951696	23.40	.998255	.19	.953441	23.58	.046559	52
9	.953100	23.32	.998243	.19	.954856	23.51	.045144	51
10	.954499	23.25	.998232	.19	.956267	23.44	.043733	50
11	8.955894	23.17	9.998220	.19	8.957674	23.37	1.042326	49
12	.957284	23.10	.998209	.19	.959075	23.29	.040925	48
13	.958670	23.02	.998197	.19	.960473	23.22	.039527	47
14	.960052	22.95	.998186	.19	.961866	23.14	.038134	46
15	.961429	22.88	.998174	.19	.963255	23.07	.036745	45
16	.962801	22.80	.998163	.19	.964639	23.00	.035361	44
17	.964170	22.73	.998151	.19	.966019	22.93	.033981	43
18	.965534	22.66	.998139	.20	.967394	22.86	.032606	42
19	.966893	22.59	.998128	.20	.968766	22.79	.031234	41
20	.968249	22.52	.998116	.20	.970133	22.71	.029867	40
21	8.969600	22.44	9.998104	.20	8.971496	22.65	1.028504	39
22	.970947	22.38	.998092	.20	.972855	22.57	.027145	38
23	.972289	22.31	.998080	.20	.974209	22.51	.025791	37
24	.973628	22.24	.998068	.20	.975560	22.44	.024440	36
25	.974962	22.17	.998056	.20	.976906	22.37	.023094	35
26	.976293	22.10	.998044	.20	.978248	22.30	.021752	34
27	.977619	22.03	.998032	.20	.979586	22.23	.020414	33
28	.978941	21.97	.998020	.20	.980921	22.17	.019079	32
29	.980259	21.90	.998008	.20	.982251	22.10	.017749	31
30	.981573	21.83	.997996	.20	.983577	22.04	.016423	30
31	8.982883	21.77	9.997985	.20	8.984899	21.97	1.015101	29
32	.984189	21.70	.997972	.20	.986217	21.91	.013783	28
33	.985491	21.63	.997959	.20	987532	21.84	.012468	27
34	.986789	21.57	.997947	.20	.988842	21.78	.011158	26
35	.988083	21.50	.997935	.21	.990149	21.71	.009851	25
36	.989374	21.44	.997922	.21	.991451	21.65	.008549	24
37	.990660	21.38	.997910	.21	.992750	21.58	.007250	23
38	.991943	21.31	.997897	.21	.994045	21.52	.005955	22
39	.993222	21.25	.997885	.21	.995337	21.46	.004663	21
40	.994497	21.19	.997872	.21	.996624	21.40	.003376	20
41	8.995768	21.12	9.997860	.21	8.997908	21.34	1.002092	19
42	.997036	21.06	.997847	.21	.999188	21.27	.000812	18
43	.998299	21.00	.997835	.21	9.000465	21.21	0.999535	17
44	.999560	20.94	.997822	.21	.001738	21.15	.998262	16
45	9.000816	20.87	.997809	.21	.003007	21.09	.996993	15
46	.002069	20.82	.997797	.21	.004272	21.03	.995728	14
47	.003318	20.76	.997784	.21	.005534	20.97	.994466	13
48	.004563	20.70	.997771	.21	.006792	20.91	.993208	12
49	.005805	20.64	.997758	.21	.008047	20.85	.991953	11
50	.007044	20.58	.997745	.21	.009298	20.80	.990702	10
51	9.008278	20.52	9.997732	.21	9.010546	20.74	0.989454	9
52	.009510	20.46	.997719	.21	.011790	20.68	.988210	8
53	.010737	20.40	.997706	.21	.013031	20.62	.986969	7
54	.011962	20.34	.997693	.22	.014268	20.56	.985732	6
55	.013182	20.29	.997680	.22	.015502	20.51	.984498	5
56	.014400	20.23	.997667	.22	.016732	20.45	.983268	4
57	.015613	20.17	.997654	.22	.017959	20.39	.982041	3
58	.016824	20.12	.997641	.22	.019183	20.33	.980817	2
59	.018031	20.06	.997628	.22	.020403	20.28	.979597	1
60	.019235		.997614		.021620		.978380	0
	Cosine.	D.	Sine.	D.	Cotang.	D.	Tang.	M.

84°

6°

M	Sine.	D.	Cosine.	D.	Tang.	D.	Cotang.	
0	9.019235	20.00	9.997614	.22	9.021620	20.23	0.978380	60
1	.020435	19.95	.997601	.22	.022834	20.17	.977166	59
2	.021632	19.89	.997588	.22	.024044	20.11	.975956	58
3	.022825	19.84	.997574	.22	.025251	20.06	.974749	57
4	.024016	19.78	.997561	.22	.026455	20.00	.973545	56
5	.025203	19.73	.997547	.22	.027655	19.95	.972345	55
6	.026386	19.67	.997534	.23	.028852	19.90	.971148	54
7	.027567	19.62	.997520	.23	.030046	19.85	.969954	53
8	.028744	19.57	.997507	.23	.031237	19.79	.968763	52
9	.029918	19.51	.997493	.23	.032425	19.74	.967575	51
10	.031089	19.47	.997480	.23	.033609	19.69	.966391	50
11	9.032257	19.41	9.997466	.23	9.034791	19.64	0.965209	49
12	.033421	19.36	.997452	.23	.035969	19.58	.964031	48
13	.034582	19.30	.997439	.23	.037144	19.53	.962856	47
14	.035741	19.25	.997425	.23	.038316	19.48	.961684	46
15	.036896	19.20	.997411	.23	.039485	19.43	.960515	45
16	.038048	19.15	.997397	.23	.040651	19.38	.959349	44
17	.039197	19.10	.997383	.23	.041813	19.33	.958187	43
18	.040342	19.05	.997369	.23	.042973	19.28	.957027	42
19	.041485	18.99	.997355	.23	.044130	19.23	.955870	41
20	.042625	18.94	.997341	.23	.045284	19.18	.954716	40
21	9.043762	18.89	9.997327	.24	9.046434	19.13	0.953566	39
22	.044895	18.84	.997313	.24	.047582	19.08	.952418	38
23	.046026	18.79	.997299	.24	.048727	19.03	.951273	37
24	.047154	18.75	.997285	.24	.049869	18.98	.950131	36
25	.048279	18.70	.997271	.24	.051008	18.93	.948992	35
26	.049400	18.65	.997257	.24	.052144	18.89	.947856	34
27	.050519	18.60	.997242	.24	.053277	18.84	.946723	33
28	.051635	18.55	.997228	.24	.054407	18.79	.945593	32
29	.052749	18.50	.997214	.24	.055535	18.74	.944465	31
30	.053859	18.45	.997199	.24	.056659	18.70	.943341	30
31	9.054966	18.41	9.997185	.24	9.057781	18.65	0.942219	29
32	.056071	18.36	.997170	.24	.058900	18.60	.941100	28
33	.057172	18.31	.997156	.24	.060016	18.55	.939984	27
34	.058271	18.27	.997141	.24	.061130	18.51	.938870	26
35	.059367	18.22	.997127	.24	.062240	18.46	.937760	25
36	.060460	18.17	.997112	.24	.063348	18.42	.936652	24
37	.061551	18.13	.997098	.24	.064453	18.37	.935547	23
38	.062639	18.08	.997083	.25	.065556	18.33	.934444	22
39	.063724	18.04	.997068	.25	.066655	18.28	.933345	21
40	.064806	17.99	.997053	.25	.067752	18.24	.932248	20
41	9.065885	17.94	9.997039	.25	9.068846	18.19	0.931154	19
42	.066962	17.90	.997024	.25	.069938	18.15	.930062	18
43	.068036	17.86	.997009	.25	.071027	18.10	.928973	17
44	.069107	17.81	.996994	.25	.072113	18.06	.927887	16
45	.070176	17.77	.996979	.25	.073197	18.02	.926803	15
46	.071242	17.72	.996964	.25	.074278	17.97	.925722	14
47	.072306	17.68	.996949	.25	.075356	17.93	.924644	13
48	.073366	17.63	.996934	.25	.076432	17.89	.923568	12
49	.074424	17.59	.996919	.25	.077505	17.84	.922495	11
50	.075480	17.55	.996904	.25	.078576	17.80	.921424	10
51	9.076533	17.50	9.996889	.25	9.079644	17.76	0.920356	9
52	.077583	17.46	.996874	.25	.080710	17.72	.919290	8
53	.078631	17.42	.996858	.25	.081773	17.67	.918227	7
54	.079676	17.38	.996843	.25	.082833	17.63	.917167	6
55	.080719	17.33	.996828	.25	.083891	17.59	.916109	5
56	.081759	17.29	.996812	.25	.084947	17.55	.915053	4
57	.082797	17.25	.996797	.26	.086000	17.51	.914000	3
58	.083832	17.21	.996782	.26	.087050	17.47	.912950	2
59	.084864	17.17	.996766	.26	.088098	17.43	.911902	1
60	.085894		.996751		.089144		.910856	0
	Cosine.	D.	Sine.	D.	Cotang.	D.	Tang.	M.

83°

7°

M.	Sine.	D.	Cosine.	D.	Tang.	D.	Cotang.	
0	9.085894	17.13	9.996751	.26	9.089144	17.38	0.910856	60
1	.086922	17.09	.996735	.26	.090187	17.34	.909813	59
2	.087947	17.04	.996720	.26	.091228	17.30	.908772	58
3	.088970	17.00	.996704	.26	.092266	17.27	.907734	57
4	.089990	16.96	.996688	.26	.093302	17.22	.906698	56
5	.091008	16.92	.996673	.26	.094336	17.19	.905664	55
6	.092024	16.88	.996657	26	.095367	17.15	.904633	54
7	.093037	16.84	.996641	.26	.096395	17.11	.903605	53
8	.094047	16.80	.996625	.26	.097422	17.07	.902578	52
9	.095056	16.76	.996610	.26	.098446	17.03	.901554	51
10	.096062	16.72	.996594	.26	.099468	16.99	.900532	50
11	9.097065	16.68	9.996578	.27	9.100487	16.95	0.899513	49
12	.098066	16.65	.996562	.27	.101504	16.91	.898496	48
13	.099065	16.61	.996546	.27	.102519	16.87	.897481	47
14	.100062	16.57	.996530	.27	.103532	16.84	.896468	46
15	.101056	16.53	.996514	.27	.104542	16.80	.895458	45
16	.102048	16.49	.996498	.27	.105550	16.76	.894450	44
17	.103037	16.45	.996482	.27	.106556	16.72	.893444	43
18	.104025	16.41	.996465	.27	.107559	16.69	.892441	42
19	.105010	16.38	.996449	.27	.108560	16.65	.891440	41
20	.105992	16.34	.996433	.27	.109559	16.61	.890441	40
21	9.106973	16.30	9.996417	.27	9.110556	16.58	0.889444	39
22	.107951	16.27	.996400	.27	.111551	16.54	.888449	38
23	.108927	16.23	.996384	.27	.112543	16.50	.887457	37
24	.109901	16.19	.996368	.27	.113533	16.46	.886467	36
25	.110873	16.16	.996351	.27	.114521	16.43	.885479	35
26	.111842	16.12	.996335	.27	.115507	16.39	.884493	34
27	.112809	16.08	.996318	.27	.116491	16.36	.883509	33
28	.113774	16.05	.996302	.28	.117472	16.32	.882528	32
29	.114737	16.01	.996285	.28	.118452	16.29	.881548	31
30	.115698	15.97	.996269	.28	.119429	16.25	.880571	30
31	9.116656	15.94	9.996252	.28	9.120404	16.22	0.879596	29
32	.117613	15.90	.996235	.28	.121377	16.18	.878623	28
33	.118567	15.87	.996219	.28	122348	16.15	.877652	27
34	.119519	15.83	.996202	.28	.123317	16.11	.876683	26
35	.120469	15.80	.996185	.28	.124284	16.07	.875716	25
36	.121417	15.76	.996168	.28	.125249	16.04	.874751	24
37	.122362	15.73	.996151	.28	.126211	16.01	.873789	23
38	.123306	15.69	.996134	.28	.127172	15.97	.872828	22
39	.124248	15.66	.996117	.28	.128130	15.94	.871870	21
40	.125187	15.62	.996100	.28	.129087	15.91	.870913	20
41	9.126125	15.59	9.996083	.29	9.130041	15.87	0.869959	19
42	.127060	15.56	.996066	.29	.130994	15.84	.869006	18
43	.127993	15.52	.996049	.29	.131944	15.81	.868056	17
44	.128925	15.49	.996032	.29	.132893	15.77	.867107	16
45	.129854	15.45	.996015	.29	.133839	15.74	.866161	15
46	.130781	15.42	.995998	.29	.134784	15.71	.865216	14
47	.131706	15.39	.995980	.29	.135726	15.67	.864274	13
48	.132630	15.35	.995963	.29	.136667	15.64	.863333	12
49	.133551	15.32	.995946	.29	.137605	15.61	.862395	11
50	.134470	15.29	.995928	.29	.138542	15.58	.861458	10
51	9.135387	15.25	9.995911	.29	9.139476	15.55	0.860524	9
52	.136303	15.22	.995894	.29	.140409	15.51	.859591	8
53	.137216	15.19	.995876	.29	.141340	15.48	.858660	7
54	.138128	15.16	.995859	.29	.142269	15.45	.857731	6
55	.139037	15.12	.995841	.29	.143196	15.42	.856804	5
56	.139944	15.09	.995823	.29	.144121	15.39	.855879	4
57	.140850	15.06	.995806	.29	.145044	15.35	.854956	3
58	.141754	15.03	.995788	.29	.145966	15.32	.854034	2
59	.142655	15.00	.995771	.29	.146885	15.29	.853115	1
60	.143555		.995753		.147803		.852197	0
	Cosine	D.	Sine.	D.	Cotang.	D.	Tang.	M

82°

8°

M	Sine.	D	Cosine.	D.	Tang.	D.	Cotang.	
0	9.143555	14.96	9.995753	.30	9.147803	15.26	0.852197	60
1	.144453	14.93	.995735	.30	.148718	15.23	.851282	59
2	.145349	14.90	.995717	.30	.149632	15.20	.850368	58
3	.146243	14.87	.995699	.30	.150544	15.17	.849456	57
4	.147136	14.84	.995681	.30	.151454	15.14	.848546	56
5	.148026	14.81	.995664	.30	.152363	15.11	.847637	55
6	.148915	14.78	.995646	.30	.153269	15.08	.846731	54
7	.149802	14.75	.995628	.30	.154174	15.05	.845826	53
8	.150686	14.72	.995610	.30	.155077	15.02	.844923	52
9	.151569	14.69	.995591	.30	.155978	14.99	.844022	51
10	.152451	14.66	.995573	.30	.156877	14.96	.843123	50
11	9.153330	14.63	9.995555	.30	9.157775	14.93	0.842225	49
12	.154208	14.60	.995537	.30	.158671	14.90	.841329	48
13	.155083	14.57	.995519	.30	.159565	14.87	.840435	47
14	.155957	14.54	.995501	.31	.160457	14.84	.839543	46
15	.156830	14.51	.995482	.31	.161347	14.81	.838653	45
16	.157700	14.48	.995464	.31	.162236	14.79	.837764	44
17	.158569	14.45	.995446	.31	.163123	14.76	.836877	43
18	.159435	14.42	.995427	.31	.164008	14.73	.835992	42
19	.160301	14.39	.995409	.31	.164892	14.70	.835108	41
20	.161164	14.36	.995390	.31	.165774	14.67	.834226	40
21	9.162025	14.33	9.995372	.31	9.166654	14.64	0.833346	39
22	.162885	14.30	.995353	.31	.167532	14.61	.832468	38
23	.163743	14.27	.995334	.31	.168409	14.58	.831591	37
24	.164600	14.24	.995316	.31	.169284	14.55	.830716	36
25	.165454	14.22	.995297	.31	.170157	14.53	.829843	35
26	.166307	14.19	.995278	.31	.171029	14.50	.828971	34
27	.167159	14.16	.995260	.31	.171899	14.47	.828101	33
28	.168008	14.13	.995241	.32	.172767	14.44	.827233	32
29	.168856	14.10	.995222	.32	.173634	14.42	.826366	31
30	.169702	14.07	.995203	.32	.174499	14.39	.825501	30
31	9.170547	14.05	9.995184	.32	9.175362	14.36	0.824638	29
32	.171389	14.02	.995165	.32	.176224	14.33	.823776	28
33	.172230	13.99	.995146	.32	.177084	14.31	.822916	27
34	.173070	13.96	.995127	.32	.177942	14.28	.822058	26
35	.173908	13.94	.995108	.32	.178799	14.25	.821201	25
36	.174744	13.91	.995089	.32	.179655	14.23	.820345	24
37	.175578	13.88	.995070	.32	.180508	14.20	.819492	23
38	.176411	13.86	.995051	.32	.181360	14.17	.818640	22
39	.177242	13.83	.995032	.32	.182211	14.15	.817789	21
40	.178072	13.80	.995013	.32	.183059	14.12	.816941	20
41	9.178900	13.77	9.994993	.32	9.183907	14.09	0.816093	19
42	.179726	13.74	.994974	.32	.184752	14.07	.815248	18
43	.180551	13.72	.994955	.32	.185597	14.04	.814403	17
44	.181374	13.69	.994935	.32	.186439	14.02	.813561	16
45	.182196	13.66	.994916	.33	.187280	13.99	.812720	15
46	.183016	13.64	.994896	.33	.188120	13.96	.811880	14
47	.183834	13.61	.994877	.33	.188958	13.93	.811042	13
48	.184651	13.59	.994857	.33	.189794	13.91	.810206	12
49	.185466	13.56	.994838	.33	.190629	13.89	.809371	11
50	.186280	13.53	.994818	.33	.191462	13.86	.808538	10
51	9.187092	13.51	9.994798	.33	9.192294	13.84	0.807706	9
52	.187903	13.48	.994779	.33	.193124	13.81	.806876	8
53	.188712	13.46	.994759	.33	.193953	13.79	.806047	7
54	.189519	13.43	.994739	.33	.194780	13.76	.805220	6
55	.190325	13.41	.994719	.33	.195606	13.74	.804394	5
56	.191130	13.38	.994700	.33	.196430	13.71	.803570	4
57	.191933	13.36	.994680	.33	.197253	13.69	.802747	3
58	.192734	13.33	.994660	.33	.198074	13.66	.801926	2
59	.193534	13.30	.994640	.33	.198894	13.64	.801106	1
60	.194332		.994620		.199713		.800287	0
	Cosine.	D.	Sine.	D.	Cotang.	D.	Tang.	M.

81°

9°

M.	Sine.	D.	Cosine.	D.	Tang.	D.	Cotang.	
0	9.194332	13.28	9.994620	.33	9.199713	13.61	0.800287	60
1	.195129	13.26	.994600	.33	.200529	13.59	.799471	59
2	.195925	13.23	.994580	.33	.201345	13.56	.798655	58
3	.196719	13.21	.994560	.34	.202159	13.54	.797841	57
4	.197511	13.18	.994540	.34	.202971	13.52	.797029	56
5	.198302	13.16	.994519	.34	.203782	13.49	.796218	55
6	.199091	13.13	.994499	.34	.204592	13.47	.795408	54
7	.199879	13.11	.994479	.34	.205400	13.45	.794600	53
8	.200666	13.08	.994459	.34	.206207	13.42	.793793	52
9	.201451	13.06	.994438	.34	.207013	13.40	.792987	51
10	.202234	13.04	.994418	.34	.207817	13.38	.792183	50
11	9.203017	13.01	9.994397	.34	9.208619	13.35	0.791381	49
12	.203797	12.99	.994377	.34	.209420	13.33	.790580	48
13	.204577	12.96	.994357	.34	.210220	13.31	.789780	47
14	.205354	12.94	.994336	.34	.211018	13.28	.788982	46
15	.206131	12.92	.994316	.34	.211815	13.26	.788185	45
16	.206906	12.89	.994295	.34	.212611	13.24	.787389	44
17	.207679	12.87	.994274	.35	.213405	13.21	.786595	43
18	.208452	12.85	.994254	.35	.214198	13.19	.785802	42
19	.209222	12.82	.994233	.35	.214989	13.17	.785011	41
20	.209992	12.80	.994212	.35	.215780	13.15	.784220	40
21	9.210760	12.78	9.994191	.35	9.216568	13.12	0.783432	39
22	.211526	12.75	.994171	.35	.217356	13.10	.782644	38
23	.212291	12.73	.994150	.35	.218142	13.08	.781858	37
24	.213055	12.71	.994129	.35	.218926	13.05	.781074	36
25	.213818	12.68	.994108	.35	.219710	13.03	.780290	35
26	.214579	12.66	.994087	.35	.220492	13.01	.779508	34
27	.215338	12.64	.994066	.35	.221272	12.99	.778728	33
28	.216097	12.61	.994045	.35	.222052	12.97	.777948	32
29	.216854	12.59	.994024	.35	.222830	12.94	.777170	31
30	.217609	12.57	.994003	.35	.223606	12.92	.776394	30
31	9.218363	12.55	9.993981	.35	9.224382	12.90	0.775618	29
32	.219116	12.53	.993960	.35	.225156	12.88	.774844	28
33	.219868	12.50	.993939	.35	225929	12.86	.774071	27
34	.220618	12.48	.993918	.35	.226700	12.84	.773300	26
35	.221367	12.46	.993896	.36	.227471	12.81	.772529	25
36	.222115	12.44	.993875	.36	.228239	12.79	.771761	24
37	.222861	12.42	.993854	.36	.229007	12.77	.770993	23
38	.223606	12.39	.993832	.36	.229773	12.75	.770227	22
39	.224349	12.37	.993811	.36	.230539	12.73	.769461	21
40	.225092	12.35	.993789	.36	.231302	12.71	.768698	20
41	9.225833	12.33	9.993768	.36	9.232065	12.69	0.767935	19
42	.226573	12.31	.993746	.36	.232826	12.67	.767174	18
43	.227311	12.28	.993725	.36	.233586	12.65	.766414	17
44	.228048	12.26	.993703	.36	.234345	12.62	.765655	16
45	.228784	12.24	.993681	.36	.235103	12.60	.764897	15
46	.229518	12.22	.993660	.36	.235859	12.58	.764141	14
47	.230252	12.20	.993638	.36	.236614	12.56	.763386	13
48	.230984	12.18	.993616	.36	.237368	13.54	.762632	12
49	.231714	12.16	.993594	.37	.238120	12.52	.761880	11
50	.232444	12.14	.993572	.37	.238872	12.50	.761128	10
51	9.233172	12.12	9.993550	.37	9.239622	12.48	0.760378	9
52	.233899	12.09	.993528	.37	.240371	12.46	.759629	8
53	.234625	12.07	.993506	.37	.241118	12.44	.758882	7
54	.235349	12.05	.993484	.37	.241865	12.42	.758135	6
55	.236073	12.03	.993462	.37	.242610	12.40	.757390	5
56	.236795	12.01	.993440	.37	.243354	12.38	.756646	4
57	.237515	11.99	.993418	.37	.244097	12.36	.755903	3
58	.238235	11.97	.993396	.37	.244839	12.34	.755161	2
59	.238953	11.95	.993374	.37	.245579	12.32	.754421	1
60	.239670		.993351		.246319		.753681	0
	Cosine	D.	Sine.	D.	Cotang.	D.	Tang.	M

80°

10°

M	Sine.	D.	Cosine.	D.	Tang.	D.	Cotang.	
0	9.239670	11.93	9.993351	.37	9.246319	12.30	0.753681	60
1	.240386	11.91	.993329	.37	.247057	12.28	.752943	59
2	.241101	11.89	.993307	.37	.247794	12.26	.752206	58
3	.241814	11.87	.993285	.37	.248530	12.24	.751470	57
4	.242526	11.85	.993262	.37	.249264	12.22	.750736	56
5	.243237	11.83	.993240	.37	.249998	12.20	.750002	55
6	.243947	11.81	.993217	.38	.250730	12.18	.749270	54
7	.244656	11.79	.993195	.38	.251461	12.17	.748539	53
8	.245363	11.77	.993172	.38	.252191	12.15	.747809	52
9	.246069	11.75	.993149	.38	.252920	12.13	.747080	51
10	.246775	11.73	.993127	.38	.253648	12.11	.746352	50
11	9.247478	11.71	9.993104	.38	9.254374	12.09	0.745626	49
12	.248181	11.69	.993081	.38	.255100	12.07	.744900	48
13	.248883	11.67	.993059	.38	.255824	12.05	.744176	47
14	.249583	11.65	.993036	.38	.256547	12.03	.743453	46
15	.250282	11.63	.993013	.38	.257269	12.01	.742731	45
16	.250980	11.61	.992990	.38	.257990	12.00	.742010	44
17	.251677	11.59	.992967	.38	.258710	11.98	.741290	43
18	.252373	11.58	.992944	.38	.259429	11.96	.740571	42
19	.253067	11.56	.992921	.38	.260146	11.94	.739854	41
20	.253761	11.54	.992898	.38	.260863	11.92	.739137	40
21	9.254453	11.52	9.992875	.38	9.261578	11.90	0.738422	39
22	.255144	11.50	.992852	.38	.262292	11.89	.737708	38
23	.255834	11.48	.992829	.39	.263005	11.87	.736995	37
24	.256523	11.46	.992806	.39	.263717	11.85	.736283	36
25	.257211	11.44	.992783	.39	.264428	11.83	.735572	35
26	.257898	11.42	.992759	.39	.265138	11.81	.734862	34
27	.258583	11.41	.992736	.39	.265847	11.79	.734153	33
28	.259268	11.39	.992713	.39	.266555	11.78	.733445	32
29	.259951	11.37	.992690	.39	.267261	11.76	.732739	31
30	.260633	11.35	.992666	.39	.267967	11.74	.732033	30
31	9.261314	11.33	9.992643	.39	9.268671	11.72	0.731329	29
32	.261994	11.31	.992619	.39	.269375	11.70	.730625	28
33	.262673	11.30	.992596	.39	.270077	11.69	.729923	27
34	.263351	11.28	.992572	.39	.270779	11.67	.729221	26
35	.264027	11.26	.992549	.39	.271479	11.65	.728521	25
36	.264703	11.24	.992525	.39	.272178	11.64	.727822	24
37	.265377	11.22	.992501	.39	.272876	11.62	.727124	23
38	.266051	11.20	.992478	.40	.273573	11.60	.726427	22
39	.266723	11.19	.992454	.40	.274269	11.58	.725731	21
40	.267395	11.17	.992430	.40	.274964	11.57	.725036	20
41	9.268065	11.15	9.992406	.40	9.275658	11.55	0.724342	19
42	.268734	11.13	.992382	.40	.276351	11.53	.723649	18
43	.269402	11.11	.992359	.40	.277043	11.51	.722957	17
44	.270069	11.10	.992335	.40	.277734	11.50	.722266	16
45	.270735	11.08	.992311	.40	.278434	11.48	.721576	15
46	.271400	11.06	.992287	.40	.279113	11.47	.720887	14
47	.272064	11.05	.992263	.40	.279801	11.45	.720199	13
48	.272726	11.03	.992239	.40	.280488	11.43	.719512	12
49	.273388	11.01	.992214	.40	.281174	11.41	.718826	11
50	.274049	10.99	.992190	.40	.281858	11.40	.718142	10
51	9.274708	10.98	9.992166	.40	9.282542	11.38	0.717458	9
52	.275367	10.96	.992142	.40	.283225	11.36	.716775	8
53	.276024	10.94	.992117	.41	.283907	11.35	.716093	7
54	.276681	10.92	.992093	.41	.284588	11.33	.715412	6
55	.277337	10.91	.992069	.41	.285268	11.31	.714732	5
56	.277991	10.89	.992044	.41	.285947	11.30	.714053	4
57	.278644	10.87	.992020	.41	.286624	11.28	.713376	3
58	.279297	10.86	.991996	.41	.287301	11.26	.712699	2
59	.279948	10.84	.991971	.41	.287977	11.25	.712023	1
60	.280599		.991947		.288652		.711348	0
	Cosine.	D.	Sine.	D.	Cotang.	D.	Tang.	M.

79°

11°

M.	Sine.	D.	Cosine.	D.	Tang.	D.	Cotang.	
0	9.280599	10.82	9.991947	.41	9.288652	11.23	0.711348	60
1	.281248	10.81	.991922	.41	.289326	11.22	.710674	59
2	.281897	10.79	.991897	.41	.289999	11.20	.710001	58
3	.282544	10.77	.991873	.41	.290671	11.18	.709329	57
4	.283190	10.76	.991848	.41	.291342	11.17	.708658	56
5	.283836	10.74	.991823	.41	.292013	11.15	.707987	55
6	.284480	10.72	.991799	.41	.292682	11.14	.707318	54
7	.285124	10.71	.991774	.42	.293350	11.12	.706650	53
8	.285766	10.69	.991749	.42	.294017	11.11	.705983	52
9	.286408	10.67	.991724	.42	.294684	11.09	.705316	51
10	.287048	10.66	.991699	.42	.295349	11.07	.704651	50
11	9.287687	10.64	9.991674	.42	9.296013	11.06	0.703987	49
12	.288326	10.63	.991649	.42	.296677	11.04	.703323	48
13	.288964	10.61	.991624	.42	.297339	11.03	.702661	47
14	.289600	10.59	.991599	.42	.298001	11.01	.701999	46
15	.290236	10.58	.991574	.42	.298662	11.00	.701338	45
16	.290870	10.56	.991549	.42	.299322	10.98	.700678	44
17	.291504	10.54	.991524	.42	.299980	10.96	.700020	43
18	.292137	10.53	.991498	.42	.300638	10.95	.699362	42
19	.292768	10.51	.991473	.42	.301295	10.93	.698705	41
20	.293399	10.50	.991448	.42	.301951	10.92	.698049	40
21	9.294029	10.48	9.991422	.42	9.302607	10.90	0.697393	39
22	.294658	10.46	.991397	.42	.303261	10.89	.696739	38
23	.295286	10.45	.991372	.43	.303914	10.87	.696086	37
24	.295913	10.43	.991346	.43	.304567	10.86	.695433	36
25	.296539	10.42	.991321	.43	.305218	10.84	.694782	35
26	.297164	10.40	.991295	.43	.305869	10.83	.694131	34
27	.297788	10.39	.991270	.43	.306519	10.81	.693481	33
28	.298412	10.37	.991244	.43	.307168	10.80	.692832	32
29	.299034	10.36	.991218	.43	.307815	10.78	.692185	31
30	.299655	10.34	.991193	.43	.308463	10.77	.691537	30
31	9.300276	10.32	9.991167	.43	9.309109	10.75	0.690891	29
32	.300895	10.31	.991141	.43	.309754	10.74	.690246	28
33	.301514	10.29	.991115	.43	.310398	10.73	.689602	27
34	.302132	10.28	.991090	.43	.311042	10.71	.688958	26
35	.302748	10.26	.991064	.43	.311685	10.70	.688315	25
36	.303364	10.25	.991038	.43	.312327	10.68	.687673	24
37	.303979	10.23	.991012	.43	.312967	10.67	.687033	23
38	.304593	10.22	.990986	.43	.313608	10.65	.686392	22
39	.305207	10.20	.990960	.43	.314247	10.64	.685753	21
40	.305819	10.19	.990934	.44	.314885	10.62	.685115	20
41	9.306430	10.17	9.990908	.44	9.315523	10.61	0.684477	19
42	.307041	10.16	.990882	.44	.316159	10.60	.683841	18
43	.307650	10.14	.990855	.44	.316795	10.58	.683205	17
44	.308259	10.13	.990829	.44	.317430	10.57	.682570	16
45	.308867	10.11	.990803	.44	.318064	10.55	.681936	15
46	.309474	10.10	.990777	.44	.318697	10.54	.681303	14
47	.310080	10.08	.990750	.44	.319329	10.53	.680671	13
48	.310685	10.07	.990724	.44	.319961	10.51	.680039	12
49	.311289	10.05	.990697	.44	.320592	10.50	.679408	11
50	.311893	10.04	.990671	.44	.321222	10.48	.678778	10
51	9.312495	10.03	9.990644	.44	9.321851	10.47	0.678149	9
52	.313097	10.01	.990618	.44	.322479	10.45	.677521	8
53	.313698	10.00	.990591	.44	.323106	10.44	.676894	7
54	.314297	9.98	.990565	.44	.323733	10.43	.676267	6
55	.314897	9.97	.990538	.44	.324358	10.41	.675642	5
56	.315495	9.96	.990511	.45	.324983	10.40	.675017	4
57	.316092	9.94	.990485	.45	.325607	16.39	.674393	3
58	.316689	9.93	.990458	.45	.326231	10.37	.673769	2
59	.317284	9.91	.990431	.45	.326853	10.36	.673147	1
60	.317879		.990404		.327475		.672525	0
	Cosine.	D.	Sine.	D.	Cotang.	D.	Tang.	M

78°

12°

M	Sine.	D	Cosine.	D.	Tang.	D.	Cotang.	
0	9.317879	9.90	9.990404	.45	9.327474	10.35	0.672526	60
1	.318473	9.88	.990378	.45	.328095	10.33	.671905	59
2	.319066	9.87	.990351	.45	.328715	10.32	.671285	58
3	.319658	9.86	.990324	.45	.329334	10.30	.670666	57
4	.320249	9.84	.990297	.45	.329953	10.29	.670047	56
5	.320840	9.83	.990270	.45	.330570	10.28	.669430	55
6	.321430	9.82	.990243	.45	.331187	10.26	.668813	54
7	.322019	9.80	.990215	.45	.331803	10.25	.668197	53
8	.322607	9.79	.990188	.45	.332418	10.24	.667582	52
9	.323194	9.77	.990161	.45	.333033	10 23	.666967	51
10	.323780	9.76	.990134	.45	.333646	10.21	.666354	50
11	9.324366	9.75	9.990107	.46	9.334259	10.20	0.665741	49
12	.324950	9.73	.990079	.46	.334871	10.19	.665129	48
13	.325534	9.72	.990052	.46	.335482	10.17	.664518	47
14	.326117	9.70	.990025	.46	.336093	10.16	.663907	46
15	.326700	9.69	.989997	.46	.336702	10.15	.663298	45
16	.327281	9.68	.989970	.46	.337311	10.13	.662689	44
17	.327862	9.66	.989942	.46	.337919	10 12	.662081	43
18	.328442	9.65	.989915	.46	.338527	10.11	.661473	42
19	.329021	9.64	.989887	.46	.339133	10.10	.660867	41
20	.329599	9.62	.989860	.46	.339739	10.08	.660261	40
21	9.330176	9.61	9.989832	.46	9.340344	10 07	0.659656	39
22	.330753	9.60	.989804	.46	.340948	10.06	.659052	38
23	.331329	9.58	.989777	.46	.341552	10.04	.658448	37
24	.331903	9.57	.989749	.47	.342155	10.03	.657845	36
25	.332478	9.56	.989721	.47	.342757	10.02	.657243	35
26	.333051	9.54	.989693	.47	.343358	10.00	.656642	34
27	.333624	9.53	.989665	.47	.343958	9.99	.656042	33
28	.334195	9.52	.989637	.47	.344558	9.98	.655442	32
29	.334766	9.50	.989609	.47	.345157	9 97	.654843	31
30	.335337	9.49	.989582	.47	.345755	9.96	.654245	30
31	9.335906	9.48	9.989553	.47	9 346353	9.94	0.653647	29
32	.336475	9.46	.989525	.47	.346949	9.93	.653051	28
33	.337043	9.45	.989497	.47	.347545	9.92	.652455	27
34	.337610	9.44	.989469	.47	.348141	9 91	.651859	26
35	.338176	9.43	.989441	.47	.348735	9.90	.651265	25
36	.338742	9.41	.989413	.47	.349329	9.88	.650671	24
37	.339306	9.40	.989384	.47	.349922	9.87	.650078	23
38	.339871	9.39	.989356	.47	.350514	9.86	.649486	22
39	.340434	9.37	.989328	.47	.351106	9.85	.648894	21
40	.340996	9.36	.989300	.47	.351697	9.83	.648303	20
41	9.341558	9.35	9.989271	.47	9.352287	9.82	0.647713	19
42	.342119	9.34	.989243	.47	.352876	9 81	.647124	18
43	.342679	9.32	.989214	.47	.353465	9 80	.646535	17
44	.343239	9.31	.989186	.47	.354053	9.79	.645947	16
45	.343797	9.30	.989157	.47	.354640	9.77	.645360	15
46	.344355	9.29	.989128	.48	.355227	9.76	.644773	14
47	.344912	9.27	.989100	.48	.355813	9.75	.644187	13
48	.345469	9.26	.989071	.48	.356398	9.74	.643602	12
49	.346024	9.25	.989042	.48	.356982	9.73	.643018	11
50	.346579	9.24	.989014	.48	.357566	9.71	.642434	10
51	9.347134	9.22	9.988985	.48	9 358149	9.70	0.641851	9
52	.347687	9.21	.988956	.48	.358731	9.69	.641269	8
53	.348240	9.20	.988927	.48	.359313	9.68	.640687	7
54	.348792	9.19	.988898	.48	.359893	9.67	.640107	6
55	.349343	9.17	.988869	.48	.360474	9.66	.639526	5
56	.349893	9.16	.988840	.48	.361053	9.65	.638947	4
57	.350443	9.15	.988811	.49	.361632	9.63	.638368	3
58	.350992	9.14	.988782	.49	.362210	9.62	.637790	2
59	.351540	9.13	.988753	.49	.362787	9.61	.637213	1
60	.352088		.988724		.363364		.636636	0
	Cosine.	D.	Sine.	D.	Cotang.	D.	Tang.	M.

77°

13°

M.	Sine.	D.	Cosine.	D.	Tang.	D.	Cotang.	
0	9.352088	9.11	9.988724	.49	9.363364	9.60	0.636636	60
1	.352635	9.10	.988695	.49	.363940	9.59	.636060	59
2	.353181	9.09	.988666	.49	.364515	9.58	.635485	58
3	.353726	9.08	.988636	.49	.365090	9.57	.634910	57
4	.354271	9.07	.988607	.49	.365664	9.55	.634336	56
5	.354815	9.05	.988578	.49	.366237	9.54	.633763	55
6	.355358	9.04	.988548	.49	.366810	9.53	.633190	54
7	.355901	9.03	.988519	.49	.367382	9.52	.632618	53
8	.356443	9.02	.988489	.49	.367953	9.51	.632047	52
9	.356984	9.01	.988460	.49	.368524	9.50	.631476	51
10	.357524	8.99	.988430	.49	.369094	9.49	.630906	50
11	9.358064	8.98	9.988401	.49	9.369663	9.48	0.630337	49
12	.358603	8.97	.988371	.49	.370232	9.46	.629768	48
13	.359141	8.96	.988342	.49	.370799	9.45	.629201	47
14	.359678	8.95	.988312	.50	.371367	9.44	.628633	46
15	.360215	8.93	.988282	.50	.371933	9.43	.628067	45
16	.360752	8.92	.988252	.50	.372499	9.42	.627501	44
17	.361287	8.91	.988223	.50	.373064	9.41	.626936	43
18	.361822	8.90	.988193	.50	.373629	9.40	.626371	42
19	.362356	8.89	.988163	.50	.374193	9.39	.625807	41
20	.362889	8.88	.988133	.50	.374756	9.38	.625244	40
21	9.363422	8.87	9.988103	.50	9.375319	9.37	0.624681	39
22	.363954	8.85	.988073	.50	.375881	9.35	.624119	38
23	.364485	8.84	.988043	.50	.376442	9.34	.623558	37
24	.365016	8.83	.988013	.50	.377003	9.33	.622997	36
25	.365546	8.82	.987983	.50	.377563	9.32	.622437	35
26	.366075	8.81	.987953	.50	.378122	9.31	.621878	34
27	.366604	8.80	.987922	.50	.378681	9.30	.621319	33
28	.367131	8.79	.987892	.50	.379239	9.29	.620761	32
29	.367659	8.77	.987862	.50	.379797	9.28	.620203	31
30	.368185	8.76	.987832	.51	.380354	9.27	.619646	30
31	9.368711	8.75	9.987801	.51	9.380910	9.26	0.619090	29
32	.369236	8.74	.987771	.51	.381466	9.25	.618534	28
33	.369761	8.73	.987740	.51	.382020	9.24	.617980	27
34	.370285	8.72	.987710	.51	.382575	9.23	.617425	26
35	.370808	8.71	.987679	.51	.383129	9.22	.616871	25
36	.371330	8.70	.987649	.51	.383682	9.21	.616318	24
37	.371852	8.69	.987618	.51	.384234	9.20	.615766	23
38	.372373	8.67	.987588	.51	.384786	9.19	.615214	22
39	.372894	8.66	.987557	.51	.385337	9.18	.614663	21
40	.373414	8.65	.987526	.51	.385888	9.17	.614112	20
41	9.373933	8.64	9.987496	.51	9.386438	9.15	0.613562	19
42	.374452	8.63	.987465	.51	.386987	9.14	.613013	18
43	.374970	8.62	.987434	.52	.387536	9.13	.612464	17
44	.375487	8.61	.987403	.52	.388084	9.12	.611916	16
45	.376003	8.60	.987372	.52	.388631	9.11	.611369	15
46	.376519	8.59	.987341	.52	.389178	9.10	.610822	14
47	.377035	8.58	.987310	.52	.389724	9.09	.610276	13
48	.377549	8.57	.987279	.52	.390270	9.08	.609730	12
49	.378063	8.56	.987248	.52	.390815	9.07	.609185	11
50	.378577	8.54	.987217	.52	.391360	9.06	.608640	10
51	9.379089	8.53	9.987186	.52	9.391903	9.05	0.608097	9
52	.379601	8.52	.987155	.52	.392447	9.04	.607553	8
53	.380113	8.51	.987124	.52	.392989	9.03	.607011	7
54	.380624	8.50	.987092	.52	.393531	9.02	.606469	6
55	.381134	8.49	.987061	.52	.394073	9.01	.605927	5
56	.381643	8.48	.987030	.52	.394614	9.00	.605386	4
57	.382152	8.47	.986998	.52	.395154	8.99	.604846	3
58	.382661	8.46	.986967	.52	.395694	8.98	.604306	2
59	.383168	8.45	.986936	.52	.396233	8.97	.603767	1
60	.383675		.986904		.396771		.603229	0
	Cosine	D.	Sine.	D.	Cotang.	D.	Tang.	M

76°

14°

M.	Sine.	D	Cosine.	D.	Tang.	D.	Cotang.	
0	9.383675		9.986904		9.396771		0.603229	60
1	.384182	8.44	.986873	.52	.397309	8.96	.602691	59
2	.384687	8.43	.986841	.53	.397846	8.96	.602154	58
3	.385192	8.42	.986809	.53	.398383	8.95	.601617	57
4	.385697	8.41	.986778	.53	.398919	8.94	.601081	56
5	.386201	8.40	.986746	.53	.399455	8.93	.600545	55
6	.386704	8.39	.986714	.53	.399990	8.93	.600010	54
7	.387207	8.38	.986683	.53	.400524	8.92	.599476	53
8	.387709	8.37	.986651	.53	.401058	8.90	.598942	52
9	.388210	8.36	.986619	.53	.401591	8.89	.598409	51
10	.388711	8.35	.986587	.53	.402124	8.88	.597876	50
11	9.389211	8.34	9.986555	.53	9.402656	8.87	0.597344	49
12	.389711	8.33	.986523	.53	.403187	8.86	.596813	48
13	.390210	8.32	.986491	.53	.403718	8.85	.596282	47
14	.390708	8.31	.986459	.53	.404249	8.84	.595751	46
15	.391206	8.30	.986427	.53	.404778	8.83	.595222	45
16	.391703	8.28	.986395	.53	.405308	8.82	.594692	44
17	.392199	8.27	.986363	.53	.405836	8.81	.594164	43
18	.392695	8.26	.986331	.54	.406364	8.80	.593636	42
19	.393191	8.25	.986299	.54	.406892	8.79	.593108	41
20	.393685	8.24	.986266	.54	.407419	8.78	.592581	40
21	9.394179	8.23	9.986234	.54	9.407945	8.77	0.592055	39
22	.394673	8.22	.986202	.54	.408471	8.76	.591529	38
23	.395166	8.21	.986169	.54	.408997	8.75	.591003	37
24	.395658	8.20	.986137	.54	.409521	8.74	.590479	36
25	.396150	8.19	.986104	.54	.410045	8.74	.589955	35
26	.396641	8.18	.986072	.54	.410569	8.73	.589431	34
27	.397132	8.17	.986039	.54	.411092	8.72	.588908	33
28	.397621	8.17	.986007	.54	.411615	8.71	.588385	32
29	.398111	8.16	.985974	.54	.412137	8.70	.587863	31
30	.398600	8.15	.985942	.54	.412658	8.69	.587342	30
31	9.399088	8.14	9.985909	.54	9.413179	8.68	0.586821	29
32	.399575	8.13	.985876	.55	.413699	8.67	.586301	28
33	.400062	8.12	.985843	.55	.414219	8.66	.585781	27
34	.400549	8.11	.985811	.55	.414738	8.65	.585262	26
35	.401035	8.10	.985778	.55	.415257	8.64	.584743	25
36	.401520	8.09	.985745	.55	.415775	8.64	.584225	24
37	.402005	8.08	.985712	.55	.416293	8.63	.583707	23
38	.402489	8.07	.985679	.55	.416810	8.62	.583190	22
39	.402972	8.06	.985646	.55	.417326	8.61	.582674	21
40	.403455	8.05	.985613	.55	.417842	8.60	.582158	20
41	9.403938	8.04	9.985580	.55	9.418358	8.59	0.581642	19
42	.404420	8.03	.985547	.55	.418873	8.58	.581127	18
43	.404901	8.02	.985514	.55	.419387	8.57	.580613	17
44	.405382	8.01	.985480	.55	.419901	8.56	.580099	16
45	.405862	8.00	.985447	.55	.420415	8.55	.579585	15
46	.406341	7.99	.985414	.55	.420927	8.55	.579073	14
47	.406820	7.98	.985380	.56	.421440	8.54	.578560	13
48	.407299	7.97	.985347	.56	.421952	8.53	.578048	12
49	.407777	7.96	.985314	.56	.422463	8.52	.577537	11
50	.408254	7.95	.985280	.56	.422974	8.51	.577026	10
51	9.408731	7.94	9.985247	.56	9.423484	8.50	0.576516	9
52	.409207	7.94	.985213	.56	.423993	8.49	.576007	8
53	.409682	7.93	.985180	.56	.424503	8.48	.575497	7
54	.410157	7.92	.985146	.56	.425011	8.48	.574989	6
55	.410632	7.91	.985113	.56	.425519	8.47	.574481	5
56	.411106	7.90	.985079	.56	.426027	8.46	.573973	4
57	.411579	7.89	.985045	.56	.426534	8.45	.573466	3
58	.412052	7.88	.985011	.56	.427041	8.44	.572959	2
59	.412524	7.87	.984978	.56	.427547	8.43	.572453	1
60	.412996	7.86	.984944	.56	.428052	8.43	.571948	0
	Cosine.	D.	Sine.	D.	Cotang.	D.	Tang.	M.

75°

15°

M.	Sine.	D.	Cosine.	D.	Tang.	D.	Cotang.	
0	9.412996	7.85	9.984944	.57	9.428052	8.42	0.571948	60
1	.413467	7.84	.984910	.57	.428557	8.41	.571443	59
2	.413938	7.83	.984876	.57	.429062	8.40	.570938	58
3	.414408	7.83	.984842	.57	.429566	8.39	.570434	57
4	.414878	7.82	.984808	.57	.430070	8.38	.569930	56
5	.415347	7.81	.984774	.57	.430573	8.38	.569427	55
6	.415815	7.80	.984740	.57	.431075	8.37	.568925	54
7	.416283	7.79	.984706	.57	.431577	8.36	.568423	53
8	.416751	7.78	.984672	.57	.432079	8.35	.567921	52
9	.417217	7.77	.984637	.57	.432580	8.34	.567420	51
10	.417684	7.76	.984603	.57	.433080	8.33	.566920	50
11	9.418150	7.75	9.984569	.57	9.433580	8.32	0.566420	49
12	.418615	7.74	.984535	.57	.434080	8.32	.565920	48
13	.419079	7.73	.984500	.57	.434579	8.31	.565421	47
14	.419544	7.73	.984466	.57	.435078	8.30	.564922	46
15	.420007	7.72	.984432	.58	.435576	8.29	.564424	45
16	.420470	7.71	.984397	.58	.436073	8.28	.563927	44
17	.420933	7.70	.984363	.58	.436570	8.28	.563430	43
18	.421395	7.69	.984328	.58	.437067	8.27	.562933	42
19	.421857	7.68	.984294	.58	.437563	8.26	.562437	41
20	.422318	7.67	.984259	.58	.438059	8.25	.561941	40
21	9.422778	7.67	9.984224	.58	9.438554	8.24	0.561446	39
22	.423238	7.66	.984190	.58	.439048	8.23	.560952	38
23	.423697	7.65	.984155	.58	.439543	8.23	.560457	37
24	.424156	7.64	.984120	.58	.440036	8.22	.559964	36
25	.424615	7.63	.984085	.58	.440529	8.21	.559471	35
26	.425073	7.62	.984050	.58	.441022	8.20	.558978	34
27	.425530	7.61	.984015	.58	.441514	8.19	.558486	33
28	.425987	7.60	.983981	.58	.442006	8.19	.557994	32
29	.426443	7.60	.983946	.58	.442497	8.18	.557503	31
30	.426899	7.59	.983911	.58	.442988	8.17	.557012	30
31	9.427354	7.58	9.983875	.58	9.443479	8.16	0.556521	29
32	.427809	7.57	.983840	.59	.443968	8.16	.556032	28
33	.428263	7.56	.983805	.59	.444458	8.15	.555542	27
34	.428717	7.55	.983770	.59	.444947	8.14	.555053	26
35	.429170	7.54	.983735	.59	.445435	8.13	.554565	25
36	.429623	7.53	.983700	.59	.445923	8.12	.554077	24
37	.430075	7.52	.983664	.59	.446411	8.12	.553589	23
38	.430527	7.52	.983629	.59	.446898	8.11	.553102	22
39	.430978	7.51	.983594	.59	.447384	8.10	.552616	21
40	.431429	7.50	.983558	.59	.447870	8.09	.552130	20
41	9.431879	7.49	9.983523	.59	9.448356	8.09	0.551644	19
42	.432329	7.49	.983487	.59	.448841	8.08	.551159	18
43	.432778	7.48	.983452	.59	.449326	8.07	.550674	17
44	.433226	7.47	.983416	.59	.449810	8.06	.550190	16
45	.433675	7.46	.983381	.59	.450294	8.06	.549706	15
46	.434122	7.45	.983345	.59	.450777	8.05	.549223	14
47	.434569	7.44	.983309	.59	.451260	8.04	.548740	13
48	.435016	7.44	.983273	.60	.451743	8.03	.548257	12
49	.435462	7.43	.983238	.60	.452225	8.02	.547775	11
50	.435908	7.42	.983202	.60	.452706	8.02	.547294	10
51	9.436353	7.41	9.983166	.60	9.453187	8.01	0.546813	9
52	436798	7.40	.983130	.60	.453668	8.00	.546332	8
53	.437242	7.40	.983094	.60	.454148	7.99	.545852	7
54	.437686	7.39	.983058	.60	.454628	7.99	.545372	6
55	.438129	7.38	.983022	.60	.455107	7.98	.544893	5
56	.438572	7.37	.982986	.60	.455586	7.97	.544414	4
57	.439014	7.36	.982950	.60	.456064	7.96	.543936	3
58	.439456	7.36	.982914	.60	.456542	7.96	.543458	2
59	.439897	7.35	.982878	.60	.457019	7.95	.542981	1
60	.440338		.982842		.457496		.542504	0
	Cosine	D.	Sine.	D.	Cotang.	D.	Tang.	M.

74°

16°

M	Sine.	D.	Cosine.	D.	Tang.	D.	Cotang.	
0	9.440338	7.34	9.982842	.60	9.457496	7.94	0.542504	60
1	.440778	7.33	.982805	.60	.457973	7.93	.542027	59
2	.441218	7.32	.982769	.61	.458449	7.93	.541551	58
3	.441658	7.31	.982733	.61	.458925	7.92	.541075	57
4	.442096	7.31	.982696	.61	.459400	7.91	.540600	56
5	.442535	7.30	.982660	.61	.459875	7.90	.540125	55
6	.442973	7.29	.982624	.61	.460349	7.90	.539651	54
7	.443410	7.28	.982587	.61	.460823	7.89	.539177	53
8	.443847	7.27	.982551	.61	.461297	7.88	.538703	52
9	.444284	7.27	.982514	.61	.461770	7.88	.538230	51
10	.444720	7.26	.982477	.61	.462242	7.87	.537758	50
11	9.445155	7.25	9.982441	.61	9.462714	7.86	0.537286	49
12	.445590	7.24	.982404	.61	.463186	7.85	.536814	48
13	.446025	7.23	.982367	.61	.463658	7.85	.536342	47
14	.446459	7.23	.982331	.61	.464129	7.84	.535871	46
15	.446893	7.22	.982294	.61	.464599	7.83	.535401	45
16	.447326	7.21	.982257	.61	.465069	7.83	.534931	44
17	.447759	7.20	.982220	.62	.465539	7.82	.534461	43
18	.448191	7.20	.982183	.62	.466008	7.81	.533992	42
19	.448623	7.19	.982146	.62	.466476	7.80	.533524	41
20	.449054	7.18	.982109	.62	.466945	7.80	.533055	40
21	9.449485	7.17	9.982072	.62	9.467413	7.79	0.532587	39
22	.449915	7.16	.982035	.62	.467880	7.78	.532120	38
23	.450345	7.16	.981998	.62	.468347	7.78	.531653	37
24	.450775	7.15	.981961	.62	.468814	7.77	.531186	36
25	.451204	7.14	.981924	.62	.469280	7.76	.530720	35
26	.451632	7.13	.981886	.62	.469746	7.75	.530254	34
27	.452060	7.13	.981849	.62	.470211	7.75	.529789	33
28	.452488	7.12	.981812	.62	.470676	7.74	.529324	32
29	.452915	7.11	.981774	.62	.471141	7.73	.528859	31
30	.453342	7.10	.981737	.62	.471605	7.73	.528395	30
31	9.453768	7.10	9.981699	.63	9 472068	7.72	0.527932	29
32	.454194	7.09	.981662	.63	.472532	7.71	.527468	28
33	.454619	7.08	.981625	.63	.472995	7.71	.527005	27
34	.455044	7.07	.981587	.63	.473457	7.70	.526543	26
35	.455469	7.07	.981549	.63	.473919	7.69	.526081	25
36	.455893	7.06	.981512	.63	.474381	7.69	.525619	24
37	.456316	7.05	.981474	.63	.474842	7.68	.525158	23
38	.456739	7.04	.981436	.63	.475303	7.67	.524697	22
39	.457162	7.04	.981399	.63	.475763	7.67	.524237	21
40	.457584	7.03	.981361	.63	.476223	7.66	.523777	20
41	9.458006	7.02	9.981323	.63	9.476688	7.65	0.523317	19
42	.458427	7.01	.981285	.63	.477142	7.65	.522858	18
43	.458848	7.01	.981247	.63	.477601	7.64	.522399	17
44	.459268	7.00	.981209	.63	.478059	7.63	.521941	16
45	.459688	6.99	.981171	.63	.478517	7.63	.521483	15
46	.460108	6.98	.981133	.64	.478975	7.62	.521025	14
47	.460527	6.98	.981095	.64	.479432	7.61	.520568	13
48	.460946	6.97	.981057	.64	.479889	7.61	.520111	12
49	.461364	6.96	.981019	.64	.480345	7.60	.519655	11
50	.461782	6.95	.980981	.64	.480801	7.59	.519199	10
51	9.462199	6.95	9.980942	.64	9 481257	7.59	0.518743	9
52	.462616	6.94	.980904	.64	.481712	7.58	.518288	8
53	.463082	6.93	.980866	.64	.482167	7.57	.517833	7
54	.493448	6.93	.980827	.64	.482621	7.57	.517379	6
55	.463864	6.92	.980789	.64	.483075	7.56	.516925	5
56	.464279	6.91	.980750	.64	.483529	7.55	.516471	4
57	.464694	6.90	.980712	.64	.483982	7.55	.516018	3
58	.465108	6.90	.980673	.64	.484435	7.54	.515565	2
59	.465522	6.89	.980635	.64	.484887	7.53	.515113	1
60	.465935		.980596		.485339		.514661	0
	Cosine.	D.	Sine.	D.	Cotang.	D.	Tang.	M.

73°

17°

M.	Sine.	D.	Cosine.	D.	Tang.	D.	Cotang.	
0	9.465935	6.88	9.980596	.64	9.485339	7.53	0.514661	60
1	.466348	6.88	.980558	.64	.485791	7.52	.514209	59
2	.466761	6.87	.980519	.65	.486242	7.51	.513758	58
3	.467173	6.86	.980480	.65	.486693	7.51	.513307	57
4	.467585	6.85	.980442	.65	.487143	7.50	.512857	56
5	.467996	6.85	.980403	.65	.487593	7.49	.512407	55
6	.468407	6.84	.980364	.65	.488043	7.49	.511957	54
7	.468817	6.83	.980325	.65	.488492	7.48	.511508	53
8	.469227	6.83	.980286	.65	.488941	7.47	.511059	52
9	.469637	6.82	.980247	.65	.489390	7.47	.510610	51
10	.470046	6.81	.980208	.65	.489838	7.46	.510162	50
11	9.470455	6.80	9.980169	.65	9.490286	7.46	0.509714	49
12	.470863	6.80	.980130	.65	.490733	7.45	.509267	48
13	.471271	6.79	.980091	.65	.491180	7.44	.508820	47
14	.471679	6.78	.980052	.65	.491627	7.44	.508373	46
15	.472086	6.78	.980012	.65	.492073	7.43	.507927	45
16	.472492	6.77	.979973	.65	.492519	7.43	.507481	44
17	.472898	6.76	.979934	.66	.492965	7.42	.507035	43
18	.473304	6.76	.979895	.66	.493410	7.41	.506590	42
19	.473710	6.75	.979855	.66	.493854	7.40	.506146	41
20	.474115	6.74	.979816	.66	.494299	7.40	.505701	40
21	9.474519	6.74	9.979776	.66	9.494743	7.40	0.505257	39
22	.474923	6.73	.979737	.66	.495186	7.39	.504814	38
23	.475327	6.72	.979697	.66	.495630	7.38	.504370	37
24	.475730	6.72	.979658	.66	.496073	7.37	.503927	36
25	.476133	6.71	.979618	.66	.496515	7.37	.503485	35
26	.476536	6.70	.979579	.66	.496957	7.36	.503043	34
27	.476938	6.69	.979539	.66	.497399	7.36	.502601	33
28	.477340	6.69	.979499	.66	.497841	7.35	.502159	32
29	.477741	6.68	.979459	.66	.498282	7.34	.501718	31
30	.478142	6.67	.979420	.66	.498722	7.34	.501278	30
31	9.478542	6.67	9.979380	.66	9.499163	7.33	0.500837	29
32	.478942	6.66	.979340	.66	.499603	7.33	.500397	28
33	.479342	6.65	.979300	.67	.500042	7.32	.499958	27
34	.479741	6.65	.979260	.67	.500481	7.31	.499519	26
35	.480140	6.64	.979220	.67	.500920	7.31	.499080	25
36	.480539	6.63	.979180	.67	.501359	7.30	.498641	24
37	.480937	6.63	.979140	.67	.501797	7.30	.498203	23
38	.481334	6.62	.979100	.67	.502235	7.29	.497765	22
39	.481731	6.61	.979059	.67	.502672	7.28	.497328	21
40	.482128	6.61	.979019	.67	.503109	7.28	.496891	20
41	9.482525	6.60	9.978979	.67	9.503546	7.27	0.496454	19
42	.482921	6.59	.978939	.67	.503982	7.27	.496018	18
43	.483316	6.59	.978898	.67	.504418	7.26	.495582	17
44	.483712	6.58	.978858	.67	.504854	7.25	.495146	16
45	.484107	6.57	.978817	.67	.505289	7.25	.494711	15
46	.484501	6.57	.978777	.67	.505724	7.24	.494276	14
47	.484895	6.56	.978736	.67	.506159	7.24	.493841	13
48	.485289	6.55	.978696	.68	.506593	7.23	.493407	12
49	.485682	6.55	.978655	.68	.507027	7.22	.492973	11
50	.486075	6.54	.978615	.68	.507460	7.22	.492540	10
51	9.486467	6.53	9.978574	.68	9.507893	7.21	0.492107	9
52	.486860	6.53	.978533	.68	.508326	7.21	.491674	8
53	.487251	6.52	.978493	.68	.508759	7.20	.491241	7
54	.487643	6.51	.978452	.68	.509191	7.19	.490809	6
55	.488034	6.51	.978411	.68	.509622	7.19	.490378	5
56	.488424	6.50	.978370	.68	.510054	7.18	.489946	4
57	.488814	6.50	.978329	.68	.510485	7.18	.489515	3
58	.489204	6.49	.978288	.68	.510916	7.17	.489084	2
59	.489593	6.48	.978247	.68	.511346	7.16	.488654	1
60	.489982		.978206		.511776		.488224	0
	Cosine	D.	Sine.	D.	Cotang.	D.	Tang.	M

72°

18°

M	Sine.	D	Cosine.	D.	Tang.	D.	Cotang.	
0	9.489982	6.48	9.978206	.68	9.511776	7.16	0.488224	60
1	.490371	6.48	.978165	.68	.512206	7.16	.487794	59
2	.490759	6.47	.978124	.68	.512635	7.15	.487365	58
3	.491147	6.46	.978083	.69	.513064	7.14	.486936	57
4	.491535	6.46	.978042	.69	.513493	7.14	.486507	56
5	.491922	6.45	.978001	.69	.513921	7.13	.486079	55
6	.492308	6.44	.977959	.69	.514349	7.13	.485651	54
7	.492695	6.44	.977918	.69	.514777	7.12	.485223	53
8	.493081	6.43	.977877	.69	.515204	7.12	.484796	52
9	.493466	6.42	.977835	.69	.515631	7.11	.484369	51
10	.493851	6.42	.977794	.69	.516057	7.10	.483943	50
11	9.494236	6.41	9.977752	.69	9.516484	7.10	0.483516	49
12	.494621	6.41	.977711	.69	.516910	7.09	.483090	48
13	.495005	6.40	.977669	69	.517335	7.09	.482665	47
14	.495388	6.39	.977628	.69	.517761	7.08	.482239	46
15	.495772	6.39	.977586	.69	.518185	7.08	.481815	45
16	.496154	6.38	.977544	.70	.518610	7.07	.481390	44
17	.496537	6.37	.977503	.70	.519034	7.06	.480966	43
18	.496919	6.37	.977461	.70	.519458	7.06	.480542	42
19	.497301	6.36	.977419	.70	.519882	7.05	.480118	41
20	.497682	6.36	.977377	.70	.520305	7.05	.479695	40
21	9.498064	6.35	9.977335	.70	9.520728	7.04	0.479272	39
22	.498444	6.34	.977293	.70	.521151	7.03	.478849	38
23	.498825	6.34	.977251	.70	.521573	7.03	.478427	37
24	.499204	6.33	.977209	.70	.521995	7.03	.478005	36
25	.499584	6.32	.977167	.70	.522417	7.02	.477583	35
26	.499963	6.32	.977125	.70	.522838	7.02	.477162	34
27	.500342	6.31	.977083	.70	.523259	7.01	.476741	33
28	.500721	6.31	.977041	.70	.523680	7.01	.476320	32
29	.501099	6.30	.976999	.70	.524100	7.00	.475900	31
30	.501476	6.29	.976957	.70	.524520	6.99	.475480	30
31	9.501854	6.29	9.976914	.70	9.524939	6.99	0.475061	29
32	.502231	6.28	.976872	.71	.525359	6.98	.474641	28
33	.502607	6.28	.976830	.71	.525778	6.98	.474222	27
34	.502984	6.27	.976787	.71	.526197	6.97	.473803	26
35	.503360	6.26	.976745	.71	.526615	6.97	.473385	25
36	.503735	6.26	.976702	.71	.527033	6.96	.472967	24
37	.504110	6.25	.976660	.71	.527451	6.96	.472549	23
38	.504485	6.25	.976617	.71	.527868	6.95	.472132	22
39	.504860	6.24	.976574	.71	.528285	6.95	.471715	21
40	.505234	6.23	.976532	.71	.528702	6.94	.471298	20
41	9.505608	6.23	9.976489	.71	9.529119	6.93	0.470881	19
42	.505981	6 22	.976446	.71	.529535	6.93	.470465	18
43	.506354	6.22	.976404	.71	.529950	6.93	.470050	17
44	.506727	6 21	.976361	.71	.530366	6.92	.469634	16
45	.507099	6.20	.976318	.71	.530781	6.91	.469219	15
46	.507471	6.20	.976275	.71	.531196	6.91	.468804	14
47	.507843	6.19	.976232	.72	.531611	6.90	.468389	13
48	.508214	6.19	.976189	.72	.532025	6.90	.467975	12
49	.508585	6.18	.976146	.72	.532439	6.89	.467561	11
50	.508956	6.18	.976103	.72	.532853	6.89	.467147	10
51	9.509326	6.17	9.976060	.72	9.533266	6.88	0.466734	9
52	.509696	6.16	.976017	.72	.533679	6.88	.466321	8
53	.510065	6.16	.975974	.72	.534092	6.87	.465908	7
54	.510434	6.15	.975930	.72	.534504	6.87	.465496	6
55	.510803	6.15	.975887	.72	.534916	6.86	.465084	5
56	.511172	6.14	.975844	.72	.535328	6.86	.464672	4
57	.511540	6.13	.975800	.72	.535739	6 85	.464261	3
58	.511907	6.13	.975757	.72	.536150	6 85	.463850	2
59	.512275	6.12	.975714	.72	.536561	6.84	.463439	1
60	.512642		.975670		.536972		.463028	0
	Cosine.	D.	Sine.	D.	Cotang.	D.	Tang.	M.

71°

19°

M.	Sine.	D.	Cosine.	D.	Tang.	D.	Cotang.	
0	9.512642	6.12	9.975670	.73	9.536972	6.84	0.463028	60
1	.513009	6.11	.975627	.73	.537382	6.83	.462618	59
2	.513375	6.11	.975583	.73	.537792	6.83	.462208	58
3	.513741	6.10	.975539	.73	.538202	6.82	.461798	57
4	.514107	6.09	.975496	.73	.538611	6.82	.461389	56
5	.514472	6.09	.975452	.73	.539020	6.81	.460980	55
6	.514837	6.08	.975408	.73	.539429	6.81	.460571	54
7	.515202	6.08	.975365	.73	.539837	6.80	.460163	53
8	.515566	6.07	.975321	.73	.540245	6.80	.459755	52
9	.515930	6.07	.975277	.73	.540653	6.79	.459347	51
10	.516294	6.06	.975233	73	.541061	6.79	.458939	50
11	9.516657	6.05	9.975189	.73	9.541468	6.78	0.458532	49
12	.517020	6.05	.975145	.73	.541875	6.78	.458125	48
13	.517382	6.04	.975101	.73	.542281	6.77	.457719	47
14	.517745	6.04	.975057	.73	.542688	6.77	.457312	46
15	.518107	6.03	.975013	.73	.543094	6.76	456906	45
16	.518468	6.03	.974969	.74	.543499	6.76	456501	44
17	.518829	6.02	.974925	.74	.543905	6.75	.456095	43
18	.519190	6.01	.974880	.74	.544310	6.75	.455690	42
19	.519551	6.01	.974836	.74	.544715	6.74	.455285	41
20	.519911	6.00	.974792	.74	.545119	6.74	.454881	40
21	9.520271	6.00	9.974748	.74	9.545524	6.73	0.454476	39
22	.520631	5.99	.974703	.74	.545928	6.73	.454072	38
23	.520990	5.99	.974659	.74	.546331	6.72	.453669	37
24	.521349	5.98	.974614	.74	.546735	6.72	.453265	36
25	.521707	5.98	.974570	.74	.547138	6.71	.452862	35
26	.522066	5.97	.974525	.74	547540	6.71	.452460	34
27	.522424	5.96	.974481	.74	.547943	6.70	.452057	33
28	.522781	5.96	.974436	.74	.548345	6.70	.451655	32
29	.523138	5.95	.974391	.74	.548747	6.69	.451253	31
30	.523495	5.95	.974347	.75	.549149	6.69	.450851	30
31	9.523852	5.94	9.974302	.75	9.549550	6.68	0.450450	29
32	.524208	5.94	.974257	.75	.549951	6.68	.450049	28
33	.524564	5.93	.974212	.75	.550352	6.67	.449648	27
34	.524920	5.93	.974167	.75	.550752	6.67	.449248	26
35	.525275	5.92	.974122	.75	.551152	6.66	.448848	25
36	.525630	5.91	.974077	.75	.551552	6.66	.448448	24
37	.525984	5.91	.974032	.75	.551952	6.65	.448048	23
38	.526339	5.90	.973987	.75	.552351	6.65	.447649	22
39	.526693	5.90	.973942	.75	.552750	6.65	.447250	21
40	.527046	5.89	.973897	.75	.553149	6.64	.446851	20
41	9.527400	5.89	9.973852	.75	9.553548	6.64	0.446452	19
42	.527753	5.88	.973807	.75	.553946	6.63	.446054	18
43	.528105	5.88	.973761	.75	.554344	6.63	.445656	17
44	.528458	5.87	.973716	.76	.554741	6.62	.445259	16
45	.528810	5.87	.973671	.76	.555139	6.62	.444861	15
46	529161	5.86	.973625	.76	.555536	6.61	.444464	14
47	.529513	5.86	.973580	.76	.555933	6.61	.444067	13
48	.529864	5.85	.973535	.76	.556329	6.60	.443671	12
49	.530215	5.85	.973489	.76	.556725	6.60	.443275	11
50	.530565	5 84	.973444	.76	.557121	6.59	.442879	10
51	9.530915	5.84	9.973398	.76	9.557517	6.59	0.442483	9
52	531265	5.83	.973352	.76	.557913	6.59	.442087	8
53	.531614	5.82	.973307	.76	.558308	6.58	.441692	7
54	.531963	5.82	.973261	.76	.558702	6.58	.441298	6
55	.532312	5.81	.973215	.76	.559097	6.57	.440903	5
56	.532661	5.81	.973169	.76	.559491	6.57	.440509	4
57	.533009	5.80	.973124	.76	.559885	6.56	.440115	3
58	.533357	5.80	.973078	.76	.560279	6.56	.439721	2
59	.533704	5.79	.973032	.77	.560673	6.55	.439327	1
60	.534052		.972986		.561066		.438934	0
	Cosine	D.	Sine.	D	Cotang.	D.	Tang.	M.

79°

20°

M.	Sine.	D.	Cosine.	D.	Tang.	D.	Cotang.	
0	9.534052		9.972986		9.561066		0.438934	60
1	.534399	5.78	.972940	.77	.561459	6.55	.438541	59
2	.534745	5.77	.972894	.77	.561851	6.54	.438149	58
3	.535092	5.77	.972848	.77	.562244	6.54	.437756	57
4	.535438	5.77	.972802	.77	.562636	6.53	.437364	56
5	.535783	5.76	.972755	.77	.563028	6.53	.436972	55
6	.536129	5.76	.972709	.77	.563419	6.53	.436581	54
7	.536474	5.75	.972663	.77	.563811	6.52	.436189	53
8	.536818	5.74	.972617	.77	.564202	6.52	.435798	52
9	.537163	5.74	.972570	.77	.564592	6.51	.435408	51
10	.537507	5.73	.972524	.77	.564983	6.51	.435017	50
11	9.537851	5.73	9.972478	.77	9 565373	6.50	0.434627	49
12	.538194	5.72	.972431	.77	.565763	6.50	.434237	48
13	.538538	5.72	.972385	.78	.566153	6.49	.433847	47
14	.538880	5.71	.972338	.78	.566542	6.49	.433458	46
15	.539223	5.71	.972291	.78	.566932	6.49	.433068	45
16	.539565	5.70	.972245	.78	.567320	6.48	.432680	44
17	.539907	5.70	.972198	.78	.567709	6.48	.432291	43
18	.540249	5.69	.972151	.78	.568098	6.47	.431902	42
19	.540590	5.69	.972105	.78	.568486	6.47	.431514	41
20	.540931	5.68	.972058	.78	.568873	6.46	.431127	40
21	9.541272	5 68	9.972011	.78	9.569261	6.46	0.430739	39
22	.541613	5.67	.971964	.78	.569648	6.45	.430352	38
23	.541953	5.67	.971917	.78	.570035	6.45	.429965	37
24	.542293	5.66	.971870	.78	.570422	6.45	.429578	36
25	.542632	5.66	.971823	.78	.570809	6.44	.429191	35
26	.542971	5.65	.971776	.78	.571195	6.44	.428805	34
27	.543310	5.65	.971729	.78	.571581	6.43	.428419	33
28	.543649	5.64	.971682	.79	.571967	6 43	.428033	32
29	.543987	5.64	.971635	.79	.572352	6.42	.427648	31
30	.544325	5.63	.971588	.79	.572738	6.42	.427262	30
31	9.544663	5.63	9.971540	.79	9.573123	6.42	0.426877	29
32	.545000	5.62	.971493	.79	.573507	6.41	.426493	28
33	.545338	5.62	.971446	.79	.573892	6.41	.426108	27
34	.545674	5.61	.971398	.79	.574276	6.40	.425724	26
35	.546011	5.61	.971351	.79	.574660	6.40	.425340	25
36	.546347	5.60	.971303	.79	.575044	6.39	.424956	24
37	.546683	5.60	.971256	.79	.575427	6.39	.424573	23
38	.547019	5.59	.971208	.79	.575810	6.39	.424190	22
39	.547354	5.59	.971161	.79	.576193	6.38	.423807	21
40	.547689	5 58	.971113	.79	.576576	6.38	.423424	20
41	9.548024	5.58	9.971066	.79	9.576958	6.37	0.423041	19
42	.548359	5.57	.971018	.80	.577341	6.37	.422659	18
43	.548693	5.57	.970970	.80	.577723	6.36	.422277	17
44	.549027	5.56	.970922	.80	.578104	6.36	.421896	16
45	.549360	5.56	.970874	.80	.578486	6.36	.421514	15
46	.549693	5.55	.970827	.80	.578867	6.35	.421133	14
47	.550026	5.55	.970779	.80	.579248	6.35	.420752	13
48	.550359	5.54	.970731	.80	.579629	6.34	.420371	12
49	.550692	5.54	.970683	.80	.580009	6.34	.419991	11
50	.551024	5.53	.970635	.80	.580389	6.34	.419611	10
51	9.551356	5.53	9.970586	.80	9.580769	6.33	0.419231	9
52	.551687	5.52	.970538	.80	.581149	6.33	.418851	8
53	.552018	5.52	.970490	.80	.581528	6.32	.418472	7
54	.552349	5.52	.970442	.80	.581907	6.32	.418093	6
55	.552680	5.51·	.970394	.80	.582286	6.32	.417714	5
56	.553010	5.51	.970345	.80	.582665	6.31	.417335	4
57	.553341	5.50	.970297	.81	.583043	6.31	.416957	3
58	.553670	5.50	.970249	.81	.583422	6.30	.416578	2
59	.554000	5.49	.970200	.81	583800	6.30	.416200	1
60	.554329	5.49	.970152	.81	.584177	6.29	.415823	0
	Cosine.	D.	Sine.	D.	Cotang.	D.	Tang.	M.

69°

21°

M.	Sine.	D.	Cosine.	D.	Tang.	D.	Cotang.	
0	9.554329	5.48	9.970152	.81	9.584177	6.29	0.415823	60
1	.554658	5.48	.970103	.81	.584555	6.29	.415445	59
2	.554987	5.47	.970055	.81	.584932	6.28	.415068	58
3	.555315	5.47	.970006	.81	.585309	6.28	.414691	57
4	.555643	5.46	.969957	.81	.585686	6.27	.414314	56
5	.555971	5.46	.969909	.81	.586062	6.27	.413938	55
6	.556299	5.45	.969860	.81	.586439	6.27	.413561	54
7	.556626	5.45	.969811	.81	.586815	6.26	.413185	53
8	.556953	5.44	.969762	.81	.587190	6.26	.412810	52
9	.557280	5.44	.969714	.81	.587566	6.25	.412434	51
10	.557606	5.43	.969665	.81	.587941	6.25	.412059	50
11	9.557932	5.43	9.969616	.82	9.588316	6.25	0.411684	49
12	.558258	5.43	.969567	.82	.588691	6.24	.411309	48
13	.558583	5.42	.969518	.82	.589066	6.24	.410934	47
14	.558909	5.42	.969469	.82	.589440	6.23	.410560	46
15	.559234	5.41	.969420	.82	.589814	6.23	.410186	45
16	.559558	5.41	.969370	.82	.590188	6.23	.409812	44
17	.559883	5.40	.969321	.82	.590562	6.22	.409438	43
18	.560207	5.40	.969272	.82	.590935	6.22	.409065	42
19	.560531	5.39	.969223	.82	.591308	6.22	.408692	41
20	.560855	5.39	.969173	.82	.591681	6.21	.408319	40
21	9.561178	5.38	9.969124	.82	9.592054	6.21	0.407946	39
22	.561501	5.38	.969075	.82	.592426	6.20	.407574	38
23	.561824	5.37	.969025	.82	.592798	6.20	.407202	37
24	.562146	5.37	.968976	.82	.593170	6.19	.406829	36
25	.562468	5.36	.968926	.83	.593542	6.19	.406458	35
26	.562790	5.36	.968877	.83	.593914	6.18	.406086	34
27	.563112	5.36	.968827	.83	.594285	6.18	.405715	33
28	.563433	5.35	.968777	.83	.594656	6.18	.405344	32
29	.563755	5.35	.968728	.83	.595027	6.17	.404973	31
30	.564075	5.34	.968678	.83	.595398	6.17	.404602	30
31	9.564396	5.34	9.968628	.83	9.595768	6.17	0.404232	29
32	.564716	5.33	.968578	.83	.596138	6.16	.403862	28
33	.565036	5.33	.968528	.83	.596508	6.16	.403492	27
34	.565356	5.32	.968479	.83	.596878	6.16	.403122	26
35	.565676	5.32	.968429	.83	.597247	6.15	.402753	25
36	.565995	5.31	.968379	.83	.597616	6.15	.402384	24
37	.566314	5.31	.968329	.83	.597985	6.15	.402015	23
38	.566632	5.31	.968278	.83	.598354	6.14	.401646	22
39	.566951	5.30	.968228	.84	.598722	6.14	.401278	21
40	.567269	5.30	.968178	.84	.599091	6.13	.400909	20
41	9.567587	5.29	9.968128	.84	9.599459	6.13	0.400541	19
42	.567904	5.29	.968078	.84	.599827	6.13	.400173	18
43	.568222	5.28	.968027	.84	.600194	6.12	.399806	17
44	.568539	5.28	.967977	.84	.600562	6.12	.399438	16
45	.568856	5.28	.967927	.84	.600929	6.11	.399071	15
46	.569172	5.27	.967876	.84	.601296	6.11	.398704	14
47	.569488	5.27	.967826	.84	.601662	6.11	.398338	13
48	.569804	5.26	.967775	.84	.602029	6.10	.397971	12
49	.570120	5.26	.967725	.84	.602395	6.10	.397605	11
50	.570435	5.25	.967674	.84	.602761	6.10	.397239	10
51	9.570751	5.25	9.967624	.84	9.603127	6.09	0.396873	9
52	.571066	5.24	.967573	.84	.603493	6.09	.396507	8
53	.571380	5.24	.967522	.85	.603858	6.09	.396142	7
54	.571695	5.23	.967471	.85	.604223	6.08	.395777	6
55	.572009	5.23	.967421	.85	.604588	6.08	.395412	5
56	.572323	5.23	.967370	.85	.604953	6.07	.395047	4
57	.572636	5.22	.967319	.85	.605317	6.07	.394683	3
58	.572950	5.22	.967268	.85	.605682	6.07	.394318	2
59	.573263	5.21	.967217	.85	.606046	6.06	.393954	1
60	.573575		.967166		.606410		.393590	0
	Cosine	D	Sine.	D	Cotang	D.	Tang.	M

22°

M	Sine.	D	Cosine.	D.	Tang.	D.	Cotang.	
0	9.573575	5.21	9.967166	.85	9.606410	6.06	0.393590	60
1	.573888	5.20	.967115	.85	.606773	6.06	.393227	59
2	.574200	5.20	.967064	.85	.607137	6.05	.392863	58
3	.574512	5.19	.967013	.85	.607500	6.05	.392500	57
4	.574824	5.19	.966961	.85	.607863	6.04	.392137	56
5	.575136	5.19	.966910	.85	.608225	6.04	.391775	55
6	.575447	5.18	.966859	.85	.608588	6.04	.391412	54
7	.575758	5.18	.966808	.85	.608950	6.03	.391050	53
8	.576069	5.17	.966756	.86	.609312	6.03	.390688	52
9	.576379	5.17	.966705	.86	.609674	6 03	.390326	51
10	.576689	5.16	.966653	.86	.610036	6.02	.389964	50
11	9.576999	5.16	9.966602	.86	9.610397	6.02	0.389603	49
12	.577309	5 16	.966550	.86	.610759	6 02	.389241	48
13	.577618	5.15	.966499	.86	.611120	6.01	.388880	47
14	.577927	5.15	.966447	.86	.611480	6.01	.388520	46
15	.578236	5.14	.966395	.86	.611841	6.01	.388159	45
16	.578545	5.14	.966344	.86	.612201	6.00	.387799	44
17	.578853	5.13	.966292	.86	.612561	6.00	.387439	43
18	.579162	5.13	.966240	.86	.612921	6.00	.387079	42
19	.579470	5.13	.966188	.86	.613281	5.99	.386719	41
20	.579777	5.12	.966136	.86	.613641	5.99	.386359	40
21	9.580085	5.12	9.966085	.87	9.614000	5.98	0.386000	39
22	.580392	5.11	.966033	.87	.614359	5.98	.385641	38
23	.580699	5.11	.965981	.87	.614718	5.98	.385282	37
24	.581005	5.11	.965928	.87	.615077	5.97	.384923	36
25	.581312	5.10	.965876	.87	.615435	5.97	.384565	35
26	.581618	5.10	.965824	.87	.615793	5.97	.384207	34
27	.581924	5.09	.965772	.87	.616151	5.96	.383849	33
28	.582229	5.09	.965720	.87	.616509	5.96	.383491	32
29	.582535	5.09	.965668	.87	.616867	5.96	.383133	31
30	.582840	5.08	.965615	.87	.617224	5.95	.382776	30
31	9.583145	5.08	9.965563	.87	9.617582	5.95	0.382418	29
32	.583449	5.07	.965511	.87	.617939	5.95	.382061	28
33	.583754	5.07	.965458	.87	.618295	5.94	.381705	27
34	.584058	5.06	.965406	.87	.618652	5.94	.381348	26
35	.584361	5.06	.965353	.88	.619008	5.94	.380992	25
36	.584665	5.06	.965301	.88	.619364	5.93	.380636	24
37	.584968	5.05	.965248	.88	.619721	5.93	.380279	23
38	.585272	5.05	.965195	.88	.620076	5.93	.379924	22
39	.585574	5.04	.965143	.88	.620432	5.92	.379568	21
40	.585877	5.04	.965090	.88	.620787	5.92	.379213	20
41	9 586179	5.03	9.965037	.88	9.621142	5.92	0.378858	19
42	.586482	5.03	.964984	.88	.621497	5.91	.378503	18
43	.586783	5.03	.964931	.88	.621852	5.91	.378148	17
44	.587085	5.02	.964879	.88	.622207	5.90	.377793	16
45	.587386	5.02	.964826	.88	.622561	5.90	.377439	15
46	.587688	5.01	.964773	.88	.622915	5.90	.377085	14
47	.587989	5.01	.964719	.88	.623269	5.89	.376731	13
48	.588289	5.01	.964666	.89	.623623	5.89	.376377	12
49	.588590	5.00	.964613	.89	.923976	5.89	.376024	11
50	.588890	5.00	.964560	.89	.624330	5.88	.375670	10
51	9.589190	4.99	9.964507	.89	9.624688	5.88	0.375317	9
52	.589489	4.99	.964454	.89	.625036	5.88	.374964	8
53	.589789	4.99	.964400	.89	.625888	5 87	.374612	7
54	.590088	4.98	.964347	.89	.625741	5.87	.374259	6
55	.590387	4.98	.964294	89	.626093	5.87	.373907	5
56	.590686	4.97	.964240	.89	.626445	5.86	.373555	4
57	.590984	4.97	.964187	.89	.626797	5.86	.373203	3
58	.591282	4.97	.964133	.89	.627149	5.86	.372851	2
59	.591580	4.96	.964080	.89	627501	5.85	.372499	1
60	591878		.964026		627852		372148	0
	Cosine.	D.	Sine.	D.	Cotang.	D.	Tang.	M.

67°

23°

M.	Sine.	D.	Cosine.	D.	Tang.	D.	Cotang.	
0	9.591878	4.96	9.964026	.89	9.627852	5.85	0.372148	60
1	.592176	4.95	.963972	.89	.628203	5.85	.371797	59
2	.592473	4.95	.963919	.89	.628554	5.85	.371446	58
3	.592770	4.95	.963865	.90	.628905	5.84	.371095	57
4	.593067	4.94	.963811	.90	.629255	5.84	370745	56
5	.593363	4.94	.963757	.90	.629606	5 83	.370394	55
6	.593659	4.93	.963704	.90	.629956	5.83	.370044	54
7	.593955	4.93	.963650	.90	.630306	5.83	.369694	53
8	.594251	4.93	.963596	.90	.630656	5 83	.369344	52
9	.594547	4.92	.963542	.90	.631005	5.82	.368995	51
10	.594842	4.92	.963488	.90	.631355	5 82	.368645	50
11	9.595137	4.91	9.963434	.90	9.631704	5 82	0.368296	49
12	.595432	4.91	.963379	.90	.632053	5 81	.367947	48
13	.595727	4.91	.963325	.90	.632401	5.81	.367599	47
14	.596021	4.90	.963271	.90	.632750	5 81	.367250	46
15	.596315	4.90	.963217	.90	.633098	5.80	.366902	45
16	.596609	4.89	.963163	.90	.633447	5.80	.366553	44
17	.596903	4.89	.963108	.91	.633795	5.80	.366205	43
18	.597196	4.89	.963054	.91	.634143	5.79	.365857	42
19	.597490	4.88	.962999	.91	.634490	5.79	.365510	41
20	.597783	4.88	.962945	.91	.634838	5.79	.365162	40
21	9.598075	4.87	9.962890	.91	9.635185	5.78	0.364815	39
22	.598368	4.87	.962836	.91	.635532	5 78	.364468	38
23	.598660	4.87	.962781	.91	.635879	5.78	.364121	37
24	.598952	4.86	.962727	.91	.636226	5.77	.363774	36
25	.599244	4.86	.962672	.91	.636572	5.77	.363428	35
26	.599536	4.85	.962617	.91	.636919	5.77	.363081	34
27	.599827	4.85	.962562	.91	.637265	5.77	.362735	33
28	.600118	4.85	.962508	.91	.637611	5.76	.362389	32
29	.600409	4.84	.962453	.91	.637956	5.76	.362044	31
30	.600700	4.84	.962398	.92	.638302	5.76	.361698	30
31	9.600990	4.84	9.962343	.92	9.638647	5.75	0.361353	29
32	.601280	4.83	.962288	.92	.638992	5.75	.361008	28
33	.601570	4.83	.962233	.92	.639337	5.75	.360663	27
34	.601860	4.82	.962178	.92	.639682	5.74	.360318	26
35	.602150	4.82	.962123	.92	.640027	5.74	.359973	25
36	.602439	4.82	.962067	.92	.640371	5.74	.359629	24
37	.602728	4.81	.962012	.92	.640716	5.73	.359284	23
38	.603017	4.81	.961957	.92	.641060	5.73	.358940	22
39	.603305	4.81	.961902	.92	.641404	5.73	.358596	21
40	.603594	4.80	.961846	.92	.641747	5.72	.358253	20
41	9.603882	4.80	9.961791	.92	9.642091	5.72	0.357909	19
42	.604170	4.79	.961735	.92	.642434	5.72	.357566	18
43	.604457	4.79	.961680	.92	.642777	5.72	.357223	17
44	.604745	4.79	.961624	.93	.643120	5.71	.356880	16
45	.605032	4.78	.961569	.93	.643463	5.71	.356537	15
46	605319	4.78	.961513	.93	.643806	5.71	356194	14
47	.605606	4.78	.961458	.93	.644148	5.70	.355852	13
48	.605892	4.77	.961402	.93	.644490	5.70	.355510	12
49	.606179	4.77	.961346	.93	.644832	5.70	.355168	11
50	.606465	4.76	.961290	.93	.645174	5.69	.354826	10
51	9.606751	4.76	9.961235	93	9.645516	5.69	0.354484	9
52	607036	4.76	.961179	.93	.645857	5.69	.354143	8
53	.607322	4.75	.961123	.93	.646199	5.69	.353801	7
54	.607607	4.75	.961067	.93	.646540	5.68	.353460	6
55	.607892	4.74	.961011	.93	.646881	5.68	.353119	5
56	.608177	4.74	.960955	.93	.647222	5.68	352778	4
57	.608461	4.74	.960899	.93	.647562	5.67	.352438	3
58	.608745	4.73	.960843	.94	.647903	5.67	.352097	2
59	.609029	4.73	.960786	.94	.648243	5.67	.351757	1
60	.609313		.960730		.648583		.351417	0
	Cosine	D.	Sine.	D.	Cotang.	D.	Tang.	M

24°

M	Sine.	D	Cosine.	D.	Tang.	D.	Cotang.	
0	9.609313	4.73	9.960730	.94	9.648583	5.66	0.351417	60
1	.609597	4.72	.960674	.94	.648923	5.66	.351077	59
2	.609880	4.72	.960618	.94	.649263	5.66	.350737	58
3	.610164	4.72	.960561	.94	.649602	5.66	.350398	57
4	.610447	4.71	.960505	.94	.649942	5.65	.350058	56
5	.610729	4.71	.960448	.94	.650281	5.65	.349719	55
6	.611012	4.70	.960392	.94	.650620	5.65	.349380	54
7	.611294	4.70	.960335	.94	.650959	5.64	.349041	53
8	.611576	4.70	.960279	.94	.651297	5.64	.348703	52
9	.611858	4.69	.960222	.94	.651636	5.64	.348364	51
10	.612140	4.69	.960165	.94	.651974	5.63	.348026	50
11	9.612421	4.69	9.960109	.95	9.652312	5.63	0.347688	49
12	.612702	4.68	.960052	.95	.652650	5.63	.347350	48
13	.612983	4.68	.959995	.95	.652988	5.63	.347012	47
14	.613264	4.67	.959938	.95	.653326	5.62	.346674	46
15	.613545	4.67	.959882	.95	.653663	5.62	.346337	45
16	.613825	4.67	.959825	.95	.654000	5.62	.346000	44
17	.614105	4.66	.959768	.95	.654337	5.61	.345663	43
18	.614385	4.66	.959711	.95	.654674	5.61	.345326	42
19	.614665	4.66	.959654	.95	.655011	5.61	.344989	41
20	.614944	4.65	.959596	.95	.655348	5.61	.344652	40
21	9.615223	4.65	9.959539	.95	9.655684	5.60	0.344316	39
22	.615502	4.65	.959482	.95	.656020	5.60	.343980	38
23	.615781	4.64	.959425	.95	.656356	5.60	.343644	37
24	.616060	4.64	.959368	.95	.656692	5.59	.343308	36
25	.616338	4.64	.959310	.96	.657028	5.59	.342972	35
26	.616616	4.63	.959253	.96	.657364	5.59	.342636	34
27	.616894	4.63	.959195	.96	.657699	5.59	.342301	33
28	.617172	4.62	.959138	.96	.658034	5.58	.341966	32
29	.617450	4.62	.959081	.96	.658369	5.58	.341631	31
30	.617727	4.62	.959023	.96	.658704	5.58	.341296	30
31	9.618004	4.61	9.958965	.96	9.659039	5.58	0.340961	29
32	.618281	4.61	.958908	.96	.659373	5.57	.340627	28
33	.618558	4.61	.958850	.96	.659708	5.57	.340292	27
34	.618834	4.60	.958792	.96	.660042	5.57	.339958	26
35	.619110	4.60	.958734	.96	.660376	5.57	.339624	25
36	.619386	4.60	.958677	.96	.660710	5.56	.339290	24
37	.619662	4.59	.958619	.96	.661043	5.56	.338957	23
38	.619938	4.59	.958561	.96	.661377	5.56	.338623	22
39	.620213	4.59	.958503	.97	.661710	5.55	.338290	21
40	.620488	4.58	.958445	.97	.662043	5.55	.337957	20
41	9.620763	4.58	9.958387	.97	9.662376	5.55	0.337624	19
42	.621038	4.57	.958329	.97	.662709	5 54	.337291	18
43	.621313	4.57	.958271	.97	.663042	5.54	.336958	17
44	.621587	4.57	.958213	.97	.663375	5.54	.336625	16
45	.621861	4.56	.958154	.97	.663707	5.54	.336293	15
46	.622135	4.56	.958096	.97	.664039	5.53	.335961	14
47	.622409	4.56	.958038	.97	.664371	5.53	.335629	13
48	.622682	4.55	.957979	.97	.664703	5.53	.335297	12
49	.622956	4.55	.957921	.97	.965035	5.53	.334965	11
50	.623229	4.55	.957863	.97	.665366	5.52	.334634	10
51	9.623502	4.54	9.957804	.97	9.665697	5.52	0.334303	9
52	.623774	4.54	.957746	.98	.666029	5.52	.333971	8
53	.624047	4.54	.957687	.98	.666360	5.51	.333640	7
54	.624319	4.53	.957628	.98	.666691	5.51	.333309	6
55	.624591	4.53	.957570	.98	.667021	5.51	.332979	5
56	.624863	4.53	.957511	.98	.667352	5.51	.332648	4
57	.625135	4.52	.957452	.98	.667682	5.50	.332318	3
58	.625406	4.52	.957393	.98	.668013	5.50	.331987	2
59	.625677	4.52	.957335	.98	.668343	5.50	.331657	1
60	.625948		.957276		.668672		.331328	0
	Cosine.	D.	Sine.	D.	Cotang.	D.	Tang.	M.

65°

25°

M.	Sine.	D.	Cosine.	D.	Tang.	D.	Cotang.	
0	9.625948	4.51	9.957276	.98	9.668673	5.50	0.331327	60
1	.626219	4.51	.957217	.98	.669002	5.49	.330998	59
2	.626490	4.51	.957158	.98	.669332	5.49	.330668	58
3	.626760	4 50	.957099	.98	.669661	5.49	.330339	57
4	.627030	4.50	.957040	.98	.669991	5.48	.330009	56
5	.627300	4.50	.956981	.98	.670320	5.48	.329680	55
6	.627570	4.49	.956921	.99	.670649	5.48	.329351	54
7	.627840	4.49	.956862	.99	.670977	5.48	.329023	53
8	.628109	4.49	.956803	.99	.671306	5.47	.328694	52
9	.628378	4.48	.956744	.99	.671634	5.47	.328366	51
10	.628647	4.48	.956684	.99	.671963	5.47	.328037	50
11	9.628916	4.47	9.956625	.99	9.672291	5.47	0.327709	49
12	.629185	4.47	.956566	.99	.672619	5.46	.327381	48
13	.629453	4.47	.956506	.99	.672947	5.46	.327053	47
14	.629721	4.46	.956447	.99	.673274	5.46	.326726	46
15	.629989	4.46	.956387	.99	.673602	5.46	.326398	45
16	.630257	4.46	.956327	.99	.673929	5.45	.326071	44
17	.630524	4.46	.956268	.99	.674257	5.45	.325743	43
18	.630792	4.45	.956208	1.00	.674584	5.45	.325416	42
19	.631059	4.45	.956148	1.00	.674910	5.44	.325090	41
20	.631326	4.45	.956089	1.00	.675237	5.44	.324763	40
21	9.631593	4 44	9.956029	1.00	9.675564	5.44	0.324436	39
22	.631859	4.44	.955969	1.00	.675890	5.44	.324110	38
23	.632125	4.44	.955909	1.00	.676216	5.43	.323784	37
24	.632392	4.43	.955849	1.00	.676543	5.43	.323457	36
25	.632658	4.43	.955789	1.00	.676869	5.43	.323131	35
26	.632923	4.43	.955729	1.00	.677194	5.43	.322806	34
27	.633189	4.42	.955669	1.00	.677520	5.42	.322480	33
28	.633454	4.42	.955609	1.00	.677846	5.42	.322154	32
29	.633719	4.42	.955548	1.00	.678171	5.42	.321829	31
30	.633984	4.41	.955488	1.00	.678496	5.42	.321504	30
31	9.634249	4.41	9.955428	1.01	9 678821	5.41	0.321179	29
32	.634514	4.40	.955368	1.01	.679146	5.41	.320854	28
33	.634778	4.40	.955307	1.01	.679471	5.41	.320529	27
34	.635042	4.40	.955247	1.01	.679795	5.41	.320205	26
35	.635306	4.39	.955186	1.01	.680120	5.40	.319880	25
36	.635570	4.39	.955126	1.01	.680444	5.40	.319556	24
37	.635834	4.39	.955065	1.01	.680768	5.40	.319232	23
38	.636097	4.38	.955005	1.01	.681092	5.40	.318908	22
39	.636360	4.38	.954944	1.01	.681416	5.39	.318584	21
40	.636623	4.38	.954883	1.01	.681740	5.39	.318260	20
41	9.636886	4.37	9.954823	1.01	9.682063	5.39	0.317937	19
42	.637148	4.37	.954762	1.01	.682387	5.39	.317613	18
43	.637411	4 37	.954701	1.01	.682710	5.38	.317290	17
44	.637673	4.37	.954640	1.01	.683033	5.38	.316967	16
45	.637935	4.36	.954579	1.01	.683356	5.38	.316644	15
46	.638197	4.36	.954518	1.02	.683679	5.38	.316321	14
47	.638458	4.36	.954457	1.02	.684001	5.37	.315999	13
48	.638720	4.35	.954396	1.02	.684324	5.37	.315676	12
49	.638981	4.35	.954335	1.02	.684646	5.37	.315354	11
50	.639242	4.35	.954274	1.02	.684968	5.37	.315032	10
51	9.639503	4 34	9.954213	1.02	9.685290	5.36	0.314710	9
52	.639764	4.34	.954152	1.02	.685612	5.36	.314388	8
53	.640024	4.34	.954090	1.02	.685934	5.36	.314066	7
54	.640284	4.33	.954029	1.02	.686255	5.36	.313745	6
55	.640544	4.33	.953968	1.02	.686577	5.35	.313423	5
56	.640804	4.33	.953906	1.02	.686898	5.35	.313102	4
57	.641064	4.32	.953845	1.02	.687219	5.35	.312781	3
58	.641324	4.32	.953783	1.02	.687540	5.35	.312460	2
59	.641584	4.32	.953722	1.03	.687861	5.34	.312139	1
60	.641842		.953660		.688182		.311818	0
	Cosine	D.	Sine.	D.	Cotang.	D.	Tang.	M

64°

26°

M	Sine.	D	Cosine.	D.	Tang.	D.	Cotang.	
0	9.641842	4.31	9.953660	1.03	9.688182	5.34	0.311818	60
1	.642101	4.31	.953599	1.03	.688502	5.34	.311498	59
2	.642360	4.31	.953537	1.03	.688823	5.34	.311177	58
3	.642618	4.30	.953475	1.03	.689143	5.33	.310857	57
4	.642877	4.30	.953413	1.03	.689463	5.33	.310537	56
5	.643135	4.30	.953352	1.03	.689783	5.33	.310217	55
6	.643393	4.30	.953290	1.03	.690103	5.33	.309897	54
7	.643650	4.29	.953228	1.03	.690423	5.33	.309577	53
8	.643908	4.29	.953166	1.03	.690742	5.32	.309258	52
9	.644165	4.29	.953104	1.03	.691062	5.32	.308938	51
10	.644423	4.28	.953042	1.03	.691381	5.32	.308619	50
11	9.644680	4.28	9.952980	1.04	9.691700	5.31	0.308300	49
12	.644936	4.28	.952918	1.04	.692019	5.31	.307981	48
13	.645193	4.27	.952855	1.04	.692338	5.31	.307662	47
14	.645450	4.27	.952793	1.04	.692656	5.31	.307344	46
15	.645706	4.27	.952731	1.04	.692975	5.31	.307025	45
16	.645962	4.26	.952669	1.04	.693293	5.30	.306707	44
17	.646218	4.26	.952606	1.04	.693612	5.30	.306388	43
18	.646474	4.26	.952544	1.04	.693930	5.30	.306070	42
19	.646729	4.25	.952481	1.04	.694248	5.30	.305752	41
20	.646984	4.25	.952419	1.04	.694566	5.29	.305434	40
21	9.647240	4.25	9.952356	1.04	9.694883	5.29	0.305117	39
22	.647494	4.24	.952294	1.04	.695201	5.29	.304799	38
23	.647749	4.24	.952231	1.04	.695518	5.29	.304482	37
24	.648004	4.24	.952168	1.05	.695836	5.29	.304164	36
25	.648258	4.24	.952106	1.05	.696153	5.28	.303847	35
26	.648512	4.23	.952043	1.05	.696470	5.28	.303530	34
27	.648766	4.23	.951980	1.05	.696787	5.28	.303213	33
28	.649020	4.23	.951917	1.05	.697103	5.28	.302897	32
29	.649274	4.22	.951854	1.05	.697420	5.27	.302580	31
30	.649527	4.22	.951791	1.05	.697736	5.27	.302264	30
31	9.649781	4.22	9.951728	1.05	9.698053	5.27	0.301947	29
32	.650034	4.22	.951665	1.05	.698369	5.27	.301631	28
33	.650287	4.21	.951602	1.05	.698685	5.26	.301315	27
34	.650539	4.21	.951539	1.05	.699001	5.26	.300999	26
35	.650792	4.21	.951476	1.05	.699316	5.26	.300684	25
36	.651044	4.20	.951412	1.05	.699632	5.26	.300368	24
37	.651297	4.20	.951349	1.06	.699947	5.26	.300053	23
38	.651549	4.20	.951286	1.06	.700263	5.25	.299737	22
39	.651800	4.19	.951222	1.06	.700578	5.25	.299422	21
40	.652052	4.19	.951159	1.06	.700893	5.25	.299107	20
41	9.652304	4.19	9.951096	1.06	9.701208	5.24	0.298792	19
42	.652555	4.18	.951032	1.06	.701523	5.24	.298477	18
43	.652806	4.18	.950968	1.06	.701837	5.24	.298163	17
44	.653057	4.18	.950905	1.06	.702152	5.24	.297848	16
45	.653308	4.18	.950841	1.06	.702466	5.24	.297534	15
46	.653558	4.17	.950778	1.06	.702780	5.23	.297220	14
47	.653808	4.17	.950714	1.06	.703095	5.23	.296905	13
48	.654059	4.17	.950650	1.06	.703409	5.23	.296591	12
49	.654309	4.16	.950586	1.06	.703723	5.23	.296277	11
50	.654558	4.16	.950522	1.07	.704036	5.22	.295964	10
51	9.654808	4.16	9.950458	1.07	9.704350	5.22	0.295650	9
52	.655058	4.16	.950394	1.07	.704663	5.22	.295337	8
53	.655307	4.15	.950330	1.07	.704977	5.22	.295023	7
54	.655556	4.15	.950266	1.07	.705290	5.22	.294710	6
55	.655805	4.15	.950202	1.07	.705603	5.21	.294397	5
56	.656054	4.14	.950138	1.07	.705916	5.21	.294084	4
57	.656302	4.14	.950074	1.07	.706228	5.21	.293772	3
58	.656551	4.14	.950010	1.07	.706541	5.21	.293459	2
59	.656799	4.13	.949945	1.07	.706854	5.21	.293146	1
60	.657047		.949881		.707166		.292834	0
	Cosine.	D.	Sine.	D.	Cotang.	D.	Tang.	M.

63°

27°

M.	Sine.	D.	Cosine.	D.	Tang.	D.	Cotang.	
0	9.657047	4.13	9.949881	1.07	9.707166	5.20	0.292834	60
1	.657295	4.13	.949816	1.07	.707478	5.20	.292522	59
2	.657542	4.12	.949752	1.07	.707790	5.20	.292210	58
3	.657790	4.12	.949688	1.08	.708102	5.20	.291898	57
4	.658037	4.12	.949623	1.08	.708414	5.19	.291586	56
5	.658284	4.12	.949558	1.08	.708726	5.19	.291274	55
6	.658531	4.11	.949494	1.08	.709037	5.19	.290963	54
7	.658778	4.11	.949429	1.08	.709349	5.19	.290651	53
8	.659025	4.11	.949364	1.08	.709660	5.19	.290340	52
9	.659271	4.10	.949300	1.08	.709971	5.18	.290029	51
10	.659517	4.10	.949235	1.08	.710282	5.18	.289718	50
11	9.659763	4.10	9.949170	1.08	9.710593	5.18	0.289407	49
12	.660009	4.09	.949105	1.08	.710904	5.18	.289096	48
13	.660255	4.09	.949040	1.08	.711215	5.18	.288785	47
14	.660501	4.09	.948975	1.08	.711525	5.17	.288475	46
15	.660746	4.09	.948910	1.08	.711836	5.17	.288164	45
16	.660991	4.08	.948845	1.08	.712146	5.17	.287854	44
17	.661236	4.08	.948780	1.09	.712456	5.17	.287544	43
18	.661481	4.08	.948715	1.09	.712766	5.16	.287234	42
19	.661726	4.07	.948650	1.09	.713076	5.16	.286924	41
20	.661970	4.07	.948584	1.09	.713386	5.16	.286614	40
21	9.662214	4.07	9.948519	1.09	9.713696	5.16	0.286304	39
22	.662459	4.07	.948454	1.09	.714005	5.16	.285995	38
23	.662703	4.06	.948388	1.09	.714314	5.15	.285686	37
24	.662946	4.06	.948323	1.09	.714624	5.15	.285376	36
25	.663190	4.06	.948257	1.09	.714933	5.15	.285067	35
26	.663433	4.05	.948192	1.09	.715242	5.15	.284758	34
27	.663677	4.05	.948126	1.09	.715551	5.14	.284449	33
28	.663920	4.05	.948060	1.09	.715860	5.14	.284140	32
29	.664163	4.05	.947995	1.10	.716168	5.14	.283832	31
30	.664406	4.04	.947929	1.10	.716477	5.14	.283523	30
31	9.664648	4.04	9.947863	1.10	9.716785	5.14	0.283215	29
32	.664891	4.04	.947797	1.10	.717093	5.13	.282907	28
33	.665133	4.03	.947731	1.10	.717401	5.13	.282599	27
34	.665375	4.03	.947665	1.10	.717709	5.13	.282291	26
35	.665617	4.03	.947600	1.10	.718017	5.13	.281983	25
36	.665859	4.02	.947533	1.10	.718325	5.13	.281670	24
37	.666100	4.02	.947467	1.10	.718633	5.12	.281367	23
38	.666342	4.02	.947401	1.10	.718940	5.12	.281060	22
39	.666583	4.02	.947335	1.10	.719248	5.12	.280752	21
40	.666824	4.01	.947269	1.10	.719555	5.12	.280445	20
41	9.667065	4.01	9.947203	1.10	9.719862	5.12	0.280138	19
42	.667305	4.01	.947136	1.11	.720169	5.11	.279831	18
43	.667546	4.01	.947070	1.11	.720476	5.11	.279524	17
44	.667786	4.00	.947004	1.11	.720783	5.11	.279217	16
45	.668027	4.00	.946937	1.11	.721089	5.11	.278911	15
46	.668267	4.00	.946871	1.11	.721396	5.11	.278604	14
47	.668506	3.99	.946804	1.11	.721702	5.10	.278298	13
48	.668746	3.99	.946738	1.11	.722009	5.10	.277991	12
49	.668986	3.99	.946671	1.11	.722315	5.10	.277685	11
50	.669225	3.99	.946604	1.11	.722621	5.10	.277379	10
51	9.669464	3.98	9.946538	1.11	9.722927	5.10	0.277073	9
52	.669703	3.98	.946471	1.11	.723232	5.09	.276768	8
53	.669942	3.98	.946404	1.11	.723538	5.09	.276462	7
54	.670181	3.97	.946337	1.11	.723844	5.09	.276156	6
55	.670419	3.97	.946270	1.12	.724149	5.09	.275851	5
56	.670658	3.97	.946203	1.12	.724454	5.09	.275546	4
57	.670896	3.97	.946136	1.12	.724759	5.08	.275241	3
58	.671134	3.96	.946069	1.12	.725065	5.08	.274935	2
59	.671372	3.96	.946002	1.12	.725369	5.08	.274631	1
60	.671609		.945935		.725674		.274326	0
	Cosine	D.	Sine.	D.	Cotang.	D.	Tang.	M

62°

28°

M	Sine.	D	Cosine.	D.	Tang.	D.	Cotang.	
0	9.671609	3.96	9.945935	1.12	9.725674	5.08	0.274326	60
1	.671847	3.95	.945868	1.12	.725979	5.08	.274021	59
2	.672084	3.95	.945800	1.12	.726284	5.07	.273716	58
3	.672321	3.95	.945733	1.12	.726588	5.07	.273412	57
4	.672558	3.95	.945666	1.12	.726892	5.07	.273108	56
5	.672795	3.94	.945598	1.12	.727197	5.07	.272803	55
6	.673032	3.94	.945531	1.12	.727501	5.07	.272499	54
7	.673268	3 94	.945464	1.13	.727805	5.06	.272195	53
8	.673505	3.94	.945396	1.13	.728109	5.06	.271891	52
9	.673741	3.93	.945328	1.13	.728412	5.06	.271588	51
10	.673977	3.93	.945261	1.13	.728716	5.06	.271284	50
11	9.674213	3.93	9.945193	1.13	9 729020	5.06	0.270980	49
12	.674448	3.92	.945125	1.13	.729323	5.05	.270677	48
13	.674684	3.92	.945058	1.13	.729626	5.05	.270374	47
14	.674919	3.92	.944990	1.13	.729929	5.05	.270071	46
15	.675155	3.92	.944922	1.13	.730233	5.05	.269767	45
16	.675390	3.91	.944854	1.13	.730535	5.05	.269465	44
17	.675624	3.91	.944786	1.13	.730838	5.04	.269162	43
18	.675859	3.91	.944718	1.13	.731141	5.04	.268859	42
19	.676094	3.91	.944650	1.13	.731444	5.04	.268556	41
20	.676328	3.90	.944582	1.14	.731746	5.04	.268254	40
21	9.676562	3.90	9.944514	1.14	9.732048	5.04	0.267952	39
22	.676796	3.90	.944446	1.14	.732351	5.03	.267649	38
23	.677030	3.90	.944377	1.14	.732653	5.03	.267347	37
24	.677264	3.89	.944309	1.14	.732955	5.03	.267045	36
25	.677498	3.89	.944241	1.14	.733257	5.03	.266743	35
26	.677731	3.89	.944172	1.14	.733558	5.03	.266442	34
27	.677964	3.88	.944104	1.14	.733860	5.02	.266140	33
28	.678197	3.88	.944036	1.14	.734162	5.02	.265838	32
29	.678430	3.88	.943967	1.14	.734463	5.02	.265537	31
30	.678663	3.88	.943899	1.14	.734764	5.02	.265236	30
31	9.678895	3.87	9.943830	1.14	9.735066	5.02	0.264934	29
32	.679128	3.87	.943761	1.14	.735367	5.02	.264633	28
33	.679360	3.87	.943693	1.15	.735668	5.01	.264332	27
34	.679592	3.87	.943624	1.15	.735969	5.01	.264031	26
35	.679824	3.86	.943555	1.15	.736269	5.01	.263731	25
36	.680056	3.86	.943486	1.15	.736570	5.01	.263430	24
37	.680288	3.86	.943417	1.15	.736871	5.01	.263129	23
38	.680519	3.85	.943348	1.15	.737171	5.00	.262829	22
39	.680750	3.85	.943279	1.15	.737471	5.00	.262529	21
40	.680982	3.85	.943210	1.15	.737771	5.00	.262229	20
41	9.681213	3.85	9.943141	1.15	9.738071	5.00	0.261929	19
42	.681443	3.84	.943072	1.15	.738371	5.00	.261629	18
43	.681674	3.84	.943003	1.15	.738671	4 99	.261329	17
44	.681905	3.84	.942934	1.15	.738971	4.99	.261029	16
45	.682135	3.84	.942864	1.15	.739271	4.99	.260729	15
46	.682365	3.83	.942795	1.16	.739570	4.99	.260430	14
47	.682595	3.83	.942726	1.16	.739870	4.99	.260130	13
48	.682825	3.83	.942656	1.16	.740169	4 99	.259831	12
49	.683055	3.83	.942587	1.16	.740468	4.98	.259532	11
50	.683284	3.82	.942517	1.16	.740767	4.98	.259233	10
51	9.683514	3.82	9.942448	1.16	9.741066	4.98	0.258934	9
52	.683743	3.82	.942378	1.16	.741365	4.98	.258635	8
53	.683972	3.82	.942308	1.16	.741664	4.98	.258336	7
54	.684201	3.81	.942239	1.16	.741962	4.97	.258038	6
55	.684430	3.81	.942169	1.16	.742261	4 97	.257739	5
56	.684658	3.81	.942099	1.16	.742559	4.97	.257441	4
57	.684887	3.80	.942029	1.16	.742858	4.97	.257142	3
58	.685115	3.80	.941959	1.16	.743156	4.97	.256844	2
59	.685343	3.80	.941889	1.17	.743454	4.97	.256546	1
60	.685571		.941819		.743752		.256248	0
	Cosine.	D.	Sine.	D.	Cotang.	D.	Tang.	M.

61°

29°

M.	Sine.	D.	Cosine.	D.	Tang.	D.	Cotang.	
0	9.685571	3.80	9.941819	1.17	9.743752	4.96	0.256248	60
1	.685799	3.79	.941749	1.17	.744050	4.96	.255950	59
2	.686027	3.79	.941679	1.17	.744348	4.96	.255652	58
3	.686254	3.79	.941609	1.17	.744645	4.96	.255355	57
4	.686482	3.79	.941539	1.17	.744943	4.96	.255057	56
5	.686709	3.78	.941469	1.17	.745240	4.96	.254760	55
6	.686936	3.78	.941398	1.17	.745538	4.95	.254462	54
7	.687163	3.78	.941328	1.17	.745835	4.95	.254165	53
8	.687389	3.78	.941258	1.17	.746132	4.95	.253868	52
9	.687616	3.77	.941187	1.17	.746429	4.95	.253571	51
10	.687843	3.77	.941117	1.17	.746726	4.95	.253274	50
11	9.688069	3.77	9.941046	1.18	9.747023	4.94	0.252977	49
12	.688295	3.77	.940975	1.18	.747319	4.94	.252681	48
13	.688521	3.76	.940905	1.18	.747616	4.94	.252384	47
14	.688747	3.76	.940834	1.18	.747913	4.94	.252087	46
15	.688972	3.76	.940763	1.18	.748209	4.94	.251791	45
16	.689198	3.76	.940693	1.18	.748505	4.93	.251495	44
17	.689423	3.75	.940622	1.18	.748801	4.93	.251199	43
18	.689648	3.75	.940551	1.18	.749097	4.93	.250903	42
19	.689873	3.75	.940480	1.18	.749393	4.93	.250607	41
20	.690098	3.75	.940409	1.18	.749689	4.93	.250311	40
21	9.690323	3.74	9.940338	1.18	9.749985	4.93	0.250015	39
22	.690548	3.74	.940267	1.18	.750281	4.92	.249719	38
23	.690772	3.74	.940196	1.18	.750576	4.92	.249424	37
24	.690996	3.74	.940125	1.19	.750872	4.92	.249128	36
25	.691220	3.73	.940054	1.19	.751167	4.92	.248833	35
26	.691444	3.73	.939982	1.19	.751462	4.92	.248538	34
27	.691668	3.73	.939911	1.19	.751757	4.92	.248243	33
28	.691892	3.73	.939840	1.19	.752052	4.91	.247948	32
29	.692115	3.72	.939768	1.19	.752347	4.91	.247653	31
30	.692339	3.72	.939697	1.19	.752642	4.91	.247358	30
31	9.692562	3.72	9.939625	1.19	9.752937	4.91	0.247063	29
32	.692785	3.71	.939554	1.19	.753231	4.91	.246769	28
33	.693008	3.71	.939482	1.19	.753526	4.91	.246474	27
34	.693231	3.71	.939410	1.19	.753820	4.90	.246180	26
35	.693453	3.71	.939339	1.19	.754115	4.90	.245885	25
36	.693676	3.70	.939267	1.20	.754409	4.90	.245591	24
37	.693898	3.70	.939195	1.20	.754703	4.90	.245297	23
38	.694120	3.70	.939123	1.20	.754997	4.90	.245003	22
39	.694342	3.70	.939052	1.20	.755291	4.90	.244709	21
40	.694564	3.69	.938980	1.20	.755585	4.89	.244415	20
41	9.694786	3.69	9.938908	1.20	9.755878	4.89	0.244122	19
42	.695007	3.69	.938836	1.20	.756172	4.89	.243828	18
43	.695229	3.69	.938763	1.20	.756465	4.89	.243535	17
44	.695450	3.68	.938691	1.20	.756759	4.89	.243241	16
45	.695671	3.68	.938619	1.20	.757052	4.89	.242948	15
46	.695892	3.68	.938547	1.20	.757345	4.88	.242655	14
47	.696113	3.68	.938475	1.20	.757638	4.88	.242362	13
48	.696334	3.67	.938402	1.21	.757931	4.88	.242069	12
49	.696554	3.67	.938330	1.21	.758224	4.88	.241776	11
50	.696775	3.67	.938258	1.21	.758517	4.88	.241483	10
51	9.696995	3.67	9.938185	1.21	9.758810	4.88	0.241190	9
52	.697215	3.66	.938113	1.21	.759102	4.87	.240898	8
53	.697435	3.66	.938040	1.21	.759395	4.87	.240605	7
54	.697654	3.66	.937967	1.21	.759687	4.87	.240313	6
55	.697874	3.66	.937895	1.21	.759979	4.87	.240021	5
56	.698094	3.65	.937822	1.21	.760272	4.87	.239728	4
57	.698313	3.65	.937749	1.21	.760564	4.87	.239436	3
58	.698532	3.65	.937676	1.21	.760856	4.86	.239144	2
59	.698751	3.65	.937604	1.21	.761148	4.86	.238852	1
60	.698970		.937531		.761439		.238561	0
	Cosine.	D.	Sine.	D.	Cotang.	D.	Tang.	M.

60°

30°

M	Sine.	D.	Cosine.	D.	Tang.	D.	Cotang.	
0	9.698970	3.64	9.937531	1.21	9.761439	4.86	0.238561	60
1	.699189	3.64	.937458	1.22	.761731	4.86	.238269	59
2	.699407	3.64	.937385	1.22	.762023	4.86	.237977	58
3	.699626	3.64	.937312	1.22	.762314	4.86	.237686	57
4	.699844	3.63	.937238	1.22	.762606	4.85	.237394	56
5	.700062	3.63	.937165	1.22	.762897	4.85	.237103	55
6	.700280	3.63	.937092	1.22	.763188	4.85	.236812	54
7	.700498	3.63	.937019	1.22	.763479	4.85	.236521	53
8	.700716	3.63	.936946	1.22	.763770	4.85	.236230	52
9	.700933	3.62	.936872	1.22	.764061	4.85	.235939	51
10	.701151	3.62	.936799	1.22	.764352	4.84	.235648	50
11	9.701368	3.62	9.936725	1.22	9.764643	4.84	0.235357	49
12	.701585	3.62	.936652	1.23	.764933	4.84	.235067	48
13	.701802	3.61	.936578	1.23	.765224	4.84	.234776	47
14	.702019	3.61	.936505	1.23	.765514	4.84	.234486	46
15	.702236	3.61	.936431	1.23	.765805	4.84	.234195	45
16	.702452	3.61	.936357	1.23	.766095	4.84	.233905	44
17	.702669	3.60	.936284	1.23	.766385	4.83	.233615	43
18	.702885	3.60	.936210	1.23	.766675	4.83	.233325	42
19	.703101	3.60	.936136	1.23	.766965	4.83	.233035	41
20	.703317	3.60	.936062	1.23	.767255	4.83	.232745	40
21	9.703533	3.59	9.935988	1.23	9.767545	4.83	0.232455	39
22	.703749	3.59	.935914	1.23	.767834	4.83	232166	38
23	.703964	3.59	.935840	1.23	.768124	4.82	.231876	37
24	.704179	3.59	.935766	1.24	.768413	4.82	.231587	36
25	.704395	3.59	.935692	1.24	.768703	4.82	.231297	35
26	.704610	3.58	.935618	1.24	.768992	4.82	.231008	34
27	.704825	3.58	.935543	1.24	.769281	4.82	.230719	33
28	.705040	3.58	.935469	1.24	.769570	4.82	.230430	32
29	.705254	3.58	.935395	1.24	.769860	4.81	.230140	31
30	.705469	3.57	.935320	1.24	.770148	4.81	.229852	30
31	9.705683	3.57	9.935246	1.24	9.770437	4.81	0.229563	29
32	.705898	3.57	.935171	1.24	.770726	4.81	.229274	28
33	.706112	3.57	.935097	1.24	.771015	4.81	.228985	27
34	.706326	3.56	.935022	1.24	.771303	4.81	.228697	26
35	.706539	3.56	.934948	1.24	.771592	4.81	.228408	25
36	.706753	3.56	.934873	1.24	.771880	4.80	.228120	24
37	.706967	3.56	.934798	1.25	.772168	4.80	.227832	23
38	.707180	3.55	.934723	1.25	.772457	4.80	.227543	22
39	.707393	3.55	.934649	1.25	.772745	4.80	.227255	21
40	.707606	3.55	.934574	1.25	.773033	4.80	.226967	20
41	9.707819	3.55	9.934499	1.25	9.773321	4.80	0.226679	19
42	.708032	3.54	.934424	1.25	.773608	4.79	.226392	18
43	.708245	3.54	.934349	1.25	.773896	4.79	.226104	17
44	.708458	3.54	.934274	1.25	.774184	4.79	.225816	16
45	.708670	3.54	.934199	1.25	.774471	4.79	.225529	15
46	.708882	3.53	.934123	1.25	.774759	4.79	.225241	14
47	.709094	3.53	.934048	1.25	.775046	4.79	.224954	13
48	.709306	3.53	.933973	1.25	.775333	4.79	.224667	12
49	.709518	3.53	.933898	1.26	.775621	4.78	.224379	11
50	.709730	3.53	.933822	1.26	.775908	4.78	.224092	10
51	9.709941	3.52	9.933747	1.26	9.776195	4.78	0.223805	9
52	.710153	3.52	.933671	1.26	.776482	4.78	.223518	8
53	.710364	3.52	.933596	1.26	.776769	4.78	.223231	7
54	.710575	3.52	.933520	1.26	.777055	4.78	.222945	6
55	.710786	3.51	.933445	1.26	.777342	4.78	.222658	5
56	.710997	3.51	.933369	1.26	.777628	4.77	.222372	4
57	.711208	3.51	.933293	1.26	.777915	4.77	.222085	3
58	.711419	3.51	.933217	1.26	.778201	4.77	.221799	2
59	.711629	3.50	.933141	1.26	.778487	4.77	.221513	1
60	.711839		.933066		.778774		221226	0
	Cosine.	D.	Sine.	D.	Cotang.	D.	Tang.	M.

59°

31°

M.	Sine.	D.	Cosine.	D.	Tang.	D.	Cotang.	
	Cosine	D.	Sine.	D.	Cotang.	D.	Tang.	M (bottom)
0	9.711839	3.50	9.933066	1.26	9.778774	4.77	0.221226	60
1	.712050	3.50	.932990	1.27	.779060	4.77	.220940	59
2	.712260	3.50	.932914	1.27	.779346	4.76	.220654	58
3	.712469	3.49	.932838	1.27	.779632	4.76	.220368	57
4	.712679	3.49	.932762	1.27	.779918	4.76	.220082	56
5	.712889	3.49	.932685	1.27	.780203	4.76	.219797	55
6	.713098	3.49	.932609	1.27	.780489	4.76	.219511	54
7	.713308	3.49	.932533	1.27	.780775	4.76	.219225	53
8	.713517	3.48	.932457	1.27	.781060	4.76	.218940	52
9	.713726	3.48	.932380	1.27	.781346	4.75	.218654	51
10	.713935	3.48	.932304	1.27	.781631	4.75	.218369	50
11	9.714144	3.48	9.932228	1.27	9.781916	4.75	0.218084	49
12	.714352	3.47	.932151	1.27	.782201	4.75	.217799	48
13	.714561	3.47	.932075	1.28	.782486	4.75	.217514	47
14	.714769	3.47	.931998	1.28	.782771	4.75	.217229	46
15	.714978	3.47	.931921	1.28	.783056	4.75	.216944	45
16	.715186	3.47	.931845	1.28	.783341	4.75	.216659	44
17	.715394	3.46	.931768	1.28	.783626	4.74	.216374	43
18	.715602	3.46	.931691	1.28	.783910	4.74	.216090	42
19	.715809	3.46	.931614	1.28	.784195	4.74	.215805	41
20	.716017	3.46	.931537	1.28	.784479	4.74	.215521	40
21	9.716224	3.45	9.931460	1.28	9.784764	4.74	0.215236	39
22	.716432	3.45	.931383	1.28	.785048	4.74	.214952	38
23	.716639	3.45	.931306	1.28	.785332	4.73	.214668	37
24	.716846	3.45	.931229	1.29	.785616	4.73	.214384	36
25	.717053	3.45	.931152	1.29	.785900	4.73	.214100	35
26	.717259	3.44	.931075	1.29	.786184	4.73	.213816	34
27	.717466	3.44	.930998	1.29	.786468	4.73	.213532	33
28	.717673	3.44	.930921	1.29	.786752	4.73	.213248	32
29	.717879	3.44	.930843	1.29	.787036	4.73	.212964	31
30	.718085	3.43	.930766	1.29	.787319	4.72	.212681	30
31	9.718291	3.43	9.930688	1.29	9.787603	4.72	0.212397	29
32	.718497	3.43	.930611	1.29	.787886	4.72	.212114	28
33	.718703	3.43	.930533	1.29	.788170	4.72	.211830	27
34	.718909	3.43	.930456	1.29	.788453	4.72	.211547	26
35	.719114	3.42	.930378	1.29	.788736	4.72	.211264	25
36	.719320	3.42	.930300	1.30	.789019	4.72	.210981	24
37	.719525	3.42	.930223	1.30	.789302	4.71	.210698	23
38	.719730	3.42	.930145	1.30	.789585	4.71	.210415	22
39	.719935	3.41	.930067	1.30	.789868	4.71	.210132	21
40	.720140	3.41	.929989	1.30	.790151	4.71	.209849	20
41	9.720345	3.41	9.929911	1.30	9.790433	4.71	0.209567	19
42	.720549	3.41	.929833	1.30	.790716	4.71	.209284	18
43	.720754	3.40	.929755	1.30	.790999	4.71	.209001	17
44	.720958	3.40	.929677	1.30	.791281	4.71	.208719	16
45	.721162	3.40	.929599	1.30	.791563	4.70	.208437	15
46	.721366	3.40	.929521	1.30	.791846	4.70	.208154	14
47	.721570	3.40	.929442	1.30	.792128	4.70	.207872	13
48	.721774	3.39	.929364	1.31	.792410	4.70	.207590	12
49	.721978	3.39	.929286	1.31	.792692	4.70	.207308	11
50	.722181	3.39	.929207	1.31	.792974	4.70	.207026	10
51	9.722385	3.39	9.929129	1.31	9.793256	4.70	0.206744	9
52	.722588	3.39	.929050	1.31	.793538	4.69	.206462	8
53	.722791	3.38	.928972	1.31	.793819	4.69	.206181	7
54	.722994	3.38	.928893	1.31	.794101	4.69	.205899	6
55	.723197	3.38	.928815	1.31	.794383	4.69	.205617	5
56	.723400	3.38	.928736	1.31	.794664	4.69	.205336	4
57	.723603	3.37	.928657	1.31	.794945	4.69	.205055	3
58	.723805	3.37	.928578	1.31	.795227	4.69	.204773	2
59	.724007	3.37	.928499	1.31	.795508	4.68	.204492	1
60	.724210		.928420		.795789		.204211	0

14 58°

32°

M	Sine.	D	Cosine.	D.	Tang.	D.	Cotang.	
0	9.724210	3.37	9.928420	1.32	9.795789	4.68	0.204211	60
1	.724412	3.37	.928342	1.32	.796070	4.68	.203930	59
2	.724614	3.36	.928263	1.32	.796351	4.68	.203649	58
3	.724816	3.36	.928183	1.32	.796632	4.68	.203368	57
4	.725017	3.36	.928104	1.32	.796913	4.68	.203087	56
5	.725219	3.36	.928025	1.32	.797194	4.68	.202806	55
6	.725420	3.35	.927946	1.32	.797475	4.68	.202525	54
7	.725622	3.35	.927867	1.32	.797755	4.68	.202245	53
8	.725823	3.35	.927787	1.32	.798036	4.67	.201964	52
9	.726024	3.35	.927708	1.32	.798316	4.67	.201684	51
10	.726225	3.35	.927629	1.32	.798596	4.67	.201404	50
11	9.726426	3.34	9.927549	1.32	9.798877	4.67	0.201123	49
12	.726626	3.34	.927470	1.33	.799157	4.67	.200843	48
13	.726827	3.34	.927390	1.33	.799437	4.67	.200563	47
14	.727027	3.34	.927310	1.33	.799717	4.67	.200283	46
15	.727228	3.34	.927231	1.33	.799997	4.66	.200003	45
16	.727428	3.33	.927151	1.33	.800277	4.66	.199723	44
17	.727628	3.33	.927071	1.33	.800557	4.66	.199443	43
18	.727828	3.33	.926991	1.33	.800836	4.66	.199164	42
19	.728027	3.33	.926911	1.33	.801116	4.66	.198884	41
20	.728227	3.33	.926831	1.33	.801396	4.66	.198604	40
21	9.728427	3.32	9.926751	1.33	9.801675	4.66	0.198325	39
22	.728626	3.32	.926671	1.33	.801955	4.66	.198045	38
23	.728825	3.32	.926591	1.33	.802234	4.65	.197766	37
24	.729024	3.32	.926511	1.34	.802513	4.65	.197487	36
25	.729223	3.31	.926431	1.34	.802792	4.65	.197208	35
26	.729422	3.31	.926351	1.34	.803072	4.65	.196928	34
27	.729621	3.31	.926270	1.34	.803351	4.65	.196649	33
28	.729820	3.31	.926190	1.34	.803630	4.65	.196370	32
29	.730018	3.30	.926110	1.34	.803908	4.65	.196092	31
30	.730216	3.30	.926029	1.34	.804187	4.65	.195813	30
31	9.730415	3.30	9.925949	1.34	9.804466	4.64	0.195534	29
32	.730613	3.30	.925868	1.34	.804745	4.64	.195255	28
33	.730811	3.30	.925788	1.34	.805023	4.64	.194997	27
34	.731009	3.29	.925707	1.34	.805302	4.64	.194698	26
35	.731206	3.29	.925626	1.34	.805580	4.64	.194420	25
36	.731404	3.29	.925545	1.35	.805859	4.64	.194141	24
37	.731602	3.29	.925465	1.35	.806137	4.64	.193863	23
38	.731799	3.29	.925384	1.35	.806415	4.63	.193585	22
39	.731996	3.28	.925303	1.35	.806693	4.63	.193307	21
40	.732193	3.28	.925222	1.35	.806971	4.63	.193029	20
41	9.732390	3.28	9.925141	1.35	9.807249	4.63	0.192751	19
42	.732587	3.28	.925060	1.35	.807527	4.63	.192473	18
43	.732784	3.28	.924979	1.35	.807805	4.63	.192195	17
44	.732980	3.27	.924897	1.35	.808083	4.63	.191917	16
45	.733177	3.27	.924816	1.35	.808361	4.63	.191639	15
46	.733373	3.27	.924735	1.36	.808638	4.62	.191362	14
47	.733569	3.27	.924654	1.36	.808916	4.62	.191084	13
48	.733765	3.27	.924572	1.36	.809193	4.62	.190807	12
49	.733961	3.26	.924491	1.36	.809471	4.62	.190529	11
50	.734157	3.26	.924409	1.36	809748	4.62	.190252	10
51	9.734353	3.26	9.924328	1.36	9.810025	4.62	0.189975	9
52	.734549	3.26	.924246	1.36	.810302	4.62	.189698	8
53	.734744	3.25	.924164	1.36	.810580	4.62	.189420	7
54	.734939	3.25	.924083	1.36	.810857	4.62	.189143	6
55	.735135	3.25	.924001	1.36	.811134	4.61	.188866	5
56	.735330	3.25	.923919	1.36	.811410	4.61	.188590	4
57	.735525	3.25	.923837	1.36	.811687	4.61	.188313	3
58	.735719	3.24	.923755	1.37	.811964	4.61	.188036	2
59	.735914	3.24	.923673	1.37	.812241	4.61	.187759	1
60	.736109		.923591		.812517		.187483	0
	Cosine.	D.	Sine.	D.	Cotang.	D.	Tang.	M.

57°

33°

M.	Sine.	D.	Cosine.	D.	Tang.	D.	Cotang.	
0	9.736109	3.24	9.923591	1.37	9.812517	4.61	0.187482	60
1	.736303	3.24	.923509	1.37	.812794	4.61	.187206	59
2	.736498	3.24	.923427	1.37	.813070	4 61	.186930	58
3	.736692	3.23	.923345	1.37	.813347	4.60	.186653	57
4	.736886	3.23	.923263	1.37	.813623	4.60	.186377	56
5	.737080	3.23	.923181	1.37	.813899	4.60	.186101	55
6	.737274	3.23	.923098	1.37	.814175	4.60	.185825	54
7	.737467	3.23	.923016	1.37	.814452	4.60	.185548	53
8	.737661	3.22	.922933	1.37	.814728	4.60	.185272	52
9	.737855	3.22	.922851	1.37	.815004	4.60	.184996	51
10	.738048	3.22	.922768	1.38	.815279	4.60	.184721	50
11	9.738241	3.22	9.922686	1.38	9.815555	4.59	0.184445	49
12	.738434	3.22	.922603	1.38	.815831	4.59	.184169	48
13	.738627	3.21	.922520	1.38	.816107	4.59	.183893	47
14	.738820	3.21	.922438	1.38	.816382	4.59	.183618	46
15	.739013	3.21	.922355	1.38	.816658	4.59	.183342	45
16	.739206	3.21	.922272	1.38	.816933	4.59	.183067	44
17	.739398	3.21	.922189	1.38	.817209	4.59	.182791	43
18	.739590	3.20	.922106	1.38	.817484	4.59	.182516	42
19	.739783	3.20	.922023	1.38	.817759	4.59	.182241	41
20	.739975	3.20	.921940	1.38	.818035	4.58	.181965	40
21	9.740167	3.20	9.921857	1.39	9.818310	4.58	0.181690	39
22	.740359	3.20	.921774	1.39	.818585	4.58	.181415	38
23	.740550	3.19	.921691	1.39	.818860	4.58	.181140	37
24	.740742	3.19	.921607	1.39	.819135	4.58	.180865	36
25	.740934	3.19	.921524	1.39	.819410	4.58	.180590	35
26	.741125	3.19	.921441	1.39	.819684	4.58	.180316	34
27	.741316	3.19	.921357	1.39	.819959	4.58	.180041	33
28	.741508	3.18	.921274	1.39	.820234	4.58	.179766	32
29	.741699	3.18	.921190	1.39	.820508	4.57	.179492	31
30	.741889	3.18	.921107	1.39	.820783	4.57	.179217	30
31	9.742080	3.18	9.921023	1.39	9.821057	4.57	0.178943	29
32	.742271	3.18	.920939	1.40	.821332	4.57	.178668	28
33	.742462	3.17	.920856	1.40	.821606	4.57	.178394	27
34	.742652	3.17	.920772	1.40	.821880	4.57	.178120	26
35	.742842	3.17	.920688	1.40	.822154	4.57	.177846	25
36	.743033	3.17	.920604	1.40	.822429	4.57	.177571	24
37	.743323	3.17	.920520	1.40	.822703	4.57	.177297	23
38	.743413	3.16	.920436	1.40	.822977	4.56	.177023	22
39	.743602	3.16	.920352	1.40	.823250	4.56	.176750	21
40	.743792	3.16	.920268	1.40	.823524	4.56	.176476	20
41	9.743982	3.16	9.920184	1.40	9.823798	4.56	0.176202	19
42	.744171	3.16	.920099	1.40	.824072	4.56	.175928	18
43	.744361	3.15	.920015	1.40	.824345	4.56	.175655	17
44	.744550	3.15	.919931	1.41	.824619	4.56	.175381	16
45	.744739	3.15	.919846	1.41	.824893	4.56	.175107	15
46	.744928	3.15	.919762	1.41	.825166	4.56	.174834	14
47	.745117	3.15	.919677	1.41	.825439	4.55	.174561	13
48	.745306	3.14	.919593	1.41	.825713	4.55	.174287	12
49	.745494	3.14	.919508	1.41	.825986	4.55	.174014	11
50	.745683	3.14	.919424	1.41	.826259	4.55	.173741	10
51	9.745871	3.14	9.919339	1.41	9.826532	4.55	0.173468	9
52	.746059	3.14	.919254	1.41	.826805	4.55	.173195	8
53	.746248	3.13	.919169	1 41	.827078	4.55	.172922	7
54	.746436	3.13	.919085	1.41	.827351	4.55	.172649	6
55	.746624	3.13	.919000	1.41	.827624	4.55	.172376	5
56	.746812	3.13	.918915	1.41	.827897	4.55	.172103	4
57	.746999	3.13	.918830	1.42	.828170	4.54	.171830	3
58	.747187	3.12	.918745	1.42	.828442	4.54	.171558	2
59	.747374	3.12	.918659	1.42	.828715	4.54	.171285	1
60	.747562		.918574		.828987		.171013	0
	Cosine	D.	Sine.	D.	Cotang.	D.	Tang.	M.

56°

34°

M	Sine.	D	Cosine.	D.	Tang.	D.	Cotang.	
0	9.747562	3.12	9 918574	1.42	9.828987	4.54	0.171013	60
1	.747749	3.12	.918489	1.42	.829260	4.54	.170740	59
2	.747936	3.12	.918404	1.42	.829532	4.54	.170468	58
3	.748123	3.11	.918318	1.42	.829805	4.54	.170195	57
4	.748310	3.11	.918233	1.42	.830077	4.54	.169923	56
5	.748497	3.11	.918147	1.42	.830349	4.53	.169651	55
6	.748683	3.11	.918062	1.42	.830621	4.53	.169379	54
7	.748870	3.11	.917976	1.43	.830893	4.53	.169107	53
8	.749056	3.10	.917891	1.43	.831165	4.53	.168835	52
9	.749243	3.10	.917805	1.43	.831437	4 53	.168563	51
10	.749429	3.10	.917719	1.43	.831709	4.53	.168291	50
11	9.749615	3.10	9.917634	1.43	9.831981	4.53	0.168019	49
12	.749801	3.10	.917548	1.43	.832253	4.53	.167747	48
13	.749987	3.09	.917462	1.43	.832525	4.53	.167475	47
14	.750172	3.09	.917376	1.43	.832796	4.53	.167204	46
15	.750358	3.09	.917290	1.43	.833068	4.52	.166932	45
16	.750543	3.09	.917204	1.43	.833339	4.52	.166661	44
17	.750729	3.09	.917118	1.44	.833611	4.52	.166389	43
18	.750914	3.08	.917032	1.44	.833882	4.52	.166118	42
19	.751099	3.08	.916946	1.44	.834154	4.52	.165846	41
20	.751284	3.08	.916859	1.44	.834425	4.52	.165575	40
21	9.751469	3.08	9.916773	1.44	9.834696	4.52	0.165304	39
22	.751654	3.08	.916687	1.44	.834967	4.52	165033	38
23	.751839	3.08	.916600	1.44	.835238	4.52	.164762	37
24	.752023	3.07	.916514	1.44	.835509	4.52	.164491	36
25	.752208	3.07	.916427	1.44	.835780	4.51	.164220	35
26	.752392	3.07	.916341	1.44	.836051	4.51	.163949	34
27	.752576	3.07	.916254	1.44	.836322	4.51	.163678	33
28	.752760	3.07	.916167	1.45	.836593	4 51	.163407	32
29	.752944	3.06	.916081	1.45	.836864	4.51	.163136	31
30	.753128	3.06	.915994	1.45	.837134	4.51	.162866	30
31	9.753312	3.06	9.915907	1.45	9.837405	4 51	0.162595	29
32	.753495	3.06	.915820	1.45	.837675	4.51	.162325	28
33	.753679	3.06	.915733	1.45	.837946	4.51	.162054	27
34	.753862	3.05	.915646	1.45	.838216	4.51	.161784	26
35	.754046	3.05	.915559	1.45	.838487	4.50	.161513	25
36	.754229	3.05	.915472	1.45	.838757	4.50	.161243	24
37	.754412	3.05	.915385	1.45	.839027	4.50	.160973	23
38	.754595	3.05	.915297	1.45	.839297	4.50	.160703	22
39	.754778	3.04	.915210	1.45	.839568	4.50	.160432	21
40	.754960	3.04	.915123	1.46	.839838	4.50	.160162	20
41	9.755143	3.04	9.915035	1.46	9.840108	4.50	0.159892	19
42	.755326	3.04	.914948	1.46	.840378	4.50	.159622	18
43	.755508	3.04	.914860	1.46	.840647	4.50	.159353	17
44	.755690	3.04	.914773	1.46	.840917	4.49	.159083	16
45	.755872	3.03	.914685	1.46	.841187	4.49	.158813	15
46	.756054	3.03	.914598	1.46	.841457	4.49	.158543	14
47	.756236	3.03	.914510	1.46	.841726	4.49	.158274	13
48	.756418	3.03	.914422	1.46	.841996	4.49	.158004	12
49	.756600	3.03	.914334	1.46	.842266	4.49	.157734	11
50	.756782	3.02	.914246	1.47	842535	4.49	.157465	10
51	9.756963	3.02	9.914158	1.47	9.842805	4.49	0.157195	9
52	.757144	3.02	.914070	1.47	.843074	4.49	.156926	8
53	.757326	3.02	.913982	1.47	.843343	4.49	.156657	7
54	.757507	3.02	.913894	1.47	.843612	4.49	.156388	6
55	.757688	3.01	.913806	1.47	.843882	4.48	.156118	5
56	757869	3.01	.913718	1.47	.844151	4.48	.155849	4
57	.758050	3.01	.913630	1.47	.844420	4.48	.155580	3
58	.758230	3.01	.913541	1.47	.844689	4.48	.155311	2
59	.758411	3.01	.913453	1.47	.844958	4.48	.155042	1
60	.758591		.913365		.845227		.154773	0
	Cosine.	D.	Sine.	D.	Cotang.	D.	Tang.	M.

55°

35°

M.	Sine.	D.	Cosine.	D.	Tang.	D.	Cotang.	
0	9.758591	3.01	9.913365	1.47	9.845227	4.48	0.154773	60
1	.758772	3.00	.913276	1.47	.845496	4.48	.154504	59
2	.758952	3.00	.913187	1.48	.845764	4.48	.154236	58
3	.759132	3.00	.913099	1.48	.846033	4.48	.153967	57
4	.759312	3.00	.913010	1.48	.846302	4.48	.153698	56
5	.759492	3.00	.912922	1.48	.846570	4.47	.153430	55
6	.759672	2.99	.912833	1.48	.846839	4.47	.153161	54
7	.759852	2.99	.912744	1.48	.847107	4.47	.152893	53
8	.760031	2.99	.912655	1.48	.847376	4.47	.152624	52
9	.760211	2.99	.912566	1.48	.847644	4.47	.152356	51
10	.760390	2.99	.912477	1.48	.847913	4.47	.152087	50
11	9.760569	2.98	9.912388	1.48	9.848181	4.47	0.151819	49
12	.760748	2.98	.912299	1.49	.848449	4.47	.151551	48
13	.760927	2.98	.912210	1.49	.848717	4.47	.151283	47
14	.761106	2.98	.912121	1.49	.848986	4.47	.151014	46
15	.761285	2.98	.912031	1.49	.849254	4.47	.150746	45
16	.761464	2.98	.911942	1.49	.849522	4.47	.150478	44
17	.761642	2.97	.911853	1.49	.849790	4.46	.150210	43
18	.761821	2.97	.911763	1.49	.850058	4.46	.149942	42
19	.761999	2.97	.911674	1.49	.850325	4.46	.149675	41
20	.762177	2.97	.911584	1.49	.850593	4.46	.149407	40
21	9.762356	2.97	9.911495	1.49	9.850861	4.46	0.149139	39
22	.762534	2.96	.911405	1.49	.851129	4.46	.148871	38
23	.762712	2.96	.911315	1.50	.851396	4.46	.148604	37
24	.762889	2.96	.911226	1.50	.851664	4.46	.148336	36
25	.763067	2.96	.911136	1.50	.851931	4.46	.148069	35
26	.763245	2.96	.911046	1.50	.852199	4.46	.147801	34
27	.763422	2.96	.910956	1.50	.852466	4.46	.147534	33
28	.763600	2.95	.910866	1.50	.852733	4.45	.147267	32
29	.763777	2.95	.910776	1.50	.853001	4.45	.146999	31
30	.763954	2.95	.910686	1.50	.853268	4.45	.146732	30
31	9.764131	2.95	9.910596	1.50	9.853535	4.45	0.146465	29
32	.764308	2.95	.910506	1.50	.853802	4.45	.146198	28
33	.764485	2.94	.910415	1.50	.854069	4.45	.145931	27
34	.764662	2.94	.910325	1.51	.854336	4.45	.145664	26
35	.764838	2.94	.910235	1.51	.854603	4.45	.145397	25
36	.765015	2.94	.910144	1.51	.854870	4.45	.145130	24
37	.765191	2.94	.910054	1.51	.855137	4.45	.144863	23
38	.765367	2.94	.909963	1.51	.855404	4.45	.144596	22
39	.765544	2.93	.909873	1.51	.855671	4.44	.144329	21
40	.765720	2.93	.909782	1.51	.855938	4.44	.144062	20
41	9.765896	2.93	9.909691	1.51	9.856204	4.44	0.143796	19
42	.766072	2.93	.909601	1.51	.856471	4.44	.143529	18
43	.766247	2.93	.909510	1.51	.856737	4.44	.143263	17
44	.766423	2.93	.909419	1.51	.857004	4.44	.142996	16
45	.766598	2.92	.909328	1.52	.857270	4.44	.142730	15
46	.766774	2.92	.909237	1.52	.857537	4.44	.142463	14
47	.766949	2.92	.909146	1.52	.857803	4.44	.142197	13
48	.767124	2.92	.909055	1.52	.858069	4.44	.141931	12
49	.767300	2.92	.908964	1.52	.858336	4.44	.141664	11
50	.767475	2.91	.908873	1.52	.858602	4.43	.141398	10
51	9.767649	2.91	9.908781	1.52	9.858868	4.43	0.141132	9
52	.767824	2.91	.908690	1.52	.859134	4.43	.140866	8
53	.767999	2.91	.908599	1.52	.859400	4.43	.140600	7
54	.768173	2.91	.908507	1.52	.859666	4.43	.140334	6
55	.768348	2.90	.908416	1.53	.859932	4.43	.140068	5
56	.768522	2.90	.908324	1.53	.860198	4.43	.139802	4
57	.768697	2.90	.908233	1.53	.860464	4.43	.139536	3
58	.768871	2.90	.908141	1.53	.860730	4.43	.139270	2
59	.769045	2.90	.908049	1.53	.860995	4.43	.139005	1
60	.769219		.907958		.861261		.138739	0
	Cosine	D.	Sine.	D.	Cotang.	D.	Tang.	M.

41

36°

M	Sine.	D	Cosine.	D.	Tang.	D.	Cotang.	
0	9.769219	2.90	9.907958	1.53	9.861261	4.43	0.138739	60
1	.769393	2.89	.907866	1.53	.861527	4.43	.138473	59
2	.769566	2.89	.907774	1.53	.861792	4.42	.138208	58
3	.769740	2.89	.907682	1.53	.862058	4.42	.137942	57
4	.769913	2.89	.907590	1.53	.862323	4.42	.137677	56
5	.770087	2.89	.907498	1.53	.862589	4.42	.137411	55
6	.770260	2.88	.907406	1.53	.862854	4.42	.137146	54
7	.770433	2.88	.907314	1.54	.863119	4.42	.136881	53
8	.770606	2.88	.907222	1.54	.863385	4.42	.136615	52
9	.770779	2.88	.907129	1.54	.863650	4.42	.136350	51
10	.770952	2.88	.907037	1.54	.863915	4.42	.136085	50
11	9.771125	2.88	9.906945	1.54	9.864180	4.42	0.135820	49
12	.771298	2.87	.906852	1.54	.864445	4.42	.135555	48
13	.771470	2.87	.906760	1.54	.864710	4.42	.135290	47
14	.771643	2.87	.906667	1.54	.864975	4.41	.135025	46
15	.771815	2.87	.906575	1.54	.865240	4.41	.134760	45
16	.771987	2.87	.906482	1.54	.865505	4.41	.134495	44
17	.772159	2.87	.906389	1.55	.865770	4.41	.134230	43
18	.772331	2.86	.906296	1.55	.866035	4.41	.133965	42
19	.772503	2.86	.906204	1.55	.866300	4.41	.133700	41
20	.772675	2.86	.906111	1.55	.866564	4.41	.133436	40
21	9.772847	2.86	9.906018	1.55	9.866829	4.41	0.133171	39
22	.773018	2.86	.905925	1.55	.867094	4.41	.132906	38
23	.773190	2.86	.905832	1.55	.867358	4.41	.132642	37
24	.773361	2.85	.905739	1.55	.867623	4.41	.132377	36
25	.773533	2.85	.905645	1.55	.867887	4.41	.132113	35
26	.773704	2.85	.905552	1.55	.868152	4.40	.131848	34
27	.773875	2.85	.905459	1.55	.868416	4.40	.131584	33
28	.774046	2.85	.905366	1.56	.868680	4.40	.131320	32
29	.774217	2.85	.905272	1.56	.868945	4.40	.131055	31
30	.774388	2.84	.905179	1.56	.869209	4.40	.130794	30
31	9.774558	2.84	9.905085	1.56	9.869473	4.40	0.130527	29
32	.774729	2.84	.904992	1.56	.869737	4.40	.130263	28
33	.774899	2.84	.904898	1.56	.870001	4.40	.129999	27
34	.775070	2.84	.904804	1.56	.870265	4.40	.129735	26
35	.775240	2.84	.904711	1.56	.870529	4.40	.129471	25
36	.775410	2.83	.904617	1.56	.870793	4.40	.129207	24
37	.775580	2.83	.904523	1.56	.871057	4.40	.128943	23
38	.775750	2.83	.904429	1.57	.871321	4.40	.128679	22
39	.775920	2.83	.904335	1.57	.871585	4.40	.128415	21
40	.776090	2.83	.904241	1.57	.871849	4.39	.128151	20
41	9.776259	2.83	9.904147	1.57	9.872112	4.39	0.127888	19
42	.776429	2.82	.904053	1.57	.872376	4.39	.127624	18
43	.776598	2.82	.903959	1.57	.872640	4.39	.127360	17
44	.776768	2.82	.903864	1.57	.872903	4.39	.127097	16
45	.776937	2.82	.903770	1.57	.873167	4.39	.126833	15
46	.777106	2.82	.903676	1.57	.873430	4.39	.126570	14
47	.777275	2.81	.903581	1.57	.873694	4.39	.126306	13
48	.777444	2.81	.903487	1.57	.873957	4.39	.126043	12
49	.777613	2.81	.903392	1.58	.874220	4.39	.125780	11
50	.777781	2.81	.903298	1.58	874484	4.39	.125516	10
51	9.777950	2.81	9.903203	1.58	9.874747	4.39	0.125253	9
52	.778119	2.81	.903108	1.58	.875010	4.39	.124990	8
53	.778287	2.80	.903014	1.58	.875273	4.38	.124727	7
54	.778455	2.80	.902919	1.58	.875536	4.38	.124464	6
55	.778624	2.80	.902824	1.58	.875800	4.38	.124200	5
56	.778792	2.80	.902729	1.58	.876063	4.38	.123937	4
57	.778960	2.80	.902634	1.58	.876326	4.38	.123674	3
58	.779128	2.80	.902539	1.59	.876589	4.38	.123411	2
59	.779295	2.79	.902444	1.59	.876851	4.38	.123149	1
60	.779463		.902349		.877114		122886	0
	Cosine.	D.	Sine.	D.	Cotang.	D.	Tang.	M.

53°

37°

M.	Sine.	D.	Cosine.	D.	Tang.	D.	Cotang.	
0	9.779463	2.79	9.902349	1.59	9.877114	4.38	0.122886	60
1	.779631	2.79	.902253	1.59	.877377	4.38	.122623	59
2	.779798	2.79	.902158	1.59	.877640	4.38	.122360	58
3	.779966	2.79	.902063	1.59	.877903	4.38	.122097	57
4	.780133	2.79	.901967	1.59	.878165	4.38	.121835	56
5	.780300	2.78	.901872	1.59	.878428	4.38	.121572	55
6	.780467	2.78	.901776	1.59	.878691	4.38	.121309	54
7	.780634	2.78	.901681	1.59	.878953	4.37	.121047	53
8	.780801	2.78	.901585	1.59	.879216	4.37	.120784	52
9	.780968	2.78	.901490	1.59	.879478	4.37	.120522	51
10	.781134	2.78	.901394	1.60	.879741	4.37	.120259	50
11	9.781301	2.77	9.901298	1.60	9.880003	4.37	0.119997	49
12	.781468	2.77	.901202	1.60	.880265	4.37	.119735	48
13	.781634	2.77	.901106	1.60	.880528	4.37	.119472	47
14	.781800	2.77	.901010	1.60	.880790	4.37	.119210	46
15	.781966	2.77	.900914	1.60	.881052	4.37	.118948	45
16	.782132	2.77	.900818	1.60	.881314	4.37	.118686	44
17	.782298	2.76	.900722	1.60	.881576	4.37	.118424	43
18	.782464	2.76	.900626	1.60	.881839	4.37	.118161	42
19	.782630	2.76	.900529	1.60	.882101	4.37	.117899	41
20	.782796	2.76	.900433	1.61	.882363	4.36	.117637	40
21	9.782961	2.76	9.900337	1.61	9.882625	4.36	0.117375	39
22	.783127	2.76	.900240	1.61	.882887	4.36	.117113	38
23	.783292	2.75	.900144	1.61	.883148	4.36	.116852	37
24	.783458	2.75	.900047	1.61	.883410	4.36	.116590	36
25	.783623	2.75	.899951	1.61	.883672	4.36	.116328	35
26	.783788	2.75	.899854	1.61	.883934	4.36	.116066	34
27	.783953	2.75	.899757	1.61	.884196	4.36	.115804	33
28	.784118	2.75	.899660	1.61	.884457	4.36	.115543	32
29	.784282	2.74	.899564	1.61	.884719	4.36	.115281	31
30	.784447	2.74	.899467	1.62	.884980	4.36	.115020	30
31	9.784612	2.74	9.899370	1.62	9.885242	4.36	0.114758	29
32	.784776	2.74	.899273	1.62	.885503	4.36	.114497	28
33	.784941	2.74	.899176	1.62	.885765	4.36	.114235	27
34	.785105	2.74	.899078	1.62	.886026	4.36	.113974	26
35	.785269	2.73	.898981	1.62	.886288	4.36	.113712	25
36	.785433	2.73	.898884	1.62	.886549	4.35	.113451	24
37	.785597	2.73	.898787	1.62	.886810	4.35	.113190	23
38	.785761	2.73	.898689	1.62	.887072	4.35	.112928	22
39	.785925	2.73	.898592	1.62	.887333	4.35	.112667	21
40	.786089	2.73	.898494	1.63	.887594	4.35	.112406	20
41	9.786252	2.72	9.898397	1.63	9.887855	4.35	0.112145	19
42	.786416	2.72	.898299	1.63	.888116	4.35	.111884	18
43	.786579	2.72	.898202	1.63	.888377	4.35	.111623	17
44	.786742	2.72	.898104	1.63	.888639	4.35	.111361	16
45	.786906	2.72	.898006	1.63	.888900	4.35	.111100	15
46	.787069	2.72	.897908	1.63	.889160	4.35	.110840	14
47	.787232	2.71	.897810	1.63	.889421	4.35	.110579	13
48	.787395	2.71	.897712	1.63	.889682	4.35	.110318	12
49	.787557	2.71	.897614	1.63	.889943	4.35	.110057	11
50	.787720	2.71	.897516	1.63	.890204	4.34	.109796	10
51	9.787883	2.71	9.897418	1.64	9.890465	4.34	0.109535	9
52	.788045	2.71	.897320	1.64	.890725	4.34	.109275	8
53	.788208	2.71	.897222	1.64	.890986	4.34	.109014	7
54	.788370	2.70	.897123	1.64	.891247	4.34	.108753	6
55	.788532	2.70	.897025	1.64	.891507	4.34	.108493	5
56	.788694	2.70	.896926	1.64	.891768	4.34	.108232	4
57	.788856	2.70	.896828	1.64	.892028	4.34	.107972	3
58	.789018	2.70	.896729	1.64	.892289	4.34	.107711	2
59	.789180	2.70	.896631	1.64	.892549	4.34	.107451	1
60	.789342		.896532		.892810		.107190	0
	Cosine	D.	Sine.	D.	Cotang.	D.	Tang.	M

52°

38°

M	Sine.	D.	Cosine.	D.	Tang.	D.	Cotang.	
0	9.789342	2.69	9.896532	1.64	9.892810	4.34	0.107190	60
1	.789504	2.69	.896433	1.65	.893070	4.34	.106930	59
2	.789665	2.69	.896335	1.65	.893331	4.34	.106669	58
3	.789827	2.69	.896236	1.65	.893591	4.34	.106409	57
4	.789988	2.69	.896137	1.65	.893851	4.34	.106149	56
5	.790149	2.69	.896038	1.65	.894111	4.34	.105889	55
6	.790310	2.68	.895939	1.65	.894371	4.34	.105629	54
7	.790471	2.68	.895840	1.65	.894632	4.33	.105368	53
8	.790632	2.68	.895741	1.65	.894892	4.33	.105108	52
9	.790793	2.68	.895641	1.65	.895152	4.33	.104848	51
10	.790954	2.68	.895542	1.65	.895412	4.33	.104588	50
11	9.791115	2.68	9.895443	1.66	9.895672	4.33	0.104328	49
12	.791275	2.67	.895343	1.66	.895932	4.33	.104068	48
13	.791436	2.67	.895244	1.66	.896192	4.33	.103808	47
14	.791596	2.67	.895145	1.66	.896452	4.33	.103548	46
15	.791757	2.67	.895045	1.66	.896712	4.33	.103288	45
16	.791917	2.67	.894945	1.66	.896971	4.33	.103029	44
17	.792077	2.67	.894846	1.66	.897231	4.33	.102769	43
18	.792237	2.66	.894746	1.66	.897491	4.33	.102509	42
19	.792397	2.66	.894646	1.66	.897751	4.33	.102249	41
20	.792557	2.66	.894546	1.66	.898010	4.33	.101990	40
21	9.792716	2.66	9.894446	1.67	9.898270	4.33	0.101730	39
22	.792876	2.66	.894346	1.67	.898530	4.33	.101470	38
23	.793035	2.66	.894246	1.67	.898789	4.33	.101211	37
24	.793195	2.65	.894146	1.67	.899049	4.32	.100951	36
25	.793354	2.65	.894046	1.67	.899308	4.32	.100692	35
26	.793514	2.65	.893946	1.67	.899568	4.32	.100432	34
27	.793673	2.65	.893846	1.67	.899827	4.32	.100173	33
28	.793832	2.65	.893745	1.67	.900086	4 32	.099914	32
29	.793991	2.65	.893645	1.67	.900346	4.32	.099654	31
30	.794150	2.64	.893544	1.67	.900605	4.32	.099395	30
31	9.794308	2.64	9.893444	1.68	9.900864	4.32	0.099136	29
32	.794467	2.64	.893343	1.68	.901124	4.32	.098876	28
33	.794626	2.64	.893243	1.68	.901383	4.32	.098617	27
34	.794784	2.64	.893142	1.68	.901642	4.32	.098358	26
35	.794942	2.64	.893041	1.68	.901901	4.32	.098099	25
36	.795101	2.64	.892940	1.68	.902160	4.32	.097840	24
37	.795259	2.63	.892839	1.68	.902419	4.32	.097581	23
38	.795417	2.63	.892739	1.68	.902679	4.32	.097321	22
39	.795575	2.63	.892638	1.68	.902938	4.32	.097062	21
40	.795733	2.63	.892536	1.68	.903197	4.31	.096803	20
41	9.795891	2.63	9.892435	1.69	9.903455	4.31	0.096545	19
42	.796049	2.63	.892334	1.69	.903714	4.31	.096286	18
43	.796206	2.63	.892233	1.69	.903973	4.31	.096027	17
44	.796364	2.62	.892132	1.69	.904232	4.31	.095768	16
45	.796521	2.62	.892030	1.69	.904491	4.31	.095509	15
46	.796679	2.62	.891929	1.69	.904750	4.31	.095250	14
47	.796836	2.62	.891827	1.69	.905008	4.31	.094992	13
48	.796993	2.62	.891726	1.69	.905267	4.31	.094733	12
49	.797150	2.61	.891624	1.69	.905526	4.31	.094474	11
50	.797307	2.61	.891523	1.70	.905784	4.31	.094216	10
51	9.797464	2.61	9.891421	1.70	9.906043	4.31	0.093957	9
52	.797621	2.61	.891319	1.70	.906302	4.31	.093698	8
53	.797777	2.61	.891217	1.70	.906560	4.31	.093440	7
54	.797934	2.61	.891115	1.70	.906819	4.31	.093181	6
55	.798091	2.61	.891013	1.70	.907077	4.31	.092923	5
56	.798247	2.61	.890911	1.70	.907336	4.31	.092664	4
57	.798403	2.60	.890809	1.70	.907594	4.31	.092406	3
58	.798560	2.60	.890707	1.70	.907852	4.31	.092148	2
59	.798716	2.60	.890605	1.70	.908111	4.30	.091889	1
60	.798872		.890503		.908369		.091631	0
	Cosine.	D.	Sine.	D.	Cotang.	D.	Tang.	M.

51°

39°

M.	Sine.	D.	Cosine.	D.	Tang.	D.	Cotang.	
0	9.798872	2.60	9.890503	1.70	9.908369	4.30	0.091631	60
1	.799028	2.60	.890400	1.71	.908628	4.30	.091372	59
2	.799184	2.60	.890298	1.71	.908886	4.30	.091114	58
3	.799339	2.59	.890195	1.71	.909144	4.30	.090856	57
4	.799495	2.59	.890093	1.71	.909402	4.30	090598	56
5	.799651	2.59	.889990	1.71	.909660	4.30	.090340	55
6	.799806	2.59	.889888	1.71	.909918	4.30	.090082	54
7	.799962	2.59	.889785	1.71	.910177	4.30	.089823	53
8	.800117	2.59	.889682	1.71	.910435	4.30	.089565	52
9	.800272	2.58	.889579	1.71	.910693	4.30	.089307	51
10	.800427	2.58	.889477	1.71	.910951	4.30	.089049	50
11	9.800582	2.58	9.889374	1.72	9.911209	4.30	0.088791	49
12	.800737	2.58	.889271	1.72	.911467	4.30	.088533	48
13	.800892	2 58	.889168	1.72	.911724	4.30	.088276	47
14	.801047	2 58	.889064	1.72	.911982	4.30	.088018	46
15	.801201	2.58	.888961	1.72	.912240	4.30	087760	45
16	.801356	2.57	.888858	1.72	.912498	4.30	.087502	44
17	.801511	2.57	.888755	1.72	.912756	4.30	.087244	43
18	.801665	2 57	.888651	1.72	.913014	4.29	.086986	42
19	.801819	2.57	.888548	1.72	.913271	4.29	.086729	41
20	.801973	2.57	.888444	1.73	.913529	4.29	.086471	40
21	9.802128	2.57	9.888341	1.73	9.913787	4.29	0.086213	39
22	.802282	2.56	.888237	1.73	.914044	4.29	.085956	38
23	.802436	2.56	.888134	1.73	.914302	4.29	.085698	37
24	.802589	2.56	.888030	1.73	.914560	4.29	.085440	36
25	.802743	2.56	.887926	1.73	.914817	4 29	.085183	35
26	.802897	2.56	.887822	1.73	.915075	4.29	.084925	34
27	.803050	2.56	.887718	1.73	.915332	4.29	.084668	33
28	.803204	2.56	.887614	1.73	.915590	4.29	.084410	32
29	.803357	2.55	.887510	1.73	.915847	4.29	.084153	31
30	.803511	2.55	.887406	1.74	.916104	4.29	.083896	30
31	9.803664	2.55	9.887302	1.74	9.916362	4.29	0.083638	29
32	.803817	2.55	.887198	1.74	.916619	4.29	.083381	28
33	.803970	2.55	.887093	1.74	.916877	4.29	.083123	27
34	.804123	2.55	.886989	1.74	.917134	4.29	.082866	26
35	.804276	2.54	.886885	1.74	.917391	4.29	.082609	25
36	.804428	2.54	.886780	1.74	.917648	4.29	.082352	24
37	.804581	2.54	.886676	1.74	.917905	4.29	.082095	23
38	.804734	2.54	.886571	1.74	.918163	4.28	.081837	22
39	.804886	2.54	.886466	1.74	.918420	4.28	.081580	21
40	.805039	2.54	.886362	1.75	.918677	4.28	.081323	20
41	9.805191	2.54	9.886257	1.75	9.918934	4.28	0.081066	19
42	.805343	2.53	.886152	1.75	.919191	4.28	.080809	18
43	.805495	2.53	.886047	1.75	.919448	4.28	.080552	17
44	.805647	2.53	.885942	1.75	.919705	4.28	.080295	16
45	.805799	2.53	.885837	1.75	.919962	4.28	.080038	15
46	.805951	2.53	.885732	1.75	.920219	4.28	.079781	14
47	.806103	2.53	.385627	1.75	.920476	4.28	.079524	13
48	.806254	2.53	.885522	1.75	.920733	4.28	.079267	12
49	.806406	2.52	.885416	1.75	.920990	4.28	.079010	11
50	.806557	2.52	.885311	1.76	.921247	4.28	.078753	10
51	9.806709	2.52	9.885205	1.76	9.921503	4.28	0.078497	9
52	806860	2.52	.885100	1.76	.921760	4.28	.078240	8
53	.807011	2.52	.884994	1.76	.922017	4.28	.077983	7
54	.807163	2.52	.884889	1.76	.922274	4.28	.077726	6
55	.807314	2.52	.884783	1.76	.922530	4.28	.077470	5
56	.807465	2.51	.884677	1.76	.922787	4 28	.077213	4
57	.807615	2.51	.884572	1.76	.923044	4.28	.076956	3
58	.807766	2.51	.884466	1.76	.923300	4.28	.076700	2
59	.807917	2.51	.884360	1.76	.923557	4.27	.076443	1
60	.808067		.884254		.923813		.076187	0
	Cosine	D.	Sine.	D	Cotang.	D.	Tang.	M

50°

40°

M	Sine.	D.	Cosine.	D.	Tang.	D.	Cotang.	
0	9.808067	2.51	9.884254	1.77	9.923813	4.27	0.076187	60
1	.808218	2.51	.884148	1.77	.924070	4.27	.075930	59
2	.808368	2.51	.884042	1.77	.924327	4.27	.075673	58
3	.808519	2.50	.883936	1.77	.924583	4.27	.075417	57
4	.808669	2.50	.883829	1.77	.924840	4.27	.075160	56
5	.808819	2.50	.883723	1.77	.925096	4.27	.074904	55
6	.808969	2.50	.883617	1.77	.925352	4.27	.074648	54
7	.809119	2.50	.883510	1.77	.925609	4.27	.074391	53
8	.809269	2.50	.883404	1.77	.925865	4.27	.074135	52
9	.809419	2.49	.883297	1.78	.926122	4.27	.073878	51
10	.809569	2.49	.883191	1.78	.926378	4.27	.073622	50
11	9.809718	2.49	9.883084	1.78	9.926634	4.27	0.073366	49
12	.809868	2.49	.882977	1.78	.926890	4.27	.073110	48
13	.810017	2.49	.882871	1.78	.927147	4.27	.072853	47
14	.810167	2.49	.882764	1.78	.927403	4.27	.072597	46
15	.810316	2.48	.882657	1.78	.927659	4.27	.072341	45
16	.810465	2.48	.882550	1.78	.927915	4.27	.072085	44
17	.810614	2.48	.882443	1.78	.928171	4.27	.071829	43
18	.810763	2.48	.882336	1.79	.928427	4.27	.071573	42
19	.810912	2.48	.882229	1.79	.928683	4.27	.071317	41
20	.811061	2.48	.882121	1.79	.928940	4.27	.071060	40
21	9.811210	2.48	9.882014	1.79	9.929196	4.27	0.070804	39
22	.811358	2.47	.881907	1.79	.929452	4.27	.070548	38
23	.811507	2.47	.881799	1.79	.929708	4.27	.070292	37
24	.811655	2.47	.881692	1.79	.929964	4.26	.070036	36
25	.811804	2.47	.881584	1.79	.920220	4.26	.069780	35
26	.811952	2.47	.881477	1.79	.930475	4.26	.069525	34
27	.812100	2.47	.881369	1.79	.930731	4.26	.069269	33
28	.812248	2.47	.881261	1.80	.930987	4.26	.069013	32
29	.812396	2.46	.881153	1.80	.931243	4.26	.068757	31
30	.812544	2.46	.881046	1.80	.931499	4.26	.068501	30
31	9.812692	2.46	9.880938	1.80	9.931755	4.26	0.068245	29
32	.812840	2.46	.880830	1.80	.932010	4.26	.067990	28
33	.812988	2.46	.880722	1.80	.932266	4.26	.067734	27
34	.813135	2.46	.880613	1.80	.932522	4.26	.067478	26
35	.813283	2.46	.880505	1.80	.932778	4.26	.067222	25
36	.813430	2.45	.880397	1.80	.933033	4.26	.066967	24
37	.813578	2.45	.880289	1.81	.933289	4.26	.066711	23
38	.813725	2.45	.880180	1.81	.933545	4.26	.066455	22
39	.813872	2.45	.880072	1.81	.933800	4.26	.066200	21
40	.814019	2.45	.879963	1.81	.934056	4.26	.065944	20
41	9.814166	2.45	9.879855	1.81	9.934311	4.26	0.065689	19
42	.814313	2.45	.879746	1.81	.934567	4.26	.065433	18
43	.814460	2.44	.879637	1.81	.934823	4.26	.065177	17
44	.814607	2.44	.879529	1.81	.935078	4.26	.064922	16
45	.814753	2.44	.879420	1.81	.935333	4.26	.064667	15
46	.814900	2.44	.879311	1.81	.935589	4.26	.064411	14
47	.815046	2.44	.879202	1.82	.935844	4.26	.064156	13
48	.815193	2.44	.879093	1.82	.936100	4.26	.063900	12
49	.815339	2.44	.878984	1.82	.936355	4.26	.063645	11
50	.815485	2.43	.878875	1.82	.936610	4.26	.063390	10
51	9.815631	2.43	9.878766	1.82	9.936866	4.25	0.063134	9
52	.815778	2.43	.878656	1.82	.937121	4.25	.062879	8
53	.815924	2.43	.878547	1.82	.937376	4.25	.062624	7
54	.816069	2.43	.878438	1.82	.937632	4.25	.062368	6
55	.816215	2.43	.878328	1.82	.937887	4.25	.062113	5
56	.816361	2.43	.878219	1.83	.938142	4.25	.061858	4
57	.816507	2.42	.878109	1.83	.938398	4.25	.061602	3
58	.816652	2.42	.877999	1.83	.938653	4.25	.061347	2
59	.816798	2.42	.877890	1.83	.938908	4.25	.061092	1
60	.816943		.877780		.939163		.060837	0
	Cosine.	D.	Sine.	D.	Cotang.	D.	Tang.	M.

49°

41°

M.	Sine.	D.	Cosine.	D.	Tang.	D.	Cotang.	
0	9.816943	2.42	9.877780	1.83	9.939168	4.25	0.060837	60
1	.817088	2.42	.877670	1.83	.939418	4.25	.060582	59
2	.817233	2 42	.877560	1.83	.939673	4.25	.060327	58
3	.817379	2.42	.877450	1.83	.939928	4.25	.060072	57
4	.817524	2.41	.877340	1.83	.940183	4.25	.059817	56
5	.817668	2.41	.877230	1.84	.940438	4.25	.059562	55
6	.817813	2.41	.877120	1.84	.940694	4.25	.059306	54
7	.817958	2.41	.877010	1.84	.940949	4.25	.059051	53
8	.818103	2.41	.876899	1.84	.941204	4 25	.058796	52
9	.818247	2.41	.876789	1.84	.941458	4.25	.058542	51
10	.818392	2.41	.876678	1.84	.941714	4.25	.058286	50
11	9.818536	2.40	9.876568	1.84	9.941968	4.25	0.058032	49
12	.818681	2.40	.876457	1.84	.942223	4.25	.057777	48
13	.818825	2.40	.876347	1.84	.942478	4.25	.057522	47
14	.818969	2 40	.876236	1.85	.942733	4.25	.057267	46
15	.819113	2.40	.876125	1.85	.942988	4.25	.057012	45
16	.819257	2.40	.876014	1.85	.943248	4.25	.056757	44
17	.819401	2.40	.875904	1.85	.943498	4.25	.056502	43
18	.819545	2.39	.875793	1.85	.943752	4.25	.056248	42
19	.819689	2.39	.875682	1.85	.944007	4.25	.055993	41
20	.819832	2.39	.875571	1.85	.944262	4.25	.055738	40
21	9.819976	2.39	9.875459	1.85	9.944517	4.25	0.055483	39
22	.820120	2.39	.875348	1.85	.944771	4.24	.055229	38
23	.820263	2.39	.875237	1.85	.945026	4.24	.054974	37
24	.820406	2.39	.875126	1.86	.945281	4.24	.054719	36
25	.820550	2.38	.875014	1.86	.945535	4.24	.054465	35
26	.820693	2.38	.874903	1.86	.945790	4.24	.054210	34
27	.820836	2.38	.874791	1.86	.946045	4.24	.053955	33
28	.820979	2.38	.874680	1.86	.946299	4.24	.053701	32
29	.821122	2.38	.874568	1.86	.946554	4.24	.053446	31
30	.821265	2.38	.874456	1.86	.946808	4.24	.053192	30
31	9.821407	2.38	9.874344	1.86	9.947063	4.24	0.052937	29
32	.821550	2.38	.874232	1.87	.947318	4.24	.052682	28
33	.821693	2.37	.874121	1.87	.947572	4.24	.052428	27
34	.821835	2.37	.874009	1.87	.947826	4.24	.052174	26
35	.821977	2.37	.873896	1.87	.948081	4.24	.051919	25
36	.822120	2.37	.873784	1.87	.948336	4.24	.051664	24
37	.822262	2.37	.873672	1.87	.948590	4.24	.051410	23
38	.822404	2.37	.873560	1.87	.948844	4.24	.051156	22
39	.822546	2.37	.873448	1.87	.949099	4.24	.050901	21
40	.822688	2.36	.873335	1.87	.949353	4.24	.050647	20
41	9.822830	2.36	9.873223	1.87	9.949607	4.24	0.050393	19
42	.822972	2.36	.873110	1.88	.949862	4.24	.050138	18
43	.823114	2.36	.872998	1.88	.950116	4.24	.049884	17
44	.823255	2.36	.872885	1.88	.950370	4.24	.049630	16
45	.823397	2.36	.872772	1.88	.950625	4.24	.049375	15
46	.823539	2.36	.872659	1.88	.950879	4.24	.049121	14
47	.823680	2.35	.872547	1.88	.951133	4.24	.048867	13
48	.823821	2.35	.872434	1.88	.951388	4.24	.048612	12
49	.823963	2.35	.872321	1.88	.951642	4.24	.048358	11
50	.824104	2.35	.872208	1.88	.951896	4.24	.048104	10
51	9.824245	2.35	9.872095	1.89	9.952150	4.24	0.047850	9
52	.824386	2.35	.871981	1.89	.952405	4.24	.047595	8
53	.824527	2.35	.871868	1.89	.952659	4.24	.047341	7
54	.824668	2.34	.871755	1.89	.952913	4.24	.047087	6
55	.824808	2.34	.871641	1.89	.953167	4.23	.046833	5
56	.824949	2.34	.871528	1.89	.953421	4.23	.046579	4
57	.825090	2.34	.871414	1 89	.953675	4.23	.046325	3
58	.825230	2.34	.871301	1.89	.953929	4.23	.046071	2
59	.825371	2.34	871187	1.89	.954183	4.23	.045817	1
60	.825511		.871073		.954437		.045563	0
	Cosine.	D	Sine.	D.	Cotang.	D.	Tang.	M.

48°

42°

M	Sine.	D.	Cosine.	D.	Tang.	D.	Cotang.	
0	9.825511	2.34	9.871073	1.90	9.954437	4.23	0.045563	60
1	.825651	2.33	.870960	1.90	.954691	4.23	.045309	59
2	.825791	2.33	.870846	1.90	.954945	4.23	.045055	58
3	.825931	2.33	.870732	1.90	.955200	4.23	.044800	57
4	.826071	2.33	.870618	1.90	.955454	4.23	.044546	56
5	.826211	2.33	.870504	1.90	.955707	4.23	.044293	55
6	.826351	2.33	.870390	1.90	.955961	4.23	.044039	54
7	.826491	2.33	.870276	1.90	.956215	4.23	.043785	53
8	.826631	2.33	.870161	1.90	.956469	4.23	.043531	52
9	.826770	2.32	.870047	1.91	.956723	4.23	.043277	51
10	.826910	2.32	.869933	1.91	.956977	4.23	.043023	50
11	9.827049	2.32	9.869818	1.91	9.957231	4.23	0.042769	49
12	.827189	2.32	.869704	1.91	.957485	4.23	.042515	48
13	.827328	2.32	.869589	1.91	.957739	4.23	.042261	47
14	.827467	2.32	.869474	1.91	.957993	4.23	.042007	46
15	.827606	2.32	.869360	1.91	.958246	4.23	.041754	45
16	.827745	2.32	.869245	1.91	.958500	4.23	.041500	44
17	.827884	2.31	.869130	1.91	.958754	4.23	.041246	43
18	.828023	2.31	.869015	1.92	.959008	4.23	.040992	42
19	.828162	2.31	.868900	1.92	.959262	4.23	.040738	41
20	.828301	2.31	.868785	1.92	.959516	4.23	.040484	40
21	9.828439	2.31	9.868670	1.92	9.959769	4.23	0.040231	39
22	.828578	2.31	.868555	1.92	.960023	4.23	039977	38
23	.828716	2.31	.868440	1.92	.960277	4.23	.039723	37
24	.828855	2.30	.868324	1.92	.960531	4.23	.039469	36
25	.828993	2.30	.868209	1.92	.960784	4.23	.039216	35
26	.829131	2.30	.868093	1.92	.961038	4.23	.038962	34
27	.829269	2.30	.867978	1.93	.961291	4.23	.038709	33
28	.829407	2.30	.867862	1.93	.961545	4.23	.038455	32
29	.829545	2.30	.867747	1.93	.961799	4.23	.038201	31
30	.829683	2.30	.867631	1.93	.962052	4.23	.037948	30
31	9.829821	2.29	9.867515	1.93	9.962306	4.23	0.037694	29
32	.829959	2.29	.867399	1.93	.962560	4.23	.037440	28
33	.830097	2.29	.867283	1.93	.962813	4.23	.037187	27
34	.830234	2.29	.867167	1.93	.963067	4.23	.036933	26
35	.830372	2.29	.867051	1.93	.963320	4.23	.036680	25
36	.830509	2.29	.866935	1.94	.963574	4.23	.036426	24
37	.830646	2.29	.866819	1.94	.963827	4.23	.036173	23
38	.830784	2.29	.866703	1.94	.964081	4.23	.035919	22
39	.830921	2.28	.866586	1.94	.964335	4.23	.035665	21
40	.831058	2.28	.866470	1.94	.964588	4.22	.035412	20
41	9.831195	2.28	9.866353	1.94	9.964842	4.22	0.035158	19
42	.831332	2.28	.866237	1.94	.965095	4.22	.034905	18
43	.831469	2.28	.866120	1.94	.965349	4.22	.034651	17
44	.831606	2.28	.866004	1.95	.965602	4.22	.034398	16
45	.831742	2.28	.865887	1.95	.965855	4.22	.034145	15
46	.831879	2.28	.865770	1.95	.966105	4.22	.033891	14
47	.832015	2.27	.865653	1.95	.966362	4.22	.033638	13
48	.832152	2.27	.865536	1.95	.966616	4.22	.033384	12
49	.832288	2.27	.865419	1.95	.966869	4.22	.033131	11
50	.832425	2.27	.865302	1.95	.967123	4.22	.032877	10
51	9.832561	2.27	9.865185	1.95	9.967376	4.22	0.032624	9
52	.832697	2.27	.865068	1.95	.967629	4.22	.032371	8
53	.832833	2.27	.864950	1.95	.967883	4.22	.032117	7
54	.882969	2.26	.864833	1.96	.968136	4.22	.031864	6
55	.833105	2.26	.864716	1.96	.968389	4.22	.031611	5
56	.833241	2.26	.864598	1.96	.968643	4.22	.031357	4
57	.833377	2.26	.864481	1.96	.968896	4.22	.031104	3
58	.833512	2.26	.864363	1.96	.969149	4.22	.030851	2
59	.833648	2.26	.864245	1.96	.969403	4.22	.030597	1
60	833783		.864127		.969656		.030344	0
	Cosine.	D.	Sine.	D.	Cotang.	D.	Tang.	M.

47°

43°

M.	Sine.	D.	Cosine.	D.	Tang.	D.	Cotang.	
0	9.833783	2.26	9.864127	1.96	9.969656	4.22	0.030344	60
1	.833919	2.25	.864010	1.96	.969909	4.22	.030091	59
2	.834054	2.25	.863892	1.97	.970162	4.22	.029838	58
3	.834189	2.25	.863774	1.97	.970416	4.22	.029584	57
4	.834325	2.25	.863656	1.97	.970669	4.22	.029331	56
5	.834460	2.25	.863538	1.97	.970922	4.22	.029078	55
6	.834595	2.25	.863419	1.97	.971175	4.22	.028825	54
7	.834730	2.25	.863301	1.97	.971429	4.22	.028571	53
8	.834865	2.25	.863183	1.97	.971682	4.22	.028318	52
9	.834999	2.24	.863064	1.97	.971935	4.22	.028065	51
10	.835134	2.24	.862946	1.98	.972188	4.22	.027812	50
11	9.835269	2.24	9.862827	1.98	9.972441	4.22	0.027559	49
12	.835403	2.24	.862709	1.98	.972694	4.22	.027306	48
13	.835538	2.24	.862590	1.98	.972948	4.22	.027052	47
14	.835672	2.24	.862471	1.98	.973201	4.22	.026799	46
15	.835807	2.24	.862353	1.98	.973454	4.22	.026546	45
16	.835941	2.24	.862234	1.98	.973707	4.22	.026293	44
17	.836075	2.23	.862115	1.98	.973960	4.22	.026040	43
18	.836209	2.23	.861996	1.98	.974213	4.22	.025787	42
19	.836343	2.23	.861877	1.98	.974466	4.22	.025534	41
20	.836477	2.23	.861758	1.99	.974719	4.22	.025281	40
21	9.836611	2.23	9.861638	1.99	9.974973	4.22	0.025027	39
22	.836745	2.23	.861519	1.99	.975226	4.22	.024774	38
23	.836878	2.23	.861400	1.99	.975479	4.22	.024521	37
24	.837012	2.22	.861280	1.99	.975732	4.22	.024268	36
25	.837146	2.22	.861161	1.99	.975985	4.22	.024015	35
26	.837279	2.22	.861041	1.99	.976238	4.22	.023762	34
27	.837412	2.22	.860922	1.99	.976491	4.22	.023509	33
28	.837546	2.22	.860802	1.99	.976744	4.22	.023256	32
29	.837679	2.22	.860682	2.00	.976997	4.22	.023003	31
30	.837812	2.22	.860562	2.00	.977250	4.22	.022750	30
31	9.837945	2.22	9.860442	2.00	9.977503	4.22	0.022497	29
32	.838078	2.21	.860322	2.00	.977756	4.22	.022244	28
33	.838211	2.21	.860202	2.00	.978009	4.22	.021991	27
34	.838344	2.21	.860082	2.00	.978262	4.22	.021738	26
35	.838477	2.21	.859962	2.00	.978515	4.22	.021485	25
36	.838610	2.21	.859842	2.00	.978768	4.22	.021232	24
37	.838742	2.21	.859721	2.01	.979021	4.22	.020979	23
38	.838875	2.21	.859601	2.01	.979274	4.22	.020726	22
39	.839007	2.21	.859480	2.01	.979527	4.22	.020473	21
40	.839140	2.20	.859360	2.01	.979780	4.22	.020220	20
41	9.839272	2.20	9.859239	2.01	9.980033	4.22	0.019967	19
42	.839404	2.20	.859119	2.01	.980286	4.22	.019714	18
43	.839536	2.20	.858998	2.01	.980538	4.22	.019462	17
44	.839668	2.20	.858877	2.01	.980791	4.21	.019209	16
45	.839800	2.20	.858756	2.02	.981044	4.21	.018956	15
46	.839932	2.20	.858635	2.02	.981297	4.21	.018703	14
47	.840064	2.19	.858514	2.02	.981550	4.21	.018450	13
48	.840196	2.19	.858393	2.02	.981803	4.21	.018197	12
49	.840328	2.19	.858272	2.02	.982056	4.21	.017944	11
50	.840459	2.19	.858151	2.02	.982309	4.21	.017691	10
51	9.840591	2.19	9.858029	2.02	9.982562	4.21	0.017438	9
52	.840722	2.19	.857908	2.02	.982814	4.21	.017186	8
53	.840854	2.19	.857786	2.02	.983067	4.21	.016933	7
54	.840985	2.19	.857665	2.03	.983320	4.21	.016680	6
55	.841116	2.18	.857543	2.03	.983573	4.21	.016427	5
56	.841247	2.18	.857422	2.03	.983826	4.21	.016174	4
57	.841378	2.18	.857300	2.03	.984079	4.21	.015921	3
58	.841509	2.18	.857178	2.03	.984331	4.21	.015669	2
59	.841640	2.18	.857056	2.03	.984584	4.21	.015416	1
60	.841771		.856934		.984837		.015163	0
	Cosine	D.	Sine.	D.	Cotang.	D.	Tang.	M.

46°

44°

M	Sine.	D	Cosine.	D.	Tang.	D.	Cotang.	
0	9.841771	2.18	9.856934	2.03	9.984837	4.21	0.015163	60
1	.841902	2.18	.856812	2.03	.985090	4.21	.014910	59
2	.842033	2.18	.856690	2.04	.985343	4.21	.014657	58
3	.842163	2.17	.856568	2.04	.985596	4.21	.014404	57
4	.842294	2.17	.856446	2.04	.985848	4.21	.014152	56
5	.842424	2.17	.856323	2.04	.986101	4.21	.013899	55
6	.842555	2.17	.856201	2.04	.986354	4.21	.013646	54
7	.842685	2.17	.856078	2.04	.986607	4.21	.013393	53
8	.842815	2.17	.855956	2.04	.986860	4.21	.013140	52
9	.842946	2.17	.855833	2.04	.987112	4.21	.012888	51
10	.843076	2.17	.855711	2.05	.987365	4.21	.012635	50
11	9.843206	2.16	9.855588	2.05	9.987618	4.21	0.012382	49
12	.843336	2.16	.855465	2.05	.987871	4.21	.012129	48
13	.843466	2.16	.855342	2.05	.988123	4.21	.011877	47
14	.843595	2.16	.855219	2.05	.988376	4.21	.011624	46
15	.843725	2.16	.855096	2.05	.988629	4.21	.011371	45
16	.843855	2.16	.854973	2.05	.988882	4.21	.011118	44
17	.843984	2.16	.854850	2.05	.989134	4.21	.010866	43
18	.844114	2.15	.854727	2.06	.989387	4.21	.010613	42
19	.844243	2.15	.854603	2.06	.989640	4.21	.010360	41
20	.844372	2.15	.854480	2.06	.989893	4.21	.010107	40
21	9.844502	2.15	9.854356	2.06	9.990145	4.21	0.009855	39
22	.844631	2.15	.854233	2.06	.990398	4.21	.009602	38
23	.844760	2.15	.854109	2.06	.990651	4.21	.009849	37
24	.844889	2.15	.853986	2.06	.990903	4.21	.009097	36
25	.845018	2.15	.853862	2.06	.991156	4.21	.008844	35
26	.845147	2.15	.853738	2.06	.991409	4.21	.008591	34
27	.845276	2.14	.853614	2.07	.991662	4.21	.008338	33
28	.845405	2.14	.853490	2.07	.991914	4.21	.008086	32
29	.845533	2.14	.853366	2.07	.992167	4.21	.007833	31
30	.845662	2.14	.853242	2.07	.992420	4.21	.007580	30
31	9.845790	2.14	9.853118	2.07	9.992672	4.21	0.007328	29
32	.845919	2.14	.852994	2.07	.992925	4.21	.007075	28
33	.846047	2.14	.852869	2.07	.993178	4.21	.006822	27
34	.846175	2.14	.852745	2.07	.993430	4.21	.006570	26
35	.846304	2.14	.852620	2.07	.993683	4.21	.006317	25
36	.846432	2.13	.852496	2.08	.993936	4.21	.006064	24
37	.846560	2.13	.852371	2.08	.994189	4.21	.005811	23
38	.846688	2.13	.852247	2.08	.994441	4.21	.005559	22
39	.846816	2.13	.852122	2.08	.994694	4.21	.005306	21
40	.846944	2.13	.851997	2.08	.994947	4.21	.005053	20
41	9.847071	2.13	9.851872	2.08	9.995199	4.21	0.004801	19
42	.847199	2.13	.851747	2.08	.995452	4.21	.004548	18
43	.847327	2.13	.851622	2.08	.995705	4.21	.004295	17
44	.847454	2.12	.851497	2.09	.995957	4.21	004043	16
45	.847582	2.12	.851372	2.09	.996210	4.21	.003790	15
46	.847709	2.12	.851246	2.09	.996463	4.21	.003537	14
47	.847836	2.12	.851121	2.09	.996715	4.21	.003285	13
48	.847964	2.12	.850996	2.09	.996968	4.21	.003032	12
49	.848091	2.12	.850870	2.09	.997221	4.21	.002779	11
50	.848218	2.12	.850745	2.09	.997473	4.21	.002527	10
51	9.848345	2.12	9.850619	2.09	9.997726	4.21	0.002274	9
52	.848472	2.11	.850493	2.10	.997979	4.21	.002021	8
53	.848599	2.11	.850368	2.10	.998231	4.21	.001769	7
54	.848726	2.11	.850242	2.10	.998484	4.21	.001516	6
55	.848852	2.11	.850116	2.10	.998737	4.21	.001263	5
56	.848979	2.11	.849990	2.10	.998989	4.21	.001011	4
57	.849106	2.11	.849864	2.10	.999242	4.21	.000758	3
58	.849232	2.11	.849738	2.10	.999495	4.21	.000505	2
59	.849359	2.11	.849611	2.10	.999748	4.21	.000253	1
60	.849485		.849485		0.000000		0.000000	0
	Cosine	D.	Sine.	D.	Cotang.	D.	Tang.	M

45°

A

TABLE,

CONTAINING THE

LOGARITHMS OF NUMBERS

FROM 1 TO 10,000.

No.	Log.	No.	Log.	No.	Log.	No.	Log.	No.	Log.
1	0.000000	21	1.322219	41	1.612784	61	1.785330	81	1.908485
2	0.301030	22	1.342423	42	1.623249	62	1.792392	82	1.913814
3	0.477121	23	1.361728	43	1.633468	63	1.799341	83	1.919078
4	0.602060	24	1.380211	44	1.643453	64	1.806180	84	1.924279
5	0.698970	25	1.397940	45	1.653213	65	1.812913	85	1.929419
6	0.778151	26	1.414973	46	1.662758	66	1.819544	86	1.934498
7	0.845098	27	1.431364	47	1.672098	67	1.826075	87	1.939519
8	0.903090	28	1.447158	48	1.681241	68	1.832509	88	1.944483
9	0.954243	29	1.462398	49	1.690196	69	1.838849	89	1.949390
10	1.000000	30	1.477121	50	1.698970	70	1.845098	90	1.954243
11	1.041393	31	1.491362	51	1.707570	71	1.851258	91	1.959041
12	1.079181	32	1.505150	52	1.716003	72	1.857332	92	1.963788
13	1.113943	33	1.518514	53	1.724276	73	1.863323	93	1.968483
14	1.146128	34	1.531479	54	1.732394	74	1.869232	94	1.973128
15	1.176091	35	1.544068	55	1.740363	75	1.875061	95	1.977724
16	1.204120	36	1.556303	56	1.748188	76	1.880814	96	1.982271
17	1.230449	37	1.568202	57	1.755875	77	1.886491	97	1.986772
18	1.255273	38	1.579784	58	1.763428	78	1.892095	98	1.991226
19	1.278754	39	1.591065	59	1.770852	79	1.897627	99	1.995635
20	1.301030	40	1.602060	60	1.778151	80	1.903090	100	2.000000

N.	0	1	2	3	4	5	6	7	8	9	D.
100	000000	000434	000868	001301	001734	002166	002598	003029	003461	003891	432
1	4321	4751	5181	5609	6038	6466	6894	7321	7748	8174	428
2	8600	9026	9451	9876	010300	010724	011147	011570	011993	012415	424
3	012837	013259	013680	014100	4521	4940	5360	5779	6197	6616	420
4	7033	7451	7868	8284	8700	9116	9532	9947	020361	020775	416
5	021189	021603	022016	022428	022841	023252	023664	024075	4486	4896	412
6	5306	5715	6125	6533	6942	7350	7757	8164	8571	8978	408
7	9384	9789	030195	030600	031004	031408	031812	032216	032619	033021	404
8	033424	033826	4227	4628	5029	5430	5830	6230	6629	7028	400
9	7426	7825	8223	8620	9017	9414	9811	040207	040602	040998	397
110	041393	041787	042182	042576	042969	043362	043755	044148	044540	044932	393
1	5323	5714	6105	6495	6885	7275	7664	8053	8442	8830	390
2	9218	9606	9993	050380	050766	051153	051538	051924	052309	052694	386
3	053078	053463	053846	4230	4613	4996	5378	5760	6142	6524	383
4	6905	7286	7666	8046	8426	8805	9185	9563	9942	060320	379
5	060698	061075	061452	061829	062206	062582	062958	063333	063709	4083	376
6	4458	4832	5206	5580	5953	6326	6699	7071	7443	7815	373
7	8186	8557	8928	9298	9668	070038	070407	070776	071145	071514	370
8	071882	072250	072617	072985	073352	3718	4085	4451	4816	5182	366
9	5547	5912	6276	6640	7004	7368	7731	8094	8457	8819	363
120	079181	079543	079904	080266	080626	080987	081347	081707	082067	082426	360
1	082785	083144	083503	3861	4219	4576	4934	5291	5647	6004	357
2	6360	6716	7071	7426	7781	8136	8490	8845	9198	9552	355
3	9905	090258	090611	090963	091315	091667	092018	092370	092721	093071	352
4	093422	3772	4122	4471	4820	5169	5518	5866	6215	6562	349
5	6910	7257	7604	7951	8298	8644	8990	9335	9681	100026	346
6	100371	100715	101059	101403	101747	102091	102434	102777	103119	3462	343
7	3804	4146	4487	4828	5169	5510	5851	6191	6531	6871	341
8	7210	7549	7888	8227	8565	8903	9241	9579	9916	110253	338
9	110590	110926	111263	111599	111934	112270	112605	112940	113275	3609	335
130	113943	114277	114611	114944	115278	115611	115943	116276	116608	116940	333
1	7271	7603	7934	8265	8595	8926	9256	9586	9915	120245	330
2	120574	120903	121231	121560	121888	122216	122544	122871	123198	3525	328
3	3852	4178	4504	4830	5156	5481	5806	6131	6456	6781	325
4	7105	7429	7753	8076	8399	8722	9045	9368	9690	130012	323
5	130334	130655	130977	131298	131619	131939	132260	132580	132900	3219	321
6	3539	3858	4177	4496	4814	5133	5451	5769	6086	6403	318
7	6721	7037	7354	7671	7987	8303	8618	8934	9249	9564	316
8	9879	140194	140508	140822	141136	141450	141763	142076	142389	142702	314
9	143015	3327	3639	3951	4263	4574	4885	5196	5507	5818	311
140	146128	146438	146748	147058	147367	147676	147985	148294	148603	148911	309
1	9219	9527	9835	150142	150449	150756	151063	151370	151676	151982	307
2	152288	152594	152900	3205	3510	3815	4120	4424	4728	5032	305
3	5336	5640	5943	6246	6549	3852	7154	7457	7759	8061	303
4	8362	8664	8965	9266	9567	9868	160168	160469	160769	161068	301
5	161368	161667	161967	162266	162564	162863	3161	3460	3758	4055	299
6	4353	4650	4947	5244	5541	5838	6134	6430	6726	7022	297
7	7317	7613	7908	8203	8497	8792	9086	9380	9674	9968	295
8	170262	170555	170848	171141	171434	171726	172019	172311	172603	172895	293
9	3186	3478	3769	4060	4351	4641	4932	5222	5512	5802	291
150	176091	176381	176670	176959	177248	177536	177825	178113	178401	178689	289
1	8977	9264	9552	9839	180126	180413	180699	180986	181272	181558	287
2	181844	182129	182415	182700	2985	3270	3555	3839	4123	4407	285
3	4691	4975	5259	5542	5825	6108	6391	6674	6956	7239	283
4	7521	7803	8084	8366	8647	8928	9209	9490	9771	190051	281
5	190332	190612	190892	191171	191451	191730	192010	192289	192567	2846	279
6	3125	3403	3681	3959	4237	4514	4792	5069	5346	5623	278
7	5900	6176	6453	6729	7005	7281	7556	7832	8107	8382	276
8	8657	8932	9206	9481	9755	200029	200303	200577	200850	201124	274
9	201397	201670	201943	202216	202488	2761	3033	3305	3577	3848	272
N.	0	1	2	3	4	5	6	7	8	9	D

N.	0	1	2	3	4	5	6	7	8	9	D.
160	204120	204391	204663	204934	205204	205475	205746	206016	206286	206556	271
1	6826	7096	7365	7634	7904	8173	8441	8710	8979	9247	269
2	9515	9783	210051	210319	210586	210853	211121	211388	211654	211921	267
3	212188	212454	2720	2986	3252	3518	3783	4049	4314	4579	266
4	4844	5109	5373	5638	5902	6166	6430	6694	6957	7221	264
5	7484	7747	8010	8273	8536	8798	9060	9323	9585	9846	262
6	220108	220370	220631	220892	221153	221414	221675	221936	222196	222456	261
7	2716	2976	3236	3496	3755	4015	4274	4533	4792	5051	259
8	5309	5568	5826	6084	6342	6600	6858	7115	7372	7630	258
9	7887	8144	8400	8657	8913	9170	9426	9682	9938	230193	256
170	230449	230704	230960	231215	231470	231724	231979	232234	232488	232742	255
1	2996	3250	3504	3757	4011	4264	4517	4770	5023	5276	253
2	5528	5781	6033	6285	6537	6789	7041	7292	7544	7795	252
3	8046	8297	8548	8799	9049	9299	9550	9800	240050	240300	250
4	240549	240799	241048	241297	241546	241795	242044	242293	2541	2790	249
5	3038	3286	3534	3782	4030	4277	4525	4772	5019	5266	248
6	5513	5759	6006	6252	6499	6745	6991	7237	7482	7728	246
7	7973	8219	8464	8709	8954	9198	9443	9687	9932	250176	245
8	250420	250664	250908	251151	251395	251638	251881	252125	252368	2610	243
9	2853	3096	3338	3580	3822	4064	4306	4548	4790	5031	242
180	255273	255514	255755	255996	256237	256477	256718	256958	257198	257439	241
1	7679	7918	8158	8398	8637	8877	9116	9355	9594	9833	239
2	260071	260310	260548	260787	261025	261263	261501	261739	261976	262214	238
3	2451	2688	2925	3162	3399	3636	3873	4109	4346	4582	237
4	4818	5054	5290	5525	5761	5996	6232	6467	6702	6937	235
5	7172	7406	7641	7875	8110	8344	8578	8812	9046	9279	234
6	9513	9746	9980	270213	270446	270679	270912	271144	271377	271609	233
7	271842	272074	272306	2538	2770	3001	3233	3464	3696	3927	232
8	4158	4389	4620	4850	5081	5311	5542	5772	6002	6232	230
9	6462	6692	6921	7151	7380	7609	7838	8067	8296	8525	229
190	278754	278982	279211	279439	279667	279895	280123	280351	280578	280806	228
1	281033	281261	281488	281715	281942	282169	2396	2622	2849	3075	227
2	3301	3527	3753	3979	4205	4431	4656	4882	5107	5332	226
3	5557	5782	6007	6232	6456	6681	6905	7130	7354	7578	225
4	7802	8026	8249	8473	8696	8920	9143	9366	9589	9812	223
5	290035	290257	290480	290702	290925	291147	291369	291591	291813	292034	222
6	2256	2478	2699	2920	3141	3363	3584	3804	4025	4246	221
7	4466	4687	4907	5127	5347	5567	5787	6007	6226	6446	220
8	6665	6884	7104	7323	7542	7761	7979	8198	8416	8635	219
9	8853	9071	9289	9507	9725	9943	300161	300378	300595	300813	218
200	301030	301247	301464	301681	301898	302114	302331	302547	302764	302980	217
1	3196	3412	3628	3844	4059	4275	4491	4706	4921	5136	216
2	5351	5566	5781	5996	6211	6425	6639	6854	7068	7282	215
3	7496	7710	7924	8137	8351	8564	8778	8991	9204	9417	213
4	9630	9843	310056	310268	310481	310693	310906	311118	311330	311542	212
5	311754	311966	2177	2389	2600	2812	3023	3234	3445	3656	211
6	3867	4078	4289	4499	4710	4920	5130	5340	5551	5760	210
7	5970	6180	6390	6599	6809	7018	7227	7436	7646	7854	209
8	8063	8272	8481	8689	8898	9106	9314	9522	9730	9938	208
9	320146	320354	320562	320769	320977	321184	321391	321598	321805	322012	207
210	322219	322426	322633	322839	323046	323252	323458	323665	323871	324077	206
1	4282	4488	4694	4899	5105	5310	5516	5721	5926	6131	205
2	6336	6541	6745	6950	7155	7359	7563	7767	7972	8176	204
3	8380	8583	8787	8991	9194	9398	9601	9805	330008	330211	203
4	330414	330617	330819	331022	331225	331427	331630	331832	2034	2236	202
5	2438	2640	2842	3044	3246	3447	3649	3850	4051	4253	202
6	4454	4655	4856	5057	5257	5458	5658	5859	6059	6260	201
7	6460	6660	6860	7060	7260	7459	7659	7858	8058	8257	200
8	8456	8656	8855	9054	9253	9451	9650	9849	340047	340246	199
9	340444	340642	340841	341039	341237	341435	341632	341830	2028	2225	198
N.	0	1	2	3	4	5	6	7	8	9	D.

N.	0	1	2	3	4	5	6	7	8	9	D
220	342423	342620	342817	343014	343212	343409	343606	343802	343999	344196	197
1	4392	4589	4785	4981	5178	5374	5570	5766	5962	6157	196
2	6353	6549	6744	6939	7135	7330	7525	7720	7915	8110	195
3	8305	8500	8694	8889	9083	9278	9472	9666	9860	350054	194
4	350248	350442	350636	350829	351023	351216	351410	351603	351796	1989	193
5	2183	2375	2568	2761	2954	3147	3339	3532	3724	3916	193
6	4108	4301	4493	4685	4876	5068	5260	5452	5643	5834	192
7	6026	6217	6408	6599	6790	6981	7172	7363	7554	7744	191
8	7935	8125	8316	8506	8696	8886	9076	9266	9456	9646	190
9	9835	360025	360215	360404	360593	360783	360972	361161	361350	361539	189
230	361728	361917	362105	362294	362482	362671	362859	363048	363236	363424	188
1	3612	3800	3988	4176	4363	4551	4739	4926	5113	5301	188
2	5488	5675	5862	6049	6236	6423	6610	6796	6983	7169	187
3	7356	7542	7729	7915	8101	8287	8473	8659	8845	9030	186
4	9216	9401	9587	9772	9958	370143	370328	370513	370698	370883	185
5	371068	371253	371437	371622	371806	1991	2175	2360	2544	2728	184
6	2912	3096	3280	3464	3647	3831	4015	4198	4382	4565	184
7	4748	4932	5115	5298	5481	5664	5846	6029	6212	6394	183
8	6577	6759	6942	7124	7306	7488	7670	7852	8034	8216	182
9	8398	8580	8761	8943	9124	9306	9487	9668	9849	380030	181
240	380211	380392	380573	380754	380934	381115	381296	381476	381656	381837	181
1	2017	2197	2377	2557	2737	2917	3097	3277	3456	3636	180
2	3815	3995	4174	4353	4533	4712	4891	5070	5249	5428	179
3	5606	5785	5964	6142	6321	6499	6677	6856	7034	7212	178
4	7390	7568	7746	7923	8101	8279	8456	8634	8811	8989	178
5	9166	9343	9520	9698	9875	390051	390228	390405	390582	390759	177
6	390935	391112	391288	391464	391641	1817	1993	2169	2345	2521	176
7	2697	2873	3048	3224	3400	3575	3751	3926	4101	4277	176
8	4452	4627	4802	4977	5152	5326	5501	5676	5850	6025	175
9	6199	6374	6548	6722	6896	7071	7245	7419	7592	7766	174
250	397940	398114	398287	398461	398634	398808	398981	399154	399328	399501	173
1	9674	9847	400020	400192	400365	400538	400711	400883	401056	401228	173
2	401401	401573	1745	1917	2089	2261	2433	2605	2777	2949	172
3	3121	3292	3464	3635	3807	3978	4149	4320	4492	4663	171
4	4834	5005	5176	5346	5517	5688	5858	6029	6199	6370	171
5	6540	6710	6881	7051	7221	7391	7561	7731	7901	8070	170
6	8240	8410	8579	8749	8918	9087	9257	9426	9595	9764	169
7	9933	410102	410271	410440	410609	410777	410946	411114	411283	411451	169
8	411620	1788	1956	2124	2293	2461	2629	2796	2964	3132	168
9	3300	3467	3635	3803	3970	4137	4305	4472	4639	4806	167
260	414973	415140	415307	415474	415641	415808	415974	416141	416308	416474	167
1	6641	6807	6973	7139	7306	7472	7638	7804	7970	8135	166
2	8301	8467	8633	8798	8964	9129	9295	9460	9625	9791	165
3	9956	420121	420286	420451	420616	420781	420945	421110	421275	421439	165
4	421604	1768	1933	2097	2261	2426	2590	2754	2918	3082	164
5	3246	3410	3574	3737	3901	4065	4228	4392	4555	4718	164
6	4882	5045	5208	5371	5534	5697	5860	6023	6186	6349	163
7	6511	6674	6836	6999	7161	7324	7486	7648	7811	7973	162
8	8135	8297	8459	8621	8783	8944	9106	9268	9429	9591	162
9	9752	9914	430075	430236	430398	430559	430720	430881	431042	431203	161
270	431364	431525	431685	431846	432007	432167	432328	432488	432649	432809	161
1	2969	3130	3290	3450	3610	3770	3930	4090	4249	4409	160
2	4569	4729	4888	5048	5207	5367	5526	5685	5844	6004	159
3	6163	6322	6481	6640	6799	6957	7116	7275	7433	7592	159
4	7751	7909	8067	8226	8384	8542	8701	8859	9017	9175	158
5	9333	9491	9648	9806	9964	440122	440279	440437	440594	440752	158
6	440909	441066	441224	441381	441538	1695	1852	2009	2166	2323	157
7	2480	2637	2793	2950	3106	3263	3419	3576	3732	3889	157
8	4045	4201	4357	4513	4669	4825	4981	5137	5293	5449	156
9	5604	5760	5915	6071	6226	6382	6537	6692	6848	7003	155
N	0	1	2	3	4	5	6	7	8	9	D.

N.	0	1	2	3	4	5	6	7	8	9	D.
280	447158	447313	447468	447623	447778	447933	448088	448242	448397	448552	155
1	8706	8861	9015	9170	9324	9478	9633	9787	9941	450095	154
2	450249	450403	450557	450711	450865	451018	451172	451326	451479	1633	154
3	1786	1940	2093	2247	2400	2553	2706	2859	3012	3165	153
4	3318	3471	3624	3777	3930	4082	4235	4387	4540	4692	153
5	4845	4997	5150	5302	5454	5606	5758	5910	6062	6214	152
6	6366	6518	6670	6821	6973	7125	7276	7428	7579	7731	152
7	7882	8033	8184	8336	8487	8638	8789	8940	9091	9242	151
8	9392	9543	9694	9845	9995	460146	460296	460447	460597	460748	151
9	460898	461048	461198	461348	461499	1649	1799	1948	2098	2248	150
290	462398	462548	462697	462847	462997	463146	463296	463445	463594	463744	150
1	3893	4042	4191	4340	4490	4639	4788	4936	5085	5234	149
2	5383	5532	5680	5829	5977	6126	6274	6423	6571	6719	149
3	6868	7016	7164	7312	7460	7608	7756	7904	8052	8200	148
4	8347	8495	8643	8790	8938	9085	9233	9380	9527	9675	148
5	9822	9969	470116	470263	470410	470557	470704	470851	470998	471145	147
6	471292	471438	1585	1732	1878	2025	2171	2318	2464	2610	146
7	2756	2903	3049	3195	3341	3487	3633	3779	3925	4071	146
8	4216	4362	4508	4653	4799	4944	5090	5235	5381	5526	146
9	5671	5816	5962	6107	6252	6397	6542	6687	6832	6976	145
300	477121	477266	477411	477555	477700	477844	477989	478133	478278	478422	145
1	8566	8711	8855	8999	9143	9287	9431	9575	9719	9863	144
2	480007	480151	480294	480438	480582	480725	480869	481012	481156	481299	144
3	1443	1586	1729	1872	2016	2159	2302	2445	2588	2731	143
4	2874	3016	3159	3302	3445	3587	3730	3872	4015	4157	143
5	4300	4442	4585	4727	4869	5011	5153	5295	5437	5579	142
6	5721	5863	6005	6147	6289	6430	6572	6714	6855	6997	142
7	7138	7280	7421	7563	7704	7845	7986	8127	8269	8410	141
8	8551	8692	8833	8974	9114	9255	9396	9537	9677	9818	141
9	9958	490099	490239	490380	490520	490661	490801	490941	491081	491222	140
310	491362	491502	491642	491782	491922	492062	492201	492341	492481	492621	140
1	2760	2900	3040	3179	3319	3458	3597	3737	3876	4015	139
2	4155	4294	4433	4572	4711	4850	4989	5128	5267	5406	139
3	5544	5683	5822	5960	6099	6238	6376	6515	6653	6791	139
4	6930	7068	7206	7344	7483	7621	7759	7897	8035	8173	138
5	8311	8448	8586	8724	8862	8999	9137	9275	9412	9550	138
6	9687	9824	9962	500099	500236	500374	500511	500648	500785	500922	137
7	501059	501196	501333	1470	1607	1744	1880	2017	2154	2291	137
8	2427	2564	2700	2837	2973	3109	3246	3382	3518	3655	136
9	3791	3927	4063	4199	4335	4471	4607	4743	4878	5014	136
320	505150	505286	505421	505557	505693	505828	505964	506099	506234	506370	136
1	6505	6640	6776	6911	7046	7181	7316	7451	7586	7721	135
2	7856	7991	8126	8260	8395	8530	8664	8799	8934	9068	135
3	9203	9337	9471	9606	9740	9874	510009	510143	510277	510411	134
4	510545	510679	510813	510947	511081	511215	1349	1482	1616	1750	134
5	1883	2017	2151	2284	2418	2551	2684	2818	2951	3084	133
6	3218	3351	3484	3617	3750	3883	4016	4149	4282	4415	133
7	4548	4681	4813	4946	5079	5211	5344	5476	5609	5741	133
8	5874	6006	6139	6271	6403	6535	6668	6800	6932	7064	132
9	7196	7328	7460	7592	7724	7855	7987	8119	8251	8382	132
330	518514	518646	518777	518909	519040	519171	519303	519434	519566	519697	131
1	9828	9959	520090	520221	520353	520484	520615	520745	520876	521007	131
2	521138	521269	1400	1530	1661	1792	1922	2053	2183	2314	131
3	2444	2575	2705	2835	2966	3096	3226	3356	3486	3616	130
4	3746	3876	4006	4136	4266	4396	4526	4656	4785	4915	130
5	5045	5174	5304	5434	5563	5693	5822	5951	6081	6210	129
6	6339	6469	6598	6727	6856	6985	7114	7243	7372	7501	129
7	7630	7759	7888	8016	8145	8274	8402	8531	8660	8788	129
8	8917	9045	9174	9302	9430	9559	9687	9815	9943	530072	128
9	530200	530328	530456	530584	530712	530840	530968	531096	531223	1351	128
N.	0	1	2	3	4	5	6	7	8	9	D.

N	0	1	2	3	4	5	6	7	8	9	D.
340	531479	531607	531734	531862	531990	532117	532245	532372	532500	532627	128
1	2754	2882	3009	3136	3264	3391	3518	3645	3772	3899	127
2	4026	4153	4280	4407	4534	4661	4787	4914	5041	5167	127
3	5294	5421	5547	5674	5800	5927	6053	6180	6306	6432	126
4	6558	6685	6811	6937	7063	7189	7315	7441	7567	7693	126
5	7819	7945	8071	8197	8322	8448	8574	8699	8825	8951	126
6	9076	9202	9327	9452	9578	9703	9829	9954	540079	540204	125
7	540329	540455	540580	540705	540830	540955	541080	541205	1330	1454	125
8	1579	1704	1829	1953	2078	2203	2327	2452	2576	2701	125
9	2825	2950	3074	3199	3323	3447	3571	3696	3820	3944	124
350	544068	544192	544316	544440	544564	544688	544812	544936	545060	545183	124
1	5307	5431	5555	5678	5802	5925	6049	6172	6296	6419	124
2	6543	6666	6789	6913	7036	7159	7282	7405	7529	7652	123
3	7775	7898	8021	8144	8267	8389	8512	8635	8758	8881	123
4	9003	9126	9249	9371	9494	9616	9739	9861	9984	550106	123
5	550228	550351	550473	550595	550717	550840	550962	551084	551206	1328	122
6	1450	1572	1694	1816	1938	2060	2181	2303	2425	2547	122
7	2668	2790	2911	3033	3155	3276	3398	3519	3640	3762	121
8	3883	4004	4126	4247	4368	4489	4610	4731	4852	4973	121
9	5094	5215	5336	5457	5578	5699	5820	5940	6061	6182	121
360	556303	556423	556544	556664	556785	556905	557026	557146	557267	557387	120
1	7507	7627	7748	7868	7988	8108	8228	8349	8469	8589	120
2	8709	8829	8948	9068	9188	9308	9428	9548	9667	9787	120
3	9907	560026	560146	560265	560385	560504	560624	560743	560863	560982	119
4	561101	1221	1340	1459	1578	1698	1817	1936	2055	2174	119
5	2293	2412	2531	2650	2769	2887	3006	3125	3244	3362	119
6	3481	3600	3718	3837	3955	4074	4192	4311	4429	4548	119
7	4666	4784	4903	5021	5139	5257	5376	5494	5612	5730	118
8	5848	5966	6084	6202	6320	6437	6555	6673	6791	6909	118
9	7026	7144	7262	7379	7497	7614	7732	7849	7967	8084	118
370	568202	568319	568436	568554	568671	568788	568905	569023	569140	569257	117
1	9374	9491	9608	9725	9842	9959	570076	570193	570309	570426	117
2	570543	570660	570776	570893	571010	571126	1243	1359	1476	1592	117
3	1709	1825	1942	2058	2174	2291	2407	2523	2639	2755	116
4	2872	2988	3104	3220	3336	3452	3568	3684	3800	3915	116
5	4031	4147	4263	4379	4494	4610	4726	4841	4957	5072	116
6	5188	5303	5419	5534	5650	5765	5880	5996	6111	6226	115
7	6341	6457	6572	6687	6802	6917	7032	7147	7262	7377	115
8	7492	7607	7722	7836	7951	8066	8181	8295	8410	8525	115
9	8639	8754	8868	8983	9097	9212	9326	9441	9555	9669	114
380	579784	579898	580012	580126	580241	580355	580469	580583	580697	580811	114
1	580925	581039	1153	1267	1381	1495	1608	1722	1836	1950	114
2	2063	2177	2291	2404	2518	2631	2745	2858	2972	3085	114
3	3199	3312	3426	3539	3652	3765	3879	3992	4105	4218	113
4	4331	4444	4557	4670	4783	4896	5009	5122	5235	5348	113
5	5461	5574	5686	5799	5912	6024	6137	6250	6362	6475	113
6	6587	6700	6812	6925	7037	7149	7262	7374	7486	7599	112
7	7711	7823	7935	8047	8160	8272	8384	8496	8608	8720	112
8	8832	8944	9056	9167	9279	9391	9503	9615	9726	9838	112
9	9950	590061	590173	590284	590396	590507	590619	590730	590842	590953	112
390	591065	591176	591287	591399	591510	591621	591732	591843	591955	592066	111
1	2177	2288	2399	2510	2621	2732	2843	2954	3064	3175	111
2	3286	3397	3508	3618	3729	3840	3950	4061	4171	4282	111
3	4393	4503	4614	4724	4834	4945	5055	5165	5276	5386	110
4	5496	5606	5717	5827	5937	6047	6157	6267	6377	6487	110
5	6597	6707	6817	6927	7037	7146	7256	7366	7476	7586	110
6	7695	7805	7914	8024	8134	8243	8353	8462	8572	8681	110
7	8791	8900	9009	9119	9228	9337	9446	9556	9665	9774	109
8	9883	9992	600101	600210	600319	600428	600537	600646	600755	600864	109
9	600973	601082	1191	1299	1408	1517	1625	1734	1843	1951	109
N.	0	1	2	3	4	5	6	7	8	9	D.

N.	0	1	2	3	4	5	6	7	8	9	D.
400	602060	602169	602277	602386	602494	602603	602711	602819	602928	603036	108
1	3144	3253	3361	3469	3577	3686	3794	3902	4010	4118	108
2	4226	4334	4442	4550	4658	4766	4874	4982	5089	5197	108
3	5305	5413	5521	5628	5736	5844	5951	6059	6166	6274	108
4	6381	6489	6596	6704	6811	6919	7026	7133	7241	7348	107
5	7455	7562	7669	7777	7884	7991	8098	8205	8312	8419	107
6	8526	8633	8740	8847	8954	9061	9167	9274	9381	9488	107
7	9594	9701	9808	9914	610021	610128	610234	610341	610447	610554	107
8	610660	610767	610873	610979	1086	1192	1298	1405	1511	1617	106
9	1723	1829	1936	2042	2148	2254	2360	2466	2572	2678	106
410	612784	612890	612996	613102	613207	613313	613419	613525	613630	613736	106
1	3842	3947	4053	4159	4264	4370	4475	4581	4686	4792	106
2	4897	5003	5108	5213	5319	5424	5529	5634	5740	5845	105
3	5950	6055	6160	6265	6370	6476	6581	6686	6790	6895	105
4	7000	7105	7210	7315	7420	7525	7629	7734	7839	7943	105
5	8048	8153	8257	8362	8466	8571	8676	8780	8884	8989	105
6	9093	9198	9302	9406	9511	9615	9719	9824	9928	620032	104
7	620136	620240	620344	620448	620552	620656	620760	620864	620968	1072	104
8	1176	1280	1384	1488	1592	1695	1799	1903	2007	2110	104
9	2214	2318	2421	2525	2628	2732	2835	2939	3042	3146	104
420	623249	623353	623456	623559	623663	623766	623869	623973	624076	624179	103
1	4282	4385	4488	4591	4695	4798	4901	5004	5107	5210	103
2	5312	5415	5518	5621	5724	5827	5929	6032	6135	6238	103
3	6340	6443	6546	6648	6751	6853	6956	7058	7161	7263	103
4	7366	7468	7571	7673	7775	7878	7980	8082	8185	8287	102
5	8389	8491	8593	8695	8797	8900	9002	9104	9206	9308	102
6	9410	9512	9613	9715	9817	9919	630021	630123	630224	630326	102
7	630428	630530	630631	630733	630835	630936	1038	1139	1241	1342	102
8	1444	1545	1647	1748	1849	1951	2052	2153	2255	2356	101
9	2457	2559	2660	2761	2862	2963	3064	3165	3266	3367	101
430	633468	633569	633670	633771	633872	633973	634074	634175	634276	634376	101
1	4477	4578	4679	4779	4880	4981	5081	5182	5283	5383	101
2	5484	5584	5685	5785	5886	5986	6087	6187	6287	6388	100
3	6488	6588	6688	6789	6889	6989	7089	7189	7290	7390	100
4	7490	7590	7690	7790	7890	7990	8090	8190	8290	8389	100
5	8489	8589	8689	8789	8888	8988	9088	9188	9287	9387	100
6	9486	9586	9686	9785	9885	9984	640084	640183	640283	640382	99
7	640481	640581	640680	640779	640879	640978	1077	1177	1276	1375	99
8	1474	1573	1672	1771	1871	1970	2069	2168	2267	2366	99
9	2465	2563	2662	2761	2860	2959	3058	3156	3255	3354	99
440	643453	643551	643650	643749	643847	643946	644044	644143	644242	644340	98
1	4439	4537	4636	4734	4832	4931	5029	5127	5226	5324	98
2	5422	5521	5619	5717	5815	5913	6011	6110	6208	6306	98
3	6404	6502	6600	6698	6796	6894	6992	7089	7187	7285	98
4	7383	7481	7579	7676	7774	7872	7969	8067	8165	8262	98
5	8360	8458	8555	8653	8750	8848	8945	9043	9140	9237	97
6	9335	9432	9530	9627	9724	9821	9919	650016	650113	650210	97
7	650308	650405	650502	650599	650696	650793	650890	0987	1084	1181	97
8	1278	1375	1472	1569	1666	1762	1859	1956	2053	2150	97
9	2246	2343	2440	2536	2633	2730	2826	2923	3019	3116	97
450	653213	653309	653405	653502	653598	653695	653791	653888	653984	654080	96
1	4177	4273	4369	4465	4562	4658	4754	4850	4946	5042	96
2	5138	5235	5331	5427	5523	5619	5715	5810	5906	6002	96
3	6098	6194	6290	6386	6482	6577	6673	6769	6864	6960	96
4	7056	7152	7247	7343	7438	7534	7629	7725	7820	7916	96
5	8011	8107	8202	8298	8393	8488	8584	8679	8774	8870	95
6	8965	9060	9155	9250	9346	9441	9536	9631	9726	9821	95
7	9916	660011	660106	660201	660296	660391	660486	660581	660676	660771	95
8	660865	0960	1055	1150	1245	1339	1434	1529	1623	1718	95
9	1813	1907	2002	2096	2191	2286	2380	2475	2569	2663	95
N.	0	1	2	3	4	5	6	7	8	9	D.

N.	0	1	2	3	4	5	6	7	8	9	D.
460	662758	662852	662947	663041	663135	663230	663324	663418	663512	663607	94
1	3701	3795	3889	3983	4078	4172	4266	4360	4454	4548	94
2	4642	4736	4830	4924	5018	5112	5206	5299	5393	5487	94
3	5581	5675	5769	5862	5956	6050	6145	6237	6331	6424	94
4	6518	6612	6705	6799	6892	6986	7079	7173	7266	7360	94
5	7453	7546	7640	7733	7826	7920	8013	8106	8199	8293	93
6	8386	8479	8572	8665	8759	8852	8945	9038	9131	9224	93
7	9317	9410	9503	9596	9689	9782	9875	9967	670060	670153	93
8	670246	670339	670431	670524	670617	670710	670802	670895	0988	1080	93
9	1173	1265	1358	1451	1543	1636	1728	1821	1913	2005	93
470	672098	672190	672283	672375	672467	672560	672652	672744	672836	672929	92
1	3021	3113	3205	3297	3390	3482	3574	3666	3758	3850	92
2	3942	4034	4126	4218	4310	4402	4494	4586	4677	4769	92
3	4861	4953	5045	5137	5228	5320	5412	5503	5595	5687	92
4	5778	5870	5962	6053	6145	6236	6328	6419	6511	6602	92
5	6694	6785	6876	6968	7059	7151	7242	7333	7424	7516	91
6	7607	7698	7789	7881	7972	8063	8154	8245	8336	8427	91
7	8518	8609	8700	8791	8882	8973	9064	9155	9246	9337	91
8	9428	9519	9610	9700	9791	9882	9973	680063	680154	680245	91
9	680336	680426	680517	680607	680698	680789	680879	0970	1060	1151	91
480	681241	681332	681422	681513	681603	681693	681784	681874	681964	682055	90
1	2145	2235	2326	2416	2506	2596	2686	2777	2867	2957	90
2	3047	3137	3227	3317	3407	3497	3587	3677	3767	3857	90
3	3947	4037	4127	4217	4307	4396	4486	4576	4666	4756	90
4	4845	4935	5025	5114	5204	5294	5383	5473	5563	5652	90
5	5742	5831	5921	6010	6100	6189	6279	6368	6458	6547	89
6	6636	6726	6815	6904	6994	7083	7172	7261	7351	7440	89
7	7529	7618	7707	7796	7886	7975	8064	8153	8242	8331	89
8	8420	8509	8598	8687	8776	8865	8953	9042	9131	9220	89
9	9309	9398	9486	9575	9664	9753	9841	9930	690019	690107	89
490	690196	690285	690373	690462	690550	690639	690728	690816	690905	690993	89
1	1081	1170	1258	1347	1435	1524	1612	1700	1789	1877	88
2	1965	2053	2142	2230	2318	2406	2494	2583	2671	2759	88
3	2847	2935	3023	3111	3199	3287	3375	3463	3551	3639	88
4	3727	3815	3903	3991	4078	4166	4254	4342	4430	4517	88
5	4605	4693	4781	4868	4956	5044	5131	5219	5307	5394	88
6	5482	5569	5657	5744	5832	5919	6007	6094	6182	6269	87
7	6356	6444	6531	6618	6706	6793	6880	6968	7055	7142	87
8	7229	7317	7404	7491	7578	7665	7752	7839	7926	8014	87
9	8101	8188	8275	8362	8449	8535	8622	8709	8796	8883	87
500	698970	699057	699144	699231	699317	699404	699491	699578	699664	699751	87
1	9838	9924	700011	700098	700184	700271	700358	700444	700531	700617	87
2	700704	700790	0877	0963	1050	1136	1222	1309	1395	1482	86
3	1568	1654	1741	1827	1913	1999	2086	2172	2258	2344	86
4	2431	2517	2603	2689	2775	2861	2947	3033	3119	3205	86
5	3291	3377	3463	3549	3635	3721	3807	3893	3979	4065	86
6	4151	4236	4322	4408	4494	4579	4665	4751	4837	4922	86
7	5008	5094	5179	5265	5350	5436	5522	5607	5693	5778	86
8	5864	5949	6035	612[illegible]	6206	6291	6376	6462	6547	6632	85
9	6718	6803	6888	6974	7059	7144	7229	7315	7400	7485	85
510	707570	707655	707740	707826	707911	707996	708081	708166	708251	708336	85
1	8421	8506	8591	8676	8761	8846	8931	9015	9100	9185	85
2	9270	9355	9440	9524	9609	9694	9779	9863	9948	710033	85
3	710117	710202	710287	710371	710456	710540	710625	710710	710794	0879	85
4	0963	1048	1132	1217	1301	1385	1470	1554	1639	1723	84
5	1807	1892	1976	2060	2144	2229	2313	2397	2481	2566	84
6	2650	2734	2818	2902	2986	3070	3154	3238	3323	3407	84
7	3491	3575	3659	3742	3826	3910	3994	4078	4162	4246	84
8	4330	4414	4497	4581	4665	4749	4833	4916	5000	5084	84
9	5167	5251	5335	5418	5502	5586	5669	5753	5836	5920	84
N.	0	1	2	3	4	5	6	7	8	9	D.

N.	0	1	2	3	4	5	6	7	8	9	D.
520	716003	716087	716170	716254	716337	716421	716504	716588	716671	716754	83
1	6838	6921	7004	7088	7171	7254	7338	7421	7504	7587	83
2	7671	7754	7837	7920	8003	8086	8169	8253	8336	8419	83
3	8502	8585	8668	8751	8834	8917	9000	9083	9165	9248	83
4	9331	9414	9497	9580	9663	9745	9828	9911	9994	720077	83
5	720159	720242	720325	720407	720490	720573	720655	720738	720821	0903	83
6	0986	1068	1151	1233	1316	1398	1481	1563	1646	1728	82
7	1811	1893	1975	2058	2140	2222	2305	2387	2469	2552	82
8	2634	2716	2798	2881	2963	3045	3127	3209	3291	3374	82
9	3456	3538	3620	3702	3784	3866	3948	4030	4112	4194	82
530	724276	724358	724440	724522	724604	724685	724767	724849	724931	725013	82
1	5095	5176	5258	5340	5422	5503	5585	5667	5748	5830	82
2	5912	5993	6075	6156	6238	6320	6401	6483	6564	6646	82
3	6727	6809	6890	6972	7053	7134	7216	7297	7379	7460	81
4	7541	7623	7704	7785	7866	7948	8029	8110	8191	8273	81
5	8354	8435	8516	8597	8678	8759	8841	8922	9003	9084	81
6	9165	9246	9327	9408	9489	9570	9651	9732	9813	9893	81
7	9974	730055	730136	730217	730298	730378	730459	730540	730621	730702	81
8	730782	0863	0944	1024	1105	1186	1266	1347	1428	1508	81
9	1589	1669	1750	1830	1911	1991	2072	2152	2233	2313	81
540	732394	732474	732555	732635	732715	732796	732876	732956	733037	733117	80
1	3197	3278	3358	3438	3518	3598	3679	3759	3839	3919	80
2	3999	4079	4160	4240	4320	4400	4480	4560	4640	4720	80
3	4800	4880	4960	5040	5120	5200	5279	5359	5439	5519	80
4	5599	5679	5759	5838	5918	5998	6078	6157	6237	6317	80
5	6397	6476	6556	6635	6715	6795	6874	6954	7034	7113	80
6	7193	7272	7352	7431	7511	7590	7670	7749	7829	7908	79
7	7987	8067	8146	8225	8305	8384	8463	8543	8622	8701	79
8	8781	8860	8939	9018	9097	9177	9256	9335	9414	9493	79
9	9572	9651	9731	9810	9889	9968	740047	740126	740205	740284	79
550	740363	740442	740521	740600	740678	740757	740836	740915	740994	741073	79
1	1152	1230	1309	1388	1467	1546	1624	1703	1782	1860	79
2	1939	2018	2096	2175	2254	2332	2411	2489	2568	2647	79
3	2725	2804	2882	2961	3039	3118	3196	3275	3353	3431	78
4	3510	3588	3667	3745	3823	3902	3980	4058	4136	4215	78
5	4293	4371	4449	4528	4606	4684	4762	4840	4919	4997	78
6	5075	5153	5231	5309	5387	5465	5543	5621	5699	5777	78
7	5855	5933	6011	6089	6167	6245	6323	6401	6479	6556	78
8	6634	6712	6790	6868	6945	7023	7101	7179	7256	7334	78
9	7412	7489	7567	7645	7722	7800	7878	7955	8033	8110	78
560	748188	748266	748343	748421	748498	748576	748653	748731	748808	748885	77
1	8963	9040	9118	9195	9272	9350	9427	9504	9582	9659	77
2	9736	9814	9891	9968	750045	750123	750200	750277	750354	750431	77
3	750508	750586	750663	750740	0817	0894	0971	1048	1125	1202	77
4	1279	1356	1433	1510	1587	1664	1741	1818	1895	1972	77
5	2048	2125	2202	2279	2356	2433	2509	2586	2663	2740	77
6	2816	2893	2970	3047	3123	3200	3277	3353	3430	3506	77
7	3583	3660	3736	3813	3889	3966	4042	4119	4195	4272	77
8	4348	4425	4501	4578	4654	4730	4807	4883	4960	5036	76
9	5112	5189	5265	5341	5417	5494	5570	5646	5722	5799	76
570	755875	755951	756027	756103	756180	756256	756332	756408	756484	756560	76
1	6636	6712	6788	6864	6940	7016	7092	7168	7244	7320	76
2	7396	7472	7548	7624	7700	7775	7851	7927	8003	8079	76
3	8155	8230	8306	8382	8458	8533	8609	8685	8761	8836	76
4	8912	8988	9063	9139	9214	9290	9366	9441	9517	9592	76
5	9668	9743	9819	9894	9970	760045	760121	760196	760272	760347	75
6	760422	760498	760573	760649	760724	0799	0875	0950	1025	1101	75
7	1176	1251	1326	1402	1477	1552	1627	1702	1778	1853	75
8	1928	2003	2078	2153	2228	2303	2378	2453	2529	2604	75
9	2679	2754	2829	2904	2978	3053	3128	3203	3278	3353	75
N.	0	1	2	3	4	5	6	7	8	9	D.

N.	0	1	2	3	4	5	6	7	8	9	D.
580	763428	763503	763578	763653	763727	763802	763877	763952	764027	764101	75
1	4176	4251	4326	4400	4475	4550	4624	4699	4774	4848	75
2	4923	4998	5072	5147	5221	5296	5370	5445	5520	5594	75
3	5669	5743	5818	5892	5966	6041	6115	6190	6264	6338	74
4	6413	6487	6562	6636	6710	6785	6859	6933	7007	7082	74
5	7156	7230	7304	7379	7453	7527	7601	7675	7749	7823	74
6	7898	7972	8046	8120	8194	8268	8342	8416	8490	8564	74
7	8638	8712	8786	8860	8934	9008	9082	9156	9230	9303	74
8	9377	9451	9525	9599	9673	9746	9820	9894	9968	770042	74
9	770115	770189	770263	770336	770410	770484	770557	770631	770705	0778	74
590	770852	770926	770999	771073	771146	771220	771293	771367	771440	771514	74
1	1587	1661	1734	1808	1881	1955	2028	2102	2175	2248	73
2	2322	2395	2468	2542	2615	2688	2762	2835	2908	2981	73
3	3055	3128	3201	3274	3348	3421	3494	3567	3640	3713	73
4	3786	3860	3933	4006	4079	4152	4225	4298	4371	4444	73
5	4517	4590	4663	4736	4809	4882	4955	5028	5100	5173	73
6	5246	5319	5392	5465	5538	5610	5683	5756	5829	5902	73
7	5974	6047	6120	6193	6265	6338	6411	6483	6556	6629	73
8	6701	6774	6846	6919	6992	7064	7137	7209	7282	7354	73
9	7427	7499	7572	7644	7717	7789	7862	7934	8006	8079	72
600	778151	778224	778296	778368	778441	778513	778585	778658	778730	778802	72
1	8874	8947	9019	9091	9163	9236	9308	9380	9452	9524	72
2	9596	9669	9741	9813	9885	9957	780029	780101	780173	780245	72
3	780317	780389	780461	780533	780605	780677	0749	0821	0893	0965	72
4	1037	1109	1181	1253	1324	1396	1468	1540	1612	1684	72
5	1755	1827	1899	1971	2042	2114	2186	2258	2329	2401	72
6	2473	2544	2616	2688	2759	2831	2902	2974	3046	3117	72
7	3189	3260	3332	3403	3475	3546	3618	3689	3761	3832	71
8	3904	3975	4046	4118	4189	4261	4332	4403	4475	4546	71
9	4617	4689	4760	4831	4902	4974	5045	5116	5187	5259	71
610	785330	785401	785472	785543	785615	785686	785757	785828	785899	785970	71
1	6041	6112	6183	6254	6325	6396	6467	6538	6609	6680	71
2	6751	6822	6893	6964	7035	7106	7177	7248	7319	7390	71
3	7460	7531	7602	7673	7744	7815	7885	7956	8027	8098	71
4	8168	8239	8310	8381	8451	8522	8593	8663	8734	8804	71
5	8875	8946	9016	9087	9157	9228	9299	9369	9440	9510	71
6	9581	9651	9722	9792	9863	9933	790004	790074	790144	790215	70
7	790285	790356	790426	790496	790567	790637	0707	0778	0848	0918	70
8	0988	1059	1129	1199	1269	1340	1410	1480	1550	1620	70
9	1691	1761	1831	1901	1971	2041	2111	2181	2252	2322	70
620	792392	792462	792532	792602	792672	792742	792812	792882	792952	793022	70
1	3092	3162	3231	3301	3371	3441	3511	3581	3651	3721	70
2	3790	3860	3930	4000	4070	4139	4209	4279	4349	4418	70
3	4488	4558	4627	4697	4767	4836	4906	4976	5045	5115	70
4	5185	5254	5324	5393	5463	5532	5602	5672	5741	5811	70
5	5880	5949	6019	6088	6158	6227	6297	6366	6436	6505	69
6	6574	6644	6713	6782	6852	6921	6990	7060	7129	7198	69
7	7268	7337	7406	7475	7545	7614	7683	7752	7821	7890	69
8	7960	8029	8098	8167	8236	8305	8374	8443	8513	8582	69
9	8651	8720	8789	8858	8927	8996	9065	9134	9203	9272	69
630	799341	799409	799478	799547	799616	799685	799754	799823	799892	799961	69
1	800029	800098	800167	800236	800305	800373	800442	800511	800580	800648	69
2	0717	0786	0854	0923	0992	1061	1129	1198	1266	1335	69
3	1404	1472	1541	1609	1678	1747	1815	1884	1952	2021	69
4	2089	2158	2226	2295	2363	2432	2500	2568	2637	2705	68
5	2774	2842	2910	2979	3047	3116	3184	3252	3321	3389	68
6	3457	3525	3594	3662	3730	3798	3867	3935	4003	4071	68
7	4139	4208	4276	4344	4412	4480	4548	4616	4685	4753	68
8	4821	4889	4957	5025	5093	5161	5229	5297	5365	5433	68
9	5501	5569	5637	5705	5773	5841	5908	5976	6044	6112	68
N.	0	1	2	3	4	5	6	7	8	9	D.

N.	0	1	2	3	4	5	6	7	8	9	D.
640	806180	806248	806316	806384	806451	806519	806587	806655	806723	806790	68
1	6858	6926	6994	7061	7129	7197	7264	7332	7400	7467	68
2	7535	7603	7670	7738	7806	7873	7941	8008	8076	8143	68
3	8211	8279	8346	8414	8481	8549	8616	8684	8751	8818	67
4	8886	8953	9021	9088	9156	9223	9290	9358	9425	9492	67
5	9560	9627	9694	9762	9829	9896	9964	810031	810098	810165	67
6	810233	810300	810367	810434	810501	810569	810636	0703	0770	0837	67
7	0904	0971	1039	1106	1173	1240	1307	1374	1441	1508	67
8	1575	1642	1709	1776	1843	1910	1977	2044	2111	2178	67
9	2245	2312	2379	2445	2512	2579	2646	2713	2780	2847	67
650	812913	812980	813047	813114	813181	813247	813314	813381	813448	813514	67
1	3581	3648	3714	3781	3848	3914	3981	4048	4114	4181	67
2	4248	4314	4381	4447	4514	4581	4647	4714	4780	4847	67
3	4913	4980	5046	5113	5179	5246	5312	5378	5445	5511	66
4	5578	5644	5711	5777	5843	5910	5976	6042	6109	6175	66
5	6241	6308	6374	6440	6506	6573	6639	6705	6771	6838	66
6	6904	6970	7036	7102	7169	7235	7301	7367	7433	7499	66
7	7565	7631	7698	7764	7830	7896	7962	8028	8094	8160	66
8	8226	8292	8358	8424	8490	8556	8622	8688	8754	8820	66
9	8885	8951	9017	9083	9149	9215	9281	9346	9412	9478	66
660	819544	819610	819676	819741	819807	819873	819939	820004	820070	820136	66
1	820201	820267	820333	820399	820464	820530	820595	0661	0727	0792	66
2	0858	0924	0989	1055	1120	1186	1251	1317	1382	1448	66
3	1514	1579	1645	1710	1775	1841	1906	1972	2037	2103	65
4	2168	2233	2299	2364	2430	2495	2560	2626	2691	2756	65
5	2822	2887	2952	3018	3083	3148	3213	3279	3344	3409	65
6	3474	3539	3605	3670	3735	3800	3865	3930	3996	4061	65
7	4126	4191	4256	4321	4386	4451	4516	4581	4646	4711	65
8	4776	4841	4906	4971	5036	5101	5166	5231	5296	5361	65
9	5426	5491	5556	5621	5686	5751	5815	5880	5945	6010	65
670	826075	826140	826204	826269	826334	826399	826464	826528	826593	826658	65
1	6723	6787	6852	6917	6981	7046	7111	7175	7240	7305	65
2	7369	7434	7499	7563	7628	7692	7757	7821	7886	7951	65
3	8015	8080	8144	8209	8273	8338	8402	8467	8531	8595	64
4	8660	8724	8789	8853	8918	8982	9046	9111	9175	9239	64
5	9304	9368	9432	9497	9561	9625	9690	9754	9818	9882	64
6	9947	830011	830075	830139	830204	830268	830332	830396	830460	830525	64
7	830589	0653	0717	0781	0845	0909	0973	1037	1102	1166	64
8	1230	1294	1358	1422	1486	1550	1614	1678	1742	1806	64
9	1870	1934	1998	2062	2126	2189	2253	2317	2381	2445	64
680	832509	832573	832637	832700	832764	832828	832892	832956	833020	833083	64
1	3147	3211	3275	3338	3402	3466	3530	3593	3657	3721	64
2	3784	3848	3912	3975	4039	4103	4166	4230	4294	4357	64
3	4421	4484	4548	4611	4675	4739	4802	4866	4929	4993	64
4	5056	5120	5183	5247	5310	5373	5437	5500	5564	5627	63
5	5691	5754	5817	5881	5944	6007	6071	6134	6197	6261	63
6	6324	6387	6451	6514	6577	6641	6704	6767	6830	6894	63
7	6957	7020	7083	7146	7210	7273	7336	7399	7462	7525	63
8	7588	7652	7715	7778	7841	7904	7967	8030	8093	8156	63
9	8219	8282	8345	8408	8471	8534	8597	8660	8723	8786	63
690	838849	838912	838975	839038	839101	839164	839227	839289	839352	839415	63
1	9478	9541	9604	9667	9729	9792	9855	9918	9981	840043	63
2	840106	840169	840232	840294	840357	840420	840482	840545	840608	0671	63
3	0733	0796	0859	0921	0984	1046	1109	1172	1234	1297	63
4	1359	1422	1485	1547	1610	1672	1735	1797	1860	1922	63
5	1985	2047	2110	2172	2235	2297	2360	2422	2484	2547	62
6	2609	2672	2734	2796	2859	2921	2983	3046	3108	3170	62
7	3233	3295	3357	3420	3482	3544	3606	3669	3731	3793	62
8	3855	3918	3980	4042	4104	4166	4229	4291	4353	4415	62
9	4477	4539	4601	4664	4726	4788	4850	4912	4974	5036	62
N	0	1	2	3	4	5	6	7	8	9	D

N.	0	1	2	3	4	5	6	7	8	9	D.
700	845098	845160	845222	845284	845346	845408	845470	845532	845594	845656	62
1	5718	5780	5842	5904	5966	6028	6090	6151	6213	6275	62
2	6337	6399	6461	6523	6585	6646	6708	6770	6832	6894	62
3	6955	7017	7079	7141	7202	7264	7326	7388	7449	7511	62
4	7573	7634	7696	7758	7819	7881	7943	8004	8066	8128	62
5	8189	8251	8312	8374	8435	8497	8559	8620	8682	8743	62
6	8805	8866	8928	8989	9051	9112	9174	9235	9297	9358	61
7	9419	9481	9542	9604	9665	9726	9788	9849	9911	9972	61
8	850033	850095	850156	850217	850279	850340	850401	850462	850524	850585	61
9	0646	0707	0769	0830	0891	0952	1014	1075	1136	1197	61
710	851258	851320	851381	851442	851503	851564	851625	851686	851747	851809	61
1	1870	1931	1992	2053	2114	2175	2236	2297	2358	2419	61
2	2480	2541	2602	2663	2724	2785	2846	2907	2968	3029	61
3	3090	3150	3211	3272	3333	3394	3455	3516	3577	3637	61
4	3698	3759	3820	3881	3941	4002	4063	4124	4185	4245	61
5	4306	4367	4428	4488	4549	4610	4670	4731	4792	4852	61
6	4913	4974	5034	5095	5156	5216	5277	5337	5398	5459	61
7	5519	5580	5640	5701	5761	5822	5882	5943	6003	6064	61
8	6124	6185	6245	6306	6366	6427	6487	6548	6608	6668	60
9	6729	6789	6850	6910	6970	7031	7091	7152	7212	7272	60
720	857332	857393	857453	857513	857574	857634	857694	857755	857815	857875	60
1	7935	7995	8056	8116	8176	8236	8297	8357	8417	8477	60
2	8537	8597	8657	8718	8778	8838	8898	8958	9018	9078	60
3	9138	9198	9258	9318	9379	9439	9499	9559	9619	9679	60
4	9739	9799	9859	9918	9978	860038	860098	860158	860218	860278	60
5	860338	860398	860458	860518	860578	0637	0697	0757	0817	0877	60
6	0937	0996	1056	1116	1176	1236	1295	1355	1415	1475	60
7	1534	1594	1654	1714	1773	1833	1893	1952	2012	2072	60
8	2131	2191	2251	2310	2370	2430	2489	2549	2608	2668	60
9	2728	2787	2847	2906	2966	3025	3085	3144	3204	3263	60
730	863323	863382	863442	863501	863561	863620	863680	863739	863799	863858	59
1	3917	3977	4036	4096	4155	4214	4274	4333	4392	4452	59
2	4511	4570	4630	4689	4748	4808	4867	4926	4985	5045	59
3	5104	5163	5222	5282	5341	5400	5459	5519	5578	5637	59
4	5696	5755	5814	5874	5933	5992	6051	6110	6169	6228	59
5	6287	6346	6405	6465	6524	6583	6642	6701	6760	6819	59
6	6878	6937	6996	7055	7114	7173	7252	7291	7350	7409	59
7	7467	7526	7585	7644	7703	7762	7821	7880	7939	7998	59
8	8056	8115	8174	8233	8292	8350	8409	8468	8527	8586	59
9	8644	8703	8762	8821	8879	8938	8997	9056	9114	9173	59
740	869232	869290	869349	869408	869466	869525	869584	869642	869701	869760	59
1	9818	9877	9935	9994	870053	870111	870170	870228	870287	870345	59
2	870404	870462	870521	870579	0638	0696	0755	0813	0872	0930	58
3	0989	1047	1106	1164	1223	1281	1339	1398	1456	1515	58
4	1573	1631	1690	1748	1806	1865	1923	1981	2040	2098	58
5	2156	2215	2273	2331	2389	2448	2506	2564	2622	2681	58
6	2739	2797	2855	2913	2972	3030	3088	3146	3204	3262	58
7	3321	3379	3437	3495	3553	3611	3669	3727	3785	3844	58
8	3902	3960	4018	4076	4134	4192	4250	4308	4366	4424	58
9	4482	4540	4598	4656	4714	4772	4830	4885	4945	5003	58
750	875061	875119	875177	875235	875293	875351	875409	875466	875524	875582	58
1	5640	5698	5756	5813	5871	5929	5987	6045	6102	6160	58
2	6218	6276	6333	6391	6449	6507	6564	6622	6680	6737	58
3	6795	6853	6910	6968	7026	7083	7141	7199	7256	7314	58
4	7371	7429	7487	7544	7602	7659	7717	7774	7832	7889	58
5	7947	8004	8062	8119	8177	8234	8292	8349	8407	8464	57
6	8522	8579	8637	8694	8752	8809	8866	8924	8981	9039	57
7	9096	9153	9211	9268	9325	9383	9440	9497	9555	9612	57
8	9669	9726	9784	9841	9898	9956	880013	880070	880127	880185	57
9	880242	870299	880356	880413	880471	880528	0585	0642	0699	0756	57
N.	0	1	2	3	4	5	6	7	8	9	D.

N.	0	1	2	3	4	5	6	7	8	9	D.
760	880814	880871	880928	880985	881042	881099	881156	881213	881271	881328	57
1	1385	1442	1499	1556	1613	1670	1727	1784	1841	1898	57
2	1955	2012	2069	2126	2183	2240	2297	2354	2411	2468	57
3	2525	2581	2638	2695	2752	2809	2866	2923	2980	3037	57
4	3093	3150	3207	3264	3321	3377	3434	3491	3548	3605	57
5	3661	3718	3775	3832	3888	3945	4002	4059	4115	4172	57
6	4229	4285	4342	4399	4455	4512	4569	4625	4682	4739	57
7	4795	4852	4909	4965	5022	5078	5135	5192	5248	5305	57
8	5361	5418	5474	5531	5587	5644	5700	5757	5813	5870	57
9	5926	5983	6039	6096	6152	6209	6265	6321	6378	6434	56
770	886491	886547	886604	886660	886716	886773	886829	886885	886942	886998	56
1	7054	7111	7167	7223	7280	7336	7392	7449	7505	7561	56
2	7617	7674	7730	7786	7842	7898	7955	8011	8067	8123	56
3	8179	8236	8292	8348	8404	8460	8516	8573	8629	8685	56
4	8741	8797	8853	8909	8965	9021	9077	9134	9190	9246	56
5	9302	9358	9414	9470	9526	9582	9638	9694	9750	9806	56
6	9862	9918	9974	890030	890086	890141	890197	890253	890309	890365	56
7	890421	890477	890533	0589	0645	0700	0756	0812	0868	0924	56
8	0980	1035	1091	1147	1203	1259	1314	1370	1426	1482	56
9	1537	1593	1649	1705	1760	1816	1872	1928	1983	2039	56
780	892095	892150	892206	892262	892317	892373	892429	892484	892540	892595	56
1	2651	2707	2762	2818	2873	2929	2985	3040	3096	3151	56
2	3207	3262	3318	3373	3429	3484	3540	3595	3651	3706	56
3	3762	3817	3873	3928	3984	4039	4094	4150	4205	4261	55
4	4316	4371	4427	4482	4538	4593	4648	4704	4759	4814	55
5	4870	4925	4980	5036	5091	5146	5201	5257	5312	5367	55
6	5423	5478	5533	5588	5644	5699	5754	5809	5864	5920	55
7	5975	6030	6085	6140	6195	6251	6306	6361	6416	6471	55
8	6526	6581	6636	6692	6747	6802	6857	6912	6967	7022	55
9	7077	7132	7187	7242	7297	7352	7407	7462	7517	7572	55
790	897627	897682	897737	897792	897847	897902	897959	898012	898067	898122	55
1	8176	8231	8286	8341	8396	8451	8506	8561	8615	8670	55
2	8725	8780	8835	8890	8944	8999	9054	9109	9164	9218	55
3	9273	9328	9383	9437	9492	9547	9602	9656	9711	9766	55
4	9821	9875	9930	9985	900039	900094	900149	900203	900258	900312	55
5	900367	900422	900476	900531	0586	0640	0695	0749	0804	0859	55
6	0913	0968	1022	1077	1131	1186	1240	1295	1349	1404	55
7	1458	1513	1567	1622	1676	1731	1785	1840	1894	1948	54
8	2003	2057	2112	2166	2221	2275	2329	2384	2438	2492	54
9	2547	2601	2655	2710	2764	2818	2873	2927	2981	3036	54
800	903090	903144	903199	903253	903307	903361	903416	903470	903524	903578	54
1	3633	3687	3741	3795	3849	3904	3958	4012	4066	4120	54
2	4174	4229	4283	4337	4391	4445	4499	4553	4607	4661	54
3	4716	4770	4824	4878	4932	4986	5040	5094	5148	5202	54
4	5256	5310	5364	5418	5472	5526	5580	5634	5688	5742	54
5	5796	5850	5904	5958	6012	6066	6119	6173	6227	6281	54
6	6335	6389	6443	6497	6551	6604	6658	6712	6766	6820	54
7	6874	6927	6981	7035	7089	7143	7196	7250	7304	7358	54
8	7411	7465	7519	7573	7626	7680	7734	7787	7841	7895	54
9	7949	8002	8056	8110	8163	8217	8270	8324	8378	8431	54
810	908485	908539	908592	908646	908699	908753	908807	908860	908914	908967	54
1	9021	9074	9128	9181	9235	9289	9342	9396	9449	9503	54
2	9556	9610	9663	9716	9770	9823	9877	9930	9984	910037	53
3	910091	910144	910197	910251	910304	910358	910411	910464	910518	0571	53
4	0624	0678	0731	0784	0838	0891	0944	0998	1051	1104	53
5	1158	1211	1264	1317	1371	1424	1477	1530	1584	1637	53
6	1690	1743	1797	1850	1903	1956	2009	2063	2116	2169	53
7	2222	2275	2328	2381	2435	2488	2541	2594	2647	2700	53
8	2753	2806	2859	2913	2966	3019	3072	3125	3178	3231	53
9	3284	3337	3390	3443	3496	3549	3602	3655	3708	3761	53
N.	0	1	2	3	4	5	6	7	8	9	D.

N.	0	1	2	3	4	5	6	7	8	9	D.
820	913814	913867	913920	913973	914026	914079	914132	914184	914237	914290	53
1	4343	4396	4449	4502	4555	4608	4660	4713	4766	4819	53
2	4872	4925	4977	5030	5083	5136	5189	5241	5294	5347	53
3	5400	5453	5505	5558	5611	5664	5716	5769	5822	5875	53
4	5927	5980	6033	6085	6138	6191	6243	6296	6349	6401	53
5	6454	6507	6559	6612	6664	6717	6770	6822	6875	6927	53
6	6980	7033	7085	7138	7190	7243	7295	7348	7400	7453	53
7	7506	7558	7611	7663	7716	7768	7820	7873	7925	7978	52
8	8030	8083	8135	8188	8240	8293	8345	8397	8450	8502	52
9	8555	8607	8659	8712	8764	8816	8869	8921	8973	9026	52
830	919078	919130	919183	919235	919287	919340	919392	919444	919496	919549	52
1	9601	9653	9706	9758	9810	9862	9914	9967	920019	920071	52
2	920123	920176	920228	920280	920332	920384	920436	920489	0541	0593	52
3	0645	0697	0749	0801	0853	0906	0958	1010	1062	1114	52
4	1166	1218	1270	1322	1374	1426	1478	1530	1582	1634	52
5	1686	1738	1790	1842	1894	1946	1998	2050	2102	2154	52
6	2206	2258	2310	2362	2414	2466	2518	2570	2622	2674	52
7	2725	2777	2829	2881	2933	2985	3037	3089	3140	3192	52
8	3244	3296	3348	3399	3451	3503	3555	3607	3658	3710	52
9	3762	3814	3865	3917	3969	4021	4072	4124	4176	4228	52
840	924279	924331	924383	924434	924486	924538	924589	924641	924693	924744	52
1	4796	4848	4899	4951	5003	5054	5106	5157	5209	5261	52
2	5312	5364	5415	5467	5518	5570	5621	5673	5725	5776	52
3	5828	5879	5931	5982	6034	6085	6137	6188	6240	6291	51
4	6342	6394	6445	6497	6548	6600	6651	6702	6754	6805	51
5	6857	6908	6959	7011	7062	7114	7165	7216	7268	7319	51
6	7370	7422	7473	7524	7576	7627	7678	7730	7781	7832	51
7	7883	7935	7986	8037	8088	8140	8191	8242	8293	8345	51
8	8396	8447	8498	8549	8601	8652	8703	8754	8805	8857	51
9	8908	8959	9010	9061	9112	9163	9215	9266	9317	9368	51
850	929419	929470	929521	929572	929623	929674	929725	929776	929827	929879	51
1	9930	9981	930032	930083	930134	930185	930236	930287	930338	930389	51
2	930440	930491	0542	0592	0643	0694	0745	0796	0847	0898	51
3	0949	1000	1051	1102	1153	1204	1254	1305	1356	1407	51
4	1458	1509	1560	1610	1661	1712	1763	1814	1865	1915	51
5	1966	2017	2068	2118	2169	2220	2271	2322	2372	2423	51
6	2474	2524	2575	2626	2677	2727	2778	2829	2879	2930	51
7	2981	3031	3082	3133	3183	3234	3285	3335	3386	3437	51
8	3487	3538	3589	3639	3690	3740	3791	3841	3892	3943	51
9	3993	4044	4094	4145	4195	4246	4296	4347	4397	4448	51
860	934498	934549	934599	934650	934700	934751	934801	934852	934902	934953	50
1	5003	5054	5104	5154	5205	5255	5306	5356	5406	5457	50
2	5507	5558	5608	5658	5709	5759	5809	5860	5910	5960	50
3	6011	6061	6111	6162	6212	6262	6313	6363	6413	6463	50
4	6514	6564	6614	6665	6715	6765	6815	6865	6916	6966	50
5	7016	7066	7117	7167	7217	7267	7317	7367	7418	7468	50
6	7518	7568	7618	7668	7718	7769	7819	7869	7919	7969	50
7	8019	8069	8119	8169	8219	8269	8320	8370	8420	8470	50
8	8520	8570	8620	8670	8720	8770	8820	8870	8920	8970	50
9	9020	9070	9120	9170	9220	9270	9320	9369	9419	9469	50
870	939519	969569	939619	939669	939719	939769	939819	939869	939918	939968	50
1	940018	940068	940118	940168	940218	940267	940317	940367	940417	940467	50
2	0516	0566	0616	0666	0716	0765	0815	0865	0915	0964	50
3	1014	1064	1114	1163	1213	1263	1313	1362	1412	1462	50
4	1511	1561	1611	1660	1710	1760	1809	1859	1909	1958	50
5	2008	2058	2107	2157	2207	2256	2306	2355	2405	2455	50
6	2504	2554	2603	2653	2702	2752	2801	2851	2901	2950	50
7	3000	3049	3099	3148	3198	3247	3297	3346	3396	3445	49
8	3445	3544	3593	3643	3692	3742	3791	3841	3890	3939	49
9	3989	4038	4088	4137	4186	4236	4285	4335	4384	4433	49
N.	0	1	2	3	4	5	6	7	8	9	D.

N.	0	1	2	3	4	5	6	7	8	9	D.
880	944483	944532	944581	944631	944680	944729	944779	944828	944877	944927	49
1	4976	5025	5074	5124	5173	5222	5272	5321	5370	5419	49
2	5469	5518	5567	5616	5665	5715	5764	5813	5862	5912	49
3	5961	6010	6059	6108	6157	6207	6256	6305	6354	6403	49
4	6452	6501	6551	6600	6649	6698	6747	6796	6845	6894	49
5	6943	6992	7041	7090	7140	7189	7238	7287	7336	7385	49
6	7434	7483	7532	7581	7630	7679	7728	7777	7826	7875	49
7	7924	7973	8022	8070	8119	8168	8217	8266	8315	8364	49
8	8413	8462	8511	8560	8609	8657	8706	8755	8804	8853	49
9	8902	8951	8999	9048	9097	9146	9195	9244	9292	9341	49
890	949390	949439	949488	949536	949585	949634	949683	949731	949780	949829	49
1	9878	9926	9975	950024	950073	950121	950170	950219	950267	950316	49
2	950365	950414	950462	0511	0560	0608	0657	0706	0754	0803	49
3	0851	0900	0949	0997	1046	1095	1143	1192	1240	1289	49
4	1338	1386	1435	1483	1532	1580	1629	1677	1726	1775	49
5	1823	1872	1920	1969	2017	2066	2114	2163	2211	2260	48
6	2308	2356	2405	2453	2502	2550	2599	2647	2696	2744	48
7	2792	2841	2889	2938	2986	3034	3083	3131	3180	3228	48
8	3276	3325	3373	3421	3470	3518	3566	3615	3663	3711	48
9	3760	3808	3856	3905	3953	4001	4049	4098	4146	4194	48
900	954243	954291	954339	954387	954435	954484	954532	954580	954628	954677	48
1	4725	4773	4821	4869	4918	4966	5014	5062	5110	5158	48
2	5207	5255	5303	5351	5399	5447	5495	5543	5592	5640	48
3	5688	5736	5784	5832	5880	5928	5976	6024	6072	6120	48
4	6168	6216	6265	6313	6361	6409	6457	6505	6553	6601	48
5	6649	6697	6745	6793	6840	6888	6936	6984	7032	7080	48
6	7128	7176	7224	7272	7320	7368	7416	7464	7512	7559	48
7	7607	7655	7703	7751	7799	7847	7894	7942	7990	8038	48
8	8086	8134	8181	8229	8277	8325	8373	8421	8468	8516	48
9	8564	8612	8659	8707	8755	8803	8850	8898	8946	8994	48
910	959041	959089	959137	959185	959232	959280	959328	959375	959423	959471	48
1	9518	9566	9614	9661	9709	9757	9804	9852	9900	9947	48
2	9995	960042	960090	960138	960185	960233	960281	960328	960376	960423	48
3	960471	0518	0566	0613	0661	0709	0756	0804	0851	0899	48
4	0946	0994	1041	1089	1136	1184	1231	1279	1326	1374	48
5	1421	1469	1516	1563	1611	1658	1706	1753	1801	1848	47
6	1895	1943	1990	2038	2085	2132	2180	2227	2275	2322	47
7	2369	2417	2464	2511	2559	2606	2653	2701	2748	2795	47
8	2843	2890	2937	2985	3032	3079	3126	3174	3221	3268	47
9	3316	3363	3410	3457	3504	3552	3599	3646	3693	3741	47
920	963788	963835	963882	963929	963977	964024	964071	964118	964165	964212	47
1	4260	4307	4354	4401	4448	4495	4542	4590	4637	4684	47
2	4731	4778	4825	4872	4919	4966	5013	5061	5108	5155	47
3	5202	5249	5296	5343	5390	5437	5484	5531	5578	5625	47
4	5672	5719	5766	5813	5860	5907	5954	6001	6048	6095	47
5	6142	6189	6236	6283	6329	6376	6423	6470	6517	6564	47
6	6611	6658	6705	6752	6799	6845	6892	6939	6986	7033	47
7	7080	7127	7173	7220	7267	7314	7361	7408	7454	7501	47
8	7548	7595	7642	7688	7735	7782	7829	7875	7922	7969	47
9	8016	8062	8109	8156	8203	8249	8296	8343	8390	8436	47
930	968483	968530	968576	968623	968670	968716	968763	968810	968856	968903	47
1	8950	8996	9043	9090	9136	9183	9229	9276	9323	9369	47
2	9416	9463	9509	9556	9602	9649	9695	9742	9789	9835	47
3	9882	9928	9975	970021	970068	970114	970161	970207	970254	970300	47
4	970347	970393	970440	0486	0533	0579	0626	0672	0719	0765	46
5	0812	0858	0904	0951	0997	1044	1090	1137	1183	1229	46
6	1276	1322	1369	1415	1461	1508	1554	1601	1647	1693	46
7	1740	1786	1832	1879	1925	1971	2018	2064	2110	2157	46
8	2203	2249	2295	2342	2388	2434	2481	2527	2573	2619	46
9	2666	2712	2758	2804	2851	2897	2943	2989	3035	3082	46
N.	0	1	2	3	4	5	6	7	8	9	D.

N.	0	1	2	3	4	5	6	7	8	9	D
940	973128	973174	973220	973266	973313	973359	973405	973451	973497	973543	46
1	3590	3636	3682	3728	3774	3820	3866	3913	3959	4005	46
2	4051	4097	4143	4189	4235	4281	4327	4374	4420	4466	46
3	4512	4558	4604	4650	4696	4742	4788	4834	4880	4926	46
4	4972	5018	5064	5110	5156	5202	5248	5294	5340	5386	46
5	5432	5478	5524	5570	5616	5662	5707	5753	5799	5845	46
6	5891	5937	5983	6029	6075	6121	6167	6212	6258	6304	46
7	6350	6396	6442	6488	6533	6579	6625	6671	6717	6763	46
8	6808	6854	6900	6946	6992	7037	7083	7129	7175	7220	46
9	7266	7312	7358	7403	7449	7495	7541	7586	7632	7678	46
950	977724	977769	977815	977861	977906	977952	977998	978043	978089	978135	46
1	8181	8226	8272	8317	8363	8409	8454	8500	8546	8591	46
2	8637	8683	8728	8774	8819	8865	8911	8956	9002	9047	46
3	9093	9138	9184	9230	9275	9321	9366	9412	9457	9503	46
4	9548	9594	9639	9685	9730	9776	9821	9867	9912	9958	46
5	980003	980049	980094	980140	980185	980231	980276	980322	980367	980412	45
6	0458	0503	0549	0594	0640	0685	0730	0776	0821	0867	45
7	0912	0957	1003	1048	1093	1139	1184	1229	1275	1320	45
8	1366	1411	1456	1501	1547	1592	1637	1683	1728	1773	45
9	1819	1864	1909	1954	2000	2045	2090	2135	2181	2226	45
960	982271	982316	982362	982407	982452	982497	982543	982588	982633	982678	45
1	2723	2769	2814	2859	2904	2949	2994	3040	3085	3130	45
2	3175	3220	3265	3310	3356	3401	3446	3491	3536	3581	45
3	3626	3671	3716	3762	3807	3852	3897	3942	3987	4032	45
4	4077	4122	4167	4212	4257	4302	4347	4392	4437	4482	45
5	4527	4572	4617	4662	4707	4752	4797	4842	4887	4932	45
6	4977	5022	5067	5112	5157	5202	5247	5292	5337	5382	45
7	5426	5471	5516	5561	5606	5651	5696	5741	5786	5830	45
8	5875	5920	5965	6010	6055	6100	6144	6189	6234	6279	45
9	6324	6369	6413	6458	6503	6548	6593	6637	6682	6727	45
970	986772	986817	986861	986906	986951	986996	987040	987085	987130	987175	45
1	7219	7264	7309	7353	7398	7443	7488	7532	7577	7622	45
2	7666	7711	7756	7800	7845	7890	7934	7979	8024	8068	45
3	8113	8157	8202	8247	8291	8336	8381	8425	8470	8514	45
4	8559	8604	8648	8693	8737	8782	8826	8871	8916	8960	45
5	9005	9049	9094	9138	9183	9227	9272	9316	9361	9405	45
6	9450	9494	9539	9583	9628	9672	9717	9761	9806	9850	44
7	9895	9939	9983	990028	990072	990117	990161	990206	990250	990294	44
8	990339	990383	990428	0472	0516	0561	0605	0650	0694	0738	44
9	0783	0827	0871	0916	0960	1004	1049	1093	1137	1182	44
980	991226	991270	991315	991359	991403	991448	991492	991536	991580	991625	44
1	1669	1713	1758	1802	1846	1890	1935	1979	2023	2067	44
2	2111	2156	2200	2244	2288	2333	2377	2421	2465	2509	44
3	2554	2598	2642	2686	2730	2774	2819	2863	2907	2951	44
4	2995	3039	3083	3127	3172	3216	3260	3304	3348	3392	44
5	3436	3480	3524	3568	3613	3657	3701	3745	3789	3833	44
6	3877	3921	3965	4009	4053	4097	4141	4185	4229	4273	44
7	4317	4361	4405	4449	4493	4537	4581	4625	4669	4713	44
8	4757	4801	4845	4889	4933	4977	5021	5065	5108	5152	44
9	5196	5240	5284	5328	5372	5416	5460	5504	5547	5591	44
990	995635	995679	995723	995767	995811	995854	995898	995942	995986	996030	44
1	6074	6117	6161	6205	6249	6293	6337	6380	6424	6468	44
2	6512	6555	6599	6643	6687	6731	6774	6818	6862	6906	44
3	6949	6993	7037	7080	7124	7168	7212	7255	7299	7343	44
4	7386	7430	7474	7517	7561	7605	7648	7692	7736	7779	44
5	7823	7867	7910	7954	7998	8041	8085	8129	8172	8216	44
6	8259	8303	8347	8390	8434	8477	8521	8564	8608	8652	44
7	8695	8739	8782	8826	8869	8913	8956	9000	9043	9087	44
8	9131	9174	9218	9261	9305	9348	9392	9435	9479	9522	44
9	9565	9609	9652	9696	9739	9783	9826	9870	9913	9957	43
N.	0	1	2	3	4	5	6	7	8	9	D.

GREENLEAF'S
New Practical Arithmetic;

AN ENTIRELY NEW WORK,

FOR SCHOOLS AND SEMINARIES

336 pp. Price 94 cents.

Especial attention is invited to its many

DISTINGUISHING CHARACTERISTICS.

1. *The prominence given to the* ENUNCIATION *of* GENERAL PRINCIPLES, (pp. 13, 18, 26, 35, 44, etc.)

2. *The simple and clear treatment of* NOTATION *and* NUMERATION.

3. *The early introduction of the* DECIMAL POINT, (pp. 15, 16,) *and the explanation of the values expressed by figures at the right of the point*, (p. 52.)

4. EXCHANGE *of* COMMODITIES, BILLS AND INVOICES, ACCOUNTS, LEDGER COLUMNS, (pp. 72, 78,) *and various useful applications*, (pp. 142, 178, 186, 187, 202, 263, 212, etc.)

5. *The discussion* of FACTORING before Multiplication by Factors, (p. 83,) or Division by Factors, (p. 84.)

6. *The simplification* of DIVISION of *Common Fractions* (p. 117,) *and of* DIVISION *of Decimals*, (p. 139.)

7. The introduction of COMPOUND DENOMINATE NUMBERS (p. 162,) *after Fractions, so as to avoid at least eight special rules in Reduction, Addition, and Subtraction of Denominate Numbers*

8. *The* METRIC SYSTEM *of* WEIGHTS *and* MEASURES *is in its proper place, in the body of the work*, (p. 155,) *and references made to the same in subsequent parts of the book*, (pp. 164, 166, 170, 187, 247, 283, etc.,) *as urged by* PROF. NEWTON, *of Yale College*, PRESIDENT HILL, *of Harvard University*, PROF. HENRY, *of Smithsonian Institute*, PROF. ROGERS, *of University of Pennsylvania*, CHANCELLOR CHAUVENET, *of Washington University*, ST. LOUIS, *and others.*